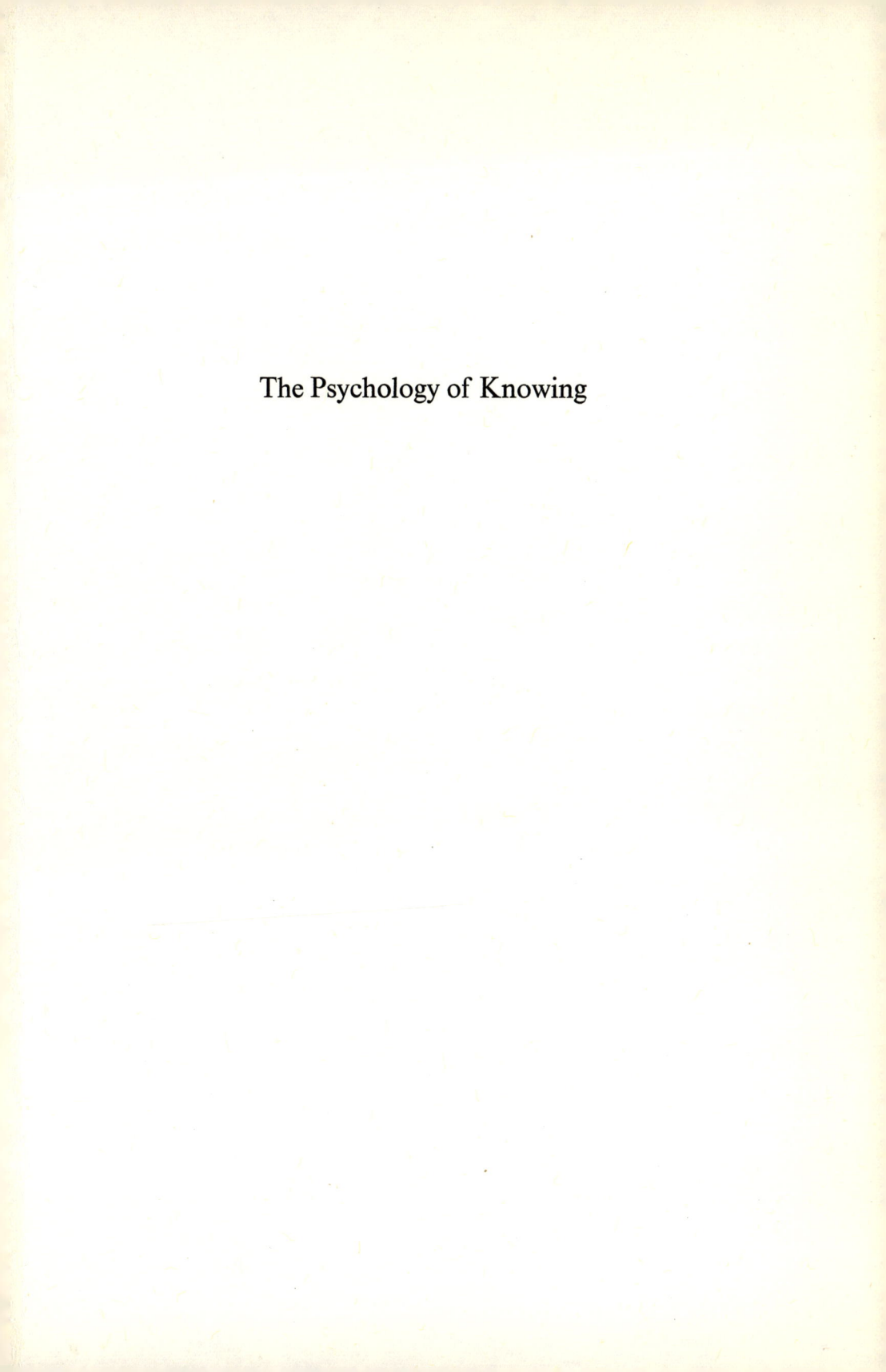

The Psychology of Knowing

Banff Conference on Theoretical Psychology.

The Psychology of
KNOWING

Edited by
Joseph R. Royce and Wm. W. Rozeboom

GORDON AND BREACH

New York   Paris   London

Copyright © 1972 by

    Gordon and Breach, Science Publishers, Inc.
    440 Park Avenue South
    New York, N.Y. 10016

Editorial office for the United Kingdom

    Gordon and Breach, Science Publishers Ltd.
    42 William IV Street
    London W.C.2

Editorial office for France

    Gordon & Breach
    7–9 rue Emile Dubois
    Paris 14ᵉ

The Second Banff Conference on Theoretical Psychology was substantially supported by the Scientific Affairs Division of the North Atlantic Treaty Organization.

Library of Congress catalog card number 75-138363. ISBN 0 677 13850 4. All rights reserved. No part of this book may be reproduced or utilized in any form or by any means, electronic or mechanical, including photocopying, recording, or by any information storage and retrieval system, without permission in writing from the publishers. Printed in east Germany.

CONTENTS

I. INTRODUCTION 1
Joseph R. Royce

II. EPISTEMOLOGY NATURALIZED 9
Willard V. Quine

III. PROBLEMS IN THE PSYCHO-PHILOSOPHY OF
KNOWLEDGE 25
William W. Rozeboom

   Comments: John D. Peyton
                Joseph R. Royce
   Rejoinder and Summary

IV. ON KNOWING WHAT ONE KNOWS NOT. WHY
THERE OUGHT TO BE A PROBLEM OF HOW TO
JUSTIFY AMPLIATION 111
Herman Tennessen

V. THE CONCEPT OF COGNITION IN CONTEMPORARY
PSYCHOLOGY 177
Myron Moroz

   Comments: John W. Gyr
               Joseph R. Royce
   Rejoinder

VI. A THEORY OF DIRECT VISUAL PERCEPTION . . 215
James J. Gibson
   Comments: Wolfgang Metzger
               T. E. Weckowicz
               John W. Gyr
               Joseph R. Royce
   Rejoinder

VII. THE PHENOMENAL-PERCEPTUAL FIELD AS A CENTRAL STEERING MECHANISM 241
Wolfgang Metzger

Comments: T. E. Weckowicz
William W. Rozeboom
Rejoinder

VIII. PERCEPTION AS REAFFERENCE AND RELATED ISSUES IN COGNITION AND EPISTEMOLOGY . 267
John W. Gyr

Comment: Karl Pribram
Rejoinder

IX. INDUCTIVE KNOWING 285
Kenneth R. Hammond

Comments: William W. Rozeboom
Rudolf Groner
Rejoinder

X. CUE UTILIZATION AND MEMORY STRUCTURE IN LOGICAL THINKING 347
Rudolf Groner

XI. MEMORY ORGANIZATION AND QUESTION ANSWERING 363
Kellogg V. Wilson

Comment: William W. Rozeboom
Rejoinder

XII. FREUDIAN DRIVE THEORY AND EPISTEMOLOGY 413
F. Xavier Plaus

Comment: Joseph R. Royce

XIII. DEPERSONALIZATION-DEREALIZATION SYNDROME AND PERCEPTION: A CONTRIBUTION OF PSYCHOPATHOLOGY TO EPISTEMOLOGY . . 429
T. E. Weckowicz

Comment: Joseph R. Royce

XIV. NEUROLOGICAL NOTES ON KNOWING . . . 449
Karl H. Pribram

    Comments: Joseph R. Royce
                  Kellogg V. Wilson
                  William W. Rozeboom
    Rejoinder

Author Index 481

Subject Index 489

I

INTRODUCTION

Joseph R. Royce

The Center for Advanced Study in Theoretical Psychology

This is the second of a projected series of Center sponsored conferences on theoretical psychology. The topic is *knowing*, particularly as seen by psychologists, but with regard for relevant philosophic issues. Why this topic? Partly because it is timely in terms of the direction late 20th century psychology is taking, and partly because it has emerged as a common theme among the Center Staff. All of us had been engaged in conceptual efforts on one facet or another of this topic for many years prior to the conference. Thus, we found it surprisingly easy to converge on a theme. We did not know about this commonality of interest, however, until the issue of major common interests was raised. It also became apparent that this would be a continuing Center theme. It is our expectation, therefore, that we will return to this topic at subsequent Center conferences, for intellectual exchange on this topic comes up repeatedly during our Center seminars, and our interest in this problem is likely to increase in the years ahead.

The First Banff Conference, dealing with the theme of unification in psychology, was held in 1965. Since that date, and especially since we officially started operating in 1967, the Center Group has been concerned about its modus operandi. One of the procedures we have evolved is our Distinguished Visiting Scholars Program. The basic idea behind this scheme is to invite world-wide leaders in theoretical-philosophical psychology to visit the Center for an extended period (from a few weeks to several months, subject to the time the scholar can spare) for the purpose of mutual exchange of ideas. We feel that a relatively extended period of residence is necessary for in-depth analysis and authentic engagement. The scheme implies thorough study of the visitor's work on the part of the Center Staff and Fellows prior to the proposed visit and a "no-holds-barred" involvement during the seminar meetings to be conducted while the visiting scholar is in residence. (We presume it is obvious that such ground rules are in the name of advancing the discipline of psychology rather than to inflict scars on our most highly respected colleagues.)

Our modus operandi involves focusing our attention on one or two themes for the entire year. We invite scholars whose work is on the forefront of an Annual Theme. The Visiting Scholars provide the substantive material (papers and books presently in print plus work in progress) for subsequent analysis and synthesis. The local Center Staff, whose participation is common to the several visitors during the year, provide critical feedback and interactions during the residence period. It is anticipated that they will also provide written material by the end of the year, either of an original substantive nature, or/and of an analytic-synthesizing nature (i.e., based on or stimulated by the material presented during the year).

The year-long activities of the Distinguished Visiting Scholars Program are subsequently coordinated with the Banff Conference Program. In fact, it would be more accurate to say that the Annual Theme and the Distinguished Visiting Scholars Program culminate in a conference, for the Distinguished Scholars are invited to return to the Center as active participants at the appropriate Banff Conference. Thus, it is anticipated that a given conference will be attended by those Distinguished Visiting Scholars who visited the Center during the previous two or three years, plus two or three additional invited participants (e.g., from among the Center Fellows and Research Associates), in addition to the Center Staff. The intent of all this is to provide an advance in our conceptual understanding of the issue in question, and to distribute this new awareness in the form of a collaborative book.

The Conference convened for four working days over the five-day period May 5–9, 1969 at the Banff School of Fine Arts, a center in the Canadian Rockies. We followed essentially the same format as the First Conference (see Royce, 1970)—that is, we pre-distributed the invited papers, and we held "seminars-in-the-round," and "auditors' hours." The only significant departure from the first conference occurred in scheduling. For the present conference we decided to meet from noon on Monday until noon on Friday, with a free afternoon on Wednesday. This procedure meant there were usually no more than two seminar sessions on a given day, and it also allowed holiday seekers the opportunity to take advantage of the week-end at either end of the conference proceedings. This procedure was well received by both the invited participants and the 75 or so auditors.

The major participants included Distinguished Visiting Scholars James

J. Gibson, Cornell University, Kenneth Hammond, University of Colorado, Wolfgang Metzger, University of Münster, and Karl Pribram, Stanford University; Center Fellows Rudolf Groner, Canada Council Fellow from the University of Berne, Switzerland, John W. Gyr, Killam Fellow from the University of Michigan, and Center Fellows Myron Moroz (Ph. D. Oregon) and F. X. Plaus (Ph. D. Windsor); and Center Staff Joseph R. Royce, William W. Rozeboom, H. Tennessen, T. Weckowicz, and Kellogg V. Wilson.

The thirteen papers can be roughly grouped under five headings according to content. The first group, by Quine, Rozeboom, Tennessen, and Moroz, is philosophically oriented. In all four cases an attempt is made to provide a conceptual analysis of a problem of wide scope—theory of knowledge for Quine, Rozeboom, and Tennessen—and the conceptual implications of the term cognition for Moroz. Quine's paper[1] sets the stage for this volume in that the author develops the theme that the future of epistemology will come from advances in psychology. On what grounds does one of the world's leading philosophers make such a claim? On the same grounds on which this volume is predicated—empirical knowledge of how we actually construct reality at least has the virtue of "telling it like it is" rather than being just another (possibly fictitious) rational reconstruction. It should be noted that such a claim does not constitute a denial of the relevance of logical and linguistic analysis—such endeavors remain in the domain of philosophy—it simply points to the relevance of a naturalistic or descriptive exposition of the underlying cognitive processes. Although this paper was not prepared explicitly for the conference, it was presented (in May 1970) at a Center Seminar-in-the-Round as part of our Distinguished Visiting Scholar Program. Rozeboom's focus is on a classic epistemology which has been referred to as "justified true belief." Although this position has received considerable elaboration in contemporary philosophic literature, such efforts have not been concerned with the relevant psychological issues. Thus, while the typical psychologist may find less substantive psychology than he would like in Professor Rozeboom's paper, he will resonate to and profit by the psychological orientation which permeates the exposition of philosophic issues.

Professor Tennessen is concerned with "the problem of induction." Psychologists, diligently working in laboratories, clinics, and the field, will be inclined to smile benignly and non-profoundly exclaim "what problem?", and swiftly move on to the next set of data. This is acceptable behavior for the psychologist and other empiricists qua science, but such a fundamental epistemological question cannot be ignored by the professional philosopher. The crucial issue has to do with justifying how we can know what we do not at a given time already know. After having examined a representative sample of contemporary attempts to prove or show that there is or cannot be any such problem—"the problem of induction is a pseudo-problem"—he concludes that all the attempts have failed most miserably. He finally points to the fundamental, methodological as well as psychological, importance of continuing to regard justification of induction (or ampliation) a *genuine* problem.

Dr. Moroz' paper is most timely, for it is becoming quite clear that the next decade or two will see a burgeoning of "cognitive" psychology. Whereas "cognitive" orientations have been relatively rare in the past,[2] there are indications that traditional *S-R* models will be relatively rare in the future. There is little to be gained by arguing with history, but there is a great deal to be gained by understanding it. It would appear that the earlier (say in the thirties and forties) *S-R* orientation was appropriate for psychology, but that the discipline is now ready to tackle the more complex issues implicit in cognition. In any event, cognition is here, and it is probably here to stay. It behooves us, therefore, to do what we can to clear up what we mean by cognitive psychology. Dr. Moroz' analysis indicates that we mean many things, and he provides a conceptual taxonomy for dealing with these several meanings. In spite of this multiplicity he comes up with two conclusions which are particularly germane to the goals of this conference. One is that we cannot equate the term cognitive with knowing, and the other is the internal-representational aspect of cognition as its most distinctive characteristic. Thus, while those psychologists who have *equated* cognition with *knowledge* have been, at best, philosophically naive, it is also clear that cognition is the place to look for whatever nuggets psychology may have in our efforts to understand the nature of knowledge.

In the next section we see this kind of concern in action, for all three authors, Gibson, Metzger, and Gyr, are concerned with how perceiving occurs, as well as the relationships between perception and knowledge. Gibson elaborates a theory of perception which involves the pick up of ecological invariants via sensory input channels. He argues that these ecological invariants are structured and constitute, therefore, information about the external world. To the extent this can occur he thereby offers a theory which is consistent with naive or direct realism. The most obvious objection to this is the mediating, representation, constructionist aspect of the cognitive processes. Professor Gibson, however, wants to maintain a clearer separation between perception per se and conception per se.

The constructionist issue came up repeatedly throughout the conference, and is one which will require considerable theoretical and empirical elaboration before it can be adequately resolved.

Professors Metzger and Gyr countered with viable alternatives and/or extensions, with Professor Metzger focusing more on the phenomenological end of the continuum, and Dr. Gyr elaborating on the importance of motor output. Professor Metzger, not surprisingly, espouses a "critical realist" epistemology in the tradition of such Gestalt notions as an isomorphism between the phenomenal and the corresponding brain field. He goes beyond classic Gestalt psychology, however, in several ways, one of them being the introduction of feedback loops which allow for constant interplay between phenomenal field forces and the underlying brain physiology—hence, the idea of a phenomenal-central steering mechanism. Dr. Gyr comes up with similar cybernetic loops at the motor output end. He then brings in the importance of afferent inputs which are consequences of these motor outputs. Such efferent-reafferent loops are seen as crucial to knowing because they provide environmental feedback. In particular, they provide external confirmation or disconfirmation of internally represented constructs.

Hammond provides us with a link between the perceptual and the conceptual ends of the cognitive continuum, for he starts with the lens model of Brunswik, extends it to two-person situations, introduces a variety of problem solving tasks, and ends with a quantitative (an adaptation of multiple R), probabilistic account of complex cognitive systems.

The next two papers go one step further along the human information processing continuum, relating the input to the organization of memory representation and retrieval processes. Dr. Groner is concerned with the cognitive processing and storing of inputs possessing varying degrees of semantic-logical redundancy. He postulates a vicarious pattern of information-utilization heuristics (determined by the redundancy of the input-sequence) and hypothesizes the corresponding storage schemes. The models (like those of Wilson) are formulated from an automata perspective allowing for computer simulation of their implications and predictions. Dr. Wilson is particularly concerned with the memory system which accounts for question answering. He rejects a hierarchical list structure and the multi-dimensional matrix approach in favor of Quillian's automata model. He argues that the power of the latter model is that it accommodates multiple entry points (for retrieval) and at the same time avoids non-existent entries (wrong answer to a question).

On the surface the next two papers do not appear to be relevant to epistemology. However, the authors have presented cogent arguments to show why their approaches cannot be ignored if the full range of reality is to be reviewed. Plaus, for example, builds his case around the differences in primary process thinking and secondary process thinking. The former is more unconscious and id oriented and manifests itself in analogical, nondiscursive, and symbolic forms (e.g., dreams). The latter is more conscious and superego oriented and manifests itself in more rational, propositional form (e.g., logical sentences). Weckowicz's paper is concerned with the relationships between psychopathology, perceptual processes, and knowing. I found this to be a particularly rewarding paper, not only because of the enlightenment we receive on the nature of the depersonalization-derealization syndrome, but also because the paper is an example par excellence of what we are trying to accomplish at the Center and at these conferences. Our concerns are with conceptual foundations, with one eye on theory per se, and the other on relevant philosophic issues, without losing sight of the fact that we are first and foremost psychologists, and are, therefore, trying to advance our understanding of the nature of man and his behavior. Professor Weckowicz does all this in his paper, and what's more he does it in the epistemologically unlikely realm of psychopathology. For what we get in this paper is an eminently sensible theory of depersonalization and an informative elaboration of relevant epistemic and philosophic issues.

The last paper is by Karl Pribram. It is the only conference paper which deals with the biology of knowing—a task even more remote from the philosophic issues than psychology. It is a difficult, and perhaps even a premature, task. The reader may, therefore, be somewhat surprised by how much hard fact can be brought to bear on this problem. He may also be surprised by the psychological and epistemological insights which emerge from this particular concatenation of neurologizing about knowing.

Although the range of these thirteen papers is considerable, they do not cover the full spectrum of epistemic-cognitive issues. Nor were they meant to. Our approach was to identify scholars who had something to say about the topic and then let them say it. Coverage of the complete spectrum would not have been possible in a single conference. It is likely we will have another meeting a few years hence, either on the same or closely related theme. If we do, we shall have to provide more complete coverage of other cognitive processes on the one hand (e.g., introspection, imagery, intuition, symbolizing), and other epistemic approaches on the other hand (e.g., humanistic, existential, metaphoric, etc.).

INTRODUCTION 7

As Conference Chairman I particularly wish to acknowledge the effort put forth by F. X. Plaus, at that time part-time Administrative Officer of the Center, who served as Conference Manager. Prior to and during the conference we were assisted by Mrs. Leola Roth, the Center Secretary, who provided general administrative and secretarial help, and later coordinated the final collation of manuscript material for this volume. We are also indebted to Mr. Leendert Mos, a Center Research Assistant, for preparation of the index, Mr. Paul DeGroot, Psychology Department Technician, who was responsible for the high fidelity recording of all the sessions, as well as the videotapes of over half the sessions, and to Mr. D. E. Becker, Assistant Director of the Banff School, who took charge of local arrangements.

We are also grateful to Michael Martin, Center Fellow, 1969–70, and Associate Professor of Philosophy, Boston University, for critical review of the paper by W. W. Rozeboom, and to W. A. Blanchard, Associate Professor, Department of Psychology, University of Alberta; J. O. Fritz, Professor, Department of Curriculum and Instruction, Faculty of Education, University of Calgary; John D. Peyton, Center Postdoctoral Fellow; Dirk Schaeffer, Assistant Professor, Department of Psychology, University of Alberta; and W. A. S. Smith, President, University of Lethbridge, each of whom chaired a seminar-in-the-round.

The conference was generously supported by two grants—one from NATO, and one from the University of Alberta. The NATO grant was of particular value in allowing us to bring several participants from Europe. These included one of the major participants, Dr. W. Metzger, University of Münster, Münster, West Germany; Dr. K. B. Madsen, Royal Danish School of Educational Studies, Copenhagen, Denmark; Dr. Manfred Wettler, University of Berne, Switzerland, and Dr. Thomas J. Berk, Associate Director, Institute for Child Therapy of the City of Amsterdam, Holland. And the University fund made it possible for us to establish 25 stipends to cover living expenses so that worthy University of Alberta graduate students could attend the conference as auditors.

REFERENCES

George, F. H., *Cognition*. London: Methuen & Co. ltd., 1962.
Moore, T. V., *Cognitive Psychology*. Philadelphia: J. B. Lippincott, 1939.
Neisser, Ulric., *Cognitive Psychology*. New York: Appleton-Century-Crofts, 1967.

NOTES

1. Reprinted from W. V. O. Quine, *Ontological Relativity and Other Essays*, Columbia University Press, N. Y., 1969, with permission of the author and the publisher.
2. While there were books on thinking and other higher mental processes, the *only* book-length effort with a cognitive perspective on a broad segment of psychology published prior to the recent books by George (1962) and Neisser (1967) is the one by T. V. Moore (1939).

II

EPISTEMOLOGY NATURALIZED

Willard V. Quine

Harvard University

Epistemology is concerned with the foundations of science. Conceived thus broadly, epistemology includes the study of the foundations of mathematics as one of its departments. Specialists at the turn of the century thought that their efforts in this particular department were achieving notable success: mathematics seemed to reduce altogether to logic. In a more recent perspective this reduction is seen to be better describable as a reduction to logic and set theory. This correction is a disappointment epistemologically, since the firmness and obviousness that we associate with logic cannot be claimed for set theory. But still the success achieved in the foundations of mathematics remains exemplary by comparative standards, and we can illuminate the rest of epistemology somewhat by drawing parallels to this department.

Studies in the foundations of mathematics divide symmetrically into two sorts, conceptual and doctrinal. The conceptual studies are concerned with meaning, the doctrinal with truth. The conceptual studies are concerned with clarifying concepts by defining them, some in terms of others. The doctrinal studies are concerned with establishing laws by proving them, some on the basis of others. Ideally the obscurer concepts would be defined in terms of the clearer ones so as to maximize clarity, and the less obvious laws would be proved from the more obvious ones so as to maximize certainty. Ideally the definitions would generate all the concepts from clear and distinct ideas, and the proofs would generate all the theorems from self-evident truths.

The two ideals are linked. For, if you define all the concepts by use of some favored subset of them, you thereby show how to translate all theorems into these favored terms. The clearer these terms are, the likelier it is that the truths couched in them will be obviously true, or derivable from obvious truths. If in particular the concepts of mathematics were all reducible to the clear terms of logic, then all the truths of mathematics would go over into truths of logic; and surely the truths of logic are all obvious or at least potentially obvious, i.e., derivable from obvious truths by individually obvious steps.

This particular outcome is in fact denied us, however, since mathematics reduces only to set theory and not to logic proper. Such reduction still enhances clarity, but only because of the interrelations that emerge and not because the end terms of the analysis are clearer than others. As for the end truths, the axioms of set theory, these have less obviousness and certainty to recommend them than do most of the mathematical theorems that we would derive from them. Moreover, we know from Gödel's work that no consistent axiom system can cover mathematics even when we renounce self-evidence. Reduction in the foundations of mathematics remains mathematically and philosophically fascinating, but it does not do what the epistemologist would like of it: it does not reveal the ground of mathematical knowledge, it does not show how mathematical certainty is possible.

Still there remains a helpful thought, regarding epistemology generally, in that duality of structure which was especially conspicuous in the foundations of mathematics. I refer to the bifurcation into a theory of concepts, or meaning, and a theory of doctrine, or truth; for this applies to the epistemology of natural knowledge no less than to the foundations of mathematics. The parallel is as follows. Just as mathematics is to be reduced to logic, or logic and set theory, so natural knowledge is to be based somehow on sense experience. This means explaining the notion of body in sensory terms; here is the conceptual side. And it means justifying our knowledge of truths of nature in sensory terms; here is the doctrinal side of the bifurcation.

Hume pondered the epistemology of natural knowledge on both sides of the bifurcation, the conceptual and the doctrinal. His handling of the conceptual side of the problem, the explanation of body in sensory terms, was bold and simple: he identified bodies outright with the sense impressions. If common sense distinguishes between the material apple and our sense impressions of it on the ground that the apple is one and enduring while the impressions are many and fleeting, then, Hume held, so much the worse for common sense; the notion of its being the same apple on one occasion and another is a vulgar confusion.

Nearly a century after Hume's *Treatise*, the same view of bodies was espoused by the early American philosopher Alexander Bryan Johnson.[1] "The word iron names an associated sight and feel," Johnson wrote.

What then of the doctrinal side, the justification of our knowledge of truths about nature? Here, Hume despaired. By his identification of bodies with impressions he did succeed in construing some singular statements about bodies as indubitable truths, yes; as truths about impressions, directly known. But general statements, also singular statements about the future, gained no increment of certainty by being construed as about impressions.

On the doctrinal side, I do not see that we are farther along today than where Hume left us. The Humean predicament is the human predicament. But on the conceptual side there has been progress. There the crucial step forward was made already before Alexander Bryan Johnson's day, although Johnson did not emulate it. It was made by Bentham in his theory of fictions. Bentham's step was the recognition of contextual definition, or what he called paraphrasis. He recognized that to explain a term we do not need to specify an object for it to refer to, nor even specify a synonymous word or phrase; we need only show, by whatever means, how to translate all the whole sentences in which the term is to be used. Hume's and Johnson's desperate measure of identifying bodies with impressions ceased to be the only conceivable way of making sense of talk of bodies, even granted that impressions were the only reality. One could undertake to explain talk of bodies in terms of talk of impressions by translating one's whole sentences about bodies into whole sentences about impressions, without equating the bodies themselves to anything at all.

This idea of contextual definition, or recognition of the sentence as the primary vehicle of meaning, was indispensable to the ensuing developments in the foundations of mathematics. It was explicit in Frege, and it attained its full flower in Russell's doctrine of singular descriptions as incomplete symbols.

Contextual definition was one of two resorts that could be expected to have a liberating effect upon the conceptual side of the epistemology of natural knowledge. The other is resort to the resources of set theory as auxiliary concepts. The epistemologist who is willing to eke out his austere ontology of sense impressions with these set-theoretic auxiliaries is suddenly rich: he has not just his impressions to play with, but sets of them, and sets of sets, and so on up. Constructions in the foundations of mathematics have shown that such set-theoretic aids are a powerful addition; after all, the entire glossary of concepts of classical mathematics is constructible from them. Thus equipped, our epistemologist may not need either to identify bodies with impressions or to settle for contextual definition; he may hope to find in some subtle construction of sets upon sets of sense impressions a category of objects enjoying just the formal properties that he wants for bodies.

The two resorts are very unequal in epistemological status. Contextual definition is unassailable. Sentences that have been given meaning as wholes are undeniably meaningful, and the use they make of their component terms is therefore meaningful, regardless of whether any translations are offered for those terms in isolation. Surely Hume and A. B. Johnson would have used contextual definition with pleasure if they had thought of it. Recourse to sets, on the other hand, is a drastic ontological move, a retreat from the austere ontology of impressions. There are philosophers who would rather settle for bodies outright than accept all these sets, which amount, after all, to the whole abstract ontology of mathematics.

This issue has not always been clear, however, owing to deceptive hints of continuity between elementary logic and set theory. This is why mathematics was once believed to reduce to logic, that is, to an innocent and unquestionable logic, and to inherit these qualities. And this is probably why Russell was content to resort to sets as well as to contextual definition when in *Our Knowledge of the External World* and elsewhere he addressed himself to the epistemology of natural knowledge, on its conceptual side.

To account for the external world as a logical construct of sense data— such, in Russell's terms, was the program. It was Carnap, in his *Der logische Aufbau der Welt* of 1928, who came nearest to executing it.

This was the conceptual side of epistemology; what of the doctrinal? There the Humean predicament remained unaltered. Carnap's constructions, if carried successfully to completion, would have enabled us to translate all sentences about the world into terms of sense data, or observation, plus logic and set theory. But the mere fact that a sentence is *couched* in terms of observation, logic, and set theory does not mean that it can be *proved* from observation sentences by logic and set theory. The most modest of generalizations about observable traits will cover more cases than its utterer can have had occasion actually to observe. The hopelessness of grounding natural science upon immediate experience in a firmly logical way was acknowledged. The Cartesian quest for certainty had been the remote motivation of epistemology, both on its conceptual and its doctrinal side; but that quest was seen as a lost cause. To endow the truths of nature with the full authority of immediate experience was as forlorn a hope as hoping to endow the truths of mathematics with the potential obviousness of elementary logic.

What then could have motivated Carnap's heroic efforts on the conceptual side of epistemology, when hope of certainty on the doctrinal side was abandoned? There were two good reasons still. One was that such constructions could be expected to elicit and clarify the sensory evidence for science, even if the inferential steps between sensory evidence and scientific doctrine must fall short of certainty. The other reason was that such constructions would deepen our understanding of our discourse about the world, even apart from questions of evidence; it would make all cognitive discourse as clear as observation terms and logic and, I must regretfully add, set theory.

It was sad for epistemologists, Hume and others, to have to acquiesce in the impossibility of strictly deriving the science of the external world from sensory evidence. Two cardinal tenets of empiricism remained unassailable, however, and so remain to this day. One is that whatever evidence there *is* for science *is* sensory evidence. The other, to which I shall recur, is that all inculcation of meanings of words must rest ultimately on sensory evidence. Hence the continuing attractiveness of the idea of a *logischer Aufbau* in which the sensory content of discourse would stand forth explicitly.

If Carnap had successfully carried such a construction through, how could he have told whether it was the right one? The question would have had no point. He was seeking what he called a *rational reconstruction.* Any construction of physicalistic discourse in terms of sense experience, logic, and set theory would have been seen as satisfactory if it made the physicalistic discourse come out right. If there is one way there are many, but any would be a great achievement.

But why all this creative reconstruction, all this make-believe? The stimulation of his sensory receptors is all the evidence anybody has had to go on, ultimately, in arriving at his picture of the world. Why not just see how this construction really proceeds? Why not settle for psychology? Such a surrender of the epistemological burden to psychology is a move that was disallowed in earlier times as circular reasoning. If the epistemologist's goal is validation of the grounds of empirical science, he defeats his purpose by using psychology or other empirical science in the validation. However, such scruples against circularity have little point once we have stopped dreaming of deducing science from observations. If we are out simply to understand the link between observation and science, we are well advised to use any available information, including that provided by the very science whose link with observation we are seeking to understand.

But there remains a different reason, unconnected with fears of circularity, for still favoring creative reconstruction. We should like to be able to *translate* science into logic and observation terms and set theory. This would be a great epistemological achievement, for it would show all the rest of the concepts of science to be theoretically superfluous. It would legitimize them—to whatever degree the concepts of set theory, logic, and observation are themselves legitimate—by showing that everything done with the one apparatus could in principle be done with the other. If psychology itself could deliver a truly translational reduction of this kind, we should welcome it; but certainly it cannot, for certainly we did not grow up learning definitions of physicalistic language in terms of a prior language of set theory, logic, and observation. Here, then, would be good reason for persisting in a rational reconstruction: we want to establish the essential innocence of physical concepts, by showing them to be theoretically dispensable.

The fact is, though, that the construction which Carnap outlined in *Der logische Aufbau der Welt* does not give translational reduction either. It would not even if the outline were filled in. The crucial point comes where Carnap is explaining how to assign sense qualities to positions in physical space and time. These assignments are to be made in such a way as to fulfill, as well as possible, certain desiderata which he states, and with growth of experience the assignments are to be revised to suit. This plan, however illuminating, does not offer any key to *translating* the sentences of science into terms of observation, logic, and set theory.

We must despair of any such reduction. Carnap had despaired of it by 1936, when, in "Testability and meaning,"[2] he introduced so-called *reduction forms* of a type weaker than definition. Definitions had shown always how to translate sentences into equivalent sentences. Contextual definition of a term showed how to translate sentences containing the term into equivalent sentences lacking the term. Reduction forms of Carnap's liberalized kind, on the other hand, do not in general give equivalences; they give implications. They explain a new term, if only partially, by specifying some sentences which are implied by sentences containing the term, and other sentences which imply sentences containing the term.

It is tempting to suppose that the countenancing of reduction in this liberal sense is just one further step of liberalization comparable to the earlier one, taken by Bentham, of countenancing contextual definition. The former and sterner kind of rational reconstruction might have been represented as a fictitious history in which we imagined our ancestors introducing the terms of physicalistic discourse on a phenomenalistic and set-theoretic basis by a succession of contextual definitions. The new and more liberal kind of rational reconstruction is a fictitious history in which we imagine our ancestors introducing those terms by a succession rather of reduction forms of the weaker sort.

This, however, is a wrong comparison. The fact is rather that the former and sterner kind of rational reconstruction, where definition reigned, embodied no fictitious history at all. It was nothing more nor less than a set of directions—or would have been, if successful—for accomplishing everything in terms of phenomena and set theory that we now accomplish in terms of bodies. It would have been a true reduction by translation, a legitimation by elimination. *Definire est eliminare.* Rational reconstruction by Carnap's later and looser reduction forms does none of this.

To relax the demand for definition, and settle for a kind of reduction that does not eliminate, is to renounce the last remaining advantage that we supposed rational reconstruction to have over straight psychology; namely, the advantage of translational reduction. If all we hope for is a reconstruction that links science to experience in explicit ways short of translation, then it would seem more sensible to settle for psychology. Better to discover how science is in fact developed and learned than to fabricate a fictitious structure to a similar effect.

The empiricist made one major concession when he despaired of deducing the truths of nature from sensory evidence. In despairing now even of translating those truths into terms of observation and logico-mathematical auxiliaries, he makes another major concession. For suppose we hold, with the old empiricist Peirce, that the very meaning of a statement consists in the difference its truth would make to possible experience. Might we not formulate, in a chapter-length sentence in observational language, all the difference that the truth of a given statement might make to experience, and might we not then take all this as the translation? Even if the difference that the truth of the statement would make to experience ramifies indefinitely, we might still hope to embrace it all in the logical implications of our chapter-length formulation, just as we can axiomatize an infinity of theorems. In giving up hope of such translation, then, the empiricist is conceding that the empirical meanings of typical statements about the external world are inaccessible and ineffable.

How is this inaccessibility to be explained? Simply on the ground that the experiential implications of a typical statement about bodies are too complex for finite axiomatization, however lengthy? No; I have a different explanation. It is that the typical statement about bodies has no fund of experiential implications it can call its own. A substantial mass of theory, taken together, will commonly have experiential implications; this is how we make verifiable predictions. We may not be able to explain why we arrive at theories which make successful predictions, but we do arrive at such theories.

Sometimes also an experience implied by a theory fails to come off; and then, ideally, we declare the theory false. But the failure falsifies only a block of theory as a whole, a conjunction of many statements. The failure shows that one or more of those statements is false, but it does not show which. The predicted experiences, true and false, are not implied by any one of the component statements of the theory rather than another. The component statements simply do not have empirical meanings, by Peirce's standard; but a sufficiently inclusive portion of theory does. If we can aspire to a sort of *logischer Aufbau der Welt* at all, it must be to one in which the texts slated for translation into observational and logico-mathematical terms are mostly broad theories taken as wholes, rather than just terms or short sentences. The translation of a theory would be a ponderous axiomatization of all the experiential difference that the truth of the theory would make. It would be a queer translation, for it would translate the whole but none of the parts. We might better speak in such a case not of translation but simply of observational evidence for theories; and we may, following Peirce, still fairly call this the empirical meaning of the theories.

These considerations raise a philosophical question even about ordinary unphilosophical translation, such as from English into Arunta or Chinese. For, if the English sentences of a theory have their meaning only together as a body, then we can justify their translation into Arunta only together as a body. There will be no justification for pairing off the component English sentences with component Arunta sentences, except as these correlations make the translation of the theory as a whole come out right. Any translations of the English sentences into Arunta sentences will be as correct as any other, so long as the net empirical implications of the theory as a whole are preserved in translation. But it is to be expected that many different ways of translating the component sentences, essentially different individually, would deliver the same empirical implications for the theory as a whole; deviations in the translation of one component sentence could be compensated for in the translation of another component sentence. Insofar, there can be no ground for saying which of two glaringly unlike translations of individual sentences is right.[3]

For an uncritical mentalist, no such indeterminacy threatens. Every term and every sentence is a label attached to an idea, simple or complex, which is stored in the mind. When on the other hand we take a verification theory of meaning seriously, the indeterminacy would appear to be inescapable. The Vienna Circle espoused a verification theory of meaning but did not take it seriously enough. If we recognize with Peirce that the meaning of a sentence turns purely on what would count as evidence for its truth, and if we recognize with Duhem that theoretical sentences have their evidence not as single sentences but only as larger blocks of theory, then the indeterminacy of translation of theoretical sentences is the natural conclusion. And most sentences, apart from observation sentences, are theoretical. This conclusion, conversely, once it is embraced, seals the fate of any general notion of propositional meaning or, for that matter, state of affairs.

Should the unwelcomeness of the conclusion persuade us to abandon the verification theory of meaning? Certainly not. The sort of meaning that is basic to translation, and to the learning of one's own language, is necessarily empirical meaning and nothing more. A child learns his first words and sentences by hearing and using them in the presence of appropriate stimuli. These must be external stimuli, for they must act both on the child and on the speaker from whom he is learning.[4] Language is socially inculcated and controlled; the inculcation and control turn strictly on the keying of sentences to shared stimulation. Internal factors may vary *ad libitum* without prejudice to communication as long as the keying of language to external stimuli is undisturbed. Surely one has no choice but to be an empiricist so far as one's theory of linguistic meaning is concerned.

What I have said of infant learning applies equally to the linguist's learning of a new language in the field. If the linguist does not lean on related languages for which there are previously accepted translation practices, then obviously he has no data but the concomitances of native utterance and observable stimulus situation. No wonder there is indeterminacy of translation—for of course only a small fraction of our utterances report concurrent external stimulation. Granted, the linguist will end up with unequivocal translations of everything; but only by making many arbitrary choices—arbitrary even though unconscious—along the way. Arbitrary? By this I mean that different choices could still have made everything come out right that is susceptible in principle to any kind of check.

Let me link up, in a different order, some of the points I have made. The crucial consideration behind my argument for the indeterminacy of translation was that a statement about the world does not always or usually have a separable fund of empirical consequences that it can call its own. That consideration served also to account for the impossibility of an epistemological reduction of the sort where every sentence is equated to a sentence in observational and logico-mathematical terms. And the impossibility of that sort of epistemological reduction dissipated the last advantage that rational reconstruction seemed to have over psychology.

Philosophers have rightly despaired of translating everything into observational and logico-mathematical terms. They have despaired of this even when they have not recognized, as the reason for this irreducibility, that the statements largely do not have their private bundles of empirical consequences. And some philosophers have seen in this irreducibility the bankruptcy of epistemology. Carnap and the other logical positivists of the Vienna Circle had already pressed the term "metaphysics" into pejorative use, as connoting meaninglessness; and the term "epistemology" was next.

Wittgenstein and his followers, mainly at Oxford, found a residual philosophical vocation in therapy: in curing philosophers of the delusion that there were epistemological problems.

But I think that at this point it may be more useful to say rather that epistemology still goes on, though in a new setting and a clarified status. Epistemology, or something like it, simply falls into place as a chapter of psychology and hence of natural science. It studies a natural phenomenon, viz., a physical human subject. This human subject is accorded a certain experimentally controlled input—certain patterns of irradiation in assorted frequencies, for instance—and in the fullness of time the subject delivers as output a description of the three-dimensional external world and its history. The relation between the meager input and the torrential output is a relation that we are prompted to study for somewhat the same reasons that always prompted epistemology; namely, in order to see how evidence relates to theory, and in what ways one's theory of nature transcends any available evidence.

Such a study could still include, even, something like the old rational reconstruction, to whatever degree such reconstruction is practicable; for imaginative constructions can afford hints of actual psychological processes, in much the way that mechanical simulations can. But a conspicuous difference between old epistemology and the epistemological enterprise in this new psychological setting is that we can now make free use of empirical psychology.

The old epistemology aspired to contain, in a sense, natural science; it would construct it somehow from sense data. Epistemology in its new setting, conversely, is contained in natural science, as a chapter of psychology. But the old containment remains valid too, in its way. We are studying how the human subject of our study posits bodies and projects his physics from his data, and we appreciate that our position in the world is just like his. Our very epistemological enterprise, therefore, and the psychology wherein it is a component chapter, and the whole of natural science wherein psychology is a component book—all this is our own construction or projection from stimulations like those we were meting out to our epistemological subject. There is thus reciprocal containment, though containment in different senses: epistemology in natural science and natural science in epistemology.

This interplay is reminiscent again of the old threat of circularity, but it is all right now that we have stopped dreaming of deducing science from sense data. We are after an understanding of science as an institution or process in the world, and we do not intend that understanding to be any better than the science which is its object. This attitude is indeed one that Neurath was already urging in Vienna Circle days, with his parable of the mariner who has to rebuild his boat while staying afloat in it.

One effect of seeing epistemology in a psychological setting is that it resolves a stubborn old enigma of epistemological priority. Our retinas are irradiated in two dimensions, yet we see things as three-dimensional without conscious inference. Which is to count as observation—the unconscious two-dimensional reception or the conscious three-dimensional apprehension? In the old epistemological context the conscious form had priority, for we were out to justify our knowledge of the external world by rational reconstruction, and that demands awareness. Awareness ceased to be demanded when we gave up trying to justify our knowledge of the external world by rational reconstruction. What to count as observation now can be settled in terms of the stimulation of sensory receptors, let consciousness fall where it may.

The Gestalt psychologists' challenge to sensory atomism, which seemed so relevant to epistemology forty years ago, is likewise deactivated. Regardless of whether sensory atoms or Gestalten are what favor the forefront of our consciousness, it is simply the stimulations of our sensory receptors that are best looked upon as the input to our cognitive mechanism. Old paradoxes about unconscious data and inference, old problems about chains of inference that would have to be completed too quickly—these no longer matter.

In the old anti-psychologistic days the question of epistemological priority was moot. What is epistemologically prior to what? Are Gestalten prior to sensory atoms because they are noticed, or should we favor sensory atoms on some more subtle ground? Now that we are permitted to appeal to physical stimulation, the problem dissolves; *A* is epistemologically prior to *B* if *A* is causally nearer than *B* to the sensory receptors. Or, what is in some ways better, just talk explicitly in terms of causal proximity to sensory receptors and drop the talk of epistemological priority.

Around 1932 there was debate in the Vienna Circle over what to count as observation sentences, or *Protokollsätze*.[5] One position was that they had the form of reports of sense impressions. Another was that they were statements of an elementary sort about the external world, e.g., "A red cube is standing on the table." Another, Neurath's, was that they had the form of reports of relations between percipients and external things: "Otto now sees a red cube on the table." The worst of it was that there seemed to be no objective way of settling the matter: no way of making real sense of the question.

Let us now try to view the matter unreservedly in the context of the external world. Vaguely speaking, what we want of observation sentences is that they be the ones in closest causal proximity to the sensory receptors. But how is such proximity to be gauged? The idea may be rephrased this way: observation sentences are sentences which, as we learn language, are most strongly conditioned to concurrent sensory stimulation rather than to stored collateral information. Thus let us imagine a sentence queried for our verdict as to whether it is true or false; queried for our assent or dissent. Then the sentence is an observation sentence if our verdict depends only on the sensory stimulation present at the time.

But a verdict cannot depend on present stimulation to the exclusion of stored information. The very fact of our having learned the language evinces much storing of information, and of information without which we should be in no position to give verdicts on sentences however observational. Evidently then we must relax our definition of observation sentence to read thus: a sentence is an observation sentence if all verdicts on it depend on present sensory stimulation and on no stored information beyond what goes into understanding the sentence.

This formulation raises another problem: how are we to distinguish between information that goes into understanding a sentence and information that goes beyond? This is the problem of distinguishing between analytic truth, which issues from the mere meanings of words, and synthetic truth, which depends on more than meanings. Now I have long maintained that this distinction is illusory. There is one step toward such a distinction, however, which does make sense: a sentence that is true by mere meanings of words should be expected, at least if it is simple, to be subscribed to by all fluent speakers in the community. Perhaps the controversial notion of analyticity can be dispensed with, in our definition of observation sentence, in favor of this straightforward attribute of community-wide acceptance.

This attribute is of course no explication of analyticity. The community would agree that there have been black dogs, yet none who talk of analyticity would call this analytic. My rejection of the analyticity notion just means drawing no line between what goes into the mere understanding of the sentences of a language and what else the community sees eye-to-eye on. I doubt that an objective distinction can be made between meaning and such collateral information as is community-wide.

Turning back then to our task of defining observation sentences, we get this: an observation sentence is one on which all speakers of the language give the same verdict when given the same concurrent stimulation. To put the point negatively, an observation sentence is one that is not sensitive to differences in past experience within the speech community.

This formulation accords perfectly with the traditional role of the observation sentence as the court of appeal of scientific theories. For by our definition the observation sentences are the sentences on which all members of the community will agree under uniform stimulation. And what is the criterion of membership in the same community? Simply general fluency of dialogue. This criterion admits of degrees, and indeed we may usefully take the community more narrowly for some studies than for others. What count as observation sentences for a community of specialists would not always so count for a larger community.

There is generally no subjectivity in the phrasing of observation sentences, as we are now conceiving them; they will usually be about bodies. Since the distinguishing trait of an observation sentence is intersubjective agreement under agreeing stimulation, a corporeal subject matter is likelier than not.

The old tendency to associate observation sentences with a subjective sensory subject matter is rather an irony when we reflect that observation sentences are also meant to be the intersubjective tribunal of scientific hypotheses. The old tendency was due to the drive to base science on something firmer and prior in the subject's experience; but we dropped that project.

The dislodging of epistemology from its old status of first philosophy loosed a wave, we saw, of epistemological nihilism. This mood is reflected somewhat in the tendency of Polányi, Kuhn, and the late Russell Hanson to belittle the role of evidence and to accentuate cultural relativism. Hanson ventured even to discredit the idea of observation, arguing that so-called observations vary from observer to observer with the amount of knowledge that the observers bring with them. The veteran physicist looks at some apparatus and sees an x-ray tube. The neophyte, looking at the same place, observes rather "a glass and metal instrument replete with wires, reflectors, screws, lamps, and pushbuttons."[6] One man's observation is another man's closed book or flight of fancy. The notion of observation as the impartial and objective source of evidence for science is bankrupt. Now my answer to the x-ray example was already hinted a little while back: what counts as an observation sentence varies with the width of community considered. But we can also always get an absolute standard by taking in all speakers of the language, or most.[7] It is ironical that philosophers, finding the old epistemology untenable as a whole, should react by repudiating a part which has only now moved into clear focus.

Clarification of the notion of observation sentence is a good thing, for the notion is fundamental in two connections. These two correspond to the duality that I remarked upon early in this lecture: the duality between concept and doctrine, between knowing what a sentence means and knowing whether it is true. The observation sentence is basic to both enterprises. Its relation to doctrine, to our knowledge of what is true, is very much the traditional one: observation sentences are the repository of evidence for scientific hypotheses. Its relation to meaning is fundamental too, since observation sentences are the ones we are in a position to learn to understand first, both as children and as field linguists. For observation sentences are precisely the ones that we can correlate with observable circumstances of the occasion of utterance or assent, independently of variations in the past histories of individual informants. They afford the only entry to a language.

The observation sentence is the cornerstone of semantics. For it is, as we just saw, fundamental to the learning of meaning. Also, it is where meaning is firmest. Sentences higher up in theories have no empirical consequences they can call their own; they confront the tribunal of sensory evidence only in more or less inclusive aggregates. The observation sentence, situated at the sensory periphery of the body scientific, is the minimal verifiable aggregate; it has an empirical content all its own and wears it on its sleeve.

The predicament of the indeterminacy of translation has little bearing on observation sentences. The equating of an observation sentence of our language to an observation sentence of another language is mostly a matter of empirical generalization; it is a matter of identity between the range of stimulations that would prompt assent to the one sentence and the range of stimulations that would prompt assent to the other.[8]

It is no shock to the preconceptions of old Vienna to say that epistemology now becomes semantics. For epistemology remains centered as always on evidence, and meaning remains centered as always on verification; and evidence is verification. What is likelier to shock preconceptions is that meaning, once we get beyond observation sentences, ceases in general to have any clear applicability to single sentences; also that epistemology merges with psychology, as well as with linguistics.

This rubbing out of boundaries could contribute to progress, it seems to me, in philosophically interesting inquiries of a scientific nature. One possible area is perceptual norms. Consider, to begin with, the linguistic phenomenon of phonemes. We form the habit, in hearing the myriad variations of spoken sounds, of treating each as an approximation to one or another of a limited number of norms—around thirty altogether—constituting so to speak a spoken alphabet. All speech in our language can be treated in practice as sequences of just those thirty elements, thus rectifying small deviations. Now outside the realm of language also there is probably only a rather limited alphabet of perceptual norms altogether, toward which we tend unconsciously to rectify all perceptions. These, if experimentally identified, could be taken as epistemological building blocks, the working elements of experience. They might prove in part to be culturally variable, as phonemes are, and in part universal.

Again there is the area that the psychologist Donald T. Campbell calls evolutionary epistemology.[9] In this area there is work by Hüseyin Yilmaz, who shows how some structural traits of color perception could have been predicted from survival value.[10] And a more emphatically epistemological topic that evolution helps to clarify is induction, now that we are allowing epistemology the resources of natural science.[11] For induction is an extrapolation by resemblance, and resemblance is subjective. Our standards of resemblance are partly acquired; however, we had to have some innate standards of resemblance too, or we never could have begun to form habits and learn things. Natural selection, then, could explain why innate standards of resemblance have been according us and other animals better than random chances in anticipating the course of nature. For me this reflection already alleviates part of the discomfort that has been vaguely classified as the problem of induction.

NOTES

1. A. B. Johnson, *A Treatise on Language* (New York, 1836; Berkeley, 1947).
2. *Philosophy of Ssience*, **3** (1936), 419–471; **4** (1937), 1–40.
3. W. V. Quine, *Ontological Relativity and Other Essays* (New York: Columbia University Press, 1969), p. 2.
4. W. V. Quine, *Ontological Relativity and Other Essays* (New York: Columbia University Press, 1969), p. 28.
5. Carnap and Neurath in *Erkenntnis* 3 (1932), 204–228.
6. N. R. Hanson, "Observation and interpretation", in S. Morgenbesser, ed., *Phlosophy of Science Today* (New York: Basic Books, 1966).
7. This qualification allows for occasional deviants such as the insane or the blind. Alternatively, such cases might be excluded by adjusting the level of fluency of dialogue whereby we define sameness of language. (For prompting this note and influencing the development of this paper also in more substantial ways I am indebted to Burton Dreben.)
8. Cf. Quine, *Word and Object*, (New York: Wiley, 1960), pp. 31–46, 68.
9. D. T. Campbell, "Methodological suggestions from a comparative psychology of knowledge processes," *Inquiry* 2 (1959), 152–182.
10. Hüseyin Yilmaz, "On color vision and a new approach to general perception," in E. E. Bernard and M. R. Kare, eds., *Biological Prototypes and Synthetic Systems* (New York: Plenum, 1962); "Perceptual invariance and the psychophysical law," *Perception and Psychophysics* 2 (1967), 533–538.
11. W. V. Quine, *Ontological Relativity and Other Essays*, (New York: Columbia Univ. Press, 1969), Chapter 5.

III

PROBLEMS IN THE PSYCHO-PHILOSOPHY OF KNOWLEDGE

William W. Rozeboom

The Center for Advanced Study in Theoretical Psychology

I had originally intended to apologize for foisting still another hyphenated barbarism ("psycho-philosophy") upon a long-suffering English language, but have decided instead to summon my *chutzpa* and demand your gratitude for not offering acronymically to improve our POK marks. You will in any event get nowhere by protesting that there can be no licit coupling of psychology and philosophy under the blanket of "knowledge"; for a major objective of this paper is to restore these unnaturally separated disciplines to their rightful intimacy in this matter. My overarching intent is to take inventory of what regarding "knowledge" there is for us to feel uncertain about, to weave a tapestry of issues within which each item of epistemic lore—theory or datum, problem or possibility—has its natural locus in relation to the whole. And psychology and philosophy are respectively the warp and the woof whose intertwining makes this fabric a cohesive unity.

To be sure, you may not have thought to doubt the legitimacy of my titular hyphenation. You are aware of how impatiently contemporary research psychologists dismiss the more intricate problems of cognition as "philosophical stuff," but have perhaps attributed this to superficial simple-mindedness or a repressive intolerance for perplexity. What you may not know is that most philosophers have become equally disdainful of psychology's relevance to the theory of knowledge. Epistemology is a *normative* discipline, the argument goes, whereas psychology (scoff) is merely a descriptive science which can emass statistics from here to doomsday on how people in fact conduct their thinking without learning a thing about how they *should* think. To suppose that psychology makes contact with the philosophy of knowledge only through confusions of *ought* with *is*, however, is to pervert a small truth into a monsterous know-nothingism. For the benefit of philosophic prudes who blanch at the sin of "psychologizing," therefore, I want to point out by way of some epistemic facts of life that here, as elsewhere, immaculate conception is neither very practical nor very satisfying.

In the first place, the main ingredients of epistemology's subject matter—cognitive acts and their constituents—are psychological entities pure and simple, albeit abstract ones. To acknowledge this is no more to confound normative statements about these entities with descriptive ones than acknowledging developmental psychology to be an empirical science is to confuse the actual behavior of your children with the deportment you wish they would display. One pattern of behavior does not become less a psychological attribute than another merely through being the more praiseworthy of the two, and neither do the prescriptive/validational aspects of a theory of knowledge diminish the psychological nature of what this is a theory *about*. As I hope to illustrate below, there are probably few significant problems of epistemology where philosophical progress is not seriously impeded by our lack of technically detailed understanding of the psychological mechanisms involved.

Secondly, although *is* and *ought* can always be distinguished in reference to any specific instance of reasoning, this does not preclude the very real possibility that how one *should* reason in a given case can in turn be adjudicated only in terms of higher-level descriptive principles. It could be, for example, that the psychology and philosophy of knowledge are like two lines of a fugue, each running through the same tonal sequence but forever out of phase. Although the actual interplay between normative and descriptive issues here greatly exceeds the reach of this simple analogy, anyone who presumes that the two classes of questions can be cleanly separated in the large just can't have thought very deeply about the logic of justifying one's beliefs (cf. Rozeboom, 1967a).

Finally, even if there were no other bond between them, normative and descriptive theories of knowledge find common cause and mutual indispensibility in practical concerns for belief management. For whenever our *de facto* habits of thought are found significantly wanting by accepted standards of sound reason, bringing the former into congruence with the latter is a job wherein the psychological engineer seeks to realize the normative epistemologist's specifications. Admittedly, philosophers and psychologists have never to my knowledge officially joined forces to pursue such a practical objective, but the source of this separation does little credit to either party: Psychological science hasn't begun to learn enough about the detailed workings of cognitive mechanisms to spin off engineering enhancements of human rationality, while traditional philosophy of knowledge can lecture schoolboys on forms of the syllogism but has little if any guidance to offer in more advanced problems where mature intellects are genuinely in need of epistemic advice. Even so, it is of some importance to recognize that a body of literature and practica in advanced epistemic engineering does in fact exist, albeit not usually characterized in quite these terms. This is the material on *scientific methodology* developed by the various natural sciences and their dilletante city cousin, philosophy of science. When as psychologists we set out to study knowledge processes in others, we should not lose sight of the fact that we already have an extensive theory of knowledge embedded in the research customs of our discipline, and that when we seek to improve our research designs, our methods of statistical analysis, the operational solidity and inferential interpretability of our data, etc., we are working the frontiers of epistemology not with the armchair disinvolvement of an academician but with an existential engagement in its real-life consequences. For psychologists of knowledge, the *de facto* methodology of the natural sciences provides a body of empirical data incomparably more saturated with real cognitive issues than anything researched to date. And any philosopher who proclaims the irrelevance of descriptive to normative theories of knowledge without first investigating whether technical science may not extensively exploit epistemic practices which have scarcely been recognized, much less thoughtfully evaluated, by extant philosophy of knowledge is living in the closed world of an arrogant fantasy.

Lest it appear from the foregoing that I have some strange antipathy toward philosophical epistemology, let me add at once that my ensuing framework for the psycho-philosophy of knowledge lies considerably closer to its philosophic grain than to the standard axes of psychological inquiry. Fifty years of peripheralist emphasis (essential as this has been to psychology's maturation as a science) has regressed psychology's comprehension of mentalistic concepts to such a primitive blur that at present, the psychology of cognition has much more to learn from philosophy than can immediately be repaid by exchange information of equal value. But with a little sophistication and effort, a resurgent psychology of cognition could suck the philosophic lemon dry and take command of advanced research in areas traditionally thought by philosophers to be their private reserve. As one who feels a professional allegiance to both disciplines, I have no special desire for psychology to usurp philosophy's epistemological birthright (nor do I expect this in fact to occur); but the dogmas of one era often seem quaintly naive a generation or two later, and philosophers who smugly continue to posit an abyss between the philosophy and the psychology of knowledge are striking epistemic postures more appropriate to this Century's beginning than to its end.

THE FORMS OF KNOWLEDGE

Foremost among the problems pertaining to any topic t is the meta-problem of clarifying what sorts of things the concept of t is intended to subsume. In the case at hand, since "knowledge" is a technical term of neither psychology nor philosophy but is imposed upon us in childhood by our mother tongue, problems of knowledge are of linguistic necessity problems pertaining to whatever it is that ordinary language denotes by this concept. The first requisite for research in the psycho-philosophy of knowledge is consequently to make sure that we are at least modestly aware of this term's commonsense usage. (I hope this preliminary need is evident to you, for unhappily it does not seem to be all obvious to a great many psychologists who apply cognition terms to their technical research with never a qualm for what, if anything, the latter has to do with the phenomena commonsensically envisioned by these concepts.*[1]) Even were space to permit, a detailed analysis of ordinary-language cognition talk would be inappropriate here; such analysis is just another of the problems which my present task is to inventory, not to solve. Rather, I shall with totally inadequate argument evoke highlights of the "knowledge" concept's linguistic commitments and then show how these unfold into a complex array of thoroughly substantive questions far beyond the reach of any additional concern for linguistic usage.

To analyze the meaning of an ordinary-language concept (i.e. one which we acquire not through stipulative definition but from immersion in our linguistic community's use of it), we must first of all identify paradigmatic contexts of its natural occurrence and then tease out what states of affairs determine the intuitive correctness of this usage. Since cognition terms in general, and especially the cognates of "knowledge," occur most fundamentally as verbs, we shall here examine just the logic of "knowing" and leave as an open question whether this word's nominal and adjectival variants involve anything of further epistemic significance. And insomuch as "know" is a transitive verb grammatically requiring both a subject and object, our first task is to determine from the linguistic nature of those phrases which properly instantiate the blanks in sentence schema

——————— knows ———————

what sorts of entities participate in the knowing-relation. That is, what, logically, can be known and who or what can know it?

---

* Numbered notes are collected at the end of the paper.

On the face of it, the nature of knowers is obvious—they are simply *persons* and perhaps other sentient beings. Thus if k is something knowable, then it is logically possible if not factually true that John Smith, 50 million Frenchmen, the Commissioner of baseball, and the greenest Martian ever to buzz Earth in a flying saucer all know k. (Contrarily, France, baseball, and green are thwarted by their logical types from ever knowing k.) Even here, however, two problems arise. One concerns the knower's implicit temporal boundaries. Since John Smith may know k at one time but not at another, it is evident that knowing k is not something attributed to a person's entire temporal extension but only to some more or less restricted segment (time slice) thereof. But how thick a time slice? Is knowing k an instantaneous property which can come and go from moment to moment? (E.g., "I don't know k just now, but I did two minutes ago and will know it again if you'll let me think for a second.") Or is knowing k a property which must apply to a person for an extended period if it is to apply at all, and if so, for how long? Trivial as this question may seem, it relates to some important complexities in the psychological mechanisms of knowing to which I shall return later (p. 39).

Secondly, in what ways if at all is a knower logically required to be humanlike or at least "person"-like (whatever that might mean)? Is it possible in principle, even if never true in fact, for a sparrow, an amoeba, a turnip, or a computer literally to know k? Although many philosophers of the ordinary-language school are disposed to answer questions like this in the negative on grounds that we just don't talk that way, I would argue to the contrary that construing the concept of knowing to be *inherently* inapplicable to sparrows, amoebae, turnips, and computers is not only anthropocentrically myopic but a strategic blunder as well. Until we are clear on just what constellation of attributes counts in humans as "knowing k," we are in no position to avow that such traits never appear in lower organisms and complex inorganic systems; while in any event, failure of such properties to grace the infrahuman cases would be an empirical generalization about these entities rather than an analytic impossibility. Taking this scientifically factual question to be a linguistic issue is the ordinary-language philosopher's way of evading the real analytic problem here, which is to determine with technical precision the psycho-physical composition of an act of knowing.

Turning now to the *objects* of knowledge, we find through inspection of everyday usage such as

1)   John knows that February 2nd is groundhog day,
2)   John knows why his sectretary left town so suddenly,

3) John knows who broke the window,
4) John knows how to swim,
5) John knows how to yawn with his mouth closed,
6) John knows double-entry bookkeeping,
7) John knows the man who broke the window,
8) John knows this woods like the back of his hand,
9) John knows pain,

that English grammar recognizes three primary kinds of knowledge. The first, illustrated by (1)–(3), takes the form

$$s \text{ knows that } p,$$

where p is a proposition, i.e. whatever it is that is conveyed by a declarative sentence. (Although (2) and (3) fill the blank in 'John knows ──' with a question rather than a statement, their obvious intent is to claim that John knows not the question as such but its answer.) The second usage instantiates d in

$$s \text{ knows how to } d$$

by description of an ability, achievement, or complex act. And the third, of form

$$s \text{ knows (it)}$$

and illustrated by examples (6)–(9), is a wildly promiscuous context in which '(it)' can be virtually any noun or noun phrase. The first two of these forms make the by-now familiar distinction between the "knowing-that" of propositional (factual) knowledge and the "knowing-how" of skills, while the third may be thought of as "knowledge by acquaintance" insomuch as 's knows (it)' usually paraphrases well as some version of 's is acquainted with (it)'.

To be sure, though ordinary language provides separate grammatical forms to discriminate among the knowings of propositions, of skills, and of things, it often botches their applications. For example, while

10) John knows that silence is golden,
11) John knows how to program a computer,
12) John knows the price of gold,

are grammatically tokened to be a knowing-that, a knowing–how, and a knowing–(it), respectively, analysis of what John would normally have to be like for us to say these things about him reveals that (12) and for the most part (11) comprise knowledge of facts, whereas (10) is largely an aspect of adroit social behavior involving little if any propositional knowledge. This sloppiness of ordinary language is why study of a concept's commonsense usage only roughs in the surface contours of its referent, so that once our linguistic intuitions have been skimmed of this initial determination they may properly be ignored with brash and cheerful irreverence as technical penetration into that referent's deeper nature begins to expose inconsistencies, ignorance, and false suppositions in everyday discourse about it. In particular, for our case at hand, it remains an open question whether one or more of the three grammatically distinct forms of knowledge may not comprise only commonsensically confused instances of the remainder. No such reductions will be insisted upon here, however. Rather, I shall be fairly articulate about problems of knowing-that, much less so about knowing-how and knowing-(it), and though I will not try to conceal my opinions about the interrelations of these I see no point to arguing their precise overlap until we learn a great deal more about the detailed mechanisms involved.

KNOWLEDGE OF SKILLS AND KNOWLEDGE BY ACQUAINTANCE

On the face of it, paradigm cases of knowing-how are so totally dissimilar to those of knowing-that—for skills have none of the primary logical features, truth, belief, and rationality (see below), of propositional knowledge—that the greatest mystery here is why the English language should ever have come to subsume both sorts under the same verb.[2] Even so, regardless of its ultimate relevance to epistemological theory, knowing-how raises a pair of issues worth at least passing mention.

For one, while '*s* knows how to *d*' is usually felt in everyday usage to be synonymous with '*s* is able (has the ability) to *d*', where '*d*' describes some activity or achievement, the equivalence is not perfect. Thus 'John has the ability to do 50 push-ups in one minute' and 'John is able to recall the names of all his grade-school teachers' do not graciously accept paraphrase as 'John knows how to do 50 push-ups in one minute' and 'John knows how to recall the names of all his grade-school teachers', respectively. And we might put down an uncreative teacher of English composition by saying "He knows how to write a best-seller, but can't actually *do* it". Why this occasional failure of the *know-how* = *ability* equation? Each of the examples just given suggests part of an answer. First, wherever common sense intuits a sharp distinction between "mental" and "physical" abilities, knowing-how cleaves to the former. Moreover, not even a mental ability counts as know-how if it is too simple. (Whether or not being able to recall a list of names is know-how depends on whether this is done by some special trick or is just dogged rote memory.) And finally, being able to produce a conceptual description of the operations which in aggregate make up a complex achievement—an engineer's knowing-that—also counts after a fashion as know-how even for someone who can't convert these words into deeds. It would appear, then, that paradigmatically someone "knows how" to d when his d-ing is a complex action synthesized out of elementary operations by a recipe which he should be able to verbalize. Could it be that ordinary language's treating some abilities as a form of knowing is simply a naive (and in most instances surely false) presupposition that such conceptual formulas do in fact guide the performance?

Actually it is a moot question whether the science of psychology has any use for ability concepts at all, any more than advanced chemistry (unlike applied geology) needs to talk about minerals. Certainly commonsense abilities are so inadequately conceptualized—for describing an ability or know-how *only* in terms of a gross performance or summary achievement, as in knowing how "to swim," "to speak Russian," "to do long division," "to treat frostbite," etc. recognizes neither the multidimensional composition of the behavior involved nor in general the stimulus conditions on which the ability-definitive behavior is dependent[3]—that even preliminary research on abilities requires a wholesale reworking of how we characterize them. It is very possible that problems of know-how will eventually see resolution in much the same fashion as have past problems in the theory of demonic possession, namely, by our becoming sufficiently sophisticated in alternative interpretations of the phenomena at issue that older conceptions thereof simply fade into the myths of our prescientific past.

Even so, heightened technical understanding of what is probably the most distinctive feature of those traits we intuitively label "skills," differentiating them from lower grades of performance dispositions, should also prove valuable for penetrating the mysteries of cognition proper. I refer, of course, to the *integrated complexity* of skills. To perform proficiently at a task, one must do just the right thing at the right time, often at a speed precluding deliberation and where the "right thing" varies from instant to instant as a complex function both of intricate momentary conditions and of what has gone before. It is relatively easy to analyze a skill as an aggregate of micro-functions, but as Lashley (1951) observed in one of his most provocative essays, the mechanisms by which these are orchestrated into a smoothly efficient molar performance are still largely a mystery. (See also Fitts, 1964.) Problems of organization, or "structure," are likewise central to the psychology of propositional knowledge; and while the kinds of structure involved in knowing-how may not be entirely the same as in knowing-that, there is reason to suspect significant overlap. In any event, our present ability even to *think* straight about problems of structure is still so rudimentary that technical progress on any one aspect of this cannot help but benefit the rest.

Apart from the generic issue of "structure," and except insofar as analysis of special cases discloses ingredients of the knowing-that sort, I am prepared to dismiss knowings-how as having no more inherent relevance for epistemology than do any other psychological functions not alleged by ordinary language to be a form a knowing. (This of course still leaves open the possibility that any or all of the latter may prove to be important ingredients of knowing-that.) I would like to say the same about knowing-(it), but this is more slippery than the other and refuses to relinquish its claim to knowledge stature without a fight.

To be sure, there are many ordinary-language knowings-(it) which seem clearly to be nothing more than loosely conceived versions of knowing-that or knowing-how. Consider, for example,

12) John knows the price of gold,
13) John knows the value of silence,
14) John knows Russian,
15) John knows Russia,
16) John knows the premier of Russia
17) John knows the Siberian winter.

In its most obvious interpretation, (12) is synonymous with

12a) John knows what the price of gold is,

a case of knowing-that; and while (12) might alternatively be intended to imply that John understands the factors which control the price of gold, the latter too can plausibly be construed as propositional knowledge. Again, (13) seems to be very much the same as (10), which is a knowing-that phrasing for what is most fundamentally a knowing-how if knowledge at all. And (14) differs from

14a) John can speak Russian

only in that the latter focuses upon John's ability to make Russian utterances, whereas (14) equally subsumes John's distinct though related abilities to speak, to understand, and to think in Russian by making explicit none of them.

But what about (15)–(17)? We might admit under pressure that a person can know Russia without ever having been there just by learning enough textbook facts and travellers' stories about the place, yet somehow that doesn't quite seem like enough. And is to know another person *merely* to possess sufficient propositional knowledge about him? Unlike (12)–(14), examples (15)–(17) press close to the core of this form's distinctive meaning, namely, as a deep version of *acquaintance-with* — "deep" in that everyday usage often distinguishes "is acquainted with" from "knows" as a contrast between "superficial" and "profound." (E.g., "I'm acquainted with Jim but I don't really know him.") To know something in this sense is to have intimate first-hand familiarity with it, an existential apprehending which mere words can never adequately convey. Thus for (17), no one truly knows the Siberian winter if he has never endured one, never felt the unrelenting cold ice the marrow of his bones, never heard the black wind hiss unceasingly of dead dreams and barren struggles, etc., etc. This is a knowing which not only can epistemological theory not afford to ignore, it is what many poets and some philosophers[4] have extolled as ultimate awareness, the blazing ineffable glory to which propositional knowledge is but warmthless moonglow.

Seeking to reduce knowing-as-deep-acquaintance to knowing-that is a thankless task, and I shall not attempt it. But I will still submit that only one form of knowing is needed to define epistemology's scope. The argument is simply that knowing-as-deep-acquaintance is not an *alternative* to propositional knowledge but an inseparable and indeed fundamental *aspect* of it. Specifically, it is the essence of the "intentionality" or "meaningfulness" of concepts. Although my brief for this will not be presented until later (p. 75), I can easily forecast the outraged protest it will evoke from existentialist/humanist quarters, namely, that existentialistic apprehension is an unmediated *oneness* of knower with the known, the very sort of intimacy which interposition of a concept between them would destroy. And as I am sympathetic to the intuition which motivates this protest even when it is vocalized in ways that seem bootless to me, I will simply leave it as a still-open question whether knowing-(it) may not after all contain a residual beyond its contribution to knowing-that, i.e. whether there is more to deep acquaintance with something than can ever be equated with a sufficiently rich conception of it.

THE COMPONENTS OF PROPOSITIONAL KNOWLEDGE

Even if I have erred in suggesting that propositional knowledge exhausts the domain of epistemological theory, this is clearly its heartland. From here on, my concern will be specifically for what is involved in a person's knowing that something is the case.

To begin, there is a standard decomposition of knowing-that into its logically necessary and sufficient conditions which is so universally agreed to by philosophers—well, not exactly *universal*, but still acceded to in most respects by a remarkably high proportion—that I shall adopt it here without argument. (Some of the argument and further references can be found in Rozeboom, 1967a.) This is the analysis which equates propositional knowledge with justified true belief; specifically, that

s knows that *p* is the case

if and only if

(a)   *s believes* that *p* is the case,
(b)   *p is* the case, and
(c)   *s* is *justified* (warranted, rational) in believing *p*.

For example, suppose that we are trying to decide whether John knows that he failed the examination. We certainly wouldn't consider it possible that he *knows* this if he doesn't even believe that he has failed. (*Not believing* here covers both the case where John actively disbelieves that he failed and where he doesn't have any opinion on the matter at all.) Neither can he know that he failed if in fact he didn't fail—a person can't know falsely, i.e. know something which isn't true. (A person can *believe* falsely, of course, but there is more to knowing than just believing.) And if John *irrationally* believes that he failed the exam—e.g., if he always leaves an examination feeling despondently sure that he blew it even though he has never in fact come close to failing before—then his failure for real on this occasion does not suffice to make his belief a case of *knowledge* until he acquires good grounds for his conviction, such as hearing the sad news directly from his examiner. Finally, if John does believe, truly and with good reason, that he failed, then nothing more seems needed for us to conclude that he knows this.

Before the justified-true-belief analysis of propositional knowledge can lay claim to technical adequacy, a number of fine points usually slighted in the philosophic literature (e.g., how strong a belief is required for knowing?) need to be worked out. When this is done, we find that *knowing* in the strict sense of the concept, like a geometrically perfect circle or a completely honest man, is so idealized that only imperfect approximations to it occur in reality (Rozeboom, 1967a; Unger, 1971). But that is of no consequence here. The important thing is that insofar as the commonsense notion of "knowledge" holds interest for advanced psychology and philosophy, it does so by way of the concepts which appear in its analysis. Accordingly, our first big step in getting on with the psycho-philosophy of knowledge is to redefine this as the psycho-philosophy of *belief*, *truth*, and *rationality*. This is, to be sure, a considerable broadening of our inquiry's scope; for I have now characterized this as the union of three topics when "knowledge" strictly lies only at their intersection. But that is precisely the aim of this essay—to dismantle the concept of knowing and see where its pieces lie within the broader framework of things. (Were we to achieve a comprehensive understanding of belief, truth, and rationality, the only epistemological problems still remaining would be linguistic nitpicking at the exact definition of 'knowledge' and its cognates in these terms.) In what follows, I shall shake down in its turn each of these three components of knowing to see what subordinate issues it comprises. In so doing we shall finally reach, or at least get near, the real frontiers of professional research in epistemology. Do not, however, expect a luxury-class excursion through this terrain. Frontiers are rough, buggy, primitive sorts of places, and the Problems to be scouted will appear less often in tidily labelled specimen jars than in evocations of uneasy confusion as poorly broken trails end in brambles and mire.

PROBLEMS IN THE PSYCHO-LOGICAL CHARACTER OF BELIEF

Of knowing's three primary constituents, *belief* lies closest to pure psychology, unintimidated by normative issues. This is probably why belief processes have been the only objects of epistemic concern to receive more than token recognition in the modern psychological literature. Even here, use of the term 'belief' and its cognates is usually shunned at the technical level; instead, one talks grandly of "cognitive processes" or "information processing" while allowing these labels to subsume virtually anything conjectured to transpire within the organism. But the literal meaning of 'cognitive' is, after all, *pertaining to knowledge*; so any version of "cognitive" psychology with a legitimate claim to this title must significantly address something which differentiates believings from infracognitive events. Much of the research so labelled has, in fact, begun to focus down upon cognition in the strict sense. But that focus is still desperately blurred, due at least in part to loss of the conceptual resources once available in classical psychology for distinguishing the specifically cognitive aspects of internal events from those which are paradigmatically *non*cognitive. An important preliminary task for technical research and theory on cognition, then, is to say in overview what there is about belief which is importantly more than—

i.e. cannot satisfactorily be reduced to—the mechanisms and regularities already familiar to modern psychology in noncognitive terms.

Cognitive Structure

Whatever the details, beliefs have two especially prominent features which set them apart at the outset from noncognitive psychological attributes: *intentionality* and *compositional complexity*. Classically, the intentionality of (some) mental states—i.e. their representing, signifying, or being *about* something else—is above all the essence of cognition, and I shall dwell upon this later. But perhaps even more significant for the role of beliefs and their cognitive kin in the organism's behavioral economy is their internal articulation. For the content of a belief—i.e. what distinguishes one belief from another—is a *proposition*; and propositions are well-structured concept complexes whose linguistic counterparts, *sentences*, consist of terms embedded at distinctive positions within a grammatical frame. Roughly speaking, *terms* are what express *concepts*, the problems of which I will get to in due course; right now I want to emphasize that there is critically more to a proposition (sentence) than just a list of concepts (terms). Thus believing *that John loves Mary* has very different behavioral import for someone who interacts with John and Mary than does believing *that Mary loves John*, while observing (perceptually believing) *that the traffic light is red and the policeman's uniform is blue* is not just a simultaneous but otherwise disjoint perceiving of *traffic light, policeman's uniform, red*, and *blue*. Philosophically elementary as this point may seem, it defines a major target for advanced psychological research insomuch as we have yet to make technically explicit any psychological mechanisms wherein a cognition's structure makes a specifiable difference for its behavioral consequences. Although some contemporary developments, notably, psycholinguistics and information-processing models, have pushed extremely close to an overt acknowledgment of propositional structure (see also Dulany, 1968, and Underwood, 1969, for important verbal-learning shifts in this direction), the basic conceptual framework and habits of theory construction developed to date by our tougher-minded research traditions do not provide the formal resources needed for this (cf. Rozeboom, 1960a, 1961a), and my own recommendation is that we first of all educate ourselves in how to *think* effectively about the psychological function of compositional structure by concentrated study of this at the lowest levels of psychological complexity (cf. Rozeboom; 1967b, 1969b) on which it contributes appreciably to the data variance.

Moreover, while cognitive psychology has scarcely begun to search out the principles by which a particular belief's causal dynamics—i.e. how it comes about and its effect on other processes—are determined jointly by its constituent concepts and propositional structure, we must further recognize that the latter is only part of a belief's full logical complexity. For the family of cognitive attributes exemplified by

———— believes that John loves Mary

is much, much larger than the array generated by letting free variable 'p' range over all propositions in predicate schema

———— believes that p.

Believing is just one of many ways in which a person can entertain a given cognitive content, such as

———— suspects that John loves Mary
———— doubts that John loves Mary
———— disbelieves that John loves Mary
———— desires that John love Mary
———— fears that John may love Mary
———— is contemplating the possibility that John loves Mary
———— wonders whether John loves Mary
———— is trying to make John love Mary
———— is dreaming that John loves Mary
———— is hypothesizing that John loves Mary
———— is imagining (as fiction) that John loves Mary
———— is pretending that John loves Mary
———— perceives that John loves Mary
———— remembers that John loves Mary
———— knows that John loves Mary

All of these and many others are subsumed by the schema

———— ϕs that p,

where 'p' is some declarative sentence and 'ϕ' is a verb describing what is variously known as a "propositional attitude," "mental act," or "intentional mode."[5] Some mental acts, like perceiving (cf. Armstrong, 1965), remembering (c.f. Rozeboom, 1965), and knowing (cf. p. 35 above), analyze as believing in a certain way or with other conditions added; others, like suspecting, doubting, and disbelieving, are alternatives to believing along a continuum of belief strengths; and still others, like hoping, dreading, imagining, and hypothesizing, do not involve any particular degree of belief at all. Modern psychology has paid some attention to variation in belief strength, notably, in work on subjective probability, cognitive dissonance and attitude change (cf. Edwards, Lindeman, and Phillips, 1965; Feldman, 1966; Rokeach, 1968) while accounts of goal-directed behavior and personality-theoretic approaches to motivation cannot totally suppress their latent concern for evaluative intentions; but that these need to be assimilated into a comprehensive theory of mental acts—a theory wherein the fuzzy act-verbs of ordinary language are refined into a multidimensional space of ways to entertain a proposition[6] and which can specify in quantitative detail the causes and consequences of shifts in a cognition's mode vector—still lies beyond the horizon of our present vision.

The contrast between momentary process stages and enduring state properties (Rozeboom, 1965, p. 339 ff.) adds still another layer of complexity to the composition of cognitions. Is knowing/believing an intermittant or an essentially sustained act? Right this moment, for example, I find myself recalling that 2 plus 3 equals 5—but did I also know/believe this ten minutes ago when I wasn't thinking about numbers at all? The commonsense answer is Yes and No, depending on whether by "belief" is meant an active awareness or merely the ready availability of this. Strictly speaking, a person can't believe that p unless he is actually thinking p; yet ordinary language seldom hesitates to presume stable versions of believing and certain other mental acts (e.g., remembering and wanting but not perceiving or imagining) whereby a person latently continues to ϕ that p even while the conscious intensity of his ϕing that p episodically ebbs and flows. Cognitions in this extended sense are dispositional attributes which potentiate activation of their process counterparts, and to be sure, a prissy insistence that only the latter properly count as cognitive would in no way absolve the psychology of cognition from its research responsibility for the internal states which underlie arousal of cognitive activity. But dispositions are characterized not merely by the results they potentiate but also by the particular input conditions which actualize this potential (see fn. 3). Commonsense predicates of form '——— latently ϕs that p', '——— is disposed to ϕ that p', and the like are thus truncated; to be technically efficacious they need a force something like '——— is in a state such that exposure to condition C will result in his ϕing that p'[7]. The main point here is not to legislate the logic of state (latent) cognitions, but to recognize that these play a very different role in the organism's psychological economy than do the process cognitions whose activation they dispose, and that how state cognitions originate, evolve, and interact with input to evoke process cognitions is logically independent of what the latter do once aroused. State changes and their process consequences have long been at issue in research on conditioning and verbal learning, with, however, dubious relevance to cognitive psychology insomuch as the output processes so studied have been exclusively overt responses or elemental ideas lacking even propositional structure much less intentional mode. Moreover, the current travail in verbal learning—nothing less than the throes of a full-scale Kuhnian revolution—inspires little confidence that its traditional doctrines deeply illuminate the mechanics of cognitive arousal.

The psychology of language

My intent for this section has been to cite research concerns linked directly to the psychologically distinctive features of cognitive acts. There is one more issue of this sort whose peripheral position in the logic of cognition has not diminished its empirical centrality in cognitive studies: How does cognition relate to *language* utilization? (Considering how profoundly we depend on verbal communication with subjects to study their "higher mental processes," it is no accident that those areas of psychology for which animal research has been most paradigmatic have also been the ones least disposed to interpret their data in cognitive terms.) In particular, is language a logical prerequisite for cognition, or can the latter occur without any linguistic concomitants at all and if so, how might language nonetheless affect the style and effectiveness of a person's cognitive functioning?

Despite the enormous literature, psychological and otherwise, which has accumulated on the theme of language, our knowledge of this extraordinary phenomenon's fundamental nature is still shockingly primitive; and one of the toughest problems in deciphering its relation to cognition is simply to say with some technical precision what a language *is*, as distinguished from nonlinguistic systems of stimulus/response interplay. It is much harder to isolate features essential to language than to dismiss ones which are not, and the latter unfortunately include most of those usually presumed to be definitive. To begin, while a language presumably requires a set of stimulus patterns such as acoustic and graphic designs to be its "expressions" or verbal "vehicles," these clearly do not by themselves constitute a language; at most they are only a language *for* someone, while reference to that person's transactions with those stimuli is needed to complete the definition. It is *not*, however, necessary for a language to be shared—it is entirely possible for a person to have a language known only to himself, as might be contrived e.g. by an institutionalized paranoic to safeguard the privacy of his soliloquies. Thus interpersonal communication is not definitive of language but is merely an important by-product of it.[8] Neither is it mandatory that a person himself be able to produce those stimuli which are language vehicles for him—the hypothesis that God counsels a select group of his northern faithful through texture changes in the aurora borealis is not logically absurd, just empirically implausible. And the fact that all acknowledged languages are *learned* is irrelevant to their nature: What disqualifies e.g. the so-called "language of the bees" from being a true language is not its innateness but (presumably) the *way* in which a bee's dance affects its audience; nor is it impossible that through some spectacular mutation a newborn infant could understand his mother tongue upon first hearing. All that is logically necessary (with a further important restriction to be added later) is for the stimuli comprised by an organism's "language" to be elicitors of cognitions in him. What language vehicles *must* do is to convey cognitive *meaning*.

That language is necessarily meaningful is not a strikingly original observation, but taken seriously it has major implications. First all, since the "meanings" words convey are some still-obscure aspect of the central processes they arouse,[9] it locates the essence of language functioning in *reception* events rather than in the performance phenomena which have been the near-exclusive study of recent psycholinguistics. (This in no way denigrates the value of research on verbal production, it merely emphasizes that this not basically what language *is*.) Secondly, it protests against an overly facile equating of meanings (i.e. cognitions) with internalized verbal vehicles. Obviously the meaning of a linguistic expression cannot be the same thing as its overt vehicle, but we are long accustomed to conjecturing the existence of central counterparts to external stimuli (traditionally sensations, percepts, ideas, or reafferent feedback from implicit responses), and it *could* be that meanings are nothing more than verbal images or words-in-thought.[10] Such a notion is implicit in many standard treatments of cognition, as when e.g. a "concept" is held to be a verbal label or mediation response conditioned to a variety of stimuli. Moreover, the most evident objections to verbal-image theories of meaning—that the meaning of a given vehicle can change, that the same word may have more than one meaning (ambiguity and homonymity) while the meanings of grossly dissimilar vehicles in different languages and sense modalities may be the same (synonymity), and still other phenomena showing beyond question that an external word-vehicle's internal sensory correlate is not the same thing as its meaning—are not nearly so conclusive as they might at first seem, for it can be argued that an overt expression's meaning is not its own central counterpart but some or all of the other verbal images or implicit word responses evoked by it. According to this view, the "same meaning" shared by synonymous expressions is not an extralinguistic entity but some word-associative equivalence between them, so that e.g. two terms are synonymous to the extent that they evoke the same verbal responses. Similarly, lexicographic characterizations of an expression's meaning in terms of phrases to which it is more or less equivalent (paraphrase theories), as typified by recent psycholinguistic incursions into semantics (e.g. Katz and Fodor, 1963), remain in effect versions of the meaning-as-internalized-language thesis unless they derive their paraphrasings from deeper non-verbal communalities among expressions.

We cannot, however, happily define cognitive meaning in terms of language if in turn the latter, as an importantly *restricted* set of stimuli, is defined in terms of meaning evocation. To bring this off credibly, it needs to be shown why a person's "language" should not then logically include *all* stimuli which for him arouse the central correlates of other stimuli. Though totally ignored in the literature, how to distinguish linguistic from nonlinguistic stimuli is one of psycholinguistics' most profound problems. Just how profound I will show in a moment, after I first submit with inconclusive argument but strong intuitive conviction that cognitive meanings—i.e., the contents of mental acts—are *not* essentially linguistic.

The strongest objective evidence that meaning is not inherently tied to verbal imagery probably lies in clinical data on the aphasias (see especially Jones and Wepman, 1961). However, what I personally find most persuasive—over and above certain semantic-theoretical considerations to be aired later (p. 55ff.)—is the introspectively evident gulf between word-thoughts and meanings. For example, as I find myself achieving increased clarity or deeper understanding of an issue, this does *not* consist in my becoming more verbally fluent about it; rather, the words at my command (and the things said by others) seem increasingly inadequate to express my grasp of the matter. When writing I often have to spend long minutes or hours crafting phrases which convey (to me) even approximately the particular multifaceted complexity of meaning I have in mind at the search's outset. And not infrequently I find myself developing new concepts which initially have no linguistic vehicle for me at all. Working out verbalizations for these is often highly instructive, but the concept is available to me in at least rudimentary form before I code it linguistically. More generally, it is hard to see how a culture or society could ever expand its cognitive horizons if experience and contemplation could not transcend the limited linguistic resources available to it at any given period. Finally, it is important to note that we can perceive, remember, and imagine the details of events—shapes, textures, colors, odors, rhythms, etc.—in far richer preciseness than we can verbalize, though we can create and train ourselves to understand verbal labels for any of these if it becomes worth our while to do so. Similarly, anyone who wishes to ascribe mental acts to at least some infrahuman organisms (e.g., who suspects that monkeys and dogs can perceive and remember to at least a modest degree) while also maintaining that only humans have genuine language is thereby committed to accept that meanings can be nonlinguistic.

If it be agreed at least provisionally that the contents of mental acts such as perceiving and remembering are nonverbal central conditions arousable by varied sensory and ideational antecedents, then it is perfectly natural to suppose further that these very same cognitive contents can also be evoked by language vehicles and that this is, in fact, what happens when the latter "convey" meanings to their recipients. So viewed, a linguistic "ex-pression" is an overt or covert verbal stimulus which "presses out"—i.e., calls forth, brings out, or otherwise activates—its meaning. This is so commonsensical a notion of language function that it would scarcely need mention had it not recently fallen into low esteem in many psychological and most philosophic circles; for psychologists through long established though rapidly waning S-R customs requiring all mediational processes to be peripheral even if covert responses, and for philosophers because the nature of meaning as something which intervenes between language and reality has remained so obdurately obscure that the preferred tactic of late has been to analyze it out of existence. I shall return to problems of meaning later. Right now, it still remains to clarify how linguistic expressions are definitively different from other stimuli.

We have already noted that for a stimulus S to qualify as a language vehicle for an organism o at time t, it must elicit a cognition (cognitive meaning, intentional content) in o at t. (To say that S elicits, evokes, or arouses effect e in o at t here means not that S is necessarily in fact doing this, but only that o's state at t is such that stimulation by S *would* elicit e in o.) Implied by this is an important formal requirement which stimuli must satisfy if they are to qualify as language. For insomuch as the full content of an intentional act is a *proposition*, stimulus S is not cognitively meaningful to o at t unless S contributes to evocation in o at t of some central process which has this degree of structural complexity. The primary linguistic stimulus is thus a *sentence* (cf. Quine, 1960, Chapt. 1), which qualifies as such regardless of its grammatical orthodoxy precisely by virtue of conveying a proposition. Relative to this sentential basis, the concept of linguistic "expression" may then also be generalized to include strings of sentences (e.g. paragraphs) as well as the subsentential units—words—which concatenate into sentences.[11] To be sure, as we become more knowledgeable about the inner organism, we will surely find that full-blooded propositional status is but a limiting ideal on several dimensions along which central processes vary, so that where we draw the line between sentences which convey propositions and not-quite-sentences which convey not-quite-propositions will be to a large extent arbitrary. But qualms about the dichotomizing of continua is a luxury which we can ill afford until their extremes become well differentiated. The important point for now, made evident by placing the fulcrum of language theory on sentences/propositions rather than on single terms, is that for all practical purposes *we have never yet had even a rudimentary psychology of language*. The reason is very simple: Except for a handful of very recent harbingers of what is to come[12], *all* past psychological accounts have treated verbal processes as elemental reactions to isolated words. These reaction elements have been variously described as implicit responses, response dispositions, overt or covert verbal associates of the stimulus word, "pure stimulus acts" or $r_g - s_g$ processes, detachable components of the response elicited by another stimulus, or (in older accounts) ideas and images; but the crucial inadequacy common to all lies in their being construed as something appropriately represented by a single term or (when the eliciting stimulus has multiple effects) by a simple list of such terms. This failure to make explicit the propositional structure of internal reactions to linguistic output is not just notational carelessness; rather, it reflects modern psychology's blindness to the nomic significance of compositional structure. Whereas the natural course of psychological events is for unrestrictedly complex environmental *facts*—i.e. entities formally isomorphic to sentences—to elicit behavior whose patterning derives from that of its input antecedents, and where the propositional articulation of mediating cognitions is required to transmit this structural influence, behavior theory has so far made formal provision only for the degenerate case of this wherein bare occurrence of a stimulus element elicits a fixed response.[13] Only when we have learned how to think about the generic import of compositional structure will the conceptual framework needed for a genuine psychology of cognition be available.

Evocation of propositional processes is the most visible watershed partitioning linguistic from nonlinguistic stimuli, but it is not the ultimate divide. For we have yet to say why *all* stimuli which evoke cognitions in a person should not count equally as linguistic expressions for him. Thus if the sight of moisture on the window, drumming on the roof and the sound of thunder, and the words 'It's raining' spoken or written by a friend in an appropriate context all induce me to believe *that it is raining*, on what grounds do these last stimuli qualify for me as language vehicles while those of the first two cases fail? (Note that even were acquisition-by-learning and self-producibility essential to language, coming to interpret wet windows and percussive noises as indices of rain is also a matter of learning, while watering windows and production of rainy sounds lies well within the range of instrumented human capability.) I shall propose a tentative solution to this problem which should not be passed over lightly despite the overidealized brevity to which I must here restrict my presentation. It is, in fact, one of the three pivotal insights into the specific behavior-theoretic character of language which I have managed to wrest from nearly a quarter century of struggle with this matter.[14] Even in rudimentary form it has no competition, for the simple reason that previous theories of language have to my knowledge never seriously addressed this issue beyond an occasional abortive[15] attempt to distinguish "signs" or "signals" from "symbols." (Cf. "Thunder is a sign of rain, 'rain' is a symbol of it.")

To begin, consider how the argument that signs (signals) are *symptoms* which produce *anticipation* of what they signify whereas symbols *represent* them (Langer, 1942; Werner and Kaplan, 1963) entirely misses the point despite its intuitive appeal. It overlooks that the anticipation of an event *e* evoked by a sign of it is an intentional act whose content represents *e*, while a symbol represents *e* only mediately by likewise evoking an intentional content—meaning—which is what most directly signifies *e*. The problem is to distinguish sign from symbol in terms of *how* they bring about central representation of the external event. A simple answer would prima facie be at hand if cognitive meaning were merely covert verbalizations. For then, presuming that symbols are essentially language vehicles[16] while signs are nonlinguistic, one might argue that when verbal expressions convey meanings, both cause and effect in this arousal sequence belong to the family of linguistic events, whereas when beliefs are aroused by nonverbal stimuli only the effect is linguistic, i.e., the sequence is a "language-entry transition" (Sellars, 1954). Denial of an inherent connection between language vehicles and meaning, however, thwarts this sortie. More generally, I submit—programmatically, since there are too many possible variants on this argument to refute one by one—that meanings are sufficiently detachable, logically and causally, from all classes of their afferent antecedents to dangle any hope that linguistic expressions differ from nonlinguistic elicitors of meaning by virtue of stimuli of the one kind evoking directly (or by an inherently shorter causal route) what the other evokes only through mediation by the former's central correlates.

But what, then *is* the language-definitive distinction between arousal of rain-belief by the sound 'It's raining' and the sound of thunder, respectively? The essence lies, I suggest, in how the cognition's *mode* is determined. In both examples, the elicited event is occurrence (in organism o at time t) of believing-that-it-is-raining, while the eliciting event is occurrence (just before t near o) of a complex stimulus configuration whose components include thunderous vibration in the one case and the acoustic pattern 'It's raining' in the other. But nonlinguistic occurrence of thunderous vibration not merely brings the it-is-raining proposition to mind but also causes it to be *believed*, rather than doubted, conjectured, hoped, or otherwise moded. In linguistic contrast, bare occurrence of the sentence 'It's raining' activates the proposition *without* determining its mode of entertainment. That the cognitive resultant is a *believing*, rather than a doubting, conjecturing, etc., is due entirely to other features of the total eliciting event such as the utterance's intonation (e.g., 'It's raining!' vs. 'It's raining?'), choice of phrasing (e.g., 'It's raining!' vs. 'Oh, for it to rain!'), and the broader context of delivery (e.g. recalling that the speaker is a notorius practical joker). Of course, the broader context also affects nonlinguistic arousal, as when the degree of rain-belief evoked by occurrence of thunderous vibration is enhanced or diminished by additional concurrent input such as the sight of lightning or heavy construction work nearby. The critical distinction here is that in nonlinguistic elicitation of an intentional act, the same stimulus configuration whose occurrence determines the intention's content *also* has a primary effect, by virtue of its occurrence, on the intention's mode. In contrast, content and mode effects are causally decoupled in linguistic arousal through their respective control by cleanly separable components of the eliciting complex. In this way, language is able to present (convey, evoke in thought) a proposition without prejudicing any particular valuation of it, while persistence of the vehicle which accomplishes this presentation insures persistence of propositional content in the teeth of modal drift. This, I propose, is the technical reality behind the often-voiced intuition that language frees our thinking from the here-and-now, or (cf. above) that signs are symptoms of events while symbols represent them. It is not that propositions with distant reference cannot be thought without words, but that when unverbalized they are likely to be evoked only by stimuli which also control the degree to which they are believed. Language is what makes *contemplative* thought a practical possibility.

Fragmentary as they are, my remarks on the psychology of language already transgress seemly proportions for this survey, and I can only hint at further issues which spark through the gap between language and cognition.

While I have protested the assumption that meanings are word bound, one need not be a dedicated Whorfian to recognize that a person's language importantly influences the character of his thinking. Detailing the specific *ways* in which this is so should prove highly educational not merely to cognitive theory but for cognitive engineering as well. Some of the more prominent of such influences:

1) That language facilitates subjunctive thought has already been noted; but detaching consideration from conviction is not its only contribution to this. Words are able to evoke abstract concepts free of the inessential, distracting, and quite possibly misleading specifics which inevitably accompany the concept's arousal by nonverbal input. Thus to redeploy a traditional example, sentences containing the word 'triangle' can sustain thought about abstract triangularity without restricting this to a particular size and angularity (e.g., right-isoceles with a 3 inch hypotenuse) as perception or visual imaging of a triangle would do.

2) The "sustaining" action just mentioned should not go underappreciated. Whereas nonverbally aroused thinking about the not-here-and-now is an ephemeral, shimmery sort of thing in which one fragmentarily activated idea flickers into another and yet another too fleetingly for effective feedback control by monitoring reactions, verbal self-stimulation prolonged indefinitely by such simple techniques as recycling through covert vocalization or repeated sensing of an enduring (e.g. printed) symbol display greatly inhances the focus and stability of thought. To be sure, evocation of meanings is no less chancy by verbal vehicles than by other forms of stimulation—the strength (probability, intensity, completeness) with which a symbol S conveys its meaning on a particular occasion depends greatly on the recipient's past training and present receptivity parameters. But this side of semantic satiation, persistent input accessibility of S optimizes the quality with which S's meaning is available when needed.

3) For reasons well worth probing in detail, we can usually perform transformations with greater ease and reliability upon external stimulus arrays than upon meanings. Symbolic transformations which correspond to significant meaning relations (e.g. valid inference) can thus enormously enhance a person's reasoning effectiveness through symbol-symbol sequencing in which meanings need be considered only for set-up of starting configurations and interpretation of results. Much of the potency of mathematics and other formal disciplines may be attributed to this capacity for trade-off between understanding and algorithmic efficiency. To be sure, the yield of meaning-free verbal thinking under less than algorithmically optimal circumstances tends toward flatulent absurdities and rote clichés. But that is another matter, albeit unhappily a familiar one.

4) While the virtues of language for interpersonal communication are too obvious for mention, what is perhaps not quite so transparently evident is that exposure to the verbal output of others also educates a person in concepts which he would acquire only much more slowly if at all from strictly nonverbal experience. Two comments on this must suffice pending some later remarks on concept formation. One is that the deeper we contemplate how a person might learn word meanings which are not already preformed in his central reactions to nonverbal stimuli, the more profoundly enigmatic this phenomenon becomes. The other is that enrichment of a person's concept repertoire through language learning may not be restricted only to concepts expressible in this language. It could be, for example, that a child whose first awareness of shape comes through his parents' use of the labels 'circle' and 'square' thereby also acquires additional shape concepts (demonstrated, say, by his ability to make form discriminations previously beyond him) for which he has no verbal expression. The extent to which this does, in fact, occur remains for future research based on theories of discrimination learning far more sophisticated than those now available.

Finally, it should be acknowledged that modern psycholinguistics, though peripheral to cognition proper, has brought to the fore some closely allied problems of considerable significance. Specifically, the syntax of a language such as English reflects a remarkable intricacy of constraints on the verbal productions of its more fluent speakers. To construct theories of the organism which countenence behavior patterning so complex as this is a very nice problem indeed, especially insomuch as a formal grammar which generates the language's syntactically *permissible* verbal strings tells little if anything about why—or how—a person emits the particular string he does on a given occasion. The needed explanation is framed by the theory of intentional acts, since presumably a person's utterance of expression E is due primarily to his ϕing that p, where in the simplest cases E expresses p while the utterance's phrasing or intonation signals mode ϕ. But as the extant abundance of grammatically distinct languages makes evident, a cognition's content determines only weakly the fine structure of its verbal coding. Unlike conscious thought, to which classical psychology has devoted much attention, the processes which discharge a preverbal cognition into phoneme-by-phoneme serial emission of a syntactically well-structured utterance have remained far beyond the ken of traditional psychologies. That they have now become appreciated—in fact revelled in—for what they are speaks well of modern psychology's readiness, at long last, to have it out with inner complexity.

PROBLEMS CONCERNING TRUTH

Although "intentional acts" have already figured prominently in this survey, we have scarcely begun to sound their psycho-philosophical depths. The full, awesome murkiness of these is visible only from the epistemic crags of "truth."

Semantic veridicality

It is simple to agree that a person cannot *know* that something is the case unless what he so believes is true (veridical, correct, accurate). Less simple is to make this provision perspicuous. Dropping the first veil is easy enough—with possible degenerate exceptions (e.g., tautologies), a proposition's truth derives from its relation to something else. To say just what this "something else" is, however, and precisely how it determines a proposition's truth value, requires sorting out one of the nastiest tangles of the significantly trivial with the obscurely unresolved ever to befuddle generations of philosophers. What is "significantly trivial" here is the correspondence principle of truth. Properly understood, this is so incontestable as to be almost vacuous, yet it must be respected with great sensitivity if one's truth theory is not to blunder into absurdity.

The correspondence principle of truth is that a proposition is true if and only if reality is as it represents; more precisely, that what a sentence '*p*' expresses is true iff (if and only if) *p*.[17] (E.g., 'John loves Mary' is true iff John loves Mary.) Such simpleminded reference to objective reality often disconcerts weekend epistemologists who have never recovered from the shock of philosophic scepticism. "Aren't you naive to assume that there is any external world at all?" the objection is likely to go. "Perhaps it's all in our minds, with truth being whatever we think it is. In any case, how could truth ever be a comparison between our thoughts and absolute objectivity when the latter is basically unknowable?" Such arguments are simply confusion compounded. In the first place, belief in external reality is not a grand metaphysical commitment, but merely some degree of confidence in one or more everyday propositions, such as 'John loves Mary', 'The traffic light is red', and 'You're standing on my foot', of form *other* than a nonrelational first-person claim. So long as I do not construe these to be shorthand for solely-first-person attributions such as 'I believe that John loves Mary', 'I'm having a red-traffic-lightish experience', and 'It seems to me that you are standing on my foot'—and to insist that a statement '*p*' is always elliptical for something like 'I think that *p*' precipitates a vicious regress[18]—I have admitted all the outside world needed for a realist ontology and correspondence analysis of truth. The latter especially does not presume that I *know* or even feel very sure that John loves Mary, that the traffic light is red, etc. It suffices to respect these propositions and their negations as genuine alternative *possibilities* on which conditional conclusions can be grounded.

Specifically, whenever I believe/am uncertain/disbelieve that p and am also aware that I believe/am uncertain/disbelieve that p—i.e. whenever my conceptual resources allow me not merely to *use* (have as content of an intentional act) the proposition that-p but also to *refer* to it—I find myself entertaining not only the proposition that-p itself but propositions *about* that-p as well.[19] It would be most surprising if the paired propositions of these two types were not analytically connected somehow, and the correspondence principle, that that-p is true if p and false if not p, acknowledges one such relation. To verify this principle I need not aspire to transcend my egocentric predicament and compare subjective beliefs with naked objectivity; it suffices merely to observe that the propositions e.g. *that John loves Mary* and *that that-John-loves-Mary is true* are so interrelated that any grounds for believing that John loves Mary are also grounds for believing that that-John-loves-Mary is true, and conversely. (How these two propositions can be analytically equivalent, or almost so, without being identical is a nice technical question, but not one which requires attention here.)

Although the correspondence principle of truth is not seriously disputable, it merely raises, not solves, the significant problems of semantics. For why should that-John-loves-Mary depend for its truth on John's loving Mary rather than on, say, ice's being cold. Clearly the proposition that-John-loves-Mary must relate to something in John's feelings for Mary which it does not find in the thermal facts of ice. But what is this relationship and to what, specifically, does the proposition bear it? The correspondence principle is totally uninformative about this—the grammatical operators which transform use into mention *presuppose* some such relation without at all illuminating its nature. The deep problem here is to formulate principles of veridicality which do not require that a problematic proposition or some paraphrase thereof be used to express its own truth conditions. Without such principles we cannot analyze truth for languages not synonymously translatable into our own.

Meaning and reference

For the most part, survey of epistemology's semantic sector is not feasible here, for the issues are all highly technical and unforgiving even of small missteps.[20] In particular, semantical theories find it especially hard to evade premature committment to a specific and inevitably dubious ontology. (E.g., do negative and disjunctive facts exist? Are there properties which have no exemplars? For every simple or complex predicate, does there exist a property which is had, or class which is belonged to, by exactly those entities which satisfy that predicate?) Whatever it allows to be the targets of semantic relatedness, a theory of semantics must on the psychological side admit at least (1) a class of meaning elements—"descriptive concepts"— which in general *designate, signify, represent, refer to, name* or *are about* certain other entities, and (2) well-structured complexes of descriptive concepts—descriptive phrases, complex predicates, and above all propositions— which signify corresponding complexes of their elements' referents if in fact the latter combine as represented. It may then be held that a proposition *p* is true iff there exists a fact (state of affairs) in which entities named by the descriptive concepts in *p* are united by the same structure that integrates their names in *p* (cf. Rozeboom, 1962a/b). That is, if the concepts *John, Mary,* and *loves* respectively designate the objects John, Mary, and the asymmetric dyadic relation of loving, then the proposition *John-loves-Mary* is true if there exists a state of affairs in which John and Mary respectively occupy the first and second pole of loving, i.e. if it is a fact that John loves Mary, and is false if no fact answers to this description. But I cannot claim even this much without entering disputed ground, so I shall turn from the semantics of intact propositions to their roots in the nature of concepts.

Although what passes for the psychology of "concepts" has recently advanced beyond simple discrimination theory towards something more genuinely cognitive, research psychology has yet to acknowledge the great functional diversities which partition the concepts we exploit in everyday life. Just how varied these are becomes evident if we assume that each word or syntactic unit in a sentence contributes a particular meaning ingredient to what the sentence expresses, and that all such word-controlled propositional components are "concepts" of one kind or another. (I would not care to argue that the combinatorial units of language and meaning, respectively, correspond quite this tidily, but something like it must surely be roughly correct.) At least four broad categories of concepts need prima facie distinguishing. Foremost on anyone's list would be the *descriptive concepts* expressed by terms such as 'John', 'Seattle', 'blue', 'hard', 'triangular', 'loves', 'hit', 'grow', 'seven', 'butter', 'tree', etc., whose semantic function is to designate objects, attributes, relations, and other (?) subfactual furnishings of the world. (Whether predicate terms—verbs, adjectives, common nouns—designate in at all the same way as do proper nouns is controversial; but then so is everything else in philosophical semantics. Any reader appalled at the crudity of my simplifications here may find consolation in the fact that they pain me too.) Secondly, there are the *logical connectives and quantifiers*, expressed by 'and', 'or', 'not', 'some', 'every', 'is', etc. Presumably these have no referents in their own right but are structural auxiliaries which combine with descriptive concepts to generate propositions and other descriptive compounds. Thirdly, syntactically inseparable from descriptive predicates though intuitively distinct from them in their semantic character, are *evaluative concepts* expressed by such terms as 'delicious', 'nasty', 'beautiful', 'petty', 'awesome', etc. A common view (e.g. Stevenson, 1944, Chapt. 3), though one I no longer find attractive (see p. 64, below), is that these are "emotive" terms which, unlike descriptive predicates, have no objective referents and merely reflect attitudes toward the objects to which they are ascribed. Finally, concepts holding special philosophic fascination are the *modal operators* expressed by 'probable', 'possible', 'should', 'must', 'because', 'necessary', and the like. Syntactically these behave like logical connectives, converting propositions into other propositions. A good proportion (all?) of the modal operators reflect intentional modes in that to modal operator M there corresponds an intentional mode ϕ_M such that if Mp is the proposition into which M transforms another proposition p, believing Mp has much the same psychological force as entertaining p in mode ϕ_M, while asserting Mp is communicatively equivalent to uttering p with context signals for mode ϕ_M. Thus instead of a moderately confident but slightly hesitant pronouncement of 'It will rain tonight', or a pleading/demanding utterance of 'you will pay back the money you owe me', it is much easier to assert firmly 'It will probably rain tonight', or 'you ought to pay back the money you owe me'.[21] Even so, there is an important logical difference between $\phi_M$ing that p and believing that Mp; for what proposition Mp purports to be *about* is not any actual $\phi_M$ing that p, but some state of affairs which *justifies* $\phi_M$ing that p. (Why should I feel considerable but not complete confidence that it will rain tonight? Because the probability of rain tonight is high but not certain. And what justifies demanding that you repay your debt to me? Because you ought to.)

Commonsensical semantic distinctions such as these challenge the psycho-philosophy of knowledge to clarify in depth and functional detail what they are all about, to dispel the mists of mystery from meaning by identifying within the fine-grained inner workings of cognizant organisms those features which show the combinatorial properties and empirical/logical outreachings already honored by the idealized abstracta of philosophical semantics. Union of the finest technical proficiencies on both sides of the psycho-philosophical hyphen is essential to this effort, for philosophically untutored psychologists are demonstrably tone-deaf to even the simplest of semantic themes while few philosophers untrained in experimental psychology seem able to comprehend either the aims, methods, or results of scientific research analyzing psychological events as natural phenomena. We may call this still-virtually-nonexistent interdisciplinary specialty "psychosemantics" to emphasize its advance beyond past psychologies of meaning in seeking to exploit, substantiate, refine, emend, and amplify the full range of distinctions and complexities recognized by philosophical semantics. I conclude this section with sketches of what I see as the main axes of its orientation.

The analysis of aboutness

In any semantic investigation, the standard query "What do we mean by 'meaning'?" will do for openers. Even though by now something of a cliché, the question is still cogent for the very good reason that the term 'meaning' has a multiplicity of ordinary-language senses which need sorting out. Previous inventories of this stock (most notably Ogden and Richards, 1923, Chapt. 7; Frankena, 1958; Black, 1968, Chapt. 7) have pushed the alleged count well into the dozens. To be sure, these have run up the score by conflating ambiguities in the meaning of 'meaning' with different varieties or theories of 'meaning' in a given sense; but even so, there exist at least four distinguishable usages whose confounding creates no end of mischief: (1) Most broadly, the "meaning" of a stimulus is any or all of the central reactions it elicits, especially ideational associates. (E.g., 'That column of smoke means that something's on fire over there.' In a variant of this sense, the "meaning" is what the associated ideas are ideas *of*, e.g., not the thought of fire but the fire itself.) An expression's "connotation" is meaning in this sense.[22] (2) Statements such as 'John had a meaningful discussion with his boss yesterday' and 'My life seems empty of meaning', in which 'meaningful' is synonymous with 'significant', 'pregnant', or 'portentful', exhibit concern for deep affective tones demarking basic values—not passive enjoyments of good-feeling but experiences of *importance*, pleasurable or otherwise. Meaning in this sense, which might be called "humanistic" meaning, is akin to the meanings expressed by evaluative predicates except for feeling too rich, too full, too ineffably personal to put into words. Finally, as illustrated by "In German 'oder' means *or*" and "The phrases '34th U.S. President' and 'Supreme W. W. II Allied Expeditionary Commander' have different meanings even though they both designate D. D. Eisenhower," in contrast to "By 'Old Bulgebottom' Herbert means his mother-in-law," both (3) the contents and (4) the objects of mental acts are commonly said to be "meanings," i.e., not only what words *express* but also what they are *about*. Of these assorted usages, only the third—"cognitive" meaning—is what semantical theory intends by this term. But unlike (1) and (2), (4) is semantically central even when it is not confused with cognitive meaning. It is, in fact, definitive to the latter; for no expression has meaning in the semantic sense unless it or some expression which includes it potentially represents something. In large measure, the theory of aboutness *is* semantics.

Historically, it has proved extremely hard for philosophers to appreciate how important it is, or psychologists how difficult, to make scientifically explicit the natural basis of the aboutness relationship. It is all very well for a philosophically "pure" semantics (Carnap, 1942, § 5) to build axiomatically upon unanalyzed reference concepts, but we still need grounds superior to naked intuition on which to judge whether the chosen axioms and their consequences are all that they should be. Once a discipline has salvaged what it can from philosophic folklore and the wisdom of ordinary language its growth must be sustained by technically refined data sources if its formal models are not to be reactionary exercises in futility; and only the advanced study of behavior mechanisms can be expected to tell what axioms correctly describe those complexities of semantic reality which exceed the grasp of traditional idealizations (see p. 72ff. below). As it is, some of our most important philosophers (e. g., Quine, 1960) have already begun to infuse philosophical semantics with do-it-yourself behavior theory. Most conspicuously, this has been true of "linguistic" philosophers beguiled by the Wittgensteinian meaning-is-use slogan. However, arguments that meanings are neither the physical objects which some words name nor ghostly inhabitants of a "third realm of nonphysical, nonpsychological entities" (Ryle, 1957) turn enlightenment into obfuscation when by sleight-of-tongue they intimate that once an expression's meaning is traced to its linguistic role or rules of employment (Sellars, 1954; Ryle, 1957) all puzzles of aboutness simply evaporate.[23] To distinguish—correctly and importantly—between meaning and reference does not do away with the latter but shows rather that we need theories of each. Moreover, to ask for the "use," "rules of employment," or "role" of an expression is to grope for what ordinary language lacks resources to conceive and only psychological science will someday provide, namely, a functionally detailed account of the events which transpire during a person's interactions with cognitively meaningful stimuli.

Meanwhile, psychology's own troubles in keeping hand and eye on the psychosemantical ball are manifest in its feckless fumblings at linguistic reference. If E is a verbal stimulus, say the visual shape *RED*, which designates an entity e, say the color red, for organism o at time t, what is the psychological nature of this semantic relationship? Clearly, since E's designative potential for o at t is determined by how it affects o then, there must be some alteration, adjustment, or reaction m (not necessarily response-like) produced by E in o at t which mediates E's reference to e for o at t,[24] while any other stimulus which also arouses m in o at t—i.e. any synonym for E—likewise designates e for o at t. That is, presentation of E (to o at t) initiates a sequence $E \to a \to b \to \cdots \to m \to \cdots$ of events[25] in o, some stage m of which "directly" designates e in the sense that (1) each stage of the sequence prior to m designates e mediately by virtue of its evoking a process which designates e, and (2) m designates e on grounds other than evoking a designator of e. The point of distinguishing m from E and the intervening precursors of m, is that while the semantic properties of verbal afferent processes are indeed to be analyzed—as the psychology of meaning has traditionally assumed—in terms of their causal effects, this is but incidental to the main problem: Since the causal sequence does *not* usually eventuate in production of the input expression's referent, we must ultimately recognize a semantically basic stage of internal arousal whose aboutness resides in something other than what it in turn elicits.

If stimulus E designates entity e (for o at t) by virtue of arousing a central process m whose own reference to e is unmediated by m's causal *consequences*, might this basic reference of m to e perhaps be explained in terms of m's causal *antecedents*? I.e. could m designate e by virtue of there existing a c such that c elicits m while c stands in some reference-criterial relation to e? Not by any antecedent of m in the arousal sequence initiated by E; for by a modest extension of the argument just offered we may stipulate that the cognitive meaning m of E is whatever event in this sequence is the one semantically closest to e. That is, construing some stages in $E \to a \to b \to \cdots \to m \to \cdots$ to designate e by virtue of arousing, or being aroused by, some other designator of e in this sequence is a recursive analysis of reference which requires one stage—call it m, or "meaning"—to form the base of the recursion and whose semantic coupling with e must hence be traced to something other than m's role in the causal sequence beginning with E. However, E is not in principle the only elicitor of m, and it is not implausible that m's reference to e (for o at t) may consist partly in m's being also a stage in the sequence of internal events initiated in o at t by an occurrence of e in some suitable context near o at t. Two versions of this approach—one major and one minor—in fact subsume essentially all psychological theories of reference proposed to date.

The minor version is the covert-speech interpretation of meaning. While views in this category seldom explicitly address the problem of reference, it is sometimes claimed (notably Skinner, 1957, Chapt. 5) that the referent of an expression E is the nonlinguistic entity to which E or its central correlate has become attached as a labeling reaction. In contrast, the major version honors our intuition that symbols are surrogates for what they signify by construing E's meaning to be some aspect of the nonlinguistic reaction produced by E's referent. So viewed, *RED* designates redness for o at t if this trigram has become conditioned (in o at t) to some detachable component of the unconditioned reaction elicited (in o at t) by the color red. (See Osgood, 1952, 1963, for the most behavior-theoretically sophisticated variant of this approach, and Morris, 1946 Appendix, for a synopsis of its history.) Covert-speech and fractional-surrogate theories of meaning agree that when verbal stimulus E designates nonlinguistic stimulus e, both E and e evoke *inter alia* a shared effect m which is a primary reaction to one of these and a secondary reaction to the other; they differ in which stimulus—symbol or referent—they take to be m's primary elicitor. I say "primary" and "secondary" here, rather than "unconditioned" and "conditioned," to avoid premature commitment to the assumed distinction's nature; for this seemingly straightforward matter in fact hooks into psychosemantics' most vital nerve.

Consider the conjecture that for some psychological effect m, a stimulus S_1 designates (represents, signifies, stands for, symbolizes, refers to, but *not* means) another stimulus S_2 for o at t when both S_1 and S_2 evoke m (i.e. if presented *would* evoke m) in o at t. This is clearly untenable as proposed, for the interchangeability of S_1 and S_2 in the analysans would make designation a symmetric relation whereby, e.g., if *RED* stands for redness, then the color also stands for the word. To achieve symbol/referent asymmetry, a common-effect theory of reference must also stipulate suitably different *ways* in which stimuli evocative of m relate to the latter. Specifically, some notion of "primary" arousal is needed to qualify a stimulus as, say, referent but not symbol, another—"secondary" arousal—to qualify it as symbol but not referent, while it must also be allowed that some conditions of arousal permit two stimuli to share an effect without either thereby signifying the other. The last case, in fact, must be the overwhelmingly prevalent one, for an organism's reactions to any two stimuli which affect him at all will always have *something* in common.

Are these rather modest requirements realizable? Perhaps—but if so, not by any approach to the psychology of language yet published. The simplest way to thwart excessive promiscuity in one's proposed reference relation is to restrict the common effects allowed to mediate it, i.e., to hold that S_1 designates S_2 iff there exists a reaction m of some special kind K such that m is a primary effect of S_2 and a secondary effect of S_1. For this restriction to be helpful, however, it must yield that two stimuli such that neither refers to the other do *not* usually have a common effect of kind K. Unlike the fractional-surrogate view of meaning, the covert-speech position at least suggests how the class of reference mediators might be limited (namely, to whatever counts as internalized language), but this and indeed any plausible suggestion for K is ineffectual for explaining the lack of referential coupling in such stimululs pairs as *RED*-blood, redness-blood, and knife-sharpness. For these and any other pair of stimuli S_1-S_2 whose central correlates are bidirectionally associated, S_1 and S_2 should have common effects of kind K no matter how brutally K is restricted.[26] The problem here is that if S_1 and S_2 (say redness and blood) both elicit an m of kind K, and if primary/secondary are the only alternatives for such arousal, it follows that either (1) S_1 designates S_2 or conversely (clearly inacceptable for redness-blood, since presumably neither of these stimuli is semantically *about* anything), (2) S_1 and S_2 both designate all primary elicitors of m (inacceptable for redness-blood for the reason already noted), or (3) S_1 and S_2 are both designated by any secondary elicitor of m (again objectionable for redness-blood, since according to standard semantic theories a word which designates one of these should not also designate the other). To escape this dilemma we need a semantically neutral way to arouse m, so that even if, e.g., blood evokes a primary effect m of redness, it does so in a tertiary manner under which blood neither designates redness nor is in turn designated by *RED* through the latter's secondary elicitation of m. But that requires what the psychology of language has not yet tried to conceive, namely, a distinction between primary and secondary meaning arousal which does not exhaust the logical possibilities, as does e.g. conditioned vs. unconditioned.

Even without tertiary complications, moreover, neither of the two interpretations of primary vs. secondary meaning arousal suggested in the literature seems at all semantically viable. Treating it as a difference in acquisition, notably as conditioned vs. unconditioned (learned vs. unlearned), will not do at all; for not only is it logically possible even if wildly contrary to fact for the effects of all semantically related stimuli, symbols and their referents alike, to be innate, we have good reason to think that virtually all effects of all external stimuli on cognitively advanced organisms are to an important degree learned. An alternative hope gleams within the notion of "fractional anticipatory response" or "detachable component" of a reaction, the thought being that m's elicitation by S_1 is secondary relative to its primary arousal by S_2 if m is the whole of S_1's K-kind effect but only a part of S_2's. This approach is in deep trouble from the outset, however, unless K is carefully restricted, because if S_1 and S_2 are discriminable (by o at t) at all, then each has some effect (on o at t) not shared by the other. Also jeopardous to it are conceptual puzzles over what is and what is not a stimulus "effect"; for if S_2 evokes reaction component r while S_1 does not, it can also be claimed that S_1, unlike S_2, has *not-r* as an effect[27]— whence it would follow, were *not-r* to be of kind K iff r is, that the K-kind effects of one stimulus (on o at t) can never be a proper subset of those of another. Worst of all, the part/whole treatment of primary vs. secondary meaning arousal has the semantic-theoretically deplorable consequence that if the K-kind effects of S_1 are a proper subset of those of S_2 while the latter are a proper subset of those of S_3, then S_2 designates S_2 while S_1 designates both S_2 and S_3, thus making semantic reference a transitive relation.

Finally, an especially ugly complication for any attempt to analyze reference in terms of shared reactions is the following: If S is a stimulus which evokes reaction m (in o at t) while for another stimulus S^* either (1) S^* is a compound stimulus which includes S (e.g., S is redness while S^* is redheadedness), (2) S is a causal consequence of S^* (e.g., S is redness while S^* is closure of certain traffic-light relays), or (3) S^* is an effect of S which causally mediates the latter's evocation of m (e.g., S is redness while S^* is the pattern of retinal firing produced by light from red surfaces), then m is also generally included in the effects of S^* on o at t. (Various qualifications such as arise from the problem of *not-r* effects complicate this argument but in no way undermine its basic cogency.) Consequently, if one stimulus were to designate another whenever the K-kind effects of the first are included in those of the second, any stimulus S would as a rule simultaneously designate (for o at t) all stimulus compounds of which S is a part, as well as all events before and after S in the causal sequence by which S, or some more distal stimulus whose behavioral import is mediated by S, produces its effects on o at t. More generally, it is extraordinarily difficult to prevent any nontrivial interpretation of "primary" arousal (nontrivial in that it does not employ an aboutness concept in the definiens) from counting as a primary elicitor of m any stimulus S^* related to another primary elicitor S of m in one of the three ways just listed, and hence from implying that any symbol which designates S also designates S^*.[28]

The present arguments are schematically abstract, and neither space allocations nor tedium tolerances approve retracing them here within the flesh of extant theories of reference.[29] Whoever carries through the application on his own, however, will soon discover not merely that these accounts are profoundly inarticulate at all the critical points but also that their unhesitant presumptions concerning which stimulus elicits *m* "primarily" and which "secondarily" rest upon an exceedingly common intuition which, made explicit, would nicely yield symbol/referent asymmetry did it not simply beg the question. I have already exploited this intuition in speaking about "central counterparts" for overt words, and it obtrudes whenever a sensation, or perception, or image, or memory, or idea, or thought, or anticipation, or (in recent jargon) coding is said to be a sensation (etc.) *of* something. It intuits a noncausal relation between internal and external events by virtue of which, e.g., the "idea" or "implicit verbal response" primarily evoked in a paired-associates experiment by nonsense syllable *BIQ* is still an idea or verbalization of the external pattern *BIQ*, rather than of the trigram *CEP* with which *BIQ* has been paired, even on trials when by learned association it is the overt stimulus *CEP* which evokes the *BIQ*-idea. Given this notion, it is straightforward to stipulate that if stimulus *S* elicits reaction *m*, the arousal is "primary" if *m* is *of S*, "secondary" if *m* is *of* something else, and neither of these if *m* is not *of* anything at all. From there it's downhill all the way home for a theory of reference—except that how to reach this *of*ness pinnacle is just the aboutness question all over again.

The ultimate heretical implication of these considerations is that language, as a distinctive system for meaning evocation, has no special psychosemantic importance. The key issues of aboutness show forth most nakedly in nonlinguistic cognitions (or at least where verbalization is not essential), notably, perception, memory, and ideation, and most specifically from the content/object polarity found therein.

What, logically, is involved in perceiving, or remembering, or thinking about something, say the first man on the moon.[30] Manifest grammar alleges these to be relations between an agent (a doer of deeds) and an object upon which the agent commits his act; yet perplexities quickly arise from so simplistic a treatment. For example, perceiving, remembering, or thinking about Neil Armstrong (say as done by his wife) does not seem to be quite the same as perceiving, remembering, or thinking about the first man on the moon, even though Neil Armstrong and the first man on the moon are the very same individual. And though we hesitate to allow that one might perceive or remember something which does not exist, no such inhibition applies to thinking about—e.g., you are now thinking about the first whale on the moon (because I have just given you the idea) even though there never has been and probably never will be any such creature. An epistemological/ontological cesspile of truly awesome grandeur has accrued from imperfect philosophic digestion of this situation, about which I shall here say only (1) that the root error has been to construe intentional acts as grasping with the mind's hand—more technically, taking persons *qua* logical particulars, rather than their attributes, to be what stand directly in aboutness relations to other entities[31]—and (2) that virtually all traditional befuddlements vanish when the content/object distinction is drawn *clearly*. For a person to perceive, remember, or think about this rather than that, his internal psychological condition obviously must be thus rather than so—which is to say that *perceiving* (*remembering, thinking about*) *x* analyzes as *having a percept* (*memory, thought*) *of x*. The percept (memory, thought) which a person *has*, i.e. some aspect of the way he *is*, is the content of his intention, while its object is what that content is *about*. What distinguishes one percept, etc. from others is not primarily its object (which can be the same for many different contents) but its character as a psychological attribute, even though—like being able to identify Jon Smyth only as "resident of Peoria," and perhaps the content/object confusion's main source—ordinary language has virtually no resources for describing an intention's content except relationally in terms of its object. Moreover, evocation of a given content does not analytically entail the existence of a corresponding object—it is perfectly possible for a man to be cognitively identical in every way to how he would be were he perceiving, or remembering, or thinking about, say, his mistress except that in fact he has never had one. (Object-free contents are hopefully infrequent, and perceptual misfires in particular may signal psychopathology; but the exceptions make clear that an intention's object is only an empirical correlate of its content.) Intentional content is thus best described as an aboutness *potential*—it is what, subjunctively, *would* have a corresponding object were external reality to be suitably cooperative. As a result, intentional predicates such as 'perceives *x*', 'remembers *x*', and 'thinks about *x*' can be interpreted to address either (1) the diadic relation which holds between a person *o* and an extant object *x* when *o* has an appropriately moded content which is about *x*, or (2) the non-relational property by virtue of which *o would* be perceiving (or etc.) another entity were one with the right qualifications to exist. In practice, 'perceives' and 'remembers' are usually understood in the stronger sense, and 'thinks about' in the weaker. In addition, both senses (1) and (2) are sometimes—but only sometimes—construed to imply that the intention to which we refer has roughly the same content as the one by which *we* are contemplating its object, i.e. that 'o perceives x' is true only if o's intentional content encorporates the concept expressed by '*x*'—which is why either assertion or denial that perceiving Neil Armstrong is the same as perceiving the first man on the moon can set off a first-class philosophic brawl.

This sketch of intentional aboutness largely reviews my previous remarks on the character of concepts, but tries to clarify the content/object distinction a bit more fully, especially the point that cognitive reference is not even remotely a matter of one stimulus assuming some of the psychological functions of another. An intention's content does not act as surrogate for its object, for nowhere in the causal dynamics of a behavior system can one replace the other—the content is within, the object is (generally) without and requires the former to be the *means* by which it has cognitive import.

So once again we run head-on into the fundamental problem of semantics: What in an intention's content makes it potentially *of* something else, and what are the factors which determine, for any intentional content c and additional entity e, whether or not c is about e? The answers will not be forthcoming here, for I do not have them—though I will, shortly, indicate the direction wherein I think they lie. It is, however, instructive to note why traditional philosophic solutions don't work. These have been strongly colored by preoccupation with perceptual aboutness, and for this it is tempting first of all to seek a causal analysis, namely, that m is a percept of x if x is the cause of m's arousal. The causal approach's allure dims, however, when extended to reactivated memories (for why then should not these be about their present recall cues just as much as about their temporally distant origins), and glows so feebly for imaginative thinking (e.g., about Pegasus, or Satan, or the first whale on the moon) that only the positivistic extremity of denying that we can literally conceive of anything we have never observed will preserve a flicker of life in it. Worse, "the" cause of a percept is hopelessly nonunique—to revive a previous example, when my percept of redness is caused by the state of a traffic light, it is also caused by a relay closure, by a retinal excitation, by a city engineer's past decision about traffic signal placement, by the turning of my head in a certain direction, and by many, many other aspects of this multiply branched and multiply mediated causal webwork. About the only hope for salvaging the causal analysis is that a percept's object might be its *immediate* (unmediated) cause. But even that doesn't achieve sufficient uniqueness of reference; for in the first place causal propagation may well be continuous (i.e., whenever c causes e there exists an m such that c causes m and m causes e), and even were causality to be discrete probably few if any events would have but a single immediate cause. What a theory of aboutness mainly gets from looking to immediate causes is a phenomenalistic squint.

Phenomenalism, or more precisely phenomenalistic positivism, holds that only ingredients *in* experience can be objects of intentional acts, i.e. that when you perceive, remember, or think about, say, your mother you are really perceiving, remembering, or thinking about something in your brain/mind, probably some activity in your sensory or post-sensory nervous system. Phenomenalism has been often discredited, but like crabgrass it sprouts forth anew wherever philosophic groundskeeping becomes lax. Its chief nutrient is a confounding of what is *in* experience with what experience is *of*[32]—i.e. the content/object confusion again—even though it takes little critical reflection to see, e.g., that your mother is not the same as any experience, or set of experiences, you have ever had. (Mothers bear children; experiences bear repeating.) Even when an object of experience really is itself part of experience, as presumably holds for introspection, the logical gap between content and object still persists unless it were to be convincingly argued (as it cannot be) that one can't be elated, or hungry, or enjoying a sunset, or engrossed in lustful reverie without being aware of his elation, hunger, sunset enjoyment, or lustful thoughts; that in fact his elation etc. *is* his awareness thereof. Once it is clear that an object of perception (or etc.), whatever it may be, is not the same thing as the percept itself, no evident semantic motive remains to stuff all such objects inside one's head. Introspective awareness may indeed be an importantly special kind of intentionality (see p. 72, below), but it is a sporadic companion to normal exterospection rather than a substitute for it.

Similar in spirit to phenomenalism but with longer referential reach is the "conceptualist" view that the meaning of a descriptive term is some set of its referent's properties, e.g., that if you are perceiving or remembering or thinking about your mother, the content of your percept/memory/thought is a collection of such properties as *grey-haired, kindly-expression, mediocre-cook, has-arthritic-hip*, etc. ("Appearance" theories of perception often suggest this interpretation.) Its fatal flaw is that properties are just as objective as the individuals which possess them (cf. Rozeboom, 1962a; Bennett, 1965). E.g., grey-hairedness and arthritic-hiphood are no more literally *in* your percept/memory/thought of your mother than she herself is. The conceptualist's half-truth is that a concept of x is often compounded out of concepts of x's properties; but even if one were to argue, like Russell (1905), that complex descriptive phrases do not really designate, it would still remain to explain how concepts which are *of* properties manage to bring off this referential achievement.

Finally, an extremely ancient and historically persistent approach to aboutness (see Brett, 1965) consists of iconic or "copy" theories which suppose that a percept/memory/thought of x must itself be rather *x*ish, i.e. that an intension's content has pretty much the same properties as its object except perhaps for such difficult-to-reproduce qualities as the object's substance, size, and location. That such a view should arise when we cannot say what a concept of x is like beyond its being *of x* is perhaps understandable, since then our description of the concept differs by only one insubstantial element (the operator "of") from our description of its object. It is nonetheless logically gratuitous, akin to supposing that when all we know of Jon Smyth is that he lives in Peoria he must somehow look a little like Peoria, and almost certainly false if—as today we have every reason to believe—mental events are features of neural activity. Even so, the copy theory of aboutness has a certain backhanded heuristic value; for once it becomes robustly clear that there need not be any resemblance whatsoever between the content and the object of an intention—e.g. that in all likelihood a percept of triangularity has itself no more geometric shape than does sourness or the Hammerklavier Sonata—then no evident restrictions remain to curtail either what in external reality is conceivable or, more psychosemantically important, what aspects of a person's inner workings can constitute his conception of a given entity.

Just how liberating this *habeus corpus* may be for semantic theory can best be appreciated by contrasting the vista of possibilities it opens upon the psychological nature of meanings with the tunnel vision of philosophic tradition. Specifically, the classic paradigm for percepts, memories, and ideas is the *sensory image*, of which modern treatments of meaning as a stimulus-producing response (see Goss, 1961) are a peripheralist echo. To be sure, this model has shown little stamina under fire, and introspective psychology's failure to field an alternative has spurred both the behaviorist revolution in psychology (wherein the imageless-thought controversy was allegedly the final intolerable ignominy to fledgling empiricists) and philosophy's latter-day reluctance to countenance meanings as natural occurrents of any sort. Yet introspection and neurophysiological psychology both testify that sensory events, whether externally or internally aroused, are just the animal acts in the circus of the mind. Passion (affect) and conation (effort) also received star billing in classical psychology; recent innovations in self-awareness training may well gain introspective access to exotic experiential flora wholly alien to past mentalistic taxonomies (Murphy, 1969); and in any event psychosemantic data of the quality provided by introspection will become increasingly unhelpful as we begin to dissect the, organism's deeper functionings with the same experimental delicacy now emerging in research on the initial stages of input processing (see e.g. Aaronson, 1967).

What I am getting at here can perhaps best be grasped through a brief return to the nature of evaluative concepts. What gives plausibility to the "emotive" interpretation of such predicates as 'pleasant', 'nasty', 'gorgeous', and 'blah' is that affect is so conspicuously a part of what these terms convey. Insofar as they convey nothing but affect, it is inevitable to conclude—*under the supposition that cognitive meaning cannot be constructed out of emotive elements*—that they have no referents at all. But if aboutness potential is not confined to internal processes just of a sensoid character, then we have no ground on which to dispute that suitably constituted complexes of affective elements may semantically *refer* to entities fully as real as and in fact perhaps identical with those designated by sensoid concepts. Thus pleasantness and blahhood *could* be perfectly good objective attributes of external things, attributes which (say) produce certain distinctive affective reactions in most persons who encounter them and which can also in principle be designated by expressions of technical physics.[33] I would not deny that the *de facto* semantic character of predicates such as 'pleasant' and 'blah' leaves much to be desired, but the same is often true of everyday sensoid concepts, e.g., 'bald', 'fat', 'smelly', 'hot', 'white', 'sticky', etc., which are quickly abandoned by any discipline attempting to deal precisely with their domain of application. I conclude, then, that contrasting "evaluative" with "descriptive" terms may well be an error. Instead, *within* the descriptive category, the meanings of some terms seem predominantly sensoid, some predominantly affectoid, some, like 'abrasive', 'bitter', and 'shrill', as much one as the other, and some which primarily mobilize internal processes of still other kinds, notably terms such as 'seat', 'handle', 'hammer', 'pliable', 'beckoning', and 'roomy', whose meanings have a strongly conative or motor character. It is no longer very original to suggest that cognitions involve motor (and motivational) functions as well as afference—one thinks especially of Piaget in this regard. (Cf. also Bruner *et al.*, 1966, on "enactive" concepts.) But even Piaget and his followers apparently allow that only sensoid images can *represent* external reality (see Furth, 1969, Chapts. 4 and 5). My emphasis here is that we have no reason to think that afferent events are any more intrinsically *of* something else than are *inter alia* affective and motor processes. For a semantic theory to suppose otherwise without argument is to signal that it has simply begged the question of aboutness.

Concept formation

What is it to "have" a particular concept? We have already noted that the focus of commonsense cognition talk wavers ambiguously between activated processes and the state properties which dispose the former's arousal. According to my own English sensitivities, "use" of a concept c is primarily an actual ϕing $P(c)$ for some intentional mode ϕ and content $P(c)$ of which c is a constituent, while the "having" of concept c is primarily a state which disposes ϕing $P(c)$ for some ϕ and P. Since many functionally distinguishable states can dispose ϕing $P(c)$, there are correspondingly many different ways to "have" concept c; but I have spoken earlier of that in general terms and need not elaborate here. Right now I want to consider the acquiring of (state) concepts.

For brevity, I would prefer just to acknowledge how people come to have the concepts they do have (especially logical concepts and the modal operators, which have received virtually no acquisition study at all) is a question well worth attention, and let it go at that. But mainstream psychology has been cheerfully researching what it has called "concept formation" for half a century, with results to show that the enterprise could well stand some sharpening of its logic. Which is not to say that philosophers have been any more astute about this. Quite the opposite: The rationalist/empiricist quarrel over concept origins has supposed that having a mindful of concepts is like having a houseful of furniture, with empiricists holding that all this furniture has been delivered by van to an originally empty house (i.e. by sensory channels transmitting miniatures of external objects into the mind) while rationalists protest that some pieces aren't of the sort that vans deliver. This stone-age view of concept formation[34] is totally obviated by two slightly more sophisticated reflections: (1) Once the copy theory of perception is dismissed, how sensory input manages to activate central percepts which are *of* a particular external entity is just as much an unsettled (and unsettling) scientific problem as is the arousal of intentional contents by nonsensory precursors. Perceptual abilities, too, generally have to be learned, and it is silly to adopt strong postures regarding which concepts can and which cannot be developed through sensory input until the machinery of perception becomes a little less mysterious. (2) It is reasonably safe to assume that cognitions can no more be activated in newly fertilized human ova than in such lowly lifeforms as beetles and potatoes. Trite as it may seem, this observation points up that you and I began life entirely devoid of conceptual resources, yet possessed from the outset a potential for developing these which seems largely unique to our particular species. At the level of slogans, therefore, rationalists and empiricists are both correct—a person's concepts all develop through his interactions with his environment, yet innate factors importantly direct the outcomes of such interactions. To explain an aspect of cognition not obviously accounted for by 1930–1950 vintage learning theory by saying only that it must therefore be innate (e.g., Chomsky, 1965, 1967) is simply to demonstrate ignorance of what a significant hypothesis in technical psychology is like. When we have some detailed dynamic models of cognitive growth, then and only then we will be in position to work out what we want to *mean* by applications of the labels 'learned' and 'innate' to this situation.

Psychology's own affair with concept formation, on the other hand, has suffered from insensitivity to essentials, like making love to one's girl friend, her mother, her brother, and her dog, and not noticing a difference. The basic concept-formative research paradigm trains subjects to discriminate one set of complex stimulus displays from another in response to some feature shared by just the concept-positive displays. It is easy to interpret such experiments as a discriminative conditioning of labeling responses to abstract stimulus elements, and until quite recently this has been the standard theoretic model—which, unhappily, is tantamount to arguing that having a concept *is* simply being disposed to make a consistent labeling response to some feature of complex stimulation. Not only does this further confuse the already obscure differences between concept-mediated responding and subcognitive discriminative behavior, neither does it distinguish concept formation as such from learning the payoff correlates in a new situation of concepts acquired previously.

A significant lurch forward, however, has recently come with awakening recognition that concepts have something intimately to do with hypotheses or "rules." Thus if the subject's task is learning to identify as "positive" or "negative" each of a number of designs differing in color, shape, and size, he is said to have acquired "the concept" when he learns (say) that a design is positive if and only if it is either red or circular. (Usually the subject is credited with attainment of the rule/concept when his behavior becomes consistent with it, though some recent studies have also required him to verbalize the rule.) Learning such a "rule" or adopting such a "hypothesis" is, with one important qualification which need not detain us[35], genuinely a cognitive acquisition by the subject, namely of *belief* to some degree in a lawlike proposition of form $(x)(Cx \supset Px \equiv Qx)$ (e.g. the generalization that any design in this experiment [C] is what the experimenter calls "positive" [P] iff it has disjunctive property of being either red or circular [Q]). Unfortunately, with few exceptions (notably Gagné, 1966), these studies have so confounded the learning of concepts with learning of the generalizations ("principles") which utilize them that some writers (e.g., Hunt, 1962, p. 29f.) explicitly claim that concepts *are* rules. Actually it is doubtful whether the new wave of concept research has been knowingly witness to any concept *acquisition* at all. A person who can already perceive redness and circularity, for example, and who also has the elementary logical operators at his avail (innately?), is thereby also capable of discerning the property of being-either-red-or-circular. (To be sure, changes in a subject's conception of being-either-red-or-circular, notably, its becoming more "integrated" or perceptually immediate, may well also occur through his exercising of it; but this possibility—a genuine and important case of concept learning—has to my knowledge not been explored in the concept-formation literature albeit work on perceptual "coding" comes close.) What these experiments have primarily addressed is not concept formation itself, but something even more richly cognitive, namely, the development of generalized beliefs by inference from observed particulars and even, where "strategies" of observation have been studied (Bruner, Goodnow, and Austin, 1956), some aspects of metabeliefs. Were this work to be explicitly recognized for what it is—the psychology of inductive reasoning—we would be immensely better positioned to appraise not merely its past accomplishements but also which directions are most significant for its future thrust.

The one sector of modern psychology wherein concept formation or something much like it really has been at issue is in work on perceptual learning, i.e. phenomena where an organism's experiences apparently alter not merely his motor habits but his afferent receptivity to certain features of the environment regardless of that input's fate in postperceptual processing (see Gibson, 1969). Perceptual learning is as much a theoretical viewpoint as it is a distinctive empirical domain, for its operational proving grounds are the principles of generalization and discrimination on which old-fashioned peripheralistic behavior theory has also fielded a considerable body of S-R speculations in which perceptual changes are not envisioned at all. It can be shown (e.g. Rozeboom, 1970, p. 123 ff.) that the empirical facts of generalization and discrimination greatly exceed the explanatory reach of S-R orthodoxies unless the latter are enriched by some nonassociative principles of perceptual differentiation or (what is nearly the same) selective attention. To date, however, perceptual difference theory's farthest advance has been its bare insistence that there is something importantly more to perceptual learning than mediation responses becoming attached to innately and unmodifiably discriminable sensory units. We still lack even the roughest conception of *mechanisms* controlling the articulation of experience. My own feeble efforts in this direction allow me to venture only (1) that unlike most of cognitive psychology, perceptual differentiation theory has nothing at all to learn from commonsense mentalism; (2) that the explanatory model which should eventually emerge here will be quite unlike past behavior-theoretic mechanisms, exploiting instead such notions as "resonance," "cancellation," and others indebted to wave physics; and (3) that this model will readily ingest, omnivorously, without strain or indigestion, *all* known behavioral phenomena; not merely generalization and discrimination but principles of action and reinforcement as well. Psychology may yet get its Newton. It remains only for the apple to strike.

While research on perceptual learning is psychology's only present handhold on concept formation, it is by no means true (unless positivism is right after all) that acquired concepts originate in perception alone. The main case in point is that of *theoretical* concepts, whose cognitive status has been perhaps the most intensely discussed issue in all of philosophy of science—and rightly so, since herein lies the ultimate confrontation between phenomenalistic and realistic epistemologies. I can speak to this best in the context of *language learning*, or more precisely the acquisition of word meanings since I shall say nothing about syntax development.

Generically, the processes by which the terms of a language become cognitively meaningful are known as "definition." While philosophers have seen fit to distinguish a rather large number of species under this genus (cf. Robinson, 1954; Leonard, 1957; Pap, 1964), the major psychosemantically distinctive types—idealized, since in practice most words enterlanguage by multiple routes—seem to me to me to be threefold: *ostensive*, *explicit*, and *theoretic* (*implicit*). Of these, explicit definition is the least problematic, involving only a synonymous transfer of meaning from one expression to another. Thus if I stipulate that 'farble' is to mean "sing in a quavery voice," 'farble' becomes a vehicle for the same concept expressed by the grammatically complex predicate 'sing in a quavery voice'—including synonymy with respect to whatever vagueness and ambiguity may reside in the latter. Terms already meaningful can also be revised by explicit definition, usually towards greater precision as when e.g. we stipulate that 'boy' is to mean "a human male under 18 years of age."

Even so seemingly innocent a process as explicit definition raises challenging psychological questions, however. For mere stipulation that a word A is to mean the same as expression B is quite insufficient to make A *in fact* synonymous with B for a given person o at time t. At the very least, o must have heard or himself issued this resolve, and even that is not enough—I could repeatedly proclaim that 'boy' is to mean "a mammal less than 65 inches tall" without this at all changing the meaning this word in fact has for me. For a definitional proposal to become a definitional accomplishment, learning must occur—just *how* being the psychological puzzle here.

Orthodox associative principles are on several grounds grossly insufficient to account for it: (1) If hearing 'A is to mean B' (or words to that effect) conditions the meaning of 'B' to verbal stimulus 'A', why doesn't the meaning of 'A' also become conditioned to 'B', ultimately resulting in a common meaning which is roughly a sum or average of the two original meanings? (As seen e.g. by considering 'B is what A is to mean', the temporal asymmetry of terms in a definition does not adequately explain this, though the time relation may not be entirely irrelevant.) (2) Why does 'A is to mean B' endow 'A' with the meaning of just 'B' rather than of the entire verbal complex with which 'A' is paired, namely, 'is to mean B'? (3) If hearing/uttering 'A is to mean B' gives 'A' the meaning of 'B', why doesn't hearing/uttering 'A does mean B' generally have this same effect? (It doesn't, of course, if 'A' and 'B' aren't synonymous at the outset; instead, it just makes a false assertion.) Apparently, explicit definition is accomplished through a special intentional mode such that when a suitably structured content is activated in this mode, the meaning component in a certain position of that structure is copied into another wherein it becomes responsive to the stimulus component which, in non-definitional mode, would evocatively control that position.

Though superficially remote from explicit definition, ostensive definition is probably much the same in underlying mechanism. Ostensive definition is the acquisition of word meanings by having referents for them pointed out in one's non-verbal experience—e.g., hearing 'This is Jon Smyth' while being introduced to him. To philosophic empiricists, ostensive definition has seemed to be the one secure base on which an epistemically creditable theory of semantics can be erected, though a common protest is that it leaves unexplained how the trainee can tell which particular prospective referent is being pointed out. (E.g., if I gesticulate in the direction of Smyth, am I pointing to him, to his shirt color, to his racial heritage, or to the wall behind him?) The objection is on target, but misses the bullseye unless it draws bead on the phenomenalistic supposition usually latent in the thinking of those to whom ostensive definition seems unproblematic, namely, that the things we "experience" are themselves *in* experience. Although the verb 'experience' is ambiguous and *sometimes* means "to have as experiential content," ostensive definition concerns the sense wherein 'to experience e' means "to have an experience containing a meaning component which is *about e*." To originate linguistic reference to an entity e, ostensive definition must attach an experiential content which is *of e* to the selected verbal vehicle. Physical pointing may be efficacious for this, but only when the learner can exploit a perceptual structure in which a relational concept of pointing supplemented by selective predication is coupled with a concept of *e*. Thus a hearer of 'Jon Smyth is the man arguing with the policeman over there' is positioned to equate the meaning of 'Jon Smyth' with whatever component of his present experience has argumentative-manhood-over-there perceptually predicated of it. The procedure here seems to be that a verbally aroused meaning complex containing, as it were, a gap corresponding to the to-be-defined term is matched against concurrent experience; and if, under definitional mode, a match is found wherein the former is congruent with a portion of the latter, then the component of the latter which fills the gap in the former under that alignment becomes the meaning of the term evocatively tied to that gap.

Up to a point, theoretic (implicit) definition is much like explicit and ostensive definition in that the to-be-defined term '*t*' is introduced via a semantic context idealizable as a more or less complex predicate '*P*( )' ascribed to '*t*'. But whereas explicit and ostensive definitions assign to '*t*' a pre-formed meaning which has already been activated under belief mode in this context, theoretic definitions *create* concepts rather than copy them. According to the most advanced judgment on this difficult and much discussed matter,[36] a theoretical term '*t*' introduced by the theory ("nomological net") '*P(t)*' derives its meaning from predicate '*P*( )' but *designates* something which satisfies the latter so long as there is any such entity. Thus if Hullian theory were correct, '$_sH_R$' would refer to whatever state of the organism grows as a function of reinforcement for doing *R* in the presence of *S* and interacts with deprivation conditions to determine the probability of *R*-responding to *S*. Similarly, when the *Random House Dictionary of the English Language* informs me that *manganese* is "a hard, brittle, greyish-white metallic element, an oxide of which, MnO_2, is a valuable oxidizing agent; used chiefly as an alloying agent in steel to give it toughness; symbol, Mn; atomic weight, 54.938; atomic number, 25; specific gravity, 7.2 at 20°C", then until such time as I acquire a superior definition of 'manganese', say through first-hand metallurgical experience, this is for me a theoretical term whose referent is, of definitional necessity, a hard, brittle, greyish-white metallic element, etc. What is most semantically remarkable about theoretical terms—a character unimaginable in traditional epistemology and still largely unassimilated by philosophical semantics—is that a theory which "implicitly defines" some of its constituent terms is *analytically* true *if* true at all (see Rozeboom, 1962b, p. 347ff.). That is, contrary to the semantic orthodoxy that a logically contingent statement '*Q(t)*' is true if entity *t* happens to have property *Q* and false if *t* does not—an account which presumes the existence of a referent for '*t*' in either case—a theoretical definition '$P(t)$' of 't' is true or false according to whether or not 't' *has* a referent, while to assume that t exists and yet be in doubt whether it has property P is like being uncertain about the marital status of bachelors.

If theoretical terms really do have the semantic traits here claimed for them, they may well be our Rosetta stone to intentionality's ultimate twin mysteries, the functional character of meanings and the nature of aboutness. The former glimmers tantalizingly within the strange quasi-analyticity of theoretic definitions. If 't' is defined by theory '$P(t)$' so that t *must*, analytically, have property P, then in some sense the meaning of 'P' has been converted into what is expressed by 't'. Yet 'P' and 't' are far from synonymous, for they differ in logical type—'P' is predicated of 't', not equated with it. Apparently at work here is a mechanism for transforming one conceptual structure into another whose referential reach exceeds that of the first. How the propositional juxtaposition of these (i.e. in present notation the proposition expressed by '$P(t)$') manages to be epistemically nontrivial, how the propositions respectively expressed by concept-definitive statement '$P(t)$' and another sentence '$Q(t)$' attributing to t some property Q not entailed by P semantically differ in kind, and what changes occur in the meaning of '$Q(t)$' if the latter is elevated to co-definitional status in this theory (i.e. if 't' is now defined by the enriched theory '$P(t) \cdot Q(t)$'), are matters on which even dim illumination at some technical depth should explain much about the understructure of meaning processes.

Moreover, the bootstraps logic by which theory formation expands a language's referential scope may be nearly the whole story of external reference. Stripped to empoverished essentials, what I have in mind is the following: Given concepts of entities $\{e_i\}$ and relations $\{R_j\}$, theoretic definition allows us to generate concepts which designate entities related by one or more of the R_j to one or more of the e_i. If, moreover, the e_i and the R_j are phenomenal objects, i.e. ingredients *in* one's experience, we see how a phenomenalistically ideal cognizer beginning only with concepts about his own experience can rework these into theoretical concepts providing referential access to the external world. (No high degree of intelligence or studied contemplation is requisite to the theorizing which performs this conceptual alchemy. The most basic moves in theory construction tend to occur compulsively at an essentially preconscious level of cognition—see Rozeboom, 1961 b, p. 368 f.) Finally, if the phenomenalistic phase of the analysis can be modified just enough to make phenomenal referents a dispensable luxury by showing how the components from which exterospective meanings are assembled can be recruited directly from nonconceptual experience (i.e. by shorting out the intermediate step of the two-stage model wherein sub-intentional experience elements are first compounded into phenomenal concepts and the latter then reprocessed into concepts with external referents), the result will be a realist theory of aboutness in which an intention's content is built out of meaning ingredients to which its object is coupled through the logical nexus of exemplification. The phenomenal scaffolding of this analysis is urged by intuition that an introspective concept of an experiential condition C is probably not much different, psychologically, from C itself—it may, for example, consist of C elaborated upon in a certain way. (I.e., introspective awareness of C may be a structure $\alpha(C)$ comprising C imbedded in a special concept schema $\alpha(\ )$.) If so, an account of external reference as mediated by phenomenal concepts should closely resemble the wanted account directly in terms of nonconceptual experience. Be this as it may, the suspicion remains that while the logic of theoretical concepts may well be the lever to pry open the secrets of distal reference, the fulcrum on which it must turn is a detailed analysis of introspective content/object relations.

Liberalization of classical semantics

From the problems of meaning and reference reviewed here so far, it might appear that for philosophers, psychosemantics is mainly a spectator sport. The wreckage of that complacency litters still another axis of psychosemantic inquiry, namely, semantic realities which will no longer tolerate the constrictive simplicities of their traditional idealizations. "Pure" semantics is overdue for a basic axiomatic overhaul.

As a preliminary, it is worth noting that conventional views on synonymy are surely wrong to construe 'X means the same as Y' or 'x is the same concept as y' as an identity equation. This is the supposition which has led some important philosophers of language (e.g., Frege, 1898, p. 59f.) to deny the psychological nature of cognitive ("logical") meaning on grounds that the mental reactions evoked by a given expression are far too inconsistent, even in the same person on different occasions much less from one person to another, for any such reaction to qualify as the common meaning conveyed by that expression to the assorted members of a given language community. Although such arguments generally presume that "psychological" (*contra* "logical") meanings are restricted to sensory images, their minor premise is undoubtedly correct—it is most unlikely that the cognitive meaning conveyed to me e.g. by the word 'red' is identical with the meaning it conveys to you, especially if one of us has color-anomolous vision. Yet in ordinary usage, 'same as' probably means "identical with" less often than it does "alike in all (or most) respects relevant to the matter at hand," as when we agree that you-today are the same person as you-yesterday, or say that sugar and salt both have the same disposition of water-solubility even though the molecular properties respectively responsible for their dissolutions in water presumably differ in some respects. For interpersonal communication, literal between-person identity of word meanings is wholly irrelevant so long as the within-person pattern of semantic *relations*—i.e. which expressions are equivalent, which sentences entail which others, which terms designate what objects—is shared by all. This is the only interpersonal "sameness" of meaning which we can operationally affirm or deny in ordinary life, and while it, too, is an ideal which linguistic reality approximates only imperfectly, the approximation seems often good enough to make this sense of interpersonal synonymy a useful notion. In any event, whatever we may ultimately choose to count as meaning-sameness, the technically important relations for interlinguistic[37] semantic comparisons, are not simple identities or (vis-à-vis analytic entailment) part-inclusions but communalities of designative potential, i.e. meaning relations which compare not what their relata intrinsically *are* but what they *do*.

That synonymy's psychological nature may be more abstractly complex than traditionally assumed does not in itself much matter for axiomatically "pure" semantics. Threats to the scope of the use/mention reciprocity underlying the correspondence principle of truth, however, are quite another matter. And regardless of any impression I may have left earlier, the correspondence principle's semantic utility is very limited indeed, for its applicability to particular cases strictly depends upon one's willingness to concede first-class cognitive status to the expression at issue. Consider, for example, the claims that

1) That-John-is-76-inches-in-height is true iff John is 76 inches in height.
2) That-John-is-tall is true iff John is tall,
3) That-John-is-zutish is true iff John is zutish.

Whereas (1) is presumably a blue-ribbon semantic verity, (3) is literally nonsense insomuch as the visual shape 'zutish' expresses no concept at all—asserting as a principle that "that-*p* is true iff *p*" is not intended to imply that this formula yields a true instantiation for any arbitrary substitution of graphic squiggles for free variable '*p*', But what about (2)? The statement 'John is tall' is certainly not meaningless, and had we no conceptual resources superior to 'tall', 'middling', and 'short' or the like for describing height we would have no grounds on which to balk at (2). But once we decide that the predicate 'tall' is *vague* with respect to more precise predicates at our command, so that we no longer care to regard sentences of form '——is (is not) tall' as describing possible states of reality logically independent of the facts described by quantitative height statements e.g. of form '_____is (is not) x inches in height',[38] we are confronted with a semantic dilemma: (*i*) For every positive real number x, deleting one of the bracketed terms in

That-John-is-tall is {true, false} if John is x inches in height

should yield an analytically true semantic conditional. However, (*ii*) in view of the meaning that 'tall' *in fact* conveys (not what it could be revised to mean), (*i*) actually holds for few if any values of x. Classical semantic dichotomies rooted in the correspondence principle just don't fit the semantic reality of vagueness; rather, this calls for a theory of *graded* aboutness which can make semantic sense out of statements of form

'Tall' refers in degree d to the property of being x inches in height.

and

That-John-is-tall is true to extent d if John is x inches in height,

in which d varies on a continuum which may well be multidimensional.

To be sure, classical semantics has long managed to endure the phenomenon of vagueness by the imperialist expedient of treating our *de facto* concepts as flawed, subcognitive approximations to the Platonic perfections which alone are the business of philosophy.[39] But problems of vagueness merely symptomatize a much deeper foundational challenge to semantics: If for a given semantic analysis it cannot usefully be assumed at the outset (say because this would beg the question at issue) that the object language synonymously translates into our metalanguage, then only the inertia of tradition requires that designation be formalized as a single-valued function mapping descriptive terms of the object language into the domain(s) of metalanguage variables. Since vagueness is not intellectually respectable, the graded multiple reference of terms which are vague relative to the metalanguage might not in itself seem sufficient reason to abandon this tradition. However, I have elsewhere argued at length (Rozeboom, 1960b, 1962b, 1964, 1971a) that an empiricist interpretation of theoretical concepts also requires admission that descriptive terms generally have multiple referents even in an ideally vagueness-free language; specifically, that if term 't' is defined by theory '$P(t)$', then 't' designates every entity e such that $P(e)$.[40] To date, the published philosophic reaction to this thesis has been a total, repressive silence. But neither has anyone deigned to point out any flaws in my argument; and if it is indeed correct that no single-reference semantic model can touch the epistemic essence of theoretical concepts, the new "pure" semantics (and perhaps even a revised logic) which will emerge from the necessary rewriting of first principles will be as profound an advance over its classical precursor as was relativity over Newtonian physics.

Finally, recognition that the relation between intentional contents and objects is not of uniform semantic quality positions formal semantics to assimilate the existentialist dimension of cognition. It is a common subjective phenomenon that one's understanding of a concept often undergoes profound changes with increased experience and maturity.[41] Few if any concepts are exempt from this effect, not just notoriously slippery notions like "love," "justice," and "freedom," but concepts of ordinary things, places, persons ("iron," "Russia," "Mother"), and even qualities familiar since infancy (e.g., "round," and "red", which are far from indifferent to education in geometry and color theory). The trend of such change is almost always towards greater precision, greater clarity, and—what is not wholly the same as clarity—an increased "depth," "fullness," or "richness" of conception. Though this last has much concerned me in my own intellectual life, there is little I can usefully say about its nature here except, to illustrate, that it is what is most lacking in the verbally fluent, overeducated student who knows all the right things to say about a thing without really understanding any of it, and reaches its highest fulfillment through intimate encounters with the concept's referent, the sort of experience which leads one to exult "Now I *really* know x!" in the deep-acquaintance sense of "know." I suspect that this is quite literally a difference in the quantity and diversity of meaning elements compounded into the concept in question. But it is enough here to acknowledge simply that it *is* an intrinsic facet of semantics that concepts having the same referent can nonetheless vary from lean to rich, and that other things equal, the richer are a proposition's concepts the choicer is its epistemic quality.

Once it is granted that richness (depth, fullness) is a factor pervading *all* of conceptual knowing—that a proposition of zero depth would be no more a proposition than a man of zero height would still be a man, and that enriching a proposition's meaning enhances rather than diminishes its status as a *conceptual* structure—there remains little basis for arguing that existential awareness (cf. p. 34, above) differs in kind from conceptual aboutness. Knowing-(it) is not, after all, the same as having-(it) *in* one's experience, at least not for most (it)s which ordinary language allows to be known, nor is knowing-(it) an all-or-none affair: Of my various acquaintances, for example, I know some much better (more thoroughly, more deeply) than I do others. If there is anything more to knowing-(it) than having a conception of (it) well advanced along the richness dimension, I for one cannot imagine what it might be. And to protest that the knowing which comes of existential involvement, the "I/thou" intimacy, is just too close, too total, too much a fusion of identities, to be strained through such coldly abstract mediaries as concepts, my reply is that were concepts only what is expressed by words now actually at our common avail, why, then I would wholeheartedly agree. But surely I have argued enough by now that meanings are basically independent of the verbal vehicles we may contrive for some of them (which is not to say that a stock of meanings once verbally domesticated cannot be evolved into a superior breed by linguistic husbandry), and that an awareness-of, no matter how existentially immediate, is just one of diverse ways for a concept to be active in one's experience. I have little doubt that limits short of perfection impair the effective transfer of nonverbally evoked meanings to language vehicles, but neither do I suspect that we often approach the asymptote of possibility in this regard. Rather than abetting anti-rational mystiques through fraudulent claims of proprietory right to the richness of immediate experience, the sincere humanist/existentialist could better seek to inject more of his most cherished meaning components into the public domain of verbalized concepts.

PROBLEMS IN THE JUSTIFICATION OF BELIEF

Due to length restrictions agreed upon by this volume's participants, ruthlessly enforced by its editors, and already exceeded by this essay, I shall be unable to say much about issues of belief justification. I can only hint, with even greater brevity than before, at those to which I attach the highest psycho-philosophical research priority.

To an epistemic traditionalist, suggesting that psychology might make any contribution at all to the theory of rationality sounds like the most flagrant confusion between the *is* and the *ought* of belief. Even so, normative belief theory needs an assist from empirical psychology in at least three ways:

1) In the first place, since few if any circumstances warrant unconditional acceptance of a given proposition, the theory of rationality is technically concerned with assertions of form, "Under circumstances C, proposition p ought to be believed in degree d." Just what alternatives there *are* for qualified belief, however, is a question in descriptive psychology. Currently popular formalizations of belief strength as subjective probability are, I would agree, useful models for this at our present stage of development; but not merely shall we eventually need to distinguish believing that-p in degree d from any degree of confidence in the proposition that that-p-has-

probability-*d*, it is doubtful that the belief-strength metric is really one-dimensional. (E.g., the grades of uncertainty which a cosmologist attaches to various theories of the universe's origin don't seem to contrast in quite the same way as do the credences he invests in the possibilities for what his wife may serve for supper tonight.) As the semantic valuation of propositions becomes recognizably more complex than a dichotomous true/false, so does the complexity of the belief-act continuum.

2) Secondly, what are the "circumstances" which determine how much belief is merited by a given proposition? Clearly this is not just the proposition's content in itself, but aspects of a particular occasion on which that content is contemplated. But which "aspects" of such occasions? The traditional philosophic paradigm for rational belief assumes that the belief in question has been inferred by the believer from other propositions which he accepts, in which case the belief strength so warranted resides in the quality of the evidence for this conclusion. But justification by inference alone must ultimately trace back to an uninferred beginning, and how are such *basic*—i.e., uninferred—beliefs then to be justified? The wistful desire of traditional epistemology, for each person to have a set of normatively *certain* beliefs (e.g. the experiential "given") which are the sole source of justification in his belief system, is hopelessly counterfactual; and we cannot effectively appraise the epistemic status of rationally uncertain basic beliefs until descriptive psychology has inventoried how, beyond inference, beliefs originate.

3) It appears moreover, that how strongly basic beliefs arising from sources of a given kind *should* be held is importantly a function of their truth likelihood (cf. Rozeboom, 1967a);[42] and estimation of these probabilities is again an empirical enterprise. I should add that while I mistrust the cogency of any normative epistemology not grounded on the *de facto* accuracy of basic beliefs under various conditions of their production, the obstacles to coherent development of such an approach are so horrendous that we may eventually have to settle for consistency as the only rationality requirement on basic beliefs. Even in that event, however, psychological categories of belief sources and their presumed reliabilities will retain normative relevance unde the egis of metabeliefs (see below).

For reasons mentioned later, the outline I would follow in a synoptic treatment of belief sources is

1. Inference
    a. deductive
    b. ampliative.

2. Observation
   a. exterospective
   b. introspective.
3. Memory.
4. Analyticity.
5. Hearsay.
6. Familiarity.
7. Desire.
8. Intuition.
9. Metabeliefs.

Though present commentary will be largely restricted to the last one of these, certain points regarding inference and observation also deserve special attention.

Concerning inference, far less is known about this than the smugness of orthodox epistemology would ever suggest. It is not even very clear what inference *is*. For example, if by *Rule Application* we mean the inference pattern

$$(R.A.) \quad \frac{\text{All } Ps \text{ are } Q,}{x \text{ is } Q,} \quad x \text{ is a } P,$$

what must occur in order for a person o at time t to deduce his belief (q) that John is queer by *Rule Application* from his beliefs (p_1) that John is a pacifist and (p_2) that all pacifists are queer? If the inference is really by $R.A.$, rather than by some other valid or invalid schema which subsumes this triplet of propositions such as

$$\frac{\text{All pacifists are } Q,}{x \text{ is } Q,} \quad x \text{ is a pacifist,} \quad \text{or} \quad \frac{\text{All } Ps \text{ are } Q,}{x \text{ is } Q,} \quad x \text{ is an } R,$$

or perhaps by no inference pattern at all, it must be that in some fashion schema $R.A.$ is instrumental in o's coming to accept q on grounds p_1 and p_2. But instrumental how? Not by virtue of metabelief in $R.A.$'s validity being included as an additional premise in the derivation; for while this could indeed occur were o to be sufficiently knowledgeable about formal logic, the inference's pattern would then be not $R.A.$ but a more elaborate schema. (More generally, construing an inference's *pattern* to be one of its *premises* precipitates an infinite regress—cf. Carroll, 1895.) Neither is it by virtue of o's having at t the property that if he believes the first two of any three *R.A.*-related propositions then he also believes the third; for not only would this bypass the intuitive requirement that the conclusion of an inference be believed *because* the premises are believed, neither is it true that in order to infer one proposition by a given pattern a person must simultaneously infer *all* conclusions which so follow from premises he believes. The correct analysis seems to me to be roughly as follows: o infers q from p_1 and p_2 at t by *R.A.* (and similarly for any other inference pattern) iff he becomes aware at t that this triplet of propositions has the *R.A.* structure and this structural awareness together with the strengths of his beliefs in p_1 and p_2 jointly cause an increment in the strength of his belief in q.

Even if correct in principle, however, this sketch of inference's nature is but prologue to deeper problems. What is it, for example, to be "aware" of logical structure in an inferentially effective sense? (E.g., how does this differ from simply having in mind an activated n-tuple of propositions which embodies this structure, and how reflectively self-conscious must the awareness be?) What are the causal dynamics of valid inference? (E.g., does "awareness" of a valid argument's structure suffice by itself to convert belief in the premises into belief in the conclusion, or is this so dependent on the person's state parameters that in principle he can be trained to reason by any arbitrary schema?) And what degree of belief is/should be conferred upon the conclusion of (*inter alia*) an *R.A.*-patterned inference by less-than-complete belief in its premises?

Insight into the generic nature of inference is a luxury which normative epistemology can perhaps afford to develop at leisure. Very much another matter is describing the specific inference patterns which in fact govern human reason. For while our technical grasp of what is and what is not a logically valid argument has by now well surpassed most needs of practical deduction, we are still unbelievably ignorant about what patterns of *ampliative* (nondemonstrative) inference should/do direct our thinking. It is not that the theory of ampliative reasoning has suffered from neglect—a chapter or two on "scientific inference" is *de rigueur* for any book on philosophy of science or research methodology. But the extant material on this divides rather cleanly into two classes; on the one hand assorted doctrines on the logic of statistical generalization which, though still disturbingly shaky at the deeper foundational levels, generally achieve considerable quantitative sophistication both at abstract theory and in practical research applications, and on the other hand a hash of tradition, mysticism, and doubletalk servicing the rest of ampliative inference with little relevance to either the problems or more advanced practices of inferential reality. Since I have reviewed the latter's more damning inadequacies elsewhere (Rozeboom, 1970, 1971 b), I shall observe here only that (1) there is no epistemic need for rational inference to be logically valid (i.e., strictly deductive) so long as the transmission of belief from premises to conclusion is more restrained (hesitant, circumspect, reserved) than is proper for deduction; (2) the inference patterns by which men reason in situations with real-life repercussions are *not* in fact typically deductive; and (3) statistical generalization from sample frequency data is merely one of several distinct ampliative patterns fundamental to all grades of intelligent thought from primitive intuition to the most advanced craftwork in scientific data analysis. I have already described two others in rather specific detail (Rozeboom, 1961 b, 1966 a, 1971 b), both of these being "ontological" or "explanatory" inductions which transform observed regularities into theories about their underlying sources, and the count may have just begun. Determinate patterns of nonstatistical induction are without acknowledged precedent in the annals of epistemology, and philosophers who would assume responsibility for their normative appraisal had best begin humbly. The first task is purely descriptive, namely, to detect and formalize those ampliative arguments which do, empirically, carry conviction for sophisticated thinkers in areas shaped by reality feedback. The habitat of these inference forms, moreover, is not primarily where philosophers most comfortably browse amid the theoretic deposits of history's Great Scientists, but in the stuff of lab reports and research strategies; not the grand syntheses which catch the imagination of an age but the technical arguments by which unromantic professionals persuade and criticize their colleagues. By no means will this inferential ore test out as uniformly high grade. The logic of scientific data analysis is still actively evolving, with good and bad theorizing closely intermingled without clear consensual standards for their separation, and its most powerful advances beyond commonsense intuition remain poorly formalized. Normative study of these arguments, if conducted with existential sensitivity to their inductive force and fine logical structure, could greatly expedite the still-amoeboid progress of "scientific method." But regardless of epistemic engineering prospects, the psycho-philosophy of knowledge now stands upon a threshold to discoveries in inductive reasoning breathtakingly vast enough to put even the past century's advances in deductive logic to shame.

Concerning observation, it is noteworthy that despite the lavish attention philosophers and psychologists have given this topic, the logical force of categorizing a given cognition as an "observation" ("percept") is still importantly obscure. For example, if I ask you why you think that John and Mary have made up their quarrel and you reply that you see (observe, perceive) them holding hands over there, just what are you asserting about your belief in their hand-holding which is distinct from asserting with equal conviction, say, that you remember or intuit this? Are you claiming that the *content* of your perceptual belief has a distinctive quality (e.g., a lively intensity) which memories and intuitions lack, so that observing that-*p* and remembering or intuiting that-*p* contain the same proposition only in an abstract (i.e. non-identitive) sense of "same"? Or do you allege a special origin for those beliefs you class as "observations," and if so, to what views on the nature of causality in general and pre-cognitive input processes in particular do you then subscribe? I would expect a person's reply to this to be importantly conditioned by his background in sensory psychology. But assuming that for most of us to "observe" is at least in part to have a belief which arises in a certain way, it remains to make explicit the mechanisms of percept production. Generically, this is of course a well known and much researched problem in mainstream psychology. Study of specifics, however, has looked to sense-mediated exterospection for its paradigms while totally neglecting *introspective* observation—not through any lack of interest in the latter but from failure to realize that anything about it needs explanation.[43] Yet once the phenomenalist confusion between having an experience and being aware that one has it is set straight, space reappears within which to puzzle over how internal realities sometimes produce beliefs about themselves. This is *not* a trivial question. It raises in pure form the fundamental cognitive problem which theories and data on the transducer functions of exterospective systems obscure to the point of irretrievability: When "information" in the modern noncognitive sense (i.e. realization by a variable of one of its possible values) arises within an organism, what else is needed to convert this into genuine cognitive information *about* its causal antecedents?

Metabeliefs

Finally, we come to epistemology's *metabelief* frontier. Broadly construed, "metabeliefs" are propositions about other propositions, including in particular semantic and rationality claims such as the correspondence principle of truth. (An alternative but inconveniently narrow use of this term would be that a "metabelief" is an entire belief act—i.e. a particular intentional event with mode on the belief/disbelief continuum—whose object is another belief act.) Viewed abstractly, metabeliefs might seem relevant to the concerns only of philosophers and others given to cognitive navel scrutiny in recoil from the real world. In fact, their practical importance is just the opposite: The more efficiently hard-headed is a person's reasoning, the more significant a role metabeliefs play in his thinking. This is because metabeliefs are the means by which normative epistemology exerts leverage on applied thinking, the machinery by which we monitor our own rationality. For example, if I am disposed to reason by an inference pattern ϱ, but through study of logic I also come to believe that ϱ-patterned arguments are deductively invalid, then when I become aware of having acquired my belief in proposition q by ϱ-patterned inference from premises $p_1, ..., p_n$, my metabelief about ϱ-coupled propositions suppresses the conviction in p which would otherwise be transmitted from my convictions in p_1 and ... and p_n. (This belief transmission will not be damped entirely, however, if ϱ is still acceptable to me as an inductive inference pattern.) Conversely, if I have come to think that pattern ϱ is valid, then even if I do not yet reason *by* ϱ I can nonetheless infer a conclusion q from my beliefs in $p_1, ..., p_n$ together with my additional beliefs that q is ϱ-related to $p_1, ..., p_n$ and that any proposition so related to an n-tuple of premises is true if the latter are.

In like fashion, metabeliefs modulate the intensities with which I would otherwise hold my basic beliefs. Thus when I introspectively detect myself *perceiving that-p*, the certainty I am tempted to feel in p is infused with a modicum of cautionary doubt by my recall of past perceivings which turned out to be not wholly veridical. Similarly, I have such modest assurance in the general accuracy of my memories that identifying a belief of mine as "memory" badly undermines my confidence in it. It is an error to suppose that when disciplined thinkers toughen the rationality of their judgments by critical self-scrutiny of form "What are my grounds for believing p?", they seek merely to review the *evidence* for p. Fully as important is to appraise the evidence itself by classifying one's basic beliefs according to their *non*evidential sources and reflecting upon the general epistemic quality of beliefs which so originate. As recognized by common sense, beliefs arise mainly in the ways listed on p. 77 f., above, but professionalized inquiry exploits much more finely discriminated if poorly verbalized belief categories. The natural sciences, especially, make intensive efforts to search out the conditions under which their basic beliefs ("data") seem most trustworthy, and then require their technical conclusions to be inferred only from evidence of this elite kind. A discipline's intramural concern for the reliability of its data is perhaps the best single indicator of its status along the continuum from hard science to soft to pseudo.

Though normative epistemology has yet to make metabeliefs an explicit object (*contra* content) of its concern, these are far too important to leave uncultivated much longer. As I will try to show, however, any serious theory of belief/metabelief interplay must aspire to vastly higher orders of sophisticated complexity than previously ventured by the philosophy of knowledge. Let us assume as a first approximation that the normative force of metabeliefs may be expressed by principles roughly of the form

α) If o at t believes that f is the relative frequency (or statistical probability) of truth in his beliefs arising from sources of kind K, and also that his belief in proposition p arises from a source of kind K, then o at t should belive in p with strength (degree of credence) $\psi(f)$, where ψ is a monotonic increasing function of truth rate f.

The "source" category K of a given belief should be construed broadly to include any introspectively detectable, epistemically relevant feature of the circumstances attendant upon the belief act in question, including aspects of the belief's own content. (E.g., o may be aware that his beliefs containing a certain concept or having a certain logical form are especially untrustworthy.) To assimilate α or its reconstructed essence into a technically coherent epistemology, however, requires attention to formidable problems on several levels of complexity.

The lowest difficulty stratum is one with which normative belief theory has already begun to skirmish in the context of statistical inference. Metabelief principle α clearly resembles the "straight rule" of instance induction widely presupposed by theories of probabilistic explanation and prediction, namely, that

β) If o at t believes that f is the relative frequency (or statistical probability) of property P among things of type Q, and also that entity x is of type Q, then o at t should feel degree of confidence $\psi(f)$ in the proposition that x has property P, where $\psi(f)$—the "subjective probability" of this proposition for o at t—increases with f. (Under the usual scaling of subjective probability, $\psi(f)$ is numerically equal to f.)

In fact, only minor changes are needed to make α a special case of β, and any boundary restrictions required to keep β plausible apply to α as well. In particular, this is true of the "total evidence" requirement that β holds only when x's Q-ness is the entirety of usable information about x. (β is obviously untenable if o at t also knows e.g. that x is an R and that all Rs are Ps). Thus α must be conditional upon K's being the narrowest (most restricted) metabelief category to which o at t assigns his p-belief. (E.g., my general perceptual accuracy is a poor standard for how much I should trust my percept that-John-is-approaching when I am further aware that the light is especially dim and that I frequently confuse John with his brother.)

6*

However, the "total evidence" requirement suffers from serious technical difficulties (see e.g. Hempel, 1965; Massey, 1968) which ultimately unfold into the problems of (i) construing the "relative frequency (or statistical probability)" of a class P relative to a class Q in a way which allows this quantity to be well-defined and non-extreme (i.e. neither zero nor unity) even when Q contains only one or no members, and (ii) developing principles of statistical inference by which we can rationally estimate the relative frequency of P in class Q from information only about P's incidence in a number of classes much broader than Q. (Problem (i) is mainly just a matter of distinguishing statistical probability from *de facto* relative frequency; but while statistical practices at estimating distribution parameters provide some preliminary intuitions about (ii), the deeper puzzles about this have scarcely been probed much less solved.) Moreover, even apart from problems of the total-evidence sort, straight rule β and hence presumably α is demonstrably more questionable than commonsense is aware (Rozeboom 1969a).

Technical refinements regarding degrees of truth and belief create a second level of complexity for metabelief theory. Contrary to the present wording of α, a belief category's epistemic merit cannot be determined strictly by the metabelieved incidence of truth therein if the correspondence of propositions to reality is not thought to be a simple true/false dichotomy. For example, it is obscure how truth frequency might be significantly predicated of a class of vague beliefs. It is probably not feasible for metabelief theory to attempt accommodation to polymorphic truth assessments until formal semantics has developed some theory of the latter. More immediately in need of remedy is the inconsistent treatment of graded belief in α. Since a person's K-kind beliefs need not all sustain equal conviction, either the unqualified "belief" cited in α's antecedent must be clarified as any degree of belief exceeding some arbitrarily stipulated threshold, or, more satisfactorily, α must be revised to read something like

α*) If o at t believes that f is the incidence of truth in his beliefs arising in strength s from sources of kind K, and also that his belief in proposition p is of strength s from a source of kind K, then o at t should believe in p with strength $\psi(f)$, where ψ is monotonic increasing in f.

But now a delicacy appears if we ask how o's belief processes can *become* rational by metabelief standards—i.e., how they might comply with a prescription like α*. To avoid even further complications, let us assume that o's metabeliefs are all correct, so that the strength and source of his belief in a given proposition are just what he thinks they are. Also let the metabelief situation stipulated in α*'s antecedent (i.e. the conjunction bracketed by 'if' and 'then' in α^*) be abbreviated as 'o at t metabelieves that $MB(p, s, K, f)$'. Then given the antecedent of α^*, two possibilities arise: One is that the strength s with which o at t in fact believes p equals the strength $\psi(f)$ with which, under his metabelief $MB(p, s, K, f)$, he should believe it. This is the rational ideal which, however, is degenerate in that were it always to obtain there would be no intellectual work for metabeliefs to do. The alternative possibility is that o's p-belief strength s at t is not equal to $\psi(f)$. In this event, rationality on p's part would presumably be to change his p-belief strength from s to s', where s' equals $\psi(f)$ or at least is closer to it than is s. But then o no longer has metabelief $MB(p, s, K, f)$ at this new time t'; instead, o at t' now believes p with strength s' on grounds which, insomuch as they include belief $MB(p, s, K, f)$, are hence no longer exclusively of kind K but are rather of a metabelief-monitored kind K' whose accuracy rate, f', at belief level s' is very unlikely to be the same as f. That is, at time t', o now believes p in strength s' while metabelieving that $MB(p, s', K', f')$—and s' will in general not equal the belief strength $\psi(f')$ called for by $MB(p, s', K', f')$ even if it is what would have been rational under $MB(p, s, K, f)$. If $s' \neq \psi(f')$ then the normative force of α^* calls for still another shift in o's p-belief to a strength s'' closer to $\psi(f')$, resulting in a metabelief change to $MB(p, s'', K'', f'')$ and so on for a recursive series which may or may not converge upon a rational ideal $MB(p, s^n, K^n, f^n)$ in which $s^n = \psi(f^n)$. If my argument here is too condensed for easy comprehension, no matter—the qualitative point is that insofar as human reason is actually guided by metabeliefs, the latter become part of the very sources whose accuracy they assess while the belief shifts they effect will be not single-stage adjustments but at best iterative approximations to an equilibrium. Whether any insurmountable difficulties lurk in this remains to be seen, but the prospect that metabelief theory may have problems of self-reference brings ominously to mind the paradoxes which are wont to gibber therein.

Still another important detail to which both α and α^* are inadequate as given is that metabeliefs themselves sustain less than perfect confidence. Even if o at t correctly feels no metabelief uncertainty about the strengths and sources of his beliefs, as for simplicity was assumed above, he will generally feel unsure of the precise incidence of truth in any one of his belief categories. Extension of α^* to cover metabelief uncertainty should be no great problem, since familiar theorems determining unconditional probabilities as a weighted mixture of conditional ones may suffice to handle this. But the issue of metabelief uncertainty also serves to introduce a still-higher level of metabelief complexity, namely, how does a person *acquire* his metabeliefs and how strongly should he believe them? In particular, how can a person learn with some degree of accuracy what proportion of his s-strength beliefs of source kind K are in fact true? To the extent that one needs to determine this empirically for himself—and while it may well be that some people get metabeliefs by hearsay, intuition, or the like, we have no reason to think that reliable appraisals of one's belief accuracies can be obtained in these ways—it would seem that this must primarily require a person to infer his truth rate for a given belief category by statistical induction from what he knows about the incidence of veridicality in a tested sample of his beliefs from this category. It is not clear, however, how one might acquire sample truth-rate data which project nontrivial metabelief generalizations. For suppose that C is some sample of the propositions in a given source category believed by o at t with strength s. If o's judgment regarding what proportion, f, of propositions in C are true were determined exclusively by his assessment of the individual propositions in C, it would be a useless analytic consequence of confidence level s: So long as o believes each p in C with strength s, he would metabelieve e.g. that $f = 1.00$ (i.e. 100% true) if his confidence s is maximal, that $f = 0$ if s is minimal (i.e. maximal disbelief), and more generally that f has whatever value is needed for s to be the belief strength o considers appropriate for a proposition metabelieved to belong to a category whose truth rate is f. Were metabeliefs always so derived, then beliefs would always have essentially the strengths which, by principle α^*, they should have. For epistemically significant tensions to arise between a person's beliefs and metabeliefs by virtue of which the latter can modulate the former, he must first acquire some s-strength beliefs from sources of kind K and then somehow re-evaluate these propositions to obtain a corrected assessment of their truth.

There appear to be at least two ways in which such reappraisals might occur. One is that o may remember at time t that he previously believed proposition p with strength s on grounds K, even though he now has reason to believe p with strength s'. (E.g., I recall feeling so sure yesterday that I saw John across the street, even though I now have hard evidence that he has been out of town all week.) The other is that o at t may be able to suppress some of the factors determining his p-belief long enough to assess how much confidence the reduced set would produce by itself, or to introspect how components of his total p-belief strength respectively trace to sources of different types, so that he can judge, in effect, "The kind-K sources of my belief in p would by themselves cause me to believe this in strength s, but due to additional influences I actually believe p with strength s'." (Thus when I look at a half-submerged stick, past experience with things in water assures me that the stick isn't really bent even though it *looks* bent—i.e. I can discern that perception alone would produce in me a much stronger conviction that the stick is bent than I actually feel.) As shown by these examples, significant metabeliefs can thus arise from manifest disparity between the belief strengths generated in the same proposition by sources of different kinds, the operational force of which is to alter the belief-strength contribution of each source kind (or more precisely, perhaps, to introduce a corresponding compensatory bias) as a function of its deviancy from the intrapersonal consensus. Since these belief adjustments in turn affect the consensual norms on which they are based, this should be a recursive process tending toward but not necessarily reaching equilibrium.

If much in this discussion of metabelief mechanisms seems confused and obscure, it is because my understanding of them is confused and obscure. I suggest, however, that anyone who professes to know the score here is probably ignorant of what the game is. For in an epistemic economy wherein even basic beliefs are in principle uncertain, *no* belief remains entirely basic. Any belief in the system is susceptible to inferential support or disconfirmation by other beliefs for or against which it, in turn, may itself serve as evidence. Rationality in such cases is not a linear progression from propositions with credibilities already established to others which these deductively or inductively imply, but a dynamic interplay within and across all layers of beliefs, metabeliefs, and meta-...-metabeliefs. Stated in such grandly qualitative terms, holistic epistemologies are by no means without precedent in modern philosophy. Serious normative study of belief systems which reorganize themselves holistically, however, has remained conspicuously nonexistent. If the present probes are not totally misdirected, the heights to be scaled, the chasms to be bridged, the depths to be plumbed, the enigmas to be unravelled, and the intricacies to be mastered have scarcely begun to impress their enormity upon our comprehension.

NOTES

1. For an all too appalling documentation of such abuses in the case of memory words, see Rozeboom, 1965.
2. Separate verbs do, in fact, generally distinguish them in other languages. Thus in German, knowing-that, knowing-how, and knowing-(it) are *wissen*, *können*, and *kennen*, respectively.
3. Since abilites are not themselves behavior but *potentials* or *dispositions* thereto, their proper conceptualization, like that of all dispositions, also requires reference to the circumstances which actualize that potential. (As evinced by the difference between

soluability in water and *soluability in alcohol*, the distinction between two dispositions may well lie not in the behavior they potentiate but only in their conditions of activation.) To be sure, commonsense conceptions of an ability's output often includes vague reference to its input requirement (e.g., one can't do long division or treat frostbite without having a long-division problem or frostbite case to work on), but this backdoor admission of stimulus conditions into our response concepts hardly counts as an official acknowledgement of their inherent relevance. For examples of the conceptual problems which arise from even the most superficial probing of commonsense ability concepts, see Rozeboom, 1966b, pp. 197ff., 206f.
4. E.g., Bergson, 1903; MacLeish, 1956.
5. Of these three equivalent expressions, the first two are well established in the philosophic vernacular. Despite its relative unfamiliarity, however, I am coming to prefer the third for the tidiness with which it allows the three primary facets of an intentional act to be identified as (*i*) a *content*, (*ii*) in general (though not always) an *object*, and (*iii*) a *mode*. Content vs. object is the meaning/referent distinction aired later, while an intention's mode is the *way* in which its content is brought to bear on other psychological processes under its influence.
6. The most important of these dimensions will undoubtedly be (*i*) degree of belief–commitment, (*ii*) valuational tone, (*iii*) intensity of arousal or awareness, and (*iv*) a passivity/activity dimension which might be called "engagement" or "salience," as in wishing for *p* vs. wanting *p* vs. striving for *p*, and in feeling unsure of *p* vs. wondering whether *p* vs. trying to determine whether *p*.
7. Under very special nomic circumstances—for example in the case of memory acts, if for any proposition *p* the only input which evokes remembering-that-*p* were to be activation of some sensation or idea resembling a component of *p*—description of a disposition's actualizer is redundant with description of its output and hence need not be made explicit in the disposition's identification. In learning theory, the interpretation of recall as a redintegration of memory traces (cf. Rozeboom, 1969; also p. 396ff. below), unlike association-theoretic views of memory, has so far been primarily of this sort. Even if recall is basically a redintegrative phenomenon, however, it is likely that items of "stored information" differ not merely in what they store but also in their manner of storage, i.e. in how they can be "retrieved," and hence cannot be characterized merely in terms of their content.
8. Influenced by certain dubious arguments of the later Wittgenstein, Terwilliger (1968, p. 20) has recently contended with some vehemence, contrary to my present claim, that communication is definitionally essential to language; specifically, that "[a] there are no private meanings for words, for if [language] were not [social], it would not and could not be a language." However, Terwilliger also observes (1968, p. 18n) that "[b] adults can, of course, invent languages which no one else can understand. [c] But in all cases these languages are derivatives of existing languages." Even were the universality of claim [c] to go unchallenged, it is wholly obscure to me how this would prevent fact [b] from demolishing thesis [a]. The only way that [a] can be made compatible with [b] even given [c], it seems to me, is to argue that a "language" is not just defined functionally in terms of what it does, but that languages must also originate in a special way which disqualifies those which are "derivatives of existing languages" from being *real* languages.
9. Although the term 'meaning' has a long and desperate history of ambiguity (see p. 53f, below), I shall here consistently use it in what I would argue is by far its most

common as well as most epistemically basic sense. Pressed for clarification, I would offer the following statements as partial definitions of this sense: (1) "Meanings" are the contents of mental acts. (2) Roughly speaking, the "meanings" of words and sentences are concepts and propositions, respectively. (3) An expression's "meaning" is what is sometimes also called its "sense," in contradistinction to its referent or designatum (cf. Frege, 1898). Thus, the two phrases 'southernmost land mass' and 'coldest continent on Earth' have different meanings (senses) even though they both refer to the same place.

10. The notion of internal counterparts for overt stimuli is, as I shall point out later, considerably more problematic than we customarily recognize. At present, when I speak of words-in-thought, I mean whatever sorts of central processes are responsible for such phenomena as generalization across homonyms, and for our construing as homonymous visual symbols so physically different as 'THREW' and 'through'.

11. Not all decompositions of a sentence into components—e.g., top half vs. bottom half—intuitively yield subsentential "expressions," however. The difference between those which do and those which don't presumably lies in the principles by which the proposition-eliciting force of a sentence is compounded out of the effects of its constituents. Were it not that in linguistic practice propositions are often conveyed by sentential fragments or even single words while, on the other hand nonlinguistically aroused cognitions are very likely evoked in general by stimulus complexes whose structural influences follow a grammar of their own, it could be convincingly argued that reference to such concatenation principles—i.e. syntax—must be included in the definition of "language." (Actually, I am willing to concede that "language" is perhaps best regarded as a cluster-concept in which not merely syntactical complexity but also communicativeness, self-producibility, and other features traditionally proposed as definitive of language have a weakly criterial status. But I would still insist that the most essential feature in this cluster is one not heretofore recognized, namely, the one described on p. 46f. below)

12. The exceptions are (*i*) Mowrer's (1954) proposal—a decade ahead of its time—that sentences are conditioning devices by which the response to one term becomes attached to another; (*ii*) semantical extensions of formal linguistics which go beyond bare syntax in seeking to model reception resolution of ambiguities in word meanings and grammatical structure (notably, Katz and Fodor, 1963); and (*iii*) Osgood's (1963) attempt to assimilate the ideas of both (*i*) and (*ii*) into his own theory of meaning. (However, (*i*) still treats specific responses to single words as the basic language process, with sentence reception being just a way to modify single-word responses. And while I suspect that development (*ii*) may indeed have the potential to become a genuine theory of cognitive language, I am not clear whether it has so far gone beyond sentence→sentence transformations into sentence→proposition activations. That is, would (*ii*) have anything nontrivial to say about a language whose terms were completely unambiguous and whose surface structure always mirrored its deep structure?) Finally, (*iv*) work on how the psychological effects of compound phrases derive from the effects of their constituent terms (Cliff, 1959; Rokeach and Rothman, 1965; Howe, 1966) though still subpropositional in concern, is a significant step in the needed direction.

13. See Rozeboom, 1961a, and especially Rozeboom, 1960a. An unpublished section of the latter, observing how the factual nature of elicitors establishes sentences rather than terms as the behavior-disposing units of language, is available upon request.

14. Although I have so far published very little explicitly on the psychology of language, it has been a central concern for me ever since the earliest days of my intellectual awakening; in fact, I first encountered hard-core behavior theory while preparing an undergraduate term paper for Charles Morris' course in semiotics, wherein I brashly undertook to set aright his theory of signification (Morris, 1946—still the most comprehensive work on the psychology of language despite its behavior-theoretic obsolescence). Then and for years thereafter, I was groping to replace the near-universal doctrine that a word arouses the same response, or propensity thereto, as the entity for which it stands—an untenable view insomuch as individual words just don't evoke specific response propensities (cf. Brown, 1958, Chapt. 3)—with an account recognizing that the psychological effects of both words and their referents are in some fundamental sense "context dependent." Realization that the linguistic/nonlinguistic determinants of specific behaviors are sentences/facts, rather than words/things (Rozeboom, 1960a, 1961a), finally illuminated this darkness for me. My second insight, a belated outgrowth of my work on the logic of theoretical concepts (Rozeboom, 1962b), was that contrary to virtually all previous views on the matter including my own, symbolic representation cannot be analyzed as the symbol's acquiring an effect on the organism akin to that of its referent. (Something like this undoubtedly happens in some phases of language learning, but it is irrelevant to the nature of aboutness—see next section.) And the revelation now to be aired became accessible to me only after I began to make explicit, rather than grudgingly parenthetical, provision in my thinking for the intentional-mode component of cognition. All of this leaves past orthodoxies far, far behind, and the distance yet to be travelled only emphasizes further the desperate inadequacy of standard views on the psychology of language.
15. Abortive in that they either emphasize the distinction without clarifying its nature (e.g., Langer, 1942; Werner and Kaplan, 1963), or tie it to some incidental feature such as the artificiality (e.g., Stebbings, 1931; Bertalanffy, 1965) or self-producibility (Morris, 1946) of linguistic symbols.
16. Clearly ordinary language does not construe "symbols" and "verbal expressions" to be entirely the same thing. (E.g., the crucifix is a Christian symbol but not, prima facie, a verbal expression.) But a strong possibility remains that when the definitive properties of language are laid bare, symbols which are not recognized words in official languages such as English will nevertheless prove to be linguistic in function, or at least to differ from true words only modestly. In any event, regardless of what "symbols" may be in an extended sense, only semantic symbols—i.e., paradigmatically language—are at issue in the "signal/symbol" contrast.
17. This principle has a long history reaching back at least to Aristotle (*Metaphysics*, 1110b 26–28 : "To say of what is that it is not, or of what is not that it is, is false; while to say of what is that it is, or of what is not that it is not, is true"). Its most advanced modern expressions are found in the Tarski–Carnap formalization of semantics, where it is sometimes known as the "semantic conception of truth" (Tarski, 1944).
18. If the logical form of every statement 'p' is really '$x\phi$s that p', then the latter analyzes as '$x\phi$s that $x\phi$s that p' which in turn really means '$x\phi$s that $x\phi$s that $x\phi$s that p', ad infinitum.
19. The English cues for distinguishing between use and mention of an expression are subtle, varied, and far from consistent. Most reliable of these is usage of form 'that p' to designate the proposition expressed by sentence 'p', while occurence of 'p'

without a 'that'-prefix signals use (e.g., assertion) rather than mention of this proposition. (Important exceptions to this rule, however, are such contexts as 'the fact that p' and 'in the event that p'.) I have not previously followed this convention rigorously but will now do so in passages wherein the distinction is especially critical.
20. Philosophical semantics' profound methodological problems have never, to my knowledge, been seriously examined in the literature. For intimations and fragments, however, see Rozeboom, 1962b and 1971a.
21. For steps toward a similar treatment of 'because', see Rozeboom, 1968. This case is especially interesting for the theory of mental acts in that the intention's mode has a relational form embracing two or more propositions as content, which is greater logical complexity than found in the acts traditionally recognized by the philosophic literature.
22. That is, in the popular sense of "connotation." Philosophically, "connotation" has meant something importantly different from this, namely, a concept's analytic entailments (cf. Ryle, 1957).
23. In his recent important excursion into the philosophy of cognition, a work whose outlook is in almost all major respects highly similar to my own despite certain devious turns of argument which spin out in directions which I find distressing, Sellars (1968) gives a virtuoso demonstration of how adroitly a brilliant philosopher can dodge and weave all around the issue of aboutness without ever coming to analytic grips with it. (Sellars makes one close pass in his notion of a "correct picture" of an external object; however, he says nothing about what determines which particular object a given picture is a picture *of*, nor by virtue of what it is "correct," beyond a brief, cryptic allusion in Chapt. V, § 30, to the causal origins of perceptual pictures.)
24. It may or may not be necessary, when E designates e, for E to occur in a special context (e.g., an asserted sentence) which evokes a reaction (e.g. a believed proposition) of which m is merely one constituent. This and similar qualifications may be appended to the present discussion wherever they feel needed.
25. More precisely, $E, a, b, ..., m, ...$ are event types (i.e. features of particular events) such that occurrence of E in a suitable context brings about an occurrence of a, which in turn brings about an occurrence of b, etc.
26. If x and y are bidirectionally associated, so that x elicits y and y elicits x, then any effect of y is also aroused by x through the mediation of y, and conversely. Moreover, this difficulty cannot be avoided by stipulating that the K-kind effects of a stimulus include only those which are unmediated, for unmediated effects probably do not exist—i.e. if causal propagation is continuous, then for any S and m such that S elicits m, there always exists some intervening process h such that S elicits h and h elicits m.
27. Psychological phenomena do indeed exist (e.g., passive avoidance, DRL response rates, go/no-go discriminations, and others traditionally explained in terms of "inhibition") wherein the withholding of action appears genuinely to be a form of behavior. In fact, there is a fairly orthodox behavior-theoretical test for distinguishing the doing of *not-r* from merely not doing r, namely, determining whether the alleged effect impedes arousal of r by other stimuli. However, I for one would not like to be stuck with responsibility for a comprehensive theory of not doing vs. *not*-doing. E.g., what are we to say about the differences among doing r, not doing *not-r*, and doing *not-(not-r)*?
28. Fodor (1965) has similarly questioned shared-effect accounts of reference on grounds of the plurality of stimuli sharing these reaction components. While it is perhaps

excessive to demand that a given *m* have only one referent (see p. 14 below), Fodor's implied accusation that contemporary mediational theories of meaning importantly fail to capture the specificity of reference is lethally on target.

29. The weakness of limiting criticism to specific theories as received is that the proffered objections, no matter how devastating, may perhaps be evaded by only minor revisions in the positions criticized. On the other hand, refutation *en masse* of all possible variants of a given approach is generally possible only in highly formalized disciplines. What I have presented here is the schema of a critique which, with high but not certain probability, will show any given common-effect theory of reference to be laughably inadequate. But psychosemanticists with an instinct for lost causes are welcome to receive it as an inventory of obstacles for their own effect-mediated theory of reference to overcome.

30. Unlike some intentional-act verbs, 'perceives', 'remembers', and 'thinks about' accept noun phrases as well as sentences for their grammatical objects. It can be argued—for the most part correctly, I think, though the analysis falters in certain marginal but psychosemantically significant cases—that *o* at *t* perceives (remembers, thinks about) *x* iff for some predicate concept *P*, *o* at *t* perceives (remembers, thinks) that *Px*. The points to be made here apply equally to intentional objects of both forms, but can be stated most compactly in terms of the noun-phrase ellipsis.

31. See my comments on Professor Metzger's paper, p. 260ff. below.

32. This is phenomenalism's *semantic* source. A second, equally important origin is the epistemic supposition that cognition must be grounded in certainty and that we can be certain only of our own experience.

33. Similarities to Locke's doctrine of "secondary qualities" will be evident here, except that I find merit neither in his primary/secondary distinction nor in his phenomenalist view of awareness. On the other hand, my proposal that evaluative terms may have external referents should not be confused with orthodox intentional treatments of feeling and emotion. In statements such as 'I feel sad about Peter's death' and 'Jimmy just loves peanut butter', the affective element is placed in the intention's *mode*, while its content (here a conception of Peter's death and of peanut butter, respectively), is essentially free of affect.

34. Not, to be sure, held by *all* philosophers. Broad (1933, p. 28ff.), for example, has already raised the second point that I am about to make here.

35. Namely, that an organism's responses to input can be consistent with a rule *p*, say through a constellation of independently conditioned S–R couplings, without necessarily being mediated by a cognitive ϕing that *p*.

36. The position described here is the analysis of theoretical concepts evolved by logical empiricism (see Feigl, 1950; Cronbach and Meehl, 1955; Carnap, 1956; Nagel, 1961; Rozeboom, 1962, 1971a) as the inadequacies of logical positivism became increasingly evident. Theoretic definitions have also been recognized under other names in older philosophic traditions (cf. Robinson, 1954, on "synthetic" and "denotative" definition). The logical empiricist account of theoretical terms has no present competitor for the simple reason that philosophies which seem to reject it—most recently, what I have elsewhere called the "omnitheoretic" movement (Rozeboom, 1970)—have proposed no serious alternative analysis.

37. Interpreting one person's words in terms of the meaning repertoire available to another is essentially the same problem when these persons employ the same overt system of language vehicles ("Does he mean what I would mean by that?") as when

they speak officially different languages. The equivocation which Quine (1960) observes in translating one language into another is at bottom a problem in translating between speakers of the "same" language—otherwise, questions about interlinguistic synonymy could be unequivocally settled by bilingually reared speakers of those languages.
38. I ignore the relational overtones by virtue of which e.g. a tall child may be shorter than a short adult. Making this explicit only compounds the vagueness of 'tall' rather than alleviating it.
39. Though a few—*very* few—serious attempts have been made to bring vagueness into the philosophic pale (e.g., Körner, 1966), they have done so only by admitting sharply bounded classes of individuals to which the application of vague predicates is still "open." This trichotomous extension of classically dichotomous *denotation* (i.e. the relation of a predicate to an object which satisfies it) is perhaps a useful preliminary probe, but it neither does justice to the essentially continuous grading of a vague predicate's applicability nor confronts the deeper problem of vague *designation*.
40. Note that such multiplicity of *reference* has an entirely different semantic character from the "multiple denotation" relation (Martin, 1958) in which a predicate stands to the various entities which *satisfy* (i.e. have the property designated by) this predicate.
41. Strictly speaking, of course, it is the concept itself which evolves for the person, not his understanding or "grasp" of it. How broad a spectrum of changes a concept can undergo and still remain abstractly the "same" is a nice question of no particular importance here.
42. Had space permitted I would have developed this point in some detail, for it is an extremely important one. Epistemically appropriate answers to the normative question "How strongly should *p* be believed under circumstances *C*?" must ultimately be grounded on judgments about how accurate beliefs arrived at under such circumstances tend in fact to be. (This holds as much for inferred beliefs as it does for basic ones.) How we can rationally arrive at such metabeliefs is perhaps the fundamental problem of normative epistemology, even though the philosophical literature has as yet recorded no thought on this matter beyond some heated but none-too-perspicacuous controversy over the justification of statistical induction.
43. However, see Natsoulas, 1970.

Postscript on Priorities

Recent exegeses on the work of Husserl (Smith & McIntyre, 1971; Willard, 1972) exhibit his theory of intentionality as strikingly similar to the one for which I have argued here, including in particular the partition of mental acts into mode, content, and (occasionally) object, with the latter two comprising the relata of *aboutness*. Also, I find that my distinction between signals and symbols has been anticipated by Ducasse (1939).

IN RESPONSE TO ROZEBOOM

John D. Peyton

Insofar as I understand what Professor Rozeboom is trying to do in his paper "Problems in the Psycho-Philosophy of Knowledge," I am in sympathy with his purpose and with his conviction that it can be done. However, I do not believe that he has done it.

Rozeboom claims that he seeks only to "take inventory of what regarding 'knowledge' there is for us to feel uncertain about" and to interrelate these problems within the whole issue of knowledge. He is, in fact, trying to establish the respective relevances of psychology and philosophy in the area of epistemology. He argues, against the majority of philosophers, that epistemology is the business of psychology as well as of philosophy. He seeks to demonstrate that this is the case through (1) some general considerations about knowledge, philosophy, and psychology (pp. 25–27), and (2) a progressive logical analysis of the concept 'knowledge,' with interpretation and argumentation to show just where and how the components of the "knowledge issue" are related to philosophical and to psychological inquiry (p. 28 ff.).

My first comment concerns the first of Rozeboom's more general arguments. He says, "The main ingredients of epistemology's subject matter—cognitive acts and their constituents—are psychological entities pure and simple, albeit abstract ones" (p. 26). This is one of many *psychological interpretations* of issues which Rozeboom gives throughout the paper. But an interpretation is, after all, just a form of hypothesis, and must be defended against alternative hypotheses and against simple skepticism. Rozeboom is not unaware of various non-psychological interpretations of propositions, concepts, inferences, etc.,[1] so I conclude that he has chosen to ignore them for some reason. Whatever the case, he offers no support for this particular hypothesis, though it certainly needs supporting. At other places, he presents other such hypotheses which need to be defended against alternative interpretations.[2]

Rozeboom's second argument for the relevance to psychology to epistemology hints at some higher-order empirical principles which might "adjudicate" normative principles of reasoning. This, he says, means that philosophy and psychology may be related as are the two lines of a fugue, which are alike but out of phase. I find this argument mystifying. It is impossible to evaluate or even understand an argument such as this without a much more explicit explication and, if at all possible, an example or two.[3]

My third comment on the paper is that many of the claims, interpretations, and arguments are simply unconvincing. For example, on pp. 44–46 Rozeboom argues that what distinguishes linguistic from non-linguistic stimuli is the "mode" of the cognition which constitutes the response. His example is the spoken linguistic stimulus "It is raining." This stimulus is to be distinguished from the non-linguistic sound of thunder, he says, because the response cognition ('It is raining.') is taken in an affirmative mode when evoked by the sound of thunder—that is, the cognition 'It is raining' is not only thought, but it is also believed—but is not affirmed in response to the spoken propositional stimulus.

I find this argument implausible, because, in the first place, it seems to me that the sound of thunder is sometimes less likely to evoke an affirmative cognition than hearing someone say "It is raining." Thunder *can* occur without rain, or the person may not be sure that that really was thunder he heard. But if a reliable person says, "It is raining," that is pretty likely to produce belief in his listeners, unless they have good reason to believe otherwise. In the second place, I fail to see why the nature of the stimulus should be *defined* by the type of response elicited. Pavlov did not wait to see what response his dogs produced before deciding whether he was using a visual or auditory stimulus. If we know, by other criteria, that a certain stimulus is linguistic, then the response of a particular subject seems irrelevant to the *definition* of that type of stimulus.

I shall leave the reader to his own judgment concerning the plausibility of Rozeboom's other interpretations and arguments. I found his critiques of other positions reasonable, but his positive statements generally left me unconvinced, if not mystified.

My final critical comment is that the whole paper, and the approach it employs, seems incapable of accomplishing the task set for it. Rozeboom wants to show that psychology is not only relevant to epistemology, but that many key problems of knowledge cannot be solved except by psychology. This is a belief I happen to share with Professor Rozeboom, but I do not see how the type of *philosophical* argumentation he presents in his paper can possibly do anything more than rebut arguments advanced against the possibility of a psychological approach to epistemology. The only really convincing evidence we could have for believing that psychology can solve problems concerning knowledge would be for psychology to actually solve some such problems. Rozeboom gives us much philosophical argument, but he rarely cites any substantive psychological theory or research. He argues for the *possibility* of psychological solutions to epistemological problems, but does not show us any actual solutions. In this area of philosophical psychology, it may not be enough to be a philosopher *or* a psychologist: perhaps one must *do* some philosophy and *do* some psychology, and let the product speak for itself.

Now that I have listed my objections to Rozeboom's enterprise, let me record what I find to be especially of value in it. The primary importance of the paper lies in the fact that it approaches the psychology of knowledge through the logical or normative structure of knowledge concepts. This approach is essential to preserve the *relevance* of whatever psychological research or theory might be applied to the real problems of knowledge. Too many psychologists have claimed to be solving problems of "learning," "language," "purpose," and even "knowledge" only by using greatly expanded meanings for these terms. Of course, psychologists *can* use terms in whatever technical way they please, but only at the expense of irrelevance to the issues and problems as originally understood. Professor Rozeboom is quite correct to insist upon a careful analysis of concepts as a first step and then to bring in psychological research and theory at those points where they are demonstrably relevant.

Rozeboom's paper is also important because of the distinctions drawn between the various questions and sub-issues of epistemology. By becoming aware of the many aspects of the problem, philosophers and psychologists should be able to think more clearly about these conceptual issues.

NOTES

1. See, for example, the interpretation given by Wilfrid Sellars in "Empiricism and the Philosophy of Mind" (in *Science, Perception and Reality.* New York: Humanities Press, 1963), that mental entities are hypothetical entities modeled after propositions, inferences, and other *linguistic* forms.
2. See, for example, pp. 51 ff., especially p. 54.
3. Other passages I found obscure occur on p. 55 ff., pp. 69–72, and p. 81 ff.

COMMENT ON ROZEBOOM'S PAPER

Joseph R. Royce

Professor Rozeboom's paper is, in my opinion, an important contribution to the growing literature on relationships between philosophy and psychology. In particular, it is an extensive elaboration of the "justified true belief" account of knowledge. As such I have no quarrel with it. What I do wish to quarrel with, however, is the claim that propositional knowledge constitutes *all* of knowledge. It seems to me that Professor Rozeboom has taken this stance, in spite of occasional rhetorical lip service to the contrary. While it is not at all necessary for anyone defending justified true belief as *a* valid epistemology to defend it as *the* valid epistemology, if the proponent insists on such a stance then it behooves him to make his case. And it seems to me that such a strong *claim* for justified true belief has, in fact, been made—but not defended. My challenge, then, to Professor Rozeboom is that he justify his claim that all knowledge is "nothing but" propositional knowledge or justified true belief.

I also wish to offer an observation. Although Rozeboom indicates a strong interest in presenting both a philosophical analysis *and* the relevant psychology, I find the presentation to be long on the former and short on the latter. This is not surprising in itself, for, as Professor Rozeboom says, psychology has more to learn on this issue from philosophy than vice versa. However, the point is that Rozeboom's view of knowledge as "propositional only" limits his attention to the psychology of beliefs. It is an expanded view of beliefs to be sure (e.g., the psychology of concepts, language, and meaning), but an impoverished view of cognition. For we get very little on perception, and nothing on imagery, symbolizing, intuition, and the developmental aspects of epistemology (e.g. Piaget).

The essence of my concerns can be summed up by saying that the content of this paper would be conveyed more accurately if it were re-titled something like "Problems in the Psycho-Philosophy of *Propositional* Knowledge."

REJOINDER AND SUMMARY

Wm. W. Rozeboom

Royce's and Peyton's criticisms are a useful foil for the summary appraisal with which I would like to put this essay into final perspective.

I quite agree that what I have produced here falls considerably short of the comprehensive survey envisioned in my opening paragraph. This is most painfully evident in my final section on the justificational aspects of belief acts, but the paper suffers throughout from shortness of breath, condensing paragraphs into clauses and making sentences go proxy for what should be extended chapters. Even so, considering the space at my avail and my stipulated purpose—which both Royce and Peyton choose to disregard—I remain uncontrite. I have sought to demark the primary logical (concept-definitive) features of "knowing," and show how and where these fit into the structure of extant and portending research in both psychology and philosophy. I have not, conversely, aspired to survey the assorted epistemic imports of all topics indexed in *Psychological Abstracts* even though I have little doubt that for each such entry some relevance could be found. Neither have I undertaken to illuminate any outstanding epistemological problems through appeal to established psychonomic data or theory. Quite apart from space prohibitions, I have had two good reasons for this abstention, the very same reasons which prompted this survey in the first place.

For one, contemporary psychology is still highly ignorant—*at the level of technical precision and evidential support which differentiates a hard science from folk belief*—about what goes on inside of sentient organisms, and is hence simply not yet positioned to answer detailed questions about the psychology of cognitive acts. (The past decade's remarkable resurgence of serious psychological concern for cognitive processes portends that this may not remain true much longer, but it is still largely true *today*.) Where are there published data or established theories, for example, which clarify the nature of symbolic representation? (I have argued above that past psychological accounts of aboutness have not even recognized the significant problems here, much less suggested a viable solution to them.) What is known or even conjectured about the psychonomic significance of propositional structure, i.e. behaviorally detectable differences between thinking, say, that *fire melts ice* on the one hand and just thinking the conjunction of terms {*fire, melts, ice*} on the other? (Apart from my own efforts, the only work I know of on this is so garbled or fragmentary as to hold only historical interest.)[1] In which research archives may we hope to find revealed the specific inference patterns which channel the main flow of ampliative reasoning in mature humans, or clues about the principles by which these forms exert their psychological force? And in what empirical studies have dimensions of propositional attitude (intentional mode) other than belief strength and to some extent desire (though values have usually been construed subpropositionally) even been recognized as significant central variables, much less ascribed a determinate nomic role in the process dynamics by which, under appropriate boundary conditions, stimulus inputs eventuate in overt behavior? When psychological science has had so little of substance to say about these and the other core issues of cognition, it is difficult for me to take seriously Royce's allegation of the wealth to be found had I but spent more time prospecting psychology's paracognitive sectors for nuggets of epistemological insight.

Moreover, while I share Peyton's impatience to get the psycho-philosophy of knowledge game out of the locker room and onto the playing field, there is an unfortunate but brutally practical reason for attempting no more than a few warm-up scrimmages on this occasion. This is that technical psychology and technical philosophy have grown so far apart in the course of their respective professional developments that the advanced *integration* of these (*not* replacement of one by the other) required to cope with epistemological puzzles is just not going to be comprehensible to most members of either discipline until they have received some preliminary exercise in the concepts of the other. (Psychologists are baffled nowadays by philosophical subtleties; it is the rare philosopher who can grasp the detailed intricacy of multivariate processes in reactive systems; and I have learned from repeated unhappy experience not to expect much appreciation for substantive contributions which do not fit smoothly into the reader's particular framework of presuppositions.) For this reason, a relatively nontechnical, prefatory juxtaposition of philosophical and psychological perspectives over a considerable range of epistemology's major issues is perhaps what is most needed just now, and that is what I have tried to provide here. I am prepared to develop many of these matters in considerably greater depth, but to do so effectively I need feedback from persons who are willing to *listen*—who will put out the effort and patience required to comprehend and improve upon an imperfect argument in an unfamiliar domain rather than seizing upon its first real or imagined flaw as an excuse to turn off—in order to advise me what specific aspects of my account are most communicatively troublesome and to suggest improvements in my formulation.

Peyton's difficulty with my proposed definitive difference between linguistic and nonlinguistic patterns of cognitive arousal well illustrates the problem to which I refer. Though a bit more technical than the psychology of language's traditional level of sophistication, the formal character of my suggestion is really quite elementary vis-à-vis modern conceptions of multivariate relatedness: When external stimulation elicits a mental act, both cause and effect in this sequence of events are structured complexes characterized by a vector of features on several dimensions. In particular, the two main dimensions (or more precisely subspaces, since both can be articulated further) which individuate cognitions are *mode* and *content*. My proposal—admittedly a dichotomous idealizing of what in real life is importantly a continuum—is simply that when cognitions are aroused by nonlinguistic input, the same dimensions of input which determine the cognition's content *also* determine its mode, whereas in linguistic communication those aspects (dimensions) of the input which determine content are distinct from those which determine mode. (To Peyton's complaint that someone's saying "It is raining" with the proper intonation can evoke a stronger belief in rain than might the sound of thunder, I can only reply "Of course." But my point has nothing to do with the comparative strengths of the convictions so aroused. Rather, it is that unlike the modal cues at a human speaker's avail, nature has no way to thunder assertively vs. queryingly vs. demandingly vs. wistfully, etc.)[2] I'm sure that there will be others who do not immediately comprehend the multivariate patterning envisioned here, and it is both appropriate and useful that I be pressed to clarify specific points like this. But until repeated interchanges on such fundaments have worked out a shared framework for technical communication, it would be autistic futility on my part (something for which my tolerance has become pretty well depleted) to dwell at length on advanced development of these basics.

Whereas Peyton protests the shallowness and/or opacity of what I say, Royce faults me for defective appreciation of the "knowledge" concept's scope. Royce's concern is an expression of his long-standing and repeatedly verbalized conviction that propositional knowledge is just one species of this genus, that in particular the humanities have their own modes of knowing which, though non-conceptual, are as fully *epistemic* in character as are the truth claims of a factual science (e.g. Royce, 1964, 1970). I have little doubt that the paradigmatic cognitions idealized by commonsense mental-act concepts, on which this essay has centered, shade off by degrees into paracognitive processes for which classical epistemology has made no provision. Neither would I be at all reluctant to acknowledge having overlooked some important paradigm cases were any such made known to me. But really now, Joe: My delimitation of the forms of "knowing" was arrived at by reviewing all grammatically distinct usages of this word which I have been able to identify. Only three alleged types of knowledge are manifest in these usages, *knowing that p*, *knowing how to d*, and *knowing (it)*, and I have given explicit arguments for my provisional conclusion that propositional knowledge includes (though is not necessarily to be equated with) all epistemic aspects of these three. Until you can describe a specific example of nonconceptual knowing and give reasons for taking it to be such,[3] you can't rightly expect me to assume expository responsibility for this, anymore than a comparative zoology text should be thought remiss for omitting Abominable Snowmen from its inventory of primates. There just may be such creatures, and the search is worth pursuing, but don't hold your breath.

I have saved for last the most serious issue raised by my critics. Peyton has correctly noted that I have not offered a very explicit defense for treating as I do the proximal stuff of epistemology, notably concepts, propositions, and inferences, to be straigthforward ingredients of psychological events. Peyton does not himself dispute this, but he feels that I have been insufficiently attentive to alternative philosophic views. To this I should say first of all that I disclaim responsibility for rebutting one by one all the foolish notions which philosophers have aired about the nature of knowledge at one time or another. The psychological status of concepts, propositions, and other intentional contents should be sufficiently evident at the outset that the case for this can rest in the success with which my account *gives* them a psychological interpretation. In particular, despite the paucity of psychonomic flesh on my review's conceptual skeleton, I have at several places (notably pp. 60–66 and 72f.) indicated how past views to the contrary have been grounded either on conceptual confusion (notably the content/object muddle) or on crude prescientific theories of mind which technical psychology has long since abandoned. Even so, lest I be accused of passing rhetoric for reason, let me belabor the obvious on behalf of those to whom it is not.

The rock on which any sane account of cognition must rest is that a person's ϕing that p (or something rather like it, if empirical reality exemplies this classical ideal only approximately) is a natural event with determinate locus in the world's causal order; in particular, that it is brought about by (*inter alia*) the peripheral stimulation which impinges upon the ϕer, and is in turn a part-cause of his subsequent movements. (We know this in the same commonsensical albeit imprecise way we know e.g. that the dryness of firewood affects how well it burns and is in turn influenced by aging, namely, by inductive extrapolation from extensive everyday experience.) Insomuch as intentional acts mediate (at times) between peripheral stimulation and overt actions, they are perforce something of which behavior theory (not just mentalistic psychology) needs to give an account, regardless of whether its assimilation of these inner events proceeds according to the constrictive model of science which some recent philosophers of mind have sought to inflict upon psychology.[4] To be sure, this still leaves some room for debate whether concepts, propositions, and other cognitive "meanings" are themselves ingredients of these internal mediators or instead inhabit some ghostly realm distinct from both the psychological attributes of cognizers and the objective referents of their cognitions. I have already (p. 60) sketched why, like many philosophers, I consider the latter interpretation to be wholly gratuitous, akin to belief in a substantival soul. But I am willing to leave the issue open a little longer if someone really does seriously want to defend a nonpsychological ontology for concepts and propositions. Most fundamental for now is simply to appreciate that despite centuries of sustained concern for the nature of meaning, philosophical understanding of this remains confused and impoverished, an asymptotic insufficiency which can be alleviated only by new insights into the detailed psychonomic character of whatever it is in a person which grounds his epistemic relation to whatever may be the objects of his cognitions.

The real issue here, it seems to me, is not whether concepts and propositions have a major psychological aspect, but whether psychological science can learn enough about them to illuminate their philosophical darks. As is true for any discipline's knowledge of its subject matter, the questions psychology can answer about the inner organism will at any one time always be a proper subset of those which can be asked. But there are no more inherent limitations on what experimental psychology can learn about this than there are on what the physical sciences can learn about e.g. the molecular basis of life or the fine structure of matter. In all advanced natural sciences, the underlying sources and causal principles behind observed events are reclaimed with ever-greater intricacy and explanatory depth through ampliative interpretation of increasingly complex data regularities, while the more quantitatively precise, reliable, and systematically varied are the science's data the more powerfully detailed is its penetration into its subject's inner mysteries. For psychology, the technically efficacious data base is behavioral, i.e. the organism's outside-of-the-skin doings and history of environmental circumstances. (Introspective reports, though often heuristically valuable, are just not firm enough to support exact interpretations,[5] and in any event give access to only a limited sector of the organism's psychonomic machinery.[6]) The forthcoming psychology of cognition to which we must look for philosophic succor will thus have a very different conceptual constitution from those psychologies with which most philosophers have yet had any working acquaintance. The concepts through which the organism's interior is to be technically described will be primarily of the sort which philosophers of science nowadays call "theoretical" or "dispositional," namely, hypothetical constructs which refer to the unobserved entities responsible for the data patterns on which the theory rests yet which characterize these underlying entities only functionally in terms of their nomic relations to the data variables. The theory of meaning afforded by such an account is nonmentalistic in that it has no commitment to, and in fact attempts to avoid, the introspectively colored concepts on which commonsense mentalistic psychology is erected; hence it escapes the charges of mysticism and unscientificality with which many contemporary philosophers reject classical mentalistic interpretations of cognition (e.g. the doctrine of "ideas"). Yet neither does it generically repudiate the mentalistic outlook, any more than modern theoretical biology entails wholesale rejection of farmers' folklore on plant growth. Rather, to the extent that the behavioral and mentalistic accounts are both correct, they will manifest an approximate isomorphism by virtue of which we can establish that both are talking *about*, albeit through markedly nonsynonymous concepts differing both in precision and experiental-richness profiles, the very same internal entities and natural principles which, moreover, are prospective referents for theoretical expressions in the language of a suitably advanced neurophysiology as well.[7]

As I see it, therefore, psycho-philosophical research on cognition needs to move simultaneously on two fronts that seek ultimately to coalesce but which cannot profitably be forced into premature intimacy. On the one hand, it is important to persist at analysis of classic mental-act conceptions, both to lay bare the structure of the intuitive theories imbedded therein and to rough in at whatever level of accuracy is appropriate to these concepts the overt behavior patterns which they project.[8] Meanwhile, it remains for behavioral research to make known the technical reality of these purported cognitive manifestations at scientifically fruitful levels of experimental design and data analysis, to quantify the detailed hierarchical[9] structure of whatever demonstrable regularities in fact govern these phenomena, to partial out of these regularities whatever aspects are plausibly accounted for by classical behavior-theoretic mechanisms (e.g., reinforcement of S-R bonds and primary stimulus generalization) of subcognitive complexity, to tease out the deeper theoretical implications of whatever residual data patterning cannot be so explained, to discern the respects in which the latter mechanisms still importantly fail to capture the distinctive logical features of mentalistically conceived cognitive functions, to trace the specific import of these still-unreclaimed mental properties for behavioral indices not yet investigated, to carry through empirical studies which determine what the new phenomena so implicated are in fact technically like, and to persist in as many iterations of this cycle as may be required for the behavioral approach to extract from our mentalistic intuitions all that proves worthy of retention therein. It is easy to underestimate—perhaps by several orders of magnitude—how difficult it is to carry through with even modest success the research program I have just described,[10] or how wide a gap still remains between our commonsense notions of mental processes and those beliefs about what goes on inside for which we have hard evidential warrant. Yet this program *can* be made productive and with patience and effort the gap *can* be closed. I submit my own past contributions as a small testimonial to the viability of this prospect.

NOTES

1. See Rozeboom, 1960a, 1967b, 1969b, and fns. 1 and 2 in the last of these for further references.
2. Peyton's second criticism here, beginning "If we know, by other criteria, that a certain stimulus is linguistic ...," is likewise far off the mark, for I have expressly argued (pp. 40f. 45) that past attempts to differentiate linguistic from nonlinguistic stimuli have been egregiously unsuccessful. If Peyton really does know of a defensible criterion for languagehood alternative to mine, it's a pity that he has not taken this opportunity to put it on record.
3. It is not enough just to name some humanistic masterpieces like *Hamlet*, *Guernica*, or the *Deutsches Requiem* and stop there, for that simply begs the question unless it can be shown that these have epistemic qualities which are lacking in, say, the Grand Coulee dam, the 72nd St. Expressway, or eggs Benedict. If it be claimed that the former, unlike the latter, say something about the "condition of man," the question still remains begged until we are given some examples of *what*, specifically, they say about this and told why we should not regard such artistic sayings simply as more or less vague (albeit perhaps extraordinarily rich—see p. 75f.) propositional beliefs evoked by means other than linguistic assertion.
4. In brief, it has been argued that psychology proper (to be distinguished from physiology) cannot be a natural science because mentalistic concepts aren't amenable to treatment in terms of causal mechanism (cf. Melden, 1966; Peters, 1960; Taylor, 1966)—in particular, that it is logically impossible for intentions to be causally responsible

for the actions to which they correspond because their relation to the latter is analytic. This view has already been shot down by, *inter alia*, Alston (1966) and Fodor (1968), so I need say no more about it here except to note that it is grounded on an astonishingly obsolete notion of causal relatedness and theoretical concepts in science.

5. Appeal to introspective data is for psychological science akin to ascertaining weight and temperature in physical research by heft and touch. Nothing is methodologically *illicit* about such observations, especially when they are the best we can do. But until we *can* do better than data this crude, our knowledge of what underlies them must inevitably remain primitive or conjectural.

6. E.g., I can introspect whether ideas A and B are co-present in my thinking, but not whether I have an association between A and B. The latter is a dispositional property which can only be inferred from my pattern of A and B thoughts or, more sensitively, from how I perform on certain technical tasks of the sort which verbal-learning research has proved ingenious at devising.

7. See Rozeboom, 1962b, p. 344ff. on the logic of "identifying" theoretical entities. I speak of "profiles" of experiental richness here because behavioral and mentalistic conceptions of internal events differ not merely in overall existential depth (however that might be measured) but also in the dimensions of experience which they emphasize.

8. With one emendation, I strongly endorse Peters' (1960, p. 50) claim that "We know *so much* about human beings, and our knowledge is incorporated implicitly in our language. Making it explicit could be a more fruitful preliminary to developing a theory than gaping at rats or grey geese." Beyond scowling at the gratuitously derogatory tone of the last phrase, I would replace "know" with "conjecture" here, since the wheat of commonsense psychology is well laced with chaff and other barnyard wastes.

9. "Hierarchical" in that scientific knowledge about the explanatory sources of observed events derives primarily from interlocked data patterns of ascending logical type in which local parameters in lower-level regularities become the variables of higher-level laws (see Rozeboom, 1961b, 1971b).

10. For a taste of the technical complexity of an even partial behavioristic reconstruction of expectations, ideational associations, and purposive acts, see Rozeboom, 1970a, Part III.

BIBLIOGRAPHY

Alston, W., Wants, actions, and causal explanation. In: Castaneda, H. (ed.) *Intentionality Minds, and Perception*. Detroit: Wayne State Univ. Press, 1966.

Armstrong, D. M., A theory of perception. In: Wolman, B. B., and Nagel, E. (eds.) *Scientific Psychology*. New York: Basic Books, 1965.

Aaronson, D., Temporal factors in perception and short-term memory. *Psychological Bulletin*, 1967, **67**, 130–144.

Bennett, J., Substance, reality, and primary qualities. *American Philosophical Quarterly*, 1965, **2**, 1–17.

Bergson, H., *An Introduction to Metaphysics*. Indianapolis: Bobbs-Merrill Co., 1949 (originally 1903).

Bertalanffy, L., On the definition of the symbol. In: Royce, J. R. (ed.) *Psychology and the Symbol*. New York: Random House, 1965.

Black, M., *The Labyrinth of Language*. New York: Frederick A. Praeger Publ., 1968.

Brett, G. S., *Brett's History of Psychology* (edited and abridged by R. S. Peters). Cambridge, Mass.: The M. I. T. Press, 1965.

Broad, C. D., *Examination of McTaggert's Philosophy*, Vol. 1. London: Cambridge Univ. Press, 1933.

Brown, R., *Words and Things*. Glencoe, Ill.: The Free Press, 1958.

Bruner, J. S., Goodnow, J. J., and Austin, G. A., *A Study of Thinking*. New York: Wiley, 1956.

Bruner, J. S. et al., *Studies in Cognitive Growth*. New York: Wiley, 1966.

Carnap, R., *Introduction to Semantics*. Cambridge, Mass.: Harvard Univ. Press, 1942.

Carnap, R., The methodological character of theoretical concepts. In: Feigl, H. and Scriven, M. (eds.), *Minnesota Studies in the Philosophy of Science*, Vol. 1. Minneapolis: Univ. of Minnesota Press, 1956.

Carroll, L., What the tortoise said to Achilles. *Mind*, 1895, **4**, 278–280.

Chomsky, N., *Aspects of the Theory of Syntax*. Cambridge, Mass.: M. I. T. Press, 1965.

Chomsky, N., Recent contributions to the theory of innate ideas. *Synthese*, 1967, **17**, 2–11.

Cliff, N., Adverbs as multipliers. *Psychological Review*, 1959, **66**, 27–44.

Cronbach, L. J., and Meehl, P. E., Construct validity in psychological tests. *Psychological Bulletin*, 1955, **52**, 281–302.

Ducasse, C. J. Symbols, signs, and signals. *Journal of Logic*, 1939, **4**, 41–52. (Reprinted in Ducasse, C. J. *Truth, Knowledge, and Causation*. London: Routledge & Kegan Paul, 1968.)

Dulany, D. E., Awareness, rules, and propositional control: A confrontation with S–R behavior theory. In: Dixon, T. R., and Horton, D. L. *Verbal Behavior and General Behavior Theory*. Englewood Cliffs, N. J.: Prentice-Hall, 1968.

Edwards, W., Lindman, H., and Phillips, L. D., Emerging technologies for making decisions. In: Barron, F., *et al.*, *New Directions in Psychology II*. New York: Holt, Rinehart and Winston, 1965.

Feigl, H., Existential hypotheses: Realistic versus phenomenalistic interpretations. *Philosophy of Science*, 1950, **17**, 35–62.
Feldman, S. (ed.) *Cognitive Consistency*. New York: Academic Press, 1966.
Fitts, P. M., Perceptual-motor skill learning. In: Melton, A. W. (ed.) *Categories of Human Learning*. New York: Academic Press, 1964.
Fodor, J. A., *Psychological Explanation*. New York: Random House, 1968.
Fodor, J., Could meaning be an r_m? *Journal of Verbal Learning and Verbal Behavior*. 1965, **4**, 73–81.
Frankena, W. K., 'Cognitive' and 'noncognitive'. In: Henle, P. (ed.) *Language, Thought, and Culture*. Ann Arbor: The Univ. of Michigan Press, 1958.
Frege, G., On sense and reference (1892). In: Geach, P., and Black, M. (eds.) *Translations from the Philosophical Writings of Gottlob Frege*. Oxford: Basil Blackwell, 1952.
Furth, H. G., *Piaget and Knowledge*. Englewood Cliffs, N. J.: Prentice-Hall, 1969.
Gagné, R. M., The learning of principles. In: Klausmeier, H. J., and Harris, C. W. *Analysis of Concept Learning*. New York: Academic Press, 1966.
Goss, A. E., Early behaviorism and verbal mediating responses. *American Psychologist*, 1961, **16**, 285–298.
Gibson, E. J., *Principles of Perceptual Learning and Development*. New York: Appleton-Century-Crofts, 1969.
Hempel, C. G., *Aspects of Scientific Explanation*. New York: The Free Press, 1965.
Howe, E. S., Verb tense, negatives, and other determinants of the intensity of evaluative meaning. Associative structure of quantifiers. *Journal of Verbal Learning and Verbal Behavior*, 1966, **5**, 147–155, 156–162.
Hunt, E. B., *Concept Learning: An Information Processing Problem*. New York: Wiley, 1962.
Jakobovits, L. A., and Miron, M. S. (eds.), *Readings in the Psychology of Language*. Englewood Cliffs, N. J.: Prentice-Hall, 1967.
Jones, L. V., and Wepman, J. M., Dimensions of language performance in asphasia. *Journal of Speech and Hearing Research*, 1961, **4**, 220–232.
Katz, J. J., and Fodor, J. A., The structure of a semantic theory. *Language*, 1963, **39**, 170–210. (Reprinted in Jakobovits & Miron.)
Körner, S., *Experience and Theory*. London: Routledge & Kegan Paul, 1966.
Langer, S. K., *Philosophy in a New Key*. Cambridge, Mass.: Harvard Univ. Press, 1942.
Lashley, K., The problem of serial order in behavior. In: Jeffress, L. A. (ed.) *Cerebral Mechanisms in Behavior*. New York: Wiley, 1951.
Leonard, H. S. *Principles of right reason*. New York: Holt, 1957.
MacLeish, A., Why do we teach poetry? *Atlantic*, March, 1956.
Martin, R. M., *Truth and Denotation*. Chicago: The Univ. of Chicago Press, 1958.
Massey, G. J., Hampel's criterion of maximal specificity. *Philosophical Studies*, 1968, **19**, 43–47.
Melden, A. I., Desires as causes of action. In: Dommeyer, F. C. (ed.) *Current Philosophical Issues*. Springfield, Ill.: Charles C. Thomas, 1966.
Morris, C., *Signs, Language and Behavior*. New York: Prentice-Hall, 1946.
Mowrer, O. H., The psychologist looks at language. *American Psychologist*, 1954, **9**, 660–694. (Reprinted in Jakobovits & Miron.)
Murphy, G., Psychology in the year 2000. *American Psychologist*, 1969, **24**, 515–522.
Nagel, E., *The Structure of Science*. New York: Harcourt, Brace & World, 1961.

Natsoulas, T., Concerning Introspective knowledge. *Psychological Bulletin*, 1970, **73**, 89–111.

Ogden, C. K., and Richards, I. A., *The Meaning of Meaning*. London: K. Paul, Trench, Trubner & Co., 1923.

Osgood, C. E., The nature and measurement of meaning. *Psychological Bulletin*, 1952, **49**, 197–237.

Osgood, C. E., On understanding and creating sentences. *American Psychologist*, 1963, **18**, 735–751. (Reprinted in Jakobovits & Miron.)

Pap, A., Theory of definition. *Philosophy of Science*, 1964, **31**, 49–54.

Peters, R. S., *The Concept of Motivation*. London: Routledge & Kegan Paul, 1960.

Quine, W. V. O., *Word and Object*. New York: Wiley, 1960.

Robinson, R., *Definition*. London: Oxford Univ. Press, 1954.

Rokeach, M., Beliefs, Attitudes, and Values. San Francisco: Jossey-Bass, 1968.

Rokeach, M., and Rothman, M., The principle of belief congruence and the congruity. principle as models of cognitive interaction. *Psychological Review*, 1965, **72**, 128–142.

Royce, J. R., *The Encapsulated Man: An Interdisciplinary Essay on the Search for Meaning* Princeton:

Royce, J. R., The present situation in theoretical psychology. In: Royce, J. R. (ed.) *Toward Unification in Psychology*. Toronto: Univ. of Toronto Press, 1970.

Rozeboom, W. W., Do stimuli elicit behavior?—a study in the logical foundations of behavioristics. *Philosophy of Science*, 1960, **27**, 159–170. (a)

Rozeboom, W. W., Studies in the empiricist theory of scientific meaning. *Philosophy of Science*, 1960, **27**, 359–373. (b)

Rozeboom, W. W., Formal analysis and the language of behavior theory. In: Feigl, H., and Maxwell, G. (eds.) *Current Issues in the Philosophy of Science*. New York: Holt, Rinehart & Winston, 1961. (a)

Rozeboom, W. W., Ontological induction and the logical typology of scientific variables. *Philosophy of Science*, 1961, **28**, 337–377. (b)

Rozeboom, W. W., Intentionality and existence. *Mind*, 1962, **71**, 15–32. (a)

Rozeboom, W. W., The factual content of theoretical concepts. In: Feigl, H., and Maxwell, G. (eds.) *Minnesota Studies in the Philosophy of Science*, Vol. III. Minneapolis: Univ. of Minnesota Press, 1962. (b)

Rozeboom, W. W., Of selection operators and semanticists. *Philosophy of Science*, 1964, **31**, 282–285.

Rozeboom, W. W., The concept of "memory". *Psychological Record*, 1965, **15**, 329–368.

Rozeboom, W. W., Scaling theory and the nature of measurement. *Synthese*, 1966, **16**, 170–233. (a)

Rozeboom, W. W., *Foundations of the Theory of Prediction*. Homewood, Ill.: Dorsey Press, 1966. (b)

Rozeboom, W. W., Why I know so much more than you do. *American Philosophical Quarterly*, 1967, **4**, 281–291. (a)

Rozeboom, W. W., Conditioned generalization, cognitive set, and the structure of human learning. *Journal of Verbal Learning and Verbal Behavior*, 1967, **6**, 491–500. (b)

Rozeboom, W. W., New dimensions in confirmation theory. *Philosophy of Science*, 1968, **35**, 134–155.

Rozeboom, W. W., New mysteries for old: The transfiguration of Miller's paradox. *British Journal for Philosophy of Science*, 1969, **19**, 245–353. (a)

Rozeboom, W. W., Compositional structure in recall. *Journal of Verbal Learning and Verbal Behavior*, 1969, **8**, 622–632. (b)

Rozeboom, W. W., The art of metascience. In: Royce J. R. (ed.) *Toward Unification in Psychology*. Toronto: Toronto Univ. Press, 1970.

Rozeboom, W. W., The crisis in philosophical semantics. In: Radner, M., and Winokur, S. (eds.) *Minnesota Studies in the Philosopy of Science*, Vol. IV. Minneapolis: Univ. of Minnesota Press, 1971. (a)

Rozeboom, W. W., Scientific inference: The myth vs. the reality. In: Brown, R. S., and Brenner, D. J. (eds.), *Science, Psychology, and Communication: Essays Honoring William Stephenson*. New York: Teachers College Press, 1971. (b)

Russell, B., On denoting. *Mind*, 1905, **14**, 479–493.

Ryle, G., The theory of meaning. In: Mace, C. A. (ed.) *British Philosophy in the Mid-Century*. London: George Allen & Unwin, Ltd., 1957.

Sellars, W., Some reflections on language games. *Philosophy of science*, 1954, **21**, 204–228

Sellars, W., *Science and Metaphysics*. London: Routledge & Kegan Paul, 1968.

Skinner, B. F., *Verbal Behavior*. New York: Appleton-Century-Crofts, 1957.

Smith, D. W. & McIntyre, R. Intentionality via intensions. *Journal of Philosophy*, 1971, **68**, 541–561.

Stebbings, L. S., *A Modern Introduction to Logic*. London: Methuen, 1931.

Stevenson, C. L., *Ethics and Language*. New Haven: Yale Univ. Press, 1944.

Tarski, A., The semantic conception of truth. *Philosophy and Phenomenological Research*, 1944, **4**, 13–47.

Taylor, R., *Action and Purpose*. Englewood Cliffs, N. Jersey: Prentice-Hall, 1966.

Terwilliger, R. F., *Meaning and Mind*. New York: Oxford University Press, 1968.

Underwood, B. J., Attributes of memory. *Psychological Review*, 1969, **76**, 559–573.

Unger, P. A defense of skepticism. *Philosphical Review*, 1971, **80**, 198–219.

Werner, H. and Kaplan, B., *Symbol Formation*. New York: Wiley, 1963.

Willard, D. The paradox of logical positivism: Husserl's way out. *American Philosophical Quarterly*, 1972, **9**, 94–100.

IV

ON KNOWING WHAT ONE KNOWS NOT
Why there ought to be a problem of how to justify ampliation

Herman Tennessen

The Center for Advanced Study in Theoretical Psychology

1. ON KNOWING THAT ONE KNOWS

A few vague and tentative preliminaries

At a modest level of ambition, there appears to be no problem of knowing. I know, say, that an imaginary number is the square root of a negative number. I may even claim to know that there are certain physical particles, *viz.* tachyons, whose masses are adequately represented solely by such imaginary numbers. And were I challenged to justify either or both of my claims, I should go about in doing so—or attempting to do so—quite confidently and without the slightest hesitation. Moreover, I shall certainly insist that I do indeed know what I am talking about: I won't have any insinuation to the contrary:

And yet: How can I possibly feel justified in contending that I know that I know, unless I know what it *is* to know? Do I know that I know *that*? In fact: can I even *pretend* to know what it is to know, if my doubts about 'knowing' were altogether seriously meant in the first place? I don't know. True enough: philosophical literature can scarcely be said to display any glaring deficiency of definition like formulations with "knowing" (or "knowledge") at the definiendum end. It is, unfortunately eqaully true that they all—even after the shallowest analyses—seem to dissolve into painful, irredeemable twaddle. The socalled "justified-true-belief" formulations, —insofar as they seek to serve as definoform sentences of sort, — may, as probably the most notorious fiasco, serve as an awful warning. And, what is worse: It seems at the face of it that there is no hope for a remedy in a steady sharpening of the concepts, a more careful and precise *formulation* of the puzzlement. On the contrary: It is rather, as Benson

Mates[1] has pointed out with regard to other typical philosophical problems: The more explicit and consistent their conveyance, the more conspicuously and unavoidably they exhibit the characters of genuine antinomies. An antinomy, according to W. v. O. Quine[2], is characterised by the fact that it "produces a self-contradiction by accepted ways of reasoning". The case at hand may, I suppose, be interpreted in a way which will show some similarities with, say, "The Barber", "The Liar" ("Epimenides"), and, possibly even with Russell's antinomy:[3]

If I claim to know that it is doubtful whether *any* knowledge claim can be justified,— *i.e.* that it is true of all knowledge claims that their justification is doubtful—then it follows that it is doubtful whether this particular knowledge claim of *mine* is justified; consequently there may well be justified knowledge claims; and hence this very knowledge claim could itself in fact be justified; in which case it follows that my claim to know that it is doubtful whether *any* knowledge claim can be justified, can indeed be justified... But, it may be argued: What about the above knowledge claim itself— if that is what it is—what guile recommends this ludicrous looking piece of ratiocination, and provides justification for my claim to *know* that all these things "*follow*" (as I say)? The traditional answer is that here we are dealing with an entirely different kettle of fish. I may doubt my claim to know that all deans are dumb. I may even question my right to claim to know that Dean Doug is dumb. But, it is argued: I *cannot* doubt that *if* I know (i.e. I am justified in claiming to know) that *all* deans are dumb, then I also know that Dean Doug is dumb. If I doubted *that*, that would not be an insult to any dean, of course, but to LOGIC itself, as it were. The distinction must be made, according to customary contentions, between two different types of claims:

Type 1 consists of claims where the claimer claims *to know what he virtually already knows:* He knows that Dean Doug is dumb whenever he already knows that all deans, including Dean Doug, are dumb. It "follows" by simple instantiation: $(x) Fx \rightarrow Fy$ [or: $(\exists x) Fx$]. But it may in most cases require considerably more efforts than in the above example to demonstrate convincingly that a given knowledge claim actually ought to be considered of type 1. Take for instance the claim introduced in the beginning of the present section, i.e. my claim to know that imaginary numbers are the square root of negative numbers; how does this claim differ from my claim to know that there are tachyons?

Type 2 are claims where the claimer, as it were, claims *to know what he does not know*, i.e., what does not "follow" from what he already assumes to know. Thus, it does not follow from anything I know about negative and imaginary numbers and their formal interrelationships that there exist physical particles whose masses may be represented by imaginary numbers (and which can travel with infinite velocity, etc. etc. ...). It is traditionally argued that the case of tachyons ought to be distinguished from that of negative and imaginary numbers by subsuming the latter under the class of type 1, the former under type 2 knowledge claims.

In what follows I shall elaborate on this dichotomy, in fact: try to make it so clear that it seems to disappear.

2. KNOWING WHAT ONE KNOWS versus KNOWING WHAT ONE KNOWS NOT

Among the many unpromising, primary and preliminary tasks confronting students of the socalled: "socalled problem of induction", the most onerous one is probably connected with the extravagant impreciseness of the standard key-notions traditionally employed, and the heinous indeterminacy of their employers semantic intentions. One notion, particularly prominent in this respect, is the notion of 'induction' itself. From the multifarious menagerie of its many meanings, I shall mention at least two *major* directions of interpretation of "induction" as it rather frequently occurs in philosophical literature (rather than, say, in mathematics, electro-statics, -mechanics, -magnetics, etc.):

(a) The more exclusively inclined, or *narrower senses* are referring to a somewhat limited, though admittedly quite general, type of procedure for knowledge acquisition where the knowledge in question, at least in the paradigmatic cases, is a knowledge of fairly general or even "universal" propositions, "universal laws", "laws of nature" ... or whatever, customarily is said to be: "reached" or: "arrived at" by a more or less elaborate enumeration of specific instances of ("evidence for") the universal propositions.

(b) In some of the *wider* (inclusive) *senses* of 'induction' "inductive inference" denotes *any* knowledge contention, universal or special (individual), which in any way may be said to transcend, transgress or *ampliate* the borderlines of what is, at a given stage of knowledge or insight perfectioning, already defined as "given" (assumed, presupposed ...) knowledge. Interpreted in the direction of the latter, wider notions of 'induction', "inductive" is then ascribed to *any* claim, where the claimer, as we have put it, *claims to know what he knows not.*

It is chiefly these wider notions of 'induction', 'inductive inference', etc. with which I shall concern myself in the present paper. However, hoping against hope to discourage a confusion of these presumably major directions of interpretation of "induction", I shall attempt to avoid the term "induction" and substitute for it, as often as I can possibly manage, the term: "*ampliation*". I shall, moreover, endeavour to confine myself to talk of "*ampliative contentions*" (or: "ampliative inferences", "ampliative reasoning" ...) as opposed to "*explicative contentions*" (resp. inferences, reasoning), to some extent in *terminological* accordance, I suppose, with Charles Sanders Peirce.[4]

The ampliative/explicative distinction, thus used, I am prepared to admit, is bound to overlap with a rich variation of usages of quite a few, more venerable distinctions from the history of philosophy, such as: nondemonstrative/demonstrative; inductive/deductive; synthetic/analytic (tauto-logical); real/formal; empirical/rational; a posteriori/a priori; universalia post rem/universalisa ante rem; contingent/necessary; accidental (existential)/essential; immanens/transcendens; questio facti/questio juris; vérités de fait/vérités de raison(nement); das Nichtzusammenglaubenkönnen/das Nichtzusammenwahrseinkönnen; ... However, the distinction at hand may typically be indicated by another set of oversimplified illustrations:

Given as knowledge (—whatever we may decide to mean by "knowledge"—) is, let us say that: "Popper and Quine are both in Banff". The inference that: "Either p or q is in Banff (is knowledge)" would, under those conditions exemplify an *explicative* contention,—i.e.: "$(p \cdot q) \supset (pvq)$". Take, on the other hand, any simple segment of this implication, and it could serve as an adequate instance of an ampliative (contention), *e.g.*: "$p!$", "$q!$", "(pvq)", "$(p \cdot q)$", "$(p \supset q)$", ... These are all explicit, and, for some "logical" or "literal" interpretations *prima facie* indubitable illustrations of the ampliative/explicative distinction, as I have decided to endeavour to use it.

A more *implicit* or covert explicativity may be demonstrated as follows: Consider the last parenthesis, "$(p \supset q)$", and let "p" stand for: "x is a teenager", and "q" for: "x is still young (—say: below 20 years old—)". For a similarly "literal" or "logical" interpretation, the contention: "$(p \supset q)$!" might well be conceived as an explicative claim.

It is, naturally, the more important to develop an awareness or preparedness for a possible explicative direction of interpretation of a contention, the more *implicit*, covert the claim conveyance. Or, in other words: the *less* overtly explicative (the more amplio*form*) the conveyance of the contention appears to be, the more momentous and indispensible is an interpreter's attitude of flexible, unbiased, attentive and suspicious vigilance with regard to the plausibility of a case of a "crypto-explicative" piece of reasoning.

A slightly puzzling borderline case is finally illustrated by an example, say, where in the formula, "$(p \supset q)$!", "p" is a proposition that could be conveyed by: "x is human", and "q" in, a similar fashion would stand for: "x is mortal". The choice seems quite arbitrary whether one would want to treat this "$(p \supset q)$" according to the same pattern as the above example where "p" symbolized: "x is a teenager", and "q": "x is young"; *or* choose to construe it as a straightforward *ampliative* contention, as in the above case where "p" was: "Popper is in Banff", and "q": "Quine is in Banff". In the teenager case, one would, I suppose, ordinarily be inclined to accept as given (knowledge) any contention to be conveyed by the following sentence, S_a: "For all x if x is a teenager, x is young, in the sense of: 'less than 20 years old' (of 'young')", or: "$x(Tx \supset Yx)$", or: $(Tx \supset 20 > x)$". The acceptance of S_a (as given knowledge) would reasonably be seen to render explicative any contention like: "$(p \supset q)$!" where "p" stands for "x is teenager", and "q" for "x is young (< 20 years old) or: "$(\exists x)(Tx \cdot Yx)$". In the man and mortality case, on the other hand, it seems more of a toss up whether to accept or reject S_b: "For all x if x is human x is mortal", or: "$x(Hx \supset Mx)$". Were S_b to be *accepted* as given (knowledge) this would render the contention explicative that: "there is (at least) one x such that x is human and x is mortal: ("$\exists x(Hx \cdot Mx)$")". A rejection of S_b as given—or rather: an acceptance of the negation of $S_b (\sim S_b)$—would, by the same token, argue *for* an interpretation of "$\exists x(Hx \cdot Mx)$" in an ampliative direction.

In other words: to conclude that "if someone, P, is teenager, P is (also) young",[5] is trivial, it "follows" by explication from the assumption (or; "given knowledge") that: "*all* teenagers are *per definitionem*, young". Whereas the claim that "if P is human, P is mortal",[6] is slightly less trivial and a trifle more audacious because, presumably, there is considerably less of an urge to accept as given (knowledge) "that all men are *per definitionem* bound to be mortal". Insofar as it is (in principle) possible for someone or something (at one time) *both* to be human *and* simultaneously *not* to be mortal, is it "interesting", "informative", to consider the claim that the person P (with whom we are concerned) does *not* happen to be such that he is both human and non-mortal. The claim, in still other words: *ampliates* what is already entailed in the given (assumed, presumed ...) knowledge.

I want to contend and even emphasize that no claim-formulation is *per se* either explicative or ampliative. Any formulation may, more or less reasonably, be interpreted one way or the other. It is particularly fatuous to attempt to judge a claim formulation solely by its external appearance. There is, as I have pointed out, most likely to be an *inverse* correlation between the ampliative (resp. explicative) *form* of a sentence and the, ampliative (resp. explicative) *contention* to be conveyed by it. One might, of course, hypothesize as to *the claimer's intentions*, taking into consideration whatever information is available (concerning the context, the claimer, his language habits, what he was up to, the total situation wherein the sentence in question occurred ... etc.). But due to the widespread, general indeterminacy of intentions—not the least with regard to what a claimer more precisely is determined to *intend* to claim by means of a given phrase or formulation—one would in most cases be well advised to *invent* and *propose* such intentions, while being as charitable as possible vis à vis the claimer, and with complete disregard of whatever claim the claimer, if ever so vigorously, may insist on having intended to convey by the claim sentence at hand. As a rule, however, I suppose it would be safe to say, that no claimer would normally *want* to convey an explicative claim—except as an example or illustration of an explicative claim (and under a few other such peculiar conditions). *All "interesting" claims are ampliative*:

The claimer, so to speak, claims to know what he knows not.

3. A VANISHING DICHOTOMY

All Non-trivial Knowledge Claims are Ampliative

A brief digression is here called for in order to emphasize how excessively wide or diluted a notion of "ampliative claim" I shall venture to introduce.

Offhand, I suppose, anyone who would want to voice any opinion in these matters, should tend to consider as explicative any typical claim within pure mathematics. This, however, is definitely not in accordance with intended usage. Only the most trivial and unambitious claims within mathematics or any other "pure", "formal" "deductive" discipline would qualify as explicative.

As a paradigmatic representation, consider *e.g.* Riemann's celebrated conjecture on the counting of primes below a given number.[7] This subject, as old as recorded history of mathematics, had its inception in Euclid's proof: "that the number of primes is greater than any given set of them". The next step beyond was Euler's who proved that the sum of the reciprocal primes diverges. For this purpose Euler introduced the series $\sum_{n=1}^{\infty} n = \zeta(S)$, which diverges for $S \leq 1$. Dirichlet extended the idea through consideration of associated functions, the socalled "L-series", in order to prove that the sum of the reciprocals of the primes in an arithmetic progression $ax + b$ diverges if a and b are without common divisor. Finally, Gauss had instituted an actual count of all primes up to three million and *experimentally* observed an approximate formula for their number $F(x)$ below a given x. Riemann set out to find an explicit expression for this function, $F(x)$, in order to compare it with the approximation. His first step was the analytic extension of the ζ-function into the whole complex plane as mesomorphic function, through derivation of a functional equation which ζ satisfies. The second step consisted of establishing the relation between $F(x)$ and the location of the non-trivial zeros of ζ. He proved that these zeros lie in the strip of the s-plane where the real part of s remains between 0 and 1. *He stated that he thought it very likely that all these zeros actually lie on the line where the real part of $x = 1/2$, but added that after several futile trials he discontinued attempts of a rigorous proof.* This constitutes the famous *Riemann's hypothesis*, unproved and uncontradicted to this day, in spite of prodigious efforts of numerous first rank mathematicians, the origin and inspiration of countless investigations, on the Dirichlet series,[8] on entire functions, on almost-periodic functions, and on the dependence of other number theoretical statements on the truth of this hypothesis.

The point here is that a claim within a deductive system is only to be fruitfully conceived as explicative insofar as the system is small, elementary, unsophisticated ... (say, a very simple logical calculus). Mathematics, on the other hand—when seen as one deductive system—, would present us with such an enormously huge and complicated calculus that the tenability of any claim within it, could only attempted to be established after the pattern of empirical research: The system may properly be said to be *explored* by means of computers, offering strengthening as well as weakening evidence pertinent to the hypothesis under consideration. The similarity with explorations of distant planets by means of self-propelled probes, "surveyors" (furnished with television cameras, etc.) is quite striking.

In this wide sense of 'ampliation' it is safe to assume that practically speaking no knowledge claim is ever *intended* as explicative. An explicative claim, it has often been contended, has an advantage over an ampliative one, *viz.*: It is more readily justifed. Provided the following two knowledge claims are *given*: (1) "One of the six keys in my pocket is a key to my office door;" (2) "keys K_1, K_2, K_4 and K_5 are *not* keys to my office door"; then, so goes the argument, I am clearly justified in making an apparently explicative claim: (3) "key K_3 is a key to my office door". Such examples are often quite deceptive, particularly when they take the character of a little crime story. But one ought to keep in mind that in order for the conclusion to be considered an explicative claim, as *I* strive to use "explicative", the conclusion would have to be entirely trivial and the whole argument rendered somewhat as follows: "If, for some reason or other (e.g. the reasons indicated by a conjunction of the two mentioned premises or "*givens*") I am justified in claiming that a certain key, K_3, is a key to my office, then I am justified in claiming that that key, K_3, is a key to my office" ("$p \supset p$"). This does not, needless to say, have any bearing whatsoever on such problems as *e.g.*: Is K_3 actually a key to my office door? ... Or: Do I (actually) *know* that key K_3 is a key to my office door? ... Or: Am I justified in believing that I know that K_3 is a key to my office door ... etc. etc. ... Such questions would seem to require an *ampliation* of the given claims in order that an answer could be provided. Or new given claims have to be added, concerning, let us say, the use of such central notions as: 'justified' 'justified in believing that I know'" etc. ...[9] In any event, the socalled justification of explicative claims (inferences, conclusions, entailments, etc.) is by no means unproblematic; it rather seems that, as I strive to use "explicative", the justification of explicative claims does itself either amount to an unenlightening redundancy or it transgresses the border into ampliation.

What then can be said about the justification of *ampliative* knowledge claims: *How can we possibly know what we know not*?

4. A SOCALLED "SOCALLED PROBLEM"

As mentioned by way of introduction: This problem—if that is what it is—is frequently dealt with under such heading as: "The Problem of Induction", "induction" occasionally being used in the direction of the above indicated sense of "ampliation", but more often in one of its narrower senses.

The most fashionable position for the last four or five decades has been to consider the problem of induction, in the wide sense of how to know what one knows not, no problem at all, or: a pseudo problem, a "socalled problem" ... I submit that this position is not (as often claimed) based on a "discovery" of the apparent problem manifesting itself as no real problem, or on a successful analysis which "disclosed", "revealed" that there *could* be no such problem. It rather rests on a quite arbitrary choice, the advantages or disadvantages of which may be argued with reference to explicit or implicit norms or general value-judgments. I shall occasionally, and mainly in conclusion, briefly touch upon a few of the advantages of *considering* "it" a problem (—i.e. how we can know what we know not—), and deal in particular with some of the disadvantages of refusing to consider it a problem.

Needless to say, it follows clearly from a combination of the excessive impreciseness of basic key words or phrases and their employers' shallow depth of intention, that it would be unforgivably naîve to approach what may be tentatively labeled: "the problem of ampliation" as though it were *a* problem.[10] To seriously endeavour to offer *a* solution to *it*, *the* problem, is sheer megalomania. More megalomaniacal are, it seems to me, only attempts to demonstrate, let alone "prove", that *it is no problem*, or that it could not *possibly* be a problem, come what may ...

Such an endeavour is nevertheless quite noticeable among many modern authors, who are themselves quite noticeable on the present scene of philosophy.

One method frequently employed for determining whether a problem formulation is bound to convey a problem or not, is ingeniously facile and painless. After a recipe of the British philosophy professor, J. O. Urmson, one simply develops a certain "acuity of ear", then listens carefully to the sound of the formulation under consideration, and, as if by magic, the final, absolutely reliable, irrevocable judgment presents itself to the listener's tympanum.

Among the tympani to test "the problem of ampliative knowledge claims", "the general (principle) problem of inductive inferences" and similar problem formulation, an overwhelming majority of Anglo-American writers seem to find that no problem could possible be conveyed by such formulations. The problem formulations are: "nonsensical", "absurd", "logically odd", or words to that effect.

One of the most noticeable and representative exponents for this attitude, and general trend in philosophy, is probably Max Black."[11] In his encyclopedia article he categorically rules out the existence of any *general* problem concerned with the possibility of inductive inferences—let alone a problem of how to know what one knows not! Its justification "can only arise as problem", Max Black—strange enough—seems to want to profess: "for somebody who is a member of the inductive institution and is therefore already bound by its constitutive rules".[12]

And he proceeds to contend that these rules "provide important general constraints" (on a reasoner) "which cannot be violated without generating nonsense". There is, Black alleges, such a thing as an "inductive language". To be in command of this "is necessarily to be subject to the implicit norms of belief and conduct imposed by the (inductive) institution". These norms, Black suggests, may be usefully thought of as "formal crystallizations into linguistic rules of general modes of response to the universe that our ancestors have, on the whole, found advantageous to survival ...".

"What is clearly impossible is the sort of wholesale revolution that would be involved in wiping the inductive slate clean and trying to revert to the condition of some hypothetical Adam setting out to learn from experience without previous indoctrination in relevant rules of inductive procedure. This would be tantamount to attempting to destroy the language we now use to talk about the world and about ourselves and thereby to destroy the concepts embodied in that language. The idea of ceasing to be an inductive reasoner is a monstrosity. The task is not impossibly difficult; rather, its very formulation fails to make sense. Yet it remains important to insist that the inductive institution, precisely because its *raison d'être* is learning from experience, is intrinsically self-critical. Induction, like the Sabbath, was made for man, not vice versa."

"... the entire institution cannot be called into question all at once without destroying the very meaning of the words in which the philosophical problems of induction are stated. Wholesale philosophical scepticism about matters of fact is senseless and must be shown to be so".

"... the sweeping question: Why should we accept *any* inductive rules? can be shown to make no sense."

"To understand induction is necessarily to accept its authority. However (to repeat), questions about the general or ultimate justification of induction *as such*, questions of the form: "Why should any induction be trusted?" must be recognized as senseless. If we persist in trying to raise them, we come, as Wittgenstein expressed it, to the limits of language, and we can see that we have done so by perceiving that what we had hoped were important and fundamental questions are no better than nonsense masquerading as sense."

There is a bit of pathos and melancholy in this Custer's last stand on induction (in The Max Black Hills). There is a sad discrepancy between (a) the bombastic grandiosity of his panicky claims, and (b) their general confidence inspiring capacities. One is resistlessly reminded of the marginal note C. A. Ewing allegedly discovered in his friend, the vicar's Sunday Sermon: "Argument weak. *Shout!!*"

Suffice it at this stage to repeat, that not only does Black's "acuity of ear" seem to permit him to sort out such "fundamental" problem formulations as "problem of ampliation", "problem of justifying induction", etc. as flagrantly absurd, but the mere posing of such problems presupposes an allegedly untenable, pyrrhonic position, its insufficient tenability, Black argues (not entirely without an air of circularity), allegedly being due to the fact or fiction that it sets itself a task such that: "Its very formulation fails to make sense". Black offers no directives for how one is expected to manage to make sense of *his* proposition: that a formulation, which, according to Black, fails to make sense, nevertheless may be employed by him—presumably even successfully so—to itemize specific attributes of a certain, if ever so preposterous task.[13] It shouldn't by any chance be *the task* that fails to make sense (to Max Black)? A task, surely, is often considered to "fail to make sense" if it is, let us say, sufficiently futile or fatuous, or excessively easy or onerous or simply: wild, crazy ... And I do think it might be safe to assume that some of the attributes Black is prepared to apply to the tasks he ascribes to socalled "wholesale" sceptics, would serve exactly that function, in fact, quite splendidly so. And as for wholesale scepticism, does it not seem rather rash to judge it solely by the sound of its formulations? A controversy on the validity of socalled "radical", "consistent", or "extreme" scepticism, would in that event be reduced to an exchange of reports on the disputant's respective adventures and experiences in dealing with relevant formulations. Speaking for myself I can but confess that my encounters with, say, pyrrhonic formulations have invariably been thoroughly enjoyable. No bad trips at all! In fact, I am bound to admit that I am rather anxious to go much further: I am convinced[14] that if by "wholesale scepticism" Max Black were referring to something along the line of "the Sextus Empiricus presentation of philosophical attitudes typical of such philosophers as Pyrrho and Carneads", then wholesale scepticism is what I most desire. And I feel certainly safe in saying that, by any standards (with regard to, for instance, clarity, consistency and tenability) I find pyrrhonism vastly superior to that petty, whimsical "retail" scepticism, so popular, particularly among British philosophers, for its compromising, moderate, down-to-earth, spinsterish reasonableness,—and, possibly, because it is so effortlessly defeated!

Were, on the other hand, Max Black's sweeping, "wholesale" tirades more charitably construed as intended to be conveyed and conceived in what we might call an *"optative"* or *"hortative" mode*, (or climate of thought) then possibilities would arise for enquiring into what could be said *for* and *against* questioning anything as fundamental and universal as: how we can know what we know not ...

There is, unfortunately, not much basis in Black's writings to support a shift in the interpretation towards such an "optative" mode. He admits, however, as we have seen, almost entirely without qualms, that, judged by the "outcome", we practice our ampliative reasoning or, as Max Black's prefers: "inductive" ratiocination with ups and downs. But he seems quite unprepared to contemplate the monstrous possibility that this might just as well be the case within a whole generation, or, for that matter, innumerable generations of ampliating individuals. Were we, however, to seriously consider such a contingency, then it would suddenly sound rather disquieting that our cognitive frames, as well as our norm—and belief—systems, in short our total "Lebenswelt", "Daseinsweise" ... all are thoroughly permeated by Max Black's "inductive language", and all our experiencing, volitions and ratiocinations are irrevocably wrapped in the conceptual scheme of inductionism.[15]

Roughly and anacrustically speaking, inductionism, as a special case of ampliative knowledge acquiring policy, is customarily characterized by a general line of reasoning, implying *inter alia*, that, everything else being equal, the fact that, for instance, a general line of reasoning has been deemed "successful" (within a frame of reference given by that same, general line of reasoning), within a time interval, $t_1 - t_n$, is to be accepted as strengthening evidence for the conjecture that the same general line of reasoning is likely to be successful (in the same sense, and as judged within the same general frame of reference) at time, t_{n+1} ... But does it not seem likely that this whole line—or better still: circle— of reasoning is not quite so liable to inspire confidence in anyone who seriously questions just this basic presupposition and for whose philosophical orientation that very question is *the* fundamental point of philosophical departure.

5. FIVE FUTILE ATTEMPTS TO SUPPORT THE PRETENSION THAT THE PROBLEM OF INDUCTION IS NO PROBLEM.[16]

5.1 Strawson's Reasonableness

It may undoubtedly be argued that, in the eyes of many a good governess, such a fundamental philosophical setting, as indicated in the concluding remarks of section 4 above, must seem rather unreasonable. And, not entirely unexpected, this is exactly the position taken by *P. F. Strawson*, who attempts to render meaningless, the whole question on how we can know what we know not. Strawson has, according to Strawson,[17] either discovered (constative interpretation) or found it recommendable (optative interpretation) that the following proposition is, or ought to be conceived as though it were, an explicative claim (or: "an analytically true proposition"): "It is *reasonable* to have a degree of belief in a statement which is proportional to the evidence in its favour". Within one, by Strawson unspecifiied, language it either *is* actually so, or it *must* or *ought to* be so that "to be reasonable" is cognitively identical with "to let one's degree of conviction vary in correlation with, what within reason, can or ought to be listed as evidence in favour of this conviction. Doing this is what reasonable means ...".[18]

If one now, still further, accepts a language—either because this is how we (according to Strawson actually do, *have* to, or *ought* to speak and think—such that "to draw inductive" (or as I would say: "ampliative") "inferences", to be inductionist" (in the same wide sense), is either synonymous with or, at least, a special case of 'being reasonable', then it would indeed seem only reasonable that anyone who desired to be reasonable (moderate, temperate, restrained, normal, sober ...) would unhesitatingly abandon himself to a blind and unquestioning faith in a strawsonian brand of inductionism. All under the condition of course, that he is also prepared to swallow whole Strawson's notions: 'reasonable', 'plausible', 'inductive', 'induction', etc.—including their alleged synonymity relationships and the whole bit.

Strawson offers no indications as to the *degree* to which his position is to be considered explicative or: the ratio of "analyticity" one may be justified in delegating to his various formulations.[19] The most impressive measure of analyticity is achieved by combining unlimited subsumability of the concept: 'to have a degree of belief in a statement which is proportional to the evidence in its favour' with an explicit introduction of absolute, cognitive identity between this concept and the concepts: 'to have confidence in inductive inferences' and: 'to be reasonable'. It would, within this exotic strawsonian language, be about as audacious to claim that: "it is reasonable to have confidence in inductive inferences" as it would be to claim that: "it is moist to be wet", "it is dangerous to have fatal accidents", "it is punctual to be on time" ...

On the other hand, not much is gained by interpreting Strawson in a more ampliative, synthetic less explicative, analytic direction.

Given are, say, two researchers, R_1 and R_2, and a claim, proposition, or statement, S, where S is conceived of in a traditional manner such that if S is true, the negation, $\sim S$, is false. Two major combinations of possibilities may then be distinguished:

1a: R_1 and R_2 are in agreement, *both* as to the degree of confidence they ought to have in S (resp. $\sim S$), *as well as* the correct foundation for this confidence which might *either* be some sort of strawsonian induction(ism), *i.e.* a *reasonable* foundation; *or*; the basis might be a non-inductionist one[20] and hence an unreasonable (fallacious, unenlightened ...) foundation.

1b: R_1 and R_2 disagree *both* with regard to their confidence in S *as well as* concerning the foundation on which such confidence ought to rest.

Neither case is apt to bother Strawson. It is, of course, perfectly possible that both R_1 and R_2 are (un)reasonable, or that none of them is; or that only one of them is reasonable while the other is unreasonable. The veridicality of S, however, is in any event—it appears from Strawson—found to be a direct function of the reasonableness exerted by the researcher who claims: "$S!$"[21]

The case for the other major types of possibilities is slightly different.

2a: R_1 and R_2 have the same (degree of) confidence in S, but only one of them on a reasonable (read: "inductionist") ground.

To mention an example: S is declared "true!" by both R_1 and R_2. But only R_1 proportions the degree of his conviction concerning S's veridicality to the strength of the evidence in favour of S'; whereas the basis for R_2's conviction differs sufficiently from R_1's "reasonableness" to qualify as: "unreasonable". He has, let us say, grossly misunderstood Feyerabend's or Kuhn's (meta-)methodological positions as an encouragement to propose wild and unlikely conjectures: the more preposterous (in the face of available evidence) the better!

2b: R_1 and R_2 are equally reasonable (in a strawsonian sense of "reasonable"), they are, in other words, both "inductionists", as Strawson would say, and quite consistently so. However, employing exactly the same "inductive" procedures they arrive at diametrically opposite conclusions with regard to the confidence they find that they ought to have in S. To R_1, for instance, all trustworthy, reliable evidence may seem to argue (mostly) *for S* (and against $\sim S$): "S is true!"; whereas R_2 may evaluated the same or a more or less different body of evidence in such a way that $\sim S$ appears to be the more tenable of the two propositions: "S is false!"

In the case-types 2a and 2b the following choice seems rather obtrusive:

Either: it is possible for a statement, S, to be false in spite of the fact that the researcher in question has consistently and conscientiously proportioned his confidence in S to the net evidence in its favour; or: S may be true (tenable, veridical ...) *in spite of* the fact that the researcher's confidence in S happens to be entirely out of proportion to the net evidence in favour of S. Neither possibility lends itself to convincing arguments in favour of strawsonian reasonableness.

Should we decide to claim the *logical* impossibility of, at least, 2b, then we have *eo ipso* returned to that same unmitigated, explicative direction of interpretation, that absolute and unrestricted degree of analyticity which we previously strived to avoid.

The ampliative claim, however: that 2a and 2b represent a real ("physical") impossibility, raises quite a few unpleasant questions—most of which will remain untouched in this connexion. Suffice it to mention the steadily increasing number of well-argued apotropaic remonstrances against the incessant perpetration of the naïve but historically significant Vienna Circle's thought model, according to which it is relatively simple to distinguish such entities as *e.g.*: 'perception'/'interpretation', 'fact'/'hypothesis', 'observation (protocol) sentences'/'theoretical sentences' ... etc. It is presumably the former of these opposition pairs which are commissioned to serve as Strawson's "evidence". And true enough, were such perception- and observation-sentences defensibly to be construed as relatively context-independent, meanings and truth—stable ... and their relevance for S plausibly seen as rather transparent and undisputable, *then* one might indeed have reasons to doubt any frequent occurrences of the case, 2b. However: this is exactly the area within the field of theories of theories where the last generations of metatheoreticians have reluctantly resigned vis-à-vis the overwhelming, available, pertinent testimonies— from theories of perception and cognition to *Grundlagenforschung* and general methodology ..., all amounting to an unconditional renunciation of the extravagant fatuity of any attempt to retain such notions as 'percepts', 'perceptions', 'sensa', 'observations', 'facts' ("that which is the case") *per se*, *i.e.*, as autonomous, self-contained entities ("things". "objects"), resting somewhere out there, patiently awaiting to be "discovered" by some brisk and assiduously enterprising scientist, for in turn to be employed as more or less crucial evidence for his hypothesis.

And even if one were—for the sake of some argument or other—to entertain the mysterious freaks of: 'percepts', 'facts', 'something which is the case' and the like, "evidence", *in vacuo* so to speak, it is hard to see what function such auxiliaries would serve with regard to *how we can know what we know not*. As has been made abundantly clear by Arne Naess:[22] Whatever quantity or quality we amass of such "evidence" in order to support a knowledge claim, S, by a person, P, (e.g.: "I, P, know that x ..."), the most widespread notion of 'knowledge' seems to preclude the likelihood or even the conceivability of P ever finding himself in the position that at a time, t', P simply *knows* that x; or: P *has* (reached) *knowledge* of x etc. on grounds of a certain amount of evidence, accumulated in the time interval between the time, t,—when he did *not* know (that) x—, and t', when he does. Not only is that *metaphor* disturbing, with which Arne Naess is concerned, *i.e.* where the reaching for knowledge is somehow seen as similar to the reaching for an apple,[23] but, more generally speaking, one needs to be convinced that one ought to accept a concept 'knowing' such that, according to this concept, P may only be said to know that x if there is available a minimum amount of "evidence" (known or unknown to P) in favour of the statement, S: (e.g.) "x is true", "x is so", "x is the case" ... (all, for all practical purposes, cognitively indistinguishable).[24] The chances are, needless to say, that at another stage of evidence accumulation, t'', P is either overendowed with evidence in favour of S, or he might have gathered some sort of informations, "facts", or whatever—which (according to the total frame of reference within which he has chosen to operate) may be most disastrous with regard to the veridicality of S. P is then confronted with the choice of *either*: (a) insisting that he, at t', knew (or: was justified in claiming to know) that x, in spite of the fact that, as it turned out at t'', x was *not* the case, or: (b) admitting that he did not, at t', know that x, in spite of the fact that his confidence in S ("x is the case" ... etc.) was conscientiously proportioned to the (alleged) net evidence in favour of S; in other words; he was in the latter case, in a position where it—according to Strawson—would be unreasonable of him *not* to claim to know that x (is true, is the case, is so ...).

It may be argued—and I should be inclined to agree—that to muster this much intricate ratiocination merely to defeat Strawson, is a dreadful waste of perspicacity. Any simple, straightforward, popperian, example is bound to expose the egregious folly of Strawson's "reasonableness": I suppose that even in the strawsonian, peculiar sense of 'reasonableness' it would be unreasonable to preclude in principle the occurrence of events which are such that their occurrence would at one time or another have been deemed: "unreasonable". What weight are we to give such unreasonable events? How is one to "proportion the degree of one's conviction" to the contention that the sun will rise tomorrow, if it did not rise today? Is "the proportion" here to be calculated in the order of something like one *dis*-confirmation to (say) $27 \cdot 10^{12}$ confirmations? That should certainly account for a pretty spectacular degree of conviction. The predicament however is obvious: Strawson may either choose to stick to his exotic notion of 'reasonableness'; in which case he should probably have to admit that there are occasions on which one ought to be *un*reasonable. The other alternative open to him is to abandon his "reasonableness" in favour of something slightly more reasonable, as it were. But how is that to be accomplished? Which are the general standards to which one might appeal if Strawson's thesis were to be accepted: that inductive reason is the same as reasonable reason? If it is envisaged to involve "proportionality", which is, "to proportion the degree of one's conviction to the strength of the evidence" and if that is what "inductive procedure" *means*, then there are no higher standards conceivable. The question will then be whether it is reasonable to be reasonable in general, that is: whether to proportion the degree of one's conviction to the evidence, is to have a degree of belief in a statement which is proportional to the strength of the evidence in its favour. From this it will be correct to draw the conclusion as Strawson does, that there is no problem of justifying induction. This is a conclusion, however, which depends entirely upon the definition of "reasonableness" that Strawson ventures to suggest. Moreover, if we say that "to have good reasons for an opinion" is "to have good inductive support for it," and we apply this to induction in general, it would be equally appropriate to ask whether we have good inductive support for induction. But is it reasonable, according to Strawson, to attempt to establish a principle of an argument by an argument which uses that very principle?

It seems that both the implicit and explicit semantics of Strawson is very weak indeed. This in turn, may have disastrous consequences for his whole argument, due to the semantical character of his premises. The existence of *use instances of the phrases*: "good reasons," "bad reasons," etc. is not a sufficient basis for verifying the existence of timeless or even periodically changing standards. And even if such standards are believed to exist and are capable of being known, the question remains why they should be ascribed an authority overriding the individual specimens of good or bad reasons. In any discussion where a person asks for a good reason, in the sense of "acceptable reason for him", a report on the sociology of "good reasons" (plus some argument or other to support that a definite one "is good") can hardly be considered compelling. The person who asks is interested in validity, one presumes, not in frequency or genesis or whatever ... Major scientific innovation and more or less radical scientific revolutions invariably lead to entirely new standards for what are to be considered "good" (resp. "bad") reasons. This may seem nonsensical from a sociological point of view, but very understandable from the point of view of validity.

Some people *may actually mean* what Strawson decides to mean by "being reasonable," that is: "to proportion the degree of one's convictions to the strength of the evidence," but others—seemingly just as competent people—would vehemently object to the proposal for such a synonymity relation. So, why on earth should we accept Strawson's semantical hypothesis? But, curiously enough, this rather negative attitude is in itself unjustified provided Strawson's doctrine on standards were to be accepted! There *are* methods available, developed by Arne Naess and his associates, for empirically testing semantical hypotheses; but "standards," if they exist, for justifiably asserting regularities in use and usage are unfortunately so low that one may safely ignore any empirio-semantical methods without being charged with superficiality. The requirements for evidence in semantical matters are, at least among Anglo-American philosophers, so low that such "hypotheses" as put forth by Strawson are bound to satisfy them.

Strawson's argumentation may more charitably be reformulated to indicate an *optative* mode. We could interpret him to *propose* that we shall in the future, in certain contexts, mean nothing else by "being reasonable" than just "having a degree of belief in a statement which is proportional to the strength of the evidence in its favour." With the additional proposal that "making an inductively justified statement" is to mean the same as 'being reasonable,' problems of how to interpret use instances of certain crucial terms such as "good reason" would then seem to disappear. But, again, it is difficult to see how any system of proposals could assist in clarifying what those philosophers may have intended to ask for, who, before the acceptance of the proposals, raised questions of the justifiability of induction. A clarification, it seems, would require a discussion of the existing texts in which these questions are posed. Strawson does not refer to any use occurrence whatsoever of "reasonable," "inductive," "justify," etc., within any such context. As regards the locution, "strength of evidence," which Strawson places at a crucial point in his explanations, there are today so many mutually inconsistent, but carefully worked out hypotheses about what this locution might conceptually signify, that nothing can possibly be gained by using the phrase: "proportional to the strength of evidence" without giving the slightest inkling as to what kind of concepts are supposed to be implied.

In short: Strawson has not been able to show that there *cannot* be any problem of justifying induction in the general sense of 'ampliation,' or 'reasoning' with any other claim than entailment, but only, at the best, hinted at the possibility that there are in fact none. And, I am bound to admit, he has supplied us most generously with our first, and first-rate, example of five futile and fatuous attempts to support the pretension that there *conld* not be a problem of how to justify that we can know what we know not.

5.2 Paul Edwards' "Good Reason"

Even less enlightening than Strawson's, is the argument advanced in an early article by Paul Edwards.[25] To bring it up at all in this connexion, can only be extenuated by the fact that Paul Edwards, inadvertently, reveals a fundamental flaw in the more general approach to philosophical problems as *exemplified* by, say, Strawson and Edwards.

The key phrase in the Edwards article is: "Good reason". By again employing something like Urmson's "acuity of ear", I suppose, the author claims to have succeeded in distinguishing three different "senses" or "meanings" of "good reason"; one of which deserves ("fittingly", "properly" ...) to be called: "the main sense". When interpreted in the direction of this alleged "main sense" the following two sentences, F_a and F_b would convey cognitively identical, synonymous, propositions. F_a: There is good reason to believe (in the report that) the phenomenon, X (has taken place?... will take place? ...). F_b: The past observations of the phenomenon, X, or of analogical phenomena, are of a certain kind viz.: they are exclusively or predominantly positive, the number of positive observations is at least fairly large, and they come in an extensively varied sets of circumstances."[26]

The formulation, F_b, is not so much "crude", as Paul Edwards suggests, but rather it is vague and imprecise to such an extent that it is extremely hard to make any sense of it whatsoever. Most plausible and charitable interpretations seem to suggest that F_b be seen more as an *argument* intended to *strengthen* F_a than as a possible, synonymic alternative to F_a. Since, I assume, of two cognitively identical propositions, one could not serve as an argument strengthening (or weakening) the other, it follows that F_a and F_b are not, under normal circumstances, likely to be judged as synonymous or even as cognitively similar by any member of any language society. In other words: No one who were to utter F_a should normally be willing to substitute F_b for F_a. No one would by F_a intend to convey anything that might as well be conveyed by F_b—or vice versa.

Furthermore—and this is the crucial point: It does not follow that what according to some—actual or fictitious—"main sense" of "good reason", is a good reason—is, as it were: *really* a good reason. It would indeed be rather wonderful if all the varying standards for 'goodness' and other values, constant or changing—were mysteriously imbedded in our everyday, ordinary, language in its stock, standard employment ..., but a trifle pollyannish, it seems, to assume that such is bound to be the case.

True enough: We often find that new value standards force us, as users of a language, to reconsider "*what we should say*"[26a] within that language, given the new standards. Thus, a change of standards of 'elementarity' with regard to physical particles leaves us with a choice as to the most appropriate designation for what has hitherto counted as paradigm cases of "elementary physical particles".

We should, by the same token, expect any (major) change in the standards of 'goodness' of reasons, to effect what we would call "good reasons". We might for example choose—in accordance with current methodological trends—to consider it a "*better* reason" for expecting a phenomenon, X, to occur, that the *non*-occurrence of X would require a drastic reconstruction of our most imaginative and inspiring, total, explanatory systems, than the mere fact that the expected occurrence of X is supported by previous, "predominantly positive" experiences. Paul Edwards could well object: "Your 'better reason' isn't even a good reason in the main sense of 'good reason'!" But the answer is obvious: *Either* we decide to adopt a different use of "good reason" than the use indicated by Paul Edwards, and suggested by him to have expressed a socalled "main sense" of "good reason". *Or* we choose to use "good reason" (more or less) in accordance with Paul Edwards' "main" sense, *in spite of the fact* that we may not think a bit of the explanatory power of good reasons which are good reasons only in Edwards' 'main' sense of "good reason",—in which case "good" would not be particularly lauditory when applied to reasons.

By way of summary: There is a more specific case of the problem of how to justify contentions that we (can) know something which is not imbedded in or entailed by our "given" body of knowledge. This specific question may be worded as follows: *How much weight should be given to previous experiences?* The people who inhabit the part of the Earth's surface between the Arctic and the Antarctic Circle, could by now—if they bothered—have accumulated a rather impressive collection of regularly experienced sunrises. And they would, I suppose, all be inclined to claim to have *good reason* to believe that there will be another sunrise tomorrow. But are their good reasons *really* good? Or have they given *too* much weight to past experiences? Maybe one ought to look elsewhere for a better reason to believe in tomorrow's sunrise? *This* is here the specific matter of contention. And to answer that most people would *call* a reason: "a good reason", when it is based primarily or exclusively on past experiences—or that this is "the main sense" of "good reason"—that is all clearly neither here nor there.

5.3 The "Futures" of F. L. Will

Some of Strawson's and Edwards' most trying troubles might have been slightly alleviated by an assurance that the future is always bound to resemble the past. Such assurance is most generously offered by Frederick Will[27] in a peculiarly perplexed piece of ratiocination, that mainly ought to attract interest as a matter of curiosity.

Relying on his "acuity of ear" two senses of "future" are revealed to

Will. *viz.*: "future-1" and "future-2". For the sake of perplexity, I suppose, Will does not confide in us what he more precisely intends to convey by "future", which ever so little hampers our attempts at understanding what these two proclaimed "senses" of "future" are alleged to be senses of. This much is clear, however, when people speak about "future" they usually speak, according to Will, of "things and events". If they are "speaking of events which have not occurred, of things which do not exist, but of events and things which, with the constant movement of the line of the present may some time occur or exist"—*then* they are talking of *future-1*. Were they, in the other hand, to speak of things which by definition could never exist, of events that could, by definition, never take place then they would be speaking of *future-2*.

Needless to say,—but Frederick Will says it:—there is no way of confirming that future-2 will be similar to (or different from) the past. Whereas this is clearly possible with regard to future-1. And what Will now wants to profess is that people who are sceptical vis à vis the suggested assurance of a necessary similarity between past and future, are using "future" in the sense of future-2. Their scepticism would dissolve, were they instead to employ the future-1 sense of "future".

The only flaw in this semantic analysis is the absolute inconceivability of any living soul ever to use either of these alleged "senses of 'future'" for any serious communication purposes.

Offhand the future-2 notion may appear most conspicuously absurd. Not only would one be at a loss to find, or even to construct, a plausible communication situation where "future-2" could be substituted for "future" in a sentence, such that this sentence still would convey what its sender intended it to convey.[28] And if this cannot be the case, in what sense of "sense" is 'future-2' then to be construed as a *sense* of 'future'?

Moreover, it is absolutely incomprehensible why anyone should ever *want* to make any conjectures, or in any other way be concerned with anything he would choose to call "future", if by "future" he were to understand something even remotely cognitively similar to what Will could plausibly have intended to express by his "future-2".

On the other hand, it may well be suggested that the notion of 'future-1' is equally incoherent. However muddled the notion, one thing seems certain: In the "sense" of 'future-1' it is supposed to be possible to confirm the general contention that the future resembles the past, by establishing past resemblances of limited sections of the past with similar definite sections of the future. But the mere suggestion of using the word "future" to designate, let alone be *used* "in the sense of", a definite period of time, say the seventies, is bound to encourage a rather peculiarly exotic language. It would for one thing permit us, say, in the eighties to look back upon the future in the seventies and agree or disagree regarding the extent to which we found the future to resemble the past.

As Arne Naess argues (in some unpublished lecture notes from the University of California, Berkeley 1961/62): "It is particularly unclear how 'sense' is to interpreted in the writings of Will so as to make sense of the proposal to regard a definite time interval as *a sense* of 'future'." The chances are that even Arne Naess should have to resign vis á vis any attempt to make sense of this position. Nevertheless, it seems to be a position to which Will is bound to be committed were he to insist on the confirmability of the claim that the future will be like the past. The alternative position, as Arne Naess has pointed out (ibid), would be to adopt a notion, let us call it: 'future-3', such that future *neither* is non-occurring, events and non-existing things, (i.e. Will's future-2), *nor* is a definite, limited period of time (Will's 'future-1') but where "future" refers to an unlimited, *open ended* period. Were Will, however, to choose *this* alternative, any attempt at a confirmation (or even corroborration) of the proclaimed "uniformity of the past with the future" would in that case meet with general prohibitive encumbrances, in particular with the perplexing quandary connected with difficulties *in principle* of confirming properties of infinite series where only properties of finite ones are known. Will could scarcely adopt 'future-3' and at the same time seriously contend that "there are beliefs about the way the future will be like the past, which have been and are being confirmed constantly by the uniform experience of countless positive instances in everyday life and in vast areas of science."

We may easily confirm the prediction that U.S.A. will still be fighting its wars in Indo-China throughout the eighties. But if and *only* if we adopt Will's exotic language (with "future"interpreted in the direction of "future-1"), would we ever be in the fortunate position of confirming a hypothesis to the effect that USA's Indo-China wars were actually fought "*in the future*". I suspect, however, that very few would feel inclined to chime in with Will when he triumphantly announces: "USA is fighting its Indo-China wars in the future, just as I anticipated!"

"The point here is", to quote Arne Naess again (ibid.), "*not* that, according to certain concepts of 'future", future things or events will never be present, but simply that open-ended intervals or classes will remain open." And he continues: "Some people seem genuinely convinced that future happenings in many ways will conform to past, even if time is unlimited. They believe they *know* this. Will has not shown that there is a hidden contradiction here, or a semantical confusion, when sceptics (zetitics) say that these convictions are groundless, that induction does not furnish even probable knowledge, and that the concept, knowledge about the future does not *necessarily* involve any contradiction or semantical confusion, but is merely a concept without denotation. Certain interesting concepts of 'knowledge of the future' may always remain without denotation, and yet involve no contradiction. Even if 'knowledge of the future' were defined in such a way that there cannot in principle be any piece of knowledge of the future, it is still left undecided whether 'knowledge of the future" is to be considered a contradiction in terms."

5.4 Black's Blunder

Seen against the backdrop of the hitherto reviewed, blandly bleating blunders, Black's is refreshingly blaring. The above section No. 4 touched tentatively upon some of Max Black's more recent exhortatory effusions[29] wherein he animadverts—and indeed with a rather heavy hand—on the unforgiveable wrongfulness of treating: "*how to justify induction in general*" as though it conveyed a genuine problem. His original and more direct attempt, however, at supporting pretensions to the effect that there cannot be a general problem of justifying induction, dates back to this *Problems of Analysis*, Chapter X, section 11.[30]

Some intrinsic difficulties in connexion with the notion of 'no problem' will be intimated in a few introductory remarks to the below section no. 6. Suffice it at this juncture to point to the suspiciously mouthwatering windfall of the no-problem-conclusion: It offers (for one thing) a *complete* and definitive relief from what might otherwise have been a nagging problem. Where no problem exists, there is no solution to seek. The inductionist has no problem!

Black's incongruous effort to justify his enravishing no-problem-judgment takes one of its major points of departure in the very same notorious remarks by Bertrand Russell which have enkindled so many an arousal (it prompted *inter alia* the retort by Paul Edwards[31], dealt with in the above subsection 5.2) viz: "We must either accept the inductive principle of ground of its intrinsic evidence or forego all justifications on our expectations about the future. If the principle is unsound, we have no reason to expect the sun will rise to-morrow."[32]

Obviously, the "natural", plain, singlehearted and straightforward response to Russell's audacious-sounding pronouncement (among "ordinary", matter-of-fact, common sense, pedestrian quotidians in general, and Edwards and Strawson in particular) is an ingenuous, simple-minded *non sequitur*, running roughly as follows:

1. We *do* have (good) reason to believe that the sun will rise tomorrow.

2. In point of fact, exactly that general sort of (good) reasons on which we base all our trust and reliance in tomorrow's sunrise constitutes *ad unquem: what is meant by "(good) reason"*. To lay one's account for convictions or predictions on that kind of grounds is precisely *what "being reasonable" means*.

3. Consequently—given Russell's mutually exclusive alternatives—: we *must* accept the inductive principle.

Briefly on this point once again:

It is perfectly possible, I suppose, to either elicit or fabricate criteria to discern, 'a good book' (from a lousy one). For instance: A book, *B*, is good if: (a) *B* is *called* "the good book" by most (English speaking) people; and/or: (b) more people *read B* than any other book; and/or (c) more people *buy B* than any other book; and/or: (d) *B excites* more people than any other book, and/or: (e) *B* raises (or solves) more important *problems* than any other book; and/or (f) more illustrious literary honours and distinguished prizes (e.g. Nobel's) have been bestowed upon *B* than upon any other book... By adopting one, or all, or any number of the above criteria (or combining them in complex and intricate manners) one might eventually stumble over or trump up a fairly precise notion of '(a) good book'. Moreover: qualified, acute, tympani could conceivably suggest that this very notion, 'good book', represents *the "main", "standard", "ordinary"* use of "good book" (within a given language society). Be this as it may, it still leaves entirely untouched the problems of *why* and *how* such a finding or fabrication can in any way prevent or even survive a change in *literary standards* (or taste). The predicament is plain: One should *either* have to adapt one's notion, 'good book', to the new standards. This would imply or presuppose a—more or less fundamental or flagrant—transgression of the alleged "main use" and "ordinary language" (in some peculiar, "main" or "ordinary", sense of these terms). The other alternative would be to lapidify the notion 'good book' at a certain level of standard (or taste) perfectioning, and carry on with the socalled "main", "stock", "standard", "ordinary" use at any cost. Which would, it seems, call for a somewhat exotic language such that "good", in the context of "good book", would have predominantly derogatory rather than laudatory connotations. And one cannot help wondering how the qualified tympani would want to react to that!

The long and short of it all might very likely best be seen in terms of the notorious, but dubious, difficulty of deriving an "ought" (interpreted chiefly in a normative, prescriptive, *optative* mode) from an "is" (interpreted in a principally descriptive, *constative* direction). Since such notions as 'good reason" and 'reasonable" as well as common uses of their conceptual designations, seem to combine some "natural" "plain", "obvious", "intuitive", "immediate", "salient" descriptions with some equally "natural", ... etc. prescriptions (evaluations, hortatations, ...) it is often contended that for this type of notions interpretations in an optative (rather than a constative) mode are strictly and unconditionally required. In other words, the claim is that no move from a constative mode—of "is"—to an optative mode—of "ought"—, ought to be justified by an appeal to any supposedly preferred use of our language. And, true enough, missing links are rather painfully felt in the chain of arguments that might have led Edwards and Strawson from the conjectured *preferred* uses of "good reason" and "reasonable" to the conclusion that these uses, provided the relevant language conjectures could justifiably be regarded as tenable—were to be considered prefer*able* as well. It goes, by the same token without saying that if a certain manner of reasoning were, *as a matter of fact*, to be found (for instance in the writings of Edwards and Strawson), this would neither argue for nor against its reason*able*ness.

The more typical and customary warnings against the general class of fallacies which the above examples may be said to illustrate would most often sound something like the following:

(1) Whether a quality, Q, is *admired* or not, is irrelevant for ascertaining whether Q is *admirable*. (2) That a book, B, is (widely) read, does not permit a conclusion as to its read*ability* (i.e. for some interpretations of "readable"). (3) It does most assuredly follow from the fact that an object, O, is actually *seen*, that O is *visible*, but *not* that O is *worth* seeing ("Sehens-*wert*" or "Sehens-*würdig*") (4) However, from the fact that O is *not* seen, it does *not* follow that O is *invisible*. (5) Many a mountain have never been climbed, but that does not imply that they are unclimb*able*. (6) Many procedures may never have worked, but are we thereby justified in concluding that they are to be considered unwork*able*? (7) If a locution, L, has never been said, are we justified in concluding that L is unsay*able*? (8) And *vice versa* for understanding: That a sentence, S, has hitherto never been understood, does *not* preclude that S may be understand*able*. (9) Consider finally a problem, R, (e.g. the celebrated Rieman's Conjecture) such that R has successfully resisted all attempts at a solution so far conceived by all students of R. How were we under these conditions to justify a conclusion to the effect that R is *insoluble* and all attempts at solution *inconceivable*?

It may admittedly be objected that only the first three of the above examples are in any unswerving way related to the venerable optative-constative (or "is"-"ought") coadunation. The last six are different. And true enough: Whereas it is surely quite irrelevant for the assessment of the degree to which Q is admir*able*, that it (Q) is in *fact* admired, the case of, say, 'inconceivability' seems slightly or essentially different. For one thing: "A solution to P is inconceivable" seems *off hand* rather more plausibly interpreted in a constative (descriptive) than in an optative (normative, prescriptive) direction. And for another: If it were the case that no solution to R had *as yet* been conceived of by any student of R, this might, not too absurdly, be construed as a *support* for (—strengthening rather than weakening—) the inconceivability claim. The contention, to take an example, that tachyons are inconceivable would undoubtedly be apt to inspire more confidence *before* than *after* the 22nd of February 1969 when Dr. Sudarshan of the University of Texas actually conceived of them. Nevertheless: just as there is at least one link or assumption missing in the argument that would lead from 'admired' to '*admirable*', so are links or assumptions missing in any argument that pretends to go from unconceived to inconceiv*able*, from unsolved to insolu*ble* ...

Which lands us right in the heart of Black's blunder.

The following reflexions follow rather closely some arguments advanced by Arne Naess.[33]

Black makes a distinction between two cases: (a) where a task is too onerous to be solved; and (b) where the seeming "task" is insoluble because it is discovered by analysis not to be a task. "Justifying the principle of induction" belongs to category (b), because it is allegedly: "obvious from the bare formulation of the problem" that none of the possible or available procedures could conceivably contribute towards its solution.

Some of the steps in Black's argumentation may, according to Naess, be restated as follows:

(1) Use of the principle of induction to justify the principle of induction must be rejected, otherwise we will have a vicious circle.
(2) Deductive proofs are not acceptable because the principles are not self-evident.
(3) Everyday methods of justification are not good enough.

Thus:

(4) *All conceivable* methods of solution are blocked in advance: The task is unreasonable.
(5) It is logically impossible to solve the task.
(6) What has been called the problem of induction is an "ancient tangle of confusion."

Max Black concludes section X,11 with a quote from C. D. Broad, who referred to inductive reasoning as "the glory of Science" and "the scandal of Philosophy." And Black adds: "Perhaps it is on the verge of becoming scandalous that this ancient tangle of confusions should still be regarded as a 'problem' in need of a solution."[34]

Arne Naess is chiefly concerned with points (4) and (5).

Against (4) he retorts: "*In what way can an argument proceed from conceived to conceivable*? Black has shown, *at best*, that certain justifications or classes of justification *he* has conceived of, do not lead to a solution. But how can he justifiably proceed to argue that all *conceivable* kinds of justification are all necessarily bound to fail? By psychological tests designed to furnish data on the limited force of human imagination? Or perhaps by a kind of induction? Neither way is attempted. Moreover: justification can indeed be conceived. For instance: justification by deduction from self-evidence propositions can both be conceived and would constitute a justification."

Against (5): Impossibility proofs such as those carried out in mathematics (*e.g.*, in 'the quadrate of the circle') are constructed to demonstrate that where certain evident axioms and certain rules governing the procedure (using only compass and ruler) are regarded as given, it will be logically impossible (result in a contradiction) to accept the existence of a solution. Nothing of this kind has been carried out or even attempted by Black as regards the principles of induction. *Black's analogy seems to Naess to reveal that Black does not distinguish empirical (or actual) impossibility and logical impossibility:* "*It is as if we were asked to go to Timbuctu, but neither by sea, nor land, nor air.*"[35] *Given some specified non-occultist physics, the impossibility can be deduced; but the truths of this physics are not necessary truths. There may be a dozen ways of going to Timbuctu other than these three.*

There is no logical contradiction in the assertions of occultists that they can go to Timbuctu, and go neither by sea, nor by land nor in the air. True enough: the travel agencies are helpless. They cannot offer any solution. Suppose the occultist leaders plan a congress in Timbuctu, but do not have money for the travel. They agree to *presuppose* that members will manage to get there by non-successive (non-consecutive) change of spatial positions, or by duplication, as certain yogis are said to do. Suddenly a duplicate body will appear in Timbuctu at the Congress opening banquet. For most of us ordinary travellers the duplication constitutes a problem, to say the least. It is no easy task. But no consolation is to be found in a claim *that it is not a problem, SINCE IT CANNOT BE DONE*. If it entails no logical contradiction (within a given system, S), but is "impossible" merely according to some specified physical theories, it still remains a problem. 'Contradictory problems' may (if indeed 'problems') be most safely conceived as a sub-class of the total class of insoluble problems. Black offers no evidence in support of the contention that the problem of induction does *not* belong to the sub-class of insoluble, non-contradictory problems. Black's arguments, if at all valid, seem on the contrary to *support this* classification, rather than his own. In other words, says Arne Naess, a tourist asking at a travel bureau for a passage to Timbuctu: "neither by sea, nor by land, nor in the air," will get different answers *not* depending upon the degree to which the travel agent is sensitive to the principle of contradiction, but upon the degree to which he is an occultist. If the bureau is run by a doctrinaire physicalist, the agent may unhesitatingly agree with Black that "nothing remains but to throw up our hands and deplore the *unreasonableness* of the original demand," exactly as he would have done, had customer thirty years ago demanded to be flown from Edmonton to Oslo in six hours.

By way of summary:

In an effort to support the rife, alamode contention that, in the wide sense of 'ampliation', there is no *problem of justifying induction*—hereafter referred to as: PJI—Max Black has lavished upon philosophical literature a singularly incongruous and truly extraordinary and exuberant piece of peculiarly paralogistic ratiocination, running roughly as follows:

(1) Efforts are known to have failed to solve the problem of *how to justify induction,* or: PJI.

(2) At one stage of insights perfectioning, S, Black reports that Black does not conceive of a solutions to PJI.

(3) Black contends that Black is unlikely to conceive of a solution to PJI at any other stage of insights perfectioning (i.e.: Black is throwing up his hands, deploring the unreasonableness of the demand for a solution to PJI).

(4) A solution to PJI is inconceivable (and unreasonable ...).

(5) Inconceivable solutions are not (apt to be) found.

(6) PJI is insoluble.

(7) "Insoluble problem' is (to be considered) a *contadictio in adjecto*.[36]

(8) Insoluble problems are (to be considered) no problems at all.

(9) *vide* (6): PJI is no problem.
Q.E.D.!

5.5 Von Wright's Meretricious Contradiction

In his forthcoming *Dialogue on Induction*, Arne Naess deals with such futile attempts *either* at establishing that there is, or is not, or *cannot* be, a problem of how to justify induction, or at "solving" or "dissolving" "the" problem—as for instance those hinted, hailed or heralded by, say, Sir Karl Popper,[37] Jerrold J. Katz,[38] H. E. Kyburg,[39] Hans Reichenbach,[40] Wesley C. Salmon,[41] and Georg Henrik von Wright.[42] von Wright's attempt is particularly pertinent in connexion with 'how to know what one knows not', as he seems more inclined than anyone else to interpret this explicative sounding sentence as though it were bound to convey a logical contradiction.

Arne Naess accredits von Wright with three theses of which W_1 is definitely von Wright's, whereas W_3, possibly also W_2, are less misleadingly seen as more specific implications of the general or basic von Wright position *viz.*:

W_1: In the sense in which Hume used the locution: "justification of the principle of induction" it would entail a logical contradiction if one were to state: "X is a justification of the principle of induction."

W_2: It is (logically) impossible to (unconditionally) guarantee (assure) that an unknown entity, X, of a class of entities defined by the property, A, will possess or exhibit the property, B, as well, if A and B are considered logically independent (cognitively different) properties; as would be the case were B not to belong to the defining properties of the class under which X is to be subsumed.

W_3: We cannot know what we don't. *I.e.*: It is impossible to guarantee that X has the property, B, if: (a) we do not know that X has the property B, and/or: (b) X does not have the property B.

von Wright's deceptively elegant argument in support of the above theses is by Naess, rendered roughly and freely as follows:

(1) An instance of A (i.e. the finding of an entity with the property A) is said to be "unknown" as long as we do not know other properties of the instance except those that are part of the definition.

(2) That an instance of A is unknown *implies* that we do not know whether A will turn out to have a property B, when $B \neq A$.

(3) A guarantee that an instance of A will turn out to be an instance of B as well can only be given if it is explicative (analytically true) that A is B, *i.e.*, that the presence of A by definition implies the presence of B, *i.e.*, that $B = A$ (which is the case to be excluded).

(4) Consequently, what Hume is looking for are conditions such that $B = A$ *under the presupposition* that $B \neq A$.

(5) "X" is a justification" (in Hume's sense of "justification") "of the principle of induction" is a logical contradiction.

Q.E.D.

Naess finds that von Wright's argumentation suffers from certain weighty weaknesses. With regard to von Wright's first point, attention is called to a rather obvious ambiguity which is of serious consequence if the argumentation is meant to show that (Hume's) requirement for justification of the thesis of induction implies or entails the acceptance of the thesis that when X is unknown X may also be known. In particular contexts, e.g. when someone, P_1, at a time, t_1, is speaking about another person, P_2, P_1 might very well by the utterance: "X is unknown" have attempted to convey the same as he could have conveyed by: "X is unknown to the person P_2 at the time t_1". If this sense is taken as the reference point for a plausible interpretation, it will not be contradictory to assert: "To P_2 at t_1 it was unknown whether the particular instance of A would also be an instance of B. However, I showed him convincingly that, with a basis in a set of "given" or true propositions about A and B, we can in fact *guarantee* that the instance of A will constitute an instance of B. Without further argumentation, or observation of additional instances, it is *now*, at time t_2, *known* to P_1, that the instance of A will be one of B." With a notion 'unknowness' appropriate to such contexts, it is *not* (at t_2) the fact that something or other was known to P_2 (at t_1) which coinstantaneously was *un*known to him.

So much for a sense of "X is unknown" which implies a relation to *persons* ('personal knowledge'). In other types of contexts, however, "X is unknown" is *not*, for any plausible interpretations related to definite persons. But in neither case will a contradiction arise: i.e. "The instance was *not* known (in sense No. 1) and *still* known (in sense No. 2)."

As for von Wright's second point, it may be observed that when we talk of ampliation with regard to future events and contend that such events are *unknown*, it may be a question of *sense* and *degree* of 'unknownness', as it were. Contentions about having the ability of prevision, or having corrigible or incorrigible knowledge of the future, can, only in the most exotic sense of "contradictory", "logically odd" etc. be rejected as contradictory, logically odd, semantically unreasonable or whatever. von Wright's second point seems to preclude any possibility of ampliation in general, and specifically that inductive inferences regarding future events could ever yield knowledge of anything unknown to the inductivist before he employed the relevant ampliative reasoning and made his inductive inference.

von Wright's third point presupposes the logical *impossibility* of a *synthetic a priori*, i.e. an ampliative inference which is (considered bound to be) true, prior to any relevant experience.

When Locke ruled that *nihil est in intellectu quod non fuerit is sensu*, Leibniz retorted: *nisi ipse intellectus*. From which, as everybody knows, Kant was led to infer or suggest the possibility or even necessity of non-demonstrative, ampliative knowledge, the truth of which is not contingent but necessary, i.e.: it is solely or primarily a function of the *form* in which all our sensing and ratiocination is aidlessly and irretrievably trapped. In spite of some of the wilder claims by semantic soothsayers like the quondam perpetrators of socalled "ordinary language philosophy,"[43] and such chimerical ideas and impressions notwithstanding, that tend to emerge, from vague and visionary suggestions, like: 'the (ultimate) limits of language, 'the deep structure of language' etc., it can safely be said that dominant trends in modern philosophy are apt to distrust all vaporous visions resembling or corresponding to 'synthetic a priori'. There is in fact a prevalent tendency to admit to a total failure to make any sense whatsoever of such or similar supposals. To believe in the meaningness, let alone existence, of 'synthetic propositions a priori', is commonly considered stupendously naive. And yet, it surely requires a good deal more credulous, optimistic enthusiasm to believe in the attainability of anything in the direction of a *proof* of such propositions logical contradictoriness. Which is exactly what von Wright demands: He seeks logical evidence, demonstrative proofs of the contradiction implied by, or entailed in, 'synthetic (propositions) a priori'. But he does not find what he seeks. He is, of course, free to fabricate or "reform" a language so as to doctor up a contradictions at will. How anything can *be* a contradiction, however, and at the same time properly be said to be *found*, still remains a mystery. An arduous or onerous task may well be found to be, for all practical purposes, *"absolutely impossible"*. But why should we want to accept such rules that they compel us to accept a language wherein 'absolute impossibility' were to be considered cognitively identical, or synomymous with 'logical contradiction'? And, in point of fact, von Wright's premise under consideration stands or falls with this very synonymity claim, since he employs a distinction: (positive) analytic/contradictory, which is quite indisputably equivalent to a distinction between 'impossibly false' 'impossibly true', respectively.

Incidentally,—although somewhat mal á propos—in *Bemerkung zu Grund-*

lagen der Mathematik,[44] von Wright's famous predecessor in Cambridge found it "understandable", that: "Die Sätze: '$a = a$', $p \supset p$'", "the word 'Bismarck' has eight letters"—etc. all be named: "synthetic a priori." Wittgenstein, moreover, speaks unhesitatingly of the synthetic (—ampliative—?) character of unforeseen appearances of prime numbers.[45] He would undoubtedly be quite intrigued by the accusation of having unwittingly bungled into proven logical contradictions!

The fourth and next to final step in von Wright's argument seems to Arne Naess, to imply that whether an instance of *A* really will (is guaranteed to) be an instance of *B* is, according to von Wright's position, *irrelevant* (for the) justification of a claim to *knowledge* (of the fact) that *A* will be *B*. Which would legitimatize, as perfectly reasonable, the following dialogue:

P_1: I know that *A* will be *B*.

P_2: No kidding: Will *A* really be *B*?

P_1: I don't understand. Why do you suddenly change the subject? Here I have barely unleashed the exciting topic of *what I know*, before you, entirely unprovoked, just wander off to a wildly unrelated question of *what there is*!

How very, very rude of you!

Briefly then: Only in a peculiarly to spectacularly forced and farfetched, non-Humean sense of all pertinent key-concepts could von Wright's pretension conceivably be viewed as tenable, viz. that the following sentence "is", or is bound to entail, a logical contradiction: "*x is a justification of the principle of induction*." And if there were any reasons to support the acceptance of such singularly exotic linguistic suggestions, as von Wright's, von Wright has neglected to inform us about them.

5.6 Goodman's Guileful Gawky Gambadas

Appendix on the riddle of a riddle

There is absolutely no merit and, in particular, not an inkling of originality in any of Nelson Goodman's ventured contributions directly relevant to the general discourse concerned with the socalled "socalled problem of justifying induction".[46] Manly and indomitably he chimes in with all the others to echo the same irksomely alamode allegation of nonsensicalness against the zetetic oriented philosophers who remain reluctant to close definitively the case for—and against—the justifiability of non-demonstrative, ampliative inferences. He even renews the unsupported and peculiarly impertinent charge that these philosophers are virtually asking for *prevision*; a demand, the absurdity of which, we are led to believe, goes entirely without saying. But why should it? Surely, neither Nelson Goodman nor Max Black—nor anyone else, for that matter— would be rash enough to suggest a language such that it would render 'prevision', 'precognition' and similar concepts logically contradictory. One may, and rightfully so, have one's serious reservations against, some of the conclusions, drawn, say, from G. N. M. Tyrrell's[47] and S. G. Soal's experiments.[48] And one is admittedly free to remain unimpressed by Basil Schackleton's steady, unceasingly, and amazingly accurate predictions, or rather "*beforehand reports*", of the order of the Zener cards, month after month, with a stunning consistency that defies even the savage attacks on psychological (and social science) statistics launched by G. Spencer Brown.[49] Or, like D. O. Hebb[50], we may openly admit to an uncompromising *prejudice* against anything that could plausibly be called "prevision", "precognition" or whatever. But no one seems to have any difficulties in imagining or conceiving of any of these phenomena whose status of existence is disclaimed. We understand what we mean, what we intend to convey, if we claim or allege that there is not and will (can) never be anything like, say, prevision or precognition. The question is only: How do we propose to go about in justifying *this* claim, *this* allegation? *What superior form of prevision, precognition or divine revelation permits Black and Goodman to foreknow the impossibility of prevision at any forseeable or unforseeable future stage of insight?* Their sources for such informations, if any remain, undisclosed.

What is it then, one may very well ask, which extenuates a separate sub-section on Nelson Goodman under the above general heading, if all we can tribute to him is another tedious repetition of the thrashed out *non-sequitur* from: (a) PJI *unsolved* to (b) PJI *insoluble* to (c) PJI *dissolved*. However, for Nelson Goodman the dissolution of what he refers to as "*the old problem of induction*" is not quite enough: No sooner is "the old problem" alleged to be dissolved, then, *mirabile dictu*, it is promply discovered that a genetic or purely descriptive, narrative account of inductive behaviour, inductively ascertained, furnishes the very basis of just such a justification! In fact, it seems that according to Goodman not only inductive, or, more generally speaking, ampliative inferences, but deductive or explicative claims as well, may unobjectionably acquire some sort of justification, proportionate to the degree to which adequate evidence has been accumulated to strengthen the contention that these inferences show a satisfactory conformity to certain (specified) rules alleged to guide such inferences.

"The point", Goodman haphazardly speculates, may possibly be: "that rules and particular inferences alike are" (—ought to be?—) "justified[51] by being brought into agreement with each other. A rule is "(—ought to be?—)" amended if it yields an inference we are unwilling to accept; an inference is "(—ought to be?—)" rejected if it violates a rule we are unwilling to amend."[52] When, armed with this strategy, we turn our attention to inductive practice, we "*discover*", Goodman contends, that all that is necessary to *justify* inductive practice, is to *observe* inductive practice, and attempt, by way of vindicable, reliable inductive practice, to arrive at tenable hypotheses concerning the rules which presumably conform to this inductive practice. The *no*-problem is really a *mere*-problem, *viz* a mere problem of *discovery* or *codification*—no problem at all!

In an attempt to make up for the pretended deficit in *genuine* problems of induction for which Goodman, I suppose, now considers himself responsible, up from the ashes of the disintegrated "old problem", he conjures a new and crazier bird: his notorious "*new riddle*", which, for mysterious reasons, temporarily received such an unaccountable attention, that *The Journal of Philosophy* found it necessary to proclaim a moratorium on articles dealing with it. And this is surely its only enigma: why was it ever considered a riddle? We are stuck with the riddle of the riddle. The solution to *that* problem, I shall maintain, is most readily found in the unparalleled muddleness and surrealistic inscrutability which characterise Goodman's suggestion for a solution to his riddle,— not the least as represented by his key-notions: 'projected', 'projectible' and 'entrenchment'.

A *hypothesis* may be said (according to Goodman) to have been "*actually projected*", if "it is adopted" (—by how many of how competent students?) "after some of its instances have been examined and determined to be true, and before the rest have been examined".[53] A *predicate* is *projected* if it occurs as a predicate in a projected hypothesis. A *projectible* predicate is one of which it is discovered (?) to be the case (?) that (according to some criteria or other) it is or *ought* to be employed in a hypothesis. As the determining criterion for projectibility, Goodman suggests: '*entrenchment*'. A predicate should be considered the more "entrenched", the more this predicate—or any predicate "coextensive" with it—has (actually) been "projected", *i.e.* (has been) employed in (actually) "projected" hypotheses. 'Entrenchment', in other words, is nothing but 'projectedness" i.e., 'being entrenched' is cognitively indistinguishable from 'being relatively often projected'.

This again suggests the same rather peculiar language found in Max Black's writings. It may well be that a tergiversating abuliac, totally lacking in stamina and perseveration, would resign after a given number of attempts at solving a problem or riddle, *R*, throw up his hands and imprecate *R* as "insoluble" and the searching for a solution as "unreasonable". But this seems a rather feeble argument for considering "insoluble" as synonymous with or cognitively tantamount to "unsolved after a number of attempts".

The case for "projectible" is only slightly different. Admittedly: What is actually understood is certainly at least intelligible, what is actually seen at least visible, what is perceived is perceptible, what is injected is injectible, etc.[54] However, Goodman should clearly have no use for "projectible" precised along this general direction of interpretation. He needs a notion to enable him to distinguish *felicitous projections* from *malprojection*, i.e. a notion 'projectible' somewhat similar to 'advisable', at least in *one* respect. That is: Not every choice of standpoint, course of action, or whatever, that has been advised is thereby to be considered advis*able*. One may be *well* or *ill* advised. The frequency of an advice being offered does not even argue for, let alone guarentee, its advis*ability*. By the same token, the frequency with which a predicate has been employed in a way that entitles it to be described as "projected", in Goodman's peculiar argot, does not, at the face of it, strengthen the contention that it *ought to be* so employed. The onerous arduousness in deriving "ought" from "is" was ridden threadbare long ago. There should be no need to expatiate more dreary repetitiousness on that subject.

It is no easy task to determine the merits and demerits of a predicate, C, employed, say, in the formulation of a hypothesis, H. An obviously determining factor is the degree to which C, within a theoretical framework, T, appears to serve H as a fertile, effective and, at the same time, precise conceptual tool. Even more crucial, is, I suppose, an estimate of the "main yielding capacity"—"Leistungsfähigkeit"—generated by C, not only in relation to H, and T but within the total explanatory system of which H and T constitute but a tiny part.

It is undeniably a disadvantage if C is "highly artificial", enormously complicated in its intricate (but precise) formulations, or if it breaks drastically with ingrained tendencies of speech and thought. But minor drawbacks like that, I think it safe to say, have never constrained—nor ought it to interfere with—the employment of an otherwise "*leistungsfähig*" conceptual tool.

It is an entirely different story when the suggested predicate is, in a shallow, simpletonian way, just inapprehensibly muddled. Such as seems to be the case with Goodman's own concoction: "*GRUE*".

Goodman contends that there are interesting problems connected with this notion when employed in a predominantly inductive or ampliative enterprise. In fact: 'grue' is contrived to exemplify some rather crucial points regarding the alleged "new problem of induction". I shall maintain that it exemplifies nothing but low-brow, blunderheaded muddleness.

The following may serve as one of an undetermined number of interpretations of Goodman's claim:

"All P are Q" can derive *no* evidential support *whatsoever* from: "x is P and x is Q". And for the following reasons: "x is P" *might* stand for "x is an emerald"; and "x is Q" *might* stand for: "x is grue", where x is said to be "grue" if and only if x has been examined before a time, t, and is green, and/or x has not been examined before t and *found to be* blue. Then, Goodman either haphazardly ventures to predict, or, for undisclosed reasons, chooses to legislate as follows: *Any x examined before t and found to be green provides a confirmation of "All P is Q" regardless of whether Q stands for "green" or Q stands for "grue"*.

Whichever way this sentence is understood, it still leaves one with the puzzle as to why Nelson Goodman should find it so advantageous to ignore one of the most basic rules in all elementary science methodology, *viz.* one which strongly stresses the fatuity of any attempt at determining the specific and/or potential weight of a piece of suggested evidence—say a proposition like: "x is P and X is Q"—entirely out of context of the total set of alternative, mutually exclusive hypotheses within a given explanatory system of theories. The rule demands clarity, explicitness of the choice situation. Indefiniteness and impreciseness in the set of hypotheses to be compared (with regard to their relative tenability) as judged within the system would in effect prevent a stipulation of the *discriminatory power* to be delegated any proposition entered as evidence and purporting to either strengthen or weaken the hypothesis concerned.

Thus, a protocol statement, S: "x is P and x is Q" would only have discriminatory power (strengthening say H_a), as long as the theoretical framework were to be construed so incomplex that the total choice situation would be exhausted by the listing of two hypothese, H_a and H_b, where H_b is to be a *straightforward* negation of H_a, and the following is to be a formulation of H_a: "All P is Q". However, add just one more hypothesis, and the situation could be drastically changed. Let e.g. H_k be a third, competing hypothesis, and let it read as follows.

H_k: "All P is Q if the conditions: c_1, c_2, and c_3 are given, while the conditions: c_4, c_5 and c_6 are *not* given; and: only a certain class of P is Q (—the rest is Q'—) given the conditions c_4, c_5, and c_6 and in the absence of conditions c_1, c_2, c_3."

It should be quite obvious that within this new choice situation (H_a, H_b and H_k) the protocol sentence, S, entered as evidence, would have a discriminatory power approaching or equal to zero with regard (at least) to the hypotheses H_a versus H_k,—and *vice versa* for the *negation* of S and the choice between H_b and H_k. Only protocol sentences with explicit references to the two sets of specific conditions should now be considered admissible as pertinent evidence, *i.e.* evidence the accumulation of which may be seen as an aid in establishing the relative tenability—veridicality/falsidicality—of the hypotheses concerned.

Imagine now an explanatory system where, within an explicit, theoretical framework, hypotheses are advanced concerning varieties of the mineral Beryl. Beryl, it is found, comes in a variety of colours, one of which is blue (i.e. Aquamarines). Let us call the blue Beryls: "Bluemeralds". Chromium, on the other hand, makes Beryl green. Let us call the green Beryls: "Greeneralds". Given a simple set of hypotheses, *e.g.* H_a: "All Emeralds are Greeneralds", and H_b: "Some Emeralds are Bluemeralds", then we might very well decide to consider every finding of an Emerald which is also a Greenerald, as evidence in support of H_a and weakening H_b. By the same token, a finding of an Emerald which is also a Bluemerald would strengthen H_b and weaken H_a. Some philosophers of science might in the latter case, even be tempted to go so far as to consider H_b *confirmed* and H_a *refuted*—dependent upon the *veridicality* of the protocol statement: "There is at least one Emerald such that this Emerald is also Bluemerald".

However the whole situation would be unrecognisably complicated, were we to throw in the following wild and exotic sounding conjecture (H_k) to the effect that, in short: All Emeralds unexamined before a time, t, will be found to be indistinguishable from Bluemeralds insofar as they are both blue Beryls. However: Bluemeralds are by definition to be *ever*-blue. Whereas the simili-Bluemeralds, or "Gruemeralds", as we may call them, will be found to be *green*: (a) when examined, and: (b) and/or after the time, t. The counter claim could be that *all* Emeralds are evergreen, or as we shall choose to say: "All Emeralds are Greeneralds", This leaves us, practically speaking, with two major hypotheses which, for simplicity reasons may be rephrased as follows:

H_a *There are no Gruemeralds*, *i.e.*: *all* Emeralds are Greeneralds, *i.e.* they do not under any circumstances appear to be like Bluemeralds. Beryls which appear to be Bluemeralds are invariably found to be Bluemeralds.

H_k *There are Gruemeralds*, *i.e.*: *not* all Emeralds are Greeneralds, *i.e.* there are conditions such that under these conditions Emeralds are like Bluemerald *viz.* "found to be blue"; hence, Beryls which under certain conditions appear to be Bluemeralds may, under different, specified conditions be found to be Emeralds, *viz.* "found to be green".

The choice situation, H_a/H_k is clearly drastically different from the H_a/H_b choice situation.

Moreover, "grue" is now presumably precise enough in the context indicated to prevent the scientists from collecting wildly irrelevant evidence to the two conflicting hypotheses.[55] Thus no x examined before t and found to be green, will strengthen, let alone provide confirmation (or weaken or provide disconfirmation) of either hypothesis. *Such a finding would have no discriminatory power pertinent to the H_a—/H_k— controversy*. To enable us to gather such findings, slightly subtler techniques would have to be developed. Virgin, friable, pegmatite dikes may be photographed *en masse*. Scientists may examine the *photographs* (rather than the Beryls themselves) in search for what would traditionally or at the face of it be classified as "Bluemeralds". A sample of the blue Beryls may be examined and then photographed. Others are not examined, but photographed after time t. Which findings would strengthen, or provide an instance of confirmation (weaken, or provide an instance of disconfirmation, respectively) of which hypothesis is thereafter child's play.

In a few words: "Grue" is far from lacking in "entrenchment". In the last eighteen years the expression has infested philosophical journals *ad nauseam*. The "grue"-some problem is merely perplexing and confusing because of its obtusive obscurity, spectacular impreciseness and its author's embarrassingly shallow depth of semantic-pragmatic intentions. What the predicate "grue" needs, rather than entrenchment, is an improvement of its subsumability and a more transparent connexion with the explicit choice of pertinent hypotheses.

All that then remains to be solved is the same old problem of how to justify induction, or: How *do* we know what we, as it were, don't. But to this problem—or to the problem (if that is what it is) as to whether it is a problem—Goodman has made no contribution whatsoever.

On the contrary, one might say: Goodman's guileful galimatias is so much the more deplorable as it, when taken seriously, is bound to divert metatheoreticians' attention from some closely related and most meritorious "*wissenschaftstheoretische*" endeavours *viz.* of *establishing reliable and justifiable grounds for testing hypotheses*, i.e. to give grounds for distinguishing: (a) strengthening (supporting) or confirming instances from: (b) weakening or disconfirming ones. Problems in this connexion are traditionally dealt with under headings like: "theories of confirmation". A more specific concern is the vacuum left by the frequently demonstrated, perspicuous and unmistakable inutility of such imperturbably pollyannish, "open-sesame" formulae as e.g. Carnap's well known: $c(P_{n+1}, P_1.P_2 - P_n)_{n \to \infty}$.

Already Duhem[56] called the intention to the apparent fatuity of attempting to test, or to devise general rules for testing, an isolated hypothesis *in vacuo*, independent of all the *other* hypotheses which constitute the theory, rather than examining it, as Duhem suggests, as an integral part of the total explanatory system to which the hypothesis in question is presumed to belong.

Arne Naess, in his forthcoming *magnum opus*[57] refers to Duhem's position as a "narrow contextual testing of hypotheses" and points to the patent necessity for a very much wider contextuality, including not only other hypotheses, but "initial conditions"—and *"Randbedingung"*— sentences etc. as well. Suffice it, in the present connexion, only to accentuate that there are indeed areas of science-theoretical endeavour that *do merit* the concern of contemporary meta-theoreticians.

Goodman's "Grue" does not.

6. A FEW FINAL REMARKS ON THE NO-PROBLEM SUBTERFUGE

6.1 On Knowing what is Unknowable

It is no doubt incredibly naive to believe in the facility of formulating a manageable problem of how to justify acquisitions of non-demonstrative knowledge. It may even be naive to ponder, with a degree of confidence, that there is, or could be shown to be, a problem here. But surely nothing quite beats the naiveté of those philosophers who *tête baissée* and without batting an eyelash launch forth to prove that *there could not possibly be any such problem*. Do they ever have problems!

One of the most popular and pernicious verbal and argumentational preferences of those who perpetrate this opprobrious exercise in fatuity, seems to suggest a sequence of points roughly along the following line:

(a) The languages we use set limits for what we can possibly know (and say and mean and understand). Moreover:

(b) Language limits can be known and fixed within the limits of those very languages which they are assumed to delimit. And:

(c) A question formulation explicitly or implicitly disputing the justifiability of *any* ampliative—and, *a fortiori*, inductive—knowledge claims, is bound to transgress such language limits. But (*vide* (a) and (b)):

(d) An intended formulation that, if formulated, would constitute a transgression of the language limits can *not* convey anything knowable (or intelligible ...). Therefore:

(e) To question, dispute or zetetically examine the justifiability of non-demonstrative knowledge claims in general, would be to betoken an inexpressible or, at least, unintelligible essay.

There is unfortunately nothing particularly confidence-kindling in either the whole or in any single segment of this *soi-disant* sequence of discursive arguments. For one thing: It is quite unclear what, if indeed anything, could conceivably argue for the choice of adopting a language such that this language sets itself impassable boundaries. Or, if the argument is rather that we do not have a choice, that the language limits are, as it were, *discovered*, if that is the model or the line of reasoning to be employed, then the inevitable question is simply: Why not transgress those limits? Surely, as soon as the boundaries are known, the crossing of them becomes a mere technical problem. We may *discover* the limits for what is, say, observable with the naked eye and a twenty-twenty vision. But it is hard to think of any convincing argument for yielding resignedly to these "natural" limits, rather than seeking technical means of transcending them. No one has, to the best of my knowledge, thought of any arguments so far. Rather to the contrary: What was considered "unobservable" at time, t, becomes observable at time t' (after, say, inventions like electron-microscope, ultra-centrifuge, cloud chamber ...); and what is unobservable at time, t', may become observable at time t'' (when the bubble chamber is invented ...) and so forth.

At any rate: Whether the limits for what we can know are *set* (by a choice of language), or *found*, the way we find limits for other human capacities, the choice is in either case ours: Do we want to accept, or do we want to transgress those boundaries?—Let us, for the sake of argument, assume that something could conceivably be said for the pretension that—given certain conditions, *e.g.*, the language or languages we presently utilize—to seriously question the justifiability of non-demonstrative inferences in general, would be tantamount to asking for an answer to something which could not possibly be known. This, certainly, would not be a decisive argument against changing these conditions, *e.g.* widening the boundaries for what is knowable so as to accommodate such a question. Hence, even if we were to accept the peculiar linguistic suggestions entailed in a refusal to call an allegedly insoluble problem "a problem", what is a no-problem then, at time, t, given *certain* conditions, a *certain* language, for instance would appear as a problem again at time t', when these conditions have been appropriately changed.

6.2 An Analogue from Computing Science

As A Final Farewell To The No-Problem[58]

Suppose we have a computer and various instructions with which we may write programmes for the computer. Further, suppose all input, output, and internal representations (memory) are binary strings (strings of 1's and 0's). Suppose we are given a programme and an input string for that programme. We would like to know if the programme, given that input string, will ever stop or halt. The problem of determining for an arbitrary programme and an arbitrary input whether or not the programme will stop, is often called the "halting problem." The question naturally arises as to whether or not the halting problem can be solved by computer. Any programme can be uniquely represented by a binary string. We would like to know if we can write a programme, P, that takes two inputs and has the following behaviour: (a) $P(n, m)$ always halts; (b) $P(n, m)$ outputs a 1 if the string n represents a programme, P'; and P' stops or halts when given input string m; $P(n, m)$ outputs a 0 otherwise. As a special case of the halting problem (I shall call it the "sc halting problem"), we would like to know if we can write a programme, P, with one input, n, with the following behaviour: (a) $P(n)$ always halts; (b) $P(n)$ outputs a 1 if the string, n, represents a programme, P'; and P' halts when given input string n; $P(n)$ outputs a 0 otherwise.

Consider two types of instruction languages for the computer. I shall call the first type a "full computability" programme language and the second type a "push down store" programme language ("PDS" for short). Without going into details, the full computability language has: (a) output and memory write instructions; (b) input and memory read, erase, and test instructions. (c) transfer control and halt instructions. The important thing about full computability is that we essentially have access at any time to any memory location. The PDS languages are similar except that we only have access to one position of memory at any given time. The PDS language makes access to memory similar to access to trays on a stack in the cafeteria, viz.— you can only put on, take off, or look at the top tray in the stack.

I. It is easy to show that the sc halting problem for PDS programmes is not soluble by a PDS programme.[59] That is, it can be demonstrated that there is no PDS programme, P, such that given input, n, P has the following behaviour: (a) $P(n)$ always halts, for all n; (b) $P(n)$ outputs a 1 if the string n represents a PDS programme P'; and P' halts when given input string n; $P(n)$ outputs 0 otherwise.

1. This does *not* mean that the *sc* halting problem for PDS programmes is no problem.

2. This does *not* mean that it is meaningless to ask for a solution to the *sc* halting problem for PDS programmes.

3. This does *not* mean that the *sc* halting problem for PDS programmes is not soluble.

4. This does *not* mean that the *sc* halting problem for PDS programmes is not soluble by computer.

II. It can be shown that the general halting problem for PDS programmes is soluble by a full computability programme. It can be shown that the *sc* halting problem for PDS programmes is soluble by a full computability programme. Let us call the problem of justifying (some particular type of, or all) inductive inferences "the problem of induction." And let us furthermore suppose the problem were for a change fairly well defined.

I'. Black has at most shown that the problem of induction does not appear to be *prima facie* soluble *by certain, specified methods* in a certain, specified language. He has not constructed a rigorous proof.

1'. This does *not* show that there is no problem.

2'. This does *not* show that it is meaningless to ask for a solution to the problem, provided the problem is well defined.

3'. This does *not* mean that the problem is unsoluble. Maybe an omniscient deity would know whether or not induction is likely to continue to work. (But then again; it might not: A god also *knows* in mysterious ways, I suppose).

4. This does *not* mean that the problem is *not* soluble by means similar or more or less dissimilar to those considered by Black.

II'. Perhaps the problem of induction can be solved by other methods than those considered by Black.

III. We can show that the general halting problem for full computability programmes is not soluble by a full computability programme.

1. This does *not* mean that it is no problem.

2. This does *not* mean that special cases are not soluble. On the contrary: the general halting problem for PDS programmes is indeed soluble by a full computability programme.

III'. Suppose it were in fact convincingly shown that not *all* inductive methods could be justified by certain procedures.

1'. This does *not* mean that there is no problem.

2'. This does *not* mean that special methods cannot be justified by those procedures.

6.3 Final Reflexions on the Existence and Essence of Philosophical Problems

When Eugene Marais[60] claims to have "*discovered*" that every termitary of *Termes bellicosus* (on the west coast of Africa) "actually has a soul", this is more charitably understood as an implicit suggestion for a basic research strategy than as a straightforward report of an actual finding. Similar thoughts may be entertained with regard to problems concerning the existence of "the nature of man", "the meaning of a word", "arts for art's sake", "a science of History", "voluntary (involuntary or deliberate) yawns" ... etc.[61]

It is indeed a question whether a majority, or possibly all of what traditionally pass under the heading: "philosophical problems" were not most charitably to be conceived in this "optative" climate of thought. Thus, when we say about a philosophical problem, P, that it *is* a problem, we do in fact intend to convey what could less misleadingly have been expressed by saying that we *ought* to treat P as though P were a problem. The problem, then, of whether there is, or could be, a problem of how to justify non-demonstrative knowledge claims in general, would in that event properly exemplify such a philosophical problem. In other words: having disposed of the pretension that, in some sort of "literary" sense, there is not or could not be a problem of ampliation, we are left with the problem as to whether we *ought* to concern ourselves with how to justify our claims to know what we do not already know. And the answer is that we ought to be concerned with *this* problem for the same reason as we ought to be concerned with *any* philosophical problem. If there "*are*" "*exist*" philosophical problems, there "*is*" "*exists*" a problem of how to justify ampliation.

Among the many reasons for believing in the "existence" of philosophical problems, one deserves a particular mention: The relationship of philosophical problems to scientific ones.

About a decade or so ago, I was once invited to address a joint meeting of a Physics and Chemistry Club, under the drab and dreary heading: "Philosophy and The Sciences". My paper was finished; but, while I was paging through a collection of Norwegian fairy tales, I was pondering upon some striking remarks for a conclusion. When, suddenly, there it was: The punch line! I had happened to come across the tales of a boy who, one night in the forest, encountered three giant trolls, wading through the woods. The trolls had only one eye between then, which they passed on to each other. The boy, scared of being stepped upon, lifts his axe as high as he can and hits the nearest troll on the shin. It so happens, of course, it is the one who carries the eye who is hit. There is a thundering roar of pain—and the troll drops the eye! The boy, as one would expect, snaps it and runs away. "And that", I ended my paper to the students of Chemistry and Physics, "is in a nutshell the relationship between Philosophy and the sciences: The sciences are the blind trolls running berserk in the wilderness. Philosophy is the boy with their eye, which *would* permit them to see and orient themselves in the world,—could they only get hold of him!"

Dedramatised and demetaphorised the point could be made[62] with less prejudice and slightly more objectively as follows: There is no scientific world orientation. There is no reason whatsoever why so-called "scientific results" should ever necessitate a change or even a modification of one's personal philosophy or general "Weltanschauung". Others would not agree. They, it appears, seem to look upon science as a mighty, monstrous machinery that produces correct views and opinions, *in vacuo*, as it were,—completely independent of its setting in society, of the interests, motives, purposes and intentions of those who attend to it, oil it, serve it, improve it, spoil it or neglect it. This vision is a delusion. There is no such science machine. More specifically speaking: It is simply nonsensically silly to attempt—for world orientation purposes—a pursuit of science totally independent of the philosophic, or even general system-building enterprise. Only insofar as a person is autonomous and articulate enough to have value-priorities, ontological priorities, can scientific results have a rational power of influencing, let alone drastically changing his basic attitudes, his "philosophy", his "world". Only under such circumstances do sentences expressing results of scientific research become sufficiently trenchant to touch, in a *rational* manner, upon personal situations. Otherwise the influence is irrational like that exerted by the weather or the phases of the Moon—a kind of coercion due to passivity, indifference, or simply—in the case on hand—to crude misconceptions concerning the nature of scientific knowledge. There is, I repeat, no such thing as a scientific world view, no established scientific knowledge in any sense of "knowledge" that can be found among the students of scientific enterprise. Consequently, their occasional efforts towards a creative philosophical world orientation should not be hampered by "science". On the contrary, they should be encouraged and enabled to utilize and participate in science—provided they, as it were: "know who they are" to the extent of having at least provisionally articulated their basic priorities of evaluation and action."

"Because at a given time in a definite society only one or a small number of views on a certain topic are considered scientifically "respectable", the "scientific" coercion will tend to induce conformity, spurious agreement, and other-directedness. In short: it is in fact: impersonalizing and dehumanizing. Let it, however, in all fairness be added that the sterility of the scientific enterprise in providing a world view should not necessarily make it less interesting. Rather to the contrary. Many who turn their backs to scientific activity do so through a misunderstanding, misconception of what it is, and lose thereby an invaluable opportunity for participating in a most central human undertaking, indeed one that in the long run may prove to be *the* collective enterprise for this remarkable species that man is".

On the other hand, a blind and blatant admiration for "scientific" methods and results are, after all, more common among philosophers. Philosophers of science are particularly prone to grovel before the sciences. Mario Bunge, for instance, has often ridiculed what he calls "the philosophy of science *fiction*". And, needless to say, philosophers of science ought to thoroughly acquaint themselves with what the scientists are in fact doing. But they would miss their calling altogether were they to confine themselves to a purely descriptive *natural wildlife study of scientists*. If the philosopher cannot at least supply the scientists with incentives for reexamining fundamental methodological problems, he is no *philosopher* of science.

But it is to be hoped that he might go even further than that ...

The image of a metatheoretician that I, in conclusion, shall attempt to conjure up—briefly, dimly and tentatively—is, I am confident, bound to appear radically different from that of the dogmatic negativists who refuse to consider as a problem-conveying formulation, such sentences as: "How can we justifiably pretend to know what we know not?" The advantage of the refusal is obvious: It offers a sigh of relief from the loathsome prospect of a multitude of tiresome undertakings. I am opposed, however, to what I have considered a light-hearted irresponsibility with regard to what kind of problem *formulations* ought to be accepted (as "reasonable", "OK", "all right") or rejected (as "nonsensical", "absurd" ...). The choice becomes particularly significant to the extent that it is decisive for the researcher's willingness to attempt to come to grips with, what, at least someone, at some time, seriously considered a (tentative) formulation of a problem. I am in the market for a science-theoretical ("*wissenschaftstheoretische*") alternative to this self confident myopic march along Black's and Strawson's *via prudentialis*. I recommend an advance on the human research front, characterized by daring expeditions by small scouting parties, while the main force moves carefully, step by step, looking and listening searchingly around, with posts in every tree, and the retreat safely guarded all the way back to the remotest cross-road where a fatal choice may once have been made. Which in turn presupposes, needless to say, a certain division of labour. A researcher with a concrete project within a well-established science discipline is not to be criticized for neglecting the problems of ampliation, induction, contradiction or whatever. His research project is "down to earth" in a sense: He is a pioneer with a geiger counter. The meta-theoreticians and the socalled "philosophers of science" are not. Their position is in the tallest, highest scouting post, where the view is ideally unlimited both forwards and backwards. The stress should here be on "scouting post" rather than on "tallest": even an ivory tower is tall ... In any event, according to such a romantic image of a meta-theoretician, no formulation of a problem or a proposition is *prima facie* to be written off as nonsensical, absurd—, including of course, this very proposition. It is an image, I admit, which is not even satisfied by a mere imitation of Otto Neurath's sailors, who, in open seas, rebuild their ship while they are sailing it. This would just be a very *difficult* task. As it is a difficult task to prove or disprove that Euler's Zeta-function, under certain conditions (complex $s = x + iy$) has all non-real zeros on the line $x = 1/2$. But neither case compares with the difficulties encountering the philosopher, say, who questions the general possibility of justifying *any* non-demonstrative knowledge acquisition—again, including, of course, knowledge about the possibility of justifying knowledge acquisition ... To take upon oneself to attempt to cope with that kind of problem (if "problem" is the word I want), is sheer megalomania, it seems. More megalomaniacal, as I have tried to argue, are only knowledge claims to the effect that it is (proven to be) *logically impossible* to cope with any such "problem", because it is logically impossible that the formulations employed to convey it could ever be uttered, and even if they were uttered, they could not possibly, under any circumstances, be understood. We *cannot*, it is traditionally maintained, transgress the language within which we perceive, feel, will, think and act (and which in turn is moulded by the way we perceive, feel, think, will, act ...). On the contrary, I should want to insist: The argument that our language, its "rules", and its "*deep structure*" in particular, is to be seen in evolutionary perspectives as representing, say, a "response to the universe that our ancestors have found advantageous to survival"[63], this argument may equally well, or possibly better, be advanced as a contra-argument to philosophical use of any natural language. There is, as *inter alia* pointed out by Bergson, no reason why a language, with its "grammar," "structure," "pragmatics" ... moulded through millennia *for survival purposes*, also should be adequate for a biologically useless, or possibly fatal, general world orientation. Philosophical problems are not necessarily, or not at all survival problems. Nor are philosophers—primarily, or at all—qua philosophers entangled in everyday, quotidian puzzles, riddles, intricacies. There is no reason, therefore, to have any confidence that whatever, within a quotidian language context, appears, "intuitively" "common sensically," "for the acute ear," to be "reasonable," "stand to reason," "make sense" ... etc., also ought to be acceptable for philosophical purposes: A trans-quotidian task may well require a trans-quotidian language—"deep structure" and all—, a complete, trans-quotidian conceptual scheme and frame of reference.

NOTES

1. Mates (1969) p. 170ff.
2. Quine (1966) p. 7.
3. *Vide* "The Ways of Paradox", Quine (1966) pp. 3–18 ("The Barber" is not considered an antinomy by Quine: It could be shown that no such barber could exist.)
4. "Ampliation" is here *not* used in any way similar to "ampliation" in medieval logic. The socalled "explicative ampliative" distinction is found in Peirce's writings, particularly in *Vol. II*, Book III (*Critical Logic. A. Explicative Reasoning, B. Ampliative Reasoning*) of *Collected Papers of Charles Sanders Peirce*, Ch. Hartshorne and Paul Weiss, editors, Cambridge: Harvard University Press, 1932. "Ampliative" as employed by Peirce, denoted (nondemonstrative) arguments the conclusion of which "ampliated" in its presuppositions the individuals whose existence was presupposed by the argument's *premises*. In the present paper *any* nondemonstrative argument shall be considered "ampliative". I find, furthermore, as it will appear, no compelling reasons for distinguishing *ampliative* and *summative* contentions (inferences, arguments, reasoning ...).
5. Or, if one prefers: to claim that "there is at least one person, P, such that P is teenager and P is young" ...
6. Or, respectively: to claim that "there is at least one person, P, such that P is human and P is mortal" ...
7. *Vide*. R. Courant: "Bernhard Riemann und die Mathematik der letzten hundert Jahre", *Naturwissenschaft*, Bd. **14** (1926) pp. 318–818. I am indebted to Professor Karl Egil Aubert, University of Oslo, for this most apt illustration of my point.
8. In the late 50th and early 60th at Princeton University, *inter alia* by the Norwegian mathematician, Atle Selberg.
9. Should I for instance succeed in using (consistently) "justified" in such a way that I could by definition be justified in claiming p if *and only if p* is actually the case then, in the above example, "key K_3 is actually a key to my office" might be considered an explicative claim.
10. Consider for one thing the rich variety of slightly more specific topics regularly treated under the heading: "the general problem of induction"; topics which on other occasions, appear to be classified just as readily under: "the problem of the frequentist analysis of confirmation"; "on confirmation of generalization"; "on (theories of) probability", "are objective predictions possible?"; "the limits of empiricism", "are objective predictions possible?", "is it possible to justify, vindicate, validate... ultimate positions, total views, world hypotheses ..." But it is chiefly, as we shall see,

the most universal of these problems which tend to be rendered "no problems", such as: "the justification of the general principles of inductive inference", "why should *any* induction be trusted?", "how are we to justify (vindicate, support ...) any non-demonstrative inference?", "is there any way to back our claim to have knowledge of what we do not already know?"

11. Max Black, (1949), (1954), and (1967).
12. Max Black (1967) pp. 178–179.
13. I do not dream of pretending, of course, to be equipped with ears as sharp or acute as Max Black; but I am bound to confess that there seems to me to be a not all too uncommon use of "fails to make sense", such that whenever a formulation, F, fails to make sense to a person, P, then P would *eo ipso* be incapable of determining what task—if indeed any task—were to be conveyed by F.
14. By Arne Naess: *Scepticism* (in the series: *International Library of Philosophy and Scientific Method*. London: Routledge & Kegan Paul, and New York: Humanities Press, 1968, published 1969).
15. "Induction" in "inductionism" again to be interpreted in one of the wider, inclusive, latitudinarian directions, cognitively akin to 'ampliation' as used in this paper.
16. Parts of section 5, resp. 5.4 and 5.5 are a more or less direct plagiarism of excerpts from some unpublished works of Arne Naess, exploited here with the blessings of the author.
17. Strawson (1952), pp. 256–258.
18. Ibid. p. 256. (It is worth noticing that Strawson quite consistently uses "induction" in what seems to be the same way in which I have endeavoured to use "ampliation".)
19. Particularly the paragraph ending as follows: "... it is reasonable to have a degree of belief in a statement which is proportional to the evidence in its favour; ... so to ask whether it is reasonable to place reliance on inductive procedures is like asking whether it is reasonable to proportion the degree of one's conviction to the strength of the evidence."
20. A counter-inductionist is hardly a non-inductionist in Strawson's sense of "induction", as a counter-inductionist only differs from the inductionist with regard to the general policy for selecting the evidence for S, according to which he then, as Strawson suggests for the inductionist, proportions his confidence in the verdicality of S.
21. It is possible that allowances should have to be made for the cases where a researcher— as suggested by a suspiciously misleading metaphor— "stumbles over the truth."
22. Naess (1961) and Naess (1968) pp. 75–108. (Cnf. also Herman Tennessen: "Comments to Arne Naess on Reaching Knowledge" and "More or Less about Knowledge", multilith from *Center for Advanced Study in Theoretical Psychology*, 1968, Edmonton).
23. Reaching for an apple may eventually lead to the reaching *of* the apple. This is where the analogy breaks down: There is no reaching *of* knowledge as a result of reaching *for* it. (Arne Naess *loc. cit.*).
24. In this sense of "knowing" it is questionable whether P could, for instance, ever claim to know that he has his clothes on, as the necessity for collecting evidence in favour of the relevant proposition(s) is not likely to arise. On the other hand, there is—even in the cases where it seems appropriate to ask for evidence—an inverse correlation between (a) P's inclination to claim: "I know that x" and (b) P's degree of acquaintance with available evidence in favour of x.
25. "Russell's doubts about induction", *MIND*, Vol. LVIII, no. 230, April 1949 pp. 141 to 163.

26. Edwards (1949), p. 152.
26a. Tennessen (1959) and (1960).
27. Will (1941).
28. If Will has informations or valid reflexions to the contrary, he has neglected to share them with us.
29. Black (1967).
30. Black (1954).
31. Paul Edwards (1949) p. 142.
32. Russell (1912) pp. 106–107, in Black (1954) p. 188, footnote 20.
33. Particularly certain critical remarks found in Naess's Berkeley Lectures (1961/62) and in his forthcoming *magnum opus*: *Metaempirical Reflexions*.
34. Black (1954), p. 190; C. D. Broad: *Ethics and the History of Philosophy*, London: Routledge & Kegan Paul, 1952, p. 143.
35. Black (1954), p. 190.
36. Black seems (for undisclosed reasons) to have a peculiar aversion against insoluble problems.
37. Popper (1935 and 59), (1963).
38. Katz (1962).
39. Kyburg (1961).
40. Reichenbach (1949).
41. Salmon (1957), (1961), (1966), (1968).
42. von Wright (1957).
43. Tennessen (1962).
44. Wittgenstein (1967), III, 39.
45. Ibid. III, 42.
46. *Vide*, in particular, Goodman (1954).
47. Tyrrell (1947) and (1954).
48. Soal and Goldney (1943).
49. Brown (1953) and (1958).
50. Hebb (1951), p. 45. "Personally I do not accept ESP for a moment, because it does not make sense. ... Rhine may still turn out to be right, improbable as I think that is, and my own rejection of his view is—in the literal sense—prejudice." D. O. Hebb here quoted after H. Schjelderup (1969) p. 256.
51. Goodman does not confide in the reader as to whether: (a) *he* thinks they *ought to be* justified, or (b) he thinks that within a competent community they *actually* will be *said* to be justified—given sufficiently acute ears.
52. Goodman (1954), p. 67.
53. Goodman (1954), p. 90.
54. The last is a borderline case. One might be hesitant in accepting x an injectible if x had been injected n number of times, but invariably caused damage to the tissue or the body into which it was injected. A similar case, I suppose, may be made for "permitted" and "permissible".
55. We shall here as elsewhere assume the possibility of conflicting hypotheses rather than subscribing to the absurd contention that such conflicts are all bound to be pseudo-conflicts due to semantic confusion.
56. Duhem, P. (1954), pp. 188–211.
57. *Metaempirical Reflexions*.

58. I am indebted to my friend and colleague, Charles Morgan, for this enlightening analogue.
59. Charles Morgan seems equally disinclined to believe in the solubility of the general halting problems for PDS programmes *by* a PDS programme, but does not at the present stage propose to deliver a formal proof of its insolubility.
60. Marais (1940), pp. 43–64, and 113–130. *Vide*, Tennessen (1969) p. 55–59.
61. *Vide* Tennessen (1958), (1959a, and b), (1960, (1961), (1964), (1969).
62. Following again Arne Naess in his *Metaempirical Reflexions*.
63. Max Black (1967), p. 178.

BIBLIOGRAPHY

The list below consists not solely of writings to which explicit references are found in the text. Included are also most of such writings on induction which I consider central for my point of view. Not, needless to say, that they all support my position, but rather that this has emerged from interactions with them. The bibliography is moreover seen and designed as a reference source for enquirers into any of the rich variety of questions concerning justification of ampliative inferences.

Abruzzi, A., Problems of inference in the socio-physical sciences. *Journal of Philosophy*, 1954, **51**, 537–549.
Ach, N., *Über die Willenstätigkeit und das Denken*. Göttingen: van den Hoeck und Rubrecht, 1905.
Achinstein, P. and Barker S. F., On the new riddle of induction. *Philosophical Review*, 1960, **69**, 236–240.
Achinstein, P., Circularity of self-supporting inductive argument. *Analysis*, 1961–62, **22**, 138–141.
Achinstein, P., Circularity and induction. *Analysis*, 1962–63, *23*, 123–127.
Achinstein, P., Variety and analogy in confirmation theory. *Philosophy of Science*, 1963, **30**, 207–221.
Ackerman, R., *Nondeductive inference*. New York: Dover, 1966.
Agassi, J., Corroboration versus induction. *British Journal for the Philosophy of Science*, 1958–59, **9**, 311–317.
Agassi, J., Empiricism and inductivism. *Philosophical Studies*, 1963, **14**, 85–86.
Agassi, J., The mystery of the ravens. *Philosophy of Science*, 1966, **33**, 394–402.
Alexander, H. G., Convention, falsification and induction. *Proceedings of the Aristotelian Society*, Supplementary Volume XXXIV, 1960, 131–144.
Ambrose, A., The problem of justifying induction. *Journal of Philosophy*, 1947, **44**, 253–272.
Amerio, F., *Epistemologi Contemporanei*. Torino: Società Internationale, 1952.
Austin, J. L., Other minds. *Philosophical Papers*, Oxford University Press, 1961, 44–84.
Austin, J. L., *Sense and sensibilia*. Fair Lawn, N. J.: Oxford University Press, 1962.
Ayer, A. J., *Language, truth and logic*. New York: Dover Publications, 1946.
Ayer, A. J., *Philosophical essays*. New York: St. Martin's Press, 1954.
Ayer, A. J., *The problem of knowledge*. Baltimore: Penguin Books, 1956.
Ayer, A. J., Philosophical scepticism. In H. D. Lewis (Ed.), *Contemporary British Philosophy. The Muirhead Library of Philosophy*. London: Allen & Urwin; New York: The Macmillan Co., 1956.
Bar-Hillel, Y., *Language and information*. Reading, Mass.: Addison-Wesley, 1964.
Bar-Hillel, Y., On an alleged contradiction in Carnap's theory of inductive logic. *Mind*, 1964, **72**, 256–267.
Bar-Hillel, Y., On alleged rules of detachment in inductive logic. In I. Lakatos (Ed.), *The problem of inductive logic*. Amsterdam: North-Holland Publishing Co., 1968.

Barker, S. F., *Induction and hypothesis: A study of the logic of confirmation*. Ithaca, N. Y.: Cornell University Press, 1957.
Barker, S. F., von Wright's "The logical problem of induction." *Journal of Philosophy*, 1958, **55**, 130–131.
Barker, S. F., Comments on Salmon's "Vindication of induction." In H. Feigl and G. Maxwell (Eds.), *Current Issues in the Philosophy of Science*, New York: Holt, Rinehart, and Winston, 1961.
Barker, S. F., Rejoinder to Salmon. In H. Feigl and G. Maxwell (Eds.), *Current Issues in the Philosophy of Science*. New York: Holt, Rinehart, and Winston, 1961.
Barker, S. F., Must every inference be either deductive or inductive? In M. Black (Ed.), *Philosophy in America*. Ithaca, N. Y.: Cornell University Press, 1965.
Bartley, W. W., III., A note on Barker's discussion of Popper's theory of corroboration. *Philosophical studies*, 1961, **12**, 5–10.
Bartley, W. W., III., Goodman's paradox: A simple-minded solution. *Philosophical Studies*, 1968, **19**, 85–88.
Bayle, P., Pyrrho. *Dictionnaire historique et critique*. Amsterdam, Leiden, LaHaye, Utrecht: P. Humbert, *et al.*, 1740.
Bennet, J. F., Some aspects of probability and induction. I and II. *British Journal for the Philosophy of Science*, 1956–57, Vol. 7, pp. 220–230 (I) and pp. 316–322 (II).
Bergson, H., *Essai sur les données immédiates de la conscience*. Huitième édition. Paris: Felix Alcan, 1889.
Bergson, H., Introduction à la métaphysique. *Revue de la métaphysique et de morale*, 1903, **11**, 1–183.
Berkeley, G., *Principles of human knowledge*. Cleveland: The World Publishing Co., 1963.
Berlyne, D. E., The motivation of inductive behavior. In H. E. Kyburg and E. Nagel (Eds.), *Induction, some current issues*. Middletown, Conn.: Wesleyan University Press, 1963.
Beth, E. W., *Semantic construction of intuitionistic logic*. Mededelingen der Koninklijke Nederlandse Akademie van Wetenschappen, Afd. Letterkunde. Nieuwe Reeks, Deel 19, No. 11. Amsterdam: N. V. Noord-Hollandsche Uitgevers Maatschappij, 1956.
Bhattacharya, K., *Philosophy, logic and language*. Bombay, New Delhi, Calcutta, Madras, London, New York: Allied Publishers Private Ltd., 1965.
Binswanger, L., "Zum Problem von Sprache und Denken" and "Über Sprache und Denken" in *Ausgewählte Vorträge und Aufsätze, Band II*, Bern: Francke Verlag, 1955.
Binswanger, L., *Grundformen und Erkenntnis menschlichen Daseins*. München: E. Reinhardt, 1964.
Black, M., Introduction. In M. Black (Ed.), *Philosophical Analysis*. Ithaca, N. Y.: Cornell University Press, 1950.
Black, M., *Problems of analysis*. London: Routledge and Kegan Paul, 1954.
Black, M., *Critical thinking*. Prentice Hall Philosophy Series. (5th ed.) Englewood Cliffs, N. J.: Prentice Hall, 1957.
Black, M., Induction and probability. In R. Klibanski (Ed.), *Philosophy in the Mid-Century, I. Logic and Philosophy of Science*. Firenze: Nuova Italia, 1958–59.
Black, M., Self-supporting inductive arguments. *The Journal of Philosophy*, 1958, Vol. LV, No. 17, 718–725.
Black, M., Can induction be vindicated? In M. Black (Ed.), *Models and metaphors*. *Ithaca*, N. Y.: Cornell University Press, 1962.

Black, M., Induction. In P. Edwards (Ed.), *The Encyclopedia of Philosophy*, Vol. 4. New York: The Macmillan Co. & The Free Press; London: Collier-Mcmillan Ltd., 1967.
Black, M., *The labyrinth of language*. New York, Washington, London: Frederick A. Praeger, Publishers, 1968.
Bondi, H., *Relativity and common sense, a new approach to Einstein*. London: Heinemann Educational Books Ltd., 1965.
Braithwaite, R. B., Models in the empirical sciences. In E. Nagel, P. Suppes, and A. Tarski (Eds.), *Logic, methodology and philosophy of science*. Stanford: Stanford University Press, 1962.
Brentano, Fr., *Psychologie vom empirischen Standpunkt*, Erster Bd. Leipzig: Duncker und Humbolt, 1874.
Brown, G. S., *Probability and scientific inference*. New York: Longmans, Green and Co., 1957.
Brown, G. S., Randomness. *Proceedings of the Aristotelian Society*, Supplementary Volume 31, 1957, 145–150.
Brown, M. S., *Theatetus*: *Knowledge* as continued learning. *Journal of the History of Philosophy*, 1969, Vol. VII, No. 4.
Brunswik, E., Scope and aspects of the cognition problem. In H. Gruber, R. Jessor and K. Hammond (Eds.), *Contemporary Approaches to Cognition*. Cambridge, Mass.: Harvard University Press, 1957.
Buchdahl, G., Induction and scientific method. *Mind*, 1961, **60**, 16–34.
Bunge, M., *Causality: The place of the causal principle in modern science*. Cambridge, Mass.: Harvard University Press, 1959.
Bunge, M., *Metascientific queries*. Springfield, Ill.: Charles C. Thomas, 1959.
Bunge, M., The place of induction in science. *Philosophy of Science*, 1960, **27**, 262–270.
Bunge, M., *Intuition and science*. Englewood Cliffs, N. J.: Prentice Hall, 1962.
Bunge, M., *Scientific research I: The search for system*. Berlin, Heidelberg, New York: Springer-Verlag, 1967.
Bunge, M. *Scientific research II: The search for truth*. Berlin, Heidelberg, New York: Springer-Verlag, 1967.
Campbell, D. T., Evolutionary epistemology. In P. A. Schilpp (Ed.), *The Philosophy of Karl Popper* (*The Library of Living Philosophers*). LaSalle, Ill.: The Open Court Publishing Co., forthcoming.
Carnap, R., Remarks on induction and truth. *Philosophy and Phenomenological Research*, 1964, **6**(4), 590–602.
Carnap, R., *The nature and application of inductive logic*. Chicago: The University of Chicago Press, 1951.
Carnap, R., *The continuum of inductive methods*. Chicago: The University of Chicago Press, 1952.
Carnap, R., *Der logische Aufbau der Welt* (zweite Ausgabe). Hamburg: Felix Meiner Verlag, 1961.
Carnap, R., The aim of inductive logic. In E. Nagel, P. Suppes, and A. Tarski (Eds.), *Logic, Methodology and Philosophy of Science*. Stanford: Stanford University Press, 1962.
Carnap, R., Answer to my critics. In P. A. Schilpp (Ed.), *The Philosophy of Rudolf Carnap*, Vol. XI (*The Library of Living Philosophers*). LaSalle, Ill.: The Open Court Publishing Co., 1963.

Carnap, R., Inductive logic and inductive intuition. In I. Lakatos (Ed.), *The Problem of Inductive Logic*. Amsterdam: North-Holland Publishing Co., 1968.

Carnap, R. and Stegmüller, W., *Induktive Logik und Wahrscheinlichkeit*. Wien: Springer-Verlag, 1959.

Castañeda, H., On a proposed revolution in logic. *Philosophy of Science*, 1960, 27, 279–292.

Castañeda, H., Knowledge and certainty. *The Review of Metaphysics*, 18(3), 1965.

Chethimattam, J. B., *Consciousness and reality*. Bangalore: The Bangalore Press, 1967.

Chisholm, R. M., *Perceiving: A philosophical study* (Part I). Ithaca, N. Y.: Cornell University Press, 1957.

Chisholm R. M., Theory of knowledge. In R. M. Chisholm, H. Feigl, and W. K. Frankena (Eds.), *Philosophy*. Englewood Cliffs, N. J.: Prentice Hall, 1964.

Chisholm R. M., *Theory of knowledge*. (Foundations of Philosophy Series) Englewood Cliffs, N. J.: Prentice Hall, 1964.

Courant, R., Bernhard Riesmann und die Mathematik der letzten hundert Jahre. *Naturwissenschaft*, vierzehnter Band, 1926.

Dingle, H., *Science and human experience*. London: Williams and Norgate, 1931.

Duhem, P., *La Theorie physique, son objet et sa structure*, Paris 1906 and 1914 (w. appendix), translated by P. P. Wiener: *Aim and structure of physical theory*. Princeton N. J.: Princeton University Press, 1954.

Ebersole, F. B., *Things we know, fourteen essays on problems of knowledge*. Eugene, Oregon: University of Oregon Books, 1967.

Edwards, P., Russell's doubt about induction. *Mind*, 1949, Vol. LVIII, No. 230, 141–163.

Ewald, O., *Welche wirklichen Fortschritte hat die Metaphysik seit Hegels und Herbarts Zeiten in Deutschland gehabt?* Gekrönte Preisschrift. *Ergänzungsband Nr. 53 der Kant-Studien*. Berlin: Reuther und Reichard, 1920.

Feigl, H., De Principiis non est disputandum ...? In M. Black (Ed.), *Philosophical Analysis*. Ithaca, N. Y.: Cornell University Press, 1950.

Feigl, H., Some major issues and developments in the philosophy of science of logical empiricism. In H. Feigl and M. Scriven (Eds.), *The Foundation of Science and Concepts of Psychology and Psychoanalysis*, Vol. I, *Minnesota Studies in the Philosophy of Science*. Minneapolis, Minn.: University of Minnesota Press, 1956.

Ferrater Mora, J., *Obras selectas* (Vol. I and II)). Madrid: Reviste de Occidente, 1967.

Feyerabend, P. K., Problems of microphysics. In R. G. Colodny (Ed.), *Frontiers of Science and Philosophy*, Vol. 1, *University of Pittsburgh Series in the Philosophy of Science*. Pittsburgh: University of Pittsburgh Press, 1962.

Feyerabend, P. K., How to be a good empiricist—A plea for tolerance in matters epistemological. In B. Baumrin (Ed.), *Philosophy of Science*, Vol. 2. The Delaware Seminar (1962–63). New York, London, Sydney: Interscience Publishers, 1963.

Feyerabend, P. K., Problems of Empiricism. In R. G. Colodny (Ed.), *Beyond the edge of certainty*, Vol. 2, *University of Pittsburgh Series in the Philosophy of Science*. Englewood Cliffs, N. J.: Prentice Hall, 1965.

Foster, M. H. and Martin M. L., *Probability, confirmation and simplicity*. New York: The Odyssey Press, 1966.

Fritz, Ch. A., Jr., What is induction? *The Journal of Philosophy*, 1960, Vol. LVII, No. 4, 126–138.

Gianonni, C., Quine, Grünbaum and the Duhemian thesis. *Nous*, 1967, 1(3), 283–299.

Gibson, J. J., *The perception of the visual world*. Boston: Houghton Mifflin, 1950.

Gibson, J. J., *The senses considered as perceptual systems*. Boston: Houghton Mifflin, 1966.
Gibson, J. J., New reasons for realism. *Synthese*, 1967, 17, 162–172.
Goodman, N., *The structure of appearance*. Cambridge, Mass.: Harvard University Press, 1951.
Goodman, N., Positionality and pictures. *Philosophical Review*, 1960, Vol. LXIX, No. 4, 523–525.
Goodman, N., *Fact, fiction and forecast*. (2nd ed.) Indianapolis: Bobbs-Merrill, 1965. (1st ed. 1954.)
Goodman N., Two replies. *The Journal of Philosophy*, 1967, Vol. LXIX, No. 9, 286–287.
Grünbaum, A., The Duhemian argument. *Philosophy of Science*, 1960, 27, 75–87.
Grünbaum, A., Professor Dingle on falsifiability. *British Journal for the Philosophy of Science*, 1961, 12, 153–156.
Gullvåg, I., *Absolutisme og relativisme i erkjennelsesteorien*, Filosofiske Problemer nr. 20. Oslo: Universitetsforlaget, 1955.
Gullvåg, I., *Knowledge, truth and reality*. Vols. I–IV. Oslo: Institute for Social Research, 1961.
Gullvåg, I., *Truth, belief and certainty*. Trondheim: Det Kgl. Norske Videnskabers Selskabs Skrifter, 1964.
Gullvåg, I., Scepticism and absurdity. *Inquiry*, 1964, 7(2), 151–163.
Gullvåg, I., *Referanse, mening og eksistens*. Filosofiske Problemer no. 34. Oslo: Universitetsforlaget, 1967.
Habermas, J., Knowledge and interest. *Inquiry*, 1966, 9(4), 285–300.
Habermas, J., *Theorie und Praxis*. Berlin: Luchterland Verlag, 1963 and 1967.
Habermas, J., Towards a theory of communicative competence. *Inquiry*, 1970, 13(4), 360–375.
Habermas, J., *Technik und Wissenschaft als "Ideologie."* Frankfurt am Main: Suhrkamp Verlag, 1970.
Hammond, K. R., *Cognition and conflict*. Program on Cognitive Processes Report 100. Mimeo., Aug. 15, 1967, Institute of Behavioral Science, University of Colorado.
Hanneborg, K., New concepts in ontology: A review of discussion of Roman Ingarden's *Der Streit um die Existenz der Welt*. *Inquiry*, 1966, 9(4), 401–409.
Hanson, N. R., *Patterns of discovery*. Cambridge, Mass.: Cambridge University Press, 1958.
Harrison, J., Knowing and promising. *Mind*, 1962, 71(284), 312–351.
Hartnack, J. Remarks on the concept of knowledge. *Inquiry*, 1961, 4(4), 270–273.
Hawkins, D., *The language of nature*. San Francisco and London: W. H. Freeman & Co., 1964.
Heidelberger, H., Knowledge, certainty and probability. *Inquiry*, 1963, 6(3), 242–250.
Hempel, C. G., Inductive inconsictencies. *Synthese*, 1960, 12, 439–469.
Hempel, C. G., Deductive-nomological vs. statistical explanation. In H. Feigel and G. Maxwell (Eds.), *Minnesota Studies in the Philosophy of Science*, Vol. III (*Scientific Explanation, Space and Time*). Minneapolis: University of Minnesota Press, 1962.
Hesse, M. B., Models and analogy in science. In P. Edwards (Ed.), *The Encyclopedia of Philosophy*, Vol. V. New York: The MacMillan Co. & The Free Press, 1967.
Hesse, M. B., Concilience of inductions. In I. Lakatos (Ed.), *The Problem of Inductive Logic*. Amsterdam: North-Holland Publishing Co., 1968.
Hintikka, J., *Knowledge and belief*. Ithaca, N. Y.: Cornell University Press, 1962.

Hintikka, J., Towards a theory of inductive generalization. In Y. Bar-Hillel (Ed.), *Logic, Methodology and Philosophy of Science* II. Amsterdam: North-Holland Publishing Co., 1964.

Hintikka, J., On a combined system of inductive logic. *Studia Logico-Mathematica et Philosophica in Honorem Rolf Nevanlinna, Acta Philosophica Fennica* Vol. 18, 1965.

Hintikka, J., A two-dimensional continuum of inductive methods. In J. Hintikka and P. Suppes (Eds.), *Aspects of Inductive Logic*. Amsterdam: North-Holland Publishing Co., 1966.

Hintikka, J., Time, truth and knowledge in ancient Greek philosophy. *American Philosophical Quarterly*, 1967, **4**(1), 1–14.

Hintikka, J. and Pietarinen, J., Semantic information and inductive logic. In J. Hintikka and P. Suppes (Eds.), *Aspects of Inductive Logic*. Amsterdam: North-Holland Publishing Co., 1966.

Hintikka, J. and Hilpinen, R., Knowledge, acceptance and inductive logic. In J. Hintikka and P. Suppes (Eds.), *Aspects of Inductive Logic*. Amsterdam: North-Holland Publishing Co., 1966.

Hoff, J. H. van't, *Imagination in science*. New York: Springer-Verlag New York, Inc., 1967.

Hönigswald, R., *Die Skepsis in Philosophie und Wissenschaft*. Schriften zur Einführung in das Philosophische Denken, No. 7. Göttingen: Vandenhoek u. Ruprecht, 1914.

Hume, D., *The philosophical works of David Hume*, Vols. I–IV. Edinburgh: Printed for Adam Black and William Tait; and Charles Tait, 63, Fleet Street, London, 1821–26.

Humphrey, W. C., *Anomalies and scientific theories*. San Francisco: Freeman, Cooper & Co., 1968.

Ingarden, R., *Der Streit um die Existenz der Welt*, I, II/1 and II/2. Tübingen: Max Niemeyer Verlag, 1964 (I) and 1965 (II).

Jaspers, K., *Psychologie der Weltanschauungen*. Berlin: Julius Springer Verlag, 1920.

Jaspers, K., *Allgemeine Psychopathologie*. Berlin: Julius Springer Verlag, 1959.

Jeffrey, H., On von Wright's *A treatise on induction and probability*. *British Journal for the Philosophy of Science*, 1952–53, **3**, 276–277.

Jeffrey, R. C., Goodman's query. *Journal of Philosophy*, 1966, **63**, 281–283.

Juhos, B., Deduktion, Induktion und Wahrscheinlichkeit. *Methodos*, 1954, **6**, 259–276.

Katz, J. J., *The problem of induction and its solution*. Chicago: University of Chicago Press, 1962.

Kemeney, J. G., On von Wright's *A treatise on induction and probability*. *Philosophical Review*, 1953, **62**, 93–101.

Kemeney, J. G., *A philosopher looks at science*. Princeton, N. J.: Van Nostrand, 1959.

King-Farlow, J., Toulmin's analysis of probability. *Theoria*, 1963, **29**(1), 12–26.

Kneale, W., *Probability and induction*. Oxford: Clarendon Press, 1949.

Kneale, W., Probability and induction. *Mind*, 1951, **60**, 310–317.

Kneale, W., Some aspects of probability and induction: A reply to Mr. Bennet. *British Journal for the Philosophy of Science*, 1957–58, **8**, 57–63.

Körner, S., *Conceptual thinking*. New York: Dover Publications, 1959.

Kuhn, T. S., The structure of scientific revolutions. *International Encyclopedia of Unified Science, Foundations of the Unity of Science*, Vol. II, No. 2. Chicago and London: The University of Chicago Press, 1962.

Kyburg, H. E., Jr., The justification of induction. *Journal of Philosophy*, 1956, **53**, 392–400.

Kyburg H. E., Jr., Recent work in inductive logic. *American Philosophical Quarterly*, 1964, **1**, 1–39.

Kyburg, H. E., Jr., Comments on Salmon's *Inductive Evidence*. *American Philosophical Quarterly*, 1965, **2**, 10–12.

Kyburg, H. E., Jr. Salmon's paper. *Philosophy of Science*, 1966, **33**, 147–151.

Kyburg, H. E., Jr., Review of Patrick Suppes and Jaakoo Hintikka (Eds.), *Aspects of Inductive Logic*. *Journal of Philosophy*, 1968, Vol. LXV, No. 10, 323–328.

Kyburg, H. E., Jr., *Probability and inductive logic*. London: The Macmillan Co., Collier-Macmillan Ltd., 1970.

Lakatos, I., Changes in the problem of inductive logic. In I. Lakatos (Ed.), *The Problem of Inductive Logic*. Amsterdam: North-Holland Piblishing Co., 1968.

Lakatos, I., Criticism and the methodology of scientific research programmes. Paper read before a meeting of the Aristotelian Society, London, October 1968.

Lenz, J. W., Carnap on defining *Degrees of confirmation*. *Philosophy of Science*, 1956, **23**, 230–236.

Madden, E. H., The riddle of induction. *Journal of Philosophy*, 1958, **55**, 705–718.

Madden, E. H., von Wright's logical problem of induction. *Philosophy and Phenomenological Research*, 1957–59, **18**, 550–551.

Marais, E. N., *Termittenes sjel* (Norwegian translation of *The soul of the white ant*). Oslo: H. Aschehoug & Co., 1940.

Margolis, J., The demand for a justification of induction. *Synthese*, 1959, **11**, 259–264.

Margolis, J., Entitled to assert. *Synthese*, 1967, **17**, 292–298.

Mates, B., Philosophical scepticism and the logical antinomies. *Akten des XIV Internationalen Kongresses für Philosophie, III. Logik, Erkenntnis- und Wissenschaftstheorie, Sprachphilosophie, Ontologie und Metaphysik*. Wien: Herder & Co., 1969.

McNabb, D. G. C., Hume on induction. *Revue Internationale de Philosophie*, 1952, **6**, 145–159.

Midgaard, K., *Communication and strategy. Filosofiske notater nr. 3*. Oslo: Universitetsforlaget, 1970.

Naess, A., *Erkenntnis und wissenschaftliches Verhalten*. Oslo: Jacob Dybwad, 1936.

Naess, A., *Filosofiske Problemer*. Oslo: H. Aschehoug & Co., 1941.

Naess, A., *Usaklighetsanalyse*. Oslo: Universitetsforlaget, 1947.

Naess, A., *An empirical study of the expressions "true," "perfectly certain" and "extremely probable."* Oslo: Jacob Dybwad, 1953.

Naess, A., *Interpretation and preciseness, a contribution to the theory of communication*, Skrifter ut gitt av Det Norske Videnskaps-Akademi i Oslo, II Hist. Filos. Klasse 1953. No. 1. Oslo: Johan Dybwad, 1953.

Naess, A., *Wie fördert man heute die empirische Bewegung*? Oslo: Universitetsforlaget, 1956.

Naess, A., *Notes on the foundation of psychology as a science*. (2nd ed.) Oslo: Universitetsforlaget, 1960.

Naess, A., *Empirisk Semantik*. Stockholm: Svenska Bøkforlaget, 1961.

Naess, A., Can knowledge be reached? *Inquiry*, 1961, **4**(4), 219–228.

Naess, A., *Symbolsk Logikk*. (3rd ed. by Jens-Erik Fenstad) Oslo-Bergen: Universitetsforlaget, 1962.

Naess, A., The inquiring mind. *Philosophy Today*, 1961, Vol. 5, No. 3/4, 184–205.

Naess, A., *Communication and argument*. Totowa, N. J.: Bedminster Press, 1965.

Naess, A., Pluralistic theorizing in physics and philosophy. *Danish Yearbook of Philosophy*, 1964, **1**, 101–111.

Naess, A., *Logikk og Metodelaere*. Oslo: Universitetsforlaget, 1966.

Naess, A., Physics and the variety of world pictures. In P. Weingarten (Ed.), *Grundfragen der Wissenschaften und ihre Wurzeln in der Metaphysik*. Berlin: Julius Springer Verlag, 1967.

Naess, A., *Filosofieus Historie*, Vols. I & II. (4th rev. ed). Oslo: Universitetsforlaget, 1968.

Naess, A., *Four modern philosophers*. Chicago and London: University of Chicago Press, 1968.

Naess, A., *Scepticism*. London: Routledge & Kegan Paul; New York: Humanities Press, 1968.

Naess, A., *Hvilken verden er den virkelige*? Oslo, Bergen, Tromsø: Universitetsforlaget, 1969.

Naess, A., Notes on a Spinoza research project. In T. Dalenius, G. Karlsson and S. Malmquist (Eds.), *Scientists at Work. Festschrift in honor of Herman Wald*. Uppsala: Almquist & Wiksells Boktryckeri AB, 1970.

Naess, A., Language of creative research and language of science: A contrast. Estratto da *Linguaggi nella societa e nella tecnica*, Edizioni di commita-Milano, 1970.

Naess, A., *Vitenskapsfilosofi*. Oslo, Bergen, Tromsø: Universitetsforlaget, 1971.

Naess, A., *A dialogue on induction*. Chicago: University of Chicago Press, in press.

Naess, A., *Die philosophische Relevanz einiger empirisch-semantischer Forschungsergebnisse*. Mitteilungen der Philosophischen Gesellschaft der Universität Graz, in press.

Naess, A., *A pluralist conception of the scientific enterprise*. In press.

Naess, A., *Meta-empirical reflexions*. In press.

Nicod, J., *Foundations of geometry and induction*. New York: The Humanities Press, 1950.

Nyman, A., Induction et intuition. *Theoria*, 1953, **19**, 21–41.

Oliver, W. D., A re-examination of the problem of induction. *Journal of Philosophy*, 1952, **49**, 769–780.

Oppenheim, P. and Hempel, C. G., A definition of degree of confirmation. *Philosophy of Science*, 1945, **12**, 98–115.

Pap, A., *Analytische Erkenntnistheorie*. Wien: Springer-Verlag, 1955.

Pap, A., *An introduction to the philosophy of science*. New York: Glencoe Free Press, 1962.

Papanoutsos, E. P., *The foundations of knowledge*. Albany, N. Y.: State University of New York Press, 1968.

Peirce, C. S., *Collected papers of Charles Saunders Peirce* (esp. Vol. II, Book III). Cambridge, Mass.: Harvard University Press, 1932.

Pettijohn, W. C., Salmon on "the short run." *Philosophy of Science*, 1956, **23**, 149.

Piaget, J., *The language and thought of the child*. London: Routledge & Kegan Paul; New York: The Humanities Press, 1959.

Polanyi, M., *Personal knowledge*. Chicago: University of Chicago Press, 1958.

Pollock, J. L., Counter-induction. *Inquiry*, 1962, **5**, 284–294.

Pollock, J. L., Non-analytic implication. *Inquiry*, 1967, **10**, 196–203.

Pollock, J. L., The structure of epistemic justification. In N. Rescher (Ed.), *Studies in the theory of knowledge*, American Philosophical Quarterly Monograph Series, Monograph No. 4. Oxford: Basil Blackwell, 1970.

Polya, G., *Mathematics and plausible reasoning*. Princeton, N. J.: Princeton University Press, 1954.

Popper, K. R., Degree of confirmation. *Mind*, 1954–55, **47**, 143–149.
Popper, K. R., "Content" and "degree of confirmation:" A reply to Dr. Bar-Hillel. *British Journal for the Philosophy of Science*, 1955–56, **6**, 157–163.
Popper, K. R., A second note on degree of confirmation. *British Journal for the Philosophy of Science*, 1956–57, **7**, 350–353.
Popper, K. R., A third note on degree of corroboration or confirmation. *British Journal for the Philosophy of Science*, 1957–58, **8**, 294–302.
Popper, K. R., *Conjectures and refutations*. London: Routledge & Kegan Paul, 1963; New York: Basic Books, 1962.
Popper, K. R., *Of clouds and clocks*. St. Louis, Missouri: Washington University, 1966.
Putnam, H., A definition of degree of confirmation for very rich languages. *Philosophy of Science*, 1956, **23**, 58–62.
Putnam, H., It ain't necessarily so. *Journal of Philosophy*, 1962, **59**(20), 658–671.
Putnam, H., The analytic and the synthetic. In H. Feigl and G. Maxwell (Eds.), *Minnesota Studies in the Philosophy of Science*, Vol. III: *Scientific Explanation, Space and Time*. Minneapolis: University of Minnesota Press, 1962.
Putnam, H., What theories are not. In E. Nagel, P. Suppes, and A. Tarski (Eds.), *Logic, Methodology and Philosophy of Science*. Stanford, California: Stanford University Press, 1962.
Putnam, H., Degree of confirmation and inductive logic. In P. A. Schilpp (Ed.), *The Philosophy of Rudolf Carnap*, Vol. XI (*The Library of Living Philosophers*). LaSalle, Ill.: The Open Court Publishing Co., 1963.
Quine, W. v. O., Truth by convention. In O. H. Lee (Ed.), *Philosophical Essay for A. N. Whitehead*. New York: Longmans, 1936.
Quine, W. v. O., Notes on existence and necessity. *Journal of Philosophy*, 1943, **40**(3), 113–127.
Quine, W. v. O., *From a logical point of view*. Cambridge, Mass.: Harvard University Press, 1953.
Quine, W. v. O., The scope and language of science. *The British Journal for the Philosophy of Science*, 1957, Vol. VII, No. 29, 1–17.
Quine, W. v. O., Speaking of objects. *Proceedings and addresses of The American Philosophical Association*, Vol. XXXI, Oct. 1958.
Quine, W. v. O., Meaning and translation. In J. Brower (Ed.), *On translation*. Cambridge, Mass.: Harvard University Press, 1959.
Quine, W. v. O., *Word and object*. New York and London: John Wiley & Sons (jointly with the Technology Press of the Massachusetts Institute of Technology), 1960.
Quine, W. v. O., *Selected logic papers*. New York: Random House, 1966.
Quine, W. v. O., *The ways of paradox and other essays*. New York: Random House, 1966.
Quine, W. v. O., *Ontological relativity and other essays*. New York: Columbia University Press, 1969.
Quine, W. v. O., *Ontological relativity*. New York: Columbia University Press, 1970.
Quine, W. v. O., *Philosophy of logic*. (Prentice Hall Foundations of Philosophy Series). Englewood Cliffs, N. J.: Prentice-Hall, 1970.
Quine, W. v. O., Epistemology naturalized. In J. R. Royce and W. W. Rozeboom (Eds.), *The Psychology of Knowing*. New York: Gordon & Breach, Science Publishers, 1972.
Radnitzky, G., Some remarks on the Whorfian hypothesis. *Behavioural Science*, 1961, **6**, 12–45.

Radnitzky, G., Reflexions on scepticism, Pyrrhonian and others. *Ratio*, 1965, 17(2), 117–144.
Radnitzky, G., *Contemporary schools of metascience*. (2nd ed.) New York: Humanities Press, 1970.
Ramsey, F. P., The foundation of mathematics and other logical essays. In R. B. Braithwaite (Ed.), *International Library of Psychology, Philosophy and Scientific Method*. Paterson, N. J.: Littlefield, Adams & Co., 1960.
Reichenbach, H., On probability and induction. *Philosophy of Science*, 1938, **5**, 21–45.
Reichenbach, H., On the justification of induction. *The Journal of Philosophy*, 1940, **37**, 97–103.
Reichenbach, H., *Theory of probability*. Berkeley and Los Angeles: University of California Press, 1949.
Rescher, N., On prediction and explanation. *British Journal for the Philosophy of Science*, 1958, **8**(4), 281–290.
Rescher, N., Non-deductive rules of inference and problems in the analysis of inductive reasoning. *Synthese*, 1961, **13**(3), 242–251.
Rescher, N., *Hypothetical reasoning*. Amsterdam: North-Holland Publishing Co., 1964.
Rickert, H., *Die Grenzen der naturwissenschaftlichen Begriffsbildung*. Tübingen, Leipzig: Verlag von J. C. B. Mohr (Paul Siebeck), 1902.
Rickert, H., *Kulturwissenschaft und Naturwissenschaft*. Tübingen: Verlag von J. C. B. Mohr (Paul Siebeck), 1926.
Rickert, H., *Der Gegenstand der Erkenntnis*. Sechste verbesserte Auflage. Tübingen: Verlag von J. C. B. Mohr (Paul Siebeck), 1928. (Erste Auflage, 1892).
Rommetveit, R., Epistemological notes on recent studies of social perception. *Inquiry*, 1957, **1**(4), 213–231.
Rosthal, R., Barker's induction and hypothesis. *Philosophy and Phenomenological Research*, 1958–59, **19**, 123–124.
Royce, J. R., The search for meaning. *American Scientist*, 1959, **47**, 515–535.
Royce, J. R., *The encapsulated man: An interdisciplinary essay on the search for meaning*. Princeton, N. J.: D. Van Nostrand & Co., 1964.
L'Uomo Incapsulato. Rome: Casa Editrice Astrolabio-Ubaldini Editore, 1970.
Royce, J. R., Rozeboom, W. W., Tennessen, H. and Weckowicz, T., On theory and metatheory. [Review of M. Marx (Ed.), *Theories in contemporary psychology*.] *Contemporary Psychology*, 1968, Vol. XIII, No. 9, 433–436.
Rozeboom, W. W., Ontological induction and the logical typology of scientific variables. *Philosophy of Science*, 1961, **28**, 337–377.
Rozeboom, W. W., Why I know so much more than you do. *American Philosophical Quarterly*, 1967, **4**, 281–290.
Rozeboom, W. W., New dimensions of confirmation. *Philosophy of Science*, 1968, **35**, 134–158.
Rozeboom, W. W., The art of metascience, or, what should a psychological theory be? In J. R. Royce (Ed.), *Toward Unification in Psychology, The First Banff Conference on Theoretical Psychology*. Toronto: University of Toronto Press, 1970.
Rozeboom, W. W., Scientific inference: The myth and the reality. In S. R. Brown and D. J. Brenner (Eds.), *Science, Psychology and Communication*. New York: Teachers College Press, 1971.
Russell, B., *The problems of philosophy*. London: Routledge and Kegan Paul, 1912.
Russell, B., *Our knowledge of the external world*. New York: W. W. Norton & Co., 1929.

Russell, B., *Human knowledge, its scope and limits*. New York: Simon & Schuster, 1948.
Ryle, G., Induction and hypothesis. *Proceedings of the Aristotelian Society*, Vol. XVI, 1937, 36–62.
Ryle, G., Comment on Mr. Achinstein's paper. *Analysis*, 1060–61, **21**, 9–11.
Rynin, D., Statements, components and extensionality. *Inquiry*, 1960, 3(3), 153–179.
Rynin, D., Evidence. *Synthese*, 1960, **12**, 6–24.
Rynin, D., Cognitive meaning and cognitive use. *Inquiry*, 1966, 9(3), 109–132.
Salmon, W. C., The uniformity of nature. *Philosophy and Phenomenological Research*, 1953, **14**, 39–48.
Salmon, W. C., The short run. *Philosophy of Science*, 1955, **22**, 214–221.
Salmon, W. C., Regular rules of induction. *Philosophical Review*, 1956, **65**, 385–388.
Salmon, W. C., Reply to Pettijohn. *Philosophy of Science*, 1956, **23**, 150–151.
Salmon, W. C., The predictive inference. *Philosophy of Science*, 1957, **24**, 180–190.
Salmon, W. C., Should we attempt to justify induction? *Philosophical Studies*, 1957, **8**(1), 33–48.
Salmon, W. C., Barker's theory of the absolute. *Philosophical Studies*, 1959, **10**, 50–53.
Salmon, W. C., Barker's induction and hypothesis. *Philosophical Review*, 1959, **68**, 247–253.
Salmon, W. C., Vindication of induction. In H. Feigl and G. Maxwell (Eds.), *Current Issues in the Philosophy of Science*. New York: Holt, Rinehart & Winston, 1961.
Salmon, W. C., Rejoinder to Barker. In H. Feigl and G. Maxwell (Eds.), *Current Issues in the Philosophy of Science*. New York: Holt, Rinehart and Winston, 1961.
Salmon, W. C., On vindicating induction. In H. E. Kyburg, Jr. and E. Nagel (Eds.), *Induction: Some Current Issues*. Middletown, Conn.: Wesleyan University Press, 1963.
Salmon, W. C., The concept of inductive evidence. *American Philosophical Quarterly*, 1965, **2**, 1–6.
Salmon, W. C., Rejoinder to Barker and Kyburg. *American Philosophical Quarterly*, 1965, **2**, 13–16.
Salmon, W. C., Rejoinder to Kyburg. *Philosophy of Science*, 1965, **32**, 152–154.
Salmon, W. C., Consistency, transivity, and inductive support. *Ratio*, 1965, **7**, 164–169.
Salmon, W. C., Day's inductive probability. Review in *Philosophical Review*, 1965, **72**, 373–378.
Salmon, W. C., *The foundation of scientific inference*. Pittsburgh: University of Pittsburgh Press, 1966.
Salmon, W. C., The justification of inductive rules of inference. In I. Lakatos (Ed.), *The Problem of Inductive Logic*. Amsterdam: North-Holland Publishing Co., 1968.
Salmon, W. C., Who needs inductive acceptance rules? in I. Lakatos (Ed.), *The Problem of Inductive Logic*. Amsterdam: North-Holland Publishing Co., 1968.
Sayre, K. M., On disagreement about perception. *Inquiry*, 1964, 7(2), 143–162.
Schagrin, M. L., An analytic justification of induction. *British Journal for the Philosophy of Science*, 1963–64, **14**, 343–344.
Scheffler, I., Inductive inference: A new approach. *Science*, 1958, **127**, 177–181.
Scheffler, I., *The anatomy of inquiry*. New York: Alfred A. Knopf, 1963.
Schick, F., Katz's The Problem of Induction and its Solution. Review in *Journal of Philosophy*, 1963, **60**, 453–462.
Schick, F., Consistency. *Philosophical Review*, 1966, **75**, 467–495.
Schjelderup, H., *Det skjulte menneske*. Oslo: J. W. Cappelens forlag, 1969.

Schmidt, S. J., *Sprache und Denken als sprachphilosophisches Problem von Locke bis Wittgenstein.* Den Haag: Martinus Nijhoff, 1968.

Schoenberg, J., Confirmation by observation and the paradox of the ravens. *British Journal for the Philosophy of Science*, 1964–65, **15**, 200–212.

Scriven, M., The principle of inductive simplicity. *Philosophical Studies*, 1955, **6**, 26–30.

Scriven, M., Definitions, explanations, and theories. In H. Feigl, M. Scriven, and G. Maxwell (Eds.), *Minnesota Studies in the Philosophy of Science*, Vol. II (*Concepts, Theories and the Mind-Body Problem*). Minneapolis: University of Minnesota Press, 1958.

Scriven, M., Explanation and prediction in evolutionary theory. *Science*, 1959, **130**, 477–482.

Scriven, M., Explanations, predictions, and laws. In H. Feigl and G. Maxwell (Eds.), *Minnesota Studies in the Philosophy of Science*, Vol. III (*Scientific Explanation, Space and Time*). Minneapolis: University of Minnesota Press, 1962.

Sellars, W., *Science, perception and reality.* London: Routledge & Kegan Paul, 1963.

Sellars, W., Induction as vindication. *Philosophy of Science*, 1964, **31**, 197–231.

Shimony, A., Coherence and the axiom of confirmation. *Journal of Symbolic Logic*, 1955, **20**, 1–28.

Simmel, G., Über eine Beziehung der Selectionslehre zur Erkenntnistheorie. *Archiv für systematische Philosophie* (Neue Folge der philosophischen Monatshefte), *Bd I* Heft 1. Berlin: Verlag von Georg Reimer, 1895.

Simon, H. A., On judging the plausibility of theories. In B. van Rootselaar and J. F. Staal (Eds.), *Logic, Methodology and Philosophy of Science* III. Amsterdam: North-Holland Publishing Co., 1968.

Skjervheim, H., Reason and modern logic. *Inquiry*, 1957, **1**(4), 243–246.

Skjervheim, H., *Objectivism and the study of man.* Oslo: Universitetsforlaget, 1959.

Skjervheim, H., *Vitenskapen om mennesket og den filosofiske refleksjon.* Oslo: Johan Grundt Tanum forlag, 1964.

Skyrms, B., On failing to vindicate induction. *Philosophy of Science*, 1965, **32**, 253–268.

Skyrms, B., *Choice and chance: An introduction to inductive logic.* Belmont, California: Dickenson Publishing Co., 1966.

Skyrms, B., Nomological necessity and the paradoxes of confirmation. *Philosophy of Science*, 1966, **33**, 230–249.

Skyrms, B., The explication of "x knows that p." *Journal of Philosophy*, 1967, **64**, 373–389.

Skyrms, B., A neglected logical lapse in Reichenbach's pragmatic justification of induction. *Methodology and Science*, 1968, **2**, 155–159.

Slote, M. A., Some thoughts on Goodman's riddle. *Analysis*, 1967, **27**(4), 128–132.

Smith, C. A. B., Consistency in statistical inference and decision. *The Journal of the Royal Statistical Society*, B, 1961, **23**, 1–7.

Smith, H. W., *Kamongo, or, the lungfish and the padre.* New York: The Viking Press, 1956 (Compass Books Edition).

Soal, S. G. and Goldney, K. M., Experiments in precognitive telepathy. *Proceedings of the Society for Psychical Research*, Vol. XLVII, 1943, 1–14.

Spilsbury, R. J., A note on induction. *Mind*, 1949, **58**, 215–217.

Stegmüller, W., *Das Wahrheitsproblem und die Idee der Semantik.* Wien, New York: Springer-Verlag, 1968.

Stern, K., Linguistic restrictionism and the idea of "potential meaning." *The Monist*, 1969, **52**(2), 246–261.

Suppes, P., Concept formation and Bayesian decision. In J. Hintikka and P. Suppes (Eds.), *Aspects of Inductive Logic*. Amsterdam: North-Holland Publishing Co., 1966.

Suppes, P., A Bayesian approach to the paradoxes of confirmation. In J. Hintikka and P. Suppes (Eds.), *Aspects of Inductive Logic*. Amsterdam: North-Holland Publishing Co., 1966.

Swinburne, R. G., "Grue." *Analysis*, 1968, **28**(4), 123-128.

Tennessen, H., The fight against revelation in semantical studies. *Synthese*, 1950, Vol. VIII, 231-267.

Tennessen, H., *Integrasjon og erkjendelse*. Filosofiske problemer nr. 18. Oslo: Universitetsforlaget, 1955 and 1959.

Tennessen, H. and Gullvaag, I. *Logical analysis and definiteness of intention*. Oslo: Universitetsforlaget, 1955 and 1960.

Tennessen, H., Note on the confusion of evidence and illustration. *The Journal of Philosophy*, 1959, Vol. LVI, No. 18, 733-736.

Tennessen, H., On worthwhile hypotheses. *Inquiry*, 1959, **2**(3), 183-198.

Tennessen, H., Evidence and illustration. *Synthese*, 1959, Vol. XI, No. 3, 274-276.

Tennessen, H., What should we say? *Inquiry*, 1959, **2**(4), 263-291.

Tennessen, H., Logical oddities and locutional scarcities. *Synthese*, 1959, Vol. XI, No. 4, 376-378.

Tennessen, H., Vindication of the Humpty Dumpty attitude towards language. *Inquiry*, 1960, **3**(2), 185-198.

Tennessen, H., Empirical semantics and the soft sciences. In *International Congress for Logic, Methodology and Philosophy of Science*. (Abstract of contributed papers). Stanford, Calif.: Stanford University Press, 1960.

Tennessen, H., On making sense. *The Journal of Philosophy*, 1960, Vol. LVII, No. 24, 764-765.

Tennessen, H., Whereof one has been silent, thereof one may have to speak. *The Journal of Philosophy*, 1961, Vol. LVIII, No. 10, 263-274.

Tennessen, H., Permissible and impermissible locutions: "Principle of tolerance" versus "Ordinary language philosophy." In B. Kazemier and D. Vuysje (Eds.), *Logic and Language, Studies Dedicated to Professor Rudolf Carnap on the Occasion of His Seventieth Birthday*. Dordrecht, Holland: D. Reidel Publishing Co., 1962 (also printed in *Synthese*, 1960, Vol. XII, No. 4, 495-508).

Tennessen, H., *Introduction to empirical semantics*. Edmonton, Alberta: University of Alberta Bookstore, 1962.

Tennessen, H., *Thirty-six lectures on topics in philosophy of science*. Edmonton, Alberta: University of Alberta Bookstore (Mimeo), 1963.

Tennessen, H., *Language analysis and empirical semantics. Eighteen essays*. Edmonton, Alberta: University of Alberta Bookstore, 1964.

Tennessen, H., Ordinary language *in memoriam*. *Inquiry*, 1965, **8**, 225-249.

Tennessen, H., History is science: Preliminary remarks towards an empirical, experimentally oriented behavioural science of history. *The Monist*, 1969, **55**(1), 116-134.

Tennessen, H., Om det finnes absurde setninger. *Norsk Filosofisk Tidsskrift*, Vol. 4, Nr. 2, 1969, 55-88.

Tennessen, H., Science of history and notions of personality. In W. Yourgrau (Ed.), *Physics, Logic, and History*. New York: Plenum Press, 1970.

Tennessen, H. *Notes on symbolic logic.* Edmonton: University of Alberta Bookstore, 3rd ed., 1970.

Tennessen, H. Five futile attempts to show that the problem of induction is no problem. Paper read before *The Boston Colloquium of Philosophy of Science*, May 1963, forthcoming.

Tennessen, H., On what there was. In R. E. Olson and A. M. Paul (Eds.), *Contemporary Philosophy in Scandinavia.* Baltimore, Md.: The Johns Hopkins Press, 1972.

Thomson, J. J., Grue. *The Journal of Philosophy*, 1966, **63**, 289–309.

Thomson, J. J., More grue. *The Journal of Philosophy*, 1966, **63**, 528–534.

Törnebohm, H., *A logical analysis of the theory of relativity.* Stockholm: Almquist & Wiksell, 1952.

Törnebohm, H., *Information and confirmation.* Göteborg, Acta Universitatis Gothoborgensis, 1964.

Törnebohm, H., Two measures of evidential strength. In J. Hintikka and P. Suppes (Eds.), *Aspects of Inductive Logic.* Amsterdam: North-Holland Publishing Co., 1966.

Tuomela, R., Inductive generalization in an ordered universe. In J. Hintikka and P. Suppes (Eds.), *Aspects of Inductive Logic.* Amsterdam: North-Holland Publishing Co., 1966.

Tyrrell, G. N. M., *The personality of man.* Melbourne, London, Baltimore: Penguin Books, 1947.

Tyrrell, G. N. M., *The nature of human personality.* (3rd ed.) Melbourne, London, Baltimore: Penguin Books, 1954.

Ullian, J., More on 'Grue' and "Grue". *Philosophical Review*, 1961, **70**, 386–389.

Ulmer, K., Die Vielfalt der Wahrheit in den Wissenschaften und ihre Einheit. In K. Ulmer (Ed.), *Die Wissenschaften und die Wahrheit.* Stuttgart, Berlin, Köln, Mainz: W. Kohlhammer Verlag, 1966.

Vendler, Z., *Linguistics in philosophy.* Ithaca, New York: Cornell University Press, 1967 (and 1968).

Vigotsky, L. S., *vide* Vygotsky, L. S.

Vincent, R. H., The paradox of ideal evidence. *Philosophical Review*, 1962, **71**, 497–503.

Vincent, R. H., The paradoxes of confirmation. *Mind*, 1964, **73**, 273–279.

Vincent, R. H., The problem of the unexamined individual. *Mind*, 1964, **73**, 550–556.

Vygotsky (or Vigotsky), L. S., Thought and speech. *Psychiatry*, 1939, **2**(1), 29–54.

Vygotsky, L. S., *Thought and language.* Cambridge, Mass.: The M.I.T. Press; New York and London: John Wiley & Sons, 1962.

Wald, A., *Statistical decisions functions.* New York: John Wiley & Sons, 1952.

Wallace, J. R., Goodman, logic, induction. *The Journal of Philosophy*, 1966, **63**, 310–328.

Watkins, J. W. N., Mr. Stove's blunders. *Australasian Journal of Philosophy*, 1959, **37**, 240–241.

Watkins, J. W. N., A reply to Mr. Stove's reply. *Australasian Journal of Philosophy*, 1960, **38**, 54–58.

Wheatley, J., Entrenchment and engagement. *Analysis*, 1967, **27**(4), 119–127.

Whiteley, C. H., On the justification of induction. *Analysis*, 1939, **7**, 68–72.

Whorf, B. L., *Language, thought and reality*, (edited by J. B. Carol). Cambridge, Mass.: The M.I.T. Press; New York, London: John Wiley & Sons, 1956.

Will, F. L., Will the future be like the past? *Mind*, 1947, Vol. LVI, No. 222, 332–347.

Will, F. L., Generalization and evidence. In M. Black (Ed.), *Philosophical Analysis.* Ithaca New York: Cornell University Press, 1950.

Will, F. L., Kneale's theories of probability and induction. *Philosophical Review*, 1954, **63**, 19–42.
Will, F. L., Justification and induction. *Philosophical Review*, 1959, **68**, 359–372.
Wittgenstein, L., *Schriften*, Vols. 1 and 2. Frankfurt am Main: Suhrkamp Verlag, 1960–63.
Wittgenstein, L., *Bemerkungen über die Grundlagen der Mathematik*. Oxford: Basil Blackwell, 1967.
Wright, G. H. von, *A treatise on induction and probability*. London: Routledge and Kegan Paul, 1951.
Wright, G. H. von, *The logical problem of induction*. Oxford: Basil Blackwell, 1965 (1st ed. 1941, *Fasc. III, Acta Philosophica Fennica*).
Yourgrau, W., Herman Bondi: Assumption and myth in physical theory. *Inquiry*, 1970, **13**(3), 332–334.
Zanstra, H., Relativity for philosophers: A brief exposition of the facts, theories and methods of thinking. *Methodology and Science*, 1969, **2**, 140–166.
Zapffe, P. W., Kategorier og virkelighets-relation. *Nordisk sommeruniversitet 1954*. København: Munksgaard, 1955.
Ziff, P., *Semantic analysis*. Ithaca, New York: Cornell University Press, 1960.
Øfsty, A., Some problems of counter-inductive policy as opposed to inductive. *Inquiry*, 1962, **5**, 267–283.

V

THE CONCEPT OF COGNITION IN CONTEMPORARY PSYCHOLOGY

Myron Moroz

The Center for Advanced Study in Theoretical Psychology

"Cognition" means "knowledge"; anyone interested in the "psychology of knowing" could expect to find some enlightenment in the numerous psychological studies of cognition or cognitive processes. This paper thus began as an attempt to explore the place and usefulness of the concepts of "cognition" and "knowledge" in psychology and to evaluate the relevance and potential contributions of psychological research on cognitive functions to the philosophical problem of knowledge. It soon became evident, however, that the concepts of cognition needed clarification before the broader problem could be approached. The present paper is, therefore, an attempt to analyze the usage of the concepts of "cognition", "cognitive process", and similar terms.

THE PROBLEM

The concept of "cognition" or "cognitive process" does not have a systematic status in psychology comparable to that of "learning", "perception", or "motivation". Instead, it is used in a variety of ways by various psychologists—if it is used at all.

It is sometimes assumed that "cognition" and "cognitive process" apply to psychological processes vaguely described as having to do with the acquisition of knowledge. Thus, a report of the Harvard University Center for Cognitive Studies states the following: "Cognition is knowing, and cognitive studies are studies of what and how people know: how we gather, categorize, store, use, communicate knowledge (Harvard University, The Center of Cognitive Studies, 1965, p. 3)." Similarly, George (1962) suggests that "cognition is primarily concerned with knowing and knowledge (p. 21)." This is, of course, justified etymologically but unless we have a definition of "knowledge" in psychological terms, the suggestion is not likely to be very helpful. Furthermore, some psychologists who are specifically concerned with the development of a "psychology of knowledge" or "knowing processes" (for example, Campbell, 1959; Royce, 1964) scarcely refer to the work of psychologists who claim to study "cognitive processes."

Disregarding the possibility that "knowledge psychologists" are unaware of the work of "cognition psychologists", this fact can mean that either the two groups are not using the term "knowledge" in the same sense or that "cognition psychologists" have little to offer to illuminate the problem of knowledge.

Other psychologists use the terms "cognition" and "cognitive process" to refer vaguely to various groups of psychological processes; still others do not use these terms at all. Even a cursory acquaintance with the psychological literature reveals two facts: (1) in spite of the fact that many psychologists use "cognitive" terms without any explicit definition, thus implying that there is general agreement on the usage of these terms, "cognitive" terms are used in several, sometimes ill-defined, senses by different writers (and sometimes by the same writers on different occasions). (2) It is possible to offer a reasonably exhaustive systematic presentation of psychology without explicitly using "cognitive" concepts. The prime example here is an operant analyst. To add to the confusion, some psychologists *seem* to be talking about processes that would be called "cognitive" by others, but refer to them by other terms (higher mental processes, complex processes, etc.).

The writer came to these conclusions after attempting to look up the words "cognitive" and "cognition" in the indices of 14 fairly recent textbooks of introductory psychology which happened to be on his shelf. The survey is admittedly incomplete, but not systematically biased. Of the 14 books surveyed, only one (McKeachie and Doyle, 1966) uses the term "cognition". It is included in the titles of two chapters: "Cognition: memory, language, and meaning;" "Cognition: reasoning, problem solving, decision making, and intelligence." Surprisingly, Krech and Crutchfield (1958) omit the term entirely, even though in their later textbook of social psychology (Krech et al., 1962) they make "cognition" one of their basic explanatory concepts and devote an entire chapter to it.[1] Five textbooks include "cognitive processes" or "cognitive functions" in their indices. In Whittaker's book (1965) this turns out to be the title of a section including chapters on thinking, the sensory basis of perceiving, and perception. In

Kendler's book (1968) "cognitive processes" is used as the title of a chapter which includes the treatment of symbolic and conceptual behavior, problem solving, etc.; together with learning, memory, verbal behavior, and frustration and conflict, it is a part of the section on "complex psychological processes." Sensation, perception, conditioning, and motivation, on the other hand, comprise "basic psychological processes." In Isaacson, Hutt, and Blum's book (1965) "cognitive functions" are compressed into one section (including organization of cognitive functions and simulation of cognitive behavior) in the chapter on verbal learning and higher cognitive functions. Similarly, in Hilgard and Atkinson's book (1967) "cognitive processes" occur in the section on simulation within the chapter on "thinking, language and problem solving." Finally, Ruch (1963) mentions "cognitive processes" briefly in connection with his discussion of field theories and "cognitive functions" in his discussion of emotions.

In addition, the adjective "cognitive" is used in a more restrictive sense in various combinations. Thus, "cognitive dissonance" occurs in eight textbooks, "cognitive map" in three textbooks, "cognitive consonance" or "cognitive harmony" and "cognitive theory" in two books each, and "cognitive development", "cognitive factor", "cognitive slippage", "cognitive strain", and "cognitive component" in one book each.

Finally, two introductory textbooks get along without mentioning "cognition" or "cognitive" at all. One (Galanter, 1966) is a somewhat unusual textbook oriented toward a systematization of psychological knowledge in terms of a few basic concepts. The other (Lewis, 1963) is a behavioristically oriented book on "scientific principles of psychology".

Even from a casual survey of this sort one can conclude that "cognition" or "cognitive process" can variously mean "sensation, perception, and thinking," or what is usually described as "thinking" or "thinking and language," or "one type of thinking or one approach to thinking." In addition, the adjective "cognitive" can be used in various combinations to describe one aspect (i.e., the cognitive aspect) of some psychological phenomena. Finally, one can write a systematic exposition of psychological concepts or scientific principles of psychology without using terms like "cognition" or "cognitive process." It would appear, then, that these terms are not particularly useful or necessary in psychology—unless we can find a more precise meaning for them.

The present paper will, therefore, attempt to analyze the meanings of "cognitive" words in more precise terms and to review possible criteria for distinguishing "cognitive" and "noncognitive" states and processes. It will also attempt to specify the important issues involved in the usage of these terms and to discuss the usefulness of the concept of "cognition" in contemporary psychology.

The following analysis will be based primarily on the work of psychologists who use "cognitive" words (or their equivalents) in their own conceptualizations and, moreover, who attempt to use them more precisely and more specifically than the examples cited above.

The writer is aware of the fact that he is attempting to deal with complex problems with many ramifications in various areas of psychology. The present paper is, therefore, regarded as an attempt to bring out and clarify some theoretical issues rather than to offer a definite solution to the problem. In the course of the following discussion references will be made to the work of various authors. These are not offered as exhaustive summaries of the work of these authors but rather as illustrations of various possible usages of "cognitive" words and various approaches to the problem.

THE USE OF "COGNITIVE" WORDS

One possible way to approach the problem might be to analyze the grammatical forms in which "cognitive" words appear in the English language—primarily in the psychological literature. This, however, seems to be only a partial solution, since, as noted above, some writers seem to be describing "cognitive" phenomena without actually using "cognitive" words. The real issue seems to be the criterion used—sometimes implicitly—by various writers to distinguish states and processes of various levels of complexity.

Cognitive words occur as nouns ("cognition"), as adjectives ("cognitive"), and—very infrequently—as verbs ("cognize"). Of these, the noun and verb forms can readily be replaced by other terms and therefore, their use does not raise any important conceptual issues by itself. The adjective "cognitive" usually cannot be replaced however, without attributing one of several possible meanings to it.

Cognition

The term "cognition" occurs in two different forms which will be called here the singular and the collective form and which parallel Rozeboom's "thing-kind" and "abstract-particular" (Rozeboom, 1965) usages of "memory". Both are used primarily by social psychologists representing the "cognitive" point of view; they can be illustrated by the following statements from Krech, Crutchfield, and Ballachey's (1962) book: "Cognition is selectively organized ... (p. 20);" "The cognition of persons, no less than the cognition of objects, is selectively organized (p. 55);" "The separate cognitions of the individual about the objects and persons in his world develop into systems of cognitions (p. 30)."

The first (the collective) usage of "cognition" can be traced to the classical tripartite division of mind into cognition, conation, and affect. Each of these three terms referred to a function or "faculty" of mind; thus "cognition" was the faculty concerned with knowing. This usage is mainly of historical interest at present, although it still occurs occasionally (see, for example, the definition of "cognition" by Drever, 1952, and the discussion of the abstract-particular usage of "memory" by Rozeboom, 1965).

In the more modern usage, "cognition" usually refers to a "totality of beliefs" or "a system of beliefs", which usage raises no specific conceptual issues (it is not implied, of course, that the terms "belief" and "system" are conceptually clear). Occasionally, the term "cognition" is used to describe certain *activities* or *processes*, as in George's (1962) book: "By cognition, we shall mean the way human beings *perceive* and *learn*, how they reason and think, even how they remember and imagine (p. 11)." In this sense, "cognition" is equivalent to the more frequent "cognitive process," which will be discussed extensively below.

In the singular form, "cognition" can be translated as "individual belief" or "individual attitude"; it is usually implied that the beliefs or attitudes are conscious. Once again, this usage raises no issues that are not inherent in the concepts of "belief" or "attitude."

Cognize

The verb "cognize" is used very infrequently and usually can be readily translated as "perceive", "understand", or "become aware of", depending on the context. Again, no specific issue peculiar to "cognizing" and absent in the other terms seems to be involved.

Cognitive

The same cannot be said, however, of the adjectival form in various combinations such as "cognitive theory", "cognitive psychology", "cognitive processes", etc. It is in this context that important conceptual issues arise.

First of all, a distinction must be made, as was done by Van de Geer and Jaspars (1966), between the use of "cognitive" to describe (1) an approach to psychology or a theory of psychology and (2) a kind of psychological process or an aspect of a psychological process.

Cognitive approach or theory

The issue of a "cognitive" versus an $S - R$ approach to psychology is a familiar one to psychologists and will not be discussed here. As Van de Geer and Jaspars (1966) note, the issue has become blurred recently, since $S - R$ psychologists do not hesitate to refer to internal mediational events any longer. Perhaps the current battle lines are drawn between "mediation" theorists on the one hand and "operant analysts" on the other (see Forehand, 1966, for a recent discussion).

Examples of this usage of "cognitive" are represented by the phrases "cognitive theory" or "cognitive psychology." A "cognitive" psychologist, of course, uses "cognitive" terms in his conceptualizations. He also asserts that his approach is the best, if not the only, approach to psychology and that it can, in principle at least, provide a relatively complete system of psychology. The term "cognitive psychology" is also used in a somewhat different though related way by Neisser (1967); this usage is discussed below.

"Cognitive" as referring to subject matter

This represents the most frequent usage of the term "cognitive". It is also the usage that is most often vague and ill-defined and, therefore, most in the need of clarification.

First of all, "cognitive" as applied to subject matter seems to be used in two different ways: (1) "cognitive" can mean an *aspect* of a psychological process; in this case it can be applied to any psychological process, or at least to any psychological process in certain organisms. (2) On the other hand, "cognitive" can mean a *kind* of psychological process; from this point of view, there are "cognitive" processes and there are other, "non-cognitive" processes in the organism.

Both of these usages raise the problem of the *criterion* of cognitive processes which would make it possible to distinguish between "cognitive" and "non-cognitive" psychological processes (or aspects of psychological processes). Various possible criteria will be discussed below; some authors state them explicitly, others only imply them in their writings.

Cognitive as an aspect

This usage of "cognitive" can be exemplified by reference to Neisser's recent book (Neisser, 1967). Judging from the title of his book (*Cognitive Psychology*) and the title of the first chapter ("The cognitive approach"), the reader might suspect that it represents another exposition of the "cognitive" point of view in psychology. A closer perusal of the first chapter, however, reveals an important difference. Neisser defines his subject matter as follows: "As used here, the term 'cognition' refers to all the processes by which the sensory input is transformed, reduced, elaborated, stored, recovered, and used (Neisser, 1967, p. 4)." He continues in the next paragraph: "Given such a sweeping definition, it is apparent that cognition is involved in everything a human being might possibly do; that every psychological phenomenon is a cognitive phenomenon. But although cognitive psychology is concerned with all human activity rather than some fraction of it, the concern is from a particular point of view. Other viewpoints are equally legitimate and necessary (p. 4)." It is apparent that Neisser's usage of "cognitive psychology" is different from that of traditional "cognitive" psychologists. "Cognitive" seems to refer to the processing of the stimulus input by the organism, including long deferred effects of stimulation. The assumption is made that such processing is involved in all psychological activities. Other possible approaches to psychology include the dynamic, behavioristic, and psychological viewpoints.

A similar usage is represented by Fowler (1962), who states that "cognition is involved in all mental processes, from conditioning, discrimination, and perception to intellective processes, concept formation and of course, cognitive functioning itself (p. 116)." In a more restricted sense, Mandler (1967) seems to suggest a similar point of view when he states that "much, if not all, of human verbal behavior is subject to the operation of cognitive Processes (p. 6)."

Cognitive as a kind of psychological process

The basic issue in this—the most common-usage of "cognitive" terms—is the determination of a criterion or criteria of "cognitive" processes which could be used to distinguish them from "non-cognitive" processes. Various criteria have been used by various writers, often without an explicit definition. In the following section a number of possible criteria will be reviewed roughly in the order of decreasing inclusiveness, and then a suggested definition of "cognitive" processes will be offered.

It should be remembered that not all writers use the term "cognitive" specifically; the following section is, therefore, not so much an analysis of "cognitive" words any longer, but rather a search for meaningful criteria which could be used to distinguish between different types ("lower" and "higher") of psychological processes.

POSSIBLE CRITERIA OF "COGNITIVE" PROCESSES

Cognitive process as any non-emotional psychological process

"Cognitive" is sometimes used to refer to a variety of psychological processes without explicitly stating their common characteristics. When used in this sense, the "cognitive" processes always include thinking and, usually, some other psychological processes: either perception or learning, or both.

For example, George's book on "cognition" (George, 1962) includes chapters on conditioned response, learning, perception, memory, thinking, and language. It is difficult to see what all these processes have in common; George's definition of "cognition" is not very helpful: "By cognition, we shall mean the way human beings perceive and learn, how they reason and think, even how they remember and imagine; and how their 'minds' work in the ordinary day-to-day activities of life (George, 1962, p. 11)." At this point one may wonder why this is a book on "cognition" and not on "general psychology." However, more clues are offered later in the book: "cognition" is described as being "primarily concerned with knowing and knowledge (p. 21)" and as dealing "with those aspects of thought that have been separated from the emotional aspect of knowledge (p. 21)". The definition of "cognition" in terms of "knowledge" is not very helpful unless we know what "knowledge" represents in psychological terms, and thus we are left with the presence or absence of the emotional aspects as the main criterion. This is, of course, reminiscent of the classical usage of "cognition" as one "faculty" of the mind. Most psychologists would find this definition too broad to be particularly useful, not to speak of the difficulty in separating emotional and non-emotional aspects of psychological processes.

Cognitive process as generalization

A similar broad definition of cognitive processes is offered by Manis (1966). His book *Cognitive processes* includes chapters on learning, memory, generalization, concept formation, language, thinking and problem solving; perception is left out, however. What do these processes have in common? "The main feature that these areas hold in common is an emphasis upon intelligent non-reflexive behavior, which typically serves to facilitate man's ability to cope successfully with his environment (Manis, 1966, pp. 2–3)". Again, the reader may wonder what distinguishes "intelligent non-reflexive behavior" from other types of behavior; in Manis' case it is the ability to generalize or "to go beyond what is (explicitly) given (p. 3)." This theme is developed in a later chapter, where the author discusses stimulus generalization, primary and mediated, and response generalization, primary and acquired. The lowest, most primitive variety of a "cognitive process" would thus be represented by any behavior exhibiting generalization, including generalization based on a "simple perceptual error (p. 37)," or, in other words, inability to discriminate. One may well wonder why this would be a case of "intelligent non-reflexive behavior." Also it is difficult to visualize an example of a "non-cognitive" process, since presumably all behavior acts, including reflexes, involve some generalization (even though we do not always take the trouble to demonstrate it).

It should be noted that the distinction between "reflexive" and "intelligent" or "higher" behavior is a common one in psychology, but it is usually based on some more specific criterion.

Cognitive process as a mediating process

A conception of cognitive processes which is worked out in greater detail and which suggests a definite criterion of such processes has been offered by Hebb. In his 1960 article (Hebb, 1960) he calls for the establishment of a "behavioristics of the thought process" and states that the term "cognitive" has "a reference to features of behavior that do not fit the $S - R$ formula (Hebb, 1960, p. 4)." As to the nature of these features—they are also called "mind" or "consciousness"—we find later in the same article that they are "loose designations of the complex interaction of mediating processes in the intact, waking higher animal (p. 6)." A mediating process, in turn, is defined in another place as "what happens between sensory event and response, linking them up (it 'mediates' the gap between them) (Hebb, 1966, p. 79)". If taken literally to mean any internal event occurring between a sensory event and a response, it could be part of almost any kind of behavior, since even simple reflexes usually involve the activity of "internuncial" neurons. But Hebb has something else in mind and the term "mediating process" may not be the best for what he suggests.

Hebb makes a distinction between two main classes of behavior: (1) lower or reflexive, which consists of straight-through connections between receptors and effectors, and (2) higher or cognitive, which involves complex closed loops of neurons in the brain (or mediating processes). Both types of behavior are affected by sensory input, but while reflexive behavior is *sense-dominated*, higher behavior can be influenced or even determined by mediating processes. Since the degree of determination by mediating processes may vary, Hebb suggests that the two classes of behavior may actually merge into each other. Hebb thus suggests the important idea that "cognitive" may be a matter of degree.

Hebb also suggests that lower or reflexive behavior can be comprised by the $S - R$ formula; higher behavior, however, is not determined by the stimulus alone. One can perhaps argue with the first half of this statement, but the distinction is a meaningful one; later, Hebb offers a more specific criterion of the two types of behavior. Immediacy and constancy of response to the adequate stimulus characterize the reflexive behavior, while the delay between stimulus and response and the ability to hold excitation are the marks of the higher type of behavior.

Two aspects of Hebb's view are important in the present context. One is his conception of cognitive processes as *internal brain events* or, more specifically, complex closed loops of neurons (his cell assembly theory is one possible explanation of how these processes work, but is not essential to his theory). This definition will later be contrasted with a definition of cognitive processes as a relation between an internal (brain) event and an external event. The other point of interest is his definition of cognitive processes as mediating *processes* rather than mediating *responses*; cognitive processes co-determine and even *initiate* behavioral acts.

The idea of systems of brain processes as determiners of behavior was expressed earlier by Lashley (1958); according to him, neurons in the brain are organized into "trace systems" and the activity of these systems constitutes "mind."

Cognitive process as a mediating representational process

Several conceptions of cognitive processes have been developed within the framework of Hullian theory, with a particular reliance on Hull's concept of "fractional anticipatory goal response" or "pure stimulus act," which means a response the sole function of which is to generate stimulation. Such responses may be used, according to Hullian theory, to anticipate or "represent" some events in the environment.

Osgood's "behavioristic analysis of perception and language as cognitive phenomena" (Osgood, 1967) represents one such conception; other similar conceptions will be mentioned in connection with the discussion of verbal mediating processes. Osgood defines cognitive processes as internal or mediating processes, but, in addition, he emphasizes the "representational" function of such processes. This is reflected in his term "representational mediating processes," which he uses frequently.

Osgood's model of behavior includes two stages and three levels of organization between stimulus and response. The *decoding* stage is concerned with input functions, the *encoding* stage with the output functions of the organism. Both decoding and encoding occur on three levels of organization.

The *projection* level is concerned with the mapping of sensory events upon the sensory cortex (on the decoding side) and the mapping of the voluntary muscle system upon the motor cortex (on the encoding side). The *integration* level is concerned with the organization of sensory input and motor skills ($S - S$ and $R - R$ connections). Finally, the level of *representation* involves the formation of mediational representational processes, which function as signs of environmental events.

Osgood suggests that sensory events and motor events can be associated at all levels of organization. Associations at the projection and integration level are single-stage connections, either innately "wired in" (unconditioned reflexes) or acquired (conditioned reflexes). But the most important type of association in human beings and probably in higher vertebrates in general, is "via a *two-stage mediation process*. The essential notion here is that in the course of associating external stimuli with overt behavior some representation of this overt behavior becomes anticipatory, producing self-stimulation that has a symbolic function (Osgood, 1957, pp. 91–92)." Rather than being defined in terms of a brain event, a cognitive process is a *relation* between an internal process and an environment event. In another sense, a cognitive process is accorded a more limited function than in Hebb's conception. Since a complete behavioral act starts with a stimulus, cognitive processes function more strictly as mediation processes rather than determiners or initiators of behavior. In fact, Osgood states that their most important function is "as the common term in mediated generalization and transfer (p. 96)."

A similar emphasis on the relational nature of cognitive processes has been expressed by Brunswik in his emphasis on the need for ecological analysis—although his theory is based on different assumptions and belongs within another tradition. The prime aspect of the cognitive problem, according to Brunswik, "would seem to be the over-all correspondence between a certain distal and a certain central variable, so that the former could be considered successfuully mapped into the latter (Brunswik, 1957, p. 8)."

Cognitive process as a categorized representational process

The mark of the conception of cognitive processes to be presented in this section is an explicit distinction between short-term and long-term psychological processes. We can speak of a cognitive process or cognitive functioning when some input process is categorized or related on a non-arbitrary basis to some more persistent internal process. This, of course, implies an "active" view of cognitive functioning—active in the sense of processing of sensory input by the organism (see Gyr *et al.*, 1966 for a relevant discussion). Thus, a distinction is made between sensory input and systems of categories, or cognitive processes and cognitive structures, or, more generally, "process" and "state" variables (Rozeboom, 1965; Spence, 1948), that is variables whose duration roughly corresponds to that of input variables and variables which remain relatively stable and constant.

Most of the conceptions included under this heading originated with the "cognitive" tradition in psychology and usually the treatment of the "input" side, or perception, is more detailed and explicit. We can perhaps look for the origin of this view to Gestalt psychology and field theory with their insistence that the behavioral environment is organized and that behavior is determined by this organized field and not directly by stimuli. But Gestalt psychologists often described the behavioral environment in phenomenological terms—a conception of cognitive processes which will be considered below. Also, their insistence on the applicability of the principles of perception to all "cognitive" phenomena makes their view an "approach" to psychology. The same can be said of Tolman's "cognitive" psychology in view of his claim that general principles of behavior can be derived from studies of lower animals. Nevertheless, some of his major concepts are worth mentioning in the present context. Tolman's distinction between experimental, intervening, and dependent variables is well known by now. A complete behavioral act is initiated by environmental stimuli and physiological states. Certain processes intervene between stimulation and response. These intervening processes include demand variables and cognitive variables, such as expectancies, cognitive maps, and belief–value matrices. Tolman's main interest was in the formation of long-term (or structural) representational processes as a result of learning.

Bruner's system makes an important use of the concept of categorization (coding) and representation. Whereas in his earlier writings Bruner was more concerned with the processes of categorization (Bruner, 1957a, 1957b), in his more recent writings he has turned to studies of various modes of representing information (Bruner 1964, 1966).

Bruner suggests that all cognitive processes involve categorization (or coding); this involves the elaboration of coding systems or schemata which are used in classifying sensory information and which represent the environment to the organism. Coding systems have the status of hypothetical constructs and are defined in functional terms. In recent years, Bruner suggests that there are three ways of coding information (enactive, iconic, and symbolic) and much of his work has been concerned with the relation among these three modes of representation.

Since Bruner stresses the inferential nature of all cognitive processes, his views may be considered a theory or approach to psychology. In fact, he is not explicitly concerned with the kind of distinctions that are being explored here. However, at least one of his collaborators (Potter, 1966) makes a distinction between "simple perceptual processes" and the "more" complex perceptual-cognitive task of recognition (p. 104)." The distinction arises in the course of ontogenetic development; the younger child's behavior in a recognition task is determined largely by the stimulus situation, while the older child makes more use of past information. Potter also makes a distinction between two phases of visual recognition, the organization of the stimulus, and its categorization. One could perhaps once again use the involvement of representational processes, this time in the form of coding systems, as the criterion of cognitive processes in Bruner's system. But it is not clear whether an uncategorized sensory input can produce a behavioral act. Also, coding systems function primarily in coding sensory input and it is not clear whether and to what degree they can initiate behavior.

A similar point of view is represented by Sarbin, Taft and Bailey (1960), who regard cognitive functioning as a process of judgment or inference. Although some simple perceptual processes may be "stimulus bound," in more complex situations relatively more information is contributed by cognitive structures. This process is described as a collocation of a major premise derived from a person's postulate system (i.e. cognitive structure) and a singular minor premise derived from observation (i.e., stimulus input) to derive a conclusion which instantiates an environmental object (i.e. allocates it to a category). Sarbin also offers a more detailed theory of "cognitive organization" of a person. He views it as a multi-dimensional space, corresponding—to a greater or lesser degree—to a multidimensional ecological space. The basic unit of cognition is the *module* (replacing the older ideas, images and schemata), which is defined as a point in the multidimensional cognitive organization. The system is described with a wealth of detail, but for the present purpose two other points are important: The inference process is not necessarily conscious; in fact, phenomenal data are often a poor guide to the description of cognitive functioning. Secondly, cognition can supplant sensory events in guiding behavior. Once again, the criterion of a cognitive process is the degree of involvement of mediating representational processes, which are conceived as organized cognitive structure.

Leeper (1963) is also concerned with the distinction between central processes "which have some heavy dependence on more or less closely preceding receptor stimulations (p. 402)" and "representational processes

(p. 403)." The latter have either limited dependence on recent stimulation or no such dependence. The main function of these representational processes is to serve as "steering or cybernetic processes." More specifically Leeper distinguishes three types of processes: (1) sensory organization processes, (2) briefer representational processes, and (3) long-sustained representational processes. Later in his paper he uses the terms "processes" and "structures" for these brief and long-sustained processes respectively. As to the relation between these processes (both sensory organizational and briefer representational) and structures, Leeper suggests the following: "We need to picture a two-way influence. In one direction, the peripherally supported processes bring changes in the long-sustained processes. The other main relation operates in the other direction, with the background representational processes doing a good deal to determine the character of the shorter phase reactions to current stimulation (Leeper, 1963, p. 409)."

Miller, Galanter and Pribram (1960) offer a conception of cognitive processes which explicitly incorporates the "cybernetic hypothesis". The greatest shortcoming of cognitive theories is, according to these authors, the failure to specify how internal representations control the actions of the organism—the "theoretical vacuum between cognition and action (Miller, Galanter and Pribram, 1960, p. 11)." Their solution is based on the distinction between "image" and the "plan". The image consists of organized representations of facts and values. The plan is a set of instructions organized hierarchically, which can control the activities of the organism. The book, broadly speaking, explores the relation between the image and the plan and, in doing so, relies on the concept of "feedback loop". "The action is initiated by an 'incongruity' between the state of the organism and the state that is being tested for, and the action persists until the incongruity (i.e., the proximal stimulus) is removed (Miller, Galanter and Pribram, 1960, pp. 25–26)."

Cognitive process as a constructed process

Cognitive processes can be viewed as basically *passive* processes of copying reality or *active* processes involving acting upon and a feedback from the environment. Gyr and his co-workers (Gyr *et al.*, 1966), in discussing computer simulation of perception, make a distinction between passive or sensory and active or sensorimotor theories of perception. Furthermore, according to these authors, "active perception" may be used in two broad senses, that of "exploration" (bodily movements and attention) and that of "processing" by the organism.

One can consider categorization as an example of active processing.

Some writers, however, go beyond categorizing and attribute an even more active role to the organism in cognitive functioning. For example, Neisser (1967) emphasizes the constructive aspect of cognition in the sense of "processing." Although he uses the term "cognition" more broadly in the "aspect" sense of the term (as mentioned above), his views are also relevant in the present context. Neisser makes a distinction among at least three levels of "cognitive" functioning: preattentive processes, focal attention, and background processes. His two higher levels of cognitive functioning seem to correspond to what is here called "cognitive types" of psychological processes. Neisser stresses the constructive aspect of all levels of cognitive functioning, but it becomes particularly important in the "analysis by synthesis" characteristic of higher levels. Briefly, he suggests that "percepts" and "images" are constructed from fragmentary cues rather than simply received or recovered from memory; in fact, what is stored in memory are traces of these constructive activities.

One can also take the point of view that cognitive functioning is more than just a processing of stimulus input, but that it involves a complete circuit of activities from sensory input through central processing to behavioral acts which result in sensory feedback. As an example of this approach, Piaget's views have been selected for discussion here—those aspects of his theory which are relevant to the present discussion. The writer relies largely on Flavell's presentation of Piaget's theory (Flavell, 1963).

Piaget starts with the central notion of *adaptation*, which includes the two complementary processes of *assimilation* of information from the environment and *accommodation* to the environment. The operation of these processes results in the development of schemata, or internal cognitive organizations; a sensory event must be related to one or more schemata before it can be said to produce "knowledge."

Piaget makes several distinctions between types of psychological processes which are relevant to the present discussion. Firstly, he regards perception and intelligence as two different types of adaptation (Flavell seems to use "cognition" as interchangeable with "intelligence"). Secondly, he describes the process of cognitive development in terms of qualitative stages. The most significant distinction for the present purpose seems to be the distinction between sensory-motor intelligence of the first stage of development and representational intelligence of the later stages. In the sensory-motor stage, the infant can be said to be concerned with present stimuli and overt actions; in the representational stages, he is concerned with the inner, symbolic manipulations of reality, at first motoric and imagistic, later verbal. These symbolic manipulations differ in complexity; thus, in the *preopera-*

tional stage, the child manipulates isolated internal events; in the *concrete operations* stage, internal events are organized into a system with limited extrapolation; and finally in the *formal operations stage*, the adolescent not only has a well-organized system of representations, but also can extrapolate them to possible events.

Throughout the course of development, the child remains an *active* agent rather than a passive recipient of stimulus input. In Flavell's words, "the cognizing organism is at all levels a very, very active agent who always meets the environment well over halfway, who actually *constructs* his world by assimilating it to schemas while accommodating these schemas to its constraints (Flavell, 1966, p. 71)." At first, this activity involves actual external actions, later it takes the form of manipulating and transforming internal events.

It is the emphasis on *activity* that distinguishes Piaget's views from those discussed in the preceding section. In his review of Bruner's recent book (Bruner *et al.*, 1966), Piaget states that the two central problems of cognitive development are "(1) to determine whether knowledge consists only in copying or imitating reality, or whether to *understand* reality it is necessary to *invent* the structures which enable us to assimilate reality, and consequently (2) to determine whether the actions performed by the subject on reality consist simply in the construction of appropriate images and adequate language, or whether the subject's actions and, later, his operations, *transform* reality and modify objects (Piaget, 1967, p. 532)."

Cognitive process as a symbolic response

This heading (perhaps not the most appropriate since it could be extended to cover other views discussed below) will include the conception of cognitive processes presented by Berlyne (1960). Although Berlyne avoids the term "cognitive" (for unstated though probably very good reasons) and prefers terms like "epistemic," "knowledge," and "thinking," his views are highly relevant to the problem under discusion.

Berlyne's views, like Osgood's and those to be discussed in the following section, represent an extension of Hullian theory. However, Berlyne confines "knowledge" to "certain highly specialized information-gathering and information-storing processes dependent on symbolic processes. It would thus be applicable principally to man, though perhaps also in some minor degree to other mammals possessed of rudimentary representational capacities (Berlyne, 1960, p. 262)." This makes these symbolic processes different from both Osgood's mediational representational responses, which are apparently typical of the behavior of higher vertebrates, and also from the conception of cognitive processes as verbal mediating responses.

"Knowledge," according to Berlyne, consists of habits, which are to be thought of as psychological dispositions demonstrated under appropriate test conditions. Not every habit is knowledge, however; "epistemic habits" can produce responses appropriate to past or absent events. Berlyne restricts the meaning of "knowledge" still further by confining it to behaviors involving "symbolic responses," which make it possible for an organism to represent to itself, and ultimately to convey to others, his future performance or possible performance.

The important distinction in Berlyne's scheme is the distinction between activities involving symbolic processes and those which do not involve such processes. The relation of Berlyne's "symbolic responses" to "mediational representational responses" is not clear; though Berlyne explains his concept of symbolic responses by reference to Osgood's definition of sign, which underlies Osgood's concept of "mediational representational responses," Berlyne's seems to use the term "symbolic response" in a narrower sense, as mentioned above.

As to the function of knowledge, Berlyne states that it "is to overcome the deficiencies of perception by providing internal stimuli, products of symbolic processes, to supplement the external stimuli that originate in outside objects (Berlyne, 1960, p. 266)." More specifically, he mentions classification, ordering, and explanation as the functions of "knowledge" and thus he seems to ascribe a more active role to it than mere mediated generalization and transfer.

Cognitive process as a verbal mediating response

As is widely known, Watson equated thinking with implicit speech and the conceptions discussed in this section may be considered to fall broadly within this tradition. More specifically, they are based—as Osgood's and Berlyne's conceptions—on the Hullian concept of "fractional anticipatory response," interpreted as a verbal response. While Osgood considers his mediational representational processes typical of higher vertebrates, and Berlyne allows his symbolic responses, to a limited degree, in higher mammals, the writers mentioned in this section restrict the use of such mediational responses to articulate humans. It is true that they do not necessarily *define* mediational responses as verbal—Kendler, for example, considers it an intervening variable (Kendler and Kendler, 1962)—but the important distinction which is made or which emerges from their experimental studies is the distinction between articulate humans on the one hand and non-articulate children and subhuman organisms on the other. Whether the behavior of the latter never involves any mediational events or whether it can be mediated by non-verbal mechanisms, is not always clear. Kendler, for one, makes a clear distinction between "single-unit" and "mediated" behavior (Kendler and Kendler, 1962) and his conception will be used as an example.

Kendler attempts to study problem-solving and concept formation within the framework of $S - R$ theory using the experimental paradigm of "reversal and non-reversal shift." In a reversal shift, a subject—after learning a discrimination such as "large" is positive—is forced to respond to another value on the same dimension ("small" is positive). In a non-reversal shift, another dimension, previously irrelevant, becomes relevant— e.g., "black" is now positive regardless of size.

Kendler finds that rats and young children perform better on a non-reversal shift, but older children and college students find a reversal shift easier to learn. The behavior of rats and younger children can be explained by a "single unit theory," but the behavior of older children requires a "mediational theory," according to which non-reversal shift requires the learning of a new mediational response and is, therefore, more difficult.

A similar approach is represented by Goss' concept of "verbal mediating response" (Goss, 1961), Maltzman's "compound habit family hierarchies" (Maltzman, 1955), Cofer's "verbal responses" (Cofer, 1957), and Staats' "verbal habit families" (Staats, 1961). In all these conceptions, the important distinction occurs between verbally mediated and non-mediated (single stage) types of behavior, verbal mediating processes are treated as responses important in generalization and transfer, and the assumption is usually made that mediating events have the same logical status as overt behavior— that of responses.

Cognitive process as a conscious process

Historically, cognition was defined as one part of the conscious mind and it was distinguished from conation and affect. This conception goes back to Kant and is still occasionally met. In modern psychology, a similar conception of cognitive processes is represented by the "phenomenological" approach stemming from Gestalt and field psychology and later represented by writers such as Snygg (1941) and MacLeod (1947, 1964). According to this view, the behavior of an individual is completely determined by his "phenomenological field," or the world as he experiences it. MacLeod, for example, states that a phenomenologist "accepts, as the subject matter of his inquiry, all data of experience (Erlebnis) (MacLeod, 1964, p. 51)." He also "begins his observation of phenomena by suspending his biases, by putting his implicit assumptions in brackets (MacLeod, 1964, p. 52)," including the assumption that there is a real world "out there." MacLeod illustrates his point of view by contrasting Koffka's statement about the central problem of perception—"why it is that we see the world as we do (MacLeod, 1964, p. 52)"—with that of Gibson— "why we see the world as it is (MacLeod, p. 52)." Gibson, according to MacLeod, "stubbornly insists that there is a real world 'out there' to which the phenomenal world can be co-ordinated (p. 52)." A phenomenologist, however, "should first ask: What are the properties of phenomena which invite a belief in the existence of the external world (pp. 52–53)?"

These quotations were included to bring out the conception of cognitive processes implied by this view: cognitive proceses are defined in absolute terms, namely as conscious experience; the fact that these may correspond to some other events is not included in the definition. If this approach is accepted as the only approach to psychology—if we define psychology in these terms—"cognition" becomes the name of an approach or a theory (some other term may of course by used instead of "cognition"). However, not all phenomenological psychologists go as far as this; Snygg (1941) suggests that behavior must also be studied objectively. MacLeod (1964) considers psychological phenomenology as "propaedeutic to a science of psychology (p. 54)." This suggests that there are other processes of importance to psychology which are inaccessible to a phenomenological psychologist; the implied criterion is the presence or absence of conscious experience.

"Cognition," in either the singular or collective sense, and "cognitive" are sometimes used by social psychologists with the meaning of "conscious belief" or a "property of conscious belief". This usage is exemplified by the use of "cognition" in Krech, Crutchfield and Ballachey (1964) and in Festinger (1957), and also by phrases such as "cognitiveh armony," "cognitive dissonance," etc.

Ausubel's views (Ausubel, 1965a, 1965b) represent a similar emphasis on conscious experience, but Ausubel differs from the phenomenological psychologists in at least two important points. Before these are discussed, it must be pointed out that Ausubel uses the term "cognitive" to denote both a viewpoint in psychology and a kind of psychological process; his theory is a "cognitive" theory of "cognitive processes." According to Ausubel, "exponents of the cognitive viewpoint ... regard differentiated and clearly articulated conscious experience (for example, knowing, meaning, understanding) as providing the most significant data for the science of psychology (Ausubel, 1965a, p. 4)." Ausubel does not mention the fact that this is not a generally accepted interpretation of the "cognitive" point of view. Cognitive psychologists such as Tolman and Leeper would certainly reject this definition of "cognitive processes." In fact, Ausubel seems to confuse the "phenomenological" with the more general "cognitive" point of view.

Ausubel differs from the phenomenologists mentioned above in (1) his greater concern with the problem of meaning, and (2) his emphasis on the inferential nature of cognitive processes. The concern with meaning implies a representational function and, therefore, a "relational" conception of cognitive processes. This is well brought out in the following statement: "Thus a symbol acquires representational properties only when it evokes an image or other ideational content in the reacting subject that is cognitively equivalent to that evoked by the designated object itself (Ausubel, 1965b, p. 64)."

The inferential nature of cognitive functioning is revealed in Ausubel's insistence on the fact that new information must be related to, incorporated within, or subsumed under an individual's cognitive structure on a non-arbitrary and substantive basis.

TOWARD A DEFINITION OF "COGNITIVE PROCESSES"

Underlying issues

To return to the original question: what conception of "cognitive processes," if any, emerges from the preceding discussion and what can be said about the usefulness of the concept of "cognition" or "cognitive process?" Perhaps one could begin by trying to reduce the diversity of views presented in the preceding section to a smaller number of underlying issues.

A few years ago, in discussing perceptual theory, O'Neil (1958) proposed five issues or bases of classification: perceiving as active or passive; the perceived as real or phenomenal; the perceived as a term or a proposition; descriptive vs. abstractive modes of analysis; central or proximal location of causal conditions. Since views on these issues tend to be associated, O'Neil found it possible to classify all perceptual theories into discrimination theories, phenomenalist theories, and judgmental theories.

In the present discussion it may be impossible to find issues that apply to all the points of view. However, an attempt will be made to specify some issues that underlie the various usages of "cognitive processes" as a kind of psychological process and to suggest—very tentatively—the position of some representatives of each point of view on each of these issues.

1. Conscious vs functional definition of cognitive processes

This is an old issue in the history of psychology; in its application to cognitive processes it was discussed at some length by Leeper (1951) who came out strongly in favor of a functional definition of cognitive processes. The arguments against restricting the concept of cognitive processes (and, more generally, the field of psychology) to conscious processes are well known; they can be grouped as follows: (1) *pragmatic arguments:* psychology as the study of consciousness limits the field to the normal human adult; (2) arguments based on the studies of the *activity of mind:* from the days of the Würzburg school to some present-day writers (e.g., Neisser, 1967) it has been argued that introspection is a poor guide to psychological processes and that some important constructive activities are not accessible to introspection; (3) arguments based on *personality* studies: apart from the psychoanalytic theory of the unconscious, it has been argued that—particularly in his personal and social relations—a human being is guided by concepts which he cannot formulate explicitly (e.g., Kelly, 1955).

Still, some psychologists prefer to define cognitive processes as conscious experience; the majority of writers reviewed here prefer a functional definition.

Actually, this problem is part of a broader issue, which may be called the *dispositional* vs *observable* definition of cognitive processes. This is obviously related to the intervening variable-hypothetical construct controversy of a few years ago. On the one hand, it is possible to regard cognitive processes as theoretical constructs or dispositional variables which merely abstract the relationships between antecedent and consequent conditions. On the other hand, one can accord cognitive processes the status of "existing" events, which can be directly observed or at least are directly observable in principle. If the latter course is taken, one can regard cognitive processes as *brain events*, or *conscious process*, or *behavioral acts* (stimulus-response connections). The issue is not as clear as might be desired, because some writers—after accepting a dispositional definition—suggest or imply a concrete interpretation.

2. Absolute vs relational definition of cognitive processes

This issue involves the representational function of cognitive processes. It is possible to define a cognitive process as an internal event (e.g., a brain process or a conscious experience), or as an internal event corresponding or related to some other event—usually, but not necessarily, some event "out there." More specifically it is asserted in the second case that cognitive processes "represent," "refer to," or "are about" other entities. Most psychologists accept such "relational" definition of cognitive processes, but the nature of the "aboutness" relationship has not been explicated (Rozeboom, 1965).

3. Mediating vs determining function of cognitive processes (responses vs processes)

Some writers conceive of cognitive processes as serving a rather passive role; a complete act of behavior is initiated by an environmental stimulus and the main function of a cognitive process is in mediated generalization and transfer. Other psychologists, on the other hand, seem to think of cognitive processes as determining or causing behavior—either in conjunction with a stimulus or as a substitute for a stimulus.

This is an important issue since it touches upon some basic assumptions of psychological theory. The distinction that is suggested here represents the distinction between the "reflex" or "reactive" and the "cybernetic" models of behavior. Behavioristic psychology, in an attempt to reject "mentalistic" conceptions, considered an organism a reactive system, with external stimuli being the causative factors. Later behaviorists introduced "intervening variables" (motivational and associative) and the effect of a stimulus is now believed to depend on both the stimulus and the internal conditions of the organism. A complete behavioral act is still presumably initiated by the external stimulus (as in Woodworth's well-known $S - O - R$ formula), which is logically and temporally prior to the response.

A "cybernetic" model, on the other hand, admits the possibility that at least some types of behavior can be inititated by the internal states of the organism—either conditions of the organism acting directly on the nervous system (i.e., without the mediation of afferent pathways) or states of the nervous system itself. The organism continues to act until some "incongruity" between the internal state and the stimulus input is removed. A clearest example of this type of behavior is represented by the appetitive behavior initiated by some internal motivational conditions (Deutsch, 1953). It is assumed by some psychologists that internal representational events can also initiate behavior in this way (Miller, Galanter and Pribram, 1960); in fact, it has been argued that the distinction between motivational and representational processes may be difficult to maintain in higher organisms (Leeper, 1963)—particularly if the latter include evaluations. Neurologically, there is nothing strange about this notion in view of the well-known fact that the nervous system and receptor tissues are spontaneously active. The effect of the stimulus is to alter the spontaneous activity of the nervous system rather than activate it. The issue can perhaps be stated by contrasting Woodworth's $S - O - R$ formula with a possible reformulation: $(S, O) - R$, where S and O could have negative (inhibition), zero, or positive values.

4. Passive vs active conception of cognitive processes

This distinction refers to the way in which cognitive processes are formed: they can be regarded as rather passive copies of environmental events or as active constructions. In the first case, they are completely determined by the input; the organism simply receives and stores stimulus information. In the second case, the organism transforms the stimulus information and cognitive processes are determined jointly by stimulus input and the activity of the organism. Furthermore, as was mentioned above, "activity" may refer to the processing of stimulus information, or to the exploration of the environment (or both).

5. Generality (or extent) of cognitive processes

What organisms can be said to be capable of "cognitive" functioning or what types of "cognitive" processes are there? This is an issue which is usually implied in the definition of cognitive processes. There must be a distinction between Osgood's "mediational representational responses," which are typical of higher vertebrates, Berlyne's "symbolic responses," which, apart from man, occur in higher mammals to a limited extent, and "verbal mediational responses," which are confined to man. It is not clear what the distinction is, particularly between the first two types of processes. Several possible bases for distinction may be suggested: complexity of structure of the representational process, time interval between the original input and re-activation, or nature of function (mediation vs determination of behavior).

It may be advisable to make a distinction between the broader concept of "mediational processes" and the narrower concept of "representational processes" and to speak of the latter when we have evidence that an internal event acts as a substitute for an external event or for an abstracted and generalized feature of the environment.

If the representational function is taken as the distinguishing mark of cognitive processes, the conception of cognitive processes as *verbal* processes seems too restrictive. The weight of evidence coming from numerous studies with animal and human subjects indicates that events can be represented by non-verbal processes.

The terms "representational," "symbolic," and "verbal" are adopted here to denote decreasing degrees of generality of representational processes.

TABLE 1

| Writer | \multicolumn{5}{c}{ISSUES} |
	1	2	3	4	5
Hebb	funct.	absol.	determ.	act.	—
Osgood	funct.	relat.	med.	pass.	repres.
Leeper	funct.	relat.	determ.	act. (proc.)	repres.?
Bruner	funct.	relat.	determ.	act. (proc.)	repres.?
Piaget	funct.?	relat.	determ.	act. (expl.)	symb.?
Berlyne	funct.	relat.	med.	pass.	symb.
Kendler	funct.	relat.	med.	pass.	verb.
MacLeod	consc.	absol.	determ.	pass.	verb.
Ausubel	consc.	relat.	determ.	act.	verb.

Toward a definition of cognitive processes

In his 1951 survey of cognitive processes Leeper (1951) suggested the following: "It is better, therefore, to avoid narrow definitions and to say that cognitive processes include all the means whereby the individual represents anything to himself or uses these representations as a means of guiding his behavior" (p. 736). The majority of writers reviewed in the present paper seem to use the term "cognitive processes" (or its equivalent) in the broad sense suggested by Leeper though they differ in their views on the nature, extent, function etc. of cognitive processes. In a few isolated instances, the term is used in a sense that is mainly of historical interest.

As commonly used, "cognitive processes" can refer to relatively short-term processes (cognitive processes?), processes of a relatively long duration ("cognitions"?), or systems of such processes ("cognition"?) ("cognitive structure"?) Furthermore, in a strict sense "cognitive processes" refers to the activity of the internal representative processes alone; in a broader sense, it refers to any behavior which presumably includes the activity of such processes. The latter is often the popular usage of "cognition" or "cognitive processes"—for example, in the introductory textbooks mentioned in the beginning of this paper.

In spite of the broad general agreement, it seems impossible to offer a precise definition of "cognitive processes" which would be acceptable to everyone concerned. The following suggestion frankly incorporates some of the present writer's views. It is suggested that—to be useful as a psychological concept—the term "cognitive process" must refer to a psychological process having the following characteristics: (1) it is an internal *brain process*, which is potentially observable, though at present usually defined functionally; (2) it is *representational*, in the sense of referring or being related to another event; the issue is complicated because the represented event does not have to be an actual event—it may be a past, future, or imaginary event; (3) it can function as a *substitute* for a stimulus event; (4) it is *actively constructed*, at least in the sense of being "processed"; (5) it is part of an organized system—"*cognitive structure.*" It would simplify matters if we agreed to use the term "cognitive processes" in the strict sense (i.e., internal representative process) and used other terms "perception, thinking reasoning" for the types of behavior which include "cognitive processes," but also have other "non-cognitive" components. The broader usage will no doubt continue, however.

In accordance with the above suggestion, the most general function of "cognitive processes" is the temporal integration of stimulus input. The simplest case of a behavior involving cognitive processes may be represented by what Hebb called "holding of excitation"—retention of stimulus input over a relatively short period of time and matching with subsequent stimulus input (e.g., delayed reaction experiment). In the more complex case, stimulus input may interact with relatively long-term internal representative processes, such as category systems (e.g., recognition of specific objects or instances of a class). And, finally the greatest degree of involvement of "cognitive processes" may be represented by manipulations or transformation of long-term processes themselves (e.g., thinking, reasoning). In addition, there may be psychological activities with a minimal or no involvement of "cognitive processes"—such as the organization of the present sensory input, reflexes, skilled motor acts.

In all of these activities, the representative function of cognition of cognitive processes becomes crucial—the fact that a cognitive process can stand for another event, past or distant or hypothetical. However, the attempt to equate "cognition" with the "acquisition of knowledge" is considered too restrictive if "knowledge" is understood in its usual philosophical sense of "justified true belief." Rather, cognition can be said to be concerned with the construction of a "model" of reality. While the "model" must be of sufficient validity to insure survival, it is easy to show that invalid perceptions and beliefs can be compelling and can influence behavior. Thus it is suggested that "cognition" and "cognitive processes" are broader terms in that they include true and false beliefs and beliefs of indeterminate truth value; "knowledge" is best restricted to "true beliefs" in keeping with the usual philosophical practice.

The above suggestion thus considers the involvement of cognitive processes as a dimension of psychological activity, ranging from zero involvement to such a considerable degree of involvement that the entire psychological activity may be described as "cognitive." The suggestion envisions a hierarchical model of psychological activity (and of the nervous system) somewhat like the models described by Attneave (1961, 1962), Neisser (1967), and Osgood (1957). The main parts of the model include a perceptual (or decoding) system, a motor (or encoding) system, a central or representative system (a "homunculus" in Attneave's words), and, possibly, affective centers. The model makes provisions for the organization of sensory input (Attneave's receptor grouping, Neisser's preattentive processes, Osgood's projection and integration level activities) and the organization of motor skills. Some behaviors are under the direct control of sensory input (Hebb's "sense-dominated" behaviors); others—while never completely free of the influence of the sensory input—involve the cognitive (representative) processes to varying degrees. The representative processes have two-way connections to the perceptual and motor systems; the place of affective centers is not clear. Perhaps, as Attneave suggests, their function is to provide affective or evaluative information to the central representative processes.

The concept of "cognitive processes" in psychology

The question of the usefulness of the concept of "cognitive processes" was raised at the beginning of the paper. In general, the concept would *of course* be useful if it could account for observations which could not be accounted for in a more parsimonious way and if it could generate testable predictions. The opinions range far and it is impossible to review the relevant data here; instead the writer will only attempt to demonstrate that at least some psychologists actively engaged in experimental investigations have found it necessary to include cognitive processes (in the sense of internal representative processes) in their conceptualizations.

First of all, it should be noted that while the original concept of "cognition" as a part of the conscious mind originated in philosophy, modern conceptions of cognitive processes were introduced by experimental psychologists in attempts to account for their data. Some psychologists accept "cognitive" concepts as a general explanation of behavior; others find them useful to designate a particular type of psychological process. It is the latter view that is particularly relevant to the view of "cognitive processes" suggested here.

In what situations would one look for evidence that discontinuities between "cognitive" and "simple" types of behavior actually exist? It seems that there are at least three situations: (1) the occurrence of different types of psychological processes in the same organism on different occasions; (2) discontinuities (or stages) in ontogenetic development; (3) discontinuities in phylogeny.

The distinction of trial-and-error vs insight learning is familiar to psychologists. No matter whether one regards them as basically one type of learning or as two distinct types of learning, the fact is that "insightful" learning does occur. Hebb considers it a "recombination of pre-existent mediating processes (Hebb, 1966, p. 293)." Other relevant distinctions are the distinction between sensory organization processes and categorizing processes in perception, e.g., Attneave's (1962) receptor grouping vs. receptor state grouping, and Neisser's (1967) pre-attentive processes vs. focal attention. On the motor side, the well-known distinction between "voluntary" and "habitual" motor skills might apply.

The best known theory of stages in ontogenetic development is Piaget's theory mentioned above. It was noted there that, for the present purpose, Piaget's distinction between non-representational and representational (symbolic) intelligence is most relevant.

Concerning the discontinuities in phylogeny, the problem engaging most attention is the difference between man and lower animals. Two views can be found in the literature. There is a tendency, on the part of some psychologists, biologists, and philosophers (e.g., Bertalanffy, 1965; Royce, 1966), to emphasize the gulf between human beings and animals based on the development of symbolism and culture by man.

People who have actually attempted to do comparative studies of intelligence on a variety of species are less convinced that such a vast gap exists as far as psychological *processes* are concerned, though they, of course, admit the differences in *achievement*. For example, Harlow (1958) finds that monkeys solve problems comparable in difficulty to items on intelligences tests and that we must differentiate between capability and achievement. The difference between apes and men may be due to "some small but critical deficiency in intellectual abilities or in specialized unlearned responses" (p. 278). Similarly, Nissen (1958) suggests that "language does not seem to introduce any really new psychological process; it may be thought of, rather, as an instrumental means or technique which enormously increases the speed and efficiency of processes already present to some extent in non-verbalizing animals" (p. 195).

Without attempting to discuss the issue of human superiority, it may be pointed out that such superiority cannot be based on the use of representational processes alone, since the use of such processes has been well-demonstrated in higher mammals at least.

The difficulties in comparing intelligence across species are well known (see, for example, Riopelle, 1960). It seems well-established, however, that classical conditioning or simple discrimination learning show no significant differences among species. Differences that arrange species in some meaningful way are usually found in the performance on tasks such as delayed reaction, learning sets and reasoning—i.e. tasks that depend on internal representational processes. It is suggested here that the increase in the capacity for such representational processes represents one important dimension of evolutionary development. A similar view was expressed by Leeper (1963). Hebb's distinction between reflexive and higher behavior (Hebb, 1966) seems to incorporate the same evolutionary development. (A similar view was expressed by Leeper (1963). Hebb's distinction between reflexive and higher behavior (Hebb, 1966) seems to incorporate the same evolutionary development.) A very similar suggestion comes from Beritov (1961) in the Soviet Union, who found the "reflex theory" insufficient as a general explanation of the behavior of higher vertebrates. He suggests that higher vertebrates exhibit two types of behavior: (1) reflex activity and (2) "image-directed" activity. Neural activity which determines behavioral acts by means of "images" (i.e., representations of earlier stimulus situations) is still based on the principles of conditioned reflexes, but cannot be reduced to it.

As a final example, Altman (1966) suggests that the mammalian nervous system consists of three functional components acquired in succession during phylogeny. The most recent system controls "cognitive instrumental activities." These activities "presuppose highly envolved receptor and afferent systems, which can provide accurate, detailed and 'objective' representation of the external world", (Altman, 1966, p. 304).

SUMMARY AND CONCLUSIONS

A conference on the "psychology of knowing" could justifiably expect to find some enlightment from studies of cognition—in view of the etymology of that term. In fact, some psychologists describe "cognition" as having to do with the acquisition of knowledge. A survey of psychological literature suggests, however, that this term is used with a variety of meanings and that it lacks a systematic status comparable to that of "perception" or "learning." A further and more detailed analysis of the uses of "cognitive" words shows that these words are used in several forms—verb, adjective, and noun—of which the adjective "cognitive" gives rise to the most interesting conceptual problems. This term is most commonly used—in phrases such as "cognitive processes"—to specify a particular kind of psychological process and in general refers to an internal process or state of the organism. These internal states or processes are variously conceptualized, for example, as non-emotional psychological processes, as mediating brain processes, as representational mediational responses, as verbal responses, and as conscious states. The following five issues seem to underlie these usages: (1) conscious vs. functional definition; (2) absolute vs. relational definition; (3) mediating vs. determining function; (4) passive vs. active formation; (5) generality.

The analysis suggests to the present author that the representational function of cognitive processes is their most distinctive characteristic. The representational function is not, however, equivalent to "knowledge;" rather, it has to do with the development of an internal model of the environment, which represents the environment with varying degrees of veridicality.

In the last section of the paper some speculations are offered on the usefulness of the concept of cognitive processes in the sense of internal representational processes. This concept seems to be useful in the attempts to account for apparent discontinuities between simpler and more complex types of behavior, as, for example, the distinction between trial-and-error and insightful behavior, and the distinction between earlier and later stages of the development of behavior in ontogeny and phylogeny.

NOTES

1. In the second edition of their book, they equate "cognition" with "thinking".

DISCUSSION OF THE PAPER BY MYRON MOROZ

John W. Gyr

Moroz begins by stating that many psychologists do not use the term cognition. This state of affairs cannot be due to the fact that cognition is only a minor part of psychology which numerous psychologists can well afford to neglect, for it becomes clear from the review by Moroz that in discussing cognition one is forced to consider most of the conceptual issues that confront psychology. The conceptual issues raised concern the nature of the organism-environment interaction: is it best represented by $S - R$, $S - O - R$, or $(S, O) - R$? Moroz seems to favor the latter.

Cognitive theory in psychology seems to be necessary because—and this is pointed out by Moroz—some generalization or mediation is involved even in the simplest conditioned reflex. That is, even at this simple level internal processes are supposed to go on which help structure both the input and the response.

There are theorists, of course, who do exclude cognition, even of this "weak" form, from certain psychological processes. The Gibsons' theory of perception would seem to be a case in point. The Gibsons contend that perception is non-cognitive and that any structure worth talking about inheres in the optic array. There is no internal structuring or "enrichment" to characterize perception. Even the weak form of cognitive structuring mentioned above, if perhaps not explicitly denied, is at least disregarded by the Gibsons.

If Moroz believes there to be an element of cognition—however minor—even in the simplest psychological process like a reflex—he would have to disagree with the Gibsons' strict definition of perception. Such, however, would not seem to be the case for, elsewhere in the paper, he argues for a differentiation between cognitive and other, non-cognitive, processes in psychology. An apparent contradiction, however, is avoided because cognition in the later part of the paper becomes a more narrowly defined process: e.g. it can function as a substitute for a stimulus event, it is representational (the meaning of this term is not very well defined, however), etc.

The strategy for defining cognition followed by Moroz is thus to divide psychological processes into those that are cognitive and those that are not, even while recognizing that, as Hebb would have it, these processes all lie on a *continuum* of *types of cognition*. Thus, Moroz has to make a somewhat arbitrary—though by no means uncommon—cutting point on this continuum. What is inherently worrisome about this procedure, however, is that it tends to become more than an arbitrary convenience and, instead, induces "cognition psychologists" and "perception psychologists" to forget that they are all working on a continuum and should be searching for common principles, etc. Piaget and Bruner are examples of researchers who have not fallen into this trap, though even the former separates these processes in a too arbitrary manner, it would seem.

The motives and experimental findings which would make $(S, O) - R$ models for psychology imperative, and which lead Moroz to favor such models, are not discussed explicitly and in detail. They could range from concerns about the relation of psychology to epistemology (e.g. Piaget, 1954), to findings concerning feedforward mechanisms (e.g. Bruner, 1957; Pribram, 1970), reafferent process in perception (e.g. Held, 1967; von Holst, 1954), the role of efference in conscious perception (e.g. Festinger *et al.*, 1965), the contribution of motor displacements to the formation of internal and higher cognitive abstractive processes (e.g. Gyr, 1970; Piaget, 1954; Poincaré, 1952), and the like.

The need not only for a cognitive theory but for a new methodology becomes acute in the case where the appropriate model for the organism-environment interaction is assumed to be of the kind $(S, O) - R$. This is the model which is favored by Moroz as well as, incidentally, by Gyr and Pribram (in this volume). In an $(S, O) - R$ type process it no longer is the case that a response and a cognitive process are ultimately triggered by an external stimulus. It becomes impossible even to state what the effective external stimulus is *and* how it will be interpreted, unless the current state of the organism is known. In this case the whole anchoring of responses purely to external stimulus events dissipates. Moroz does not contrast $S - O - R$ with $(S, O) - R$ models but, rather, cites representative theories from each. Hence the above important implication of the various models does not stand out in his discussion. In fact, Moroz indicates somewhere that the differences between, say, Hullian concepts and theories and "cognitive" theories (including, presumably, his own) may be merely "verbal". Clearly, the differences go deeper than the "verbal" level. A fairly incisive discussion of the methodological point raised above has been given by Chomsky (1957) in his discussion of Skinner's attempt to bring behaviorist concepts and techniques to bear on the problem of language learning.

Moroz has left the issue of the relationship of cognition to knowing open, except to say that since cognitions can be both true and false (in the sense of justified true belief), the term cognition had best be kept separate from the term knowledge. Even through the intent of the paper by Moroz was to leave these general issues unexplored for the moment, a few general remarks will be made in view of the fact that the $(S, O) - R$ model favored by Moroz throws new light on the problem of knowledge. That is, the notion of true belief itself would seem to depend for its meaning on the model of the organism-environment interaction which is assumed. If the psychological and philosophical assumption one starts out with is that of a complete dichotomy between subject and some kind of absolute reality, it is reasonable also to think in terms of absolute knowledge and absolute truth. (This kind of thinking is congruent with a $S - R$ and, to an extent, with a $S - O - R$ model of organism-environment relationship.) That is, it is congruent with the idea that observation is the simple reception of an outside existent. In an $(S, O) - R$ model, on the other hand, perception is defined as a relation between an organism's actual or potential activity and an ensuing feedback from the environment. Outside reality as a concept is thus not defined as an absolute outside existent. Rather, it is anchored to a given set of (sensorimotor or mental) operations of the subject. It changes as the set of operations change. It is therefore impossible, at any one moment, to talk of anything but a relative reality; one defined in terms of a given but highly particular set of operations.

The above model of perception is beginning to have wide repercussions in philosophy and especially in science where it has been discovered as it were independently. Thus, Bohm (1965) prefers to consider science as a way of heightening our perceptions of an ever-increasing segment of the world with which we are in contact, rather than as a way of gaining absolute truth. If this is the way in which science and perception both ought to be conceived, the distinction between cognition and knowledge in terms of justified true belief becomes less pure—if indeed the distinction can be made at all—than at the time it was formulated, when a type of $S - R$ model guided the assumptions of philosophers and psychologists. A quote by Heisenberg (1958) summarizes the issue: "... Thus even in science the object of research is no longer nature itself, but man's investigation of nature. Here, again, man confronts himself alone."

COMMENT ON MOROZ' PAPER

J. R. Royce

I wish to offer a brief comment on the phylogeny of cognition. On page 203 Moroz quotes Bertalanffy and myself as accounting for the discontinuities between humans and animals on the basis of "development of symbolism and culture by man." He then goes on to suggest that there still may be fundamental phylogenetic continuity of underlying psychological *processes* in spite of the obvious differences in *achievement*.

Unfortunately, Moroz' subsequent discussion begs the issue, as the evidence he quotes for evolutionary continuity is focused on learning and problem solving tasks, *not* symbolizing tasks (i.e., in the sense of being able to do things like write poems and music and create paintings, etc.).

As a student of comparative-physiological psychology, I find the overall principle of continuity extremely valuable in my efforts to understand the evolution of behavior, particularly if I utilize the concept of emergents. Evolution, after all, means change. And our best understanding of such change is via recombinations of the gene pool (in interaction with the environment, of course). If we look at biological forms which are sufficiently far apart on the phylogenetic scale, it is obvious that new phenotypes have "emerged" as a function of changes in the underlying genotypes. In short, the notion of "emergent traits" implies both continuity and discontinuity. However, presently available evidence (i.e., about the evolution of homo sapiens, and about cognitive processes) is simply inadequate to fill in the details of the "continuity" principle.

In short, while certain cognitive processes have been demonstrated in lower animals, this is not the case for *all* human cognitive processes. Thus, if Moroz' major point is that we psychologists can learn about certain aspects of cognition by studying animals there is no argument. On the other hand, the context of all this is that "we cannot expect to learn *all* about the laws which govern human behavior by such study." (Royce, 1966, p. 68). For the fact still remains that only man has developed a culture. On the basis of the presently available evidence, therefore, I am forced to the conclusion that *some* human cognitive processes (especially those relevant to "culture", e.g., language, and symbolizing in general) are *not* adequately manifested in infrahuman organisms.

REBUTTAL

M. Moroz

The intent of my discussion of the phylogeny of cognition was to suggest that the representational function is the main, if not the defining, aspect of all cognitive processes, including "language and symbolizing in general," and that the increasing ability to use internal representational processes is believed (at least by some psychologists) to characterize cognitive development in phylogeny. This does not preclude the possibility that there may be different *ways* of representing events internally—as suggested by Bruner (1964), for example—or that typically human cognitive processes may have particular characteristics of their own. Whatever these characteristics are, they cannot be simply a matter of the ability to use representational processes, since some animals at least have been found to possess this ability.

Thus I find myself in agreement with Royce's point that one can study certain aspects of cognitive processes in animals, but that there may be other aspects of such processes which can only be studied in humans. Whether the differences between humans and lower animals are due to a different use of processes which are basically similar (e.g., in their representational function) or to the development of qualitatively different traits, is, it seems to me, an open question at the present time. As I tried to point out, both views have their advocates.

Gyr considers—and then rejects—the possibility that I believe "there to be an element of cognition—however minor—even in the simplest psychological process like a reflex." The primary justification for such a belief would seem to be the fact (mentioned by him earlier) that "some generalization or mediation is involved even in the simplest conditioned reflex."

I discuss the conception of cognitive processes based on the ability to generalize and find that it is not a useful conception, if under "generalization" we include primary generalization involving an inability to discriminate. Such a conception of cognitive processes would be too general, in my opinion, to be useful.

Thus I do not suggest that "cognitive theory in psychology seems to be necessary because ... some generalization or mediation is involved even in the simplest conditioned reflex" (though such a view is possible and has in fact been proposed). Rather, the point of my discussion is that the concept of "cognitive processes" is useful because some types of psychological processes are distinct—for reasons discussed in the paper. This may well involve the necessity to make an arbitrary—for the time being, at least— cutting point on the continuum of psychological processes and I fully appreciate the difficulties pointed out by Gyr. Nevertheless, the distinction between levels of the organization of behavior seems to me to be a useful one in principle; several writers cited in my paper have also found it useful to make such a distinction—e.g., Beritov (1961), Hebb (1960, 1966), Neisser (1966), and Osgood (1957).

BIBLIOGRAPHY

Altman, J., *Organic foundations of animal behavior*. New York: Holt, Rinehart & Winston, 1966.

Attneave, F., In defense of homunculi. In W. A. Rosenblith (Ed.) *Sensory communication*. Cambridge, Mass.: MIT Press, 1961, pp. 777–782.

Attneave, F., Perception and related areas. In S. Koch (Ed.) *Psychology: A study of a science*. New York: McGraw-Hill, 1962. pp. 619–659.

Ausubel, D. P., Introduction. In R. C. Anderson and D. P. Ausubel (Eds.), *Readings in the psychology of cognition*. New York: Holt, Rinehart & Winston, 1965, pp. 3–17(a).

Ausubel, D. P., A cognitive structure view of word and concept meaning. In R. C. Anderson and D. P. Ausubel (Eds.), *Readings in the psychology of cognition*. New York: Holt, Rinehart and Winston, 1965, pp. 58–75. (b)

Beritov, I. S., *Nervnyie mekhanismy povedeniia vysshykh pozvonochnykh zhivotnykh* (*Neural mechanisms of higher vertebrate behavior*). Moscow: Academy of Sciences of the USSR, 1961.

Berlyne, D. E., *Conflict, arousal, and curiosity*. New York: McGraw-Hill, 1960.

Bertalanffy, L., On the definition of the symbol. In J. R. Royce (Ed.), *Psychology and the symbol*. New York: Random House, 1965, pp. 26–72.

Bohm, D., *The special theory of relativity*. New York: W. A. Benjamin, 1965.

Bruner, J. S., On perceptual readings. *Psychol. Rev.*, 1957, **64**, 123–152. (a)

Bruner, J. S., Going beyond the information given. *In Contemporary approaches to cognition*. Cambridge, Mass.: Harvard Univ. Press, 1957, pp. 41–69. (b)

Bruner, J. S., On perceptual readiness. *Psychological Review*, 1957, **64**, 123–152.

Bruner, J. S., The course of cognitive growth. *Amer. Psychologist*, 1964, **19**, 1–15.

Bruner, J. S., On cognitive growth. In J. S. Bruner *et al.*, *Studies in cognitive growth*. New York: Wiley, 1966, pp. 1–29.

Brunswik, E., *Scope and aspects of the cognitive problem*. In *Contemporary approaches to cognition*. Cambridge Mass.: Harvard Univ. Press, 1957, pp. 5–31.

Campbell, D. T., Methodological suggestions from a comparative psychology of knowledge processes. *Inquiry*, 1959, **2**, 152–182.

Chomsky, N., Review of B. F. Skinner's book Verbal Behavior. *Language*, 1957, **33**, No. 3, 26–58.

Cofer, C. N., Reasoning as an associative process: The role of verbal responses in problem solving. *J. gen. Psychol.*, 1957, **57**, 55–68.

Deutsch, J. A., A new type of behavior theory. *Br. J, Psychol.*, 1963, **44**, 304–317.

Drever, J., *A dictionary of psychology*. London: Penguin Books, 1952.

Festinger, L., The relation between behavior and cognition. *Contemporary approaches to cognition*. Cambridge, Mass.: Harvard Univ. Press. 1957, pp. 127–150.

Festinger, L., Burnham, C. A., Ono, H., and Bamber, D., Efference and the conscious experience of perception. *Journal of Experimental Psychology Monograph*, 1965, **72**, 373–384.

Flavell, J. H., *The developmental psychology of Jean Piaget*. Princeton, N. J.: Van Nostrand, 1963.

Fodor, J. A., *Psychological explanation.* New York: Random House, 1968.
Forehand, G. A., Epilogue: Constructs and Strategies for problem-solving research. In B. Kleinmunz (Ed.), *Problem solving: Research, method, and theory.* New York: Wiley, 1966, pp. 355–383.
Fowler, W., Cognitive learning in infancy and early childhood. *Psychol. Bull.*, 1962 **59**, 116–152.
Galanter, E., *Textbook of elementary psychology.* San Francisco: Holden-Day, 1966.
George, F. H., *Cognition.* London: Methuen, 1962.
Goss. A. E., Verbal mediating responses and concept formation. *Psychol. Rev.*, 1961, **68**, 248–274.
Gyr, J. W., Perception as reafference and related issues in cognition and epistemology. (In this volume.)
Gyr, J. W., Brown, J. S., Willey, R., and Zivian, A. Computer simulation and psychological theories of perception. *Psychol. Bull.*, 1966, **65**, 17–192.
Harlow, H. F., The evolution of learning. In A. Roe and G. G. Simpson (Eds.), *Behavior and evolution.* New Haven: Yale Univ. Press, 1958, pp. 269–290.
Harvard University, The Center for Cognitive Studies. *Fifth Annual Report*, 1965.
Hebb, D. O., The American revolution. *Amer. Psychologist*, 1960, **15**, 735–745.
Hebb, D. O., *A textbook of psychology.* Philadelphia: Saunders, 1966.
Heisenberg, W., *Physics and philosophy: The revolution in modern science.* New York: Harper, 1958.
Held, R. E., and Hein, A., On the modificability of form perception. In W. Wathen-Dunn (Ed.). *Models for the perception of speech and visual form.* Cambridge, Mass.: M.I.T. Press, 1967.
Hilgard, E. R. and Atkinson, R. C., *Introduction to psychology.* New York: Harcourt, Brace and World, 1967.
Holst, E. von, Relations between the central nervous system and the peripheral organs. *British Journal of Animal Behavior*, 1954, **2**, 89–94.
Isaacson, R. L., Hutt, M. L., and Blum, M. L., *Psychology: The science of behavior.* New-York: Harper & Row, 1965.
Kelly, G., *The psychology of personal constructs.* New York: Norton, 1955.
Kendler, H. H., *Basic psychology.* New York: Appleton-Century-Crofts, 1968.
Kendler, H. H. and Kendler, T. S., Vertical and horizontal processes in problem solving. *Psychol. Rev.*, 1962, **69**, 1–16.
Krech, D. and Crutchfield, R. S., *Elements of psychology.* New York, Knopf. 1958.
Krech, D., Crutchfield, R. S., and Ballachey, E. L., *Individual in society.* New York: McGraw-Hill, 1962.
Lashley, K. S., Cerebral organization and behavior. In *The brain and human behavior*, *Res. Public. Assoc. Res.nerv. ment. Dis.*, 1958, **36**, 1–18.
Leeper, R. W., Cognitive processes. In S. S. Stevens (Ed.), *Handbook of experimental psychology.* New York: Wiley, 1951, pp. 730–757.
Leeper, R. W., Learning and the fields of perception, motivation, and personality. In S. Koch (Ed.), Psychology: *A study of a science.* New York: McGraw-Hill, 1963, pp. 365–487.
Lewis. D. J., *Scientific principles of psychology.* Englewood Cliffe, N. J.: Prentice-Nall, 1963
McKeachie, W. J., and Doyle, C. L., *Psychology.* Reading, Mass.: Addison-Wesley, 1966.
MacLeod, R. B., The phenomenological approach to social psychology. *Psychol. Rev.*, 1947, **54**, 193–210.

MacLeod, R. B., Phenomenology: A challenge to experimental psychology. In T. W. Wann (Ed.), *Behaviorism and phenomenology*. Chicago: Univ. of Chicago Press, 1964, pp. 47–74

Maltzman, I. M., Thinking: From a behavioristic point of view. *Psychol. Rev.*, 1955, **62**, 275–286.

Mandler, G., Verbal learning. In *New directions in psychology III*. New York: Holt, Rinehart, Winston. 1967, pp. 1–50.

Manis, M., *Cognitive processes*. Belmont, Calif.: Eadsworth, 1966.

Miller, B. A., Galanter, E., and Pribam, K. H., *Plans and the structure of behavior*. New York: Holt, Rinehart and Winston, 1960.

Neisser, U., *Cognitive psychology*. New York: Appleton-Century-Crofts, 1967.

Nissen, H. W., Axes of behavioral comparison. In A. Roe, and G. G. Simpson (Eds.) *Behavior and evolution*. New Haven: Yale Univ. Press, 1958, pp. 183–205.

O'Neil, Wm., Basic issues in perceptual theory. *Psych. Rev.*, 1958, **65**, 348–361.

Osgood, C. E., A behavioristic analysis of perception and language as cognitive phenomena. In *Contemporary approaches to cognition*. Cambridge, Mass.: Harvard Univ. Press, 1957, pp. 75–118.

Piaget, J., Review of J. S. Bruner et al. Studies in cognitive growth. *Contemp. Psychol.*, 1967, **12**, 532–533.

Piaget, J., *The construction of reality in the child*. New York: Basic Books, 1954.

Poincaré, H., *Science and hypothesis*. New York: Dover 5221, 1952.

Potter, M. C., On perceptual recognition. In J. S. Bruner et al., *Studies in cognitive growth*, New York: Wiley, 1966. pp. 103–134.

Pribram, K. H., **Neurological notes on knowing.** (In this volume.)

Riopelle, A. J., Complex processes. In R. H. Waters, D. A. Rehlinghaffer, and W. E. Caldwell (Eds.), *Principles of comparative psychology*. New York: McGraw-Hill, 1960, pp. 208–249.

Royce, J. R., *The encapsulated man*. Princeton, N. J.: Van Nostrand, 1964.

Royce, J. R., Animal psychology. In Guilford, J. P. (Ed.), *Fields of psychology*, New York: Van Nostrand, 1966, pp. 66–103.

Rozeboom, W. W., The concept of "memory." *Psychol. Rec.*, 1965, **15**, 329-269.

Ruch, F. L., *Psychology and life*. Chicago: Scott, Foresman & Co., 1963.

Sarbin, T. R., Taft, R., and Bailey, D. E. *Clinical inference and cognitive theory*. New York: Holt, Rinehart & Winston, 1960.

Snygg, D., The need for a phenomenological system of psychology. *Psychol. Rev.*, 1941, **48**, 404–424.

Spence, K. W., The postulates and methods of behaviorism. *Psychol. Rev.*, 1948, **55**, 67–78.

Staats, A. W., Verbal-habit families, concepts and the operant conditioning of word classes. *Psychol. Rev.*, 1961, **68**, 190–204.

Van de Geer, J. P. and Jaspars, J. F. M., Cognitive functions. *An. Rev. Psychol.*, 1966, **17**, 145–176.

Whittaker, J. O., *Introduction to psychology*, Philadelphia: Saunders, 1965.

VI

A THEORY OF DIRECT VISUAL PERCEPTION

James J. Gibson
Cornell University

The theory to be outlined is partly developed in *The Senses Considered as Perceptual Systems* (Gibson, 1966), especially in chapters 9–12 on vision. It is related to, although a considerable departure from, the theory presented in *The Perception of the Visual World* (Gibson, 1950). Some of its postulates go back 20 years to that book, but many are new.

What is "direct" visual perception? I argue that the seeing of an environment by an observer existing in that environment is direct in that it is not mediated by visual sensations or sense data. The phenomenal visual world of surfaces, objects, and the ground under one's feet is quite different from the phenomenal visual field of color–patches (Gibson, 1950, Ch. 3). I assert that the latter experience, the array of visual sensations, is not entailed in the former. Direct perception is not based on the having of sensations. The suggestion will be that it is based on the pickup of information.

So far, all theories have assumed that the visual perception of a stable, unbounded, and permanent *world* can only be explained by a process of correcting or compensating for the unstable, bounded, and fleeting sensations coming to the brain from the retinal images. That is to say, all extant theories are sensation-based. But the theory here advanced assumes the existence of stable, unbounded, and permanent stimulus-information in the ambient optic array. And it supposes that the visual system can explore and detect this information. The theory is information-based, not sensation-based.

PERCEPTION AND PROPRIOCEPTION

Simplifying a distinction made by Sherrington, the term *perception* will be used to refer to any experience of the environment surrounding the body of an animal, and the term *proprioception* for any experience of the body itself (including what Sherrington called *interoception*). Far from being one of the senses, then, proprioception is a kind of e perience cognate with perception. Proprioception *accompanies* perception but it is not the same thing as perception.

An awareness of the body, however dim, does in fact seem to go along with an awareness of the world. Conversely, an awareness of the body, however intense, even an experience of pain, is never wholly without some awareness of the environment. And this reciprocity is only to be expected since the very term "environment" implies something that is surrounded, and the term "observer" implies a surrounding world.

The difference between perception and proprioception, then, is one of function, not a difference between the receptors stimulated as Sherrington assumed, that is, the exteroceptors and the proprioceptors. Perception and proprioception both depend on stimulation, but the visual system, for example, can isolate from the flux of stimulation that which is exterospecific (specifies the world) from that which is propriospecific (specifies the body). Vision, in other words, serves not only awareness of the environment but also awareness of self.

For example, the motion of an object relative to the stationary environment can be detected by vision, and this is a case of *perception*. Likewise the motion of one's body relative to the stationary environment, whether active or passive, can be detected by vision, and this is a case of *proprioception*. Locomotion, as distinguished from object motion, is specified by transformation of the ambient optic array as a whole. An observer can ordinarily distinguish the two cases with no difficulty, and so can animals, even species with very simple eyes.

Note that proprioception, as here defined, it not to be confused with *feedback* in the modern usage of the word, that is, a return input to the nervous system from a motor action. The movements and postures of the body are detected (in several independent ways) whether they are imposed by outside forces or are obtained by an action of the observer himself. Proprioception can be passive or active, just as perception can be passive or active. The above hypothesis is elaborated in Chapter 2 of *The Senses Considered as Perceptual Systems*. The classical doctrine that proprioception is one of the sense modalities is familiar, and is still taught, but it simply will not work. The evidence is against it.

It should already be evident that this theory of perception does not accept the usual analogy between the brain and a computer, and rejects the idea that perception is a matter of processing the information fed into a computer. No one has suggested that a computer has the experience of being "here."

OPTICAL STIMULATION AND OPTICAL INFORMATION

The theory distinguishes between stimulation by light and the information in light. The difference is between light that is seen and the light by which *things* are seen. Light as energy is treated by physical optics. Light as information is treated by an unfamiliar discipline called ecological optics (Gibson, 1961; 1966, Chapter 10). The facts of physical optics are sufficient for a psychophysics of the light sense, and of the elementary visual sensations. But the facts of ecological optics are required for an understanding of direct visual perception.

The relation between optical stimulation and optical information seems to be as follows. The stimulation of photoreceptors by light is a necessary condition for visual perception. The activity of the visual system depends on ambient light; there is no vision in darkness. But *another* necessary condition for visual perception is an *array* of ambient light. It must be structured or differentiated, not homogeneous. With homogeneous ambient light, perception fails although the sensation of light remains. Such is the case in dense fog, empty sky, or in the experiment of wearing plastic diffusing eye-caps, an experiment that we repeat every year at Cornell. In homogeneous darkness, perception fails because stimulation is absent. In homogeneous light, perception fails because stimulus *information* is absent although stimulation is present. We conclude that stimulus energy is a necessary but by no means sufficient condition of stimulus information.

The meaning of the term "information". There are currently two radically different usages of the word "information" in psychology. One I will call *afferent-input information* and the other *optic-array information*. The former is familiar; it is information conceived as impulses in the fibers of the optic nerve. Information is assumed to consist of *signals*, and to be *transmitted* from receptors to the brain. Perception is a process that is supposed to occur *in* the brain, and the only information for perception must therefore consist of neural inputs *to* the brain.

Optic-array information is something entirely different. It is information in light, not in nervous impulses. It involves geometrical projection to a point of observation, not transmission between a sender and a receiver. It is outside the observer and available to him, not inside his head. In my theory, perception is *not* supposed to occur in the brain but to arise in the retino-neuro-muscular system as an activity of the whole system. The information does not consist of signals to be interpreted but of structural invariants which need only be attended to.

It has long been assumed by empiricists that the only information for perception was "sensory" information. But this assumption can mean different things. If it means that the information for perception must come through the senses and not through extrasensory intuition, this is the doctrine of John Locke, and I agree with it, as most of us would agree with it. But the assumption might mean (and has been taken to mean) that the information for perception must come over the sensory nerves. This is a different doctrine, that of Johannes Müller, and with this we need *not* agree. To assume that visual information comes through the visual sense is not to assume that it comes over the optic nerve, for a sense may be considered as an active system with a capacity to extract information from obtained stimulation. The visual system in fact does this. Retinal inputs lead to ocular adjustments, and then to altered retinal inputs, and so on. It is an exploratory, circular process, not a one-way delivery of messages to the brain. This hypothesis is elaborated in Chapters 2 and 3 of *The Senses Considered as Perceptual Systems*.

THE MAIN PRINCIPLES OF ECOLOGICAL OPTICS

The term *ecological optics* was introduced in a paper (Gibson, 1961) and the subject was further developed in a chapter on environmental information (Gibson, 1966, Ch. 10). But the concepts and postulates are not yet wholly established, and what follows must be regarded as tentative.

Ecological optics attempts to escape the reductionism of physical and geometrical optics. It introduces a new concept, *ambient light*, which goes beyond the physicist's conception of radiant light, and it postulates a notion of space-filling illumination that extends the classical meaning of illuminance.

1 The unlimited reflecting of light waves

In a medium of water or air, in which animals live and move and have evolved, light not only propagates as it does in empty space but also reverberates. It is rapidly reflected back and forth between earth and sky, and also between the facing surfaces of semi-enclosed spaces. Given the speed of light and the fact of sunlight, it almost instantly reaches an equilibrium in the medium, that is, a steady state. The light moves in all directions at once. This steady state of multiply reflected light has very interesting properties. First, at every point in the medium there is ambient light and, second, the ambient light at every such point will be structured by the reflecting surfaces facing that point.

2 Projection to a point

At any point in a medium there will exist a bundle of *visual solid angles* corresponding to the components or parts of the illuminated environment. The *faces* and *facets* of reflecting surfaces are such components; what we call *objects* are others; and the *patches of pigment* on a flat surface are still others. Note that the bundle of *solid angles* postulated above is not the same as a pencil of rays, which is a concept of *geometrical* optics. The cross-section of a solid angle always has a "form," no matter how small, whereas the cross section of a ray is a formless point. And the cross section of a *bundle* of solid angles always has a pattern whereas the cross section of a pencil of rays does not.

3 The ambient optic array

A bundle of visual solid angles at a point (a point of observation) is called an *ambient optic array*. Such an array is invariant under changes in the illumination from noon to sunset. It is an arrangement of components, not an assemblage of points, and the components are nested within others of larger size. It is analyzed by topology or perspective geometry, not by analytic geometry. The array can be said to exist at a point of observation whether or not an eye is stationed at that point. In this respect the array is quite unlike a retinal image, which occurs only if a chambered (vertebrate) eye is put there and aimed in a certain direction. The array is also unlike an image inasmuch as the image is usually said to be an assemblage of focus points each corresponding to a luminous radiating point (presumably an atom) in the environment.

4 Projected surfaces and occluded surfaces at a point of observation

Given that surfaces are in general *opaque*, not transparent, some of the surfaces of the world will be hidden at a given point of observation (occluded) and the remainder will be unhidden (projected at the point). This holds for any layout of surfaces other than a flat plane unobscured to its horizon. But any hidden surface may become unhidden by a change of the point of observation. The occlusion of one surface by another entails an *occluding edge*.

5 Connected sets of observation points

A path of locomotion in ecological space consists of a connected set of observation points. To each connected set of observation points there corresponds a unique family of perspective transformations in the ambient optic array. In short the changing optic array at a moving point of observation specifies the movement of the point (i.e., the path of locomotion of the observer).

The optical transition between what I call two "vistas" of the world (as when an observer goes from one room to another) entails the progressive occlusion of some parts of the world and the disocclusion of others. The transition, however, arises from a path of locomotion which is reversible, and the transition is itself reversible. What went out of sight in going comes back into sight on returning. This reversible optical transition is to be distinguished from an *irreversible* transition such as occurs when an object is melted or dissolved or destroyed. The study of the two different ways in which an object can go out of sight, by being hidden or by being destroyed, suggests that they are clearly distinguishable on the basis of optical information.

6 The family of perspectives for an object

Given an illuminated object with several faces (a polyhedron for example) it will be surrounded by an unlimited set of points of observation. Each *perspective* of the object (its projection in each optic array) is unique at each point of observation. The family of perspectives is unique to the object. An observer who walked around the object (looked at it "from all sides") would obtain the whole family.

The features of the object that make it different from other objects have corresponding features in the family of perspectives that are *invariant* under perspective transformations. These invariants constitute information about the object. Although the observer gets a different form-sensation at each moment of his tour, his information-based perception can be of the same object. This hypothesis provides new reasons for realism in epistemology (Gibson, 1967).

7 Correspondence of structure between an ambient optic array and the environment

There is evidently some correspondence between the structure of the environment and the structure of the ambient light at a stationary point of observation. It is by no means a simple correspondence. It is not point-to-point but component-to-component. There are subordinate and superordinate components of the world and corresponding subordinate and superordinate forms in the array, each level of units being nested within larger units. But some components of the environment are missing from a frozen array, because of occlusion. All components of the environment, however, could be included in the changing array over time at a moving point of observation.

8 Invariant information in an ambient optic array

A list of the *invariants* in an array as the amount of illumination changes, as the type of illumination changes, as the direction of the prevailing illumination changes, and (above all) as the point of observation changes cannot yet be drawn up with any assurance. But a few facts seem to be clear. The *contours* in an array are invariant with most of the changes in illumination. The *textures* of an array are reliably invariant with change of observation-point. The property of a contour being *closed* or *unclosed* is always invariant. The *form* of a closed contour in the array is independent of lighting but highly variant with change of observation point. A great many properties of the array are *lawfully* or *regularly* variant with change of observation point, and this means that in each case a property defined by the law is *invariant*.

9 Summary

Eight main principles of ecological optics have been outlined. They are perhaps enough to show that the new optics is not just an application of the accepted laws of physical and geometrical optics, inasmuch as different laws emerge at the new level. And it should now be clear why ecological optics is required for a theory of direct visual perception instead of what is taught in the physics textbooks.

THE SAMPLING PROCESS IN VISUAL PERCEPTION

The theories of sensation-based perception presuppose the formation of a retinal image and the transmission of it to the brain. The theory of direct perception presupposes the sampling of the ambient array by the ocular system. What is this sampling process?

No animal has wholly panoramic vision (although some approximate to having it) and therefore no animal can perceive the whole environment at once. The successive sampling of the ambient array is carried out by head-movements, the eyes being stabilized to the structure of the array by compensatory eye-movements (see Gibson,1966, Ch. 12, for an explanation of head-movements and compensatory eye-movements). The point to be noted is that vertebrate animals with chambered eyes must perform *sample-taking* in order to perceive the environment. Invertebrates with compound eyes probably do the same, although very little is known about visual perception in arthropods. The sampling of the optical environment is a more general process than the fixating of details. The latter arises in evolution only when the eyes develop concentrated foveas.

Along with the taking of stabilized samples of the spherical array there goes a process of optimizing the pickup of information in the sample. Accommodation of the lens, the centering of the retinal fovea on an item of the sample, and the adjustment of the pupil for an optimal level of intensity, together with the adaptation of the retina, are all cases of the adjustment of the ocular system to the requirements of clear vision.

From the earliest stage of evolution, therefore, vision has been a process of exploration in time, not a photographic process of image registration and image transmission. We have been misled about vision by the analogy between eye and camera. Physical optics, and the physiological optics that depends on it, do not now conceive the eye in any way except as a camera. But a camera is not a device with which one can perceive the whole environment by means of sampling, whereas an eye does perceive the environment by sampling it.

If the visual system is exploratory we can assume that it extracts the information in successive samples; we do not have to speculate about how the brain could "store" the sequence of images transmitted to it and combine them into a total image of the world. The experience of the visual world is not compounded of a series of visual fields; no one is aware of the *sequence* but only of the total *scene*. Presumably this is because the ocular system detects the invariants over time that specify the scene.

I once assumed (Gibson, 1950) that the only way one can be aware of the environment behind one's back is to remember it, in the sense of having a *memory image* of it. Similarly, I supposed that, when I look out of the window, my lawn, only part of which is projected through the window to my eyes, must be filled out by images of the remainder. But I no longer believe this theory. Awareness of the room behind my back and the lawn outside my window cannot depend on imagery. I doubt if it depends on *memory*. I apprehend part of the room as *occluded by my head*, and part of the lawn as *occluded by the edges of the window*. And the perception of occlusion, it seems to me, entails the perception of *something* which is *occluded*.

A memory image of a room or of a lawn is something quite different from the perception of surfaces that are temporarily hidden from sight. I can summon up a memory image of the house and the lawn where I lived as a child. This is not at all like the awareness I have of the room behind my back and the lawn outside my window. The theory of information-based perception differs from the theory of sensation-based perception in many ways but in none more radical than this: it does not require the assumption that memories of the past must somehow be mixed with sensations of the present.

THE FALSE PROBLEM OF DEPTH PERCEPTION AND THE TRUE PROBLEM OF ENVIRONMENT PERCEPTION

For centuries, the problem of space perception has been stated as the puzzle of how "depth" or the "third dimension" could be seen when the sensations for the perception were depthless or two-dimensional. Three kinds of solution have been offered, one by nativism (intuition), one by empiricism (past experience), and a third by Gestalt theory (spontaneous organization in the brain). But none of them has been convincing. In the light of the present theory the puzzle of depth perception is insoluble because the problem is false; we perceive the layout of the environment, not the third dimension of space. There is nothing special about "depth" in the environment. As Merleau-Ponty somewhere pointed out, "depth is nothing but breadth seen from the side." We have been misled by taking the third dimension of the Cartesian coordinate system to be a phenomenal fact of perception. And if the flat patchwork of visual sensation is not the basis of visual perception in any case, a third dimension does not *have* to be added to the two dimensions they already possess.

Perception of the *environment* differs from a perception of *space*. An environment implies points of observation in the medium, whereas a space does not. The points of geometrical space are abstract fictions, whereas the points of observation in an environment are the positions where an observer might be stationed. Perception of the environment is thus accompanied by an awareness of the perceiver's existence in the environment (and this is what I call proprioception) whereas a perception of space in its purest form need not be accompanied by any awareness of the thinker's existence in that space.

Geometrical optics is based, of course, on geometrical space. This is everywhere transparent, and it is composed of ghostly points, lines, and planes. It is impersonal and lifeless. Ecologocal optics is based on a space of solid opaque surfaces with a transparent medium in which living animals get about, and which permits the reverberation of reflected light. The surfaces are textured and pigmented. They are flat or curved. They have corners and occluding edges. There are objects and the interspaces between objects. In short, the environment has a layout.

The so-called *cues* for the perception of depth are not the same as the *information* for the perception of layout. The former are called *signs* or *indicators* of depth, or *clues* for an inference that depth exists in the world. Their meaning has to be learned by association. They are sensations in the visual field of the observer, noticeable when he introspects. The latter, the available kinds of information, are *specifiers* of layout, not signs or indicators or clues. They have to be distinguished or discriminated, but their meaning does not have to be learned by association. They are not sense impressions or sense data. When the information for occlusion of one surface by another is picked up there is no sensation for the occluded surface but it is nevertheless perceived. And the information for the occlusion of one surface by another *is* picked up by vision.

The surface layout of the world is thus perceived *directly* when the information is available and when the cycle of action from retina to brain to eye to retina again is attuned to this information. The information must be *attended to*, of course, and this may depend on the maturation of the system, and on practice in looking, and even on the education or training of attention. But the meanings of an edge, of a falling-off-place, of an obstacle in one's path, or of the solid ground under one's feet are given in the ambient optic array and do not have to be memories of past experience attached to present sense-data, or memories of touching aroused by sensations of seeing.

False questions in the perception of the environment

We have seen that the old question of why the phenomenal environment has depth whereas the retinal images are depthless is a false question. There are other false questions of this same sort. One is the question made famous by Stratton's experiment in 1897, *why is the phenomenal world upright whereas the retinal image is inverted on the retina*? Another, going back at least to Helmholtz, is *why is the phenomenal world stationary when the retinal image continually moves with respect to the retina*? Still another (connected with the fact of sampling) is, *why is the phenomenal environment unbounded when each retinal image is bounded by the margins of the retina*? In another form, this is the question, *why does the phenomenal world seem to persist when the retinal images are impermanent*? The answer to all the above questions is this: we do not *see* our retinal images. We see the environment. The doctrine of Müller that all we can see is our retinal images (or at least all we can ever see *directly*) is quite false. If we saw our retinal images we would perceive two worlds, not one, since there is a separate image of it in each eye.

THE FALSE PUZZLE OF THE CONSTANCY OF PHENOMENAL OBJECTS

The so-called "constancy" of objects in perception despite changing stimulation and changing sensation has long been considered a puzzle. For the past century, experimenters have studied the perceived size of an object with retinal size variant, the perceived form of an object with retinal form variant, and the perceived surface-color of an object with variation of the intensity and wavelength of the light in the retinal image. There is always some tendency to perceive the "real" size, form, and color of the surface of the object, the amount of constancy depending on experimental conditions. Explanations of this result differ with different theorists but they all begin with one assumption, namely, that the perceived size, form, and color are based on retinal size, form, and color respectively—that the process of perception must *start with* these stimulus variables of the image.

According to the present theory this assumption is mistaken. There is information in the optic array for the size, shape, and color of a surface in a layout of other surfaces. The information is a matter of complex invariant ratios and relations; it is not easy to isolate experimentally. But the size, the form, and the color of the image impressed on the retina, when they are experienced at all, are not relevant to and not commensurable with the dimensions and slant and pigmentation of the surface. If I am right, a whole century of experimental research on the *amount* of constancy obtained by an observer is pointless. Insofar as these laboratory experiments have impoverished the stimulus information for perception they are not relevant to perception.

THE EFFECT ON PERCEPTION OF IMPOVERISHING THE STIMULUS INFORMATION

If perception is a process of operating on the deliverances of sense, it has seemed obvious that one way of investigating the process is to *impoverish* the stimulation, to *minimize* the cues, and observe what happens. Visual perception is supposed to come into its own when the input is reduced. Perception then has more work to do. Experiments with a tachistoscope, or with blurred pictures, or with very faint images on a screen are therefore common in the psychology laboratory.

According to the present theory, however, this is not the best way of investigating the process, for perception is frustrated when the stimulus information is impoverished. If the visual system is not allowed to "hunt" for the external specifying information, all sorts of internal processes begin to occur. They are very interesting processes, worthy of investigation, but they should not be confused with the normal process of perceiving.

The situation is similar when contradictory information in the same display is presented to an observer, "conflicting cues." The ambiguous figures and reversible perspectives that have been so frequently studied are of this sort. Ink blots are a combination of impoverished and inconsistent information. I argue that the *guessing* that goes on in these experiments, the attempt to fill out or complete a perception by supplementing the almost meaningless data, is not indicative of what goes on in ordinary perception. The process does not reach an equilibrium state of *clarity* as it does in ordinary perception. And the achieving of precise awareness is the aim of perception.

Orthodox theories assume that there is always an "objective contribution" to perception (the sensations) and a "subjective contribution" to perception (innate ideas, or memories, or field-forces in the brain), the two contributions being combined in various proportions. I reject this assumption. If unequivocal stimulus information is made available to an observer in an experiment, his perception will be determined by it and by nothing else. When *ambient* stimulus information is available to an observer outside the laboratory he can *select* the information that interests him; he can give attention to one part instead of another, but his perception will be determined by the information he attends to.

When *no* stimulus information is allowed to reach the eyes of an observer, as when the eyes are covered by diffusing plastic caps (which can be made of halved ping-pong balls) he is *deprived* of visual perception, although not of sensation. The subject does not like the situation; it is worse than being blindfolded. The only visual experience is that of "nothing." His perceptual system acts a little like a motor running without a load. If he is not allowed to go to sleep, experiences resembling hallucinations may arise.

SUMMARY AND CONCLUSIONS

This theory of vision asserts that perception is direct and is not mediated by retinal images transmitted to the brain. Most theories assume that perception of the world is *indirect*, and that all we ever *directly* perceive is our retinal images.

Now it is perfectly true that when an observer looks at a painting, photograph, sculpture, or model, he gets an *indirect* visual perception, a *mediated* experience, an awareness *at second hand*, of whatever is represented. A human artifact of this sort is an *image* in the original meaning of the term. It is a light-reflecting object in its own right but it displays *information* to specify a quite different object (Gibson, 1966, Chapter 11). An image in this straightforward meaning of the term is something to be looked at, and it has to be looked at, of course, with eyes. Thus there can be a direct perception of a man's portrait accompanied by an indirect perception of the man himself.

The fallacy of the standard theories of perception consists of taking as a model for vision the kind of indirect visual perception that uses pictures as substitutes for things. The false analogy should now be evident. Direct perception of a retinal image implies an eye inside the head, in the brain, with which to look at the image. But there is no little man anywhere in the brain who can do this. We do not look at our retinal images and perceive the world in the way that we look at a portrait and perceive the sitter. Putting the objection another way, the so-called image on the retina is not an image at all, properly speaking, since it cannot be looked at, as a picture can be looked at, and cannot therefore mediate perception. The famous experiment of looking at the back of the excised eye of a slaughtered ox and observing an image is profoundly misleading. The eye is a biological device for sampling the information available in an ambient optic array. The vertebrate eye does it in one way and the insect eye does it in another way but both register differences of light in different direction at a point of observation.

The availability of information in ambient light and the possibility that it can be picked up directly have implications for epistemology. They lend sophisticated support to the naive belief that we have direct knowledge of the world around us. They support direct realism (Gibson, 1967). If these hypotheses prove correct, they justify our deep feeling that *the senses can be trusted*. At the same time they explain the seemingly contrary conviction *that the senses cannot be trusted*. For a distinction has been drawn between what might be called the *useful* senses, the perceptual systems, and the *useless* senses, the channels of sensation.

A DISCUSSION OF GIBSON'S PAPER

T. E. Weckowicz

Professor Gibson's paper, in which he presented his very original theory of perception and the possible epistemological implications of it, is of great interest not only to psychologists but also to philosophers.

His theory is really a revolutionary one. It proposes sensationless perceptual processes which extract directly the information, in the form of abstract invariances, from the ambient energy flux impinging on a moving organism. It does away with such hoary and cherished concepts of experimental psychology and empiricist philosophy as the retinal image, sensation, sense datum and indeed the percept itself. It makes a clear break with the Empiricist and Associationist tradition of philosophy and psychology. This is an old tradition going back to the English empiricist philosophers of the seventeenth and eighteenth centuries and their nineteenth century associationist successors in philosophy and psychology. With regard to the specific theories of perception in this tradition one has only to mention Johannes Müller's doctrine of specific nerve energy and Helmholtz theory of unconscious inferences. These empiricist philosophies and psychologies either did not really come to grips with the problem of knowledge or ended with epistemological conclusions of Solipsism or Scepticism.

There have been many attempts to break the impasse, such as Kant's contention that the contents of mind did not constitute knowledge. This required a transcendental act of knowing on the part of the subject.[1] Thus *a priori* categories of reason and synthetic *a priori* propositions were introduced to break the impasse. Another example which can be mentioned is the concept of intentionality as introduced by Brentano and Husserl. The contents of consciousness became objects of knowledge and acquired the appropriate meaning only by an intention of the subject. Intending was conceived as a mental act. The problem of meaning, a step-child of psychology, was solved by referring contents of mind: such as words, or propositions to various real and ideal entities. This solution of the problem of meaning fit very well the symbolic indirect knowledge processes, but it did not answer the problem of immediate knowledge acquired by perceiving. What did the perceived, meaningful objects refer to? Well, they could refer only to themselves, unless one postulated a ghostly observer inside one's head who observed percepts or retinal images which referred to real objects. Thus one again ended in the blind alley of phenomenalism. There was an impasse, which was only bypassed but not resolved, by Behaviourism which abandoned the whole area of perception and replaced it with that of discrimination behaviour. This, of course, did not answer the epistemological problem. The so-called common language philosophers tried to solve the problem by adopting the position of Naive Realism on the basis of the analysis of common language usages, but at the cost of dissociating themselves from scientific psychology. As far as the psychology of perception is concerned, the impasse has remained unresolved.

There have been many examples in the history of science when an impasse was resolved by somebody putting forward a revolutionary idea, which appeared to be quite preposterous in the framework of the existing body of knowledge. When one reads about Professor Gibson's "sensationless" perceptions one cannot help thinking of another group of men who at the turn of the century, not being able to solve the problem of thinking, put forward an idea which appeared to be preposterous within the then existing framework of psychological knowledge. "Sensationless" perception brings to mind the shades of Würzburg and the idea of *unanschauliche Bewußtheit* or *Bewußtseinslage*, translated by Titchener as "impalpable awareness" or "impalpable conscious attitude." The idea of awareness without sensations, in those days when it was believed that sensations were the very stuff mind or consciousness were made of, was as preposterous as the idea of matter without volume or mass. Now, Professor Gibson suggests that perceptions are not composed of sensations but consist of direct awareness of the external objects and one's body. Perhaps actively extracting information from the ambient energy, which according to Professor Gibson constitutes perception, is an act like raising one's arm and is as directly experienced and as free of awareness of sensations as the raising of one's arm is directly experienced and is free of awareness of the contractions of individual muscles. These are philosophical implications of Professor Gibson's theory of direct perception as I see them.

As a conclusion of this discussion I would like to query two points in Professor Gibson's paper. The first point concerns information. Professor Gibson when he talks about information does not mean the concept of information as it appears in Shannon's information theory. Some other theory of information is required. When invariances in the structure of the energy array are extracted some grammar (perhaps a topological grammar) is implied. These notions will eventually require formalization. The second point also concerns extracting information from the ambient stimulus array.

An active exploration is postulated. The question which can be asked is whether it is a random exploration. It it is not random, then a certain circularity between the sensory input and sensory organ adjustment is implied, pointing to a possibility of such mechanisms as groupings and reversible set mechanisms postulated by Piaget.

NOTES

1. This contention of Kant was to some extent adumbrated by Locke's notion of reflections.

COMMENTS ON GIBSON'S PAPER

John W. Gyr

It can be shown that not all perceptual information resides in the optic array, as Gibson claims. Rather, the organism monitors not only what happens in terms of input but what happens *as a result of what the organism does*. This introduces a role for efference, feedback, and feedforward into perceptual process and requires an extension of the Gibsonian perceptual paradigm.

The role of motor movement in perception as a means to disambiguate or structure the input from an optic array has been stressed by Gibson. This is the minimal role which the motoric plays in perception. Even this limited role forces the theoretician—if he is to construct an integrated theory of perception—to inquire into the problem of how efference and reafference, interact, i.e., into the relation between perception and attention or search. By and large, Gibson's theory says very little about how attention and perception can be derived from an interconnected set of principles. In Gibson's theory about perception, the main and in essence the sole stress is on principles of ecological optics. Attentional mechanisms are treated essentially as a separate phenomenon. What is needed is a theory in which perception itself is regarded as involving the intercorrelation between sensory and motor functions. In such a theory it is natural to tie motor movements to perceptual phenomena and to consider abstraction, filtering and search within a common conceptual framework.

It can be argued that the role of the motoric in perception considerably exceeds that assigned to it by Gibson; that the efferent-reafferent *relation* carries information in the perceptual process, and that sensorimotor feedback and feedforward processes are a natural part of perception. Such a conception allows, at least in principle, an integrated treatment of abstraction, filtering and search. The following considerations can be brought forward as favoring this kind of theory. First, the structure of the brain is such that orderly relations exist between events in brain and events in *behavioral* space. This fact makes an efferent-reafferent theory of perception at least a legitimate candidate. Second, there is evidence for the fact that a number of perceptual processes—both of space and of pattern—do involve some kind of feedback and comparison between efferent and reafferent events and that such processes are *necessary* to perceptual functioning. Third, there is some evidence for mechanisms, variably labeled feedforward, predictive tuning or gating, which tell the sensory system what is going to be done. These processes too are under some kind of motoric control.

The advantages of the kind of theory of perception which can built on the above considerations are several. One has already been mentioned. It concerns the possibility to build a theory of perception in which processes of abstraction, filtering and search interdigitate. A second advantage is that in such a theory, perception and perceptual development are one and the same thing since perception as an efferent-reafferent feedback process in a complex environment is, in principle, forever changing. Thirdly, by having informational feedback, an efferent-reafferent perceptual system which possesses "knowledge" of the results of its own activity is self-reinforcing and not depend on concrete rewards and punishments. As such it is a system more in line with the true character of perceptual development of organisms in natural surroundings. Fourthly, by including motoric events as a necessary part of the perceptual process, some of the mathematical structures, such as mathematical *groups*, which purportedly underly transformations by displacement may become useful conceptual tools for describing perceptual events, for understanding higher-order invariants, for arriving at analytic notions of perceptual organization, and the like. Finally, the characteristic of motoric systems—such as the fact that motions are indefinitely repeatable—have been linked not only to, say, the perception of space, but to fundamental properties of cognition, language and epistemology. The general nature of the above are, theoretically, still very uncertain. It is possible that a perception theory based on efferent-reafferent principles could help facilitate the approaches made to some of these problems.

CRITICAL REMARKS TO J. J. GIBSON'S CONCEPTION OF "DIRECT" VISUAL PERCEPTION, i.e., OF REVIVED PREPHYSIOLOGICAL REALISM

Wolfgang Metzger

I shall deal with three points:

1) Realism;
2) The ecological world;
3) Information and optic array.

FIRST POINT: REALISM

1. Gibson and I agree in being realists. But I should not say "naive" Realism vs. sophisticated Realism because "naive" has a kind of contemptuous connotation. I would rather use the terms *"prephysiological* vs. *postphysiological* Realism".

2. In the sense of Tennessen, Gibson tries to jump back to the moment where critical realism originated.

3. This moment was when it was found that there is no single phenomenon to be found in the surroundings of a normal adult in the state of being awake without a process beginning at a source of stimulation (I do not say "distant" stimulus, which is a contradiction in itself), travelling to a sense organ, stimulating this organ, i.e. arousing excitations that go on travelling to some center in the cortex, and without this cortical region working undisturbedly. If this is true for any single phenomenon (as the color of this neck-tie) it is at once true for the whole world around us.

4. This implies a pluralistic view, in which there is assumed a single and common transphenomenal world of sources of stimulation among others of experimental sets, to which correspond as many phenomenal worlds as there are living beings with distance–receptors.—
This world of the immediately given is *not* identical with the world of stimulation sources, but an effect of it in the organism that is allowed for by the way the sensory organs and the nervous system work: it has

the characteristics of an image (except its reality-character) or, if you prefer, of a copy.

5. Psychology of perception is, among others, occupied with the degree of correspondence or conformity between the transphenomenal world of sources of stimulation and the world of the immediately given, the only world acknowledged by James J. Gibson.

6. The deviations between the two worlds have in everyday cases proved to be not so *diverse* that agreement between different observers is prevented from occurring. Thus subjects can practically identify or consider as identical their different phenomenal worlds.

7. But at the same time these *deviations* are in every case so systematic that it has proved suitable to replace the study of fortuitous illusions by a systematic quantitative comparison between "phenogram" and "ontogram" in every possible percept, which in no case are congruent in every regard.

8. Yet, as these deviations have the same direction in all subjects of the same species the information and communication value of the percepts is not impaired by this: The structures of percepts in diverse phenomenal worlds will be more similar to each other than any of them is to the underlying structure in the physical world.

Under normal conditions the correspondence between subjective worlds is astonishing but it is in no case sufficient for Gibson's jump to the hypothesis according to which the immediately given is numerically the same for any possible observer at the same viewpoint.

If percepts are assumed as numerically—not only structurally—identical with the sources of stimulation, they should be as independent from the subject or organism as these.

From this follows a series of questions. I would be happy to hear the answers to the following:

1) How is the phenomenon of phantom limbs possible?

2) How is it possible that by the change of view or attitude obvious changes in the environment take place?

3) How is it possible that by the affective state and by prevailing needs the environment may be thoroughly changed, too? This being the fundamental problem of the relation of drive and knowledge!

4) How can psychological phenomena be found outside ourselves: as feelings and mood of others (cf. Freudian projection)?

5) What about the exterior localization of dreams, apparitions, phantoms, hallucinations, after-images, eidetic phenomena, stroboscopic movements?

6) What about the normal deviations of the immediately given depending on differences of species, of personality characteristics, and of momentary states of the organim?

7) What about the specific deviations, modifications, distortions, alterations of the outer world including one's own body by psychoses, nervous diseases, poisoning, and cerebral lesions?

SECOND POINT: THE PROBLEM OF ECOLOGY

That the physical correlates of phenomena in the transphenomenal world are not atoms or molecules but objects whose magnitude is on the order of the human organism does not arouse difficulty. No new physics need to be founded in order to account for that: The ecological physics of Dr. Gibson is already a part of existing physical science. Physics itself has problems that are related to very *different orders of magnitude*: if the question is e.g. whether this chair will remain standing or will be tilted by a push of a certain intensity, direction, and point of impact, or whether the most adequate form of the wings of an airplane has to be found, or if the question is which is exactly the orbit and the time in which the moon finishes one circuit round the earth, no physicist will bother about atoms and molecules.

THIRD POINT: INFORMATION AND OPTIC ARRAY

Of course what happens in the sensory organs can be described as picking up and processing of information. But first any information must be carried by a physical process, which in the case of vision is electromagnetic oscillation, and second any process of this kind must arrive at a receiver and bring about changes in it. How much of the information will be forwarded to the regions in which the processes corresponding to having percepts go on depends on characteristics of the receptor, in this case the two-dimensionally distributed elementary retinal cells. If these are not believed to mediate decisive information, another organ must be named as their substitute. Due to this two-dimensionality of the receiving and forwarding apparatus no tri-dimensional array can be perceived directly. Rather, for the eye there exists nothing but the two-dimensional *distribution* of stimulation, including their changes in time which must not be considered as sequences of static cross sections but as continuous changes, the sequence of which can only be understood as transitions in the sense of infinitesimal calculus.

If there are such things as tri-dimensional optic arrays, there are but two possibilities: Either they are physical in the sense that they exist—in terms of the causal process—on this side of the retina. In this case they cannot play any role for the phenomenal distribution of visual percepts, because the light-waves have to pass through the retina, that is, through a two-dimensional filter, in which all tri-dimensional features of sources of stimulation, including those of optic arrays (if any were left in electromagnetic oscillation), are definitely extinguished. Or they are phenomenal, that mean,—in terms of the causal process—they come into existence beyond the retina only. In this second case they must have been reconstructed on the basis of characteristics of the two-dimensional spatio-temporal distribution of retinal stimuli. Some principles according to which this reconstruction may occur, have been known since Kopfermann; others have been described by the author and later on, among others, by Hans Wallach, and above all by Gibson himself. Even in this case, optic arrays, without being physical facts, can account for all the phenomena for which this factor was introduced by Gibson, as has been shown by Hering, Gelb, Koffka, Kardos, and many others.

COMMENT RE GIBSON'S PAPER

J. R. Royce

I am interested in pursuing the epistemological issues which are embedded in Gibson's position. In particular, I've come up with an insight, and I'd appreciate Dr. Gibson's reaction to it.

The insight has to do with the interpretation of veridicality and how it relates to realism. The standard position says veridicality means we have perceived so accurately that we "know" the "real object." But, of course, there are problems concerning what's "really out there." As so often happens with intractable problems, we may be asking the wrong question. Instead of asking how the subject can "know" the "real object," perhaps it is more appropriate to ask in what way the object is "real" to the subject. When put in this way the "probabilistic functionalism" of Brunswik and Gibson's "ecological invariants" provide us with powerful linkages to "reality out there." For Gibson is saying there are aspects of the ecology the organism can detect, and I am suggesting that, regardless of its "objective reality," the fact that the organism can pick up ecological invariants means there is at least some kind of match between "internal order" or "world-view" and "external order" or "the object."

Professor Gibson claims his theory provides support for direct (or naive) realism because the pickup of ecological invariants allows the subject to "know" the "real object." The interpretation I am putting forth is probably more consistent with a critical or constructive realism wherein the subject can be said to be dealing with reality *because of* the invariance of what is perceived. The point here is that reality comes from invariance, *not* from veridicality in the traditional sense.

REPLY TO GYR

J. J. Gibson

He and I seem to agree that specific movements of the head, limbs, and body correspond to specific transformations of the optic array or specific optical motions within the array. Far from underplaying this fact, I have emphasized it and studied its manifestations. The difference between us is that I call it simply visual kinesthesis or visual proprioception whereas Gyr, following von Holst, says that these inputs have to be "monitored" and "compared with a copy of the output." Von Holst gets into all sorts of muddles with active *vs.* passive movements whereas I simply postulate that specific optical transformations correspond to the specific movements of the animal (or the events in the world) that caused them. Von Holst assumes distinct channels of sense whereas I assume perceptual systems.

So I do not believe that motor action helps to "produce optic structure" and "contributes" to perception. *Exploratory* motor action helps to isolate the *invariants* of optical structure under transformation. The information for perception of the world resides in these invariants while information about the body's motor action resides in the transformations. My theory takes account of both perception and proprioception at the same time.

I never said that "all the perceptual information resides in the optic array." I said it was available to the visual system in a group or set of optic arrays, and that it has to be picked up by the exploratory activity of the observer.

No one has shown that "perception is affected by changes in the efferent state of the organism even when there is *no* change in afferent input from the optic array," not Sperry or Festinger or Held or anyone else. There is a confusion of thought here, for Gyr seemed to agree at the outset that a bodily response always made a difference in the ambient optic array and that all the observer had to do to get an afferent input from it was to keep his eyes open.

REPLY TO ROYCE

J. J. Gibson

There are, surely, all degrees of richness of perception from the simplest detections to the most elaborate and detailed awarenesses. The environment is inexhaustible in its complexities and in its details. Thus I do not claim that we ever "perceive so accurately" that we "know" the "real object," and I do not think I ever claimed that perception was veridical except in the ordinary-language sense of the term *perception* meaning one thing and the term *misperception* meaning another. I never intended to say that the pickup of ecological invariants allows one to "know the real object", so perhaps my kind of realism does not fall into one of the academic types. I don't know what "critical" or "constructive" realism would be. But I am convinced that invariance comes from reality, not the other way round. Invariance in the ambient optic array over time is not constructed or deduced; it is there to be discovered.

BIBLIOGRAPHY

Gibson, J. J., *The perception of the visual world.* Boston: Houghton Mifflin, 1950.
Gibson, J. J., Ecological optics. *Vision research*, 1961, **1**, 253–262.
Gibson, J. J., *The senses considered as perceptual systems.* Boston: Houghton Mifflin, 1966.
Gibson, J. J., New reasons for realism. *Synthese*, 1967, **17**, 162–172.
Hering, E., Beiträge zur Physiology. 2. Heft. Leipzig: Engelmann 1862.
Köhler, W., Ein altes Scheinproblem. Naturwiss., 1929, *17*, 395–401.
Köhler, W., *The Place of Value in a World of Facts.* New York: Liveright 1938.
Kopfermann, Herta, Psychologische Untersuchungen über die Wirkung zweidimensionaler Darstellung körperlicher Gebilde. *Psychol. Forsch.*, 1930, **13**, 291–364.
Lauenstein, Lotte, Über räumliche Wirkungen von Licht und Schatten. *Psychol. Forsch.*, 1938, **22**, 267–319.
Metzger, W., Tiefenerscheinungen in optischen Bewegungsfeldern. *Psychol. Forsch.*, 1935, *20*, 195–260.
Metzger, W., Gesetze des Sehens. Frankfurt: Kramer ²1953.
Metzger, W., Das einäugige Tiefensehen. In: Metzger, W. und H. Erke (Hrsg.): Wahrnehmung und Bewußtsein. Hdb. d. Psychol., Bd. I/1. Göttingen: Hogrefe 1966, 556–589,
Metzger, W., Zur anschaulichen Repräsentation von Rotationsvorgängen und ihrer Deutung durch Gestaltkreislehre und Gestalttheorie. *Z. Sinnesphysiol.*, 1940, **68**, 261–279.
Metzger, W., Über die Notwendigkeit kybernetischer Vorstellungen in der Theorie des Verhaltens. *Z. Psychol.*, 1965, **171**, 336–342.
Metzger, W., Psychologie. Darmstadt: Steinkopff ⁴1968.
Überweg, F., Zur Theorie der Richtung des Sehens. *Z. rationelle Med.*, 1858, 3, V., 268.282.
Wallach, H., Über visuell wahrgenommene Bewegungsrichtung. *Psychol. Forsch.*, 1935, **20**, 325–338.
Wallach, H., and O'Connell, D. N., The kinetic depth effect. *J. exp. Psychol.*, 1935 **45**, 205–217.

VII

THE PHENOMENAL-PERCEPTUAL FIELD AS A CENTRAL STEERING MECHANISM

Wolfgang Metzger

University of Münster

It requires some courage to speak on consciousness to an American audience, for the phenomena any study of consciousness must rely on are too questionable for them. Strictly speaking they only consist of a sum of verbal reactions whose relation to the underlying observations as reported by the informant is highly complicated and whose reliability in any case remains uncertain.

Theoretically, all contents of consciousness have a certain chance of manifesting themselves somehow in overt nonverbal behavior. But American psychologists in general do not trust very much in the value of behavior as representing what goes on in the mind of a subject. So many of them try to get along without any knowledge about consciousness except for sensory discrimination which can be represented without uttering a single word simply by running to the left or to the right in a choice experiment. As for the rest, they consider a human being to be a "black box" that after suffering certain impacts from the outside at a certain spot of its surface reacts on its surroundings at another spot. They seem to feel safe only in studying the familiar $S-R$ relation.

But Europeans who cannot abandon their old love also have their difficulties with it. The phenomena of consciousness are, we might say, quite reluctant about being brought into a consistent system. To give an instance: from physical as well as physiological knowledge it follows undeniably that processes underlying those phenomena must go on in the cerebrum, that means, within the skull of the subject. But on the other hand, no subject can be found who is ready to admit having found the effects of stimulation of any sense organ within his skull. In extreme cases—as in auditory or visual sensation—they are not even localized at his own body, as e.g., in the region of the mediating sense organs, but far from it—as a color (yet as an afterimage) at the opposite wall, or as a noise even beyond the room, somewhere outside.

From a previous era, when some of you were still occupied with conscious phenomena, you will remember the way in which H. v. Helmholtz and J. v. Kries attempted to solve this dilemma. They introduced a hypothetical process by which they believed sensations were transferred from their original place within the skull to that place in the surroundings of the body where they were actually found by the observer. I refer to the assumption designated as the projection-hypothesis in the sense of an exteriorization of elementary sensations—which, by the way does not, in principle, differ very much from the projection hypothesis used in the psychoanalytic sense, that refers to feelings, emotions, and intentions, as projected from the subject into other persons.

The dilemma intrinsic to this assumption, which at first seemed to be insoluble, consists in the following:

1) The process of exteriorization must, for its greater part, take place outside the organism and therefore cannot be a physiological process.
2) On the other hand, physical processes of such a kind are not known and it is most unlikely that they will ever be found.

But $S-R$ psychologists also had their difficulties. $S-R$ relations have not always proved to be as simple and unambiguous as was first supposed when Watson and his friends began preaching the gospel of objective psychology nearly sixty years ago. There are many different responses that can be called forth by one and the same stimulus. And on the other hand, there are many stimuli that can be followed by one and the same response. Auxiliary concepts such as 'covert behavior'—i.e. a behavior that is not objectively observable and therefore must not be an object of behavioristic psychology—could not be dispensed with, and these were soon followed by Tolman's 'intervening variables' and by the 'hypothetical constructs' of MacCorquodale and others.

From the very first it seemed to me most probable that at least a great many of those intervening events or factors which had to be postulated in order to develop a consistent theory of overt behavior could be immediately ascertained as observable contents of consciousness. In this way it appeared likely that the wide gap between stimulus and response could at least partially be filled in by observation and we could hope that by these means some light would fall into the darkness of the behavioristic black box after all.

There were two more facts that encouraged some of us to take up again the inquiry into consciousness. First a methodological fact: The role of speech or verbal behavior as a means of communicating subjective phenomena can be reduced to the extent that must be tolerated in *every* science. The method is simple. Instead of taking some other person as the subject of examination, the psychologist himself has to assume the role of the subject, while assigning the role of experimenter to his assistant. When doing so, the information of the psychologist is first hand information, just as that of the physicist when observing the hand of a voltmeter. True, no second observer can look at his phenomena as such. But this methodological deficiency can be overcome by repeating the observation by another person under exactly the same conditions. While obviously the observation of single sensations (such as the reddish hue of a color) cannot be "repeated" in this fashion, this repetition and verification by another observer is quite possible with regard to organization, structures, and structural characteristics, as Oskar Graefe has shown. And even reliable measurement has been shown to be possible within the realm of consciousness by Stevens, Ekman, and others.

Besides this methodological justification there is another achievement by fundamental reflection on consciousness, which has produced a new situation. Forty years ago, in 1929, Wolfgang Köhler succeeded in demonstrating that the projection hypothesis need not be necessary, if we assume that not only (1) the image of the objects but also (2) the image of the subjective bodily ego and (3) the image of the relations between the object and the subject, are correlated with cerebral processes of a corresponding dynamic structure and distribution. This is, indeed, the only assumption about conscious phenomena that is consistent with itself, and with the scientific world concept, as it is generally accepted.

The non-identity of "distant stimuli" or, expressed more logically, of the source of stimulation with the conscious phenomenon must also be assumed for the observer's own body exactly as for other perceived objects. As soon as this is recognized, the whole dilemma between the localization of sensory processes and the localization of objects and their qualities turns out to be a mere fallacy. For "inside" in this connection refers to the organism which as such is no conscious phenomenon but rather a complicated source of "proximal" stimuli,—while "outside" refers to the bodily self, which is in no way identical with the organism but is itself an "image" or percept, i.e., a complex of sensations emergent upon the total excitation originating from the diverse proprioceptors of the organism together with the images of parts of his own body as seen by the subject himself. (See Fig. 1, from Metzger, *Psychologie*, 4. ed. 1968, p. 283.) Seen in this way, the

16*

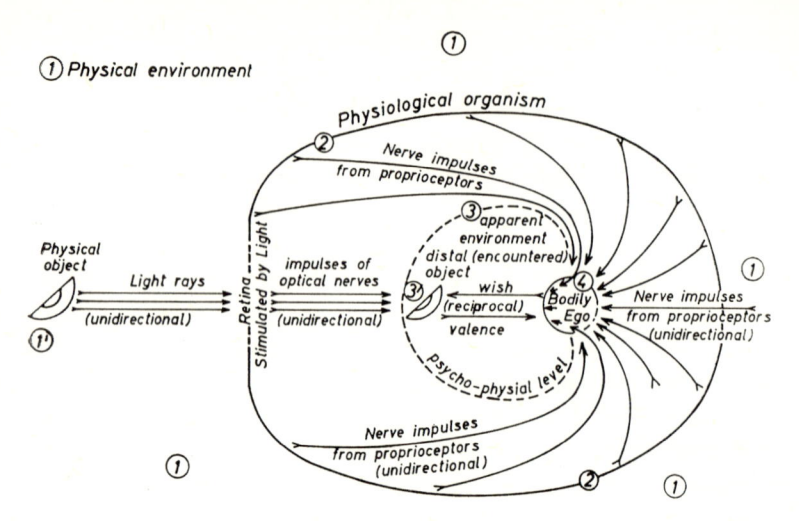

FIGURE 1 Relationship between physical world including physiological organism (= Macrocosm) and phenomenal-perceptual world including experienced bodily Ego (= Microcosm)

1 = physical environment of organism
1' = physical object, reflecting light rays
2 = physiological organism, as part of the physical world
3 = apparent (perceived) environment of bodily Ego
3' = apparent (distal) object or percept, representing the physical object
4 = bodily Ego, as part of the phenomenal-perceptual world, representing the organism

apparent relations between perceived objects and the subject exactly correspond to the objective relations between the "distant stimuli" and the organism. Instead of being localized within the ego, seen objects appear to be opposite or vis-s-vis the ego, just as complexes of distant stimuli are opposite or vis-a-vis the organism. (This means, by the way, that secondary processes of "objectivation" of an original purely subjective experience, as they are developed in neo-Kantian literature, e.g. by Ernst Cassirer, need not be assumed.) I know these statements are highly redundant. But I have learned from experience that without a relatively high degree of redundancy these matters will never be understood. So I shall go on describing some consequences of what I said above.

What results for the problem of *voluntary action* if we apply to it the outcome of the line of thinking followed so far? What happens if, e.g., a person lifts his hand and puts it on the table again? In order to avoid misunderstandings, we must keep in mind that the fact of "two worlds" applies to every single trait or content of experience and therefore is also valid for my own hand that I feel, see, and influence by my will, whose behavior we are now going to analyse. In this case, too, it is indispensable to discriminate strictly between the "objective" arm as a member of my organism, and the conscious image of it, which is a part of my bodily ego that I can feel and see. As was said already, only this image can be influenced immediately by our voluntary intentions. This discrimination follows conclusively from the fact that, on the one hand, by anesthesizing the afferent nerve tracks originating in a subject's arm and by simultaneously letting him shut his eyes the arm disappears for the subject, while for another observer it is just as perceivable as before; and on the other hand, if a subject loses his objective arm by an accident, his limb may persist being a more or less clearly perceptible part of the bodily ego in the so-called phantom limb experiences. In the first case the phenomenal, in the second the anatomical member of the two normally associated counterparts is lacking. Furthermore, the decisive fact of two-ness is necessarily also valid for the *relations* between the acting subject and the actions following from his intentions as compared with the processes going on at the same time within his organism as a result of efferent processes between his brain and its anatomical extremities. My intention to lift up my right hand, e.g., can only be directed to the phenomenal hand as a part of my phenomenal bodily ego but never directly to the anatomical part of my organism that is related to the former and bears the same name. Only by assuming this can the totality of phenomena involved in voluntary action be accounted for without contradiction. To these belongs, among others, the discrepancy between the region of the bodily ego on which our will immediately acts, and the region of the organism that, at the same time, is subject to innervation. As Julius Pikler has shown long ago, the former region lies unmistakeably within the hand itself as a part of the bodily ego, whereas the latter just as unmistakeably lies within the muscular system of the upper arm and the shoulder of the anatomical organism. In general, from the control of movement of the phenomenal arm there follows a secondary control of the arm as part of the organism which corresponds to the former with admirable accuracy. But this precise reduplication of the phenomenal motion by the objective motion is in no way a matter of course; on the contrary, it borders on the miraculous. Nor does it work in every case. Under certain conditions it fails. This is the case, among others, when a person acts in a dream, in the hallucinations of motion due to affections of the brain by psychoses, lesions, or poisoning, as well as in the illusory movement of phantom-limbs after amputation In this connection an observation I made sometime ago while awaking from a very lively dream may be of interest. I had been rather active in that dream and when I began to wake up my right arm was above my head. My theoretical interest awoke more quickly than my body, so I could observe what now happened. The arm above my head dissolved without moving, while another arm came into existence resting on my stomach, an arm which obviously had objectively been there all the time.

This duplication of the environment as both a physical world of stimuli, distal and proximal, and a phenomenal world of percepts—and also of one's own person as both a physiological organism and a bodily ego—as has been said above already, also refers to the mutual interaction between a person and his environment. But as can be recognized from the prevailing use of the terms 'stimulus' and 'response' in experimental psychology as well as in physiology and ethology, this reduplication has not been taken into account in most cases. In practice we are compelled by the facts to differentiate the concept of stimulus into two clearly distinguishable sub-concepts. The first sub-concept of stimulus means the physico-chemical processes that act on the receptor-cells of the organism; the second is a little more intricate, as we shall see immediately.

The response of the organism to a stimulus in the first sense may be of two different types. The first type consists in an organic change or process (such as the production of saliva or the contraction of the pupil), frequently without any concomitant conscious phenomena. In the second type of response two phases must be distinguished. In the first phase, something happens in the phenomenal world (a new percept appears, an existing one changes or moves or disappears etc.). In the second phase this new phenomenon acts upon the ego or subject, e.g. attracts his attention or scares him away. It may also invite him to handle it in a certain manner. For these characteristics of percepts (not of stimuli in the first sense!) Kurt Lewin introduced the German term "Aufforderungscharakter", which was translated into English by "valence". This action of a percept on the ego may also be called stimulation, though not in a physiological but only in a psychological sense. In everyday German, we also use for this the term "Reiz", the literal translation of stimulus (as in "ein reizendes Mädchen") while in English, expressions such as 'attractiveness', 'enticement', 'lure', or 'appeal', are preferred. One thing must be kept in mind: the events I have just been dealing with occur between the percept and the ego within the phenomenal world and not between the physical surroundings and the organism; in other words, not between stimuli in the first sense and perceptors. If, notwithstanding, it is customary in behaviorist psychology to call "stimulus" a female, or an enemy, or a mate, or an offspring, or some prey animal, it must be clear that in doing so the objective level of physico-chemical and physiological processes, with which it was supposed to deal exclusively, has been left behind.

We must treat the concept of response in exact analogy with what has been said above. This term also has two meanings. In the first sense, it refers to the changes in positions of various parts of the phenomenal bodily ego, including any preceding changes of attitudes, emotions, and intentions; in the second sense, to the execution by the extremities of the organism of the intended movement which, as we have already mentioned, does not occur when a person dreams and therefore must logically be distinguished from the response in the first sense.

I come now to my crucial point, namely to the question: what is the use of this duplication of the world into a physical and a perceptive one, of the person into an organism and a bodily ego, of stimulation into configurations of physico-chemical impacts upon receptors and valences affecting the ego, and of reaction into intended changes of the bodily ego and motions executed by parts of the organism? What relevance can all this have? It is extremely improbable that so highly complicated an organization could have developed during evolution and preserved without a considerable survival value. And it seems to me that this value can clearly be demonstrated.

We begin with the action side of the picture. Here we find a striking similarity to the well-known technical servo-mechanisms, e.g., the mechanical steering of a large vessel. To illustrate this by the simplest parallel: Instead of a direct connection between the steering-wheel and the rudder there is a two-step connection. The first step connects the bridge with the steering machine, the second the machine with the rudder. Instead of the wheel it suffices to have a small lever that can be turned easily, while the hard work of turning the heavy rudder through highly resistant water is done by the machine according to the information given it by the lever.

The phenomenal arm as perceived by the subject which is dependent on his will corresponds to the lever as handled by the helmsman. The arm as part of the organism corresponds to the rudder, and the musculature bringing the organismic arm into the position prescribed by the motion intended for the phenomenal arm corresponds to the steering-machine that moves the rudder according to the position of the lever.

It is true there is a difference between the nervous and the technical servomechanisms, which I will try to point out now. Mechanically it is possible to fix on the shaft of the first lever a second one that indicates the actual position of the rudder and its deviation from the intended position, coinciding with the first lever when the intended position is reached by the rudder.

In the neural mechanism there is no second lever. The lever is constructed in such a way that it indicates the true effect of the intention to move at the same time. This comes about by the following trick. This lever—we mean always the arm as part of the bodily ego—cannot move independently from the "rudder" viz. the arm as part of the organism and therefore cannot run ahead of it. That means that even the least "pressure" acting upon the "lever" puts the organismic arm in motion, and the lever is brought into its intended position by the activity of the organismic arm in moving to the intended position. This, of course, presupposes that the reactions of the "steering machine" are extraordinarily quick, in other words, that it reacts to minimal dislocations of the lever, and practically without delay. Some years ago I discussed this principle of construction with a group of specialists in cybernetics and, according to their judgment, such a construction is theoretically possible. Considering the variety and variability of active human (and vertebrate) motion, its advantages are obvious. Perhaps under the conditions of human action it is the only one that works.

So far I have discussed a rather simple but relatively unnatural case, a case in which the subject is alone with one of his limbs and the intended position of this limb is fixed arbitrarily by the subject. In order to transfer the idea to a more important situation, viz. the subject's interaction with other things or beings, above all with those objects which serve to gratify his needs or to carry out his intentions, we have to take a glance at the other side of the matter, at the side of the objects. Here, too, the analogy of orienting oneself in his surroundings by using a periscope is obvious to the engineer. This periscope differs from the normal type by the fact that the observer does not look outward through a set of lenses and prisms but observes an image that is projected on a plane inside the whole system just as is the image of the sun in the well known Einstein-tower at Potsdam. But this image differs from the image of the sun in the astronomical device in that its parts are more than a mosaic whose elements reflect light more or less apart from any dynamic interaction. In consciousness these parts are units dynamically segregated from each other and coherent in themselves, tightly packed within a narrow cerebral field, one of them being the unit representing one's own ego. Hereby, dynamic interaction of a nature not yet sufficiently known becomes possible between these units corresponding to the organism and the objects of its environment, interaction that is unmistakeably lacking in the space between the physiological organism and its physical objects but is necessary for a meaningful and biologically beneficial interaction between the person and his environment.

The function of the phenomenal world, then, would be to make possible just those dynamic interactions and to transfer them to the organism through an intricate system of circular conductors that allow for the necessary feedback in such a way that the organism itself is made to behave "with regard to" the objects encountered in its environment and relevant for its survival.

The following considerations aim at developing some of the fundamental features of this idea. They start from three facts that are characteristic both for the satisfaction of needs and for the execution of intentions. I shall try to make these clear by a second diagram (Figure 2) in which you see various symbols for phenomenal objects related to different needs at the upper left, the phenomenal ego with some patterns of action correlated to these needs at the lower left, and on the right the subcortical centers of needs. Now, when the tension of a need (n_i) increases above its threshold, or when the time of execution of an intention approaches, several things happen.

1) Given certain circumstances, a pattern of action (m_i) is activated and put into readiness within the phenomenal ego. Therefore, the system of needs exerts an influence on the motor or executive system—which is quite plausible.

2) In the phenomenal environment the objects (D_i) that correspond to certain needs (or, more exactly, the IRMs by which they are characterized as such)—or the objects to which a given intention refers—are accentuated. They begin to attract attention. That means that there is also an influence from the centers of need on the system of perception. The objects to which a need refers seem to be activated by something like resonance. Whether these objects are determined by heredity, or by imprinting, or by conditioning—or are established deliberately by an intention—does not make a difference.

The two effects just described do not exist independently from one another. Rather

3) the field between the phenomenal ego and the phenomenal object of the need or intention is being polarized, so that attracting or repelling forces come into existence between them. These are experienced more or less strongly as appeal or threat, and are often irresistible. This polarization of the field between the phenomenal object and the subject underlies the directed component of all instinctive or intentional behavior, without which

250 W. METZGER

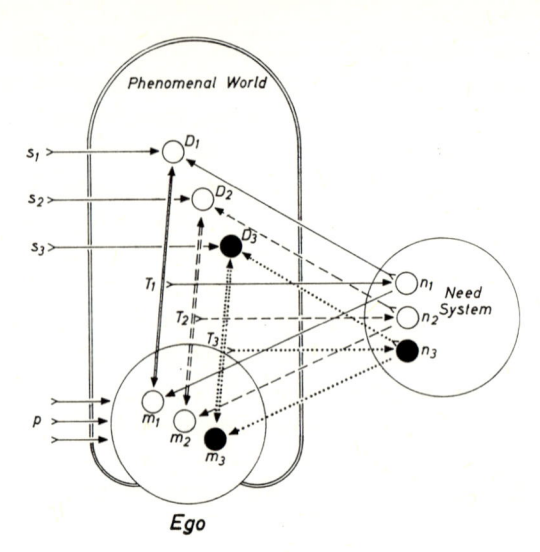

FIGURE 2 Relations between need-system, perceptual system, and action-system

s_{1-3} = Impulses from *sense*-organs, underlying the perception of drive-objects (d)

D_{1-3} = Drive-objects within the perceptual field

p = Impulses from *Proprioceptors*, building up the bodily Ego (E) within the perceptual field

m_{1-3} = *Motor* action-schemes

n_{1-3} = *Needs*

○ = Latent need, neutral object, dormant action-scheme

● = Aroused need, outstanding (valent) object, activated action-scheme

⇢ = Nervous impulses from sense-organs underlying phenomenal objects, including the bodily Ego

⇠ = Nervous impulses from need-centers to phenomenal field conferring a valence to the pertaining drive-objects

⇙ = Nervous impulses from need-centers to pertaining action-schemes, underlying their "readiness for action"

$T_1\updownarrow\ T_2\updownarrow\ T_3\updownarrow$ = Tensions (attractions or repulsions) between Ego and drive-object

⇢ = Inforcement of successful activity

The relation between bodily Ego and action-schemes is oversimplified and needs further elaboration no activity can ever reach its aim. The interrelations between the subject and the object, as described above, become themselves a steering mechanism, in which—in the case of attraction—the place of the phenomenal object represents the value aimed at, the position of the subject the actual value, and consequently the distance between them represents the difference between these two values by which the human steering machine viz. the muscular system is set in motion so that in the physical world the distance between the organism and the object diminishes and finally disappears.

In the case of negative polarization or repulsion, the situation is somewhat different. Repulsion merely causes flight or retreat of the subject, that is, an increase in the distance between the subject and the object, until the threat becomes subliminal. In this moment the whole affair is settled and nothing more happens. (It seems to me to be significant that—as has been observed repeatedly—repulsion goes on along the force lines originating in the threatening object, even if another direction of movement would be more suitable.)

But let us return to the case of attraction. Here the approach toward the object is but the first phase of the whole process. At its completion, in the moment when the distance disappears, a second phase is immediately initiated viz. the execution of the innate or learned pattern of performance—or the intended activity—which up to this moment was ready for action but had been blocked, is now set free. Not until then could the tension caused by the need or intention be definitely released—provided that the object is appropriate. If this is the case, the much discussed reinforcement takes place, that is to say the connection between the pattern of the object and the pattern of action by which the accentuation of the object in the field of perception and the subsequent polarization will be intensified later on while at the same time it will be restricted to a class of objects that will become more and more sharply defined. This coupling and its storage I have localized hypothetically in the region of the center of need. But possibly this hypothesis will have to be revised some day.

I shall drop the subject at this point, hoping that in the not too far distant future a cybernetician who is better than I will succeed in developing a more detailed model from which inferences can be drawn that are open to experimental verification. But it seems to me to be pertinent to add some remarks on the epistemological standpoint that is implied in these considerations. The standpoint in question is *strict critical realism*. True, this construction contains a dogma, i.e., an assertion that can neither be verified nor disproved. I mean the assumption that behind the world of the immediately given, behind the world of percepts, the presumed reality of the naive realist, there exists another world that to the phenomenal world has the relation of the original to its image but in itself is metaphenomenal or transphenomenal. That means that by its very nature it evades every direct observation and is therefore excluded from scientific thinking by positivism. However we are compelled to grant its existence as the link X by which the experiences of all subjects, or more generally living beings equipped with distance receptors can be coordinated, or, to put it more exactly, by which the existing and demonstrable coordination of their experiences can be explained. Without this coordination any formation of coherent groups and cooperation would be impossible, if we do not return to the absurd assumption of preestablished harmony in Leibniz's sense.

Without the assumption of this coordinating principle neither a theory of perception consistent in itself nor a theory of social intercourse and supra-individual grouping would be possible. And without the supplementary assumption that the world, as immediately given, is constituted by processes that go on within our own—transphenomenal—organism, no consistent pathology of perception is possible, as we shall see a little later.

First I have to add that both diagrams I showed you before were only partial representations of the critical realistic construction. In order to exclude any misunderstanding I shall now exhibit the complete diagram as it can be found in a contribution by Norbert Bischof to the first volume of the large German handbook of psychology. This diagram differs from the foregoing ones in various respects. First: all elements that refer to the steering function of the field of perception are omitted. Second: the so called psychophysical level of the cerebrum and the world of perception were represented as coinciding in the first and second diagrams, while in Bischof's scheme they are separately represented as parallel, somewhat better corresponding to the present state of our knowledge. To the left, within the transphenomenal organism, the cerebral body-pattern (Körperschema after Paul Schilder) appears inside the cerebral world-pattern. To the right, beyond the double line that separates the physiological from the phenomenal, the phenomenal bodily ego appears inside the phenomenal surroundings which is identical with the reality of the naive realist. Third: Bischof's diagram contains some hint to the connection existing between the tendencies of the bodily ego and the state of the motor system within the transphenomenal organism which for the sake of clarity had been omitted in the preceding diagrams. But the fourth and decisive feature of this third diagram of Bischof's is that on the side of the conscious phenomena—to the right—below the representation of the naive-phenomanal world it also contains a representation of the critical-phenomenal world

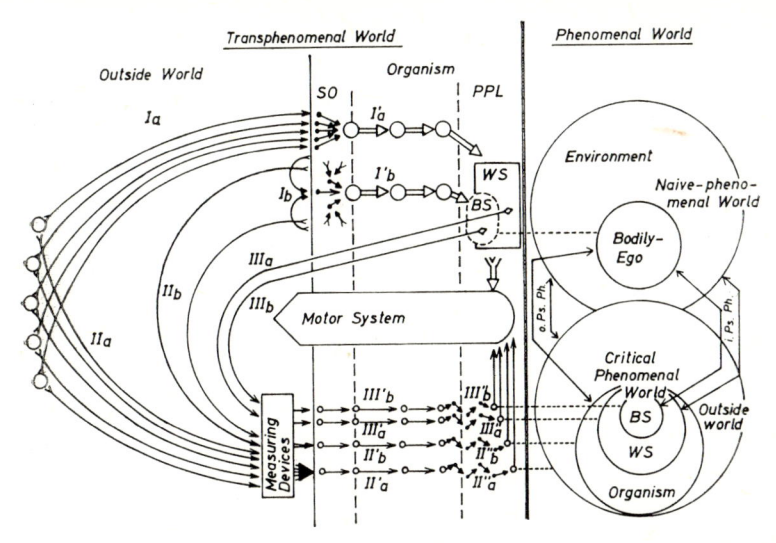

THE PHENOMENAL-PERCEPTUAL FIELD AS A STEERING MECHANISM 253

FIGURE 3 Diagram representing the relations between phenomenal world, transphenomenal world, and critical phenomenal world according to the critical realistic view

SO = Sense Organs
PPL = Psychophysical Level (in the cortex)
WS = World Scheme
BS = Body Scheme
$oPsPh$ = Outer Psychophysics
$iPsPh$ = Inner Psychophysics

Roman Numbers

I = Perception
II = Physical Investigation
III = Neurophysiological Investigation

Subscripts

$(\ )_a$ = Referring to Outside World resp. World Scheme
$(\ )_b$ = Referring to Organism resp. Body Scheme

Strokes

no stroke = Physical Transmission Processes
one stroke' = Perceptual Processes
two strokes " = Rational Processes

'Scheme' is used here in the Sense of a Cortical Dynamic Structure corresponding immediately to a 'Percept', an 'Image' or a 'Perceived Object' (including the Ego) in the Phenomenal World in which, corresponding to the above discussion, the bodily ego and the whole world of perception appear inside the organism and the organism within the physical environment which, together with the organism, is *thought to be* the transphenomenal reality.

While the naive-phenomenal world of the immediately given (above) originates directly from the unselected stimulation of the sense organs, including the after-effects of preceding stimulation stored in memory, the critical phenomenal world (below) in its distinctive features originates from "scientific findings"—above all from the observation of coincidence between pointers and lines on the scales of various measuring instruments—which are also sensory phenomena but a kind of such phenomena that are preferred in science because they have proved to be most invariant against any kind of disturbance in transmission. This makes them the most reliable basis for theoretical reflection. The critical-phenomenal world that is constructed on this basis is the quintessence of the scientific picture of the world. Or, to put it more exactly: the world as it looks to the scientist who is relatively the most advanced among his colleagues for the time being at any given phase of scientific development. This "world as it looks" sometimes changes rather rapidly, while the "world as it is" is much more permanent. It contained atoms and electrons when nobody thought of them, it never contained a matter like phlogiston, and the number of planets has not increased in it since the 16th century, when nobody dreamed of the existence of Neptune or Pluto. This is one of the reasons why the philosophical reduction of the "world as it is" to the "world as it is believed to be" (by the scientist), a reduction that belonged to the main endeavors of the neo-Kantian philosophy and is still maintained e.g. by K. Holzkamp, is finally not possible. There is still another reason. The impingements upon our organism by which our phenomenal world comes into existence must stem from a transphenomenal world. They cannot come from the stock of scientific knowledge we have drawn from the totality of our everyday and systematic experiences. It is true, this stock of knowledge may substitute for the transphenomenal reality in our discussions concerning the world. But if reality corresponded to this simplification, it would be unconceivable how anything new and unexpected should ever occur or appear in our phenomenal world. In other words, it would be incomprehensible how every spot of our phenomenal world could be so obviously open to ever-changing influxes coming from a sphere X that cannot lie in it, as Oskar Graefe has contended against the phenomenalism of Kurt Lewin.

Our own actions, too, must have effects on a transphenomenal reality and cause changes there. Otherwise it would be inconceivable how these actions can, together with their effects or consequences, appear in the phenomenal worlds of other persons, and that these consequences need not be observed there at the same time but their observation can be separated from our own activity by time intervals of any length. This possibility presupposes an X that preserves the effects of my activity long beyond their existence in my own phenomenal world. To give an instance: I may build a footbridge in the desert; and another person may find it and pass over it many years later.

There remains the naive-realistic objection that the world immediately experienced by us as supporting us is characterized by such traits of firmness, stability, and independence from ourselves that it appears to be an unreasonable demand that we should consider it as a correlate of ever changing cerebral processes, processes that occur within our own organism. But this objection is invalidated by the fact that the independence of the outer environment from the subject is only very approximately true. Let me mention briefly the facts that can be understood only by assuming that their immediate correlates are to be localized within our own organism:

1) The change of view, i.e. of the mode of apperception as a means of mentally modifying the outer environment.

2) The occurrence of strictly psychical phenomena, as feelings or moods etc. outside the subject, in the extreme instance in so-called Freudian projection.

3) The exterior localization of dreams, apparitions, phantoms, and hallucinations, yet even in the so-called eidetic phenomena, after-images etc., not to forget the objects of thought and their modifications within the thought process.

4) The structural discrepancies, as, e.g., in camouflage.

5) The metric deviations, as in visual illusions which are not a laboratory affair, i.e. not an affair of paper and pencil but a universal phenomenon found in any tridimensional object as soon as we make the measurements necessary to discover them.

6) The modifications, distortions, alterations of the outer world—including one's own body—during psychoses, poisoning, and cerebral lesions, which have been frequently described.

What concerns the two fundamental and indispensable theses of critical realism, namely

1) that the world of what is immediately given is of an organismic nature, and

2) that there exists a transphenomenal world which, among other things, embraces our own organisms and becomes the means by which the perceptive worlds of different observers are coordinated,

we may finally say: The second at least is not verifiable; but the multitude of findings that can be derived from both and understood by them is so immense and so various that they are absolutely sufficient to get the facts in focus that are postulated in the above statements, even in the face of great demands concerning their trustworthiness.

SUMMARY AND CONCLUSIONS

The phenomenal world has been described in my presentation as a central steering organ in the sense of cybernetics.

In this organ, duplicates of the outer objects and the organism can interact in a way which, as a consequence of their very nature, is not possible for the originals. This interaction is transferred to the effector organs by circular processes so that the organism is enabled to move in its environment just as if it were immediately controlled by field forces, which do actually not exist there.

Thus the phenomenal world must be considered as *the* decisive intervening variable in behavior as observed from outside.

DISCUSSION OF METZGER'S PAPER

T. E. Weckowicz

Professor Metzger's stimulating paper deals with some psychological questions which have baffled both philosophers and psychologists for centuries and yet are the crucial questions concerning ourselves and the world we are living in. An attempt has been made to deal with the mind-body problem, the nature of the experienced world and the basis for a possible knowledge of external reality. These problems are tackled from the phenomenalistic and organismic point of view in the tradition of the *Gestalt* school of psychology. Professor Metzger embraces a Critical-realist epistemological position. My comment with respect to it is that the view Professor Metzger propounds could be better classified as a Representationist epistemological position: the external world and the body are represented in the nervous system, presumably as some kind of a field of energy configuration, such as Köhler's isoelectric cortical medium field or Pribram's holograms. There is an isomorphism between these cerebral events and the experienced phenomena. The cerebral field also to a certain extent reflects the external world and the self. However because of the nature of the medium, there is in it a greater preponderance of cohesive forces than restraining forces and also presence of the bodily needs. The resulting representation is to some extent distorted and slanted by certain field dynamisms such as the occurrence of closure, figure-ground organization, valencies, and so on, towards becoming an *Umwelt*, a behavioral or phenomenal environment rather than a faithful representation of physical world. The dynamic changes which occur in this isomorphic mind-brain field result in a behavior of the organism in relation to the physical world. Thus certain changes first occur in a medium with relatively low restraining forces. They are directly influenced by the organismic need centers and presumably by memory traces. Secondly the energy of the organism is mobilized and certain behavioral acts initiated in the physical world where the restraining forces are stronger. The purpose of these behavioral acts is to bring about the state envisaged by the blueprint in the isomorphic mind-brain field. The fact that organisms survive, that they can cooperate and influence one another and themselves through the medium of the physical world, is used as a philosophical argument for the existence of objective reality. I suppose this is a fair summary of Professor Metzger's statement, in any case of his statement as I understand it. My reaction to it can be summarized briefly. Professor Metzger is entitled to his epistemological position although I find it difficult to see how he can avoid the pitfalls of phenomenalism and dualism with a ghostly observer watching a ghostly spectacle and moving a ghostly arm connected by a system of strings and pulleys with a real arm. However his position, although it is that of phenomenalism, does not necessarily imply dualism and interactionism. It is quite compatible with a monism or a double-aspect theory.[1] In the latter case the problem becomes that of a relationship between the brain representation of the external world and the self and the things represented. This becomes an empirical question requiring the finding of some evidence for the postulated brain mechanisms. Another problem of a more philosophical nature is the problem of isomorphism between brain events and mental phenomena. It is quite obvious that not all brain events are represented in consciousness. Even some dispositional behavioral characteristics such as sets or various intervening variables and theoretical conctructs may have no representation in consciousness. There are probably some brain events corresponding to them, unless these characteristics are purely mental although unconscious occurrences. It is quite clear that unless the dualist and interactionist position is adopted, a position quite respectable and adopted by such men as Sherrington, Sir Russell Brain and Smythies, the problem to be solved is that of distinguishing between the brain events which are accompanied by conscious phenomena and those which are not. This may be an empirical question. Finally a few words may be said regarding the problem of projecting experienced subjective phenomena into the objective space of the physical world. Professor Metzger deals with this problem adequately by suggesting the existence of a space representation in the brain corresponding to phenomenal space; however I would like to add a few more words. The mechanism of projection was postulated by von Helmholtz and von Kreis in relation to sensory experiences and by Freud in relation to emotional experiences. I think that this formulation of the problem was a result of a confusion between the phenomenal and the physical spaces. One cannot subscribe to the doctrine of phenomenalism as far as the experienced objects are concerned and then place these objects in a physical space which is experienced directly. What is sauce for the goose is sauce for the gander. If one adopts the Phenomenalist position then the experienced phenomenal objects are perceived in the phenomenal space. On the other hand, if one adopts the Realist position then one perceives physical objects in the physical space. J. R. Smythies in his book, *Analysis of Perception*, discusses the problem in great detail. The recent experiments of von Békésy may throw some light on the nervous mechanisms responsible for locating some sensations outside the organism and other sensations inside the organism. This does not answer the epistemological question but points to some interesting nervous system function correlates of the experienced phenomena.

NOTES

1. Herbert Feigl has put forward a version of double-aspect theory called by him "identity theory." He has proposed to establish the identity of contents of consciousness ("raw feels") and brain states by describing them in the terms of common universals within the same logical space. The *Gestalten* or some categories like them are good candidates for the required universals.

COMMENTS ON PROFESSOR METZGER'S PAPER

William W. Rozeboom

There is so much I like about Professor Metzger's paper that I am loath to say anything critical about it. Yet it perpetuates a philosophic error which invites total disaster upon any theory of cognition which makes it. Insomuch as nothing significant in Metzger's contribution rests on this blemish, I can best show my respect for the former by attempting to free it from the latter.

Although the error to which I refer is prime contender for epistemology's Original Sin, it is certainly not original with Professor Metzger. In fact, it so thoroughly saturates the mother's milk of his intellectual heritage—the brilliant Germanic tradition of act-psychology—that he many never have had occasion to reflect that an alternative is conceivable. Consider, for example, the seminal views of Brentano and Köhler:

"Every mental phenomenon is characterized by ... the intentional (and also mental) inexistence of an object, and ... reference to a content, a direction upon an object (by which we are *not* to understand a reality in this case), or an imminent objectivity. Each one includes something as object *within itself*, although not always in the same way. In presentation something is presented, in judgment something is affirmed or denied, in love [something is] loved ... The hypothesis that a physical phenomenon like those which exist intentionally *in us* exists outside of the mind [is not logically self-contradictory]. It is only that when we compare one with the other, conflicts are revealed which show clearly that there is no actual existence corresponding to the intentional existence in this case ... We will make no mistake if we quite generally deny to physical phenomena any existence other than intentional existence." (Brentano, 1874, pp. 50, 55; italics added.)

"The Behaviorist tells us that observations of direct experience is a private affair of individuals, whereas in physics two physicists can make the same observation, for instance, on a galvanometer. I deny the truth of the latter statement ... If somebody observes a galvanometer, he observes something different from the galvanometer as a physical object. For the object of his observation is the result of certain organic processes, only the beginning of which is determined by the physical galvanometer itself. In a second person, the observed galvanometer is again only the final result of such processes, which now occur in the organism of this second person. By no means do the two people observe the same instrument then, although physically the processes in one and the other are started by the same physical object." (Köhler, 1929 p.20.)

With such illustrious precedents as these, it is scarcely surprising to find Metzger asserting that

... "behind the world of the immediately given, behind the world of percepts, the presumed reality of the naive realist, there exists another world that to the phenomenal world has the relation of the original to its image but in itself is metaphenomenal or transphenomenal. That means that by its very nature it evades every direct observation and is therefore excluded from scientific thinking by positivism" (Metzger, p. 252 above).

Despite Metzger's labeling of his position here as "strict critical realism," it is in fact an orthodox phenomenalism. (I would have liked to call it a "crypto-phenomenalism," but there is nothing at all crypto about it.) A *real* critical realist would hold that what we observe directly is (in general) not mental phenomena but objects in Metzger's transphenomenal world.

It might seem a bit arrogant of me to stigmatize phenomenalism as a pure-and-simple error when so many first-rate thinkers have held this view and my earlier arguments against it (p. 62 above) are so skimpy. So I shall merely point out that *if* one distinguishes a mental act's content from its object sufficiently well to see that what intends the object most directly is not the act's nominal subject (i.e., a person) but its content, *then* it becomes evident that phenomenalism is both gratuitous and strongly counterintuitive. The realistically natural view here—the only one which now makes any sense to me although clarity in this matter was for me no simple overnight attainment— is that when physicist o observes galvanometer g, this analyzes as o's having a mental content m_g (in this instance a percept) such that m_g is about (represents, signifies, is *of*) object g, whatever the latter may ontologically be. But if the property of *having* m_g is misconstrued as an *experience of* m_g—and note that the familiar verb-form "to experience x" is treacherously ambiguous between "to have an experience of x" and "to have x in experience"— the result is a phenomenalism which sees m_g as the *object* of o's mental act, behind which may (Metzger) or may not (Brentano) lurk a corresponding "real" but unobserved entity g.[1]

If I wished to amplify my objections to phenomenalism here, I would probe with such questions as why having a percept should require being aware of that percept when e.g. having a brain tumor in no way requires awareness of that tumor, and what in the analysis of 'o perceives object x' should necessitate that x be something within o's mind. But I am content just to note that if Professor Metzger can be tempted to try on a genuine critical realism for size, he will discover that nothing in his paper needs amendment beyond a few labels and phrasings. He will still want to recognize two realms of being, the outer physical vs. the inner experiential, but what was formerly called the "apparent environment" or "phenomenal world" is now seen as a configuration of representations, or meanings, which are generally *of* the outer physical world. Similarly, his "world of percepts" (cf. quotation above) remains just as before except for the assumption that a person perceives his percepts. Instead, the latter are the *means* by which one perceives something else.

NOTES

1. Such a view is obviously going to have trouble separating intentional contents from objects. With evident reluctance to make much of it, Brentano construed the distinction as that of a proposition vs. the nominative term therein—e.g., that "if I make the judgement 'A centaur does not exist', then ... the object is a centaur [while] the content of the judgement is that a centaur does not exist" (Brentano, 1874, p. 71f.)—so that the content "includes the [object] within itself, and likewise exists within the subject" (Brentano, 1874, p. 71). Köhler, on the other hand, ignores the content/object distinction altogether.

REBUTTAL

Wolfgang Metzger

My comment to Rozeboom's comments on my paper can only refer to one single but crucial point.

I do not see any connection between my statements and those of Brentano as quoted by Rozeboom. In accordance with Brentano I should deny to physical *phenomena* any existence other than intentional existence. But *against* Brentano it is my contention that physical *phenomena* are the correlates of brain processes and that these are aroused by stimulation of sense organs by impacts coming from transphenomenal "real" physical objects that are *not* identical but different from the physical *phenomena*. Without assuming the existence of those transphenomenal physical objects it is impossible to understand that analogous (not identical) physical phenomena can occur for two or more different observers, as W. Köhler points out. If this is "pure" phenomenalism our languages must be too different for a mutual understanding.

Regarding the discussion of my paper by Weckowicz, I have the impression that I have been thoroughly understood by him and that the comments given by him deal with unavoidable consequences of my approach, consequences that should be followed in further consideration and research. There is only one tiny correction I have to propose: The observer and his arm etc. are just as ghostly as we perceive or experience them, i.e., they are as substantial as matter can be, considering that matter is a phenomenal and not a physical affair.

BIBLIOGRAPHY

Bischof, N., Erkenntnistheoretische Grundlagenprobleme der Wahrnehmungspsychologie. In Metzger, W. und Erke, H. (Hrsg.), Wahrnehmung und Bewußtsein. *Hdb. d. Psychol. Bd. I/1.* Göttingen: Hogrefe, 1966, 21–78.

Brentano, F. [Excerpts from *Psychologie vom empirischen Standpunkt*, 1874.] In: Chisholm, R. M. (Ed.) *Realism and the Background of Phenomenology.* Glencoe, Ill.: The Free Press, 1960.

Cassirer, E., *Das Erkenntnisproblem in der Philosophie und Wissenschaft der neueren Zeit,* Berlin, 1911. (Trans. by Woglom, W. H. and Hendel, C. H.) New Haven: Yale University Press, 1950.

Ekman, G., Psychophysik und psychophysische Meßmethoden. In Meili, R. und Rohracher, H. (Hrsg.), *Lehrbuch der experimentellen Psychologie.* Bern: Huber, 1963, 19–52.

Graefe, O., Über Notwendigkeit und Möglichkeit der psychologischen Wahrnehmungslehre. *Psychol. Forsch.*, 1961, **26**, 262–298.

Helmholtz, H. v., *Treatise on Physiological Optics.* Rochester, New York, 1924–1925. Ed. by James P. C. Southall, Optical Society of America, 1924–1925.

Hering, E., *Beiträge zur Physiologie*, 1862. (Trans. by Hurvich, L. M. and Jameson, D.) Cambridge: Harvard University Press, 1964.

Holzkamp, K., *Theorie und Experiment in der Psychologie.* Berlin: de Gruyter, 1964.

Holzkamp, K., *Wissenschaft als Handlung*, Berlin: de Gruyter, 1968.

Köhler, W., Ein altes Scheinproblem. *Naturwiss.*, 1929, **17**, 395–401.

Köhler, W., *The place of value in a world of facts.* New York: Liveright, 1938.

Köhler, W., *Gestalt Psychology.* New York: Mentor Books, 1959 (originally 1929).

Kries, J. v., *Allgemeine Sinnesphysiologie.* Leipzig: Vogel, 1923.

Lewin, K., Untersuchungen zur Handlungs- und Affektpsychologie. I und II. *Psychol. Forsch.*, 1926, **7**, 294–358.

Lewin, K., *Die psychologische Situation bei Lohn und Strafe.* Leipzig: Hirzel, 1931.

Lewin, J., Der Richtungsbegriff in der Psychologie. *Psychol. Forsch.*, 1934, *19*, 249–299.

Lewin, K., *Dynamic Theory of Personality.* (1st ed.) (Trans. by Adams, D. K. and Zener, K. E.), New York and London: McGraw-Hill, 1935.

Lewin, K., *Principles of Topological Psychology*, (1st ed.) (Trans. by Heider, F. and Heider, G. H.), New York and London: McGraw-Hill, 1936.

Lewin, K. The conceptual representation and measurement of psychological forces. *Contr. Psychol. Theory*, Vol. 1, No. 4, 1938.

Lewin, K., Field theory and experiment in social psychology; concepts and methods. *Am. J. Sociol.*, 1939, **44**, 868–897.

Lewin, K., Field theory of learning. *Yearbook Nat. Soc. Stud. Educ.*, 41, Part II, 1942, 215–242.

Lewin, K., Defining the "field at a given time." *Psychol. Rev.*, 1943, **50**, 292–310.

Lewin, K., Behavior and Development as a Function of the Total Situation. In L. Carmichael (Ed.), *Manual of Child Psychology.* New York: Wiley, 1946, 791–844.

MacCorquodale, K. and Meehl, P. E., On a distinction between hypothetical constructs and intervening variables. *Psychol. Rev.*, 1948, **55**, 95–107.

Metzger, W., Über die Notwendigkeit kybernetischer Vorstellungen in der Theorie des

Verhaltens. *Z. Psychol.* 1965, **171**, 336–342.
Metzger, W., *Psychologie*. Darmstadt: Steinkopff ⁴1968.
Pikler, J., Über die Angriffspunkte des Willens am Körper. *Z. Psychol.*, 1929, **110**, 288.
Schilder, P., *Das Körperschema*. Berlin: Springer, 1923.
Stevens, S. S., Mathematics, Measurement, and Psychophysics. In S. S. Stevens (Ed.), *Handbook of Experimental Psychology*. New York: Wiley, 1951, 1–59.
Stevens, S. S., To honor Fechner and repeal his law. *Science*, 1961, **133**, 80–86.
Stevens, S. S. and Galanter, E. H., Ratio scales for a dozen perceptual continua. *J. exp. Psychol.*, 1957, **54**, 377–411.
Tolman, E. C., Operational Behaviorism and Current Trends in Psychology. *Proceedings of the 25th Anniversary Celebration of the University of Southern California*, 1936, 89–103.
Tolman, E. C., A Psychological Model. In T. Parsons and E. A. Shils (Eds.), *Toward a General Theory of Action*. Cambridge, Mass.: Harvard University Press, 1954, 277–361.
Überweg, F., Zur Theorie der Richtung des Sehens. *Z. rationelle Medicin*, 1853, 3, V, 268–282.
Watson, J. B. *Psychology from the Standpoint of a Behaviorist*, Philadelphia: J. B. Lippincott Co., 1919.

VIII

PERCEPTION AS REAFFERENCE AND RELATED ISSUES IN COGNITION AND EPISTEMOLOGY

John W. Gyr

The Center for Advanced Study in Theoretical Psychology

A number of years ago Gibson (1962) published a paper on the concept of the stimulus in psychology. In that paper Gibson equated perception, not with events happening in the retina at a given moment in time, but with events happening in the *visual system* at a given time and over time. By the visual system is meant the visual apparatus as a whole, which consists, among other things, of an eye that is not stationary but moving and which causes a continuously changing input to the retina of the eye. Gibson (1963) states: "We had to suppose that the role of the senses, their sole function, was not to yield sensations. Instead of mere receptors, i.e. receivers and transducers of energy, they appear to be systems for exploring, selecting and searching ambient energy ... This new picture of the senses includes attention as part of sensitivity, not as an act of the mind upon the deliverances of the senses" (p. 12). Gibson thus suggested that the information in molar stimuli results from the structure and sequence of stimulus energy which characterizes the input to a motorically active perceptual system.

It was pointed out by Gyr, Brown, Willey, and Zivian (1966), that Gibson, although he has made much of motor exploration, has not emphasized the role of efferent or proprioceptive feedbacks in perception. Because of much research stressing such feedback (see Gyr, 1971) which has become available in the interim, the time seems ripe to suggest a further important refinement of the conception of the stimulus provided earlier by Gibson and of the theory of perception itself.

Many authors, including Gibson, see perception as a process in which fixation-motion-fixation, etc. constitutes an integrated process. It is generally agreed that for such a process it is arbitrary to separate the information obtained during a prior fixation from that obtained at the end of a movement leading to a further fixation, etc. (Jeannerod, Gerin and Pernier, 1968; Ingle, 1967). However, something additional can be said about a perceptual process in which fixation-movement-fixation, etc. constitute a molar unit. In such a process stable correlations may be formed between the specific *efferents* underlying specific movements and specific resulting *reafferents*. The perceptual process which results has been diagrammed in a simplified form in Figure 1. There is an environment and an organism, the latter is

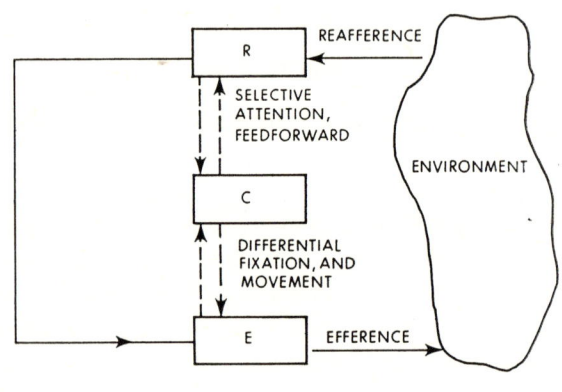

FIGURE 1

composed of boxes R (Receptors), E (Efferents), and C (Correlators-Comparators) and their interconnections. It may be assumed that the organism-environment relations are such that specific built-in connections exist, such as, for example, a tendency for the eye to focus on pattern, as opposed to empty space (Fantz, 1965). These relations are indicated by the solid directed lines. As a result of learning, during perceptual (visuo-motor) development, it is assumed further that, by certain processes to be discussed later, the correlator, C, can find certain correlations between the efferent signals issued and the ensuing reafference. This in turn will allow the system to differentially, or systematically, fixate, move its head, locomote, etc., depending on prior reafference, and to selectively attend, depending on prior efference. The latter is effected, in part at least, by the feedforward mechanism discussed by Pribram in this volume (See also, Pribram, 1969). In this kind of a system both efference and afference become interconnected during the process of perceptual development to produce both attention and selective fixation, etc. as part of sensitivity (Gibson, 1963). In this view it is completely arbitrary to dissociate efference and afference (see

Festinger, 1967; Gyr, 1969; Gyr, Brown, Willey and Zivian, 1966; Held and Hein, 1967; Sperry, 1952, 1958; Trevarthen, 1968a, 1968b, etc.). Yet, this is, in fact, what has been done by a great many theorists of perception who have stressed input (afference) while being totally unconcerned about or underplaying and leaving vague the role of output (efference). What is suggested by the studies cited above is that for the development of the various constancies, the perception of absolute straightness, curvedness, perpendicularity (Held and Hein, 1967)—in fact for all perceptual capacities other than simple discrimination between pairs of stimuli—*exafference,* that is, impulses resulting from external stimuli, exclusive of impulses resulting from bodily movement (von Holst, 1954), is not enough to generate perception. This is especially true during perceptual development and under conditions in which input is systematically distorted. What is required is the information provided to the organism by a correlation between its efference and the ensuing reafference. There is reason to believe that this is true for both focal and ambient vision (Trevarthen, 1968a, 1968b), though the motor mechanisms involved will be different. (See also Festinger, 1967; Gyr, 1971.) In this conception then, a molar stimulus includes both efferent and reafferent signals. The perceptual information is not wholly contained in the ambient optic array.

This conception of the perceptual process as an efferent-reafferent system, as illustrated in Figure 1, in addition to having interesting implications for research in perception—to be reported later—has important consequences for the unification of perceptual with cognitive and even epistemological problems. Thus, for example, Piaget (1954), Inhelder and Piaget (1964), and Furth (1969) have long argued the point that thinking processes result from the "interiorization" and "internalization" of the generalized features of the transformations (movements) and their results (reafferences) which characterize the earliest adaptive processes.

"Interiorization" should not be confused with "internalization." Both processes, it would seem, are in some way involved in thinking but Piaget would insist on their conceptual distinction (Furth, 1969). The distinction comes about due to Piaget's notion that to know is to act and that an action involves both steering and being steered by the environment. That is, an action is founded on "hypotheses" and "expectations" about the environment (the kind of process which goes on in box C of Figure 1). In turn, the processes in box *C* may be modified by reafference ensuing from the environment as a result of a motor transformation of the environment caused by the action. Herein, indeed, lies the similarity between Piaget's theory and the theory of perception which forms a major topic of this paper. Knowing thus involves an acting and transforming of a reality state. "Interiorization" is the process of doing this without overt concrete action. However, it should be remembered that the process of knowing is internal from the beginning: it finds its representation in box *C*, Figure 1. "Interiorization" thus does not involve "internalization". Nevertheless to aid the process of "interiorization" (Furth, 1969) it is helpful to use symbols, linguistic signs, imagery, etc. Piaget wants to remind the reader however, that symbols, used as a representation of outside reality and attained by "internalizing" that reality, have a figurative or *static character*. Therefore, they can aid in the process of "interiorizing" the dynamic acting-on features of knowing and sensorimotor processes only if these static or figurative aspects of symbolizing become assimilated with the significate or meaning or dynamic features of the processes they might denote. The process described here has some similarity to the discussion by Pribram (in this volume) on the interdigitation between Images-of-Events and Images-of-Achievement. Both Pribram and Piaget seem to be concerned here with a psychological reality which ensues when dynamic processes and external inputs interact. Pribram discusses the latter under the notion of *sign*. It is clear, of course, that to handle this kind of reality a theory has to be more than mediational; more than $S-O-R$.

As mentioned already, these "interiorization" and "internalization" processes discussed by Piaget are the ones with which the Correlator is concerned in Figure 1. E.g. the Correlator in Figure 1 can determine whether an efferent-reafferent sequence generated by the system has, say, *closure*, whether it is *reversible*, whether there are successive *powers* of a given transformation, etc. These are examples of the generalized features of acts Piaget is concerned with (Furth, 1969) and which are specifiable for the kind of cybernetic system (Ashby, 1966) which the efferent-reafferent perceptual system specifies. Thus the theory of perception summarized here allows, indeed requires, the consideration and specification of these very important but, at times, unspecified Piagetian notions and, in this way, it has important consequences for the unification of perceptual with cognitive and even epistemological problems.

Other theorists who have drawn implications of an epistemological nature from precisely this kind of a theory of perception are Bohm (1965), Platt (1962), and Poincaré (1952).

In the following the theory of perception which has been put forward will be spelled out in greater detail and its empirical support will be indicated. Following this, the bearing of this theory of perception on cognitive and epistemic problems will be presented.

The Perceptual Theory

Perception as a reafferent process, or the role of efference in the consciousness of perceptual experience, have been in one form or another the central theme of numerous studies (Bower, 1965; Festinger, Burnham, Ono, and Bamber, 1967; Hein and Held, 1963; Held, 1968, 1967, 1964, 1961; Held and Bossom, 1961; Riesen, 1947; Rock, 1966; Trevarthen, 1968a, 1968b; von Holst, 1954; von Holst and Mittelstaedt, 1950, etc.). These studies tend to show that under many conditions in which perceptual learning is involved—as in ontogenetic development or in the case where the perceiver wears distorting prism or where early perceptual deprivation is involved—afference alone does not lead to certain perceptions of space (e.g. Held and Hein, 1963) or pattern (e.g. Festinger, Burnham, Ono and Bamber, 1967). Rather, perception seems to depend on having an "active" perceiver and consequent efferent activity, and on the establishing of efferent-reafferent correlations. In this framework efferent signals and reafference are both required before the organism can make a perceptual judgment. Moreover, there is centrally controlled feedforward which facilitates and inhibits input at the receptor level (Pribram, in this volume). There is thus an *internal structure* which compares "predicted" with obtained input and which "prepares" itself to receive certain inputs. This inner structure can itself be examined for its properties, as discussed later.

The same structure is implied in studies on early perceptual preferences in monkeys and infants (Fantz, 1965), especially in regard to the perception of solidity, of the object, and of certain complex forms. For a review of some of the literature see Gyr, Brown, Willey and Zivian, 1966, and Gyr, 1971.

The above is not to suggest that movement is the only way to adapt to prism-induced distortions (Rock, 1966; Singer and Day, 1967). But movement tends to be the more effective method and, as Bower (1965) suggests, the effectiveness of movement-produced cues tends to be ontogenetically prior to stationary "picture" cues. Other evidence seemingly contradictory to the reafferent thesis for perception is the discovery by Meyers (1964), and Meyers and McCleary (1964) that there is form and motion discrimination in kittens deprived both of patterned light and self-produced motion, and the findings by Fantz (1965) of form preferences even in one-day old monkeys and human infants. However, Fantz (1965) suggests changes in such preferences over time which result, at least in part, from the development of systematic eye scans and other visuo-motor mechanisms. To quote Fantz (1965): "What is perceived and what is learned is effected by this self-produced stimulation as much as by the environment."

The available evidence led Fantz (1965) to suggest a number of things about perception and perceptual development. On the one hand he states that "... experience and learning have their main effect on behavioral processes other than the recognition and discrimination of patterned stimuli." However, he also states that "... normal developmental changes in selective attention increase the correspondence between perceived characteristics of the environment and those physical characteristics consequential for behavior," (such as, presumably, solidity, space, the notion of an object, etc.). This is to suggest that certain percepts at least *are* dependent on reafferent processes, whereas certain others, especially simple discriminations are not. This is similar to a conclusion reached by Held and Hein (1967) that there are two main areas of perception which are primarily affected by, and dependent on, reafferent processes.

1) Absolute judgments of straightness, curvedness, perpendicularity, etc.

2) Judgments involving the various *constancies* such as those of size, object, and space. Percepts in this category—and they include most of the percepts ultimately useful to the active living organism—can be egocentrically defined (Rock, 1966). I.e., they can be defined by the transformations imposed on them by an actively moving organism.

The Relation Between a Theory of Perception as a Reafferent Process and Certain Issues in Cognition and Epistemology

1. First, there are theories by psychologists such as Piaget (1954), Inhelder and Piaget (1964), Furth (1969), Berlyne (1965), Bruner (1968), Pribram (in this volume) and Pribram (1969) that deal with issues relevant to epistemology, such as the origins and the nature of the concepts of space, the objective as related to the subjective, causality, notions of class and serial order, the notion of logical necessity, mathematical (formal) reasoning, etc. It is Piaget's thesis that such concepts cannot be derived from a process which merely abstracts, generalizes, and differentiates afferent sense data. Preferring, on the other hand, not to be driven into the arms of an overly simple *a priorism*, Piaget seeks an explanation of the origin of the aforementioned concepts in the "internalization" and especially the "interiorization" (Furth, 1969) by the organism of his own actions. The assumption is made by Piaget, similar to the theory of reafference proposed earlier for perception, that action is an integral part of all perceptual and cognitive, that is, of all adaptive processes. Piaget then borrows from Poincaré

(1952) the idea that there is an inherent logic, (such as the structure of the mathematical *group*), in the acts of an organism. By "interiorizing" its own actions at the time when imagery and symbolic processes become possible, the subject can in due time, accordinng to Piaget, cognize the logical-mathematical structure inherent in its own activity.

Imagery, the first step to aid the "interiorization" process, consists according to Piaget of "internalized" activity. A number of studies on imagery (Hebb, 1949; Jacobson, 1932; Piaget, 1945; Rey, 1948; Schifferli, 1953) indeed suggest that imagery involves "internalized" responding. Thus, Schifferli (1953) found that in imagining a geometric object subjects showed the same pattern of saccadic eye movements which they had shown earlier when examining figures. Berlyne (1965) also suggests that classificatory and relational thinking is, in its development, especially dependent on the kind of imagery which is based on the "internalization" of receptor adjusting and instrumental activities .These, in turn, presumably aid the process of "interiorization". He states in this regard that *words* do not, in this sense, change the stimulus field and that verbal thought must visually be of a non-transformational kind. Berlyne admits that children can be taught to multiply and perform other mathematical operations by purely verbal means. However, unless more active operational methods involving, say, receptor-adjusting responses are used (see Zaporozhets, 1960) the "understanding" of the children will suffer. Here is a recognition, perhaps, that an Inner Structure and its associated processes of "interiorization" are required as well as linguistic signs.

Bruner (1968), discussing predication as a rule of language (e.g. "John is a boy"), suggests that this same form may be found in ontogenetically prior systems, such as that of human sensorimotor *skills*. He then proposes the possibility that this earlier form may have predisposed language to the form of predication. That is, sentences such as "John is a boy," "John caused a riot," says Bruner, may be analyzed in terms of a *topic* and *comment*. He then argues that in perception the extraction of features (in scanning) from a general sensory input is also describable by the notions of comments and topic. Bruner expands this analysis to other human skills and, in addition to the form of language, also discusses the growth of a phonology. He describes the delineation of modular sound production from the mouth as a funnel opened *outward* for the voiced (a), and a funnel opened *inward*, for the unvoiced (p). This formation of *binary oppositions*, he suggests, can be seen in a cruder form in human skills development. As an example he mentions the development of the infant's hand movements which "grows from the babble of athetoid movement of the fingers, to a sharp contrast of 'hand wide open' and 'hand tight-fisted' during reaching." Note that Bruner's analysis and speculation here is very much in accord with Piaget's discussion of "interiorization" of acts, leading to true *operations* (Furth, 1969). Bruner also mentions the modularization of part acts into roughly equal time segments and how coordination of these into different sequences may take place which, he says, Lashley (1951) likened to *syntactic structures*. Bruner concludes: "It seems to be a not unreasonable hypothesis that human skill, human information processing, and human language might conceivably be a set of related responses that differentiated man as he evolved from his hominid ancestors." Clearly Bruner accepts the possibility that the generalized nature of the organism's own acts— such as the relation of binary opposition, their sequential character, etc., themselves can become descriptors of a psychological reality.

The theories proposed by Piaget, Berlyne, Zaporozhets, Bruner, and others, clearly depend on conceiving of ontogenetically early adaptive processes as "active" processes in which efference-reafference correlations are built. Thus, a reafferent theory of perception as sketched earlier is the type of theory that is required. Any one of the more "passive" theories of perception would have nothing to contribute to the above theories of cognition, nor to the epistemological position to which they relate, i.e., a position which is neither purely Empiricistic nor purely Idealistic. Conversely, it could be argued that if perception is indeed the kind of reafferent process suggested in this paper, the validity of theories such as those of Piaget, Bruner, Pribram, etc. would be enhanced inasmuch as they assume the kind of perceptual or sensorimotor system in which there is a decided Inner Structure which "examines" its own transformations on the world, whereas other theories such as Osgood's (1953) and possibly even Berlyne's do so to a lesser extent. To put it another way, the difference between the former and the latter is the difference between $\begin{smallmatrix} S & & O \\ & \searrow \swarrow & \\ & R & \end{smallmatrix}$ theories and $S - O - R$ theories. In the former S and O are *both* inputs to R, whereas in the latter O is merely a mediating system. (See also Moroz and Pribram in this volume.)

Processes of "interiorization", which form a central part of all these theories of cognition may, perhaps be illustrated more easily at the relatively earlier and simpler levels of the organism's perceptual sensorimotor development than later on when highly complex cognitive processes appear. Even in perception, the process of "interiorization" which would be sufficient to explain, say, the development of the notion of *space* is probably already enormously complex. (In regard to the task of building a conceptual language to describe the building of internal structures it is interesting to note that Berlyne (1966) regards Piaget's construct of the mathematical *group* as more fundamental than the learning theorists' notion of *habit family hierarchy*.)

An illustration of how even, at the earliest perceptual level, notions of "activity" and of "interiorization" become important in a reafferent model—and hence how a study of these processes can aid the theorist who is interested in cognitive or epistemological issues—will now be sketched. This may help to provide some concreteness to a domain of psychological processing that is still understood only vaguely.

The illustration is taken from work which attempted to formulate theoretically a process of pattern perception which was based very heavily on reafferent principles. This work has been reported in Gyr, Brown, Willey and Zivian (1966) and Gyr, Zivian and Brown (1967). The attempt in this work was to have a computer program "find" efferent-reafferent correlations, say, in connection with such perceptual inputs as straight lines and curves. What the program notes in the case of a straight line is that for this kind of an input, and only for this kind of an input, it is true that a straight line scan, and only a straight line scan, by the eye parallel to that input—if repeated identically several times—can produce identical retinal firing patterns (Platt, 1962). By finding this "law" the program begins to discriminate between straight lines and curves, straight line movements and curved movements, to scan systematically straight line contours, etc.

Parenthetically, the fact that saccadic motion is systematically related to certain types of perception has been shown for movement by Yarbus (1967), for the position of a point by Festinger and Canon (1965) and for pattern by Fantz (1965), Festinger, Burnham, Ono and Bamber (1967), Gaarder (1967), and Jeannerod, Gerin and Pernier (1968). Moreover, based on his findings in neuropsychology, this same relationship has been proposed by Trevarthen (1968a, 1968b).

In order to show how "activity" and "internalization" become important even at this level of perceptual processing and to illustrate a concrete case of "interiorization", the concepts involved in the computer program just discussed will now be defined somewhat more rigorously.

Definitions of a straight line of given orientation, parallel line, and straight line of any orientation

(i) Let $l\alpha$ be a stimulus line which makes an angle α with the observer's horizontal

(ii) Let vector *a* be the linear, non-topological, representation of the fovea. It is a vector of 0's and 1's, where the n-th component is 1 or 0 depending on whether the n-th foveal cell has been hit by $l\alpha$ or not.

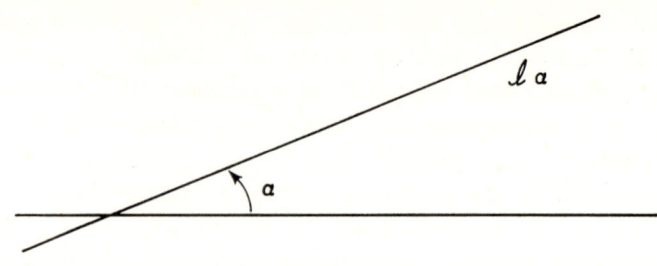

(iii) Let $t\alpha$ be a movement of the eye parallel to $l\alpha$. Equation (1) should now hold:

$$t\alpha(a) = a \qquad (1)$$

This equation is more symbolic than mathematical for what it shows is that at time ψ, the cells represented by the vector a were *among* those hit, then a movement $t\alpha$ was made, and at time $\psi\alpha$ these same cells were *among* those hit.

(iv) As can be seen, there are an infinite number of stimulus lines with the same orientation, α. Each stimulus line l_α^1 will generate a (not necessarily different) foveal vector a_i, but all the a_i will satisfy equation (1). In other words, two parallel lines, l_α^1 and l_α^2, will generate foveal vectors a_1 and a_2 respectively, which remain invariant under the same movement, $t\alpha$.

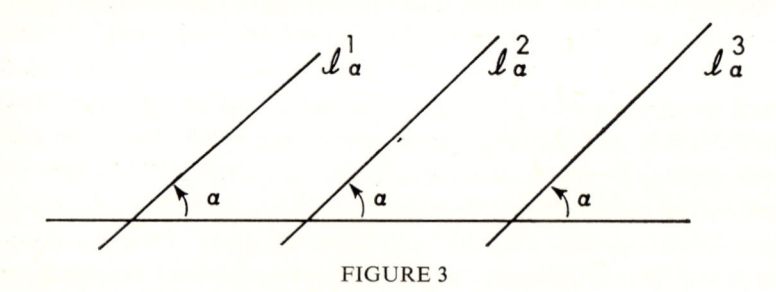

FIGURE 3

(v) Once a foveal vector a_i is recognized (by a subroutine, *Sl*) to be invariant with respect to a movement, $t\alpha$, it is stored in the vector form $(a_i, t\alpha, Sl)$.

(vi) All stimulus lines of orientation α will generate a storage vector whose second component is $t\alpha$. That is, the concept of *parallelism* is embodied in the sameness of this second component.

(vii) In a similar manner *all* straight lines, *regardless of orientation*, have the same third component, *Sl*. This is the perception of *lineness*. The third component, *Sl*, be it remembered, is the subroutine which causes the program to scan in a straight line and which causes it to note a specific invariance, see formula (1). In Berlyne's (1965) terms *Sl* consists of transformational responses and stimuli, as opposed to situational responses and situational stimuli. Moreover, *Sl* consists of certain higher order processes which record systematic changes or non-changes in the transformational sequences. *Sl* in essence carries on processes for which box *C* (Correlator-Comparator), Figure 1, is designed.

Be it thus noted that the percept of a general straight line regardless of orientation is an abstraction *referring to a set of operations* on the environment. What unites all lines into a class is not something common about the exafferent firings of all straight lines, but about the actions which the organism performs on them and the outcomes of these actions.

This notion of the importance of the act *per se* is the one—as discussed earlier—which is applied by Piaget and others to the area of thought. For example, the discovery of logical operations of classification and seriation derives, according to Piaget, from an abstraction by the child of his own operations of behaviorally grouping and regrouping things in his environment. In either case the system "turns around" on its own actions and uses them as a criterion for an abstraction. It is interesting to note, therefore, that even at the most primitive levels of perception the "data" are organized by the system in a way such that operations form a central part of the data base.

The above idea of using an operation or subroutine as a datum in an abstraction process is thus one with very general application throughout perception and cognition. The idea of using operations by the system as data to the system also has an analogue in John von Neumann's (1956) principle that instructions to the computer and data to the computer can be put in the same memory bank, thereby allowing the computer to use its instructions (operations) as data.

Another interesting feature of *Sl* as an element in the definition of a percept is its complete generality. The "law" incorporated in *Sl* in effect "reads": "if there is a straight line, a given operation *Sl* can always be performed with the same outcome, regardless of the unlimited variety of possible environmental straight line inputs". As Hebb (1969) also points out in relation to the problem of imagery "there is a classical view going back to Berkeley that a percept (or an image) must be of a *specific* object and cannot have generalized reference. Hebb then proposes that *super-*

ordinate cell assemblies, unlike simple cell assemblies, need not be specific to a given stimulus situation but that they can be quite general. Be the "neurophysiological" base for generality what it may, it is evident that in an "active" or reafferent theory, generality of a percept or any process can be attained by reference to an act or an *operation*. In fact, Piaget suggests (Beth and Piaget, 1966) that the problem of how the notion of (logical) *necessity* could arise might be explainable in this manner.

Computer simulation models such as the above can be used to specify various transformational processes of efferent-reafferent perceptual systems. Higher-order variables in these processes can be studied, for example, in terms of their *group* characteristics. It is from such characteristics, at least according to the theories of Piaget, Poincaré, and others, that highly general notions of space, class, etc. will ensue. An attempt might be made, via computer simulation, to study what could be involved in such a developmental process.

2. The relation between theories of perception as a reafferent process and certain issues in cognition and epistemology has been pointed out as well by people other than psychologists. For example, Bohm (1965) appended fifty pages on the topic of Physics and Perception, to a book on the Special Theory of Relativity.

Bohm (1965) reminds us that the Einsteinian solution of the conceptual crisis in physics at the time amounted to showing that time, space, mass, etc. are relative rather than absolute. Thus time, far from being an absolute notion, denotes an invariant relationship between an observer and a given velocity with which the observer moves. Given different velocities for two observers, they cannot agree on a time coordinate to be ascribed to distant events. Bohm then observes that theories of perception such as Gibson's— i.e. theories which belong to the class which has been called in this paper reafferent theories of perception—also stress that the world is perceived through abstraction of invariant relationships. These relationships can be forever expanded and modified and they are in no sense absolute. For example, as experiments with distorting prisms have shown, straightness, radial direction, etc. are not absolutely defineable in terms of the properties of the optic array as such, but only egocentrically defineable. Far from agreeing with the common belief that Newtonian concepts are in complete agreement with everyday psychological experiences, Bohm stresses the extensive similarity between modern theories of perception and Relativity Theory. Bohm suggests that science is mainly a way of extending our *perceptual* contact with the world. To quote: "... scientific research does not lead to absolute truth, but rather (as happens in ordinary perception) to an awareness and understanding of an evergrowing segment of the world with which we are in contact."

This conception of science as a way of perceiving (active, reafferent perceiving) suggests that psychology in general, and the psychology of developmental processes in particular, can contribute to the natural scientist in this examination of the nature of his fundamental concepts.

In this regard it is also worth noting the similarity between the three irreducible mathematical structures which have evolved independently from the work of Bourbaki in the case of mathematics and from the work of Piaget and his collaborators for psychological processes (Beth and Piaget, 1966). These structures are algebraic structures, ordered structures, and topological structures. Here again there seems to be an interesting parallel between the constructs of the formal discipline of mathematics and of the psychological concepts of the individual.

SUMMARY AND CONCLUSIONS

It is apparent that a theory of perception as a reafferent process has important implications, not just for the field of perception, but for cognition and epistemology as well. This circumstance should lend added impetus to further work on problems in this area of perceptual processes. Of particular importance is the continuing study of the kinds of internal processes, subroutines, or transformational sequences which accompany these perceptual processes and which, when abstracted, form the foundation or part of the foundation of extremely general notions, such as that of the class of all straight lines, space, the notion of a particular object (object constancy), etc. Ultimately, this kind of process can also probably form the basis of thought. A host of sub-problems need to be tackled before the latter problems can be fully understood and it is the thesis of this paper that to work on problems of reafferent perception is a good and feasible beginning.

One final remark which supports the notion that theoretical psychology is worthwhile can be made. It is apparent that considerations of a cognitive and epistemological nature which seemingly far transcend the field of perception can help to give guidance or support to the kind of work one might want to carry out as a perception-psychologist.

DISCUSSION OF GYR'S PAPER

Karl Pribram

There is one comment I want to add to Dr. Gyr's remarks. Whenever "perception" is discussed in terms of a neural response mechanism three processes tend to become mixed up. There is first the process of feedback initiated by the input. Feedback is corrective of mismatch between input and the response mechanism. Second, there is the motor copy or exclusively efferent process. This process, though triggered by input, is a more or less self-sufficient mechanism corresponding to the percept. Finally, there is a feedforward process which presets the perceptual mechanism, readies it for a particular input.

Feedforward and feedback can be conceived together to place biases on input. The feedforward mechanism needs only to rough-in the general contexts to be explored. Input is then correctively adapted to this context by feedback.

The idea that perception is a *purely* motor mechanism does not appeal to me very much. Introspectively, if perception were *solely* a triggered output I should be able to see pretty young ladies in a state of undress if I were so inclined, etc. Also, the mechanisms necessary to build up a "motor copy" from input would in themselves be sufficient to explain the perceptual process—so what is to be gained by positing such an additional mechanism?

REBUTTAL OF THE COMMENTS BY PRIBRAM

John W. Gyr

I find Pribram's differentiation between feedback, the motor copy, and feedforward instructive. I also agree that feedback and feedforward can be conceived together to place biases on input.

I wonder, however, what it is in my paper, what it is in Pribram, or both, that leads him to suggest that the theory proposed by me is a *purely* motor theory of perception. To quote from the body of my paper, I state (p. 271): "Rather, perception seems to depend on having an 'active' perceiver and consequent efferent activity, and on the establishing of efferent-reafferent correlations. In this framework, efferent signals and reafference are *both* required before the organism can make a perceptual judgment." (Italics added.)

I wonder also how Pribram would classify, say, the work of von Holst, cited in my paper. This work was intended to show that, with afferent input held constant, variations in efferent commands would produce changes in perceptual judgments. Von Holst explored three efferent experimental conditions for the fly: no efference, efference in regard to moving left, and efference in regard to moving right. These three efferent conditions in turn lead to the following three perceptions on the part of a fly: (1) motion by the environment, (2) movement by the fly, and (3) motion of the environment and movement by the fly. Is Pribram going to say that von Holst's theory puts all the emphasis for perception on motor output signals because von Holst happens to vary only efferent signals in this particular series of experiments? It is obvious that a theory which, among its many predictions, has one which says that perception will vary with efference is not necessarily a purely motor theory of perception. Any theory of perception which stresses feedback, and hence the importance of an efferent-reafferent correlation, would be concerned both with afferent and efferent processes in perception and with the manipulation of each of these variables singly or in combination. This is true for von Holst and, I would like to argue, it is true for me.

BIBLIOGRAPHY

Ashby, W. R., *Introduction to cybernetics.* New York: Wiley Science Editions, 1966.

Berlyne, D. E., *Structure and direction in thinking.* New York: John Wiley, 1965.

Beth, E. W. and Piaget, J., *Mathematical epistemology and psychology.* (Translated by W. Mays.) Dordrecht, Holland: D. Reidel Publishing Co., 1966.

Bohm, D., *The special theory of relativity.* New York: W. A. Benjamin, 1965.

Bower, T. G. R., Stimulus variables determining space perception. *Science*, 1965, **149**, 88–89.

Bruner, J. S., *Processes of cognitive growth: Infancy.* The Heinz Werner Lecture Series. Reprinted in the Eight Annual Report 1967–1968 of the Center for Cognitive Studies, Harvard University, pp. 1–75.

Fantz, R. L., Ontogeny of perception. In A. M. Schrier, H. H. Harlow and F. Stollnitz (Eds.) *Behavior of nonhuman primates.* Vol. II. New York: Academic, 1965.

Festinger, L., Burnham, C. A., Ono, H., and Bamber, D., Efference and the conscious experience of perception. *Journal of Experimental Psychology Monograph*, 1967, **74**, 1–37.

Festinger, L. and Canon, L. K., Information about spatial location based on knowledge about efference. *Psychological Review*, 1965, **72**, 373–384.

Furth, H., *Piaget and knowledge: Theoretical foundations.* Englewood Cliffs, N. Y.: Prentice Hall, 1969.

Gaarder, K., Mechanism in fixation saccadic eye movements. *British Journal of Physiological Optics*, 1967, 28–44.

Gibson, J. J., The concept of the stimulus in psychology. *American Psychologist*, 1962, **17**, 694–703.

Gibson, J. J., The useful dimensions of sensitivity. *American Psychologist*, 1963, **18**, 1–16.

Gyr, J. W., Brown, J. S., Willey, R., and Zivian, A., Computer simulation and psychological theories of perception. *Psychological Bulletin*, 1966, **65**, 174–192.

Gyr, J. W., Zivian, A. and Brown, J. S., Computer simulation of perceptual development (paper delivered at the Conference for Models of Perception and Learning, Stanford University, 1967). Mental Heatlth Research Institute, University of Michigan, *Communication* No. 215.

Gyr, J., Is a theory of direct visual perception adequate? *Psychological Bulletin*, 1971, in press

Hebb, D. O., *Organization of behaviour.* New York: Wiley, 1949.

Hebb, D. O., Concerning imagery. *Psychological Review*, 1968, **75**, 466–477.

Held, R., Exposure history as a factor in maintaining stability of perception and coordination. *Journal of nervous and mental disease*, 1961, **132**, 26–32.

Held, R., The role of movement in the origin and maintenance of visual perception. In *Procedures XVII International Congress of Psychology.* Amsterdam: North Holland, 1964.

Held, R., Dissociation of visual functions by deprivation and rearrangement. *Psychologische Forschung*, 1968, **31**, 338–348.

Held, R. and Bossom, J., Neonatal deprivation and adult rearrangement. *Journal of Comparative and Physiological Psychology*, 1961, **54**, 33–37.

Held, R. and Hein, A., On the modifiability of form perception. In Wathen-Dunn, W. (Ed.), *Models for the perception of speech and visual form*. Cambridge, Mass.: MIT Press, 1967.

Ingle, D., Two visual mechanisms underlying the behavior of fish. *Psychologische Forschung*, 1967, **31**, 44–51.

Inhelder, B. and Piaget, J., *The early growth of logic in the child*. New York: Harper and Row, 1964.

Jacobson, E., Electrical measurements of neuromuscular states during mental activities. Imagination and recollection of various muscular acts. *American Journal of Physiology*, 1930, **94**, 22–34.

Jeannerod, M., Gerin, P., and Pernier, J., Deplacements et fixations du regard dans l'exploration libre d'une scene visuelle. *Vision-Research*, 1968, **8**, 81–97.

Lashley, K. S., The problem of serial order in behavior. In Jeffress, L. A. (Ed.), *Cerebral mechanisms in behavior: The Hixon Symposium*. New York: John Wiley & Sons, 1951, pp. 112–146.

Meyers, B., Discrimination of visual movement in perceptually deprived cats. *Journal of Comparative and Physiological Psychology*, 1954, **57**, 152–153.

Meyers, B. and McCleary, R. A., Interocular transfer of a pattern discrimination in pattern deprived cats. *Journal of Comparative and Physiological Psychology*, 1954, **57**, 16–21.

Piaget, J., *Play, dreams and imitation in childhood*. New York: Norton, 1951.

Piaget, J., *The construction of reality in the child*. New York: Basic Books, 1954.

Platt, J. R., Functional geometry and the determination of pattern in mosaic receptors. *General systems*, 1961, **7**, 103–119.

Poincaré, H., *Science and hypothesis*. New York: Dover, 1952.

Pribram K. H., The neurophysiology of remembering. *Scientific American*, 1969, **220**, 73–85.

Rey, A., Les images mentales en psychophysiologie. *Dialectica*, 1958, **12**, 130–145.

Riesen, A. H., The development of visual perception in man and chimpanzee. *Science*, 1947, **106**, 107–108.

Rock, I., *The nature of perceptual adaptation*. New York: Basic Books, 1966.

Schifferli, P., Etude par enregistrement photographique de la motricite oculaire dans l'exploration, dans la reconnaissance et dans la representation visuelle. *Monatschrift für Psychiatrie und Neurologie*, 1958, **126**, 65–118.

Singer, G. and Day, R. H., Spatial adaptation and after effect with optically transformed vision: Effects of active and passive responding and the relationship between test and exposure responses. *Journal of Experimental Psychology*, 1966, **71**, 725–731.

Sperry, R. W., Neurology and the mind-brain problem. *American Scientist*, 1952, **40**, 291–312.

Sperry, R. W., Physiological plasticity and brain circuit theory. In Harlow, H. F. and Woolsey, C. N. (Eds.), *Biological and chemical bases of behavior*. Madison: University of Wisconsin Press, 1958, pp. 401–424.

Trevarthen, C. B., Two mechanisms of vision in primates. *Psychologische Forschung*, 1968a, **31**, 299–337.

Trevarthen, C. B., The origin of the visual frame for action in vertebates. In Ingle, D. (Ed.), *The central nervous system and fish behavior*. Chicago: University of Chicago Press, 1968b, pp. 61–94.

von Holst, E., Relations between the central nervous system and the peripheral organs. *British Journal of Animal Behaviour*, 1954, **2**, 89–94.

von Holst, E. and Mittelstaedt, H., Das reafferenez prinzip. *Die Naturwissenschaften*, 1950, **20**, 464–476

von Neumann, J., The general and logical theory of automata. In Newman, J. R. (Ed.) *World of mathematics*, Vol. IV. New York: Simon and Schuster, 1956.

Yarbus, A. L., *Eye movements and vision*. New York: Plenum Press, 1967.

Zaporozhets, A. V., The development of voluntary movement. Moscow: Academy of Pedagogical Sciences, 1960.

IX

INDUCTIVE KNOWING

Kenneth R. Hammond

Institute of Behavioral Science
University of Colorado

1   PROXIMAL-DISTAL SEPARATION

This paper treats the problem of inductive cognition as one in which the organism somehow utilizes the data *given* to make an inference about data *not given*; one in which the organism makes an induction from palpable, proximal data, to some impalpable, distal state-to-be-inferred. Once the from-to distinction is made, the question immediately arises as to what the nature of the relations might be between proximal and distal variables—a question never given its due in the history of psychology (but see Polanyi, 1966).

Although this is not the place to pursue the reasons why such a significant problem was overlooked, it is worth noting briefly that the traditional "schools" of psychology failed to recognize the importance of this distinction. Psychophysicists concentrated on sensory data, gestaltists spent their energies insisting upon the patterning of proximal data, while the classical behaviorists analyzed the relation of proximal stimulus events to proximal response events. If the distal region was not completely ignored, its relation to the proximal region was conveniently assumed to be one-to-one.

Although modern stimulus-response psychologists have made the distinction in one form or another, the nature of the relation between the two regions never became the focus of attention. This oversight occurred, I think, because $S-R$ theorists chose to arrange proximal-distal conditions with a view toward testing theories about organismic behavior; the laboratory task was arranged not with regard to the characteristics of proximal-distal relations but in order to test a specific theoretical proposition about organismic constructs. From our point of view, however, proximal-distal relations in the environment are essential elements of the inductive task, and the wide variety of forms they take can be overlooked only at the peril of developing a science whose results are trivial and artifactual. To avoid such risks, proximal-distal relations in laboratory tasks presented to subjects should be *representative* of proximal-distal relations in tasks which subjects are likely to encounter in their environment. Otherwise, the theory and the results of the laboratory experiments will be irrelevant with respect to organism-environment relations (Brunswik, 1956; Hammond, 1966b). It is our judgment that it is precisely at this point that the charges of ecological irrelevancy directed toward modern $S-R$ theory carry significance.

2 SUBSTANTIVE AND FORMAL REPRESENTATION OF PROXIMAL-DISTAL RELATIONS

If the investigator should choose to arrange proximal-distal relations so that they represent those which might be expected to be found in the environment (or some subset of environments) he immediately faces a second choice: should such relations be represented in a *formal* sense or in a *substantive* sense? By *formal*, we refer to the mathematical/statistical properties (e.g., redundancy) of proximal-distal relations; by *substantive*, we refer to the environmental thing-content of the inductive task.

Substantive representation has hardly been attempted for two reasons: a) we apparently lack the technical ability to discover and to bring into the laboratory in a representative fashion those cognitive tasks which various complicated environmental situations present to us, and b) traditional methodology has never inspired the effort.

Formal representation of proximal-distal relations, on the other hand, is clearly feasible. That is, it is easy enough to abstract the various relations which are *possible* from substantive tasks—and to decide whether it is reasonable to include these in a cognitive task. It is, for example, immediately obvious that the relation between the data given and the state to-be-inferred can be a positive linear one or a negative linear one. And of the near-infinite choice of forms of nonlinear relations, one can imagine at least two forms which are common, which are distinctly different from each other, and distinctly different from linear forms. These are the two halves of the *sine* function—roughly, an inverted U-shaped curve (∩) and a U-shaped curve (U). Thus, on a purely formal basis we can choose relations which we assume can and will be present in cognitive tasks in the human ecology, and include such relations in the cognitive tasks we present to our subjects.

In the study to be described below, we have chosen to include the four kinds of proximal-distal relations which are likely to be encountered in *any* cognitive task. As indicated above, these are: 1) a positive linear relation, 2) a negative linear relation, 3) an inverted U-shaped relation (∩) and 4) a U-shaped relation. Not only does it seem reasonable to find such relations between proximal and distal data in cognitive tasks, it also seems reasonable that *all* other possible relations would be a close approximation to these. For purely formal reasons, then, and without regard to the substantive materials of the task, these four relations were the ones with which we began our investigation of the effects of differences in function-form with respect to inductive knowing.

In order to make the significance of this choice clear, it should be noted that orthodox approaches to the problem of cognition have proceeded otherwise. Bruner, Goodnow, and Austin, for example, in their "Study of Thinking" (1956) which set the direction for contemporary concept-learning and concept-formation studies, arranged the function-forms in their principal study to be categorical, linear and orthogonal—a practice established by Hull in 1920 and still followed in virtually all studies of knowing.

Statistical Nature of Induction

It is perhaps unnecessary to point out that, by definition, any inductive task presented to the Knower must be statistical in character. For, if the proximal data set presented exhausts the distal data set (e.g., if the sample observed constitutes the entire population), then the problem of inductive knowing ceases to exist; we have what Cohen and Nagel have called a *perfect* induction. It is precisely those cases in which our subjects must deal with an *imperfect* induction—that is, in which they must make an inference from a sample to a large population-that we are concerned with here.

The two points presented above form the cornerstone of the theory to be presented here. Proximal-distal relations are a critical aspect of inductive tasks; yet their effects on cognition have hardly been studied. Nearly all psychological research has been based on the implicit assumption that (1) proximal-distal relations are *simple*(that is, linear), (2) proximal-proximal relations are orthogonal, and (3) such relations are either randomly or perfectly determined. Our point of departure rejects these assumptions; we turn now to the exploration of certain theoretical and empirical consequences of rejecting them.

3 A MODEL OF INDUCTIVE KNOWING

During the 1930's, Brunswik presented a model of inductive knowing which was intended to represent the perceptual process. And in the 1950's he also applied the model to the more cognitive aspects of knowing (see

Hammond, 1966); aside from some powerful but very general insights, however, Brunswik died before he was able to complete the effort. Our own work takes up from where Brunswik stopped.

Brunswik called his model of perceptual processes the "lens model" (see Figure 1) because it resembles the focusing process of a lens. Conceptually, however, the lens model is intended to depict a situation in which some remote cause (or distal state of affairs) scatters its effects more or less irregularly; the behaving organism must somehow detect and integrate these effects in order to achieve a stable relation with the cause or distal state of affairs to which the organism does not have direct access.

It can be seen from Figure 1 that the lens model depicts a probabilistic environment which provides uncertain, corrigible (cf., Campbell, 1966), information in the form of cues (X_i) about a remote or otherwise impalpable state of affairs (Y_e) and a probabilistic organism which combines, integrates, or otherwise makes use of this information in order to achieve, or "know" the task-relevant variable (Y_e).

The lens model need not be restricted to the case of a single Knower, however, and in 1965 we (Hammond, 1965; Rappoport, 1965) were able to illustrate its application to the situation where two or more Knowers (or two or more environmental tasks) are present (see Figure 2). In addition in 1964 a formal mathematical analysis of the data produced by the lens model became available (Hursch, Hammond, and Hursch, 1964). Happily, it turned out that both task and Knower could be analyzed in terms of the same mathematical logic, and, therefore, both task(s) and Knower(s) could be treated alike from a formal, mathematical point of view. This, in turn, meant that task(s) and Knower(s) could be seen as *systems*, since the same concept can be applied to both Knower and task. Brunswik's remark in 1957 that "Both organism and environment will have to be seen as systems, each with properties of its own, yet both hewn basically from the same block ..." has been vindicated by these two extensions of his work.

We turn now to an examination of four kinds of systems: (a) single-systems, (b) double-systems, (c) triple-systems, and (d) N-systems. Each will be described in terms of the parameters of the system in question.

4 TYPES OF SYSTEMS AND THEIR PARAMETERS

Single-System Parameters

These refer to the parameters of the cognitive system of a Knower attempting to make inductive inferences about a task, the properties of which

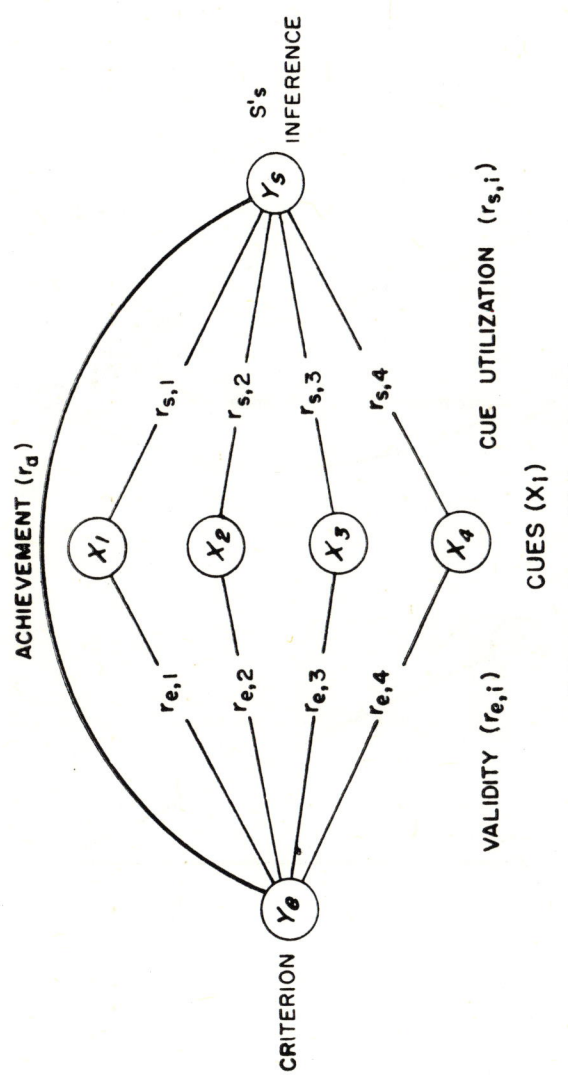

FIGURE 1 Brunswik's Lens Model

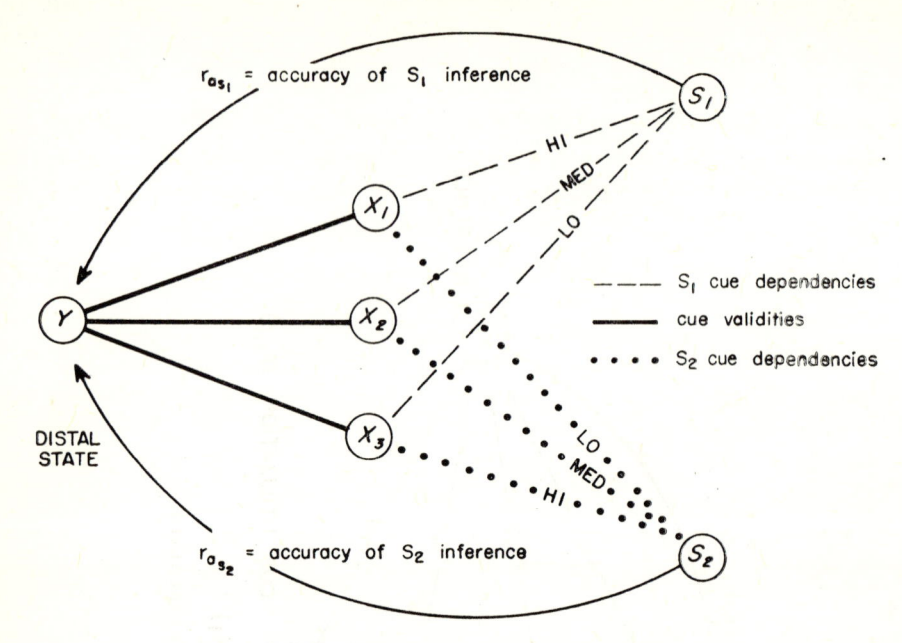

FIGURE 2 The Two-person Lens Model

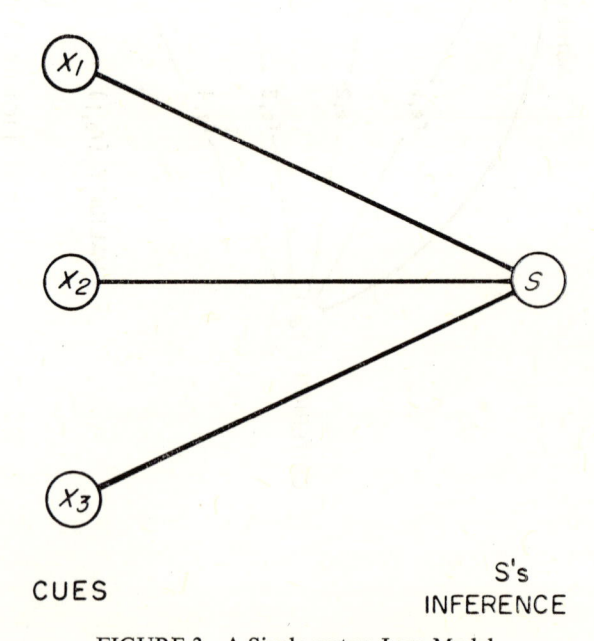

FIGURE 3 A Single-system Lens Model

remain unspecified (see Figure 3). Following the lens model conception of inductive tasks, we specify the following parameters: (a) a *number* of cues which vary in (b) their *intersubstitutability*, (c) the *form* of their relation to the Knower's judgment, (d) the *parameters* of such forms, (e) their *indeterminacy* and (f) the extent to which they are linearly *integrated* within the system, and the extent to which they *integrated* in nonlinear ways. Each is discussed in turn.

Number

The number of cues which influence the inductive judgment of a Knower will, of course, vary from occasion to occasion. Although the lower limit of the number of cues which can be considered by a Knower is one, seldom will an occasion arise in which the Knower's judgment is so restricted. The upper limit of the Knower's capacity to incorporate information from several cues remains unknown, although, of course, it has been suggested by Miller that it is roughly 7 (plus or minus 2).

Intersubstitutability

In addition to the human Knower's capacity to respond to several cues simultaneously, he is able to respond to cues which are substitutable for one another. The human Knower can respond to a warm handshake as well as a warm smile as an indicator of friendliness. When a cue which is ordinarily depended upon for information is unavailable, a second cue which is highly correlated with (redundant with) the first cue can be utilized with ease. The process of substitution was labeled "vicarious functioning" by Brunswik and was given a highly important place in his description of cognitive processes. One of the reasons that man's inductive processes have proved to be so elusive to the student of cognition is precisely because of man's capacity to allow several different cues to influence his judgment in the same way. Not only does this appear to be true in the case of visual perception, but it seems to be equally true with respect to language; various words are intersubstitutable with respect to affective meanings as well as with respect to denotative meanings.

Indeterminacy

The uncertainty in the Knower's cognitive system lies in the relation between cue and judgment. The Knower's allocation of uncertainty to the various cues that enter his judgment is a distinctive feature of his inductive process. Postulating uncertainty in this relation has never become a firm part of modern theoretical psychology.

Function-form

Here we refer to the form of the relation between a cue-variable and the Knower's judgment. Such relations may be linear in form, or may take on various nonlinear forms. Positive linear function-forms are, of course, most common; also common are inverted-U function-forms.

The nonlinear use of cues has been a prominent issue in the literature concerning clinical inference for over 20 years and bears closely on the question of the unique contribution of the clinician to the inference process. For if it is found that the clinical psychologist (or any other clinician) can be replaced by simple linear equations, then, of course, the clinician can hardly be said to have been using clinical data in the complex fashion he claims.

Function-parameters

The concept of function-form described above is rather broad in that it denotes the general form of the relation between each cue and the Knower's judgment. The concept of function-parameters is more precise for it specifies the *details* of the relation between each cue and the Knower's judgment. Thus, if the relation were a linear one between a given cue-judgment relation, the parameters of the function would be indicated by the intercept (a) and the slope (b) in the equation $y = a + bx$ where y equals the Knower's judgment and x equals the specific value of a cue. Nonlinear equations would, of course, require further specification.

Integration of cue-data

The information from several cues must somehow be "put together" since there are several inputs from the several cues but only one judgment. The nature of the integrative process, or processes, remains an open question, and several models of cognitive integration have been offered (see, for example, Feldman, 1966). This question is much more complex than the preceding one in the same sense that multiple regression analysis is more complex than the analyses of the relation between just two variables. Not only must the *form* of integrative function (adding, averaging, etc.) be determined, but its generality over tasks, and the consistency of its application also must be considered.

Double-System Parameters

A double-system includes both a task and a Knower (see Figure 4; cf. Figure 3). As indicated above, inductive tasks can be described in terms of the same parameters used to describe the Knower's cognitive system. Thus proximal and distal variables in the task are related by (a) *many* channels which are (b) *intersubstitutable* and which vary in their (c) *dependability*, (d) *function-form*, (e) *function-parameters*, and (f) *degrees of integration*.

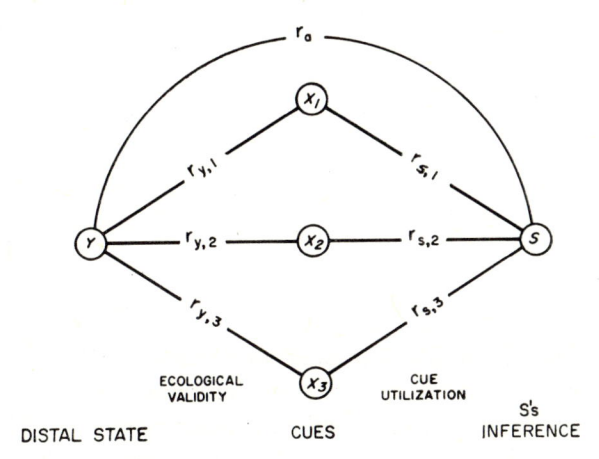

FIGURE 4   A Double-system Lens Model

The above task parameters not only differentiate inductive tasks from one another; they provide concreteness and specificity for the over-all concept of *texture*. They mark the first step toward operational recognition of the conceptual implications (and the increased differentiation of) the concept of entangled causality since Hume's remarks about the probability of causes. If this statement appears extravagant, it must be remembered that the concept of *causal texture* was not introduced into psychology until 1935 by Brunswik and Tolman. It was done in this fashion:

"Each of us has come to envisage psychology as primarily concerned with the methods of response of the organism to two characteristic features of the environment. The first of these features lies in the fact that the environment is a causal texture in which different events are regularly dependent upon each other. And because of the presence of such causal couplings actually existing in their environments, organisms come to accept one event as a local representative for another event.

"The second feature of the environment to which the organism also adjusts is the fact that such causal connections are probably always to some degree equivocal."

Although their remarks make the concept of causal texture intuitively clear, they also create the necessity for the type of explication provided by the above task parameters. We turn now to a description of these parameters as they apply to the task-system.

Multiple mediation

The relation between distal and proximal regions is a one-many relation; a given distal event will result in many proximal events. Put otherwise, any distal event will have many proximal offshoots. Thus, information from remote layers of a cognitive task can teach us via many channels, or cues. Although inductive tasks may present us with a minimum of one cue, in general there will be many. *How* many, on the average, we do not know and will not know until ecological surveys of inductive tasks are carried out.

Intersubstitutability

The distal-proximal relation is an intersubstitutable one. That is, cues may substitute for one another in conveying information. If one cue is not present, or fails to provide information, another may do so. Thus, it may be said that cues function vicariously for one another. In the language of information theory, to the extent that two cues substitute for one another, they may be considered redundant. Thus, it is not only the multi-channeled character of the environment which must be taken into consideration, but the intersubstitutability of these channels must be considered as well. Almost no research has been done on intersubstitutability.

Function-form

The functional relation between distal and proximal variables may, of course, take on various forms. There are two broad classes of function-forms to be considered. One class includes all those functional relations which are linear in form and the other includes those which are nonlinear in form. In the first group we find only two principal relations. That is, a positive linear relation and a negative linear relation between proximal and distal variables. In the second group, however, there are, of course, a wide variety of non-linear forms which may occur. Hardly any research has been done with respect to function-form, although we shall report in detail on one such study below.

Function-parameters

A further concept to be applied to the theory of environments concerns the parameters of the functional relations between proximal and distal variables. These parameters constitute the laws of the system. That is to say, they specify the relation between the distal variable and each of the proximal variables that would exist if the system were a completely dependable one. (If we were to use the language of correlational statistics we would say that the dependability of the proximal-distal relation is specified by the correlation between the proximal variable and the distal one, whereas the functional relation between the proximal variable and the distal one is indicated by the b coefficient of the regression equation.) Thus, one proximal-distal relationship may be similar to another in terms of its dependability, yet each may have different function parameters, e.g., their slopes may be different. Similarly two proximal variables may have different function parameters but may be similar with respect to dependability.

Dependability

Fundamental to the theory of probabilistic functionalism, is the idea that the data of inductive tasks are less than completely dependable because of the probabilistic or uncertain relations between proximal events and distal events. Thus, various inductive tasks will differ in their overall uncertainty depending upon the magnitude of the probability relation (e.g., correlation) between proximal and distal events.

Integration

Environmental systems will differ in the extent to which the systems are integrated. A highly integrated system will be one in which the proximal variables denote, or predict, or determine, the distal variable with a large degree of certainty. Highly integrated systems will permit one to be certain about the value of the distal variable, given the data from the proximal variables. Poorly integrated systems will be those in which the value of the distal variable can be predicted from knowledge of proximal events only with a large degree of error.

System compatibility

Here we refer to the extent to which the distal regions of any two systems co-vary, given the same sets of proximal data. If the distal regions of two systems co-vary highly under these circumstances, they are said to be highly compatible. If two systems are highly compatible, they have a stable relation with one another; they have "come to terms" with one another. System compatibility will depend upon the internal features of both systems—indicated by the seven parameters described above.

The Triple-System (and N-System) Case: Knowing the Cognitive System of the Other

The triple-system case and the N-system case will be discussed together. A triple-system case is illustrated in Figure 2; it may include a single Knower and two environmental tasks, or two Knowers and a single environmental task. We shall consider only the latter, principally because research involving interpersonal *learning* is almost wholly non-existent. Thus, we will direct our attention to the problem of two Knowers attempting inductively to learn about one another as they learn a common task.

The addition of a second organic system—a second Knower—to the double-system of Knower and task creates a new, and complicated, set of circumstances. In the double-system case, considered above, only one system (the Knower) *monitors* its behavior in relation to the second system (the task). (This is not a necessary condition; the task-system may, in principle, be one which is self-monitoring; its output, for example, might be contingent upon the behavior of the Knower.) When a second Knower is added as the third system, however, *two* self-monitoring systems, *two* systems capable of producing behavior contingent upon the behavior of another, are brought into contact with one another. In the study to be described below, two Knowers, together, attempt to learn an environmental task, and each learns about the cognitive system of the Other in the process of learning about the task. In other words, in this form of the triple-system case, S_1 attempts to learn the task as he learns about the cognitive system of S_2; also, S_2 attempts to learn the task as he learns about the cognitive system of S_1. Two of the three systems, then, are in a dynamic, *interactive* relation to one another, for S_1 is changing as he learns about S_2, who is also changing as he learns about S_1. The experimental analysis of these circumstances is undertaken in the latter part of this chapter. First, however, we need to distinguish between two sets of materials in this triple-system case.

The basic materials of inductive knowing in the triple-system case

There are two sets of basic materials in these inductive tasks. One set involves the content of the task; it is *substantive* in nature. The other set involves the relations between various parameters of the task; it is *formal* in nature. These two sets of materials provide the analytical properties and intuitive properties (respectively) of quasi-rationality.

Substantive materials

Language provides the substantive material in the communication effort between the two organismic systems. It is substantive because it consists of tangible materials—words, sentences, etc. These are the *noticeables* of the process and they form a set of cues (in addition to the Other's judgmental response) to the cognitive system of the Other. These substantive objects (e.g., sentences, words) carry meanings, of course, but they do not carry unequivocal meanings. They prevent the Knower and the Other from unequivocally presenting, or communicating, the characteristics of their cognitive systems because of the indeterminacy, referential opacity, idiosyncratic connotations, differential denotations, etc. of words and sentences (see Quine, 1960).

Equally important, the quasi-rational logic of the Knower and Other are as equivocal as their semantics. Abelson and Knouse (1966) show, for example, that:

1) Verbs representing negative subjective states have very high deductive power and low inductive power.

2) Verbs representing manifest negative actions have fairly high power both inductively and deductively.

3) Verbs representing positive subjective states have fairly high inductive power and low deductive power.

4) Verbs representing positive episodic interactions have very high inductive power and low deductive power.

In short, the substantive materials of communication ordinarily are confusing and inefficient.

Formal materials

In addition to the substantive materials of a cognitive system, there are *formal* aspects to be considered as well; these include the parameters of the cognitive systems of the Knower and the Other and their relation to one another. Such parameters cannot be made explicit by the Other, and although they are *detectable* by the Knower, they can be made *explicit* only with the aid of instruments. That is, although S_1 might detect certain formal aspects of S_2's cognitive system, S_1 cannot describe accurately and completely the formal properties (e.g., the form of the relation between each cue and S_2's judgment, the parameters of such relations, their indeterminacy, the extent to which the cue-data are integrated in a consistent manner, etc.) of S_2's cognitive system.

Neither subject, of course, thinks in such terms; they are not a part of his language or culture. It is becoming apparent, however, that technical aids interfaced with computers can now provide information about the formal properties of the cognitive system of the Other in an intelligible, ordinary language form. But even if such technical aids are developed, we need to explore the extent to which the formal properties of the cognitive system of the Other may be detected without aids (although such properties cannot be described) by the Knower.

Of course, the Other, the person whose cognitive system is being learned about, can offer the Knower little help in an inductive task. First, as we have noted above, the substantive materials of communication are inefficient (and often misleading) sources of information, and, second, the Other cannot provide accurate descriptions of the formal properties of his own cognitive system for reasons mentioned above. Although the substantive aspects of the Other's cognitive system may be clarified to some extent without technical aids, *only* by means of technical aids can the *formal* properties of the Other's system be made accurately and completely explicit. In short, the formal properties of the cognitive system of the Other are detectable implicitly rather than explicitly.

In summary, we have tried to be specific about the relations between palpable, proximal data and the impalpable, distal state-to-be-inferred. Most important, we have indicated that both aspects of the problem—the materials representing the inductive task and the materials representing the organism—could be analyzed in terms of the same mathematical logic, and, therefore, both task(s) and Knower(s) could be treated alike from a formal, mathematical point of view. This meant that task(s) and Knower(s) could be treated as systems. We have described four types of systems; we turn now to the mathematics which makes the relations between systems precise, and which makes empirical investigation possible.

V. THE LENS MODEL EQUATION

The lens model equation was first presented in 1964 by Hursch, Hammond, and Hursch in the following form:

$$r_a = \frac{R_e^2 + R_s^2 - \Sigma d}{2} + C\sqrt{(1 - R_e^2)(1 - R_s^2)} \tag{1}$$

where

r_a = the correlation between subject's judgments and the variable estimated
R_e = the multiple correlation between the cues and the variable estimated
R_s = the multiple correlation between the cues and the subject's judgments
Σd = the sum of the products $(r_{e_i} - r_{s_i})(\beta_{e_i} - \beta_{s_i})$ where r_{e_i} = the correlation between cue$_i$ and the variable estimated, r_{s_i} = the correlation between cue$_i$ and the subject's judgment, β_{e_i} = the beta weight for

the correlation between cue$_i$ and the variable estimated and β_{s_i} = the beta weight for the correlation between cue$_i$ and the subject's responses.

C = the correlation between the variance unaccounted for by the multiple correlation in the ecology and the variance unaccounted for by the multiple correlation in the subject's response system.

The following alternate form was provided by Tucker (1964),

$$r_a = GR_e R_s + C\sqrt{1 - R_e^2} \sqrt{1 - R_s^2} \qquad (2)$$

where G is a component comparable to C; G indicates the amount of linear co-variation between two systems, just as C indicates the amount of nonlinear co-variation between two systems. Both terms are modified by the amount of linearity (R^2) in each system.

The Lens Model Equation and System Parameters

It is important to note that the lens model equation is not a theoretical statement in the sense that equations of Hull or Lewin were: it is simply a logical (mathematical) statement; it cannot be falsified by empirical data derived from the behavior of subjects. The lens model equation provides the precise mathematical relations between the parameters of quasi-rational systems; it was developed for this purpose from the logic of multiple regression statistics by Hursch et al. (1964).

The lens model equation shows that the degree of co-variation (r_a) between the terminal foci (Y_e, Y_s) of the systems is a function of each parameter in the two systems. Thus, if the linear integration of the task-systems (R_e) is small, then the subject will have to detect and make correct use of the nonlinear relations between cues and the distal variable (terminal focus) of the task-system. This rather obvious conclusion is indicated in the lens model equation in the following way; when R_e^2 is small, then the linear component term ($R_e^2 + R_s^2 - \Sigma d$) will be small and r_a will vary directly with C (the extent to which the nonlinear relations in the task-system are matched by the nonlinear relations in the cognitive system of the Knower). Not so obvious is the fact that the same relation also holds in the three-system case, an observation that has direct consequences for the study of interpersonal learning, to be discussed below.

But high accuracy in inductive knowing depends on the correct allocation of uncertainty to various aspects of the task system. For, if the Knower assumes that the relation between cue$_i$ and the distal variable is highly uncertain when, in fact, it is highly dependable, then the Σd term will be larger than necessary and r_a will be smaller than it need be.

It is important to note that in the three-system case the two Knowers could reach (or fail to reach) a high degree of co-variation, or achievement (r_a) with respect to the same quasi-rational task-system for *different reasons*. And, of course, the same can be true in the case of N-systems; two Knowers could reach (or fail to reach) the same degree of predictive ability with respect to a third person (-object) for different reasons—and not be aware of this fact. The possibility of similar achievement (or lack of it) as a result of different processes was described in detail by Hursch, *et al.* (1964) and several examples were provided from the data of an experiment by S. A. Summers (1962).

A second type of information concerns the limits (and the source of limits) of the extent to which two quasi-rational systems can achieve a stable, co-varying relation. More precisely, the lens model equation indicates the conditions under which limits are imposed. For example, if the task system has only linear properties, then the maximum achievement which can be reached is defined by the multiple regression coefficient of the task-system. This topic is of sufficient importance to require detailed treatment; all that can be said here, however, is that a second type of information provided by the lens model equation concerns the *limits* of inductive cognition and the conditions which specify such limits—an entirely new concept in the field of inductive knowing, where heretofore it has been assumed that perfect achievement was always possible.

We turn now to a discussion of the function of each of the parameters of the lens model equation. Although these parameters have been discussed above, our discussion here will focus on their role in the lens model equation.

The first point to be noted is that the equation maintains the theme of distal-proximal separation. Both the lens model and the lens model equation lend concreteness to our emphasis on the separation between surface and depth (between boundary conditions and central conditions) in inductive systems. Although the end term of the equation (r_a) expresses the degree of relation between the two foci in depth of the two (or more) systems, the remaining terms (with one exception) express relations between surface and depth.

Thus, the two multiple regression coefficients indicate relations between various surface conditions (e.g., proximal stimuli, or cues) and terminal foci (distal variables and central variables). The beta coefficients indicate relation between rate of change in surface conditions and terminal foci, and the correlation coefficients indicate the degree of co-variation between surface and depth. The exception referred to above concerns the term C, which indicates the degree of nonlinear covariation between central conditions, without regard to surface conditions. It should be noted, however, that the term C is multiplied by two terms involving the multiple regression coefficient. Thus, the effect of C on r_a is modified by the values of R_e and R_s, both of which include surface-depth relations.

Multiple mediation

The lens model equation takes account of multiple mediation in both the environmental system and the organismic system. More broadly, it takes account of multiple relations between surface and depth in any two of several interacting systems.

Intersubstitutability

The lens model equation also takes account of the concept of intersubstitutability. This is a key concept, and once more the choice of multiple regression statistics makes clear the importance of the possibility that one set of boundary or surface conditions (cues) may bear the same relation to central focal conditions as another.

Equally important is the fact that the lens model equation indicates quite specifically how substitution takes place. As indicated above, a high degree of co-variation between the terminal foci of two quasi-rational systems can take place for different reasons. Thus, a high degree of performance in the detection of nonlinear features of a task-system could substitute for failure to detect the proper distribution of uncertainty in the task-system. Mathematically, a high value of C may compensate for a high value of the Σd term.

Function-form

Both linear and nonlinear function-forms may, of course, occur in either the task-system of the organismic system and both are included in the lens model equation. Linear systems are denoted and expressed in quantitative form by the multiple R, and the co-variation between nonlinear aspects of the system *in any form* are denoted and expressed in quantitative form by C.

Function-parameters

Function-parameters are denoted and expressed in quantitative form in the lens model equation in the second parenthetical term of the Σd term. Thus, two quasi-rational systems may fail to achieve stable relations not only because of the failure to allocate uncertainty between boundary and central conditions appropriately, but also because of a failure to develop matching slopes (rates of change) in the regression equations linking such conditions in both systems.

Dependability

Here, of course, we refer to the probabilistic relation between surface and depth (boundary and central) conditions within each quasi-rational system. Such probabilistic circumstances are also reflected in the theme of the analytical technique; it is for this general reason that the statistical technique is used to evaluate relations between quasi-rational systems. Specifically, the dependabilities of surface-depth relations are indicated by correlation coefficients (r_{e_i} and r_{s_i}). Covariation between nonlinear relations in the two systems is, of course, indicated by C.

Linear Integration

The linear integration of the two systems is indicated by the value of the multiple regression coefficient (R). This statistic provides a precise measure of the predictable linear variance in a given quasi-rational system. This measure has a key conceptual role in the entire analysis. R_e, for example, indicates degree of linear integration which exists between the distal condition which gives rise to various boundary conditions of an environmental surface (ordinarily conceived of as proximal stimuli). A low value of R_e indicates a low degree of linear integration within an environmental system. A low degree of linear integration has two immediate implications: (1) such environmental systems will require a more complex method of description than that afforded by linear multiple regression statistics, and (2) such environmental systems will require the organismic system to develop a more complex function than a linear one if a *maximally* stable relation is to be developed.

It should be noted, however, that it is not necessary for the adapting system to develop a nonlinear system in order to achieve a satis*factory* (as opposed to *maximal*) relation with a nonlinear environmental system. On the other hand, if an environmental system has a high degree of linear integration, the adapting organismic system will be most efficient if it also employs a highly linear method of integrating its boundary conditions with its central conditions.

The above equation meets all the requirements for analyzing the interaction of environment and organism within the framework indicated above; it is appropriate to our conceptual scheme. Thus,

1. The task-system and the organismic system have equal status in the equation; the terms of the equation are symmetrical and thus provide a measure of the inter-relation of the two systems.

2. There are comparable terms relating to the linear integration of the environmental system (R_e) and the organismic system (R_s).

3. There are (a) terms relating to the slope (β_{e_i}) of the regression plane and variation (r_{e_i}) about the regression plane for the cue-distal variable relations of the task-system, and (b) terms relating to identical parameters (β_{s_i}) relations and the variation (r_{s_i}) about them in the cognitive system of the Knower.

4. There is a term (C) which indicates co-variation of the non-linear aspects of the two systems.

The above equation has been tested analytically by Tucker (1964) and Naylor (1966, 1967); both have suggested alternate forms of the above equation which not only widen its applicability, but add to the clarity of its logic. In addition Björkman (1967) has shown that the lens model equation is applicable to the non-metric case as well as the metric case.

There have been criticisms of the multiple regression approach to the analysis of inductive inference (Anderson, 1962; Green, 1968) the main point of which is that multiple regression techniques are too coarse. More specifically, Anderson has indicated that the correlation approach falsely indicates a good fit between model and data, and Green has indicated (for much the same reason) that the nonlinear use of cues will fail to be detected; in short, linear models will appear to be appropriate when they are in fact inappropriate. As we shall show in detail below, however, both arguments fail to hold in the case of the lens model equation; empirical tests show conclusively that poor linear fits and nonlinear relations are in fact detected when the data are analyzed in terms of the lens model equation.

4 APPLICATION: A STUDY OF (INDUCTIVE) INTERPERSONAL KNOWING

We turn now to the analysis of the *triple-system* case; it represents the first serious empirical investigation of inductive knowing involving two Knowers and a task-system in which one Knower inductively comes to know the Other.

This study is a first of its kind in several respects: (a) it investigates the inductive, cognitive processes whereby one person comes to know another; (b) it investigates such processes in a situation involving dynamic, contingent systems—that is, in a situation in which each system is *changing*, and in which the changes in one system are *contingent* upon the changes in another; (c) it rejects the traditional *tabula rasa* condition in which the subject supposedly comes to the experiment with a "blank mind"; rather, it investigates interpersonal learning under conditions in which the subject brings a stable cognitive system to the experiment—one, however, which is specified precisely *in advance* by the investigator; (d) it includes specific nonlinear as well as linear properties.

Purpose of the Study

The study of the triple-system case was carried out for both theoretical and substantive reasons: that is, to evaluate the utility of the application of the general theory, the model and its associated mathematics, and to discover whether knowledge could be gained about two substantive problems; (a) the extent to which one person can learn *from* another person with a similar or different cognitive function-form; and (b) the extent to which one person can learn *about* another person with a similar or different cognitive function-form. In short, our substantive interest concerned the effects of variations in function-form with respect to two problems of considerable human significance—both fundamentally related to the problem of inductive knowing.

Plan of the Study

The results of our previous experiments made it clear that it would be possible to establish the appropriate function-forms in the cognitive system of the subjects (and, of course, in the task-systems) with the necessary precision (see, for example, Hammond, 1965; Hammond, Todd, Wilkins, and Mitchell, 1966). A series of experiments were therefore devised in which it would be possible to study the empirical effects of variations in the four function-forms described above (linear positive, linear negative, inverted U-shape, U-shape) with respect to interpersonal learning. It was found necessary to conduct ten experiments in order to make the necessary comparisons. These ten experiments were arranged as indicated in Table 1.

The general plan involved three stages:

Stage 1: A *Training Stage* in which subjects were trained to develop precisely one of the four cognitive function-forms required by the study;

Stage 2: An *Interactive Stage* in which pairs of subjects were brought together to work on a common task;

TEN-EXPERIMENT STUDY OF COGNITIVE FUNCTION FORM

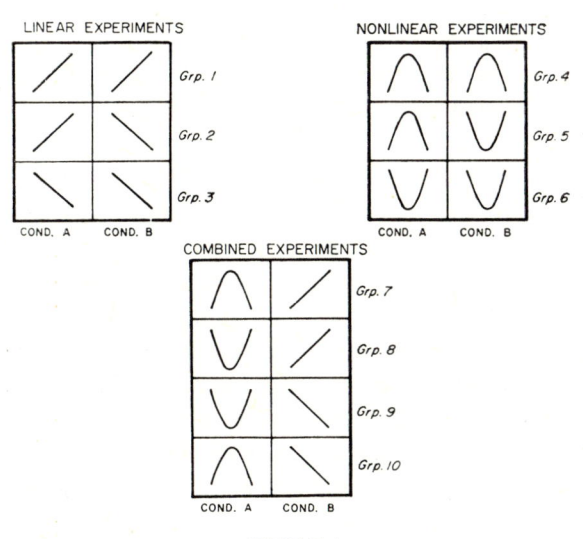

TABLE 1

Stage 3: An *Interpersonal Learning Test Stage* in which each subject made a judgment of the task outcome (but received no feedback) and estimated the judgments the other person would make to each stimulus presentation.

The relative difficulty of learning each of the four function-forms in the task was ascertained in the Training Stage (but will not be described here). The extent to which each person learns from the Other is analyzed in the Interactive Stage, and the extent to which each subject has learned about the Other is measured in the Interpersonal Learning (IPL) Test Stage.

In order to evaluate the effects of the four function-forms described above, ten experiments were arranged as indicated in Table 1. Each of the four function-forms was paired with one another by bringing together pairs of subjects to work on a common task. In this way it was possible to compare the interactive processes produced by pairs of persons with similar *linear, positive* function-forms with the interactive process produced by pairs with similar *linear, negative* function-forms, and with similar *nonlinear* (e.g., inverted U-shaped) function-forms, as well as the effects of pairing subjects with *different* function-forms.

In addition to inducing various function-forms in the cognitive systems of the subjects in the Training Stage, subjects also learned to develop different cue-dependencies. The task involved two cues; subjects were brought together in pairs in such a fashion that S_1 had a high dependence on Cue A, and a zero dependence on Cue B, whereas S_2 was trained in the reverse way; that is, S_2 developed a high dependence on Cue B and a zero dependence on Cue A. Of course, the function-form was specified with respect to the cue the subject learned to depend on—since the other cue was randomly related to the criterion.

For example, in Experiment 2 (Table 1) Subject 1 came to the experiment trained to depend on Cue A in a *positive* linear manner and to ignore Cue B; Subject 2 of the pair came to experiment trained to ignore Cue A but to depend on Cue B in a *negative* linear manner.

Differential cue-dependencies were constant over the ten experiments, thus providing a constant cognitive difference between subjects over experiments and a constant condition for the Interactive Stage. This procedure insured interpersonal cognitive differences, and also made certain that in every condition subjects would have something to learn *from* and *about* the Other, and that the investigators would know exactly what it was.

Procedure

Subjects

Two hundred male introductory psychology students served as subjects; 20 in each of the 10 experiments. Within each experiment, the 20 subjects were randomly assigned to the experimental groups.

Materials

The materials used consisted of sets of 5 × 8 inch cards, on which were printed two bar graphs; one graph was labeled "A" (Cue X_1) and the other was labeled "B" (Cue X_2). The graphs were contentless. Within any one of the ten experiments, Graphs A and B co-varied with the criterion, Graph "C", according to the combinations of functions-forms shown in Table 1.

Each *training* deck consisted of 60 such cards, with the heights (values) of each bar graph varying from card to card. Each *interactive* task deck consisted of 20 trials. Four interactive task decks, composed of the same cards in different serial orders, were presented in a rotating sequence to the 10 pairs of subjects. Each *interpersonal learning test* deck consisted of 10 cards, with the values of each bar graph, as in the training decks, varying from card to card.

Training Stage

Differential cue-dependencies

Within each pair of subjects in the ten experiments, one subject, S_1, was trained on a task in which cue X_1 (Graph B) accounted for 98% of the variance in the criterion, Y (Graph C); the second cue, X_1 (Graph A), was randomly related to Y for this subject. The other subject within a pair of subjects, S_2, was trained on a task in which cue X_2 accounted for 98% of the variance in the criterion, Y; the second cue, X_1, was randomly related to Y for this subject.

The multiple correlations within all training tasks were less than unity ($R^2 = 0.98$); the tasks, therefore, were *uncertain*, inductive tasks. Subjects completed the Training Stage after they had reached a predetermined level of performance. The Training Stage resulted, then, in half the subjects, S_1, depending on cue X_1 and ignoring cue X_2, and half the subjects, S_2, depending on cue X_2, and ignoring cue X_1.

Only those subjects who achieved at least a correlation of 0.75 with the cue-to-be-dependent-on and no larger correlation than 0.25 with the cue-to-be-ignored were included in the Interactive Stage.

Differential Function-forms

The above-described training procedure was also employed to induce the subject's acquisition of the appropriate function-forms specified by the experimenter as follows:

1. Positive linear policy—the greater the cue value, the greater the criterion value. (Mathematical expression: $y = 2x$)

2. Negative linear policy—the greater the cue value, the less the criterion value. (Mathematical expression: $y = 20 - 2x$)

3. Inverted U-shaped policy—the greater the cue value up to some point, the greater the criterion value; beyond this point, the greater the cue value the less the criterion value. (Mathematical expression: $y = \sine ax$)

4. U-shaped policy—the greater the cue value up to some point the less the criterion value; beyond this point, the greater the cue value, the greater the criterion value. (Mathematical expression: $y = 20 - \sine ax$)

The subjects were told that their task was to make a judgment about the value of the Graph "C" on the basis of the value of Graph "A" and "B". They were further informed that *one* of the graphs was far more important than the other, and given specific information about the function-form involved; for example, "the higher the value of the important graph, the *higher* the value of C (linear positive)"; or "the higher the value of the important graph, the *lower* the value of C (linear negative)." The detailed specification of the function-form was provided for the subject on the basis of previous research, Hammond and Summers (1965) and Summers and Hammond (1966) which indicated that such specification reduced learning time, yet provided a learning task of appropriate difficulty.

Interactive Stage

The properties of the interactive task were different from the training tasks, although the subjects were not made aware of this. The interactive task was arranged so that both cues, X_1 and X_2, now had equal validity ($r_1^2 = r_2^2 = 0.49$); they remained uncorrelated, however, and the multiple correlation remained, as in training, less than unity ($R^2 = 0.98$). The subjects were not told that the task properties had changed; they were merely asked to "work together" on the problem. Thus, the new task presented to both S_1 and S_2 was one for which neither subject was adequately prepared and one which involved inductive learning—both *from* and *about* the Other.

The task consisted of a series of 20 trials on each of which the two subjects were required to judge the level of the criterion, Y, on the basis of the levels of cues X_1 and X_2. On every trial each subject made a personal judgment (S) as to the level of Y; also, on every trial the two subjects made a joint judgment (J) of Y, after revealing their personal judgments to one another. Subsequent to the joint judgment, the two subjects were shown by the experimenter the correct criterion value, Y.

It should be noted that on each trial the subjects were *required* to come to a joint judgment upon which they could agree; this requirement insured discussion and exchange of information which provided the base for interpersonal learning.

Interpersonal Learning Test Stage

Subsequent to the Interactive Stage, the subjects were asked to make ten more judgments. The task properties were exactly the same as in the Interactive Stage. However, in the IPL Test Stage, each subject was required to look at a stimulus card and to record not only his own judgment, but also to record the judgment that he thought the Other would make in response to that stimulus card. No feedback was given on these trials. By means of this procedure it was possible to evaluate the accuracy of subject's judgment with respect to the *task* which had a function-form which was different from, or similar to, his, after his interaction with an Other who had a function-form different from, or similar to, his. In addition, it was possible to evaluate the accuracy of a subject's prediction of the *Other's* judgment—thus obtaining a measure of the extent to which he had learned *about* Others who had similar or different cognitive function-forms, as well as different cue-dependencies in every case.

Establishment of Appropriate Experimental Conditions

The establishment of appropriate experimental conditions requires that:

1. Pairs of subjects must come to the Interactive Stage with cognitive systems which are *equally* different over the ten experiments. That is, differential cue-dependencies must be established to the same degree across all 100 pairs of subjects;

2. subjects must come to the Interactive Stage with the appropriate function-form required for a specific experiment;

3. the potential amount of learning *from* and *about* the Other must be comparable across experiments;

4. the interpersonal learning task involving learning *from* and *about* the Other must be of an appropriate level of difficulty; the task must not be so easy or difficult that IPL cannot be measured.

These conditions were met for all 100 pairs of subjects, although space does not permit the presentation of proof.

7 CHANGE IN LENS MODEL PARAMETERS IN THE INTERACTIVE STAGE

It will perhaps be useful to remind the reader of the complexity of the analysis we are about to present. Our experimental conditions have established an Interactive Stage in which two Knowers with different (as specified by the investigator) inductive systems will confront a task-system for which neither inductive system is perfectly adequate (nor totally inadequate). The specification of the formal properties of the subject's cognitive system, in contrast to the *tabula rasa* researchers ordinarily attempt to create, is representative of circumstances in which inductive knowing does in fact take place. For when persons ordinarily confront one another, they have moderately successful (but different) functional cognitive systems which they must bring to bear on a task not quite like that for which their experience has prepared them. What *is* unrepresentative of life-conditions in this study is the immediate presentation of feedback concerning the right answer in the new task. If anything, then, these laboratory circumstances err on the side of oversimplifying the (physical) learning task. Yet the situation does permit analysis of dynamic, contingent change (interpersonal learning) in the cognitive systems of two Knowers—*analysis of change in one system as it occurs in relation to change in the Other*. We know of no other approach to the problem of inductive knowing which has attempted to cope with a problem of this complexity.

The analysis begins by showing changes in cue-dependencies, since these are a fundamental aspect of the theoretical model described above.

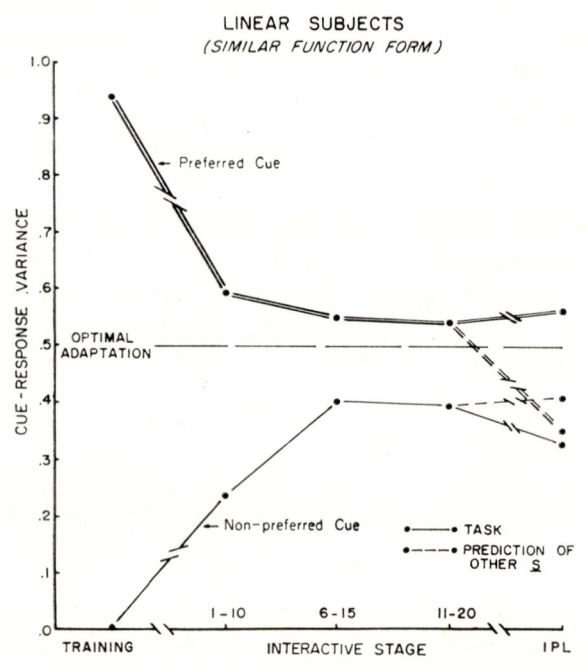

FIGURE 5 Cue-dependencies measured in terms of r^2 between cue and Subject's judgment. Groups 1 and 3 from Table 1

Cue dependencies ($r_{s_i}^2$)

The results show quite clearly that subjects' cue-dependencies in *all* groups changed markedly during the Interactive Stage (see Figures 5, 6, 7, and 8). Moreover, their cue-dependencies approach the value required for optimal adaptation to the new (physical) inductive task in the Interactive Stage. This parameter of the lens model equation, then, appears to provide a measure of cognitive functioning which is sensitive to the interaction between subjects, as well as to information provided by the new physical task.

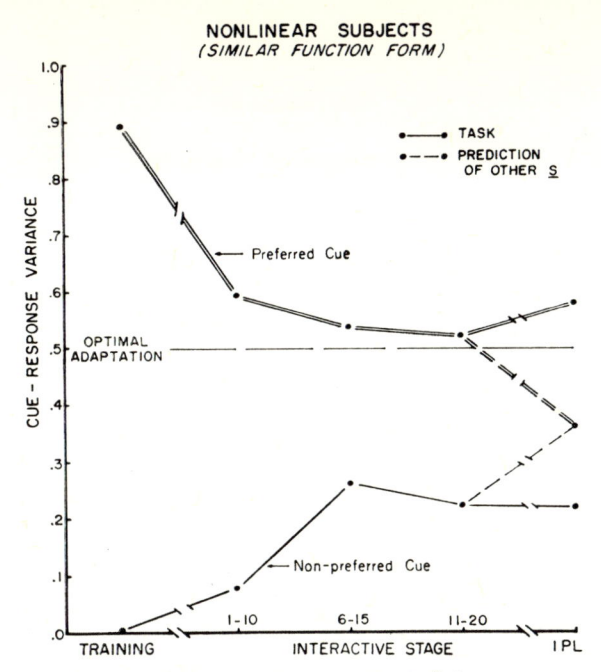

FIGURE 6 Cue-dependencies measured in terms of r^2 between cue and Subject's judgment. (Note: appropriate transformation made for nonlinear relations so as to provide r^2 comparable for linear relations.) Groups 4 and 6 from Table 1

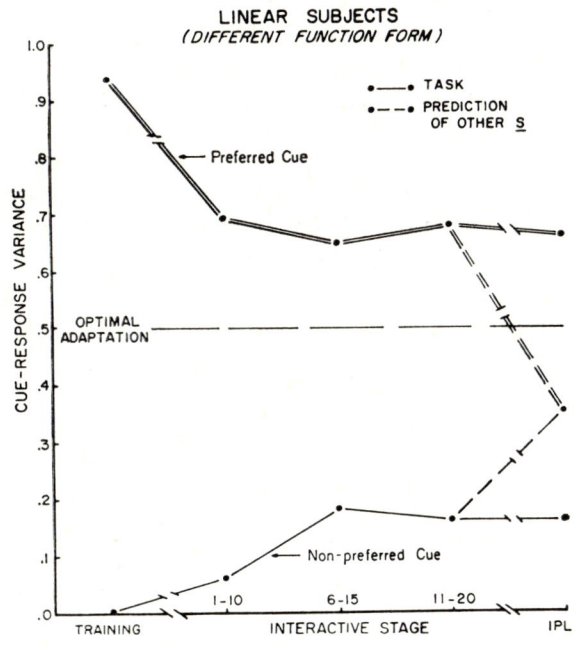

FIGURE 7 Cue-dependencies measured in terms of r^2 between cue and Subject's judgment. (Note: appropriate transformation made for nonlinear relations so as to provide r^2 comparable for linear relations.) Groups 2, 7, 8, 9, and 10 from Table 1

NONLINEAR SUBJECTS
(DIFFERENT FUNCTION FORM)

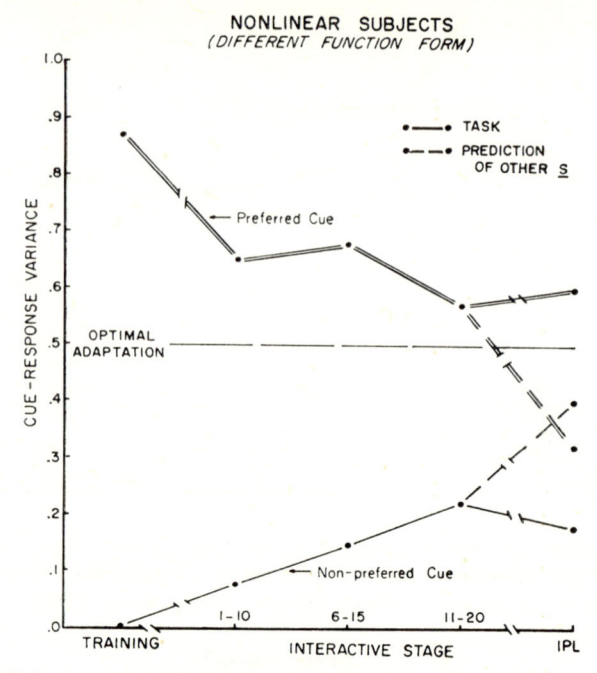

FIGURE 8 Cue-dependencies measured in terms of r^2 between cue and Subject's judgment. (Note: appropriate transformation made for nonlinear relations so as to provide r^2 comparable for linear relations.) Groups 5, 7, 8, 9, and 10 from Table 1

We turn now to the question of the effect of a second important parameter of the lens model; what is the effect of similarity and difference of subjects' function-forms on changes in cue-dependencies?

Dissimilar function-form

The effect of dissimilarity between subjects' function-form on change in cue-dependency may be clearly seen by comparing Figures 5 and 6 with Figures 7 and 8. These graphs indicate that when the subjects have *similar* function-forms (Groups 1, 3, 4, and 6 in Table 1), they acquire the cue-dependency of the Other to a greater degree than when function-forms are *different* (Groups 2, 5, 7, 8, 9 and 10 in Table 1). Persons who use data in similar ways learn from one another more rapidly than those who use data in different ways—a finding which holds over four different function-forms.

The analysis of change can be pursued in greater detail. For example, we can examine the effect of the function-form of both Subject and Other with respect to both preferred and non-preferred cues.

Effect of Subject's function-form (preferred cue)

The data concerning cue-dependencies can be subjected to statistical test by arranging them in a Subject by Other by Blocks design. Thus, the effect of the *Subject's* function-form, the effect of the *Other's* function-form, as well as *trials* can be evaluated with respect to change in dependency (r_i^2) on the preferred cue. The results of such tests show that change in preferred cue-dependencies is determined by (a) the function-form of the Subject as well as (b) the function-form of the Other—but there were no statistically significant interaction effects.

More specifically, the magnitude of decrease in the Subject's preferred cue-dependency occurred in the following order: (1) those subjects with an inverse U-shaped function-form changed most, (2) those with a U-shaped function-form next, (3) those with a negative linear function-form next, and (4) those with a positive linear function-form changed least. In brief, the nature of the function-form determines the rate at which one gives up dependence on a preferred cue of decreased validity.

Effect of the function-form of the Other (preferred cue)

Change occurred as a result of the function-form of the Other (as well as the function-form in the cognitive system of the Subject) as follows: (1) when the Other had a U-shaped function-form, the Subjects changed most, (2) when the Other had a linear positive function-form, the Subjects changed somewhat less, (3) when the Other had an inverse U-shaped function-form, somewhat less, and, (4) when the Other had a negative linear function-form the Subjects changed least—with respect to their preferred cue, the cue on which they had been trained to place the greatest weight.

In short, both main effects were statistically significant (across all four function-forms)—both the function-form of the Subject had an effect and the function-form of the Other had an effect on changes in the rate of giving up dependence on the preferred cue. These results show the importance of both the cue-dependency parameters as well as the function-form parameter of the lens model equation.

Effect of Subject's function-form on non-preferred cue-dependency

There were no differences among Subjects with different function-forms with respect to the rate at which they increased their dependency on the cue they had been trained to ignore. In other words, variations in the function-form of the Subject had no effect on the rate at which they acquired dependence on the cue which was previously invalid and was now valid, and which was the cue the Other considered valid.

Effect of the function-form of the Other

The specific function-form of the *Other* did have an effect, however: (1) if the Other had a linear positive function-form, Subjects acquired a dependency on the formerly ignored cue most rapidly, (2) if the function-form of the Other was U-shaped, somewhat less rapidly, (3) if the function-form of the Other was inversely U-shaped, somewhat less rapidly, and (4) if the function-form of the Other was negatively linear, the Subjects changed least with respect to the acquisition of the formerly ignored cue.

In addition, there is a clear indication from the above graphs, confirmed by statistical analyses, that there is a further *differential* rate of change in cue-dependencies. That is, subjects *give up* their dependencies on the preferred cue (the cue on which they were trained) more rapidly than they *acquire* dependency on the cue on which the Other was trained. In short, *relinquishment of a prior cognitive system occurs before the successful acquisition of a second system*. These results suggest a three-stage process: (a) *relinquishment* of a prior system, (b) a *search* for a new system, and (c) *adaptation* of a new system.

Again, it should be noted that these results are general across four different function-forms, both with respect to Subject and Other, thus carrying out our intention (stated earlier) to sample, in a *formal* sense, various proximal-distal relations.

To summarize, having specified one lens model parameter (cue-weights) in the cognitive systems of pairs of subjects, we investigated the effect of variations in a second lens model parameter (function-form) on the first (cue-weights) in an interactive situation in which each Subject learned from the Other as the Other and the Subject himself was learning about the task. Under these complex (two persons and a task) dynamic, (changing) and contingent (the judgment by one subject affected the judgment of another) circumstances, we found that the function-form of both Subjects (the learner) and Other (the person learned from) had an effect on changes in cue-dependencies. We take this result to indicate that both parameters of the lens model carry empirical significance for the study of inductive knowing in the process of interpersonal learning.

Interpersonal Learning About the Other

The same graphs (Figures 5, 6, 7 and 8) also illustrate two significant findings with respect to the process whereby one person inductively learns *about* another (as distinct from learning *from* another). At the right of the graph are four points which illustrate the results from the IPL Test Stage. Note first that in all four graphs the judgments made for the *task* are usually continuous with the curve during the final 10 trials of the Interactive Stage; when they are not continuous, the curve *reverts* to the level of trials 6–15. Therefore, we conclude that the new task learning in the Interactive Stage was stable. Secondly, note that when the Subject is asked to predict the judgment the *Other* would make, the subject's prediction is always in the correct direction; moreover, the linear subjects are highly accurate in predicting the usage of the preferred cue of the Other.

These two findings taken together indicate that (1) the Subjects maintain their cognitive systems (as modified by the interactive process) but (2) clearly distinguish the Other's judgmental policy from their own. The Subjects, therefore, have learned two different inductive systems, one to be applied to predicting task outcomes, one to be applied to predicting the responses of the Other (differently thinking) person.

It should also be noted that the interpersonal learning illustrated here is incidental (or latent) in that the subjects were not instructed during the Interactive Stage to learn *about* the Other. Yet they obviously did and this result is true over four different function-forms in the learner, the person learned about, and in the task system.

A Third Parameter: Subjects' Integration of the Data (R^2)

We turn now to the question of the degree to which the subjects in the Interactive Stage integrate the data from the two cues in a consistent manner—over the ten combinations of function-form. As may be seen from Figures 9, 10, 11, and 12, the subjects entering the Interactive Stage did so with a very high degree of consistent data integration (high R^2) in the appropriate (linear or nonlinear) manner.

We turn now to examining the effect of similarity and difference of function-form between Knower and Other on the consistency of data integration (R^2).

Groups with similar function-forms

Figures 9 and 10 illustrate two interesting results: irrespective of the function-form of Subject or Other, in the Interactive Stage, subjects with similar function-forms maintain the function-form they were trained to develop in the Training Stage; interaction with another subject with different cue-dependencies did not lead to a change in the manner in which the data are integrated. In other words, when the subjects have similar function-forms, they recognize the fact of similarity; notice that the differences between the task-predictions and the predictions for the Other are trivial with respect to the manner of integration of data. Combining this result with the fact that subjects recognize differences in cue-dependencies, we conclude that, despite perceived *differences* in cue-weighting systems, subjects recognize a *similarity* in the form of data integration—a finding which could hardly be demonstrated without the lens model research paradigm.

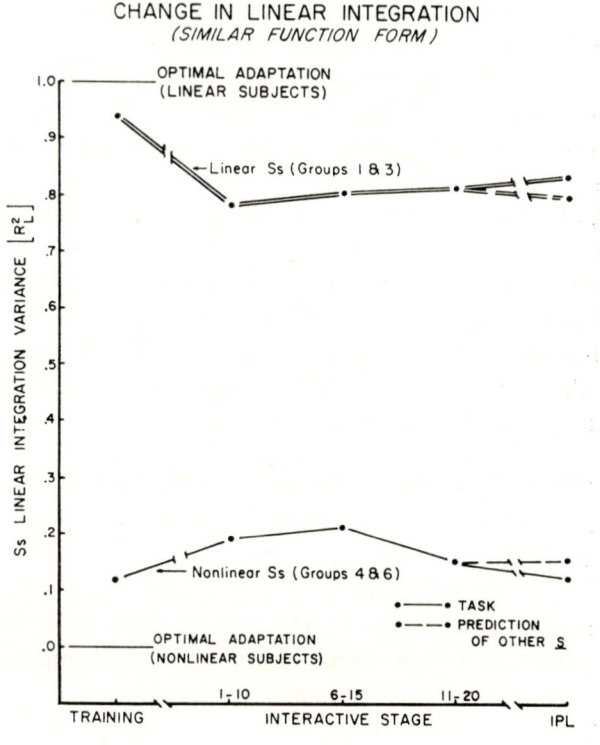

FIGURE 9 Integration of Data (R^2); Subjects with Similar Function-Form. Groups 1, 3, 4, and 6 from Table 1

It is worth making note of the wide separation of linear and nonlinear subjects in Figures 9 and 10 at the beginning of the Interactive Stage; this separation confirms the establishment of different function-forms in the Training Stage. And it is worth noting in Figure 10 that although the linear subjects begin the Interactive Stage with more systematic nonlinear variance than they should, the interaction between the subjects reduces the nonlinear variance to a trivial amount. Thus, even though the subjects are depending on different cues, the fact that they have learned similar function-forms evidently facilitates their integration of the data in the appropriate manner.

CHANGE IN NONLINEAR INTEGRATION
(SIMILAR FUNCTION FORM)

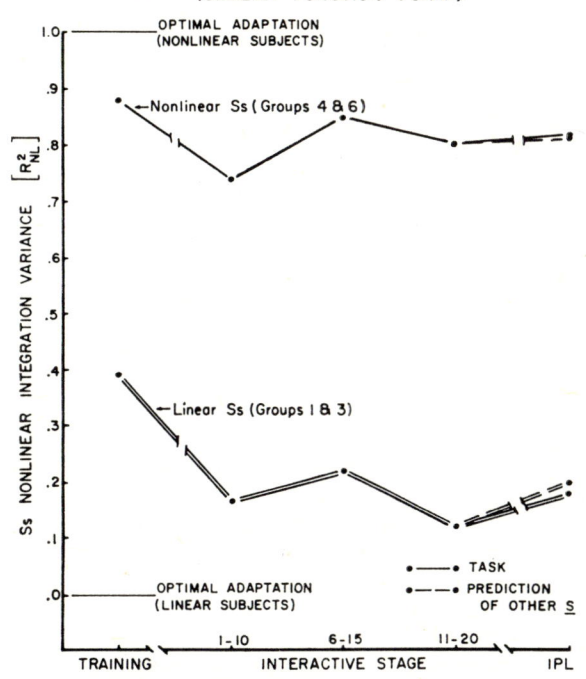

FIGURE 10 Integration of Data (R^2_{NL}); Subjects with Similar Function-Form. (Note: appropriate transformation made for nonlinear relations so as to provide comparable to R^2 for linear relations.) Groups 1, 3, 4, and 6 from Table 1

Groups with different function-forms

The first point to be noted is the difference between Figures 9 and 10 and Figures 11 and 12; the former show stable curves, whereas the latter show change. Moreover, Figures 9 and 10 show that subjects perceive the similarity which does in fact exist between them, whereas Figures 11 and 12 show that the subjects perceive the differences which do in fact exist between them—again, *irrespective of four types of function-form.*

It is clear that the change in the form of the integration of the data is in the direction of optimal adaptation, although it is equally clear that while dependence on the preferred cue decreases to optimal level, dependence on the cue-to-be-learned does not increase to optimal level—particularly in the case of the linear subjects. This result parallels the observation made earlier, that relinquishment of prior cue-dependence occurs before acquisition of new cue-dependence, a finding which, if replicated, holds considerable significance for understanding the dynamics of interpersonal interaction.

318 K. R. HAMMOND

CHANGE IN LINEAR INTEGRATION
(DIFFERENT FUNCTION FORM)

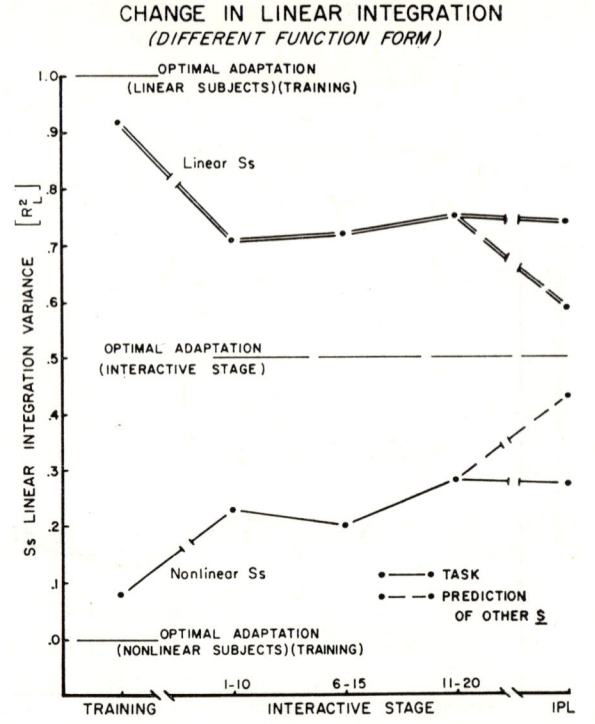

FIGURE 11 Integration of Data (R_L^2); Subjects with Different Function-Form. Groups 2, 4, 7, 8, 9, and 10 from Table 1.

8 DISCUSSION AND SUMMARY

Despite the fact that the conference upon which the present volume is based concerned itself with theoretical psychology, a large amount of empirical data was presented in this Chapter. This was done simply because of the desire to substantiate the theoretical argument presented, which is simply this: the opening of a new region—the distal-proximal region—to theoretical analysis can lead to new empirical research in psychology. Specifically, Parts 1 and 2 make the argument that closer conceptual examination of task characteristics can lead to the study of organismic-environment interaction processes, as well as inter-organism interaction processes, which have never before been brought under empirical scrutiny—processes which are life-relevant as well as theory-relevant.

Brunswik's lens model was introduced in Part 3 for the purpose of indicating the symmetry of such relations, and to illustrate the necessity for developing a theory which reflects this symmetry. The development of such a theory was described in Part 4, where the conceptual parameters

CHANGE IN NONLINEAR INTEGRATION
(DIFFERENT FUNCTION FORM)

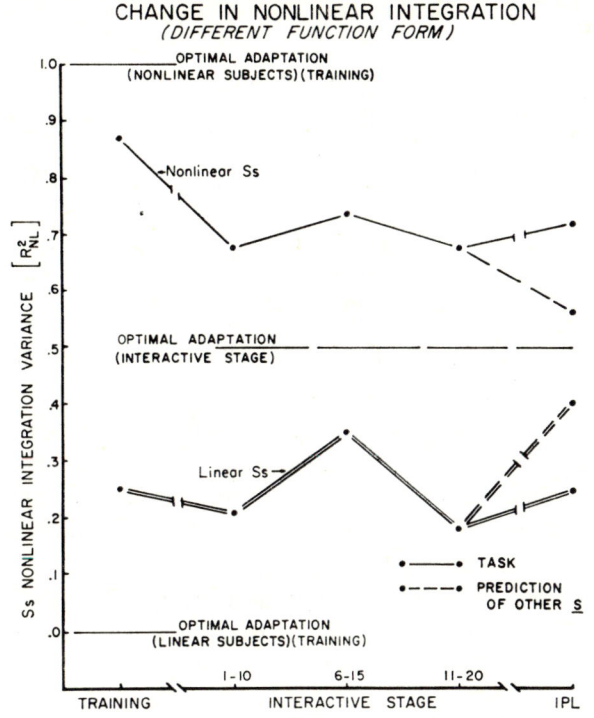

FIGURE 12 Integration of Data (R^2_{LN}); Subjects with Different Function-Form. (Note: appropriate transformation made for nonlinearrelations, so as to provide R^2 comparable to R^2 for linear relations.) Groups 2, 4, 7, 8, 9, and 10 from Table 1

of four types of organismic-environment relations (systems) were set forth. In addition, in Part 5, the mathematics associated with these systems were presented.

Having pointed to a region—that is, a set of relationships—heretofore hardly touched by theory, and having presented a set of concepts concerning these relationships, as well as their mathematical linkages, Part 6 turns to the application of these concepts. The specific problem chosen to illustrate the fruitfulness of the approach outlined here—interpersonal learning—is an important one which has gone largely unnoticed.

Although the theory described at the outset can hardly claim strong predictive power, it does indicate what we should look for. When, for example, in Part 7 we investigate the changes in cognitive systems which occur as a result of the interaction between two persons who bring different cognitive systems to a common task, the lens model equation indicates that we should examine changes in (a) cue-dependencies, and (b) integration-systems as a result of (c) the interaction between various function-form relations between proximal and distal variables. The results show that all three are important characteristics of inductive knowing.

Furthermore, the research paradigm developed from the theory shows that it can provide substantive, as well as theoretically relevant, data. The results from the study reported here, if replicated and generalized, will advance our knowledge about inductive knowing—both with respect to tasks and interpersonal learning. They confirm earlier results obtained by Hammond and Summers (1965) and Summers and Hammond (1966) that humans can not only learn nonlinear (configural) relations, but, in addition, can learn to *combine* both linear and nonlinear relations. Moreover, the present study extends the above findings in several ways: first, it shows that the Hammond and Summers results hold over ten combinations of linear and nonlinear relations; second, that persons can learn *from* one another to combine such relations; and third, that persons can learn *about* another person's use of various linear and nonlinear relations even though not specifically instructed to do so.

It is in the sense of demonstrating how a theory, model and their associated mathematics can be brought to bear on a new problem that this Chapter conforms to the theme of the conference.

COMMENTS ON PROFESSOR HAMMOND'S PAPER

William W. Rozeboom

Ever since I first read Hursch, Hammond, and Hursch (1964) some years ago, the multiple-regression embodiment of Brunswik's lens model has seemed to me to be an outstanding example of the small but significant technical advances which in aggregate transform intuitive speculations into a hard science. And since I have no serious quarrel with anything Hammond has said here, I would like to take this opportunity to clarify some features of the model which its past literature has left unpleasantly obscure.

First, I had best briefly derive the basic lens-model equations. (I will assume some elementary knowledge of multiple regression and the covariance statistic as set forth, e.g., in Rozeboom, 1966, Chapter 4.) Let $X_1, ..., X_m, Y_1, Y_2$, (and $Y_3, ..., Y_n$ for the n-system case) be a set of variables jointly distributed over some population of events. Then variable Y_i ($i = 1, ..., n$) can be partitioned as a sum of three mutually orthogonal components

$$Y_i = \dot{Y}_i + \tilde{Y}_i + E_i,$$

where $\dot{Y}_i$ is the linear regression of Y_i upon $X_1, ..., X_m$, $\dot{Y}_i + \tilde{Y}_i$ is Y_i's curvilinear regression upon $X_1, ..., X_m$ (i.e., $\tilde{Y}_i$ is the curvilinear regression's residual after the linear regression is partialled out), and E_i is the residual of Y_i unaccounted for in any way by the X_k. It is then easily shown that the covariance between Y_1 and Y_2 (and similarly for any others of the Y_i) analyzes as

$$\text{Cov}(Y_1, Y_2) = \text{Cov}(\dot{Y}_1, \dot{Y}_2) + \text{Cov}(\tilde{Y}_1, \tilde{Y}_2) + \text{Cov}(E_1, E_2) \quad (1)$$

Now, for any two variables A and B, $\text{Cov}(A, B) = \sigma_A \sigma_B r_{AB}$; while if $\hat{A}$ is the linear, or curvilinear, regression of A upon a set of predictor variables, $\sigma_{\hat{A}}$ equals σ_A times the linear, or curvilinear, correlation of A with those predictors. Hence if the relation between focus variables Y_1 and Y_2 is mediated entirely by cue variables $X_1, ..., X_m$, while for simplicity and without loss of generality the variables are scaled to have unit variances, we have

$$\text{Cov}(E_1, E_2) = 0,$$

$$\text{Cov}(Y_1, Y_2) = r_{Y_1 Y_2},$$

$$\text{Cov}(\dot{Y}_1, \dot{Y}_2) = R_1 R_2 r_{\dot{Y}_1 \dot{Y}_2},$$

$$\text{Cov}(\tilde{Y}_1, \tilde{Y}_2) = \sigma_{\tilde{Y}_1} \sigma_{\tilde{Y}_2} r_{\tilde{Y}_1 \tilde{Y}_2} = r_{\tilde{Y}_1 \tilde{Y}_2} \sqrt{\eta_1^2 - R_1^2} \sqrt{\eta_2^2 - R_2^2},$$

where R_i and η_i are respectively the multiple linear and curvilinear correlations of Y_i with the X_k. Hence from (1),

$$r_{Y_1 Y_2} = r_{\dot{Y}_1 \dot{Y}_2} R_1 R_2 + r_{\tilde{Y}_1 \tilde{Y}_2} \sqrt{\eta_1^2 - R_1^2} \sqrt{\eta_2^2 - R_2^2}, \tag{2}$$

which is Hammond's second equation (p. 299) except for an improved analysis of the nonlinear residual.[1]

A second way to analyze the linear component of Cov (Y_1, Y_2) is to note that the variance of the difference between any two variables A and B is $\sigma_{A-B}^2 = \sigma_A^2 + \sigma_B^2 - 2$ Cov (A, B), whence Cov $(A, B) = (\sigma_A^2 + \sigma_B^2 - \sigma_{A-B}^2)/2$. Hence with unit-variance scaling for Y_1 and Y_2 as before,

$$\text{Cov}(\dot{Y}_1, \dot{Y}_2) = \tfrac{1}{2} (R_1^2 + R_2^2 - \sigma_{\dot{Y}_1 - \dot{Y}_2}^2), \tag{3}$$

while

$$\Sigma d =_{\text{def}} \sigma_{\dot{Y}_1 - \dot{Y}_2}^2 = \sum_{R=1}^{m} (\beta_{1k} - \beta_{2k})(r_{1k} - r_{2k}) \tag{4}^2$$

in which β_{ik} is the β-coefficient for predictor X_k in Y_i's linear regression upon the cue variables, r_{ik} is the linear correlation between Y_i and X_k, and "Σd" is Hammond's abbreviation for the variance of the linear-regression difference. Substitution into (1) then yields

$$r_{Y_1 Y_2} = \tfrac{1}{2} (R_1^2 + R_2^2 - \Sigma d) + r_{\tilde{Y}_1 \tilde{Y}_2} \sqrt{\eta_1^2 - R_1^2} \sqrt{\eta_2^2 - R_2^2}, \tag{5}$$

which, apart from the improvement already noted in (2), is Hammond's first equation (p. 298). The Σd term in (5), however, tends to be misleading. It *seems* from (4) and (5) that in order for achievement correlation $r_{Y_1 Y_2}$ to be maximal, Σd should be zero (since it is a variance it cannot be negative), which in turn requires that $\beta_{1k} = \beta_{2k}$ and $r_{1k} = r_{2k}$ for each cue X_k, i.e., that the cue-utilization coefficients exactly match the cues' ecological validities. But in fact, $\Sigma d = 0$ is optimal *only* when there is no error variance in the distal variable's total regression upon the cues. For with the parameters of Y_1's relation to the X_k held constant, $r_{Y_1 Y_2}$ is maximal when $\dot{Y}_1$ and $\dot{Y}_2$ are positively collinear (i.e., when $r_{\dot{Y}_1 \dot{Y}_2} = 1$) *and* all the variance in Y_2 not needed for an optimal $\tilde{Y}_2$ is invested in $\dot{Y}_2$, i.e. when $\sigma_{E_2} = 0$. But if $\sigma_{E_1} > 0$ under these optimal circumstances, Y_2's projection into linear cue space is longer than Y_1's (i.e., $\sigma_{\dot{Y}_2} > \sigma_{\dot{Y}_1}$), whence the difference-variable $\dot{Y}_1 - \dot{Y}_2$ necessarily has nonzero variance. That is, if $\sigma_{E_1} > 0$, Σd must be positive if the quantity $R_2^2 - \Sigma d$ in (5) is to be maximal.

Moreover, the more that the cues are redundant, the more a good match between $\dot{Y}_1$ and $\dot{Y}_2$ can tolerate large discrepancies between cue-utilization coefficients and ecological validities. To illustrate this by means of an extreme example, suppose that there are just two cue variables and that their correlation is unity. Then $\dot{Y}_1$ and $\dot{Y}_2$ are perfectly collinear regardless of what values the β-coefficients may have, including the case where X_2 has zero weight for Y_1 while X_1 has zero weight for Y_2. This point has considerable significance for triple systems in which two persons judge the same distal variable. For given considerable cue redundancy, the judges could reach close, accurate agreement in their judgments, yet differ markedly in their cue utilizations. This shows how, in real life, persons who have achieved consensus and mutual trust on certain public issues could nonetheless dissipate their accord in acrimonious dispute over the bases for their conclusions. Contrary to the spirit of Hammond's 2-person studies, perhaps, sometimes it doesn't pay to let the right hand know how the left hand is doing it.

Next, it is worth noting the lens model's formal scope. This is in no way limited to cognitive or even psychological systems, for the model applies to any two variables Y_1 and Y_2 whose relation is mediated by one or more variables X_k. In particular, it is *not* requisite that Y_2 be a perception or judgment about distal variable Y_1. Y_2 could just as well be, say, degree of pupillary dilation aroused by miniskirt brevity Y_1. Neither need the X_k be proximal variables in Brunswik's sense, namely, aspects of events at the organism/environment interface. In fact, as is true of Hammond's own work, the X_k can themselves be distal variables or central percepts thereof such that the S first judges the values of $X_1, ..., X_m$ (or, alternatively, $X_1, ..., X_m$ are his judgments of the distal cues) and from there tries to infer the value of an even-more-distal variable Y_1.

On the other hand, the lens model's capacity to analyze "inductive knowing" has severe limitations, for the only inference pattern it subsumes is the statistical enthymeme:

> The value of X_1 on this occasion is —,
> the value of X_2 on this occasion is —,
> ....
> the value of X_m on this occasion is —;
>
> ---
>
> therefore, the value of Y on this occasion is probably —.

(This argument is enthymematic because it lacks a major premise supplying probabilities for Y given the values of the cue variables.) The lens model does *not* cover even inductive inference of population parameters from observed sample frequencies, much less confirmation of theories by tests of their observational consequences.

Another aspect of the lens model which is highly susceptible to misunderstanding is the multiplicity of cue mediation (Brunswik's "vicarious functioning"). Mathematically, the number of cue variables mediating between focus variables Y_1 and Y_2 can always be reduced to two, while more generally, an n-system can be parsed to have no more than n relevant cues. This is because the curvilinear regression of each Y_i is some exact function $\phi_i(X_1, ..., X_m)$ of the cues and is hence itself a cue; consequently, if $X' =_{\text{def}} \phi_i(X_1, ..., X_m)$ for $i = 1, ..., n$, the pair X_i' and X_j' of transformed cue variables suffices to mediate the relationship between focus variables Y_i and Y_j ($i, j = 1, ..., n$). The maneuver I am describing here is a familiar one in multivariate analysis, where for linear transformations it is known as "rotation of axes." Basically, the point is that cue space (curvilinear as well as linear) can be spanned in any number of ways, and how we choose to span it for a given analysis is mathematically arbitrary albeit this very much affects the number of relevant cue variables. Consequently, with one important qualification, use of the lens model to study e.g. how judgment is affected by the number of relevant cues is a meaningless enterprise. The qualification is that some ways to span cue space may well have greater "psychological reality" than do others—e.g., $X_1, ..., X_m$ may correspond to S's direct perceptions in a way that rotated cues $X_1', ..., X_n'$ do not. (Thus when I simultaneously perceive the height and distance of an object, I do not also perceive e.g. its height-times-its-distance.) What differences in "psychological reality" may in fact exist among transformationally equivalent sets of cue variables is an exceedingly interesting research question which to date has been virtually untouched.[3] However, the theory of this must be *added to* the lens model, not sought within it, even though this issue could well profit from lens-modeled research on how the accuracy and ease of acquiring distal/central correlations vary as a function of the particular axes in cue space along which input information is distributed.

The point just made about the number of cue variables also holds for linear vs. nonlinear cue utilization. The extent to which the relation between cues and focus variables is linear rather than curvilinear is very much an artifact of how we choose to span cue space. For example, the rotation from $X_1, ..., X_m$ to $X_1', ..., X_n'$ described above guarantees that all cue/focus relations are linear (though of course it does not also insure that the X_k' themselves are related only linearly), while it is an old and much practiced tradition in sensory psychology to reduce nonlinearities in the system by scaling input intensities as decibels. Admittedly, some of the nonlinearly alternative scalings of a given cue variable are intuitively more "natural" than are others, but until we learn more about what underlies this intuition and how to assess it empirically, it is hard to know how seriously to take recent work on linear vs. nonlinear cue utilization (cf. Goldberg, 1968).

Finally, under what circumstances does the lens model yield interpretively *significant* parsings of multivariate data? This occurs, I propose, when and only when the particular parameterization chosen for the model's application to a given phenomenon corresponds to the latter's second-level sources of variation, i.e., when the parameters most directly reflect factors in the phenomenon's underlying mechanism. What I mean by this can best be clarified by a highly oversimplified example. Consider a single-system with one cue variable X and judgment variable Y; specifically, suppose that X is distance-in-inches between eyebrow and hairline in a series of life-sized facial photographs, that Y is the S's estimate of *IQ* for a person whose photograph he is shown, and that the experimental design restricts X to only three values, 1 inch, 2 inches, and 3 inches. Then the regression of Y upon X for S at any given moment can be described by three parameters, two alternative choices for which are

$$\text{Parameterization } A: M_{Y|X_i} = a_1 + a_2 X_i + a_3 X_i^2,$$

$$\text{Parameterization } B: M_{Y|X_i} = b_i \quad (i = 1, 2, 3),$$

where X_i is value i of X and $M_{Y|X_i}$ is the contingent mean of Y given X_i, i.e. the average *IQ* which S guesses for photographs with an i-inch forehead. Suppose also that S has previously been trained (by methods which need not concern us here though in practice this would be an important detail) to have the judgment function $M_{Y|X_i} = 80 + 20X_i$; i.e., for parameterizations A and B, respectively,

$$a_1 = 60, \; a_2 = 20, \; a_3 = 0;$$

$$b_1 = 80, \; b_2 = 100, \; b_3 = 120;$$

but that now, working *only* with photographs having one-inch foreheads, S is retrained to give the response $Y = 85$ to X_1-stimuli. Our touchstone question now is: How does this retraining on X_1 modify S's responding to stimuli with cue values X_2 and X_3? In terms of the B-parameterization, one S—call him "linear"—might have post-retraining response parameters of

$$\text{Linear } S: b_1 = 85, b_3 = 110, b_3 = 135,$$

whereas another S might have post-retraining parameters of

$$\text{Hullian } S: b_1 = 85, b_2 = 97, b_3 = 119.$$

I call the second S "Hullian" because I intend him to generalize more or less according to the Hull-Spence model under which a new response (here the judgment $Y = 85$) learned to stimuli with feature X_1 should transfer in some degree to other stimuli to the extent they have features similar to X_1, but that apart from primary stimulus generalization, reconditioning on one stimulus leaves responding to other stimuli basically unaltered. Consequently, parameterization B, which has no built-in connections between S's response tendencies to the various stimuli, is most appropriate for the Hullian case. In contrast, the linear S generalizes by a pattern best characterized by parameterization A; namely, his cue-utilization function tends to maintain an invariant linear form whose slope coefficient is the primary manifestation of S's learning experiences, in this case changing from $a_2 = 20$ to $a_2 = 25$.

In short, a phenomenon's parameterization should be chosen to reflect the nodes at which it is modulated by changes in background constancies, for this is when the parameters give inductive access to the phenomenon's underlying sources (cf. Rozeboom, 1961). Since Hammond's work with the lens model has until now emphasized linear parameters (as shown e.g. by his parameterizing curvilinearity only as a residual), it would be desirable to determine whether his S's really do tend to generalize linearly in these situations. And if they do, what then is the theory—so strongly at odds with traditional models of learning—which explains *how* Ss are able to profit from past experience in this way?

NOTES

[1] The difference lies in my having analyzed the part of Y_i linearly unaccounted for by the cue variables into Y_i's curvilinear-residual regression $\tilde{Y}_i$ upon the cues plus its component E_i entirely unrelated to the latter, whereas Hammond does not separate these. The improvement is important for the model's application to study of nonlinear systems, for the original version confounds inefficiency of curvilinear cue utilization with the distal variable's intrinsic unpredictability.

[2] *Proof:* Let $D =_{\text{def}} \dot{Y}_1 - \dot{Y}_2$ and assume unit-variance, zero-mean scales for all the Y_i and X_k. Then $\dot{Y}_i = \sum_{k=1}^{m} \beta_{ik} X_k$ ($i = 1, 2$), so $D = \sum_{k=1}^{m} (\beta_{1k} - \beta_{2k}) X_k$. Also, since any linear combination of the X_k has zero covariance with any component of Y_i orthogonal to the X_k, $\text{Cov}(D, Y_i) = \text{Cov}(D, \dot{Y}_i)$. Hence $\sigma_D^2 = \text{Cov}(D, D) = \text{Cov}(D, \dot{Y}_1 - \dot{Y}_2) = \text{Cov}(D, Y_1 - Y_2) = \text{Cov}\left[\sum_{k=1}^{m} (\beta_{1k} - \beta_{2k}) X_k, Y_1 - Y_2\right] = \sum_{k=1}^{m} (\beta_{1k} - \beta_{2k}) \text{Cov}(X_k, Y_1 - Y_2) = \sum_{k=1}^{m} (\beta_{1k} - \beta_{2k})(r_{1k} - r_{2k})$. To complete the proof, note that σ_D is invariant under all arbitrary linear rescalings of the variables so long as Y_1 and Y_2 retain unit variance.

[3] To my knowledge, nearly all the extant research bearing on this lies in multidimensional psychophysical scaling, where non-euclidian distance metrics introduce anisotropies in perceptual space. (See Garner, 1970.)

SOME ASSUMPTIONS UNDERLYING HAMMOND'S FORMULATION OF THE LENS MODEL

Rudolf Groner

If one compares the sophisticated philosophical and statistical treatment of inductive inference with the undeniable lack thereof in psychology, one must indeed be grateful to Kenneth Hammond and his research group for their attempt to close at least some of these gaps. Among the many sources of uncertainty in inductive inference (lack of logical conclusiveness, sampling fluctuation, error of measurement) Hammond concentrates, via Egon Brunswik's probabilistic functionalism, solely on one component, namely the error of measurement. The basic model is the lens model which "depicts a probabilistic environment ... and a probabilistic organism ..." (Hammond, this volume, p. 288).

Such a probabilistic treatment, however, may miss the point on the side of the achieving organism on two grounds: First, what often is observed as probabilistic behavior by merely recording response sequences can be revealed to be pseudo-probabilistic (as it was nicely demonstrated by Feldman 1959, 1963): interactional decison rules, though absolutely deterministic, simulate a quasiprobabilistic behavior. Furthermore, analysis of unconstrained response emission with the tools of information theory have repeatedly demonstrated (e.g. Miller and Frick, 1949; Hick, 1953) that the human organism is a very poor random number generator violating in many respects the assumptions of basic probability theory (and certainly also of regression theory as applied by the lens model). Second, following Brunswik's line of argument in Darwinian terms for a functionalistic psychology (Brunswik, 1952), it can easily be demonstrated that the survival value of any probabilistic strategy is intrinsically inferior to a deterministic (though still multiply-mediated) maximization strategy.

However, if we are ready to make a more subtle distinction between different aspects of theoretical emphasis, we might conclude that the lens model—though not the best *interpretive* model on various psychological grounds (some of them mentioned above and some more, but not all, below)—does an excellent job in *describing* two systems, task and subject, and their interrelationships in terms of the same statistical language. This language, multiple regression analysis, can be described as an extremely robust method, hard to falsify as a psychological model for information integration (Groner, 1968, 1970) but with powerful methodological properties which have been nicely demonstrated by Goldberg (1970) as a "bootstrapping" trick: Even assuming that in reality a different model of cue integration holds (e.g. non-compensatory lexicographic ordering), when the data are made probabilistic by superposing a large enough error component, the multiple regression analysis yields better predictions than does the "true" model! Of course, in such a case and probably not only in this case the multiple regression model entails a multiplicity of possible interpretations. It is (as Hoffman, 1960, put it) a "paramorphic representation of human judgment."

Nevertheless, there are limits to the possible interpretations by the model, and it therefore may be quite useful to re-analyze the Hursch, Hammond and Hursch (1964) formulation of the lens model, making explicit some of the psychological implications which here rest mainly on mathematical assumptions necessary to allow for and simplify the process of derivation (as is always the case with sufficiently mathematicized models in psychology). This analysis will emphasize mathematical possibilities and their interpretive psychological counterparts which are *excluded* by the lens model. I realize that the complementary arguments on the positive, constructive side concerning what the lens model *is capable* of doing have already been given by Hammond and his research group covering an impressive multitude of different psychological areas such as clinical psychology (Hammond, 1955), cognitive functioning (Hammond and Summers, 1965) and conflict resolution (Hammond, 1965).

First, let us present a complete deductive proof of Hursch, Hammond and Hursch's (1964) formulation of the lens model, an endeavor which may be justified by the necessity of underpinning the present arguments and by the difference in proceeding to Hursch *et al.* (since they proceeded "inductively" from selected special cases to the most general formulation where it is sometimes difficult to follow the justification of the added generality). We follow the symbols used by Hursch *et al.* and for the sake of simplicity also assume standardized variables. The model starts from the "achievement" defined as the correlation between the distal variable Y_e with the subject's estimate Y_s:

$$r_a = \frac{1}{N} \sum_{j=1}^{N} Y_{ej} Y_{sj} \qquad (1)$$

Each variable is decomposed into a linear combination of weighted cues plus a linearly unpredictable residual Z using the same cue values in both the environmental and subject's system (Assumption I).

$$r_a = \frac{1}{N} \sum_{j=1}^{N} (\beta_{e1} Y_{1j} + \beta_{e2} Y_{2j} + \cdots + \beta_{en} Y_{nj} + Z_{ej})$$
$$\times (\beta_{s1} Y_{1j} + \beta_{s2} Y_{2j} + \cdots + \beta_{sn} Y_{nj} + Z_{sj}) \qquad (2)$$

Multiplying this equation leads to the following product matrix:

$$\frac{1}{N} \sum_{j=1}^{N} \begin{array}{l} (\beta_{e1}\beta_{s1} Y_{1j}^2 + \beta_{e1}\beta_{s2} Y_{1j} Y_{2j} + \cdots + \beta_{e1}\beta_{sn} Y_{1j} Y_{nj} \\ + \beta_{e2}\beta_{s1} Y_{1j} Y_{2j} + \beta_{e2}\beta_{s2} Y_{2j}^2 + \cdots + \beta_{e2}\beta_{sn} Y_{2j} Y_{nj} \\ \vdots \qquad\qquad \vdots \qquad\qquad \vdots \\ + \beta_{en}\beta_{s1} Y_{1j} Y_{nj} + \beta_{en}\beta_{s2} Y_{nj} Y_{2j} + \cdots + \beta_{en}\beta_{sn} Y_{nj}^2 \\ \hline + Z_{ej}\beta_{s1} Y_{1j} \quad + Z_{ej}\beta_{s2} Y_{2j} \quad + \cdots + Z_{ej}\beta_{sn} Y_{nj} \end{array} \left| \begin{array}{l} + \beta_{e1} Y_{n1} Z_{sj} \\ + \beta_{e2} Y_{2j} Z_{sj} \\ \vdots \\ + \beta_{en} Y_{nj} Z_{sj} \\ \hline + Z_{ej} Z_{sj} \end{array} \right.$$

First of all we note that the marginal vectors (on the lower left and upper right separated by the double line) vanish, since $\frac{1}{N} \sum_{j=1}^{N} Z_{ej} \sum_{i=1}^{n} \beta_{si} Y_{ij} = 0$ (by virtue of the property that any linear function of the variables $Y_1 \ldots Y_n$ and hence in particular $\sum_{i=1}^{n} \beta_{si} Y_i$ has zero correlation with the residual Z_e. For details see Rozeboom, 1966, p. 163) and from the same reason $\frac{1}{N} \sum_{j=1}^{N} Z_{sj} \sum_{i=1}^{n} \beta_{ei} Y_{ij} = 0$. The upper left of the matrix (representing the crossproducts of the linearly predictable components of both systems $= L$) contains all cue intercorrelations $r_{ik} \left(= \frac{1}{N} \sum_{j=1}^{N} Y_{ij} Y_{kj} \right)$. It can be rewritten in much less clumsy form using matrix notation (where R is the symmetric matrix of cue-intercorrelations, r_e the column vector of cue-validities and r_s the vector of cue-utilization coefficients, β_e and β_s the column vectors of the environmental and subjective cue weights, obtained as the least-square estimates by $\beta_e = R^{-1} r_e$ and $\beta_s = R^{-1} r_s$). We note first that to give the subjective cue weights *and* cue-utilization coefficients a psychological interpretation the individuals have to utilize the cue intercorrelation in some manner (Assumption II) and second that in order to arrive at a unique solution for β the intercorrelation matrix must be non-singular (Assumption III). This method of assessing weights guarantees a maximum of linear predicted covariance, therefore, leaving only the non-linearly-predictable residual for estimating the not-linear component (Assumption IV), introducing a bias towards L. Eventually, we note that all non-linear residuals attributable to the n cues are summed into a single compound component Z_e and Z_s (Assumption V).

We now are ready to rewrite the crossproducts of the linear components:

$$L = \beta'_e R \beta_s \tag{3}$$

which may be restated by virtue of the above given solution of multiple regression weights in some interestingly equivalent ways

$$L = \beta_e r_s \tag{4}$$

$$L = r'_e \beta_s \tag{5}$$

or since,

$$L = r'_e R^{-1} R R^{-1} r_s$$

$$L = r'_e R^{-1} r_s \tag{6}$$

Recall that the coefficient of multiple correlation is defined $R^2 = \sum_{i=1}^{n} \beta_i r_i$.
In order to express L in terms of the pairwise differences of the coefficients (expressing the degree of matching) consider the crossproducts of those differences designed Σd

$$\Sigma d = \sum_{i=1}^{n} (\beta_{ei} - \beta_{si})(r_{ei} - r_{si})$$

$$= \sum_{i=1}^{n} \beta_{ei} r_{ei} - \sum_{i=1}^{n} \beta_{ei} r_{si} - \sum_{i=1}^{n} \beta_{si} r_{ei} + \sum_{i=1}^{n} \beta_{si} r_{si}$$

$$= R_e^2 + R_s^2 - 2L$$

Solving for L leads to the multiple linear term in the lens model:

$$L = \frac{R_e^2 + R_s^2 - \Sigma d}{2} \tag{7}$$

The sum of the crossproducts of the nonlinear residuals (here named M, figuring in the lower right part of the crossproduct matrix) divided by N gives us a covariance term (not a correlation, since the residuals of standardized variables are not in standard form). However, the covariance can be expressed as the product of the correlation between the residuals ($= C$

times the standard deviations of the residuals of the two variables:

$$M = \frac{1}{N} \sum_{j=1}^{N} Z_{ej} Z_{sj} = C \sqrt{(1 - R_e^2)(1 - R_s^2)} \tag{8}$$

which completes the derivation of the lens model

$$r_a = \frac{R_e^2 + R_s^2 - \Sigma d}{2} + C \sqrt{(1 - R_e^2)(1 - R_s^2)} \tag{9}$$

Tucker (in his alternative formulation, 1964) uses the same logic as applied in formula (8) for building up the linear term (instead of the matching differences Σd).

Let us now discuss in some detail the five assumptions. It may be noted that I did not make explicit the assumptions already stated by Hammond in his present paper such as function-form, intersubtitutability, etc. This means only that I admit their importance but don't want to be repetitious.

ASSUMPTION I: EXISTENCE OF A LINEAR PSYCHOPHYSICAL FUNCTION

The lens model does not distinguish between the representation of cues in the environment and its perceptual counterpart, which probably is transformed by some psychophysical function. However, the derivation of the multiple regression model would not be affected by a linear transformation (which still preserves the cue intercorrelation matrix). There is little question about the great psychological and philosophical impact of this assumption (for a discussion of the philosophical implications of Brunswik's earlier work see Ness, 1936, p. 71–84). Unless falsified, it may be maintained as a working hypothesis with neat mathematical properties.

ASSUMPTION II: SUBJECTIVE UTILIZATION OF CUE INTER-CORRELATIONS

If somebody wants to interpret the subjects' β-weights *and* cue-utilization coefficients both as psychologically meaningful system-parameters (which is usually done by most authors), it is also necessary to assume that the subjects utilize the cue-intercorrelations.[2] Otherwise, only one parameter can be interpreted leaving the other as a statistical artifact.

Since there is no other "cue for cue-correlation" than the relative frequencies of cue-value combinations (for details see Groner, 1970), Assumption II becomes even more dubious, considering that these cue-intercorrelations are usually introduced as independent variables by the experimenter. Simulating the actual, "environmental" correlations after Brunswik's (1956) postulate of representative design may somewhat mitigate the situation. There is also an experimental way to analyze the subjective correlations (Groner, 1968): Assume we want to analyze the subjective intercorrelation between the cues "intelligence," "sympathy" and "handsomeness." First we sample randomly one of the cues from the three possibilities, and its level. Let us assume we have got "highly intelligent." We use this piece of information for evoking a response on one of the two other cues, which one is again decided by random sampling, asking the subject "how handsome would you expect somebody to be who is highly intelligent?" In a subsequent run, the subject's response is used as an independent variable for evoking his response on the one remaining cue. This rather unorthodox procedure using the subject's response later as an independent variable has been named DIFF (*d*ependent–*i*ndependent variable *f*lip-*f*lop), and it might be especially useful for the investigation of single systems. In the case of the double-system unfortunately its applicability is limited by Assumption I.

ASSUMPTION III: NONE OF THE CUES IS LINEARLY DEPENDENT ON THE REMAINING $n - 1$ CUES

If this were not so, the solutions for R^{-1} would not be uniquely determined, and therefore most of the parameters of the lens model could not be assessed. This assumption eliminates the case of extreme cue intersubstitutability; it is particularly relevant for one of Brunswik's favorite paradigms, for the case of spatial perception.

Which alternative solutions are left if some of the cues are linearly dependent? The easiest way is simply to eliminate all cues which are linearly dependent on some others, but it may be difficult to decide on psychological grounds which ones should be omitted. Another way to assure linear independence is the extraction of *factors* instead of regressing on variables where the factor loadings represent the correlation between the factor and the distal object (= "cue-factor validity"). However, in spite of the statistical equivalence of the two solutions, this shift from directly measurable variables (= proximal cues) to internal constructs (= cue-factors) has important interpretive implications and should not be made without considerations about the underlying model.

ASSUMPTION IV: THE SOLUTION IS HIERARCHICAL, EXTRACTING FIRST A MAXIMUM OF LINEAR PREDICTABLE COVARIANCE

This very mathematical looking property has a peculiar effect on any non-symmetrical curvilinear function form: it gets split up partly into the linear term (according to its asymmetry) *and* into the non-linear residual. Again, it is quite unlikely that psychological information processing works in such a way; much more reasonable would be to assume that the functional units of the cue is preserved. Non-linear regression techniques (Ezekiel and Fox, 1959) might, in some instances, offer a solution here. Another way to avoid the problem is (as it was done in the present experiments) to introduce only symmetrical function forms.

ASSUMPTION V: THE NON-LINEAR RESIDUALS ARE CARRIED BY A SINGLE COMPONENT

This is the most beautiful trick of Hursch *et al.'s* formulation: The covariance of the two residuals carries (except for correlated error) whatever the two systems have in common and cannot be attributed to a linear prediction rule. In one powerful stroke it sweeps in whatever non-linear co-functioning there is between the two systems which can be interpreted as curvilinear function-forms or as con-figurational judgment or possibly some other sources of variation which sometimes are difficult to assess. The great advantage (but also the limitation) of such a procedure is that one is not obliged to specify the source of non-linearity; by appropriate subsequent analysis, however, it might be detected.

There are two ways of dealing with the restrictions imposed by the above mentioned assumptions. One way is to directly test these assumptions, deciding whether or not they can be justified on empirical grounds and (if not) how large an error component is introduced by their retention. The other way, suitable for Assumption III, IV, and V, is to avoid pitfalls through restriction in the experimental design. Clearly, the first way is superior insofar as empirical testing broadens the psychological foundation of the descriptive model.

NOTES

1. I acknowledge the opportunity of discussing most of this presentation with the participants of my graduate seminar in "Mathematical Models in Cognition" at the Department of Psychology, University of Alberta, Winter 1969/70.
2. What happens if the subject is "insensitive" to the cue-intercorrelations (R) and he is exposed to two ecologies, everything being equal, except that the cue-intercorrelations change? We can distinguish two possible cases.
    1. The subjective β-weights are the psychologically relevant system-parameters (with the operational assumption that they remain constant). Then the effects due to the non-orthogonality of the design are reflected in changes of cue-utilization coefficients:

    $$R_1 \neq R_2; \beta_{s1} = \beta_{s2} = \beta_s. \text{ Then } \beta_s = R_1^{-1}r_{s1} = R_2^{-1}r_{s2}; r_{s2} = R_2\beta_s;$$
    $$\text{and } r_{s2} = R_2 R_1^{-1} r_{s1}. \tag{10}$$

    2. The cue-utilization coefficients are the psychologically relevant system-parameters and are remaining constant. (Note that this assumption imposes restrictions on the allowable differences between R_1 and R_2).

    $$R_1 \neq R_2; r_{s1} = r_{s2} = r_s. \text{ Then } r_s = R_1\beta_{s1} = R_2\beta_{s2}; \beta_{s1} = R_1^{-1}r_s;$$
    $$\text{and } \beta_{s1} = R_1^{-1} R_2 \beta_{s2}. \tag{11}$$

    Note that in (10) and (11) the same matrix $K = R_1^{-1}R_2$ applies "correcting for non-orthogonality" but in different directions, allowing for testable predictions (Groner, 1970).

REPLY TO ROZEBOOM AND GRONER

Kenneth R. Hammond

First I want to express my appreciation to Rozeboom, not only for his sophisticated criticism of my paper, but for his positive, constructive contributions to it. His improvement of the Lens Model Equation (LME) will replace the original formulation of it in much (but not all) of our work in the same way that Tucker's (1964) reformulation provided a highly useful alternative. Not only is Rozeboom's reformulation generally useful, it also provides a constructive answer to Groner's well-taken criticism contained in his remarks under Assumption V. Seldom is an author in the enviable position of having one critic provide him with an answer to another! I must add, however, that the original formulation, mathematically clumsy as it may be, has some advantages which make it useful for the analysis of certain experiments—particularly studies involving triple-system (e.g., two-person policy-conflicts) a point to which I will return.

One of Rozeboom's criticisms of the original formulation is that the Σd term "tends to be misleading". He maintains that a cursory examination of this equation (his equation (5)) would lead one to assume that in order to maximize the achievement correlation (his $r_{Y_1 Y_2}$), Σd should be zero, an assumption which he notes is false. Rozeboom is, of course, quite correct about this: the Σd term *does* tend to be misleading; the assumption *is* false. But he should have known that even in our original presentation of the LME (Hursch, Hammond and Hursch, 1964) we dealt with the relation of Σd to maximal achievement and pointed out that "matching cue utilization coefficients (implying $\Sigma d = 0$) will give as an upper limit $r_a = R_e^2$ while a completely linear response system ($R_s^2 = 1.00$) will give the subject an upper limit of $r_a = R_e$, which, of course, is higher than R_e^2 ..." (p. 50). In a second paper also, (Hammond, Hursch and Todd, 1964) we gave considerable attention (nearly two pages) to the Σd term of the LME, being careful to point out that "Σd ... is a highly complicated concept, and its relation to the use and misuse of cues is not unambiguous ..." (p. 447). We then discussed the role of the Σd term in maximizing $r_{Y_1 Y_2}$ and presented several examples of its differential effects.

Irrespective of our previous treatment of this matter, however, it would be fair to ask "why continue to employ a formulation of the LME which can give rise to misunderstanding?" The answer is that it does have its uses in specific experiments. Indeed, it is useful in precisely the cases Rozeboom mentions, where, as he puts it, "... in real life, persons who have achieved concensus and mutual trust on certain public issues could nevertheless dissipate their accord in acrimonious dispute over the bases for their conclusions." Precisely. We have discussed this matter at length elsewhere (Hammond and Brehmer, in press; Hammond and Boyle, 1970) in somewhat plainer terms, simply by noting that the LME makes it clear how persons could agree in principle yet disagree in fact, or in other cases, disagree in principle yet agree in fact.

FIGURE 1

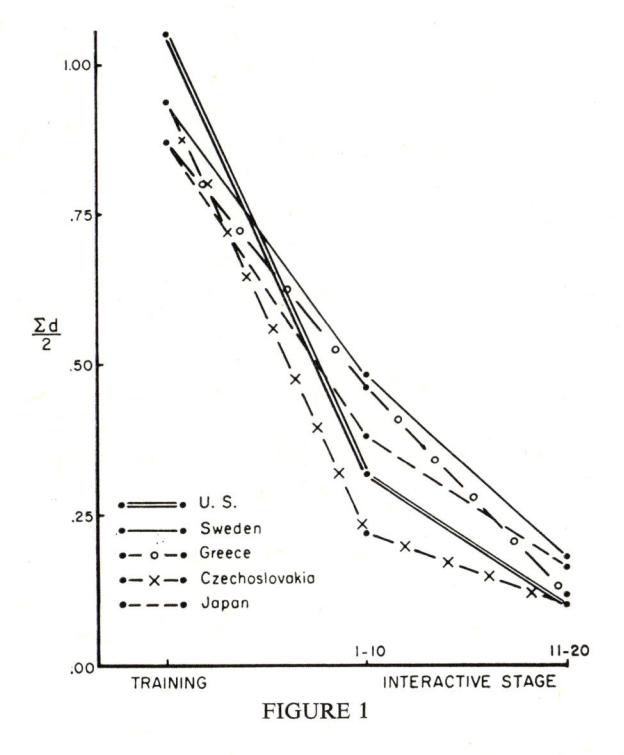

Figure 1 provides an example; it shows the change in the value of the Σd term between two quarreling persons. In the case illustrated, Σd approached zero, indicating nearly perfect agreement in cue-utilization by both persons; in other words, indicating nearly perfect agreement in principle. The persons involved, however, never discovered that agreement in principle had evolved because the inconsistency ($R^2 < 1.00$) in their LME's led to disagreement in fact, that is, in their judgments. Note that it was the use of the Σd term in the original LME which made it easy for us to locate the nature of the quarrel (see Hammond and Brehmer, 1970, for a detailed treatment of this phenomenon). These results, then, not only show the usefulness of the Σd term, but they bear out Rozeboom's insightful suggestion.

It must be emphasized, however, that such results are not at all "contrary to the spirit of Hammond's 2-person studies"; quite the opposite—they evolve from the nature of our approach inasmuch as our description of the course of a 2-person quarrel evolves directly from our use of the LME. Indeed, it is the Σd term in particular in the LME which makes it possible to observe agreement in principle and disagreement in fact, or the "dissipation of accord in acrimonious dispute".

Now I wish to treat the next two arguments together, for they are undoubtedly correct, yet it seems to me, neither are central.

1) Rozeboom points out that the lens model deals with only *one* "inference pattern." True; our rejoinder, however, is that this is the only *important* inference pattern. The lens model represents the inferences most of us make most of the time. (The proof of this assertion will have to meet an empirical test neither Rozeboom nor I am prepared to put forth in this context.) Moreover, it is an "inference pattern" which psychology has somehow missed. (In the early pages of my chapter I suggest why.) A survey of 14 contemporary introductory psychology textbooks showed that *none* included a discussion of the process of inductive inference. Worse, inductive inference was not even indexed! Under these circumstances I refuse to be embarrassed because the lens model approach does not cover *all* cases of inductive inference. (Incidentally, our approach *does* concern itself with the problem of inferring population parameters from sample data; see, for example, Brunswik, 1956, p. 80–82.)

2) When Rozeboom argues that the "number of cue variables ... can always be reduced to two ..." I must agree, which is to say that I agree that a cue-matrix *can* be factor-analyzed. But for what purpose? If the investigator wishes to analyze an environmental task-system (or any suitable matrix) by means of factor analysis for whatever purpose, he certainly can do so. Our purpose is specific to the behaving organism, however. We need to know much about how cue-distal variable matrices, *specified by the behaving organism*, are dealt with by him. Our survey of textbooks indicates that psychologists know little about this. Contrary to Rozeboom it is *not* a "meaningless enterprise" to discover how judgment is affected by "the number of relevant cues ..." when those cues are specified by the organism making the inference. What psychologists may do later in order to understand judgment phenomena is a different matter. (I trust that this

comment includes Rozeboom's qualification. The reader should also consult Groner's conclusion relating to this point contained in his comments on "Assumption III".)

But when Rozeboom argues that the theory of "this must be *added* to the lens model not sought within it," I am not so sure. Consider the general question of the nature of the cue-distal variable matrix in light of Groner's remarks about cue-intercorrelations. Groner has put his finger on one of the most important contributions of lens model theory, for it is this theory which insists on including cue-intercorrelation as a parameter of the inference process which must be dealt with—not factored away or set aside by means of traditional orthogonal-factor design. Cue-intercorrelations are of essential importance to the behaving organism; on the positive side they provide security through redundancy, on the negative side they provide the potential for confusion and mistrust in policy-quarrels. For example, Person *A* will argue that his judgments are based on *this* dimension (cue) of the problem, Person *B* will insist that *A* is lying because it is clear to *B* that *A*'s judgments are based on *that* dimension (cue), whereas it is the intercorrelations between the dimensions which provide the honest justification for the confusion. This is a feature of interpersonal conflict exposed so far only by the lens model approach *together with* its multiple regression statistics which form the bases of the LME. And this is as good a place as any to point out that, however distasteful multiple regression statistics may be to psychologists (mathematical or otherwise) they do produce insights of the sort just mentioned—which I have yet to see appear from more "sophisticated" phenomenological *or* mathematical theorists, despite all the promissory notes.

Finally, Rozeboom takes it for granted (not without a certain justification, I admit) that I am in favor of a linear model as the "best" representative of the inference process. He derives that conclusion from the nature of the LME which does, in fact, treat "curvilinearity only as a residual"—a fact which I find partly, but not wholly, regrettable. (See also Groner's comments in relation to Assumption IV.)

I am glad to have the opportunity to address this question, albeit briefly, for whenever our work is discussed by cognitive theorists, its unhappy fate is to be assigned to the group of models labelled "linear, additive"—an assignment I heartily resent inasmuch as I have taken pains to argue otherwise.

Indeed, the Hursch, Hammond and Hursch (1964) paper was the first to introduce analytical techniques for detecting non-linearity in judgmental systems, and David Summers and I did the first empirical work on non-linear judgmental systems. In fact, we emphasized the role of non-linearity in an article in the *Psychological Review* (1965) entitled "Cognitive Dependence on Linear and Non-Linear Cues", and in an article in the *Journal of Experimental Psychology* entitled "Inference Behavior in Multiple-Cue Tasks Involving Both Linear and Non-Linear Relations" (1966). Moreover, I believe it is folly to pursue the question of whether a linear *or* non-linear (configural) model, or an additive *or* weighted average model, best represents the form of man's cognitive processes—despite the fact that many reputable psychologists are chasing this will-o'-the-wisp. The plain fact is that man can make inferences in a wide variety of ways, linear, additive, non-linear, configural, interactive, etc. Humans use data in *any* way that is necessary in order to successfully make the inference. The question is, under what conditions does what occur, and why?

Admittedly, there is evidence that linear additive processes have a high preference rating in human priorities for information processing. But if humans are allowed to discover that they should use data in other ways, they will, and rather successfully, too. The experiments described in my paper support this generalization.

To be sure, matters of scaling enter into this question, and no one as yet has pursued such scaling problems very far. My own intuitive judgment, however, is that scaling problems will not seriously affect our understanding of cognitive processes in general; rather, they will make their presence felt in connection with highly specific judgmental problems in applied contexts.

But Rozeboom's final sentence is certainly a challenge: "...what then, is the theory—so strongly at odds with traditional models of learning—which explains ...?" The paper presented at this Conference is by no means an adequate reply. I will do better, however, if Rozeboom will continue to give our efforts his valuable criticism.

Because of the partial overlap in the remarks of Groner and Rozeboom I have already referred to some of Groner's points. He gets to the heart of matters at the very beginning, however, when he challenges the probability view as artifactual ("pseudo-probabilistic"). Whether the human organism can best be described as probabilistic or as deterministic, however, may well be a matter which can never be resolved, inasmuch as the determinist can always (as even in modern physics) argue that the probabilistic behavior observed is due to technical inadequacies, rather than a product of a fundamental principle—a matter discussed in my original presentation of the lens model as a representation of cognitive processes (Hammond, 1955).

But I would like to point out that when Groner points to studies such as those by Feldman, he (and everyone else) fails to make a distinction between the *various* phenomena involved in human cognitive processes; these include (among others) a) hypothesis *formation* (general rules purporting to describe the behavior of external systems) and b) *control* of cognitive function (application of these rules in specific instances).

This distinction is implicit in the lens model equation. Consider Tucker's formulation in which the relation between two systems is described as

$$r_a = GR_eR_s + C\sqrt{1 - R_e^2}\sqrt{1 - R_s^2}$$

Now, assume that all non-linear relations are transformed in such a way that all the systematic co-variance (linear and non-linear) between the two systems can be represented by G. We can then represent the situation between an independent system (say, an environmental task, S_1) and an adapting system (say, a learner, S_2) in the following way:

$$r_a = GR_1R_2$$

where degree of adaptation (r_a) of System$_2$ to System$_1$ is a function of S_2's ability to detect (G) the general principles controlling S_1 despite the less than perfect control which may exist in System$_1$ (R_1). Of course, the imperfect cognitive control which may exist in System$_2$ (R_2) also affects r_a. Now it may well be that many environmental tasks include perfect control systems, the processes of which are communicated unequivocally to the behaving organism—that is, $R_{s_1} = 1.00$. Nearly all psychologists seem to think so, for virtually all research until Brunswik (the first probabilist) involved tasks with $R_{s_1} = 1.00$. (The partial reinforcement studies can be considered exceptions in technique, but not in principle). Brunswik's argument was that even when environmental systems are perfectly controlled (for example, macro-physical systems controlled by Newtonian physics), these processes are *not* communicated unequivocally to man; R_{s_1} for the organism *outside* the physical laboratory is less than 1.00.

If it were otherwise it would be puzzling as to why man has had to resort to laboratories (where he can set R_{s_1} to 1.00) to learn the laws of physics, and why he has gone to all the trouble to devise instruments to circumvent nature's effort to hide these laws from him. Psychologists, however, seem to believe that knowledge lies on the surface of the environment, or at least, that the laws which control environmental systems are communicated directly, unequivocally and without error to the organism and that it is the psychologists' special responsibility to discover why it takes so long for the organism to learn what is so obvious to the investigator.

The lens model provides a different point of departure. We start with the premise that insofar as the unaided organism is concerned, environmental task systems have an R less than 1.00, that an irreducible uncertainty exists (irreducible *unless* instrumentation is used) with which man has always had to cope, which in turn has encouraged the development of cognitive systems which function with less than perfect control ($R_{s_2} < 1.00$), for perfectly good functional reasons, which we shall now consider briefly.

Why, asks Groner, should any functionalist who takes Darwin seriously fail to see that survival requires a *maximizing*, that is to say, a deterministic, organism? Why should R_{s_2} fail to approach unity, irrespective of the irreducible uncertainty in the task (R_{s_1})? Our reply is that survival requires *better*, not *best*, solutions. That point is crucial. It is not necessary for the surviving species to have best solutions; solutions which are simply better than their competitor's are good enough.

Now it may well be that a new organism with best, i.e., maximizing capabilities, could drive *homo sapiens* from Earth. Possibly. But current technological man certainly has recognized the advantages of maximizing solutions and seeks them. He does not, however, achieve maximal solutions by relying on the interpretative theories of psychologists which insist that man somehow really is a maximizer. Rather, technological man proceeds by removing the uncertainty from environmental *tasks* (making $R_{s_1} \to 1.00$) and thereby developing S_1 systems which allow R_{s_2} to approach unity by matching as well as other means, and thus allowing achievement (r_a) to approach unity. (The development of air safety is a perfect example of this technique, which involves coping with (a) nature's imperfect communicability between law and surface data by providing perfectly dependable signals, $R_{s_1} = 1.00$, and (b) man's lack of perfect control by providing instrumentation with pointer-reading devices that can be read with virtually no error, $R_{s_2} \to 1.00$.)

Before leaving the topic of maximizing I want to refer briefly to two further points: (1) note that it is *lower-order* organisms which maximize; they pursue a given strategy in a wholly deterministic manner—a phenomenon formerly referred to as "instinct", now referred to as an "innate releasing mechanism". That is, a lower order organism will make the same response, irrespective of the probability relations relating the cue and the distal variable. This point was nicely illustrated by Brunswik (1956, p. 62) when he referred to the sea urchin which responds to a shadow cast across it either by a fish, a ship, or a cloud. That is maximizing behavior; and the further down the phylogenetic scale one goes, the more likely he is to encounter it, which suggests to me that a more differentiated concept of maximizing must be considered, a point which must be developed elsewhere. (See Campbell (1966, p. 84–88) for a similar point of view.)

The direction which this development will take can be suggested, however, by referring to Brunswik's description of the distinction between perception and thinking (1956, p. 89 ff.), in which he notes that the "'stupidity' (matching rather than maximizing behavior, K.R.H.) of perception thus is by no means to be construed as maladaptiveness; as we all know, life has survived on relative stupidity from time immemorial, and if threatened in its existence it is so by malfunctioning of the intellect rather than by malfunctioning of perception" (p. 92–93). All the reader needs to do to grasp this point is to picture in his mind's eye the thousands of missiles standing ready, at the command of those pitiful humans whose "malfunctioning of the intellect" will lead them to that maximizing solution that will destroy life as we know it.

BIBLIOGRAPHY

Abelson, R. P., and Knouse, D. E., Subjective acceptance of verbal generalizations. In S. Feldman (Ed.), *Cognitive consistency*. New York: Academic Press, 1966, pp. 117–197.

Anderson, N. H., Application of an additive model to impression formation. *Science*, 1962, **138**, 817–818.

Björkman, M., Stimulus-event learning and event learning as concurrent processes. *Organizational Behavior and Human Performance*, 1967, **2**, 219–236.

Brown, LaRue, and Hammond, K. R., A supra-linguistic method for reducing intragroup conflict. Program of Research on Cognitive Processes Report No. 108, University of Colorado, Institute of Behavioral Science, 1968.

Bruner, J., Goodnow, J., and Austin, G., *A study of thinking*. New York: Wiley, 1956.

Brunswik, E., Scope and aspects of the cognitive problem. In H. Gruber, R. Jessor, and K. Hammond (Eds.), *Cognition: The Colorado Symposium*. Cambridge, Mass.: Harvard University Press, 1957, pp. 5–31.

Brunswik, E., *The conceptual framework of psychology*. Chicago: University of Chicago Press, 1952.

Brunswik, E., *Perception and the representative design of psychological experiments*. Berkeley, California: University of California Press, 1956.

Campbell, D., Pattern matching as an essential in distal knowing. In K. R. Hammond (Ed.), *The psychology of Egon Brunswik*. New York: Holt, Rinehart & Winston, 1966, pp. 81–107.

Ezekiel, M., and Fox, K. E., *Methods of correlation and regression analysis*. New York: Wiley, 1959.

Feldman, J., *An analysis of predictive behavior in a two-choice situation*. Unpubl. doct. diss. Pittsburgh: CIT.

Feldman, J., Simulation of behavior in the binary choice experiment. In: Feigenbaum, E. A. and Feldman, J. (eds.) *Computers and Thought*. New York: MacGraw-Hill, 1953.

Feldman, S. (Ed.), *Cognitive consistency*. New York: Academic Press, 1966.

Garner, W. R., The stimulus in information processing. *American Psychologist*, 1970, **25**, 350–358.

Goldberg, L., *Personal communication*, February 1970.

Goldberg, L. R., Simple models or simple processes? Some research on clinical judgments. *American Psychologist*, 1968, **23**, 483–496.

Green, B. F. Jr., Descriptions and explanations: A comment on papers by Hoffman and Edwards. In B. Kleinmuntz (Ed.), *Formal representation of human judgment*. New York: John Wiley & Sons, 1968, pp. 91–98.

Groner, R., A statistical test of linearity in multiple regression, applied to a multidimensional impression formation task. Paper at the 1968 Conference of the Society for Multivariate Experimental Psychology in Manchester, England, April, 1968.

Groner, R., Deciding between a multiple regression approach versus an orthogonal analysis of variance approach in linear models of human judgment. Paper at the 1970 Conference on Human Judgment at the Institute of Behavioral Science, Boulder, Colorado, 1970.

Hammond, K. R., New directions in research in conflict resolution. *Journal of Social Issues*, 1965, **21**, 44–66. Reprinted in *Bulletin of British Psychological Society*, 1966, **15**, 49–69.

Hammond, K. R., Probabilistic functioning and the clinical method. *Psychological Review*, 1955, **62**, 255–262.

Hammond, K. R., Hursch, Carolyn, and Todd. F. J., Analyzing the components of clinical inference. *Psychological Review*, 1964, **71**, pp. 438–456.

Hammond, K. R., and Brehmer, B., Distrust among nations: A challenge to scientific inquiry. To appear as Quasi-rationality and distrust: Implications for international conflict. In L. Rappoport and D. Summers (Eds.) *Human Judgment and Social Interaction*. New York: Holt, Rinehart, in press.

In J. Hellmuth (Ed.), *Cognitive Studies*, Vol. 2, *Deficits in Cognition*. New York: Brunner/Mazel, Inc., 1970, in press.

Hammond, K. R., and Boyle, P. J. R., Quasi-rationality, quarrels, and new conceptions of feedback. *Bulletin of the British Psychological Society* 1971, **24**.

Hammond, K. R., Todd, F. J., Wilkins, Marilyn, and Mitchell, T. O., Cognitive conflict between persons: Application of the "lens-model" paradigm. *Journal of Experimental Social Psychology*, 1966, **2**, 343–360.

Hammond, K. R., and Summers, D. A., Cognitive dependence on linear and nonlinear cues. *Psychological Review*, 1965, **72**, 215–224.

Helenius, M., Disagreement over child rearing: A case of socially induced cognitive conflict. In L. Rappoport and D. Summers (Eds.) *Human Judgment and Social Interaction*. New York: Holt, Rinehart, in press.

Hick, W. E., Why the human operator, *Trans. Soc. Instrument Technol.*, 1952, **4**, 67–77.

Hoffman, P. J., The paramorphic representation of clinical judgment. *Psychological Bulletin*, 1960, **57**, 116–131.

Hursch, Carolyn, Hammond, K. R., and Hursch, J. L., Some methodological considerations in multiple-cue probability studies. *Psychological Review*, 1964, **71**, 42–60.

Miller, G. A., and Frick, F. G., Statistical behavioristics and sequences of responses. *Psychological Review*, 1949, **56**, 311–324.

Naylor, J., Some comments on the accuracy and the validity of a cue variable. *Journal of Mathematical Psychology*, 1967, **4**, 154–161.

Naylor, J., and Schenck, E. A., Pm as an "error-free" index of rater agreement. *Educational and Psychological Measurement*, 1966, **26**, 815–824.

Ness, A., Erkenntnis und wissenschaftliches Verhalten. Skrifter utgitt av Det Norske Videnskaps-Akademi I Oslo, II Hist.-Filos. Klasse. 1936, No. 1.

Polanyi, M., *The tacit dimension*. Garden City, N. Y.: Doubleday, 1966.

Quine, W., *Word and object*. Cambridge, Mass.: MIT Press, 1960.

Rappoport, L., Interpersonal conflict in cooperative and uncertain situations. *Journal of Experimental Social Psychology*, 1965, **1**, 323–333.

Rozeboom, W. W., Ontological induction and the logical typology of scientific variables. *Philosophy of Science*, 1961, **28**, 337–377.

Rozeboom, W. W., *Foundations of the Theory of Prediction*. Homewood, Ill.: Dorsey, 1966.

Summers, D. A., Conflict, compromise, and belief change in a decision-making task. *Journal of Conflict Resolution*, 1968, **12**, 215–221.

Summers, D. A., and Hammond, K. R., Inference behavior in multiple-cue tasks involving both linear and nonlinear relations. *Journal of Experimental Psychology*, 1966, **71**, 751–757.

Summers, S. A., The learning of responses to multiple weighted cues. *Journal of Experimental Psychology*, 1962, **64**, 29–34.

Todd, F., J. and Hammond, K. R., Differential feedback in two multiple-cue probability learning tasks. *Behavioral Science*, 1965, **10**, 429–435.

Tolman, E. C., and Brunswik, E., The organism and causal texture of the environment. *Psychological Review*, 1935, **42**, 43–77.

Tryon, R. C., and Bailey, D. E., The BC Try computer system of cluster and factor analysis. *Multivariate Behavioral Research*, 1966, **1**, 43–77.

Tucker, L. R., A suggested alternative formulation in the development by Hursch, Hammond, and Hursch and by Hammond, Hursch, and Todd. *Psychological Review*, 1964, **71**, 528–530.

X

CUE UTILIZATION AND MEMORY STRUCTURE IN LOGICAL THINKING

Rudolf Groner

The Center for Advanced Study in Theoretical Psychology

A frequent error in the psychology of thought processes is the naive, straightforward application of concepts from the field of formal logic to psychological problems. The basic thesis of the present approach is a clear distinction between the structure of a problem defined in terms of traditional formal logic, and its psychological counterpart which may be called "Paralogic" after DeSoto *et al.*, 1965.

One might argue that it is unnecessary and misleading to distinguish between those two systems, because both are products of human reasoning and deal with the same part of the reality perceived and constructed by the human senses. This is certainly true insofar as the difference between the two systems is not ontological: the division is rather of usefulness in distinguishing between different aims and manifestations in the two systems. The discipline of formal logic can be understood as the product of a scientific endeavor which originated in the everyday reasoning here called Paralogic, but has gradually diverged from the latter in the direction of certain formal ideals such as content independence and pure axiomatisation. Paralogic occurs and is reflected essentially in the medium of language, where linguistic transformations can be expected to coincide with the paralogical operations (for further discussion see Clark, 1969). In contrast, the discipline of formal logic has created its own miniature language of primitives and axioms, has focused upon general properties and theorems, and has been relatively unconcerned with the information processing and storage aspect of inference (Its younger sister-discipline, automata theory, sheds more light on these latter questions, and for this reason is more interesting and useful for psychologists).

Beside the difference in historical roots, the following facts show that a distinction between formal logic and paralogic is necessary:

1 There is no mutual implication between the two systems in the sense that knowledge of formal logic is necessary for solving a problem or that the ability to solve particular problems is a sufficient prerequisite to derive the formal logical structure.

2 Experimental observations, properly designed, show discrepancies between the problem-solving algorithms derived from formal logic and subjective problem-solving heuristics.

3 The algorithms of formal logic often make unrealistic assumptions about psychological variables such as memory load and information processing capacity.

The present paper concerns the last two of these points applied to a rather simple (from the logical point of view) task environment. The chosen tasks consist of sentences like the following:

"Joe is smaller than Teddy, Kellogg is smaller than Bill,
Joe is smaller than Bill, Teddy is smaller than Kellogg;
who is the smallest, second-smallest ... and largest"?

While such tasks persist among the favorite questions on intelligence tests, they have been neglected for some decades in work on the psychology of thinking, after a short period of considerable interest half a century ago (Burt, 1919a, b; Piaget, 1921).

The following presentation begins with a short introduction to some formal logical properties of this class of problems and continues with a brief recapitulation of some important experimental results. Subsequently, theoretical interpretation of these findings will draw some conclusions about the structure of the paralogical system.

SOME LOGICAL PROPERTIES OF SERIAL ORDER PROBLEMS

Let us examine the simplest non-trivial case of such a problem:

1. $a \varrho b$
2. $b \varrho c$
3. $a \varrho c$

Following the nomenclature of trasitional logic (e.g., Stebbing, 1958; Hunter, 1957) we call a, b, c, *terms*; if a term is on the left side of the *relation* ϱ, it is called *referent*; if it stands to the right of ϱ, it is the *relatum*. The number of different terms may be expressed by k (in the special case above $k = 3$). The terms are considered as elements of a set A, on whose Cartesian Product $A \times A$ a binary relation ϱ is defined with the properties of transitivity (for every x, y, and z in A, if $x \varrho y$ and $y \varrho z$, then $x \varrho z$), asymmetry (if $x \varrho y$ then not $y \varrho x$), and connectedness (for every x and y in A, $x \varrho y$ or $y \varrho x$. A special case of connected terms may be named "*adjacency*": Two terms x, y in A are called adjacent if there exists no z in A such that either $x \varrho z$ and $z \varrho y$, or $y \varrho z$ and $z \varrho x$.

It is possible to divide the set S of all order premises into two disjoint subsets, one of them containing the premises about adjacent terms only, the other one the remaining premises about non-adjacent terms. Because A is fully ordered, the number of premises with adjacent terms ("adjacent premises") equals $k - 1$, while the number of non-adjacent premises increases with positive acceleration according to the formula $(k - 2)(k - 1)/2$. Since all non-adjacent premises can be derived from the adjacent by virtue of the transitivity property, the words "non-adjacent" and "transitively determined" can be used synonymously.

It can be proved that the adjacent premises alone are necessary and sufficient conditions for the construction of a series. From this feature, we can state an interesting simple problem-solving algorithm which solves our k-order series problem with a relatively small and simple storage device (push-down storage with k slots under some restricted conditions as shown below).

Let us first assume that the problem makes available either (a) the complete set S of all premises, or (b) the subset with the $(k - 1)$ adjacent premises (in both cases the premises are not arranged in any particular succession). In condition (a), the algorithm is essentially a counting device, which makes use of some combinatorial properties of the pairing of the terms. It works in the following way (I am omitting the details here):

1) Search for the term on the extreme left. It is the one which is the referent $(k - 1)$ times (i.e., on the left side). Store it in the first slot.

2) Search for the second term from the left. It is the one which is the referent $(k - 2)$ times. Store it in the second slot.

$\vdots$

k) Search for the term on the extreme right. It is the one which is the referent $(k - k)$ times (i.e., none, of course). Store it in the k-th slot.

Now let us consider case (b). We make use of the necessary and sufficient condition of adjacency in all premises for series construction.

1) Search for the term on the extreme left. It is the one which is one times a referent and never a relatum. Store it in the first slot and keep its relatum.

2) Take this relatum and search for the premise where that relatum is the referent. Store it in the second slot and again keep its relatum.

⋮

k) Store in the k-th slot the relatum of the premise which you have found on the $(k - 1)$th trial.

The method gets somewhat more complicated, and also our push-down storage breaks down, if we have a mixed case of (a) and (b), i.e., that case which contains all adjacent and also some (but not all) transitively determined premises. I will not elaborate the whole algorithm here; it is essentially an extension of our second "chaining" algorithm, but it has built in some decision cycles every step after the first, which eliminate the transitively determined premises. It is unnecessary here to develop still further the logical background of this class of problems. More important for the subsequent theoretical interpretation is the presentation of some experimental results, since the literature has reported very little data relevant to the present paradigm.

SOME EXPERIMENTAL RESULTS

In order to gain some knowledge about the paralogical operations of human subjects, an experiment was designed around the task described above starting with the simplest nontrivial ordering task, i.e., one with three logical terms ($k = 3$). The exhaustive relating of every binary combination of terms results in three premises, two of them adjacent and one transitively determined. The independent variable of our experiment was the temporal succession of the three premises whose six alternative values determined a 3×2 factorial design (three alternative positions of the transitively determined premise times two alternative positions of the remaining premises). The design is presented in detail in Table 1. Sixty-six subjects were tested individually. The premises were printed on a sheet of paper in horizontal succession, using three names and the relation "smaller than". The instructions did not specify in which order the premises were to be used; the subjects could, at least in principle, go through the premises in any way they preferred.

The dependent variables were latency scores for the correct solution (defined as appropriate ordering of all three terms) and some coded evaluation of the solving-aloud protocols of the first 30 subjects[2]. For the evaluation of these protocols, a simple coding key was developed to assign each of the subject's spoken sentences to one of four distinct classes of utterances.

TABLE 1 The experimental groups G1–G6 (a), and (b) their particular differentiation scheme according to Heuristic 3 (S I)

	G1	G2	G3	G4	G5	G6
a:	1. a<b 2. b<c 3. a<c	1. a<b 2. a<c 3. b<c	1. b<c 2. a<b 3. a<c	1. b<c 2. a<c 3. a<b	1. a<c 2. a<b 3. b<c	1. a<c 2. b<c 3. a<b

b: (diagrammatic differentiation schemes for each group G1–G6, showing steps 1, 2, 3 with tree structures over terms a, b, c)

1) "Reading in" of the i-th premise.
2) Partial results.
3) Complete results.
4) Remarks falling in none of the categories 1–3 (most often critical comments, or statements about strategy changes).

The first striking result was the fact that none of the 30 subjects appeared to change the given sequence of premise, i.e., they always used the premises in the left-right order, in spite of the simultaneous representation. That means that the simple algorithm cited earlier, which may run several times in different directions through the premises and utilize the information selectively, is fundamentally inappropriate for the explanation of the subject's problem-solving heuristics.

From solution protocols, I have hypothesized three different problem-solving heuristics, which should explain the solution process of all subjects. Applying the above proposed categorization, the particular heuristics can even be operationally defined and distinguished by a particular pattern of input-output sequences. Here I want only to describe these heuristics briefly and rather informally. (A completeness proof via computer simulation for the mathematical sufficiency of the proposed mechanisms has been given elsewhere.)

First Heuristic: Successive Logical Conclusion

In the first two premises, one term necessarily figures twice (because there are four logical positions and only three terms). A partial conclusion can be drawn about the serial position of this term. In the next step, this partial conclusion and the third premise are evaluated together, which leads to the desired complete result. The particular input-output-patterns of this and the other two heuristics are shown in Table 2.

TABLE 2 Input-output sequences of the three heuristics

HEURISTIC 1 (SLC): READ IN 1st PREMISE → READ IN 2nd PREMISE → 1st PARTIAL RESULT → READ IN 3rd PREMISE → FINAL RESULT

HEURISTIC 2 (T&E): TRY i^{th} TERM → READ IN 1st PREMISE → READ IN 2nd PREMISE → READ IN 3rd PREMISE → Kth PARTIAL RESULT → FINAL RESULT

HEURISTIC 3 (SI): READ IN 1st PREMISE → 1st PARTIAL RESULT → READ IN 2nd PREMISE → 2nd PARTIAL RESULT → READ IN 3rd PREMISE → FINAL RESULT

Second heuristic: Trial and Error

Here, the subject picks out one term, usually the referent of the first premise, and tries it as the left-hand term successively through all premises. If there is any contradiction, the next term, usually the referent of the second premise, is utilized in the same way until no inconsistency occurs.

Third Heuristic: Spatial Image

The two terms of the first premise are picked up and placed, according to the relation between them, on an imagined row or column. Then, the second premise is arranged on the same line in a similar manner, buth with respect to the common term already placed from the first premise. The operation is performed with the third premise, again considering the terms which occured previously.

The exact description of these hypothetical problem-solving heuristics were arrived at by evaluation of the solution protocols. Using our operational criteria, it was possible to identify the heuristic used by each subject. If we relate our independent variable (the six different orders of premises) to the particular heuristics chosen by the subjects, we get some evidence of interaction (see Table 3a) between input sequence and chosen strategy; when combined appropriately (Table 3b) we get a χ^2 of 7.73, which is significant at the 5% level ($df = 2$).

TABLE 3 Relation between experimental groups G1–G6 and chosen heuristics

a) EXPERIMENTAL GROUPS SINGLE	G1	G2	G3	G4	G5	G6
HEURISTIC 1: S L C	2	3	1	5	3	5
HEURISTIC 2: T & E	0	1	2	0	0	1
HEURISTIC 3: S I	2	1	3	0	1	0

b) GROUPS COMBINED	TRANSITIVELY DETERMINED PREMISE IN 1. OR 2. POSITION (G2, G4, G5, G6)	TRANSITIVELY DETERMINED PREMISE IN 3. POSITION (G1, G3)
HEURISTIC 1: S L C	16	3
HEURISTIC 2: T & E	2	2
HEURISTIC 3: S I	2	5

TABLE 4 Means (●) ± 1 SD (⊢⊣) of the latency scores in experimental group G1–G6

LATENCY (in sec.)

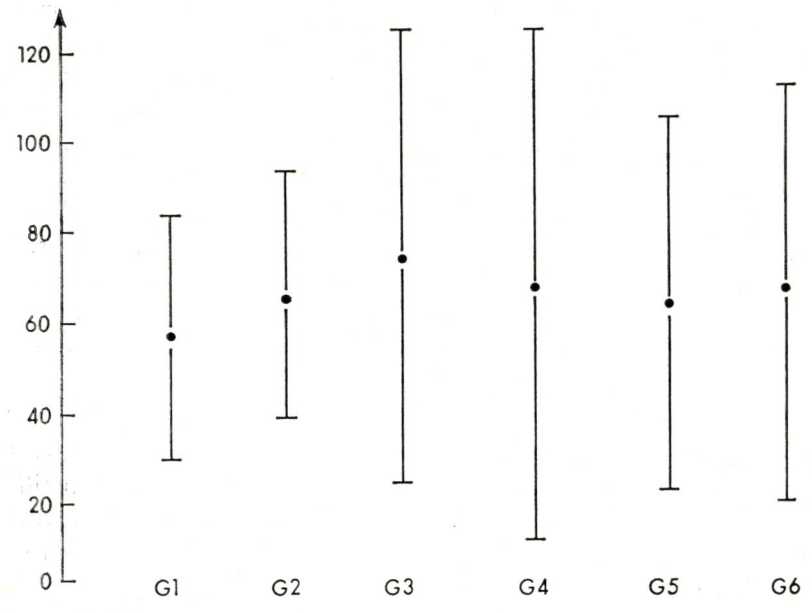

If we compare the latency scores of the six experimental groups we find a striking similarity of means, together with a large variance within the groups (see Table 4). The difference between the groups is (as it is obvious from the figures) not significant.

THEORETICAL INTERPRETATION AND DISCUSSION

Let us first consider the rather strange finding that the interaction between premise succession and chosen heuristic is significant in spite of the small number of subjects and the weak scale level, while the latency scores seem to converge to a common mean over all experimental groups with the increasing number of subjects.

We might have expected that solution time would depend on the position of the "redundant" premise, in the sense that if the transitively determined premise occurs in the first or second position, the final result is inhibited because of the indeterminacy of the solution at this point. Stated more concretely, if you apply heuristic 1 to the first two premises of experimental groups 2, 4, 5, and 6, you can solve only for one object (i.e., for the left-most one in groups 2 and 5, and for the right-most one in 4 and 6); while in the case of groups 1 and 3, the heuristic automatically changes into the algorithm of "chaining" (because here the premises accidentally happen to be in an appropriate order). Thus the right solution can be produced after the second premise. The third premise, if evaluated at all, would function here as additional reinforcement for the correct solution, but would not require any additional drawing of conclusions.

If heuristic 3 is rigidly applied to the groups with the transitively determined premise in the first or second position, still stranger things happen. The subject arrives under some conditions (more on this below) at a wrong conclusion which has to be cancelled in the evaluation of the last premise, and he gets into trouble in each case because of the successive nesting and overlapping of the terms on the imagined line. On the other hand, under the neat conditions of experimental groups 1 and 3, with the transitively determined premise in the last position, heuristic 3 degenerates again into the "chaining" algorithm.

Latency-enhancing troubles may thus be predicted for certain combinations of heuristic and premise order, especially for heuristic 3 when the transitively determined information is in the first or second position. However, a look at Table 3b reveals that this combination is rare, occurring less often than independent distribution of heuristics across experimental conditions would predict.

In light of this result, we can solve the riddle of missing group differences. Somehow the subjects compensated for the handicap of the nonoptimal arrangement of premises by selecting the most appropriate heuristic for the particular case. However, this explanation, which is supported both by the significant correlation between premise order and selection of heuristic and by the lack of appreciable group differences, still suffers two shortcomings: First, how can the subjects decide in advance, before they know the whole problem structure, the appropriateness of a particular heuristic; and second, why did the subjects undertake the more complicated solving procedures instead of simply changing the input order of premises as suggested in our logical algorithm.

An explanation of the second point, which stresses the obvious fact that we grow up in a culture which very strongly emphasizes and reinforces the left-to-right order of written language, I do not find satisfactory. More plausible, it seems to me, is that we usually (or at least quite often) *hear* the relevant information, and under those conditions a continued rearrangement of the perceived information is, if not impossible, quite costly (taking into account the limitations of short term memory and of simultaneous operation capacity).

The astonishing phenomenon of heuristics pre-selection has also been demonstrated in another context (Groner, 1969), where it was argued that superficial scanning of a problem structure's "evident features" could determine quite accurately a good choice of problem-solving strategies. In the present problem, the "evident feature" could be "common term either twice referent or twice relatum" which leads automatically to a Successive Logical Conclusion Strategy, while the feature of connectedness leads to the Spatial Image Strategy.

Of much greater theoretical importance seems to me the general "environmental" situation of our problem. I think we can draw some analogies here to Brunswik's (1934, 1956) concepts, although it shouldn't be overlooked that our problem is fundamentally different from Brunswikian inference in a *probabilistic* situation so that many of his terms may change their original meaning in the present deductive-deterministic situation.

The essential point, held in common with Brunswik, is the notion that the individual has to construct his own model of the environment by an active process, putting together pieces of previously unrelated information. This process is maintained by operations and processes of the subject's paralogical system. (The discipline of formal logic at best can provide us a useful framework for describing the "environmental side" of the whole process.)

23*

One important environmental precondition for a successful application of Brunswik's (1956) concepts is his requirement of a "representative design": To arrive at valid conclusions about the subject's adaptive mechanisms, the experimental design should representatively simulate the environmental conditions with respect to both completeness and relative importance of the independent variables. Our experimental approach comes somewhat closer to this goal than other similar experiments in the literature since it includes the important and hitherto neglected variable of transitively determined versus adjacent premises. This additional inclusion seems to be the principal source for the variegated pattern of different heuristics not previously found in other experiments (e.g., Hunter, 1957; De Soto, et al., 1968; Huttenlocher, 1968; Clark, 1969).

Let us briefly review some of Brunswik's most important concepts. Not-immediately-perceived objects (distal variables) are reflected with varying degrees of cue validity by the proximal stimuli which are transformed and possibly distorted mappings of the original distal stimuli impinging on the organism. If there is a one-to-many mapping from the distal to the proximal stimuli, Brunswik speaks of vicarious mediation, which is utilized for achievement by the organism through an sctive process of vicarious functioning.

The present paradigm of logical relations can perhaps be fitted into this environmental model of organismic adaptation, though, by some *tour de*

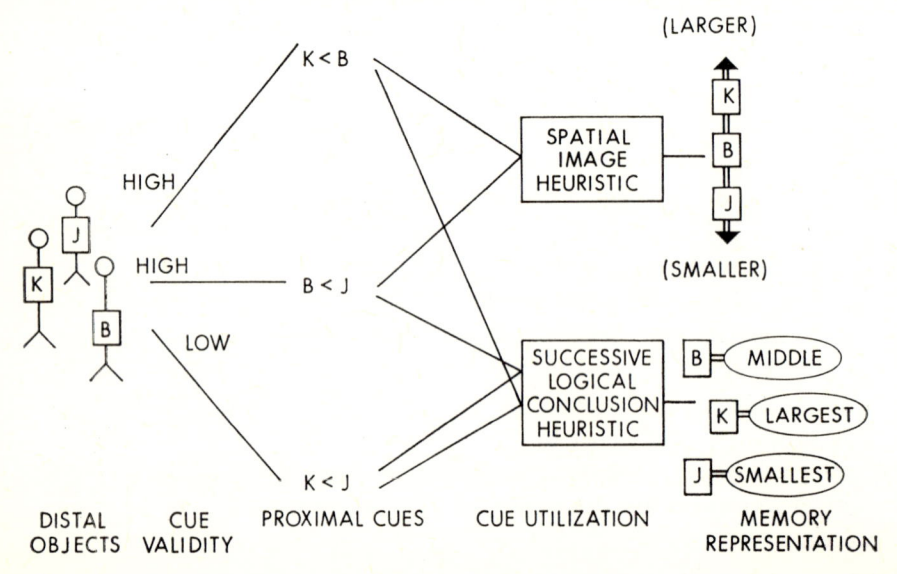

TABLE 5 Modified lens model adapted from Brunswik (1956) to the three term problem

force. If we look at the environmental side of our situation (see Table 5 for an illustration), we have as distal objects some outside representation of the terms, initially unknown to the subject. Their order is partially reflected in the binary premises which are the only information directly available to the subject and representing the proximal variables. Considering their relation to the distal objects, either they can be transitively determined, in which case they represent a low degree of cue validity, or they are adjacent, making them of higher cue validity. In the restricted situation of three-term problems, the transitively determined premise together with one of the adjacent premises fixes only the position of one of the extreme terms, while the two adjacent premises together give the solution about all three terms.

This presents a complication for the subject since he does not know in advance whether a premise is adjacent or transitively determined. Our model assumes that there is some kind of "validity detector" pre-scanning of the first two premises. So it is possible that the presentation of the two highly valid proximal cues gives rise to the Spatial Image Heuristic, which would be inappropriate in the presence of one cue with low validity because of the indeterminacy for a spatial representation. In the latter case, the (most often chosen) Successive Logical Conclusion Heuristic handles the smaller amount of available information much more effectively. Thus the adaptation of the subject to proximal information with different degrees of cue validity takes place through a process of selection of the applied heuristics.

To summarize our proposals, we assign to the distal variables the logically ordered terms, and to the proximal variables the premises, given in some accidental succession. As a logical counterpart to vicarious mediation in Brunswik's situation, we have the possibilities of mediation either through adjacent premises with a higher cue validity or "partially redundant" (i.e., transitively predetermined) premises representing a lower cue validity in the sense that they imply a weaker logical connection to the distal variables. The process of vicarious functioning is maintained by the subjects through a process of selecting different heuristics dependent upon the cue validity of the proximal stimuli.

Now let us have a closer look at some of the subjects' heuristics, beginning with the Spatial Image strategy. Similar strategies have already been reported in the literature by DeSoto, *et al.* (1965), Handel *et al.* (1968), Huttenlocher (1968). However, the absence of transitively determined premises and the additional conversion of the order relation, including for instance "smaller" and "larger" make those experiments not directly comparable to the present one.

Successive differentiation of the respective positions of new incoming terms according to the previously placed objects can be considered as a rewriting rule: If a and b are already placed on the line, the additional information $a \varrho c$ replaces a by the ordered pair ac, while the term b may be assumed to remain stored without any change. Taking the Spatial Image hypothesis seriously, we could expect a resulting line with the elements acb in that order, even though the result is indeterminate from the logical viewpoint represented by the SLC heuristic.

From a formal point of view, the rewriting procedure of the Spatial Image Heuristic can be represented as a context-free constituent-structure grammar (Chomsky, 1957; Chomsky and Miller, 1963). But this relatively simple generative system breaks down if the transitively determined premise is in the second position and the third premise changes the order (for an illustration of this point see Table 1b, especially experimental groups 2 and 4). However, if the third, order-reversing premise is suppressed, we could expect a certain spatial ordering of the terms which can be accurately predicted and experimentally tested (under experimental condition 2: $a < c < b$, and under condition 4: $b < a < c$).

Yngve (1960) has shown that a grammatical structure of the present type (and with finite recursions) can be simulated by a relatively simple finite automaton with push-down storage as a short term memory device. In agreement with the conventions about written language in our culture (and also in agreement with the stubborn information utilization of our subjects!) the automaton proceeds, in a strict left-right order, in that its rewritings are always on the right side. Self-embedding and left-recursive constructions (see Miller, 1962, on this point) are maintained by buffering the short term memory, whereby the load is considerably increased by left-recursive writings. Counting the minimal number of necessary short term memory positions, Yngve was able to quantify the memory requirements for different recursive schemes.

If we fit our Spatial Image Heuristic into Yngve's model and additionally assume that the main difficulty for human subjects lies in short term memory utilization (cf. Groner, 1969), we could predict the relative difficulties under different conditions of premise representations. It also could be predicted that there is a fixed point where the Spatial Image Heuristic ceases to work because of the limitations of human short-term memory capacity (Miller, 1965; Atkinson and Shiffrin, 1968). However, the present three-term-series problems place little burden on human short-term storage capabilities, so further experiments with $k > 3$ should be carried out to test the latter predictions. It should also not be overlooked that these left-recursive constructions constitute only a part of the memory load; additional burdens are imposed by storing partial results, and it is an open question whether the execution of a heuristic itself doesn't require some short-term memory space (for some supporting experimental evidence on this point see Süllwold, 1964). Finally, as G. A. Miller (1956) has pointed out, storage capacity might be considerably extended by coding the terms and their relations into chunks containing a greater amount of information.

Since very little is actually known about the coding process involved in logical thinking, I would like to take this opportunity to speculate a bit about some coding processes possibly involved here. Two different coding processes are already implicit in the reported heuristics, though they may be hidden by the laconic shortness of the descriptions.

The first coding scheme is embodied by the Spatial Image Heuristic and may be labeled "*relational coding*". The important characteristic of this coding scheme is an ordering performed on the internal representations of the elements, allocating and replacing them according to every new incoming premise. Drawing an analogy to the software of a computer, the *address* of each element is used to represent its degree of the relevant dimension. The order of the addresses is taken as the key for coding and recording the information, thus providing a fixed framework for the storage of the ordered results. The whole process can be characterized as actively producing some kind of an isomorphism between an order in the environment and its internal representation.

Our one-dimensional "imagined line" is a rather simple special case for the possibilities of such a relational coding scheme. Simply extending the dimensionality of the address system would open many more capabilities of such a coding scheme, not only processing information such as "Bill is taller and thinner than Kellogg", but possibly also capturing (if we are willing to unleash our speculation still more) very complex processes like imagination.

To sum up, the relational coding scheme is organized as a simultaneous representation of all objects having their relations represented by the coordinates of that scheme.

The second kind of coding is achieved by the Successive Logical Conclusion and Trial and Error Heuristics, and may be named "*categorical coding*". The result of the logical operation can be expressed in an *nonrelational statement*, i.e., one of subject-predicate form. The basic principle of this coding scheme is the utilization of a single verbal label, the predicate, capturing the essential properties of the relative position of the term within the group of all other terms. Naturally, it works best in a situation where strong properties can be captured by the predicate. This is especially the case with the extreme elements "c = largest" and "a = smallest", which are very efficiently coded in respect to all the other elements. The validity of such a statement is, of course, relative to the referential group of terms from which this coding has been deduced.

There seems to be a limitation imposed on the categorical coding scheme by language: Apparently only one grammatical transformation exists transforming adjectives into order predicates: The superlative. This observation may indicate that the usefulness and actual application of the categorical coding scheme in ordering problems is restricted $k < 3$ (with the predicate "middle" characterizing the non-extreme element). For cases with $k > 3$, however, ordinal numbers could in principal be used as predicates ("Joe is the fourth-largest"). But we have to be careful that with such an extension the difference between the two coding schemes does not become merely academic: The system of ordinal numbers can equally well be interpreted either as an ordered set of predicates or as an efficient address system providing locations for the terms.

Other cognitive models, where (with some generosity in overlooking specific differences) there is also some evidence for such a categorical coding scheme, are the Concept Learning System of Hunt, Marin, and Stone (1966) and the learning heuristics of sequential patterns (Simon and Kotovsky, 1963; Groner, 1969). Also, Piaget's (1949) concept of "intensive quantification" seems related to this coding scheme.

The main difference between the two coding schemes lies in the fact that the relational coding scheme is a compact representation of all terms in a coherent framework wherein change of a single element would affect the whole representation quite drastically, while the categorical coding scheme consists of many association-like subject-predicate connections which probably better resist intrusions. From a formal-logic point of view both coding schemes are equivalent in the sense that both are capable of representing the same logical structure and both can be mapped isomorphically into each other (i.e., the categorical code "a = smallest" implies all relational statements "$a < x$", "$a < y$" etc., and vice versa).

Discussion of these two coding schemes may sound highly speculative (but apparently not above the threshold of liberality for this conference). However, both schemes can be made explicit enough to formulate in strict mathematical language, i.e., in a computer program. Whether these schemes are useful in task environments broader than the one characterized by three-term logical problems is another question which only future empirical work can answer.

SUMMARY

To distinguish between the structure of a problem defined in terms of formal logic and the "paralogical" representation in human cognition, an example was worked out in which both aspects could be studied and compared. To get some information about the paralogical aspect, an experiment was carried out varying the order of three binary relational statements (premises), one of them being determined by the other two through logical transitivity. There was some evidence that even in this relatively homogeneous situation no single mechanism was capable of explaining the solution processes. From the input-output sequences of the subjects' protocols, it was possible to identify and define operationally three different problem-solving mechanisms (heuristics), which were then simulated on a computer.

In an attempt at a theoretical interpretation, three main experimental results were dealt with simultaneously: (1) None of the subjects rearranged the given (but changeable) order of premises. (2) There was no significant difference between the latency scores for solutions (although the variability within each group was large). (3) The interaction between the independent variable (the order of the premises) and the chosen heuristic was significant. Drawing some analogies to Brunswik's lens model, it was suggested that the subjects utilized a pattern of vicarious strategies, controlled by the particular input sequence.

Deeper analysis of the three heuristics revealed in one of them a recursive scheme in the form of a constituent-structure grammar leading to some empirically testable predictions. Finally, two different memory coding schemes were hypothesized and related to other cognitive processes.

NOTES

1. This paper was carried out when the author was a fellow at the Center for Advanced Study in Theoretical Psychology, University of Alberta, supported by a cultural exchange postdoctoral fellowship of the Canada Council. I gratefully acknowledge the helpful discussions with my wife Marina, William W. Rozeboom, and Kellogg Wilson. Myron Moroz, Xavier Plaus, Rheva Frank, and Bill Rozeboom were kind enough to go through a preliminary draft, taking away some of the "Horrors of the German Language" (Mark Twain, 1910, pp. 43-52) however, I am afraid, not all. Of course, no one is responsible for any errors in logic, experimentation, or interpretation, preferably myself included.
2. I am gratefully indebted to Miss Dina Stern, University of Berne, Switzerland, for administering the experiments, sending me some results, and desisting from sending me solution protocols of the remaining 36 Ss. Perhaps, that was the only way to keep the results significant.

BIBLIOGRAPHY

Atkinson, R. C., and Shiffrin, R. M., (1968) Human memory: A proposed system and its control processes. In: *The Psychology of Learning and Motivation*, vol. 2, New York: Academic Press.
Brunswik, E., (1934) *Wahrnehmung und Gegenstandswelt: Grundlegung einer Psychologie vom Gegenstand her.* Leipzig und Wien: Deuticke.
Brunswik, E., (1956) *Perception and the representative design of psychological experiments* (2nd ed.) Berkeley and Los Angeles: University of California Press.
Burt, C., (1919a) The development of reasoning in school children I. *J. exp. Ped.*, **5**, 68–77.
Burt, C., (1919b) The development of reasoning in school children II. *J. exp. Ped.*, **5**, 121–127.
Chomsky, N., (1957) *Syntactic Structures*. Den Haag: Mouton.
Chomsky, N., and Miller, G. A., (1963) Introduction to the formal analysis of natural languages. In Luce, R. D., and Bush, R. R., and Galanter, E.: *Handbook of Mathematical Psychology*, vol. 2, New York: Wiley.
Clark, H. H., (1969) Linguistic processes in deductive reasoning. *Psychol. Rev.*, **76**, 387–404.
De Soto, C., London, M., and Handel, S., (1965) Social reasoning and spatial paralogic. *J. Pers. Soc. Psychol.*, **2**, 513–521.
Groner, R., (1969) Beiträge zur Computersimulation kognitiver Prozesse auf dem Niveau interindividueller Differenzen. In Irle, M. (ed.): *Bericht über den XXVI. Kongreß der Deutschen Gesellschaft für Psychologie in Tübingen*, pp. 279–286, Göttingen: Hogrefe.
Handel, S., London, M., and De Soto, C., (1968) Reasoning and spatial representations. *J. verb. Learn. verb. Behav.*, **7**, 351–357.
Hunt, E. B., Marin, J., and Stone, P. J., (1966) *Experiments in induction*. New York: Academic Press.
Hunter, I. M. L., (1957) The solving of three-term series problems *Brit. J. Psychol.*, **48**, 286–298.
Huttenlocher, J., (1968) Constructing spatial images: A strategy in reasoning. *Psychol. Rev.*, **75**, 550–560.
Miller, G. A. (1956) The magic number seven, plus or minus two; some limits on our capacity for processing information. *Psychol. Rev.*, **63**, 81–97.
Miller, G. A., (1962) Some psychological studies of grammar. *Amer. Psychol.*, **17**, 748–762.
Piaget, J., (1921) Une forme verbal de la comparaison chez l'enfant. *Arch. Psychol.*, **18**, 141–172.
Piaget, J., (1949) *Traité de logique*. Paris: Colin.
Simon, H. A., and Kotovsky, K., (1963) Human acquisition of concepts for sequential patterns. *Psychol. Rev.*, **70**, 534–546.
Stebbing, L. Susan, (1958) *A modern introduction to logic*[7]. London: Methuen.
Süllwold, F., (1964) *Das unmittelbare Behalten und seine denkpsychologische Bedeutung.* Göttingen: Hogrefe.
Suppes, P., (1957) *Introduction to logic*. Princeton, Toronto, London: Van Nostrand.
Twain, Mark, (Clemens, S. L.) (1910) *Speeches*, New York: Harper.
Yngve, V. H., (1960) A model and a hypothesis for language structure. *Proc. Amer. Phil. Soc.*, **104**, 444–466.

XI

MEMORY ORGANIZATION AND QUESTION ANSWERING

Kellogg V. Wilson

The Center for Advanced Study in Theoretical Psychology

For a considerable number of years academics have been attempting to assess the knowledge of their students by asking questions. Many students expect and instructors demand nearly verbatim repetition of material in text or lecture but we often attempt to determine the "deeper" forms of knowledge by asking for information in a form which differs considerably from that of the original information. For example, consider the following doctoral preliminary type questions:

What are the relations between Information Theory and von Bertalanffy's concept of the Open System?

What form of information storage about past experience is represented by the Hullian habit family hierarchy?

Describe the probable form of the Freudian theory of psychosexual development if three sexes were required for human production?

It is worth noting that in all three cases, and especially the last, that there is no objectively correct answer but that the more acceptable answerr should manifest some kind of "sophistication". The purpose of this papes is to describe the kind of structure of memory that might be associated with such "sophistication" which is based on the forms of memory organization developed for computer programs which answer questions and process semantic information, to present some speculations about the mode of operation of the human brain which might enable it to function in this way and, finally, to describe two experiments on the effects of the organization of sentences. The use of computer programs as models of psychological processes has been defended quite cogently by Reitman (1965, Chapter 1) and the points he raises shall not be repeated here. The emphasis in this paper will be on the potentialities of different kinds of memory structure rather than on the details of computer simulation and is an attempt to describe more or less rigorously what properties might be exhibited by the alternative memory structure.

The position taken in this paper is that knowledge consists of information which is stored in memory in a form which permits retrieval in a variety of different contexts. Simple storage of information is not enough—the medical records of a hospital's files do not "know" as much as an intelligent and experienced physician, even though a larger range of "experience" is codified therein, simply because the ordinary alphabetic file by patient name does not permit direct answering of questions about the significance of symptoms of a particular sort for a patient with a particular history.

The principal form of "knowing" to be discussed in this paper is verbal, which should not be taken to deny the possibility of other forms of knowledge. Rather, the "units" of verbal knowledge are more easily discussed at present and there is a hope that the forms of memory organization associated with other forms of knowledge will be essentially similar.

QUESTION ANSWERING AND MEMORY ORGANIZATION

The principal problem in the development of a computer question answering system is to structure the information in a form that will permit retrieval in a variety of ways. Implicit in this statement is a rejection of a concept of "knowledge" as sequences of $S - R$ connections. Such a form of memory organization would have the same limitations as the alphabetic file of patient information mentioned above in that each informational "item" (or R) could be retrieved by only one "input" (or S). The obvious flexibility of even ordinary human retrieval processes would not be possible. Somewhat greater flexibility can be introduced by permitting inputs to the system and output from the system to have the structure of vectors where input vector components have a fixed relationship to those of the output vector (such as a linear regression equation) but since the coding would not permit interactions or contextual dependencies, even this is not enough. A multivariate $S - R$ system would be equivalent to the matrix structure considered below.

Matrix Structure

If the information stored is in a very limited domain—say that of the teams, scores, locations and dates of games played by Canadian football teams during the last season—the most obvious form of information structure would be a matrix—in this case, possibly, a winning team name by losing team name by number of game (1st, 2nd, etc.) matrix where each cell contains a vector with the location, date and pair of scores. With some sort of syntactic analysis subroutines the following questions could be answered:

What was the winning and losing score when Edmonton first defeated Calgary?
Where did Winnipeg first defeat Edmonton?

With some additional subroutines the following questions sould be answered:[1]

What are the point totals for Edmonton and Calgary when playing against each other?
How often did Winnipeg win against Calgary?
Did Edmonton defeat Calgary more often when playing in Edmonton than in Calgary?

The first set of questions can be answered by selecting the appropriate vector component while the second can be answered from fairly obvious operations on the contents of selected rows and columns (corresponding to winning and losing team names). However, the following questions can only be answered by processing the entire contents of the data matrix:

What team scored six points most often?
Which are the cities for which the score totals are even?

With a limited domain of information to be stored, it will often be possible to design a matrix that will have a small number of empty cells that will answer the most probable questions easily. However, if we attempted to make all aspects of the information in the matrix for the example above equally accessible by adding dimensions to the matrix corresponding to the city where the game was played, the date of the game, the winning and losing scores with ones in the cells corresponding to the combinations which occurred and zeroes in the scores which didn't, there would be a great many cells without content (i.e., most of memory would record the events which didn't happen) and it would be questionable whether either, and particularly the second, of the last pair of questions would be answerable with much less processing.

The point of this rather simple example is that even with a fairly limited information domain, it is difficult to design an information structure which is reasonably compact that will permit answering of conceivable questions with approximately equal difficulty. Thus, it is necessary to organize the information in memory in a form which will permit relatively easy answering of questions which are more probable and/or more "important" but which will render some information retrievable only with difficulty if at all, even though the information is "known" in the sense that all the relevant "facts" have been entered into the information processing device. If the example above is not convincing, consider the difficulty or impossibility of your answering the following questions:

What did you do on April 21, 1957?
How many people have you met in the last five years who have last names containing a "p" or "b"?

The storage of information in matrix form is not especially effective if the information stored does not share a large number of characteristics in common so that at least reasonably approximate representation can be made by assigning a value on some small number of dimensions. The difficulties of such matrix orderings of word meanings are evident in the work of Osgood, Suci and Tannenbaum (1957) and Deese (1965). Even given the restricted information about meaning available from the semantic differential, the common factor dimensions only account for about 50% of the variance of the responses to the concepts. The common conclusion that the semantic differential measures connotative but not denotative meaning seems justified if we make the plausible assumption that many concepts can share common connotations but few can share common denotations. Deese's approach, which orders words in a space defined by words with shared verbal associations, is simply not suitable to represent the semantic structure or relations between, sets of words which differ considerably in meaning and hence share no common associates. Thus, Osgood's semantic differential would be able to answer the question "How do humans differ from cattle?" by comparing the positions of the positions of the *human* and *cattle* in the space of the "evaluative," "activity" and "potency" dimensions while Deese's procedure would probably not order those two words in a common space of even three dimensions. In any case, neither system would probably be capable of representing the important differences in, say, the digestive systems of these two organisms.

Hierarchical List Structures

The representation of information structures in which the shared characteristics of subordinate categories differ considerably from one subset to another can be achieved in a computer by a list structure[2] which resembles the familiar hierarchical classification of animals in traditional biology or Piaget's concept of the "grouping" (see Flavell, 1963, pp. 168–172). Such hierarchies are organized so that each element except the highest is a member of a list whose name is a higher element and, except for the lowest, the name of a list of lower order elements—e.g., *animals* is the name of a list which includes *mammals* and *reptiles*, *mammals* is the name of a list which includes *canines* and *felines*, *felines* is the name of a list which includes *lions*, *tigers*, *cats*, etc. If logical connectives are inserted between the elements of this list, this could serve as a definition of the name of the list in much the same manner as traditional students of concept formation view the form of a concept (e.g., Hunt, Stone and Martin, 1965). Unlike the matrix which has multiple entry points, the hierarchical list has but one entry point and the branches followed down the tree until the desired level is reached. Such a structure could obviously be used to yield a list of *felines* but, assuming that the lowest layer is the list of characteristics of the animal strains named, it would be quite awkward to construct a list of small animals. That such structures can be used to facilitate serial learning in free recall has been demonstrated by Bower (1968), who found that familiarization with a hierarchical structure of minerals greatly facilitated the learning of the lowest order elements even thought the names of only some of these elements were presented during training. In an earlier paper (Wilson, 1968), it was suggested that greater flexibility could be given to such structures if they terminated in matrices ordered by shared characteristics. However, a more sophisticated form of memory organization has been proposed by Quillian (1967a and 1967b) for dictionary word definitions.

Quillian Memory Structure

Two definitions of the noun form *air* are represented in Figure 1.[3] The boxed nodes are *type* nodes which are each entry points into a list structure, but not necessarily a hierarchical list, and the remainder are *token* nodes. The type node *AIR* is a header and the type nodes *AIR*1 and *AIR*2 are the entry points to the *planes* of linked token nodes which correspond to the alternative definitions of the word. The vertical arrows pointing in one direction are links to associated *properties* such as modifying adjectives (e.g., *invisible*, *tasteless*). The double-headed vertical arrows from the type nodes are to be interpreted as equals relations and can serve as an entrance or exit from the plane of the token nodes. The pairs of terms such as *contains* and *comprise* are relational terms which are in a kind of inverse relation (indicated by the double-headed arrow labelled *inv.*) where each member of the pair corresponds to a different direction of motion through the associational network.[4] These links essentially constitute modifying phrases where the subject of the relation is linked to one of the relational

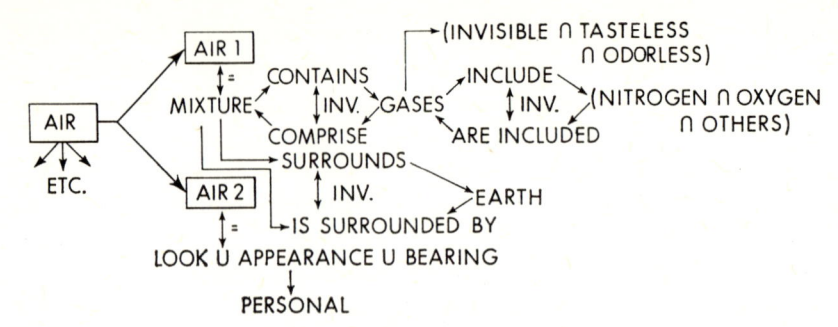

FIGURE 1 Representation of dictionary meaning in modified Quillian notation of the definitions:

Air 1: The mixture of invisible, tasteless, odorless gases (as nitrogen and oxygen) which surrounds the earth

Air 2: The look, appearance or bearing of a person

terms which is, in turn, may serve as the subject of another such phrase (e.g., the token node *gases* in the plane of Air_1). The principal distinction between the relational and property modifiers is that the relational modifiers contain an object term and that the relation can be expressed in two directions. The ∩ symbols in strings of words have the usual meaning of logical *and* the ∪ symbols refer to the weak logical *or*. The links from the header node to the type nodes are meant to indicate a strong *or* relation (i.e., neither *A* or *B* but not both). In practice, the alternative planes correspond to the alternative meanings which would be differentially activated by context.

Each of the token nodes in the plane of a type node is, in turn, linked by a bidirectional equal relation to a corresponding token node, each with its own definitional plane. The power of this system is a result of this network of interconnections which permits a network of definitional and conceptual relationships to be activated from one or more entering nodes. In effect, Quillian's memory organization provides a form of content addressable memory described by Shiffrin and Atkinson (1969) as essential for long term memory organization

In processing inquiries using such a memory, Quillian states that the words of the question activate nodes and that the paths in the planes activated may eventually intersect on an answer which consists of information in doubly activated nodes—a process which Quillian describes principally with reference to finding similarities or differences between word concepts. For example, the question "what gases does air contain?" would hopefully converge on *oxygen* and *nitrogen* (and *others*) but it is well at this point to examine how this might occur. If the pre-processing of the question before memory were entered were to identify *air*, *gases* and *contain* as the words whose type nodes are to be entered and if the *what* term is interpreted as being satisfied by the objects of the relation contain, it seems likely that an answer would be found fairly quickly. Now let us consider some possible limitations. If the question asked were "What gases does air include?" the answer might not be found unless the near synonymity of the *include* and *contain* relational nodes were recognized. Simmons *et al* (in AFIPS, 1966) emphasize the importance of appropriate coding of relational terms and it would seem not too difficult to produce an appropriate coding for relations like set inclusion.[5] This raises the question of how the problems of synonyms or near synonyms can be dealt with. Perhaps some coding in terms of semantic distinctive features (see below) would be helpful and it seems plausible that closely related words will have a substantial number of corresponding token nodes and hence would be linked through a substantial number of type nodes. A somewhat more difficult point concerns questions which are somewhat vague. The question "What substances does air contain?" can be regarded as having an answer which includes the answers to the questions "What gases does the air contain?", "What substances from industrial smokestacks remain in the air?", and "What levels of radioactive material from nuclear testing still remain in the air?". Given an ideal memory organization, links to the nodes which would supply all this information, and more, might be reached from the type node of *substances* (and other type nodes) but the chains of association would be quite long and complex and, in practice, probably only the information about the gases of air would be retrieved. This is not an especially serious fault, especially since the performance of all but the most pedantic of humans is likely to do the same but it appears that vagueness of the question would permit conceptual biases associated with the interpretation of *substances* to operate.

One important implication of this form of memory organization would seem to be that extensive preprocessing of questions to reduce them to a standard format, such as is described by Simmons (1965), would probably not be required but that extensive processing would be required to store information extracted from sentences. Thus, there would seem to be a considerable economy in the unfortunate human propensity towards providing a large number of answers to questions from a memory system which is substantially unaltered by experience.

In summary, the Quillian semantic word memory structure differs from a hierarchical list structure in that word concepts can be connected to other concepts through a relation whose nature differs according to the direction of entry in addition to connections to a string of properties joined by logical connectives. This additional kind of relation plus the provision for multiple entry points into the structure gives it a flexibility that a hierarchical list structure does not have. The relational connections give a definition a form essentially like other sentences in which a concept is used and it is worth noting that word meanings can be learned as effectively through examples of their use in sentences as through formal definitions (Johnson, 1969). Such considerations lead us to believe that the Quillian structure can incorporate information from sentences.

Summary of Formal Properties of Memory Structures

Before proceeding to the problem of incorporating information from sentences, it would be well to restate what has been implied about the formal properties of the three forms of memory organization discussed above. A matrix structure orders information in terms of shared properties and is effective to the extent that properties are shared. If the properties are binary or two valued (e.g., true-false, present-absent) five properties will be sufficient to code 32 alternative informational items but ten properties will be sufficient for 1024 items. However, the number of items which can be stored will be effectively much less if only a few items have a non-null value for each property. This situation is entirely analogous to that of applying factor analysis where the variables (i.e., the items) have very low communalities. If the informational items can be divided into sets and subsets corresponding to superordinate and subordinate characteristics then a hierarchical list structure is an appropriate form of memory organization. This reduces the necessity for finding shared characteristics when items are quite diverse, as seems to be the case for word meanings (see the discussion above of the work of Osgood and Deese), but the flexibility associated with the multiple entry points of the matrix is lost since the superordinate and subordinate categories of an item must be known before it can be found. Also, such structures are somewhat arbitrary in that a particular concept such as "tree" or "air" can often be placed in a large number of superordinate or subordinate categories quite easily—e.g., "air" is a member of the set of "mixtures" and also of "gases". If we permit hierarchical lists of qualitatively different sorts to terminate in the same items we can escape this kind of arbitrariness and this is possible within the Quillian memory. However, another critical feature of the Quillian memory is that relations between items are codified as well as properties which correspond to the sets of which the items are members. In both the matrix and hierarchical lists, relations are treated as properties so that a relationship could be entered up to three times, once for each of the two terms and once for the relation—e.g., "John loves Mary" would be represented by "loves Mary" as a property of John, "is loved by John" as a property of Mary and "John, Mary" as an element of the set of ordered pairs where the first member "loves" the second. It is possible to regard the Quillian memory as an important generalization of the hierarchical list and a later section shall show that all three forms of memory organization are compatible with list processing languages used by computers.

Structures of Information from Sentences

Quillian does not consider the problem of incorporating information from sentences but there are systems which work to some degree of adequacy in question answering which seem to incorporate similar, though less explicitly described, memory organizations (see papers by Craig, *et al.*, Simmons, *et al.*, Thompson in AFIPS, 1966) that reduce sentences to minimal kernel assertions about the properties or relations of concepts or entities which are then stored in the same manner as the dictionary items. For example, the sentence "The Second Conference sponsored by the Center was held at Banff, Alberta on May 5-9, 1969 on the theme of 'Knowing'" might be stored under the node of the *Center for Advanced Study in Theoretical Psychology, University of Alberta* (the later ample identifying material being hopefully obvious from context) as in Figure 2. (For the sake of simplicity the paired relational nodes of Figure 1 are replaced by single nodes marked with *R*.) While every token node in a dictionary definition should be connected by two-way links to type nodes but this is not so obvious for nodes like the full name of the Center. Similarly, the terms *second* and *conference* should lead through one-way links to the appropriate dictionary type nodes but links from these nodes back to the type

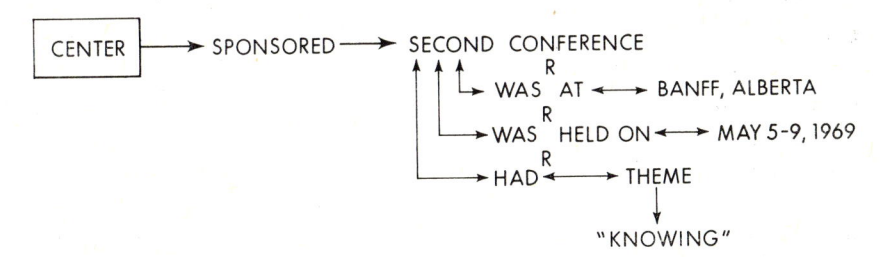

FIGURE 2 Representation of sentence "The second conference sponsored by the Center was held at Banff, Alberta on May 5-9, 1969 on the theme "knowing"

node *second conference* are not needed unless we desire the capacity to answer questions like "Was there a Conference held in Banff, Alberta on May 5-9 whose number was a prime?" Also, the location and dates might be listed as modifiers rather than relations which would make it more difficult but not impossible to answer questions about them. Finally, it is difficult to know what "Knowing" might be linked to, but perhaps this conference will yield that knowledge.

One form of association not commonly incorporated into question answering systems is a relational link which involves a kernel sentence or proposition instead of a word concept. Such kernels are indicated by the bracketing in the sentences below:

John believes that (his mother hates him).

The fact that (evil and injustice abound in the world) leads me to believe that (a just God cannot exist).

Weinrich (in Greenberg, 1963) refers to this form of association as *nesting* and Abelson and Carrol (1965) have incorporated this form of association into their simulations of individual belief systems. In addition to increased complexity of memory structure, such sentences pose some problems for the incorporation of new informations into the system. Greater objectivity and fewer internal contradictions can be obtained by organizing information under nodes corresponding to the sources but the increased complexity of memory will probably cause some problems in retrieval and some duplication of information in memory if several sources say the same thing (though this could be avoided by some sort of memory search and storing a statement of equivalence of belief if one is found). If we wish to incorporate such information into the memory structure without coding by source (in addition to or instead of coding by source), we would probably want to code the credibility of the information by the credibility of the source or change both the credibility or other attitudes towards both the information and the source so they are more nearly like each other as Osgood and Tannenbaum (1955) and Abelson and Carrol (1965) suggest. Such features are obviously desirable to the degree that we wish to simulate or emulate human performance.

One deliberate omission in this paper is an extended discussion of how the question answering system would report back the information retrieved. In their present forms, the question answering systems referred to above will report back a string of properties or a simple relational phrase, or in some systems, simple sentences generated from these elements. In general, future systems can be expected to retrieve linked kernels of properties or relational phrases and, in reporting this output to the user, these kernels will be embedded in some suitable grammatical frame. This system will probably differ considerably from the system of modern generative grammars (e.g., Chomsky, 1965) in that semantics would be introduced at the highest level of the generative process, a plausible assumption for humans also.

The Quillian system may seem at fault as it is presented here since the structural form of storage is somewhat arbitrary and some variations in this form are clearly possible. However, it will probably result that alternate forms of storage will result in inability or difficulty in answering certain types of questions and that these difficulties will increase with the degree to which all possible links are not formed. This feature makes the Quillian memory structure especially attractive as a model for human long term memory since these alternative forms of storage may be useful in the analysis of errors in answering questions and perhaps such aspects of cognitive style as "category width." Quite obviously, the model would have to be extended to deal with such questions and with the fact that some forms of organization of information into sentences in books or lectures are apparently more effective than others—the subject of the experiments reported in the last section of this paper. Finally, it should be appreciated that the Quillian model describes only the final result of learning and says nothing about how this learning occurs or how the capacities to develop such structures are themselves developed—a subject which should be of considerable interest to the Piagetian.

Another inadequately considered property of a Quillian system is the importance of the rate of activation of linked nodes in the structure relative to the duration of activation. If a memory structure is entered from two nodes in question answering, it is doubtful that the to-be doubly activated node containing the answer will be reached at exactly the same instant so that some persistence of activation is required to permit double activation through paths of different length. Hence the rate of activation relative to duration will determine the range of different path lengths possible for double activations. Too low a relative rate can result in a considerable restriction of associational diversity as is described by Rimland (1964, esp. Chapter 9) for infantile autism. Too high a relative rate could result in an excess of associations such as has been attributed to schizophrenics by Rimland. The effects of the psychedelic drugs such as LSD and Rimland's treatment of memory could be considered in terms of such a parameter. Proponents of "creativity" might argue for a high rate (e.g., Guilford's divergent thinking, Guilford, 1967) but such diversity might require some sort of "editor" to be built into the system.

The above limitations of the Quillian system are probably reflections of its current relatively recent development but there are other limitations which may be more serious. One is that all concepts are defined in terms of relations to other concepts but that none are related to the elementary sensory-perceptual features (e.g., size, shape, color) which are so beloved by students of "concept formation". While sensory primitives probably don't play an entirely basic role in conceptual behavior in the sense that all concepts can be defined, eventually, as logical equations of primitives (a perhaps debatable point), some recognition of their special status should be made. If such students' account of concept formation is to be taken literally, conceptual structure would consist of strings of elementary features joined by logical connectives with the name of the concept as the name of the list and, perhaps, serving as an elementary feature for a "higher" concept. This structure would be much like the hierarchical list structure described above and would share its limitations. This view would also imply that all concepts could be eventually defined as logical operations on primitives obtained through substitution for the definition for non-primitive concepts. Such a view ignores the importance of relational associations between concepts as in Quillian's model.

Another possible defect is the lack of semantic distinctive features[6] (Katz and Postal, 1964, and Osgood, in Dixon and Horton, 1968) which would permit the economical description of some subsets of words in terms of values of vectors of shared characteristics. Also, the use of such features could be used to reduce the number of type nodes since alternative word meanings are often analogic extensions of some common "core". For example, the meaning of *air* in "to air a blanket" and in "to air a grievance" appear somewhat similar. Similar considerations apply to metaphor.

Before concluding this section, it would be well to discuss some phenomena from the field of verbal learning which are of interest in connection with the views on structural memory organization in this paper. First, there is the phenomenon of clustering in "free recall" which has been interpreted as implying a hierarchical form of memory organization (Mandler, in Dixon and Horton, 1968) which would be used to generate the words in the string to be learned much as in a context-free phrase structure grammar.[7] Second, there is the important effect of context on word associations (see Pollio, in Dixon and Horton, 1968) which is quite compatible with the Quillian model and which should imply the futility of attempting to represent a word as a point in some multi-dimensional space independent of verbal context.[8] Finally, there are the measures of "associative strength" of

Pollio (1964) and Nobel (1952) which would be rough measures of the centrality of words in a network such as Quillian's.

At this point, three somewhat radical proposals shall be made. The first is that extensive empirical comparisons of the Quillian model in its initial stages with human experimental data is probably not needed since its initial goal is to simply provide a form of memory organization that is capable of answering questions which are well within ordinary and familiar human capacities. If and when this is achieved (and it should be appreciated that Quillian has claimed less than the more visionary portions of this paper seem to imply), an obvious next step will be to develop systems containing such memories that can store information read in the form of sentences, answer questions by initiating intersecting paths of activity in its memory and asking questions to elicit information which might be required to complete these paths. Here, comparisons with human data would be useful. The second proposal is that the organizational structure of the information taken in (and organization here refers to that of an outline or summary of the information, not syntactic structure) will largely determine superordinate and subordinate nodes in the memory structure (and here superordinate refers to the richness of interconnection to other richly connected nodes) and hence a kind of conceptual bias in processing further information and in answering questions. It is worth noting that systems intended to simulate some forms of human cognition (Abelson and Carrol, 1965; Colby, 1965) such biases are more or less deliberately developed.[9] If they should accidentally develop[10] in a computer system not intended to simulate human performance (and hence lacking "defense" mechanisms) that input information which will result in a radical restructuring might be selected by "conceptual therapists"—a process similar to some conceptions of psychotherapy and the effects of psychedelic drugs. The third proposal is that at least some of the characteristics of generative grammars (Chomsky, 1963) might be derivable from the structure of long term memory and that some additional constraints not recognized in such grammars, such as the limited number of embedded constructions ordinarily generated and the greater frequency of right branching constructions (Miller, 1962), might be derivable from the structure of short and long term memory. Also, the claims for linguistic "universals" (Greenberg, 1963) and innate forms of linguistic "competence" (Chomsky, 1965) could well be considered in this light.

In closing this section, one of the most important implications of the Quillian model should be noted—its use of contextual dependencies. Since the meaning of a word at the level of the type nodes, and possibly token nodes in extensions of the model, depend on the other token planes which are excited in near temporal contiguity. Such contextual dependencies in coding are one of the most pervasive features of human language and may be found even at the level of the phonetic coding of the phoneme (Liberman, et al., 1967).[11] While context free grammars are very common in computers (e.g., most rewriting rules of compilers), contextual dependencies seem generally important in the information processing of animal brains (Pribram, 1963 and this Conference). This constitutes an important difference between the brain and the usual form of digital computer which shall be discussed in the next section.

SOME NEUROPHYSIOLOGICAL SPECULATIONS

The three forms of memory organization considered above each require a form of associational structure differing considerably from our usual concepts of $S - R$ associations in behavior, of synaptic associations in nerve nets, and of numerically addressed contents of a computer memory. The computer or the brain, of course, does not incorporate the pictures which are given in Figures 1 and 2 but the nodes in these figures can be interpreted as some kind of locus, and the arrows indicate some sort of associational link to another node (although the bidirectional arrows labelled *inv.* for the pairs of relational terms have a somewhat special status in that they indicate a correspondence). Before proceeding to the neurophysiological speculations, we shall examine the kind of associational links in list structures in computer memories. In figure 3(a) the word structure for the list processing language LISP is shown (Woodward, 1966). The most important feature of this word structure is that there are associational links to the next word down and the next word to the left[12] and that the selection of the next word is under the control of some executive program. The link to *nil* means that there are no further words in the string while the link to *etc.* means there are links to other words not in the figure. The representation of a matrix structure is given in figure 3(b). To enter this matrix, the address of the head of the row and column string would be obtained from the label of the row and column (not shown) and to find the contents of a cell of a particular row and column, the contents of the row and column strings would be compared by the executive processor until words with the same contents are found—i.e., the single word intersection of the row and column.[13] In Figure 3(c) a hierarchical structure is made up from LISP words. Here, the links to the left are to subsequent words in the list and the links down

```
                    ┌─────────┬────────┬─────────┐
                    │ADDRESS OF│        │ADDRESS OF│
            (a)     │NEXT WORD │CONTENTS│NEXT WORD │──▶
                    │DOWN      │        │LEFT      │
                    └─────────┴────────┴─────────┘
                                  │
                                  ▼
                    WORD STRUCTURE IN LISP
```

(b) [2 × 3 matrix of linked LISP word structures]

2 × 3 MATRIX STRUCTURE OF LISP WORDS

(c) [Hierarchical tree: ANIMAL → NIL; REPTILE → MAMMALS → ETC.; CANINES → FELINES; SNAKES → LIZZARDS → ETC.]

REPRESENTATION OF A HIERARCHICAL
STRUCTURE OF LISP WORDS

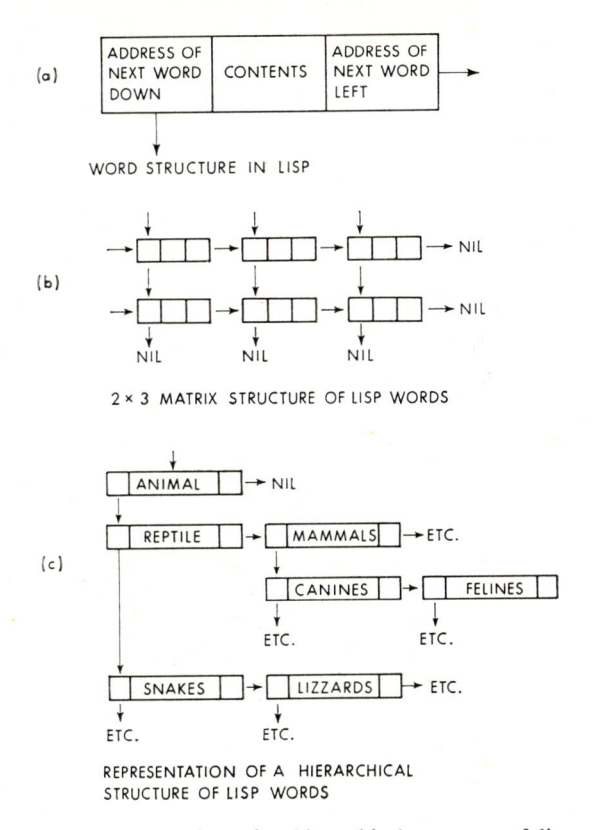

FIGURE 3 Representation of a hierarchical structure of lisp words

are to the first word in the list whose name is the contents of the higher word (e.g., *reptile* is the name of the list *snakes, lizards*, etc.). To search this list, the executive processor would either have to "know" the location of the desired item or examine the contents of all words below the lowest order node which is known to contain the information. This kind of search could be somewhat difficult since a completely unguided search would require some sort of "backing up" the structure to examine yet unexplored branches.

If we examine the Quillian type structures in Figures 1 and 2, neglecting the *and* (∩) and *or* (∪) links which will be treated as unitary nodes for now and the *inv.* links which have a special status (noted above), no token node has more than two links out to other nodes in the plane plus an additional link to the corresponding type node. Thus, the token nodes could be represented by word structures like those in Figure 3(a) with one additional address. The type nodes would constitute a special problem since the type node of a dictionary entry could have up to, say, 20 or more links to the type nodes of the alternative meanings but nodes of the alternative meanings would need up to several hundred links to corresponding tokan nodes in other planes in addition to the link into its own plane.

While the structures required by a Quillian type memory seem not especially difficult to represent in a computer with appropriate list processing software, they do seem to pose some problems for the nervous system. If we assume that each token node corresponding to a distinctive word meaning corresponds to a specific locus or a chain of interconnected loci, the nervous system would have to have the capability of establishing links to arbitrarily specified loci (from the standpoint of neural geometry)[14] without interfering with intervening loci. Perhaps, Landauer's hypothesis (1964) concerning the function of chemical structures in the cortex as tuned resonators which can selectively contact other suitably tuned structures could explain how this might be achieved by the cortex.

Frequency coded associational links on the cortex would also permit a kind of memory search implied by the Quillian model which is quite difficult for the computer with a single central processing unit. A search of memory initiated from two or more type nodes would require that branches from nodes be explored and compared, as would be the case of the hierarchical list structure, and, unless the processor somehow "knows" in which "directions" an intersection would be found, there would be no choice other than conducting a very long and exhaustive search. However, a brain with frequency coded associational links could, in effect, carry out parallel processing since the frequencies produced could be continued until an intersection is found or until they elicit other frequencies from intervening nodes in the path until an intersection is found.[15] (In this connection, the discussion above of the rate of activation relative to that of propagation should be kept in mind.) This, again, brings us back to the very strong role that contextual dependencies play in human information processing in comparison to the computer.

Conceptual Organization beyond the Sentence

In linguistic theory of grammatical or syntactic structure the sentence is regarded as the most complex level of organization and, aside from such phenomena as tense agreement and pronoun referents, there is little recognition of structural units beyond the sentence. To be sure, syntactic theory to date has largely avoided semantics (for probably good reasons) and it seems difficult to define the structure of a paragraph without some sort of semantic considerations and the division of sentences into paragraphs is somewhat arbitrary just as the decision to express kernel propositions in one or several sentences is arbitrary. However, the importance of semantic structure beyond the sentence is indicated by such phenomena as tables of contents, headings of sections and the topic outlines which some participants in these meetings used to complete their initial incomplete drafts. Such structures can be regarded as having a function like the non-terminal symbols in a grammar from which the terminal symbols can be derived by the rewriting rules (Chomsky, 1963).

It is possible that Quillian type structure might hold for such organization but a hierarchical list structure organization be approximated. These kinds of structures are a meeting ground between psycholinguistics and the cognitive structures or belief systems so frequently discussed by educational, social and clinical psychologists and which have been simulated by Abelson and Carrol (1965), Colby (1965) and Colby and Gilbert (1964). Since further knowledge of the nature of such structures will probably result from psycholinguistic research, it seems more appropriate to introduce two such experiments at this point rather than to propose or advocate such research. The first experiment is concerned with the effects of context of questions asked on question answering performance and was intended to determine the effects of question asking on retrieval. The second experiment is concerned with the effects of sentence order on memorization and of transfer of training from one type of order to another. Both are concerned with the effects of structure beyond the sentence and neither was intended as a test of the Quillian model. However, an effect of question context on performance in recall was obtained in the first experiment which implies that question context has an activation effect on retrieval processes much like that described in the discussion above of information retrieval from the Quillian memory.

In the first experiment, sentences describing the geological history of Uranium deposits and the changing concepts of mental illness were alternated in order of the dates of the events described (some of which were altered to fit the pattern). The second to the sixth of the 14 sentences used will illustrate this pattern.

200 million years ago a great inland sea covered almost the whole of the southwest U.S.

The plight of the mentally ill during primitive times was one of brutality and persecution, a plight which continued into more civilized times.

In 12,000 B.C., the land beneath the great sea slowly rose and the waters receded leaving behind them vast salt beds beyond which were the highlands.

The ancient learned men (150 B.C.) thought that mental disease was due to being perverse, wicked and possessed of the devil.

In 950 A.D. hot solutions were bubbling up from deep within the earth's crust—solutions bearing Uranium and other metals.

Two sets of 14 multiple choice questions (five alternatives) were used consisting of eight common items and six questions which were either Temporal (T) or Causal (C). The Temporal questions asked for information about what happened on a particular date as in the two examples below.

What does the year 1489 make you think of?

1793 is an important date. What happened then?

The Causal questions could be answered from information in separate sentences on the same topic which were always separated by a sentence about the outer topic. Two examples are given below.

What succeeded the noticing of uranium traces in the river beds?

Was Pinel's work continued? Who, if anyone, continued his work?

If the sentences were entered into a memory structure in the order in which they were given, we would expect that a date would be an effective entering node for information retrieval. However, if the sentences are entered into a relational structure, we would expect that the Causal questions would be more easily answered.

The T (temporal) set of questions contained six temporal questions unique to that set and the C (Causal) set contained six unique causal questions. In addition, both sets contained two T questions and two C questions which were common to both so that 8 out of the 14 questions in the C set were of the C type and eight out of the 14 T set questions were T type. In addition, both sets contained two common *Intra* questions which could be answered from information within single sentences and, hence, should be less affected by the organizational mode of the information given or the other questions. Finally, each set contained two *Control* questions which were unanswerable from the information given which were used to establish a base rate for the "don't remember" alternative (common to all questions) and for guessing. Thus, the T questions contained six T questions unique to that set, two T questions also in the C set (for a total of eight T questions), and six additional questions in common with the C set, two of which were C questions, two of which were *Intra* questions and two of which were *Control* questions. The contents of the C set consisted of six unique C questions and the eight questions shared with the T set.

A majority of the questions (eight out of 14) were of the type corresponding to the set label while the three remaining types were represented by two questions each. Thus, the question sets seemed potentially capable of inducing a different "set" during recall (an assumption supported by the data) while the eight questions shared by the two sets provided a common basis for comparison of performance under the different "sets" induced by the two question sets.

The T and C questions were each administered twice to the S's by projecting them one at a time on a screen for 18 seconds. The five response alternatives (but not the questions) were on forms given the S's. Four different orders of presentation were used, $TTCC$, $CCTT$, $TCCT$ and $CTTC$, with groups of 19, 21, 24 and 22 S's respectively. The set of sentences was played twice on a tape recorder before the first and third presentation so that the $TTCC$ and $CCTT$ groups received homogeneous sets of questions before the sentences were repeated while the $TCCT$ and $CTTC$ groups received heterogeneous question sets. By not repeating the sentences before the second and fourth question sets it is possible to determine the effect of asking the questions alone on subsequent retrieval.

The means of the number of questions correctly answered associated with statistically significant effects are given in Tables I and II. Table I contains the mean number of C type questions correctly answered in the C set and T type questions answered in the T set (a maximum of eight) in both cases). The difference between question types was significant at

TABLE I Mean No.'s of Correct Answers, to C Questions in C Sets and T Questions in T Sets Associated with Significant Effects

	\multicolumn{3}{c}{Order}	
Type	1st	2nd	Mean
C	3.9	4.4	4.2
T	3.2	3.2	3.2
Mean	3.5	3.8	

the 0.1% level, the differences between first and second presentations at the 0.5% level and the interaction at the 2.5% level but inspection of this table indicates that improvement from the first to the second presentation is confined to the C questions. Thus, Table I indicates that performance on the C questions was superior to that on the T questions, which is not especially surprising, and that performance on the C questions improved on the second presentation while that for the T questions did not.

The frequencies correct for the eight questions common to each set were analyzed separately for each question type (*T, C, Intra* and *Control*) and the means associated with significant effects are presented in Table II. Two main effects involving differences between groups were found for the *C* and

TABLE II   Mean No.'s of Correct Answers (out of 2) for Common Questions Associated with Significant Effects

(a)

Question Type	TTCC	CCTT	TCCT	CTTC
C	0.8	1.2	1.3	1.1
Intra	0.9	0.8	1.3	1.3

(b)

Question Type	Question Set C	Question Set T
C	1.2	1.0
T	1.7	0.9

(c)

Question Set	C, C_1	C, C_2	C, T_1	C, T_2	T, C_1	T, C_2	T, T_1	T, T_2
Group TTCC	0.8	0.8	0.7	0.8	1.7	1.8	0.8	1.0
CCTT	1.3	1.3	1.1	1.1	1.3	1.6	0.8	0.8
TCCT	1.4	1.4	1.1	1.2	1.7	1.8	0.8	0.9
CTTC	1.2	1.0	1.0	1.2	1.7	1.8	0.9	0.8
Mean	1.2		1.0		1.7		0.9	

Intra questions (significant at the 2.5% level in both cases) which are presented in Table II(a). The relatively inferior performance of the *TTCC* group for the *C* questions might be attributed to the fact that the *C* question sets were presented for the first time with this group only after the sentences were presented for the second time so that the *S*'s might be assumed to be using a causal conceptual framework less well. The relatively better performance of the *S*'s in the *TCCT* and *CTTC* groups for the *Intra* questions could seem due to the heterogeneity of the question types between the first and second repetitions of the sentences which might lead to a conceptual organization which is not exclusively causal or temporal. However, this is most likely due to sampling error since the performance of the *TCCT* and *TTCC* groups and the *CTTC* and *CCTT* groups on the first question set should have been equivalent since each pair had not been treated differently up to that point while, in fact, differences were essentially the same as in Table II(a).

The most interesting effects found were for the differences in performance in the *C* and *T* sets for the common *C* (2.5% level) and *T* (0.1% level) questions shown in Table II(b). Both types of questions were answered more effectively in the context of the *C* set but it is remarkable that the *T* questions are answered correctly more often than the *C* questions when presented in a context of predominantly *C* questions. This effect occurred quite uniformly and without noticeable (or any significant) interaction effects for all four groups as is easily seen in Table II(c) with the possible exception being the slightly lower mean of 1.3 for the *T* questions with the *CCTT* group in the first *C* set. The performance of the *CCTT* group is the most interesting of all since the decrement in performance on the common *T* questions in the *T* set followed better performance previously on the same questions in the *C* set and two further repetitions of the sentences. This result implies that it is not simply the organization of information in memory which leads to ability to answer questions but that the organization of information which is activated by the question context which is effective as well and that the activation produced by a "superior" context (*C* questions) can produce better performance on "inferior" questions (*T* type). This result seems quite compatible with the Quillian memory model and it might be hypothesized that the *T* questions activated but one critical node in addition to those activiated by the previous *C* questions so that search involved less competition between intersecting paths than the two or more nodes activated by the *C* questions. An experiment which is deliberately designed to test such hypotheses in which question order and timing are controlled and where response latencies are obtained is required to more exactly test this hypothesis.

One final significantly insignificant result is that no significant effects were found for the *Control* questions which means that differences in performance cannot be attributed to differences in guessing rates. The "don't remember" alternative for these questions was chosen at an average rate of 1.8 out of 2 times which means that the "false positive" rate per question was only 0.1.

In the second experiment, which was part of the M.Sc. thesis research of Mr. Ralph Sasson, the *S*'s were played a group of sentences twice on a tape recorder before each of eight trials and on each trial, they were asked to anticipate the next sentence before it was projected on a screen. As before, the sentences concerned two different themes, the history of the concepts of mental illness and of light, and the same set of sentences were given in two different orders. In the Temporal (*T*) order the sentences were arranged in order of the date of the event and alternated in theme while in the Causal (*C*) order, the sentences were arranged into two groups according to theme and secondarily arranged in chronological order. The *TC* group received four trials on the Temporal order followed by four trials on the Causal order while the *CT* group received the opposite order of trials. There were two control groups, *IC* and *IT*, who received four trials on an irrelevant group of sentences (*I*) whose theme was unrelated to either theme in the other sentences, followed by four trials of either the Temporal or Causal order. The repetitions of the *S*'s were scored by counting the number of correctly repeated phrases (with synonyms and reversals of adjective orders being accepted as correct) and the percentages of correct repetitions are given in Figure 4.[16] (The performances of the *IC* and *IT* groups on the *I* sentences on the first four trials were almost identical and are omitted from this graph because they are not especially informative.)

In comparison with the performance of the *TC* and *CT* groups on the

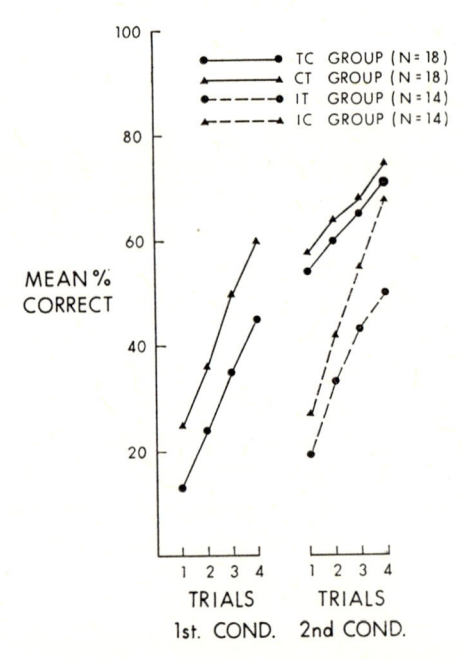

FIGURE 4   % correct repetition of phrases

first four trials, the *IC* and *IT* groups' performance on the last four trials is slightly elevated but no significant difference was found in the statistical analysis. Of greater interest is the better performance of the *IC* and *CT* groups with the Causal order in comparison of that of the *IT* and *TC* groups with the Temporal order (effect significant at 0.1% level) which agrees with the results of the first experiment. Perhaps of greatest interest is the fact that the performance of the *CT* group remains essentially the same as the *TC* group following the change in condition (no significant difference) which implies that the learning of material with a "superior" organizational structure will facilitate the further learning of the same material with another structure.

Together, these experiments imply that a relational structure, when "activated" by suitable questions or prior context, will result in superior recall in comparison to structures which order information in terms of a (perhaps arbitrary) property such as the temporal order of the events. However, the first experiment shows that relational structures can be extracted from a temporal ordering and the second shows that ordering in terms of a property can be facilitated if a relational ordering is established first. The primacy of the relational ordering may be a result of past training but the Quillian model implies that it can lead to superior recall since causal questions, at least, will initiate activity at two nodes "close" to the answer while the temporal questions will initiate activity at but one. However, the later property may have lead to superior recall in a context of causal questions in the first experiment.

The fact that sequences of sentences can have an organizational structure is not especially surprising—after all, a random permutation of sentences of "connected" discourse (pronoun correspondences and tense agreements aside) would not be especially intelligible and the inexperienced writer is often advised to make this structure manifest by preparing an outline of what he is preparing to write. As was mentioned before, such an outline is like the non-terminal symbols of generative grammars (Chomsky, 1963) which are rewritten into the final string of sentences (i.e., the terminal symbols) by the rules of the grammar. This process has built-in semantic constraints which will prevent the generation of some sentences which are "anomalous" in the sense that they are outside the conceptual system associated with the memory structure.[17] The examination of points of uncertainty in the serial recall of sentences, much as Johnson (in Dixon and Horton, 1967) examined points of uncertainty in recall of words within sentences, may shed considerable light on this generative process. Research into the details of conceptual structure may well lead to a new area of cognitive psychology which might be called "verbal learning" or, perhaps, "educational psychology."

Some Final Remarks

Again, it should be pointed out that the area of concern of this paper is almost entirely with verbal knowledge. The relations of the kind of structures considered in this paper to the various sensory-perceptual "primitives," such as color and shape, were mentioned briefly and it should be evident that such entities would be regarded as embedded in the conceptual structure rather than as its foundation.

Another point which has been neglected are the motivational and emotive aspects of cognition which have been discussed by Pribram (1963, 1967 and in this Conference). Finally, some recognition should be made of those who are concerned with knowing as an "experience." The seemingly "mechanistic" treatment of knowledge in this paper is not due to a rejection of the reality of "experience" so much as to the author's "conceptual bias" which leads him to feel that he doesn't have very much that is useful to say about this aspect of "knowing."

SUMMARY AND CONCLUSION

Question answering requires that information not merely be stored but that it be stored in a form which permits retrieval for a variety of input contexts. A multidimensional matrix form of organization has been adopted for some descriptions of meaning by psychologists and this form has the advantage of providing multiple entry points. However, it was rejected as unsuitable on the grounds that the dimensions of classification of information can differ considerably with context (e.g. the semantic distinctive features of rocks have little in common with those of graduate students) so that most cells in a matrix classification of information would be devoted to non-existent entities (e.g. intelligent, red haired apple trees). A hierarchical list structure was considered in which each entity was defined or described in terms of a list of entities. This is consistent with the implicit definition of a concept in psychological studies of concept formation in which subjects learn the definition of "concepts" in terms of a string of properties joined by logical connectives (e.g. the GAX category contains non-red and triangular or square objects). Such systems do provide for differences in the composition of subordinate classes dependent on the superordinate class so non-existent classes are avoided but such systems are rather inflexible in practice since information can be reached through a route consisting of one particular order of superordinate categories and may not be available easily if that route is not known (e.g. it would be difficult to obtain case histories of patients with a rare disease from hospital records arranged by patient name unless there was a list of the patients with that disease). Finally, a form of memory organization for semantic concepts developed by Quillian was considered which consists of interconnected nodes with directed associational links between nodes (i.e. a directed graph structure). Retrieval in this system consists of initiating activation of a string of nodes at two or more points and with the retrieved information lying at the intersection of the lines of activation. This system seems to offer the best available representation of a memory system for question answering since it provides for multiple entry points (unlike the hierarchical list structure) and does not represent non-existent entities (unlike the multidimensional matrix).

The Quillian memory also seems appropriate for the representation of belief systems in which the objects of belief are names of concepts and since the concepts themselves are defined in terms of propositional relations similar in structure to beliefs. Finally, the role of conceptual organization of sets of sentences was considered and two experiments were described, one of which showed an effect of the organization of a set of sentences on learning and another which showed effects of the form and the context of questions on information retrieval.

NOTES

1. This example is essentially similar to a program written for the author's course in artificial intelligence by Michael J. Grohn. This form of memory organization is also used by several of the systems described in the first part of a review paper by Simmons (1965).
2. Actually, as a later section of this paper demonstrates, a list structure representation is compatible with all three forms of memory organization described in this paper. The concept is introduced here because list structures are particularly well suited to represent hierarchical tree-like classification systems.
3. The definitions used were taken from the Webster's Seventh New Collegiate Dictionary (1967). The notation used is a considerable modification of Quillian's, but since Earl Hunt (personal communication) has said that the notation has been changed from last published accounts (Quillian, 1967a and b) and since the system is still very much in a developmental stage, such liberties don't seem very reprehensible.
4. This pairing of relational terms in a kind of inverse relation was suggested by Simmons et al. (in AFIPS, 1966) in a somewhat different form.
5. Quillian evidently recognizes this point also and the vagueness in coding of *include* and *contain* in figure 1 is not representative of his work. Rather, it was done deliberately to make this point and the subsequent one about synonymity.

6. Semantic distinctive features correspond to the distinctive features of phonemes (Jacobson, *et al.*, 1952) which, roughly are perceived characteristics of speech sound which, in various combinations, can specify the categories of speech sounds which are associated with differences in meaning within a language system (i.e. the phonemes). While not all combinations are present or even possible, it is possible to code the phonemes of a language in terms of considerably smaller number of characteristics. Katz and Postal's (1964) proposed extension of this coding to semantic features does not provide any very clear method of identifying such features and it is possible that some psychological scaling techniques might aid intuition in this effort. One criteria used in the identification of phonemic distinctive features is that a *minimal contrast* which requires that a proposed distinctive feature be the sole difference between at least one pair of phoneme categories. Word pairs regarded as being in "opposition" such as man-woman or man-boy might be regarded as being in minimal contrast—i.e. differing in but one semantic distinctive feature. Also, it is worth noting the bipolar factors found by Deese (1965) in his factor analyses of measures of word association similarities could be regarded as semantic distinctive features.

7. The names of the higher order levels in the hierarchy would correspond to the nonterminal symbols in the grammar which would be 'rewritten' as the list names—a process which would continue until the lowest order elements are generated. This process was erroneously referred to by the author as a context dependent grammar in an earlier publication (Wilson, 1968). Also, see footnote 11 of this paper.

8. The congruity principle of Osgood and Tannenbaum (1955) and Cliff's (1959) finding that adverbs can be regarded as "multipliers" of the lengths of adjective vectors might be regarded as effective counterarguments to this position since they indicate that formulation of workable laws for the prediction of vectors of word combinations as functions of vectors of individual words. However, there still remains the fact that words very often have multiple meanings which are dependent on context and that judgments of words which results in a point representation in space can be misleadingly precise without specification of context (or knowledge of the context supplied by the subjects).

9. Such biases result from an attempt to make certain that "central" beliefs or propositions—e.g. "I love my father.," "America is always good"—are not contradicted or substantially modified. The prevalance of such phenomena is too great to require documentation and it is significant here because it implies some tendency towards logical consistency of a sort within the memory system. Such tendencies constitute an important subject of study for modern social psychology.

10. One way this could develop would be through the processing of contexts involving word distinctions not embodied in the dictionary like portions of memory. For example, if the system were to process extensive psychoanalytic material there may be some strange things done with phases including the word *dynamics* in a physical science context.

11. This distinction is an important part of the theory of formal grammars (Chomsky, 1963). In a context free grammar, the permissible substitutions (i.e. recodings) of a symbol do not depend on any other part of the sequence while such dependencies to be found on context dependent grammars.

12. The choice of the terms *down* and *left* is quite arbitrary and was made to conform to the structure of figure 3(c).

13. This is not usually the best method of locating a matrix element in a computer memory and is given here only to demonstrate that the matrix can be represented as a list structure. Also, it should be evident that more links with the words would be needed for more than two dimensional matrices.
14. While early information that is related might be stored in spatially adjacent loci, the diversity of (some) adult experience is such that it seems doubtful that this could continue indefinitely.
15. One attractive feature of frequency coding is that wave form of the excitation pattern could contain several frequency components and that a specific functional locus could be sensitive to any one of several frequency components or to a combination of components.
16. The data for this experiment have also not been completely analyzed. In particular, the attempted identification of structure through points of relative uncertainty in recall suggested later in this paper has not been done.
17. This may be the only sense in which the Whorf hypothesis about the relation of culture to language "structure" might be true.

COMMENTS ON PROFESSOR WILSON'S PAPER

William W. Rozeboom

I am delighted by this opportunity to root around in Wilson's pea patch, for the formal properties of his memory model illustrate why information-processing, cybernetic, systems-theoretical or computer-oriented approaches to psychology—call these "automatistic" theories for short—are both my joy and my despair.

The brief history of automatistic psychology nicely demonstrates how a movement founded on naivete, bad metaphor, and word magic can nonetheless evolve into a powerful and legitimate force within its discipline. First came post-war advances in control-systems engineering (notably, signal transmission and computer theories) which, needing verbal labels for new technical concepts, expropriated commonsense cognition talk for this purpose. The resulting mechanistic marvel with its spray-on cognitive complexion was promptly embraced by psychonomically frustrated onlookers as the Lochinvar who could at last breach the mind's maidenhead to inner mysteries, and from this seduction was born automatistic psychology in the back alley of psychological science. Initially, automatistic theorizing was little more than a revelling in the licence to speak cognition words out loud once more, not knowing or caring whether this touched any substantive issue not already well-assimilated in other terms by the older behavioristic/associationistic traditions. By the late '50s, however, its awe-eyed panting after systems engineering to disclose the essence of human cognition was giving way to simulation programs built upon genuinely psychological if still ingenuously introspective hypotheses about problem-solving processes. Thereupon it found congenial companionship in the re-cognitization underway in most orthodox sectors of psychology, especially math models, concept formation and psycholinguistics, until today its concepts have become familiar throughout much of the psychological mainstream.

Automatistic theories have two major strengths. One is their emphasis on explanatory models that really work, i.e. which do in fact have the data implications ascribed to them, unlike so many past theoretic proposals especially in the S-R tradition. The other is their avid willingness to acknowledge the detailed complexity of inner events, both in diversity of process stages and nonlinearity of the functions by which one leads to another. (In retrospect, we can see how unbelievably empoverished—though in part deliberately so—orthodox behavioristic and associationistic theories have been in this regard.) But offsetting these virtues are two equally serious debilities. One is a strongly hypothetico-deductive[1] outlook which takes the main automatistic goal to be creation of computer programs (or programmable models) simulating commonsense human competences with indifference to whether organic systems work in at all the same way. Even worse—because it is more insidious—is that while the intended scope of automata theory includes all reactive systems, organic as well as artificial, its past development has been massively preoccupied with computer programming, thus restricting its repertoire of technical concepts largely to structures and functions practical for computer engineering. Consequently, if neural action has a fundamentally different organization from the unit-by-unit discrete serial activation schematized by flow diagrams—as we have good reason to suspect—it is a moot question whether the basic formal properties of higher organisms can be effectively captured by current styles of automatistic thinking. For automatistic theories to make the serious psychological contributions now within their grasp, they must learn how to conceive of system structure in terms dictated wholly by psychological considerations, unconstrained by the zeitgeist in computer-theoretic software. It is from the perspective of this latter point that I want to discuss automatistic models of memory.

The automatistic use of memory words, though often an outrage to this concept's cognitive core (cf. Rozeboom, 1965), nonetheless addresses an important general feature of adaptive systems likewise central to memory phenomena proper, namely, re-activation of processes in a system by stimuli which would be ineffective for this had not these processes or something like them been active in the system previously. More specifically, the matter at issue is "information storage and retrieval," for analysis of which we may usefully think of the organism's (system's) properties as being of two kinds, *states* and *process stages* (Rozeboom, 1965, p. 339 ff.). Process stages are those conditions of the organism which vary as a function of input and hence share the latter's moment-to-moment instability, notably sensations, ideation, and behavior—i.e., psychological *activities*. In contrast, an organism's state properties—habits, preferences, traits, and other dispositional attributes—are stable though by no means unchanging characteristics which are relatively independent of the organisms's momentary process condition. The organism's moment-to-moment process activity is governed by process laws whose parameters are set by the organism's state properties, while the latter in turn are determined by state laws whose independent variables generally include certain features of the organism's process history. (Thus in traditional association theory, how likely it is that arousal of idea x reminds a person of idea y is given by the strength of his $x \to y$ association, where the latter is a state property determined in part by his past frequency of thinking x and y jointly.) Idealistically speaking, moreover, once a process m becomes activated in a system s, it often occurs that s thereby acquires a state property μ whose presence subsequently enables m to be activated in s by process antecedents ("recall cues") not previously capable of this. In automatistic jargon, such an m is an item of "information," formation and retention of μ is "storage" of m, and subsequent re-activation of m through μ's agency is its "retrieval."

The problem most explicitly confronted by past theories of memory has been mechanisms for efficient storage and retrieval of information. Crucial to any such theory, however, is its implicit conception (scarcely ever examined critically) of what *logical kinds* of items are to be stored and retrieved. The Quillian-Wilson model makes an important advance in the latter respect, and I shall speak to this first.

Quillian (1967) and Wilson make clear that their model is specifically intended to handle *propositional* information, i.e. to store, retrieve, and make derivations from input in the form of declarative sentences. This would seem only natural for work on cognition were it not for the fact that virtually all past theories of psychological mechanism, traditional and automatistic alike, have treated process stages as unstructured aggregates of units lacking internal composition relevant to the system's function, so that a system's process condition at any given moment can be expressed by a simple list of *terms* naming which process elements are currently active. In contrast, processes which carry propositional information must be described by well-structured configurations of terms able to differentiate e.g. the process complex {*John loves Mary, John plays football*} from {*John loves John, Mary plays football*} even though the set of process elements is the same in both, namely {*football, John, loves, Mary, plays*}. Since Wilson does not detail how his model embodies and exploits this propositional structure at the process level (it should, for example, be able to extract {*a football player loves Mary*} from the first but not the second of the information complexes just mentioned), I cannot evaluate its success at this. From what I know of Quillian's version (wherein process structure is represented by a "tag" on each process element noting where in the state structure its activation came from), it should be possible to show that processing of propositions has important limitations in this model dues specifically to its psychonomically unnecessary flow-diagram construction (see below). Neither does the model make any provision for degrees of belief, much less for other dimensions of propositional attitude. But modern psychology has elsewhere recognized the propositional aspects of cognition in scarcely any way at all, and I cannot find it in my heart to fault a theory for not having attained mecca when it is struggling to get leg up on the highway thereto which most other pilgrims have never even thought to tread.

At first glance, information storage in the Quillian-Wilson model appears to be accomplished by a more-or-less orthodox associative structure whereby if the organism's state properties include an associative linkage from element x to element y, arousal of process x interacts with state property $x \rightarrow y$ to bring about activation of process y.[2] But Quillian-Wilson memory differs from true associationism in three fundamental respects. One is that the Q-W system does not form unmediated associations among all co-experienced process elements, but only those which reflect the grammatical structure of input sentences. Thus where classical association-theoretic principles imply that input of *John loves Mary* should produce the associative network

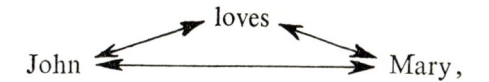

$$\text{John} \rightleftarrows \text{loves} \rightleftarrows \text{Mary},$$

Wilson's version of the Q-W model converts this into the state structure

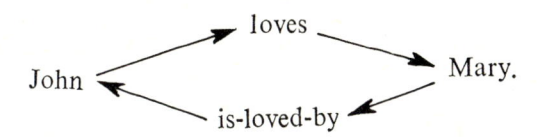

$$\text{John} \underset{\text{is-loved-by}}{\overset{\text{loves}}{\rightleftarrows}} \text{Mary}.$$

(Wilson does not say how his model manages to parse received sentences correctly, and to insert the verb's passive transformation, but it should not be difficult for an auxilliary input-processing routine to do this so long as the grammar of the input strings is carefully standardized. How such a routine differs from traditionally conjectured perceptual mechanisms, and in what respects humans might really work like this, is an instructive bit of analysis for another occasion.)

Secondly, the Q-W model contains no provision for generalization and graded arousal. Orthodox association theory draws heavily upon the principle that an association $x \rightarrow y$ will also interact with a process z to evoke y in strength which is an increasing function of z's similarity to x. In contrast, activation in the Q-W model is all-or-none, and z can directly arouse y

only if a z-node has been specifically linked to a y-node, regardless of how similar z may be to other processes linked directly to y.

The Q-W model's third critical departure from association-theoretic orthodoxy is that the elements coupled by activational linkages are not themselves process elements (or state surrogates thereof), but something else which might be called "containers" of process elements. Since this point touches upon the model's most basic structural properties, it is worth reproducing a portion of Wilson's Figure 1 (p. 368) augmented by additional information planes not made explicit there. For Wilson, the input information {*Air is a mixture of gasses, Birds fly in air, Humans breathe air*} is stored in a network something like Memory Structure *A*, in which the dotted arrows are between-plane connections which Wilson has added to Quillian's model. In this structure, *air* occurs in two token nodes and one type node; what "*air*" represents in the diagram is not itself joined to other process terms by association arrows, but is *carried by*, and can hence be common to more than one of, the entities ("nodes") which the arrows connect. In contrast, were process elements themselves to be the system's

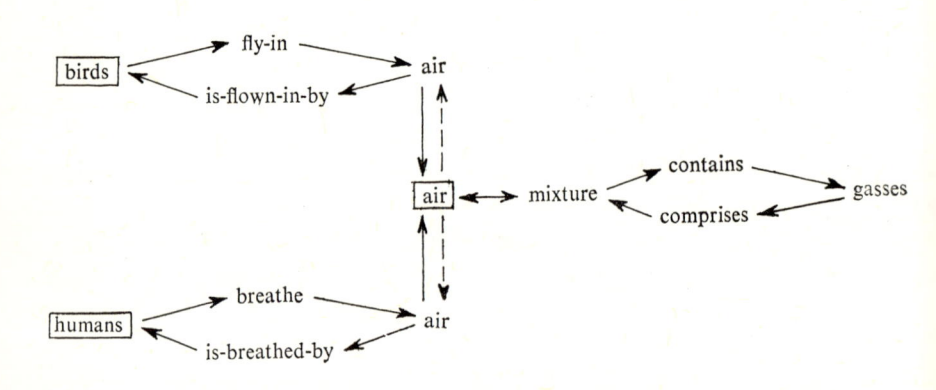

Memory Structure A

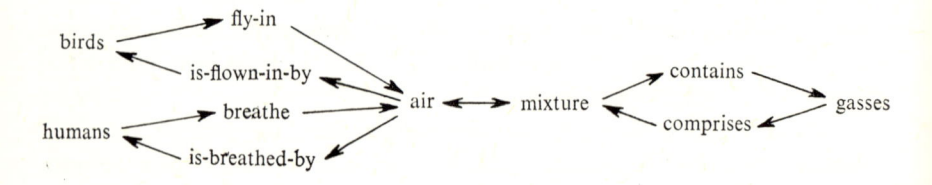

Memory Structure B

memory nodes, as is true of orthodox association theory, the state diagram most like *A* would be Memory Structure *B*. (There are no boxed nodes in *B* because the type/token distinction here lacks significance.)

What functional differences are there between structures *A* and *B*, and why should Quillian and Wilson have proposed the first rather than the second? Regarding the latter, *A* is the legacy of computer-oriented thinking. Programming concepts are understandably geared to the practicalities of computer hardware; and to date the latter require routing of activity from one *place* to another in the system, while each separate item of information is stored at a different location which must be reached before this item can be acted upon. As for the difference between structures *A* and *B*, this depends very much on whether Quillian's or Wilson's version of *A* is at issue. For Quillian (1967), the class of between-plane connections comprises only one-directional links from token nodes to type nodes with the same content (e.g., from *air* in the top and bottom planes of *A* to $\boxed{air}$ in the second), so that a plane can be entered only through its type node. Consequently, starting with activity in the top plane of *A*, Quillian can reach the information plane whose type node contains *air*, but cannot retrieve the non-typal information about *air* in the bottom plane. In contrast, because Wilson's between-plane links are bidirectional, any two planes tokening the same content *x* are mutually accessible through *x*'s type node; hence activation of a given plane *P* permits retrieval of all information stored elsewhere about all process elements tokened in *P*.

More generally, any two nodes which are *n* pulses of activation apart in structure *B* are at most *n* + 2 pulses apart in Wilson's version of struture *A*. While this still leaves some minor differences in formal potential between *B* and Wilson's *A*, we have insufficient detail about the intended functioning of the latter to tell whether *A* would be appreciably superior to *B* for this purpose. In short, then, Wilson has labored to make the location-addressable memory structure presupposed by automatistic theories yield content-addressable memory function. But *psychological* theories of memory have always assumed content addressability at the outset, without much hang-up over how this occurs in the organism. And if, as I am inclined to believe, the most pressing task for the psychology of memory is to learn more about the *functional* intricacies of recall (for only then will we know what our conjectured mechanisms are supposed to *do*), automatistic struggles to devise more efficient shuttle circuits for retrieving information scattered throughout a maze of locations are for psychology (*contra* computer theory) largely waste motion. I hasten to add, however, that the psychological relevance of such models would be greatly enhanced by careful comparative study of the formal differences among e.g. structure B and the two versions of A to lay bare what corresponding differences they entail for discernable memory phenomena which empirical psychology has not yet thought to research.

Another automatistic conceptual bias more likely to obscure than to illuminate the bases of organic behavior lies in the essentially *seriatim* character of computer operations. That is, computers still do only t things at a time, where t is seldom greater than unity. If Wilson's model concurs in this (unlike Quillian, he does not explicitly commit himself to it), then problems of selection arise whenever a type node is activated. For if the total memory structure contains n token nodes for process element x, each of which is linked bi-directionally with type node $\boxed{x}$, there are then $n + 1$ different exits from the latter. If only one of these exits can be followed at a time, is the choice made randomly or is there some logic of selection? Whichever exit is initially chosen, does activation immediately press onward from the new node thus reached, or are all exits from $\boxed{x}$ somehow scanned before action is propagated unconditionally; and if the latter, what determines the final choice? The technical points at issue here cannot be made clear without more detail about the model's intended functions and their manner of execution; but it is abstractly evident that if only a small fixed number of nodes can be activated at once, then the greater the average number of exits per node, the smaller should be the probability that the system will accomplish a given task within a specified period of time. For temporal efficiency, it should be possible for all exits from an activated node to be followed simultaneously, but I doubt that this is compatible with the Q-W model's projected routines for processing the information so activated.

Perhaps the best way to highlight the logical suppositions of automatistic views on storing and retrieving propositionally structured information is by contrast with the most natural psychonomic approach to this—"natural" in being an old intuition of classical psychology albeit one never well developed technically. This is the notion that activation of a process $R(x_1, ..., x_n)$, wherein elements $x_1, ..., x_n$ stand in relation R, strengthens a relatively permanent "memory trace" τ of $R(x_1, ..., x_n)$ given which the probability, intensity, and/or latency with which another process $S(y_1, ..., y_m)$ revives ("redintegrates") the structured complex $R(x_1, ..., x_n)$ is a function jointly of τ's strength and the extent to which $S(x_1, ..., x_m)$ resembles the process $R(y_1, ..., y_m)$ of which τ is the trace. (The detailed nature of this "resemblance" needs to be worked out by future research, but its primary determinants are presumably (a) the proportion of elements in $R(x_1, ..., x_n)$

and $S(y_1, ..., y_m)$ common to or, more weakly, similar in both, and (b) structural similarity whereby, e.g., $R(x_1, ..., x_n)$ is more similar to itself than it is to an elementwise identical process $R(x'_1, ..., x'_n)$ in which the x'_i are a permutation of the x_i.) At this level of the trace model's conception, an organism's memory state is characterized simply as a set $\{\tau_i\}$ of memory traces. Nothing is said about linkages or other relations among the τ_i because there is so far no work for between-trace connections to do (which of course in no way precludes later postulation of these if need arises). Moreover, nothing in the trace model's initial conception suggests that memory traces are differentially *accessible* to various recall cues. That is, the basic postulate concerning how an active process S interacts with a trace τ_i to revive the latter's process counterpart does not view this as dependent upon whatever additional traces are also present (though it is entirely open with respect to whether τ_i's strength is influenced by other traces). Hence in this first approximation to whatever more sophisticated version of the theory may eventually evolve, a given input S is conceived to operate upon all traces simultaneously, with a corresponding propensity to concurrent revival (in degrees respectively appropriate to the individual traces) of all processes from whose traces S can get any action. Finally, in light of this press to simultaneous arousal of indefinitely many processes, some principles of process concatenation are needed (e.g., formation of a composite by superimposition of constituents), the details of which again remain open for future research but wherein concepts of "competition," "summation," and others long exploited to this end in the verbal learning and behavior-theoretic literature may be expected to figure prominently.

I do not suggest any inherent incompatibility between trace theory and automatistic approaches to memory, for there is no reason why functional properties envisioned by the former cannot be reasonably well approximated by some ingeniously contrived computer-theoretic mechanism. My point is that those functions which are most basic in trace theory's initial conception are still alien to automatistic thinking and will undoubtedly remain so until automatistic models shed their conceptual dependency on computer programming or computers become designed around physical principles vastly different from their present "digital" construction. For now, the physical analogies most appropriate to trace theory are not switching circuits with all-or-none seriatim action and discrete channels of arousal established apart from the contents of their termini, but wave phenomena in which state structures are swept by a complex wavefield to which these resonate in degrees determined by the intensity of field components in or near the bands to which the resonators are tuned and whose joint emissions modulate the wavefield's character by cancellation and enhancement. To be sure, analogies are merely heuristic for scientific theory, and as memory research progresses we may well discover phenomena more readily modelled by switching circuits than by wave physics (or, more likely, not well modelled by either). But it would be unfortunate if the pre-packaged technical sophistication of contemporary computer programming were to occlude our access to those explanatory concepts which extrude most naturally from empirical work on memory phenomena.

NOTES

1. See Rozeboom, 1970, pp. 90ff., for arguments against hypothetico-deductivism as a proper mode of scientific inference.
2. More precisely, when x and y are process elements, what the terms "x" and "y" refer to in the associative concept "$x \to y$" are state surrogates of x and y in the way, e.g., the wiggles on a phonograph record are state surrogates of the acoustic processes they help activate. This distinction is a fine point which I will not try to keep verbally explicit here.

REJOINDER TO ROZEBOOM'S COMMENTS

Kellogg V. Wilson

AUTOMATA THEORY, COMPUTER SIMULATION AND PSYCHOLOGICAL THEORIZING

Rozeboom was evidently delighted by his "opportunity to root around in Wilson's pea patch" but, like the real life counterpart of his metaphor, his expedition does not strike me as being especially discriminating. In particular, he launches a very broad attack on computer simulation which, however, he concedes has progressed to "genuinely psychological ... hypotheses about problem solving processes." While he sees some virtues to these efforts, he seems preoccupied with the mode of approach rather than the ideas involved. A computer simulation program is a set of hypotheses and the use of computer simulation makes it possible to explore the consequences of the hypotheses and examine alternatives to a much fuller extent than is possible using mathematical or logical proof procedures. Hypotheses which lead to obviously contrary to fact consequences can be eliminated—a fact that Rozeboom concedes when he states such models "really work." Simmons (1970) has characterized work on question answering systems, like much of the scientific endeavor, as a search for a good paradigm and the Quillian model of memory was offered in my paper as a significant but not final step in that direction, particularly in comparison with the memory structures described earlier.

Before proceeding to defend the Quillian model, I would like to clarify a confusion arising from Rozeboom's unfortunate statement that "automata theory has been massively preoccupied with computer programming." Formal automata theory is an area which is quite distinct from computer technology or simulation and is not even so much a theory of computers as a theory of abstract computing entities, such as Turing machines, which are rarely ever constructed and which correspond to modern electronic computers in only a very abstract and general way. Automata theory, beginning with the work of Turing, predates effective modern computers by about 10 years and was and is still largely concerned with abstract and mathematical theoretical questions quite apart from technology. Arbib (1969) provides a comprehensive summary of the current state of automata theory. While much more can be said automata theory and its potential contributions to psychological theorizing, I shall not do so here since the contents of my paper are not closely related to automata theory.

In effect, Rozeboom implies that discussions of memory or other psychological phenomena in terms associated with computer simulation are prone to be misleading since they are based more on computer technology than on psychological hypotheses. However, the first form of memory organization discussed in my paper, the matrix structure was used by the psychologists Osgood and Deese and is a slightly more general form of the semantic distinctive features of the linguists Katz and Postal. While the matrix organization of memory was used in early computer question answering systems, it is certainly misleading to say this hypothesized form of memory stems from computer technology since the concept of the matrix has a history in mathematics and multivariate psychology (especially factor analysis) which considerably predates the advent of modern electronic computers. Similarly, the concept of the hierarchical list structure also has a considerable history independent of computer technology and I pointed out it has been used by Piaget. Also it is implicit in the definition of a concept, long used in concept formation experiments in psychology, as a logical function of more primitive concepts. Also, the list processing languages used to incorporate such structures in a computer memory (and which can be used with other structures as my paper indicates) were developed to carry out computer simulation of various problem solving and game playing processes which were based on psychological hypotheses. (See Ernst and Newall, 1969 and the various papers by Newall, Shaw and Simon in Feigenbaum and Feldman, 1963). The form of memory postulated by Quillian has been largely associated with computer simulation but it has an independent formal status as a directed ordered graph structure (Arbib, 1969, pp. 31–32) and it is worth noting that Quillian's work was part of a Ph.D thesis in Psychology and that his model has led directly to at least one psychological experiment (Collins and Quillian, 1969). The emphasis in my paper was on the form of memory organization, not on the source of the ideas, and I don't think any attitude other than openness to ideas regardless of their source and freeness of exchange between individuals in different areas will lead to any progress in the difficult problems associated with the analysis of human intellectual performance.

SERIAL VS. PARALLEL PROCESSING

Perhaps, the best defense against the accusation that Quillian's model is somehow limited by available computer technology is that retrieval in this form of memory is quite difficult to simulate on a conventional serial processing computer—a point emphasized in my paper and partially understood by Rozeboom who points out a computer "can do only t things at a time and t is seldom greater than unity." In retrieval, the memory network is entered from two or more nodes (ordinarily) and the information located is at the intersection of the multiple paths of activation from these nodes. This form of search is difficult to simulate on a serial processing computer since at each stage rapidly growing lists of activated nodes would have to be compared to determine if they have common members. Since an activated node activates all nodes to which it is connected (rather than some as Rozeboom assumes), efficient simulation in a reasonable amount of time requires parallel processing with interconnections between the processing units. Rozeboom is simply wrong when he states that "those functions which are most basic in trace theory's initial conception are still alien to automatistic thinking and will undoubtedly remain so until automatistic models shed their conceptual dependency on computer programming or computers become designed around physical principles vastly different from their present 'digital' construction." In fact, digital computers can approximate continuous functions quite accurately and automata theory already contains discussions of computers vastly different in principle from those existing today which have interconnected parallel processing modular units with self-organizing adaptive properties (Arbib, 1969, Chapter 10; Holland, 1968). I do not wish to claim that such automata are immediately useful as psychological models but they well may prove to be rich sources of ideas for such models and quite effectively refute the contention that automata theoretic conceptions are limited by computer technology. If we have the ideas for simulation before they are implemented on a computer (and this is generally the case for the better simulations), we shall avoid the pitfalls which Rozeboom describes.

SOME SPECIFIC POINTS

Before proceeding to Rozeboom's trace theory, I would like to discuss some points he raises in connection with Quillian's model and some points he should have raised in connection with inadequacies in my presentation.

1 PROCESSING OF SENTENCES, DEGREES OF BELIEF AND INFERENCE PROCESSES

My presentation was sketchy about the processes involved in the extraction of information from sentences. I felt that I was not prepared to solve all problems at once and that it is better to delineate the form of what is stored in memory before describing the processes of storage. Briefly and crudely, I think that each sentence is analyzed into one or more kernel propositions which are essentially like Chomsky's deep structures. However, I don't think this analysis proceeds from surface to deep structure by using the rules of generative grammars but that parsing is conceptually directed by the memory system, perhaps as activated by previous sentences (a *process* in Rozeboom's terms), and propositions extracted from sentences are stored in memory if they are plausible. Strictly syntactic processing of sentences like "Time flies like an arrow," lead to anomalous analyses consistent with the sentences, "You should time flies like you time an arrow," "You should time flies like an arrow times flies," and "The variety of flies called 'time flies' like an arrow," which are not consistent with our conventional beliefs. Also, we can process sentences or brief statements which are not strictly grammatical such as, "You hadn't better do that notime" and "Daddy, bye-bye" because they elicit appropriate conceptual structures. Thus, the sentence, or better, the sentence in context, elicits some preliminary understanding (which may be revised) prior to final analysis and storage and there may be some conscious deliberation and formulation of an interpretation of the sentence prior to storage. Such views are largely taken from the work of Schank *et al.* (1970; Schank and Tessler, in Walker and Norton, 1969). Since this analysis presumably proceeds with the aid of a conceptual system which is previously activated, we find that memorization of sentences proceeds better when sentences concerning related topics are contiguous as was demonstrated by the thesis research of Sasson described in my paper. Since the results of the processing of sentences rather then the details of surface structure are ordinarily stored, the semantic content of previously processed sentences is more accurately recognized after interviewing material than the particular version of surface structure previously encountered (Sachs, 1967).

Implicitly, at least, the acquisition of information is assumed to be on an all-or-none basis but it would be hard to distinguish between gradual acquisition and initial storage of sentences with a low degree or belief. The degree of belief attached to a sentence was not dealt with in my paper, as Rozeboom points out, but is dealt with in the papers by Abelson and Colby referred to in my paper and whose more recent work is described in papers by these authors in Walker and Norton (1969). One problem mentioned in my paper is the storage of contradictory sentences from different sources which may be stored with a modifying tag indicating the source or may somehow be combined.

Rozeboom seems to take the position that information is stored as "unstructured aggregates" and that structure and inference both arise from processes which operate on the unstructured state information. I agree that inference is a process but hold that it is directed by structure of memory states. The problem of inference is very lightly touched on in my paper. In terms of Rozeboom's example, if the propositions "Mary loves John" and "John is a football player" have been stored, the question "Does Mary love a football player?" would be answered in the affirmative since a link between "Mary" and "football player" would be found through the node of "John." Such inferences, of course, are fairly direct and Collins and Quillian (1969) have shown that human subjects take longer to answer questions like "Does a pigeon fly?" than "Does an ostrich fly?", even though they presumably have seen pigeons more often, since the tag "doesn't fly" is directly attached to the "ostrich" node while the information that a pigeon flies can be reached only through the intervening mediating node of "bird." For reasons I won't attempt to develop here, I believe that such inferences which follow directly from the structure of information stored in memory are different from inference processes like those of formal mathematics and logic in which sub-goals and directed search processes are constructed consciously and which have been simulated in various game playing, problem solving and theorem proving simulations (Feigenbaum and Feldman, 1963; Ernst and Newall, 1969). For recent work on inference in structured memories see Simmons (1970), Schwarcz et al. (1970) and Quillian (1969).

2 NODAL STRUCTURE AND SEARCH PROCESSES

Rozeboom makes a distinction between Memory Structure A, in which "type" and "token" nodes are distinguished and Memory Structure B, in which they are not. Since all "type" nodes are connected in both directions to a corresponding "token" node, the primary difference would be in the search times but a behavioral experiment to test this hypothesis would have to be very precise and be based on an assumption of uniform transmission times. I distinguished between the two types of nodes since the structure of the associational network is made more clear and since the two types of nodes may have different anatomies in the computer or the nervous system because the type nodes are more heavily interconnected than the token nodes. In any case, I doubt that this question is an important one.

In my discussion of the memory search processes, I pointed out that memories where node activation is long relative to transmission speed are prone to retrieve large amounts of very indirectly related information since the intersecting paths generated can be very long while memories where node activation is relatively short are liable to produce no answers or very commonplace replies. I neglected that a node can be doubly activated through very short paths such as those connecting synonyms, type and token nodes or subjects and objects of verb relations. A possible solution is to assume some sort of minimal refractory period for nodes so that double activation from directly connected nodes would not be possible.

3 A "NEW NOMINALISM"

One valid criticism of a Quillian type memory is that it seems based on a kind of "new nominalism" in which the name of a concept is confused with the concept itself. The node labels should be regarded as only labels and not "ideas." Some such nodes such as words which refer to perceptual experience, like color and shape names, must be linked to non-verbal nodes but it is assumed that the bulk of our concepts are defined in terms of other concepts. Schank *et al.* (1970) have taken a somewhat different position and assume that concepts are embedded in a previously existing conceptual system like a Kantian synthetic *a priori*. The work of Piaget could be regarded as partial support for this view for terms relating to the child's concepts of time, space, causality and to the more objective aspects of interpersonal relations but it seems hard to support this view for concepts like "justice" and "love" which are defined in terms of other relatively abstract concepts or personal experience (often as interpreted by the person) and which obviously differ appreciably from one person to another. Schank has made strong claims for a simple conceptual scheme in which English verbs can be expressed but it is hard to see how a conceptual coding in terms of semantic distinctive features could be developed without considerable prior experience. It is possible that such codings could be developed through some sort of memory re-organization in the experienced language user.

4 SIMILARITY, GRADED AROUSAL AND "ORTHODOXY"

Rozeboom has pointed out that "orthodox association theory draws heavily on the principle that an association $x - y$ will also interact with a process z to evoke y in strength which is an increasing function of z's similarity to *y"* while the Q-W (Quillian-Wilson) model does not provide for graded arousal or any generalization processes (as described by the generalization gradients of orthodox S-R learning theory) which are dependent on similarity. I think the Quillian model does have provision for graded arousal of at least a statistical nature which depends on the length of path or some randomness of background and diffuse activation. Also, graded arousal could be produced by variations in degrees of belief. Generalization involving linguistic material has long been regarded by some S-R psychologists as involving chains of mediating stimuli and responses which are learned and no two entities can be "similar" unless there is some kind of relational association between them. To speak of similarity in other terms requires that the entities be embedded in some sort of multidimensional space or be codified in terms of a vector of semantic distinctive features. (The difficulties with both types of rather similar systems have been commented on in my paper.) In addition, such dimensional orderings involve a co-ordinate system not necessarily developed through association but whether this constitutes a deviation from "orthodoxy," I shall leave to those of a theological bent to decide.

5 EMPIRICISM AND COMPUTER SIMULATION

I remarked in my paper that use of experimental data to test simulations of verbal behavior such as those of Quillian would probably not be necessary in the initial stages as long as the systems involved seem capable of exhibiting "ordinary" verbal behavior. This runs counter to the empiricist orientation of most experimental psychologists but I think it is defensible since ordinary verbal behavior is relatively standardized and familiar and its simulation is no mean task. Once such simulation has been achieved, and I don't think this has happened yet for the Quillian model or any other model of question answering, then more detailed comparisons involving use of human data will be in order.

Of course, it would be naive to postulate that successful simulation proves an exact correspondence to the human nervous system as Rozeboom points out. However, one can argue that there has to be some formal similarity of the functional properties of such different systems and formal automata theory has shown the equivalence of systems such as certain classes of formal automata and grammars which seem quite different on an intuitive level (Arbib, 1969; Hopcroft and Ullman, 1969). Moreover, a description of a complex system at an abstract level may be more comprehensible and in that sense more "real" than a detailed description of operations in the most elementary form. Digital computer operations are commonly understood in terms of the languages and operating systems involved rather than in terms of the detailed circuitry or electrical changes in the computer. Also, it is worth noting that Pribram in this volume and elsewhere refers to brain operation in experiential terms or in terms of macrosystem operation and has rarely referred to chemical events which are certainly "basic."

While I do not claim that the Quillian system should or could be extensively empirically tested at this stage using empirical data, there is a fair amount of evidence which argues for some sort of structured memory system. There has been a substantial amount of work in social psychology on the relation of beliefs to the interpretation of written material and experience and the view that some beliefs are more central than others is widely held. The work of Abelson and Colby mentioned above on the simulation of belief systems in computers has been designed to reproduce some of the phenomena (Abelson being a social psychologist and Colby a psychiatrist) and Schank's work mentioned above was initiated in connection with that of Colby. Again, the bias allegedly associated with computer software developments is far from evident.

Additional evidence for a retrieval process like that described by Quillian was found in the question answering experiment reported in my paper in which the "priming" associated with the asking of causal questions improved performance on temporal questions—an effect which clearly was associated with a "process" rather than a "state" as Rozeboom uses those terms. Finally there is other evidence for effects of structure in memory on recall, in addition to the already cited study of Collins and Quillian (1969). Blumenthal (1967) compared the effectiveness of the initial and final nouns as probes for recall in sentences with identical surface structures but different deep structures in Chomsky's sense and so with different structural representations in a Quillian type memory. Examples are, "Gloves were made by tailors" and "Gloves were made by hand." In the first, the propositional information would be represented in memory by a link from "gloves" to "tailors" through "made by" and a link from "tailors" to "gloves" through "made." In the second, no agent making the gloves is specified and "made by hand" is an adjective phrase describing a property of the "gloves" made. Blumenthal found that the initial and final nouns were equally effective as probes in the recall of passives with an agent named such as "Gloves were made by tailors" and were equal in effectiveness to the initial noun in sentences with an unnamed agent such as "Gloves were made by hand" but that the final noun in such sentences was substantially less effective as a probe. It is very hard to reconcile data such as these and the earlier mentioned results of Sachs (1967) with models which do not involve structural analysis of sentences. However, a model such as Quillian's must permit the option of storing surface structure information or of two way links to modifying words or phrases, such as "made by hand" in the example mentioned above, to account for any recall at all in Blumenthal's study from probes such as "hand" in the second example.

The Quillian Memory, Matrix Memory and Rozeboom's Trace Model

In the final section of his remarks on my paper, Rozeboom describes a trace model in which a process $R(x_1, x_2, ..., x_n)$ strengthens a relatively permanent corresponding memory trace when it occurs. This process can be revived or "redintegrated" by another process to the degree that the trace is strong and the initiating process resembles the process associated with the memory trace. Since the process R is characterized by n component values of x, this form of memory seems similar to the multivariate S-R, matrix and semantic distinctive feature memory structures commented on above and in my paper. His zeal to defend the orthodoxy of the "natural psychonomic approach" which is described as "an old intuition of classical psychology" ("classical" referring no doubt to the Greeks or perhaps to Mozart and Haydn) leads him to bottle old wine in old bottles.

Rozeboom's analysis also hardly does justice to the evidence for structural organization in language memory and recall which is cited above and the analysis of language structure associated with structural linguistics particularly the analysis by Fillmore (1968) of the differential role of parts of speech in language structure. In this connection it is worth noting that the Quillian model as I presented it represents nouns and verbs as names which can be modified by tags and that one elementary form of a proposition consists of a $noun_1$-verb-$noun_2$ relationship in which the verb is the name of the relationship between the nouns. Also, it is worth recalling the phenomena of "nesting" described in my paper in which propositions or their names serve as nouns in higher-order propositions. In addition to the network of interrelated concepts, the Quillian model has a somewhat hierarchical character as well, more evident as discussed in Collins and Quillian (1969) and Quillian (1969) than in references in my paper. (In my remarks on Pribram's paper in this volume, I criticized what I felt was the overly hierarchical character of his view of knowledge. My remarks above constitute a partial retreat from that position.)

Rozeboom's comments on computers and the operation of recall imply that recall has a multi-processes and almost Gestalt "field" quality. In my view, the multiple path form of retrieval of the Quillian model provides for context effects as is noted above but at the same time embodies discrete associational links. While field like properties can be postulated for the nervous system as in Landauer's hypotheses referred to in my paper or in Pribram's use of the hologram concept, the bulk of knowledge about the nervous system implies a discrete form of conduction. Field like properties can in all probability emerge from the parallel processing associated with multiple paths of conduction and there is good reason to believe that effective computer simulation of such processing (which is difficult given present hardware) will exhibit such contextually dependent results.

BIBLIOGRAPHY

A.F.I.P.S. (Amer. Fed. of Information Processing Societies) conference Proceedings, v. 29 *Fall Joint Computer Conference* Washington, D. C.: Sparton Books, 1966.

Abelson, R. P. and Carrol, J. D., Computer simulation of individual belief systems. *Amer. Behav. Sci.*, 1965, **8**, 24–30.

Arbib, M. A., *Theories of Abstract Automata* Englewood Cliffs, N. J.: Prentice-Hall, 1969.

Blumenthal, A., Prompted recall of sentences. *J. Verb. Learn. Berb. Behav.*, 1967, **6**, 203–206.

Bower, G. H., Address given at Western Psychological Association, San Diego, Calif., April, 1968.

Chomsky, N., Formal properties of grammars. In R. D. Luce, R. R. Bush and E. Galanter (Eds.) *Handbook of Mathematical Psychology* N. Y.: Wiley, 1963.

Chomsky, N., *Aspects of the Theory of Syntax*. Cambridge, Mass.: M. I. T. Press, 1965.

Cliff, N., Adverbs as multipliers. *Psychol. Rev.*, 1959, 66, **27–44**.

Colby, M. K., Computer simulation of the neurotic process. In R. Stacy, B. Waxam (Eds.) *Computers in Biomedical Research* I, N. Y.: Academic Press, 1965.

Colby, M. K., and Gilbert, J. P., Programming a computer model of neurosis. *J. Math. Psych.*, 1964, **1**, 405–417.

Collins, A. M. and Quillian, M. R., Retrieval time form semantic memory. *J. Verb. Learn. Verb. Behav.*, 1969, **8**, 240–247.

Deese, J., *The Structure of Associations in Language and Thought*. Baltimore, Md.: John Hopkins Press, 1965.

Dixon, T. R., and Horton, D. L. (Eds.), *Verbal Behavior and General Behavior Theory*. Englewood Cliffs, N. J.: Prentice-Hall, 1968.

Ernst, G. W. and Newall, A., *G. P. S.: A Case Study in Generality and Problem Solving*. New York: Academic Press, 1969.

Feigenbaum, E. A. and Feldman, J. (Eds.) *Computers and Thought*. New York: McGraw-Hill, 1963.

Fillmore, C. J., The case for case. In Bach, E. and Harms, R. T. (Eds.) *Universals in Linguistic Theory*. New York: Holt, 1968.

Flavell, J. H., *The Developmenttal Psychology of Jean Piaget*. Princeton, N. J.: Van Nostrand, 1963.

Guilford, J. P., *The Nature of Human Intelligence*. N. Y.: McGraw-Hill, 1967.

Greenberg, J. H. (Ed.), *Universals of Language*. Cambridge, Mass.: M. I. T. Press, 1963.

Holland, J. N., *Hierarchical Descriptions, Universal Spaces and Adaptive Systems*. Ann Arbor, Mich.: Computer and Communication Sciences Dept., Univ. of Mich., 1968.

Hopcroft, J. E. and Ullman, J. D., *Formal Languages and their Relations to Automata*. Reading, Mass.: Addison-Wesley, 1969.

Hunt, E. B., Martin, J. and Stone, P. J., *Experiments in Induction*. N. Y.: Academic Press, 1966.

Jacobson, R., Fant, C. G. M. and Halle, M., *Preliminaries to Speech Analysis*. Cambridge, Mass.: M. I. T. Press, 1952.

Johnson, D. M., Presentation at the Theoretical Psychology Center, University of Alberta, 1969.

Katz, J. J., and Postal, P. M., An *Integrated Theory of Linguistic Description*. Cambridge, Mass.: M. I. T. Press, 1964.

Landauer, T. K., Two hypothesis concerning the biochemical bases of memory. *Psychol. Rev.*, 1964, **71**, 167–179.

Liberman, A. M., Cooper, F. S., Shankweiler, D. P. and Studdert-Kennedy, M., Perception of the Speech Code. *Psychol. Rev.*, 1967, **74**, 431–461.

Miller, G. A., Some psychological studies of grammar. *Amer. Psychologist*, 1962, **17** 748–762.

Noble, C. E., An analysis of meaning. *Psychol. Rev.*, 1952, **59**, 421–430.

Osgood, C. E., Suci, G. J., and Tannenbaum, P. H., *The Measurement of Meaning*. Urban, Ill.: Univ. of Illinois Press, 1957.

Osgood, C. E., and Tannenbaum, P. H., The principle of congruity in the prediction of attitude change. *Psychol. Rev.*, **62**, 1955, 42–55.

Pollio, H. R., Composition of associative clusters, *J. Exp. Psychol.*, 1964, **67**, 199–208.

Pribram, K. H., Reinforcement revisited: A structural view. In M. Jones (Ed.) *Nebraska Motivation Symposium*, **1963**. Lincoln, Nebr.: Univ. of Nebr. Press, 1963.

Pribram, K., The new neurology and the biology of emotion. *Amer. Psychologist*. 1967, **22**, 830–838.

Pribram, K., The neurophysiology of remembering. *Scientific American*, 1969, **220**, 73–86.

Quillian, M. R., Semantic memory. Ph. D. thesis Carnegie Institute of Technology, 1967a.

Quillian, M. R., The teachable language comprehender. *Communications of the A.C.M.*, 1969, **12**, 459–476.

Quillian, M. R., Word concepts: A theory and simulation of some basic semantic capabilities. *Behav. Sci.*, 1967, **12**, 410–430.

Reitman, W. R., *Cognition and Thought.*, N. Y.: Wiley, 1965.

Rimland, B., *Infantile Autism*. N. Y.: Appleton-Century, 1964.

Rozeboom, W. W., The concept of "memory." *Psychological Record*, 1965, **15**, 329–368.

Rozeboom, W. W., The art of metascience. In: Royce, J. R. (ed.) *Toward Unification in Psychology*. Toronto: Univ. of Toronto Press, 1970.

Sachs, J. M., Recognition memory for syntactic and semantic aspects of connected discourse. *Percept. and Psychophysics*, 1967, **2**, 437–442.

Schank, R. C., Tesler, L., and Weber, S., Spinoza II: *Conceptual Case-Based Natural Language Analysis*. Stanford, Calif.: Stanford Univ. Artif. Intell. Proj. Memo AIM-109, 1970.

Schwarcz, R. M., Burger, J. F., and Simmons, R. F., A deductive question-answerer for natural language inference. *Communications of the A. C. M.*, 1970, **13**, 167–183.

Shiffrin, R. M., and Atkinson, R. M., Storage and retrieval processes in long-term memory. *Psychol. Rev.* 1969, **76**, 179–193.

Simmons, R. F., Answering English questions by computer. *Comm. A. C. M.*, 1965, **8**, 53–70.

Simmons, R. F., Natural language question answering systems: 1969. *Communications of the A. C. M.*, 1970, **13**, 15–30.

Simmons, R. F., Storage and retrieval of aspects of meaning in directed graph structures. *Comm. A. C. M.* 1966, **9**, 211–219.

Walker, D. E., and Norton, L. M. (Eds.), *Proceedings of the International Joint Conference on Artificial Intelligence: May 7–9, 1969, Washington, D. C.* Bedford, Mass.: The MITRE Corp., 1969.

Webster's Seventh New Collegiate Dictionary, Springfield, Mass.: G and C. Merriman, Co., 1967.

Wilson, K. V., On the importance of grammars and lists in pattern recognition. In Proceedings of the International Conference on Pattern Recognition: The Retina and the Machine. University of Manitoba, May, 1968. (In Press).

Woodward, P. M., List programming. In Fox, L. (Ed.) *Advances in Programming and Non-Numerical Computation*, N. Y.: Pergamon, 1966

XII

FREUDIAN DRIVE THEORY AND EPISTEMOLOGY

F. Xavier Plaus
The Center for Advanced Study in Theoretical Psychology

From the perspective of psychoanalysis, the central issue of epistemology could be said to be "how thinking progresses from the drive-determined autism of the infant to the socially adaptive and veridical thinking of the adult (Gill and Klein, 1967)". This quotation expresses the intent and focus of the present discussion, which will be concerned with a central concept of psychoanalysis, the instinctual drives, and their relationship to knowledge, focusing on some epistemological aspects of psychoanalytic theory. Before getting into the issues, some justification of the title appears in order.

Psychoanalysis has always been concerned with its biological underpinnings and has used biological or physiological concepts in its attempt to delineate psychological phenomena—not always, however, without some confusion. A case in point is the principle of instinctual drives. Although it has the implication of a physiological concept and is said to be "on the frontier between the mental and the somatic (Freud, 1915)", in point of fact the phenomena that it refers to are psychological. That is to say, the instinctual drives are defined as the *mental representatives* of stimuli originating within the organism. Rapaport (1960b) specifically points out that the phenomena conceptualized are not somatic processes but forces which initiate and regulate behavior. However, the important aspect of concern here is that the psychotherapeutic data about drives are thought products (Klein, 1967). This theoretical conception of the origins of knowledge processes leads us right into epistemology.

Most philosophers would consider epistemology to be concerned with (a) the nature and (b) the criteria of knowledge. Being equally concerned with *a* and *b*, they arrive at definitions of knowledge such as "justified true belief". However, I am blissfully ignoring all the problems concerning the validity of knowledge, and will take solace in Lorenz's position that "adaptation has provided our thought with an innate structuralization which corresponds to a considerable degree to the reality of the external world (Lorenz, 1962)". This position is adopted in the belief (whether justified and true or not) that the separation of philosophical and psychological approaches to a theory of knowledge is both barren and artifical; and that questions of validity should be delayed until the genesis of the psychological processes involved is delineated. Since my concern is with certain psychological approaches to the nature of knowing processes, knowledge will be defined, for my purposes, as the "structuralization of experience".

Two issues on the relationship between drives and knowledge will be considered under the headings of (a) the structuralization of experience, and (b) the relationship between primary process ideation and secondary process thinking. In the first section, I will (a) consider Freud's theory of thinking; (b) evaluate two positions on memory structure and knowledge; and (c) give several examples from psychological theory of primitive categories of thought. Section two will deal with the implications of primary and secondary processes; Freud's attempt to delineate the nature of knowing processes.

THE STRUCTURALIZATION OF EXPERIENCE

Psychoanalytic Theory of Thinking

Although Freud never explicitly delineated a theory of knowledge, it is unavoidably implied in his propositions on the development of thinking.[2] The essential element in this latter theory is that ideation (primary process thinking) develops as a result of the frustration of instinctual drives. That is, in the infant, when a need or tension (associated with an instinctual drive) reaches a critical point, if the need-satisfying object is present, there is a discharge of tension. However, if the object is not present, the discharge of tension is delayed. One result of this delay (after the initial occasion) is that the infant hallucinates the absent need-satisfying object. These hallucinatory images are seen as wish fulfillments of instinctual drives.

"The hallucinatory image is the archetype of thought. Its appearance in consciousness is determined by drive tension; it is the fundamental element in the primary process; it represents that special case of the pleasure principle which is conceptualized as wish fulfillment" (Rapaport, 1950, p. 316).

However, this hallucinatory image likewise does not satisfy the need and as a result the infant turns to reality and develops reality-oriented (secondary process) thinking.

"This attempt at satisfaction by means of hallucinations was abandoned only in consequence of the absence of the expected gratification experienced. Instead, the mental apparatus had to decide to form a conception of the real circumstances in the outer world and to exert itself to alter them. A new principle of mental functioning was thus introduced; what was conceived of was no longer that which was pleasant, but that which was real, even if it should be unpleasant" (Freud, 1911, p. 219).

Thus Freud assumed that from primary process ideation (and its drive-determined organization of memory) develops secondary process thinking with a new conceptual organization of memory. Although it is not obvious from the above, these two knowing processes can be distinguished either in terms of mode of discharge (psychic energy) or in terms of organizational properties. I will digress momentarily to deal with the concept of psychic energy; the discussion will then, turn to my primary concern—the structuralization of experience, by examining the concepts of representation and memory.

Holt, in a series of papers (1962, 1965, 1967a), has demonstrated that Freud never abandoned his neurological assumptions, even after he gave up the attempt to formulate a psychology from neurology ("The Project"). He points out that Freud's assumptions were: (a) that the nervous system tries to rid itself of stimulation); (b) that it only reacts to stimuli to discharge them; and (c) that there are quantitative changes in stimulation—whether internal or external. This latter assumption shows up later as the concept of psychic energy. Holt goes on to posit five biological discoveries as refuting Freud's "model of a passive-reflex mechanism". They are

1) the nervous system is perpetually active ...;

2) the effect of stimulation is primarily to modulate the activity of the nervous system; ...

3) the nervous system does not transmit energy; ...

4) the energies of the nervous system are different in kind from the impinging external stimuli; ...

5) the tiny energies of the nerves bear encoded information and are quantitatively negligible (Holt, 1965, pp. 108–109).

For these and other reasons, there seems to be a growing consensus, in some circles, that the concept of psychic energy is no longer tenable and should be abandoned (Kubie and Holt in Modell, 1963; Apfelbaum, 1965; Rubinstein, 1965, 1967; Loevinger, 1966; Holt, 1965, 1967a, 1967b; Berger, 1967, 1968; and Grinker, 1968). It is this position that is adopted here;

the focus is on the structural aspects of the theory rather than any energic ones.

As the beginning to an alternative to Freud's energic theory, Berger postulates a new set of assumptions:

"We may begin by conceiving of the mind as an active system. The direction of an ongoing system is determined by the way it is structured; that is the mind as an information-processing apparatus, which interprets (perceives) input and guides output (behavior), functions according to the way it is organized. This organization or structure, in turn, is the result of innate factors that result from evolutionary selection, interacting with factors that result from specific experiences encountered during development" (Berger, 1967, p. 10).

Adopting the assumption that the mind functions according to the way it is structured leads us to a consideration of the concepts of representation and memory in psychoanalytic theory.

Representation and Memory

Although much of the psychoanalytic literature is concerned with memory from the perspective of repression, we are focused on the positive aspects—registration and storage (Klein, 1966). This aspect is not generally dealt with by Freud beyond statements to the effect that memory traces of experience are laid down.

It is necessary to be first clear on what might be meant by memory traces. For example, Paul (1967) states that "according to the strong form of trace theory, an experience generates a replica of itself". On the other hand, Gomulicki (1953), in his review of the concept, employed the term to signify "nothing more specific than an acknowledgment that memory does have a physical basis ..." The important point for our discussion is that, as Wolff (1967) makes clear, Freud implied a direct correspondence between the objective event and that which was stored in memory and later recalled. Thus, issue is not taken with any general conception that simply posits traces as stored information, but rather with the position that memory traces are copies of earlier experience.

Neisser (1967) has pointed out the prevalence of this assumption in psychological theories and he labels it "the reappearance hypothesis of memory". It is the assumption that ideas are nothing but faded copies of sensory experiences. Neisser argues for a constructivist position on perception, memory and thought—which position he terms the "utilization hypothesis". To make the importance of this assumption clear, I will summarize

Furth's (1968) distinction between representational (copyist) and constructivist theories of knowledge.

Furth indicates that representation has been used in a narrow passive sense to mean imaginal representation in which there is an inherent correspondence between the image and external reality, or in a wide sense where there is no intrinsic relation to the real thing. Furth contends that English empiricism employed representation in the former sense with the result that ideas are simply seen as imaginal representations. The French-German idealist tradition, however, since it employed representation in the wide sense, did not conceive of representational thinking as necessarily or simply involving sensory representations. Furth goes on to demonstrate that for such psychological theorizing "knowledge is conceived of as coextensive with the internalized representations (Furth, 1968)". Although the copyist theory of knowledge and the reappearance hypothesis of memory may not necessarily be coextensive, it would appear that they describe Freud's implicit epistemological position.

An important consideration, in this regard, is that children apparently see schematically, whereas adults see realistically.

"Observations by Granit (1921), by Werner (1948), by Piaget (e.g. 1936, 1937a) and by virtually anybody who watches children, have shown that children's perception of objects tends to be abstractive and syncretic-schematic rather than veridical and objective" (Paul, 1967, p. 253).

The conclusion that thus appears warranted is that, at least in early childhood, the main explanation for the development of thought can not rest on a strong form of memory traces. Although rejecting Freud's use of memory traces does not require that the copyist theory of knowledge be treated to the same fate, I feel that there is a more plausible alternative.

As Furth (1968) demonstrates, an alternative to a copyist theory of knowledge is a constructivist one; an important example of this position is Piaget's theory of knowledge, where he employs representation in the wide sense.

"For Piaget's theory, at all developmental levels, knowledge is basically linked to the biological internal organization. Knowledge does not merely derive from taking in of external data, the organism in interacting with the environment transforms or constructs external reality into an object of knowledge" (Furth, 1968, p. 153).

The essential point in Piaget's theory of knowledge is that "operative thinking ... does not represent[3] but implicitly transforms a reality state according to its own structure (Furth, 1969)"—this structure is referred to as schemes[4]. What both Piaget and Neisser seem to be emphasizing in their approach is the contribution of the subject in the development of knowledge. Knowledge of an object is just as much constructed from the prior internal organization of the knower as from external stimulation. Cassirer seems to be taking the same position when he writes "it is now the function of knowledge to build up and constitute the object, not as an absolute object but as a phenomenal object, conditioned by this very function (Cassirer, 1957)".

Primitive Categories of Thought

Although the specific stages of sensorimotor development are beyond the scope of this paper, Piaget traces the development of adult intelligence from reflex patterns in the newborn. Wolff cogently summarizes the implication of the reflex scheme as a "congenital structure of memory organization, or a primitive category of thought; it is the mental representation of an action pattern which we infer from the fact behavior is stable and repeatable (Wolff, 1967)". Through experience, by the infant acting on his environment, these global schemes differentiate and slowly become transformed and integrated into schemes of representation (in the wide sense).

Piaget's work on the sensorimotor stage of development has important implications for Freud's concept of drive representations. In this regard, let me quote at length Wolff's criticism of the origin of ideation in Freud's theory:

"If the wealth of Piaget's empirical observations is correct and his interpretations are valid, it follows that the infant cannot hallucinate the absent object or prolong his experience of it beyond the duration of physical encounter. He can conserve the object only by activating the motor anticipation pattern by which he "knows" the object. Until the end of the first year at least, the psychic representation of the object is either action in progress (stages one through three) or the anticipation of past "successful" action (stages four and five). Until the end of the first year "hallucination" of the absent object occurs only in a context of action, and is equivalent to empty repetition of action (for example, empty sucking, grasping, or babbling). According to Piaget's formulation, when the child conserves the object by motor anticipation patterns, permanence may be extended beyond the ongoing action, but the "hallucination" of the object remains the product of sensorimotor activity and is not the activation traces of isolated sensory impressions" (Wolff, 1967, p. 325).

In addition to this formulation of representation and memory structure and its implications for the development of thinking, there are extant in the psychoanalytic literature theories with similar conceptualizations. They are Spitz's "organizers of the psyche" (Spitz, 1959, 1965) and Erikson's conception of "instinctual modes" (Erikson, 1950).

Rapaport (1967) and Wolff (1967) have pointed out the similarities between Erikson's conception of organ modes and Piaget's sensorimotor schemes. Erikson's position is that the erogenous zones (as delineated by Freud) have modes or formal properties that refer to their manner of operation; e.g. the mouth takes in and/or rejects. The similarity to Piaget is that the instinctual modes refer to mental representatives of actions.

"The significance of the modes is that they were conceived of as the generalizations of concrete and phylogenetically determined action patterns which ... constitute categories of experience and thought organization" (Wolff, 1967, p. 332).

To continue the comparison, where Piaget contends that (in the developmental process) the schemes become relatively disassociated from external actions and refer to operative thinking, so also the instinctual modes become estranged from their zones of origin to become behavior and thought modalities.

Spitz's analogous concept is the "organizer of the psyche". Each organizer represents a level of increasing complexity of psychic structure. In considering the first year of life, Spitz delineates three stages, or three organizers of the psyche. For example, the first organizer is indicated by the infant's "smiling response" and usually occurs around three months of age. For Spitz, this indicates that in the way of organization the following has taken place:

1) the infant turns from inner sensation to outer perception; ...
2) reality testing begins; ...
3) memory traces are laid down; and ...
4) directed object relations take their inception (Spitz, 1959, pp. 23–24).[5]

Spitz elaborates the implications for each level of organization in economic terms and employs the concept of memory traces in the same terms as Freud. However, I believe these concepts are not essential to his argument. Rather, both Erikson's and Spitz's conceptualizations are amenable to the constructivist-structural position adopted here and exemplified by the work of Piaget. This position, once again, is that the organism constructs its world-as-known, both in accordance with its own psychic structure or organization and by acting upon its environment. The focus of development is the organizational structures out of which our knowledge of reality is constructed and experienced as "out there". The significance of the instinctual modes and organizers of the psyche is that they constitute attempts to delineate organizational schemes for the development of interpersonal relations (Spitz, 1965) and personality (Erikson, 1962).

In summary, within his representational world (representation being used in the wide sense) the child constructs the organizations of his internal and external environment. This structuralization of experience we refer to as knowledge. Leaving aside memory traces and psychic energy, the essence of Freud's theory of instinctual drives is that there are mental representatives (schemes) of physiological functions that organize experience. The further assumption is that these schemes (congenital categories—Wolff, 1967) become relatively disassociated from the original action patterns to become categories of thought. This delineation of instinctual drives as operative schemes of action patterns and primitive categories of thought brings us to the distinction between primary and secondary process.

PRIMARY AND SECONDARY PROCESS

In section one, I pointed out that primary process ideation (operating according to the pleasure principle) is unable to discharge the tension (accumulation of energy) associated with a physiological need. As a result of this proposition, Freud postulated that the infant turns to reality and develops reality-oriented thinking. Hartmann (1939) made some conceptual advance by postulating that we must assume ego-apparatuses which have an inborn capacity to relate to reality (these are referred to as apparatuses of primary autonomy and include perception, memory, motility, and language capacity), presumably the development of ideation (primary process) and thinking (secondary process) are contemporaneous.

The explanatory concepts that Freud used for this delineation of the development of thinking are the pleasure principle and psychic energy. Since I an focusing on the structural aspects of thinking, I will turn to the structural mechanisms that Freud has suggested characterize primary process ideation, i.e. condensation and displacement.[6] However, I must first digress and consider the pleasure principle.

The Pleasure Principle

On several occasions Freud appears to insist that an initial experience of a need-satisfying object is necessary for it to be subsequently hallucinated.

"As a result of the link that has been established, next time this need arises a psychical impulse will at once emerge which will seek to recathect the mnemic image of the perception and to re-evoke the perception itself, that is to re-establish the situation of the original satisfaction (Freud, 1900, p. 566).

"This satisfaction must have been previously experienced in order to have left behind a need for its repetition (Freud, 1905, p. 184).

"All images originate from perceptions and are repetitions of them. So that originally the mere existence of the image serves as a guarantee of the reality of what is imagined" (Freud, 1925, p. 237).

From this, the infant must respond to experience for even primary process ideation to develop, and is thus adaptive and, in this sense, operates according to the reality principle. Thus, primary process ideation is not exclusively established by the pleasure principle. This conclusion, Wolff (1967) contends, is also supported by Piaget's observations.

This conclusion becomes particularly important when considered in the light of Holt's criticisms of Freud's basic conception of the human organism. If the organism is not essentially passive and does not seek to avoid stimulation, the concept of the pleasure principle may also no longer be viable. In his discussion on the distinctions between primary process and the pleasure principle, Wolff (1967) suggests that the latter be reserved for the "primitive distributions and dispositions of psychic energies." If this was its only interpretation, then rejecting psychic energy would also imply rejecting the pleasure principle. However, another interpretation is also part of psychoanalytic theory.

"The more thought (and also affect and behavior) can be characterized as an unrealistic seeking for immediate gratification, the more it is to be considered primary process; ... and the more thought or behavior is organized by adaptive considerations of efficiency in the search for realistic gratification, the more it approximates the ideal of secondary process" (Holt, 1967; fn. p. 394).

This characteristic of striving for immediate gratification is an essential aspect of the pleasure principle, however it does not need to be interpreted in terms of psychic energy. A recent formulation of the preemptoriness of behavior, that avoids the concept of psychic energy, is Klein's (1967). The preemptoriness of motives and thought that Klein tries to conceptualize in a structural model is an attempt to deal with the aspects of behavior that are usually subsumed under the pleasure principle. The present discussion, on the other hand, will undoubtedly seem barren to the psychoanalytically-oriented reader, since the primary orientation of psychoanalytic theory, namely motivation, is disregarded. However, I am concerned with the structural aspects of primary process ideation, which are not logically synonymous with the pleasure principle, even though these two processes tend to be concomitant. The value of Klein's approach is his attempt to account for motivation and thought in one conceptual model.

Condensation and Displacement

Many of those concerned with psychoanalytic theory seem to concentrate on one formal property of primary process ideation, i.e. the drive determined organization of experience—considered as primitive organizational structures. Primitive usually refers to the proposition that primary process is the initial thought process of the infant out of which develops secondary process. However, there is no justification for assuming that, in the first year of life, the two processes are distinct.[7] Piaget's concern has been with demonstrating that intelligence and thought have a logical structure and thus he concentrated on the attempt to trace the development of logical thought from early action patterns.[8] However, a high proportion of ordinary thought does not appear to be rational and symmetrical as Piaget contends, and thus the value of Freud's distinction between primary and secondary process. The assumption adopted here is that both forms of thought develop from the primitive categories of thought, the schemes of action discussed in section one. Thus knowing, as the structuralization of experience, can take place in the context of organizational structures (schemes) that are not necessarily logical.

Following the work of Cassirer, Langer suggests this aspect of primary process ideation:

"Non-discursive form in art has a different office, namely to articulate knowledge that cannot be rendered discursively because it concerns experiences that are not formally amenable to the discursive projection. Such experiences are the rhythms of life, organic, emotional and mental (the rhythm of attention is an interesting link among them all), which is not simply periodic, but endlessly complex and sensitive to every sort of influence. All together they compose the dynamic pattern of feeling. It is this pattern that only non-discursive symbolic forms can present, and that is the point and purpose of artistic construction" (Langer, 1953, pp. 240–241).

In addition, the kind of distinction that I am trying to point to is also made by Watzlawick, Beavin and Jackson (1967).[9] They delineate two basic modes of communication—"one by a self-explanatory likeness, the other by a word". The former they refer to as analogical communication, and the latter as digital communication.

"Human beings communicate both digitally and analogically. Digital language has a highly complex and powerful logical syntax but lacks adequate semantics in the field of relationships, while analogic language possesses the semantics but has no adequate syntax for the unambiguous definition of the nature of relationship" (Watzlawick et al., 1967, pp. 66–67).

What these two quotations point to are two thinking processes, one characterized by logical, discursive thought, which is amenable to syntactic description, and the other, analogical, non-discursive thought whose expression must be symbolic. The question becomes is this kind of distinction relevant to the primary–secondary process distinction? The important question is whether they are distinct modes of thought with different structural properties.

Gill (1967) has suggested that the primary process mechanisms of condensation and displacement are not discontinuous with secondary process thinking in that he links displacement with differentiation and condensation with integration. Holt[10] goes on to suggest that these mechanisms are not suitable for defining the primary process and suggests that the distinction between these two processes should be made in terms of the pleasure principle (Holt, 1967).

I suggest that Holt is correct in stating that there are two criteria involved in the distinction between primary and secondary process, and they are not logical opposites. These criteria have, in the past, been wishfulness and realism. Wishfulness, taken in the context of the pleasure principle, has the quality of preemptoriness. This latter defines the pleasure principle, however, since I have contended (in line with psychoanalytic theory) that the definitions of the pleasure principle and primary process are not coextensive, wishfulness and preemptoriness are not coextensive. Thus, wishfulness would appear to be a valid criterion for distinguishing these forms of thought, although not a structural property. The second criterion of realism, however, is not unique to secondary process thinking in that primary process ideation also functions according to the reality principle, particularly as the origins of creativity. Secondary process thinking is felt to be realistic because it is logical, and it is this latter quality which appears to be the distinguishing characteristic.

The most cogent and persuasive example of logical properties of secondary process thinking is Piaget's attempt to demonstrate a relationship between fundamental matrix structures (e.g. the Bourbacki structures–algebraic structures, structures of order and topological structures, Beth and Piaget, 1966), and the structures of the subject's actions. Edelheit (1969), on the other hand, suggests that the ego, and by implication secondary process thinking, is characterized by vocal-auditory organization.

"I have tried to show that a dialectic relationship exists between speech and psychic structure. The maturation of the physiological speech apparatus, the coordination of vocal-auditory experience, and the organization of that experience in specific linguistic patterns and categories, are concomitant with and correlated to the ontogenesis of the ego" (Edelheit, 1969; p. 410).

Piaget contends, however, that the operational structures are more fundamental and that, although language may be a necessary condition for the achievement of logico-mathematical operations, it is not a sufficient condition for their formation. In any case, the powerful logical syntax of linguistic structures does not appear to characterize primary process ideation, whose structural properties seem analogical and non-discursive, and (following Cassirer) can not be rendered discursively. The possibility of the genesis of primary process ideation, in terms of operative schemes of the subject's actions, awaits delineation.

SUMMARY AND CONCLUSION

I have tried to demonstrate that, when we discard Freud's assumptions on memory traces and psychic energy, the essential aspect of his theory of instinctual drives is mental representations of physical functions which organize experience. These mental representations were then related to Freud's distinction between primary and secondary process. The distinction between these two thinking processes postulated is in terms of their organizational structures. Primary process functions more in terms of operative schemes which are non-discursive and analogical, demonstrated by the mechanisms of condensation and displacement, and represented (narrow sense) more in the form of symbolic schemas. Secondary processes, on the other hand, function more in terms of operative schemes that are discursive and digital, demonstrated by the mechanisms of differentiation and integration, and represented more in the form of linguistic schemas.

NOTES

1. Now at the Royal Ottawa Hospital, Ottawa, Ontario.
2. Rapaport (1967) did define knowledge as the "product of our minds" methods of organizing stimulation into experience and further organizing it into more global units".
3. Here Furth is using representation in the narrow sense.
4. I am following Furth's (1968) practice of using the term scheme for the operative process by which we know, and the term schema for the symbolic process by which we represent known reality.

5. It is of more than passing interest that the contemporaneous stage in Piaget's system is the second stage (the period of "primary circular reactions" and "first acquired adaptations") during which there is the first clear indication that experience influences behavior.
6. By the process of displacement, one idea may surrender to another the whole quota of cathexis; by the process of condensation, it may appropriate the whole cathexis of several ideas (Freud, 1915b).
7. Cf. the quotation from Wolff (1967) on page 418.
8. "In the first place there is the fact that actual thought develops (if circumstances are favourable) in conformity with the principles of logic; in the second place, in its later reflections the mind shows itself capable of noting this conformity, and even to a certain extent of justifying the acceptance of the percepts of logic as 'laws of thought' (in the sense, naturally, of normative laws) (Beth and Piaget, 1966; pp. 305–306)".
9. Both Langer and Watzlawick *et al.* point out the similarity between their formulations and Freud's.
10. In a footnote to Gill (1967), p. 294.

COMMENT ON PLAUS' PAPER

J. R. Royce

While Plaus offers a disclaimer to the effect that he is "blissfully ignoring all the problems concerning the validity of knowledge", he, nevertheless, goes on to define knowledge as "the structuralization of experience", and subsequently elaborates on an essentially constructivist position. He justifies this stance on the grounds that he is primarily concerned with the psychological aspects of the knowing process, but, in my opinion, he goes further, and at least *seems* to equate modes of cognition with knowing.

This practice is not limited to Plaus—it is characteristic of most psychologists, and it is so prevalent that it has, in fact, achieved the dubious distinction of having received a label—psychologism. What is bothersome about psychologism is that it fails to deal with the problem of truth criteria—that is, the bases for deciding what shall be acceptable as "true" and what shall be rejected as "false". More specifically, in Plaus' case it surely follows that *any* "structuralization of experience" is as valid as any other. Appeal to the reality testing of secondary process thinking will not do because the analysis is still at the psychological level—that is, we still have not been offered an epistemological basis for truth claims.

Plaus, and other psychologists of a "psychologistic" persuasion, have an easy answer to my objections by simply relaxing their claim. All that is required is that cognizing not be equated with knowing. However, if they insist on the strong claim that all cognitive processing—thinking, perceiving, symbolizing, intuiting, imaging, etc.,—whether it be logical or illogical, illusory or veridical, pure fantasy, completely autistic, logical but paranoid, etc., is *ipso facto*, knowledge, then I submit that they are, at best, philosophically naive.

I presume it is clear that there is no objection whatsoever to Plaus limiting his analysis to cognitive processes related to knowing and, as such, I am in complete sympathy with the effort he has made. In fact, I applaud the manner in which he has contrasted the symbolic-analogical with the linguistic-discursive modes of *thinking* implicit in psychoanalytic theory. The implications of this for *epistemology* per se, however, have not been adequately elaborated.

BIBLIOGRAPHY

Apfelbaum, B., Ego Psychology, Psychic Energy, and the Hazards of Quantitative Explanation in Psycho-analytic Theory. *Int. J. Psychoan.*, 1965, **46**, 168–181.

Berger, L., Function of Dreams. *J. Abn. Psych. Mono.* 1967, **72**, 1–28.

Berger, L., Motivation, Energy and Cognitive Structure in Psychoanalytic Theory. In: Judd Marmor (Ed.) *Modern Psychoanalysis.* New York: Basic Books, 1968; 44–65.

Beth, E. W. and Piaget, J., *Mathematical Epistemology and Psychology.* Dordrecht-Holland: D. Reidel, 1966.

Cassirer, E., *The Philosophy of Symbolic Forms.* Vol. 3: The Phenomenology of Knowledge. New Haven: Yale University Press, Inc., 1957.

Edelheit, H., Speech and Psychic Structure: The Vocal-Auditory Organization of the Ego. *J. Amer. Psychoan., Assoc.*, 1969, **17**, 381–412.

Erikson, E. H., *Childhood and Society.* (1950), rev. ed. New York: Norton, 1962.

Freud, S., The Interpretation of Dreams, (1900). *Standard Edition*, 5. London: Hogarth Press, 1953.

Freud, S., Three Essays on the Theory of Sexuality (1905). *Standard Edition*, 7. London: Hogarth Press, 1953.

Freud, S., Formulations on the Two Principles of Mental Functioning (1911). *Standard Edition*, 12. London: Hogarth Press, 1958.

Freud, S., The Unconscious (1913). *Standard Edition*, 14. London: Hogarth Press, 1957.

Freud, S., Instincts and Their Vicissitudes (1915). *Standard Edition*, 14. London: Hogarth Press, 1957.

Freud, S., Negation (1925). *Standard Edition*, 19. London: Hogarth Press, 1961.

Furth, H. G., Piaget's Theory of Knowledge: The Nature of Representation and Interiorization. *Psych. Rev.* 1968, **75**, 143–154.

Furth, H. G., *Piaget and Knowledge.* New York: Prentice-Hall, 1969.

Gill, M. M., The Primary Process. In: R. R. Holt (Ed.) *Motives and Thought.* New York: International Universities Press, 1967, 260–298.

Gill, M. M. and Klein, G. S., The Structuring of drive and reality: David Rapaport's contribution to Psychoanalysis and Psychology. In: M. M. Gill (Ed.) *The Collected Papers of David Rapaport*, 1967, 8–34.

Gomulicki, B. R., *The Development and Present Status of the Trace Theory of Memory.* Cambridge: Cambridge University Press, 1953.

Granit, A. R., A Study of the Perception of Form. *Bri. J. Psych.*, 1921, **12**, 223–247.

Grinker, R. R., Conceptual Progress in Psychoanalysis. In: Judd Marmor (Ed.) *Modern Psychoanalysis.* New York: Basic Books, 1968, 19–43.

Hartmann, E., *Ego Psychology and the Problem of Adaptation* (1939). New York: International Universities Press, 1958.

Holt, R. R.,A Critical Examination of Freud's Concept of Bound vs. Free Cathexis (1962). *J. Amer. Psychoan. Assn.*, 1962, **10**, 475–525.

Holt, R. R., A review of some of Freud's biological assumptions and their influence on his theories. In: N. S. Greenfield and W. C. Lewis (Eds.) *Psychoanalysis and Current Biological Thought.* Madison: University of Wisconsin Press, 1965, 93–124.

Holt, R. R., Beyond Vitalism and Mechanism: Freud's Concept of Psychic Energy. In: J. H. Masserman (Ed.) *The Ego.* New York: Grune and Stratton, 1967a, 1–41.

Holt, R. R., The Development of the Primary Process: A Structural View. In: R. R. Holt (Ed.) *Motives and Thought*. New York: International Universities Press, 1967b, 345–383.

Klein, G. S., The Several Grades of Memory. In: R. M. Loewenstein, Lottie M. Newman, M. Schur, and A. J. Solnit (Eds.) *Psychoanalysis—A General Psychology*. New York: International Universities Press, 1966, 377–389.

Langer, Suzanne, *Feeling and Form*. New York: Scribner, 1953.

Loevinger, Jane, Three Principles for a Psychoanalytic Psychology. *J. Abn. Psych.*, 1966, **71**, 432–443.

Lorenz, K., Kant's Doctrine of the a priori in the light of Contemporary Biology. In: L. von Bertalanffy and A. Rapaport (Eds.) *General Systems*, Yearbook of the Society for General Systems Research, Vol. 7; Bedford Mass.

Miller, G. A., Galanter, E. H., and Pribram, K. H., *Plans and the Structure of Behavior*. New York: Holt, 1960.

Modell, A. H., The Concept of Psychic Energy. *J. Amer. Psychoan. Assn.*, 1963, **11**, 605–618.

Neisser, U., *Cognitive Psychology*. New York: Appleton-Century-Crofts, 1967.

Paul, I. H., Schema in Memory Theory. In: R. R. Holt (Ed.) *Motives and Thought*. New York: International Universities Press, 1967, 219–258.

Piaget, J., *The Origins of Intelligence in Children*, 2nd. Ed. New York: International Universities Press, 1952.

Piaget, J., Principal Factors Determining Intellectual Evolution From Childhood to Adult Life. In: D. Rapaport (Ed.) *Organization and Pathology of Thought*. New York: Columbia University Press, 1951, 154–175.

Rapaport, D., On the Psychoanalytic Theory of Thinking (1950). In: M. M. Gill (Ed.) *Collected Papers of David Rapaport*. New York: Basic Books, 1967, 313–328.

Rapaport, D., Dynamic Psychology and Kantian Epistemology (1947). In: M. M. Gill (Ed.) *Collected Papers of David Rapaport*. New York: Basic Books, 1967, 289–298.

Rapaport, D., Psychoanalysis as a Developmental Psychology (1960). In: M. M. Gill (Ed.) *Collected Papers of David Rapaport*. New York: Basic Books, 1967, 820–852.

Rapaport, D., On the Psychoanalytic Theory of Motivation (1960). In: M. M. Gill (Ed.) *Collected Papers of David Rapaport*. New York: Basic Books, 1967, 853–915.

Rubinstein, B. B., Psychoanalytic Theory and the Mind-Body Problem. In: N. S. Greenfield and W. C. Lewis (Eds.) *Psychoanalysis and Current Biological Thought*. Madison: University of Milwaukee Press, 1965, 35–56.

Rubinstein, B. B., Explanation and Mere Description: A Metascience Examination of Certain Aspects of the Psychoanalytic Theory of Motivation. In: R. R. Holt (Ed.) *Motives and Thought*. New York: International Universities Press, 1967, 20–77.

Spitz, H., *A Genetic Field Theory of Ego Formation*. New York: International Universities Press, 1959.

Spitz, R., *The First Year of Life*. New York: International Universities Press, 1965.

Watzlawick, P., Beavin, Janet, and Jackson, D. D., *Pragmatics of Human Communication*. New York: Norton, 1967.

Werner, H., *Comparative Psychology of Mental Development* (1948) rev. ed. New York: International Universities Press, 1957.

Wolff, P. H., Cognitive Considerations for a Psychoanalytic Theory of Language Acquisition. In: R. R. Holt (Ed.) *Motives and Thought*. New York: International Universities Press, 1967, 300–343.

XIII

DEPERSONALIZATION — DEREALIZATION SYNDROME AND PERCEPTION: A CONTRIBUTION OF PSYCHOPATHOLOGY TO EPISTEMOLOGY

T. E. Weckowicz

The Center for Advanced Study in Theoretical Psychology

Since at least the time of Husserl modern philosophers have tended to reject empirical psychology. It is said that psychology as a science cannot answer the questions philosophers are asking. It cannot furnish ultimate criteria of truth, ultimate criteria of knowledge of the external world or explain what being a person really means. Scientific psychology deals with contingent facts while philosophy deals with necessary logical implications. Thus the twain, like West and East in Kipling's poem, will never meet.

In no other area of mutual interest do psychology and philosophy overlap to a greater extent than in the area of inquiry into the sources of human knowledge, although the points of view may differ. Historically, the traditional philosophy of mind was developed as a part of epistemology. To answer the question of how knowledge of the external world was possible it was necessary to know how the human mind was working. The psychology of knowledge became particularly important when, as the result of the seventeenth century discoveries about the nature of light and sound, the "naive realism" of previous centuries became untenable. This concern of philosophers was only rivalled by their interest in the springs of human motivation which was necessary for understanding of the workings of human society, no longer regarded as an imperfect reflection of the Kingdom of Heaven. When in the nineteenth century experimental psychology had separated from philosophy, both disciplines continued their inquiry into the way knowledge is acquired, however, the approaches became quite different. Philosophy continued to be preoccupied with absolute criteria of truth, with certainty of knowledge and with the ultimate meaning of the proposition "I know that," e.g. the old problem of Plato in "Thetetus" of the difference between knowledge and true opinion. The experimental introspectionist psychology was concerned with contents of consciousness, conceived as sensory data, and their relationship to the external world. The external world was known through sensory data. However the question "how it was known" through sensory data was relegated to the limbo of apperception or "mental act." These higher processes tended to be analysed philosophically rather than experimentally. As a result philosophers following Husserl (Husserl, 1900) were inclined to reject the contributions of experimental psychology or any psychological explanation as irrelevant to solving the problem of human knowledge. For Husserl and the influential phenomenological movement in continental Europe the "act of knowing" consisted in "intentionality" of transcendental subject towards transcendental object and was thus beyond the reach of empirical science. Even "Gestalten" proposed by Wertheimer, Köhler and Koffka as a replacement for sensory data were rejected as mere contents of consciousness which did not explain the act of knowing. In the pure act of knowing both transcendental essences of subject and object were revealed to human knowledge, thus going beyond (transcending) the contents of consciousness.

In more recent times in England and America the so called "philosophy of mind", although it apparently has given up the quest for absolute knowledge and instead has examined such problems as that of perception, memory, cognition and motivation—problems familiar to psychologists, has had a tendency to avoid any connection with experimental psychology. The Anglo-American philosophers of mind do not seem to be concerned with the empirical facts uncovered by experimental psychology but with the linguistic implications of using certain words or sentences in common language when describing psychological occurrences.

The question: is psychology of cognition relevant to theory of knowledge, remains unanswered in spite of the prevailing opinions of philosophers. There are many examples from the more remote and recent past when the scientific discoveries and theories were quite relevant to philosophical questions. One needs to give only a few examples. Newtonian physics and the arising problem of the discrepancy between the "real world" and "experienced world," and hence some of the most burning problems of epistemology provides one example. More recently, Einstein's theory of relativity, Bohr's principle of complementarity and Heisenberg's principle of uncertainty, provide other examples. All these theories in physics are concerned with such concepts as identity, simultaneity, abstract space, and time, or the question whether the universe is deterministic or probabilistic, once considered to be in the domain of logic or intuitive knowledge beyond the reach of empirical science. If discoveries and theories of physics are relevant to philosophy and theory of knowledge, surely then there is no *a priori* reason why the discoveries and theories of experimental (empirical) psychology could not also be relevant. On the whole the reluctance of philosophers to psychologize (using this word with reference to scientific psychology) was reciprocated by psychologists who eschewed philosophizing. It was felt that the status of the young science as a science depended on carefully avoiding philosophical entanglements. However, there are a few exceptions. In the area of epistemology, traditionally regarded as a domain of philosophy, some contemporary psychologists have staked claims. Jean Piaget and his collaborators provide one striking example, Donald T. Campbell (1959) provides another. Piaget (1965) argues that both logic and epistemology "tend to dissociate themselves from general philosophy and increasingly unite with scientific problems" (1965, p. 29). Thus, different sciences encounter specific epistemological and logical problems. Psychology is in a special position because, apart from the specific epistemology of psychology as a pursuit of scientific knowledge, there is a psychology of epistemology as there is, Husserl and most other philosophers to the contrary notwithstanding, a psychology of logic. While both logic and epistemology are concerned with implicative relations which are the domain of philosophy, psychology is concerned with causally related events which are parallel to the implicative relations. The latter when abstracted and formalized constitute the subject matter of logic and epistemology. Thus, although neither logic nor epistemology can be reduced to psychology, psychology can throw some light on necessary and sufficient causes of human behaviour from which relations described in the language of philosopy can be abstracted, even if they "exist" in a Platonic universe of ideas apart from this behaviour. Piaget is particularly concerned with what he calls "genetic epistemology," with the process of growth of knowledge of the external world which a child acquires in its interaction with the environment. Developmental psychology is particularly relevant to the understanding of the genesis of man's epistemological presuppositions about the world and the logic of his thinking. The obvious criticism which can be levelled against Piaget is that he commits the so called "genetic fallacy," that he tries to explain a formal system, which can only be analysed logically, by reconstructing its evolution in the history of the individual or the history of the species. This touches on a very difficult problem of the nature of explanation whether it is formal, functional or historical (genetic). It is a "sticky" problem and I do not want to get involved myself with it in this essay. It is sufficient to say that there are several kinds of explanations and I prefer a convergent approach, with several kinds of explanations bearing on the same problem, to a "closed system" type of explanation. Thus, Piaget, in my opinion, is not concerned with logical explanation within a system of logic or epistemological explanation within a philosophical system, but with a genetic explanation of concomitant behaviour from which these systems can be abstracted. Perhaps a quotation from a collaborator of Piaget, Jean–Blaise Grize, will throw some light on the problem: "Genetic epistemology is thus seen in a double aspect. It is scientific by its usage of psychology, but it is philosophic by the questions that it poses and by the kind of responses that it gives to these questions. It thus offers certain incontestable analogies with current logical empiricism with respect to which it will be useful to situate the position of genetic epistemology" (Jean–Blaise Grize, 1965, p. 469). If I understand the author correctly, he means that in both cases there are two parallel systems, one of empirical observations and the other of a logical (formal) structure. These two systems interact with one another.

If developmental psychology is allowed to make a contribution to the problems of logic and epistemology, because it is concerned with the genesis and growth of psychic structures, there is a distinct possibility that a branch of psychology concerned with disintegration and dissolution of such structures can also make contributions to both logic and epistemology. This branch of psychology is, of course, psycho–pathology. In this essay I would like, as a psychopathologist, to discuss the syndrome of "depersonalization–derealization" in relation to the problem of knowledge, particularly to that of immediate knowledge of the external world and the self, given by perception. This syndrome, although relatively rare, is very interesting from a theoretical point of view.

Let me state at the outset that psychopathology is an experimental science to a much lesser extent than experimental psychology. Only a small proportion of the knowledge of psychopathological phenomena is based on the classical scientific procedure of experimentation. Most of it is based on naturalistic observations, as in descriptive zoology and botany. Nevertheless, it is an empirical discipline and can be contrasted with philosophy. Many attempts have been made, particularly on the European continent, to use philosophical concepts, particularly from philosophical phenomenology and existentialism, to gain some understanding of the strange observations made by psychopathologists. In contrast, the psychiatric phenomena of hallucinations and illusions provide favourite material for philosophers when they are discussing various theories of knowledge of the external world through sensory perception. As I have said before I shall not attempt to cover the whole field of psychopathology but shall limit myself only to rather a rare but extremely interesting syndrome of "depersonalization–derealization," the syndrome touching indirectly on some of the perennial philosophical problems, namely that of "reality," "existence," and the status of the knowledge of the external world obtained through sensory perception. Because of the philosophical implications of this syndrome many philosophically minded psychiatrists on the European continent used philosophical categories from Phenomenology and Existentialism in attempts to explain it. I propose to use a different strategy, namely, to see whether this syndrome can throw some light on some problems of epistemology.

Let me briefly describe the syndrome; further details and various theories explaining it will be found elsewhere (Weckowicz, 1970). Depersonalization, which we can call "depersonalization–derealization," since usually it is accompanied by a feeling of unreality of the surrounding world, is a loosely associated group of symptoms occurring in psychiatric patients. It can be induced experimentally and also occurs spontaneously in normal subjects. To quote Schilder: "The individual feels totally different from his previous being; he does not recognize himself as a person. His actions seem automatic, he behaves as if he were an observer of his own actions. The outside world appears to him strange and new and it has lost the character of reality. The 'self' does not behave any longer in its former way." (Free translation from German, Schilder, 1914, p. 54.) From this definition it can be seen that the core of the syndrome is a change in the *immediately given experience*, a "strangeness" and "unreality" of the object of experience: either the self or the external world or both. There is a disturbance in the subject–object relationship producing perplexity and interfering with the smooth flow of conscious experience. There is a feeling of change. The subject feels himself changed completely in comparison with his former state. This change extends to both himself and the external world. There is a feeling of unreality, the self and the body appear unreal as if the subject were dreaming and were conscious of having a dream. The external world looks unreal, as if it existed in the imagination of the subject. People and the subject himself, apart from appearing or feeling unreal, have a robot like quality. The subject has a feeling of being passive, watching his behaviour which is occurring completely automatically. These experiences are very unpleasant for the subject, who at the same time experiences that he is not capable of emotional responses. He feels subjectively unable to experience affect. The most interesting feature and most important for our subsequent theoretical discussion is the non-delusional quality of the experiences. The true depersonalization–derealization experience in contrast to nihilistic delusions, has an interesting "as if" quality. The subject is *rationally aware that his body is real* and that the *external world is real*. They only appear as if they were not real. The individual finds the perceptual experience quite perplexing and in conflict with his system of beliefs. Only when he becomes deluded do his immediate experiences and his beliefs become congruent with each other. These experiences are very strange indeed, and the subject resorts to metaphors, "as if" expressions and figures of speech to describe them. Because of the consistency with which they occur they cannot be regarded as playacting. For the sake of our discussion of the epistemological significance of this syndrome I shall single out only one aspect of it: the immediate, perceptual experience of unreality of one's self, one's body, and of the external world, accompanied by a belief, a rational knowledge, that they are real.[1] It is as though the subject were filled with Cartesian doubts. As in Descarte's *Meditations* (Descartes, 1931) the subject feels that he may be deceived by a malicious demon (although he does not need to express it in these words) and the light he sees, the noise he hears, the heat he feels, may be false, not real. It may only seem to him that he sees light, that he hears noise, or that he feels heat. His body may not be real. He may be dreaming. However, the doubts are not rational as they are in Descarte's *Meditations*; they are on the perceptual level. It is as if his percepts were lacking in a certain quality which distinguishes real percepts from imaginary percepts. Not only the external world and his body seem to be unreal and therefore non-existent, but also the inner core of his experienced self is unreal and does not exist, at least in the immediate experience, if not in the reflective knowledge. Of course, in cases of nihilistic delusions there is not only an immediate experience of non-existence but also a belief (reflective knowledge) of non-existence. The patients, as it were, "think, but they do not exist." This does not agree with Descartes' feeling of certainty that even if he is deceived by a malicious demon and things only seem to him, at least he is certain that they seem to him and he can think of them, therefore, he is certain that he exists. This deduction has of course been criticized by philosophers belonging to the English empiricist tradition, such as Hume and Russell, who tended to reject the derivation of the transcendental ego from the Cartesian argument.

However, on the European continent it became the corner stone of Husserlian Phenomenology. Philosophically minded European psychiatrists explain the depersonalization–derealization syndrome in philosophical terms as a disturbance in intentionality of mental acts, particularly that of perception, leading to distortion of the relationship between the subject conceived as the transcendental ego or self and the objects of a mental act such as the perceived or phenomenal self, the perceived body and the perceived external world. There is a disturbance of what Husserl calls *noesis* or "being in consciousness."

Since the words "real" and "unreal" are concerned with the existence of something or its "being," I would like to clarify a certain issue before I proceed any further. The term existence has three meanings: ontological, which means existing absolutely outside human experience, phenomenological,[2] which means existing in human conscious experience, and transcendental, which means *a priori* entailed by the act of experiencing. Traditionally philosophers were concerned with the status of ontological objects causing the appearance of phenomenological objects in subjective experience. They were also concerned with the transcendental (ontic) self which was the experiencer, but was not experienced in contrast to the phenomenological, the perceived self. When the terms "real," "unreal," "does not exist" or "appears to not exist" are used in the phenomenological sense they are used as descriptions of experience. The phenomenological sense may be broader when it refers to the totality of conscious experience, when we say that a particular object is red, or narrower, when we say that a white object may appear red, in red illumination, or that a conjurer by a clever trick may produce an illusion that a thing has disappeared. The narrower sense refers to a particular experience, usually in naive perception. If such terms as "real," "exist," "does not exist" are used in an ontological sense, their meaning is metaphysical, such as the Solipsist's statement that the external world is not real. It is concerned with existence (being) in the absolute sense. For the purpose of this essay I shall limit myself to the "phenomenological" meaning of the word existence. Continental Existential and Phenomenological psychiatrists are mainly concerned with the transcendental and ontological meaning of the term existence.[3] From now on my essay will be concerned with psychology of knowledge in its perceptual aspects and only peripherally with epistemology proper.

To subjects experiencing the "depersonalization–derealization" syndrome, the surrounding world, their bodies, and even their experienced selves, *appear* to be unreal against their beliefs that this is not true. These subjects are very perplexed by their experiences and they are not completely satisfied with their rational beliefs. It is as if there were two kinds of knowledge; one supplied by the immediate perceptual experience and the other by rational judgment. These two kinds of knowledge conflict with one another. But, what is it that makes this conflict so strange? When I experience the Müller-Lyer illusion I see that one half of a black line on the paper is longer than the other one although I know that they are equal. I can describe my perception in terms of sensory data: extension of a thin patch of blackness on a white background. Can the "unrealness" of something seen be reduced to the traditional sensory data of patches of colour and contours postulated by empiricists? Apparently not, although some attempts to do it were made in the past. Hume (1962) distinguished between impressions (modern sensations or perceptions) and ideas (modern images). Impressions were supposed to be more "vivid", presumably more intense than ideas, which were supposed to be faint. However, we perceive a dim light while we can imagine a very bright light. Does it mean that the perceived dim light is brighter than the imagined bright light? This statement somehow seems to contradict common sense; the two perceptions are not on the same dimension. This was the opinion of Thomas Reid (Boring 1957), a countryman and a contemporary of Hume. According to him an instantaneous conviction of objective existence is an ingredient of every percept. Thus, the quality of "reality" becomes something like perceived redness or roundness. This became an important issue of the nineteenth century introspectionist psychology and the last attempt to solve it experimentally was that of Perky (1910) in Titchener's laboratory. The results of the experiment seemed to support Hume. However, Perky did not take into account the induced set and expectancy. When psychologists started to investigate the influence of these factors on perception the attempts to find the quality of reality in the sensory data as such were abandoned. A subjective judgment as to the reality or unreality of a certain experience depended on the frame of reference of this experience, on the system of beliefs and expectancies. This view, starting with James (1890) and the functionalists, was recently put forward forcefully by Neisser (1967) and Kolers (1964). From the epistemological point of view the "coherence theory of truth" is implicit in this view. To illustrate by a fanciful example what is meant a proponent of the theory would say: if a man had completely coherent dreams, continuing as coherent sequences in time from one night to another, he would have difficulty, in retrospect, in telling the difference between the states of wakefulness and dreaming.

However, patients suffering from the "depersonalization–derealization" syndrome believe that the world and their bodies are real, and yet perceive them to be unreal. Have we to go back to Hume and Reid and look for the quality of reality in sense data? Apparently not, if we abandon the Empiricist theories of perception and the Empiricist tradition of epistemology. The characteristic of the Empiricist epistemology, starting with Locke, Hume, and Berkeley, including the two Mills, Helmholtz, Titchener and Mach, and ending with such contemporary philosophers as Russell and Ayer, is a "two stage" or "two level" theory of knowledge. It is assumed that there is raw material of experience: sense data, given by perception, from which the existence of external objects is inferred by some kind of secondary higher judgmental process. The details of these views, of course, vary depending on which particular theory the philosopher or the psychologist espouses. If he follows a "representative" theory of perception he believes, together with Helmholtz, that the existence and the properties of the external objects are inferred from the sensory data plus their associations. On the other hand, if he opts for the more recent "phenomenalist" theory, he believes, together with Mach, James, Bentley, Ames and perhaps even Berkeley, that the external objects are logically constructed from the sensory data in a mentalistic or physicalistic universe, depending on his particular metaphysical predilection.

The most important feature of this approach is that perception (sensation) as such is not considered as a knowledge acquiring process. Perception is separated from cognition. If the necessary conditions for stating that A knows p are (1) A believes that p, (2) p is true, (3) A has good evidence for p, sensory perception furnishes only some of the evidence. The actual judgment process of squaring the evidence with the belief occurs at the cognitive level. The only evidence on which these judgments are based are sense data and their associations in memory. Immediately there arises in one's mind an image of a homunculus watching screens on which sense data are projected, trying to decipher them and to infer their meaning.

There have been many critics of this type of epistemology and theory of perception. The best known among philosophers are members of the English common language school like Ryle (1963), Austin (1964), and Armstrong (1961, 1962, 1965), and, among psychologists, Gibson (1966, 1967). The criticism from the philosophical point of view includes such arguments as in correct usage of the term "see" or "perceive" with reference to the sense datum, the predicament of the homunculus with an infinite regressus of homunculi inside homunculi, and the specter of the blind alley of Solipsism. More interesting is empirical evidence furnished by experimental psychologists that sensory organ functioning and perception should be regarded not as a passive reflexion of the external world, but as an active process of information extraction (Gibson, 1966; Piaget, 1952, 1954; Armstrong, 1965). As a result, these workers tend to adopt some form of Realism, either naive or critical, in their epistemological orientation.

I think that a very important feature of anti-empiricist theories of perception and epistemologies of Realism is a view of sensory processes and perception as, *sui generis*, knowledge establishing processes. This point was stressed forcefully by Armstrong (1965). Following the common usage, we can divide knowledge into two kinds: "knowledge by acquaintance" and "knowledge about." Sensory processes and perception (they are really descriptions of basically the same process) provide non-reflective, immediate knowledge by acquaintance, while conceptual, judgmental processes provide reflective, more abstract and verbalized "knowledge about" or "propositional knowledge." "Knowledge about" or "propositional knowledge" can be characterized by stating: If A knows that p is true then (1) A believes that p, (2) p is true and (3) A has good evidence for p. However, that cannot be said about "knowledge by acquaintance", the concrete, non-reflective, non-verbal, immediate knowlege supplied by perceptual processes. According to Armstrong (1965), in the case of this type of knowledge: if A knows that p, then (1) A believes that p, (2) p is true, (3) A's belief is reliably correlated with the truth of p. Perception as such is the evidence for itself. An infinite number of other propositions pertaining to perception have to be brought as evidence for p. Armstrong, while rejecting the doctrine of logically incorrigible datum, accepts a reliable correlation, holding a belief in the existence of a perceived object and beliefs of that sort being true. He postulates a direct causality between a true belief about the environment and the feature of the environment about which this belief is held. Translated into the language of empirical psychology it means that valid information about an object is extracted by sensory processes and given in immediate awareness. This information is not a sense datum, but some concrete knowledge about a concrete object. Thus, we usually perceive "that something is the case" and not just "something." We "see that there is a horse at a certain distance before us" and not simply "see a horse" (Armstrong, 1965).[4] Perception gives us immediate knowledge that the object we see is real, but this quality of reality is not provided by sensory data but by a complex process of extracting information from the environment. Gibson's (1966) theory of "senses considered as perceptual systems" is very useful in this connection.[5] If the complex information about surrounding objects and one's body in relation to these objects existing in the array of energy impinging on the sensory organs is, by an active exploration over time, extracted in the form of certain invariances, the significance of which depends on this active exploration, then the whole complex process may be responsible for the feeling of reality normally attaching to the perceived world and the perceived self. It is not a characteristic of a sensory datum and it does not depend primarily on the non-perceptual, reflective, conceptual, cognitive processes. This would explain why the patients suffering from "depersonalization–derealization" syndrome have a feeling that the world around them and their bodies seem to be unreal while they believe that it is not true. Armstrong (1965) calls such a type of perceptual process a *"belief-acquiring sort*, but without the actual acquiring of a belief." Apparently the arising perceptual belief is contradicted by the existing systematized cognitive beliefs. The Müller-Lyer illusion experienced by a sophisticated observer provides a relevant example. Armstrong gives an example of a man who knows that he has turned off the gas, yet he is still unable to shake off the feeling that he has not done so. Piaget (1952, 1954), Inhelder and Piaget (1958), and Brunswik (1954) provide support for the view that perceptual processes are different from cognitive processes. According to Piaget perception originates in the sensorimotor period of infancy and remains to a great extent autonomous from the conceptual–cognitive processes developed in the stages of concrete and formal operations.

If it is accepted that it is possible to believe rationally that the world and one's body are real and yet to perceive them as unreal, the question to be answered next is: what makes certain perceptions appear real and other perceptions unreal? It cannot be the cognitive framework, since the "reality" characteristic to a great extent is independent of the concomitant beliefs and expectancies. At the present stage one can offer only certain speculations. First, it would be profitable to ask what kind of physiological and experimental conditions can induce "depersonalization–derealization–like" states in patients and normal subjects. This condition has been described quite often in cases of many organic diseases of the brain, particularly those involving the parietal, the temporal lobes, and the limbic systems, the areas of the brain designated by Pribram (1960) as the posterior intrinsic systems and playing an important role in providing meaning to perception. These states were occasionally obtained by Penfield and Rasmussen (1950) by electrical stimulation of various areas of the temporal lobe in conscious patients. Hallucinogenic drugs like LSD_{25} very often produce symptoms similar to depersonalization and derealization, sometimes indistinguishable from the depersonalization symptoms occurring in psychiatric patients and occasionally lasting several days. There are some reports of the occurrence of depersonalization–derealization phenomena, or similar to them, produced by experimental means in psychological laboratories. Thus, sensory deprivation experiments occasionally have produced depersonalization-like experiences in subjects (Wexler, Mendelson,

Leiderman and Solomon, 1958). Similar effects are sometimes produced by delayed auditory feedback and "white noise" (Cattell, 1966). Thus, it seems that a disruption of the normal input of information into the brain and its matching with some processes going on in the brain, and also some lasting changes in arousal, could produce depersonalization. Experiments in which subjects received conflicting information occasionally produced symptoms somewhat resembling depersonalization–derealization. Witkin and Asch (1948a, b) reported that conflicting vestibular and visual stimulation for the orientation of the body in space, as in the tilted room or tilted chair situation, occasionally produce symptoms somewhat resembling depersonalization and derealization. Weightlessness, as in space travel, was also reported to produce some perceptual disturbance and ego disorientation which were similar to those occurring in the syndrome in question (Mercury Project Summary, 1963). All these findings indicate that depersonalization–derealization is related to some ongoing complex information-processing by the organism. Weckowicz (1969), after reviewing various theories of depersonalization–derealization existing in the past and current psychiatric literature, particularly those within the framework of psychoanalysis and Phenomenological–Existential psychiatry, pointed out some convergence of the views. Contemporary psychoanalysts stress in connection with depersonalization the impairment of the integrative function of the ego, the separation of the representation of the self from the representation of the object, and a disturbance of relationship between individual experiences and their frame of reference. Similarly, the Existential psychiatrists stress a lack of the activity of the ego, a lack of the active integration of experience, a split between the self and the external world and fragmenting of experience, with a disruption of its continuity as the factors which produce depersonalization and derealization. The notions of activity and construction in the act of knowing go back to Brentano and Husserl. These philosophers were referring to acts in pure intentional consciousness which organized and objectified sensory materials. Brentano (Boring, 1957) differentiated acts of "ideating," involving sensing and imagining, from acts of "judging," which were concerned, among other things, with perception of real objects. To what extent these purely philosophical speculations are relevant to empirical evidence it is difficult to say. However, there is no doubt that modern experimental psychology stresses very much either active construction of the perceived world or an active exploration and extraction of the incoming information, or possibly both. The Lockean *tabula rasa* idea of the human mind or that of a block of wax with the environment acting like a seal, or the idea of a mirror or a photographic plate are all definitely out, except in cases of a special attitude, such as the one assumed by a realist painter or an introspectionist psychologist.

Gibson (1966) stated that perception of real objects in the world depends on active "obtaining," active extracting of information contained in the array of the energy impinging on the organism by its perceptual systems. Stimulation input, which is "imposed" and passively received, does not lead to the perception of real objects but only to experiences of sensations. Thus, he stressed active exploration of the environment and active extraction of information (Gibson, 1962) as determining the degree of reality of the perceived, meaningful objects. Passive perception of "imposed" as contrasted to "obtained" stimulation could lead to meaningless sensation. In an earlier publication Gibson (1950) differentiated two types of visual experiences: "visual world" and "visual field." The "visual world" is three dimensional, has depth, and obeys the constancy of perception laws. The "visual field" is flat, two-dimensional, and obeys the laws of perspective drawing. Meaningful objects are contained in the "visual world," while meaningless sensations, unless they play a representational role, belong to the "visual field." Since depersonalized subjects complain of a lack of depth, of flatness of the perceived world, it is likely that they tend to see more in terms of the "visual field" than the "visual world." The fact that in schizophrenic patients, frequently subject to depersonalization, constancy of perception is impaired, points in the same direction (Weckowicz, 1964). Piaget (1954) also stresses the importance of active sensory-motor operations and schemas in perception. The environment is explored according to certain schemas, which are built during the interaction between the organism and the environment. If we attempt to bring together the views of Gibson and the workers who stress not only the active extraction of information from the environment but also an active construction of a model of the environment sometimes referred to as "analysis-by-synthesis" (Hebb, 1949; Piaget, 1954; Neisser, 1967), we must point out that it is not likely that the exploration of the environment by the sensory organs is a random affair. It must go on according to a certain plan or a schema. Construction of a model of the environment does not necessarily mean that an icon of the environment is produced, although there is some evidence for it. The relationship may be complementary, like the relationship between a lock and key. A movement of an eye has to compensate or even anticipate a movement of an object in the visual field. If there is some kind of model or schema building on the part of the organism exploring the environment then there are certain interesting possibilities for mechanisms responsible for greater or lesser experienced reality of the perceived environment. Suppose there is a system like a TOTE (Miller, Galanter and Pribram, 1960) which is responsible for matching the information obtained from the environment with the constructed schema of the environment. In this case the apparent reality of the perceived object may depend on such temporal factors as the amount of time the constructed schema anticipates the received information or the amount of discrepancy between the anticipatory schema and the feedback of information from the environment. Perhaps there are some optimal values for the time interval and also for the optimal amount of mismatch, which are related to the mechanisms of attention and the experienced reality of an event. A complete mismatch of the constructed schema and the obtained environmental information could produce an unpredictable world of dreams with a fluctuating sense of reality, while a perfect match would produce something like controlled daytime imagery with no "hard facts" of external reality opposing the imaginings. In the latter case the matched information would not come directly from the environment but from the memory store.[6] It is interesting that a "good trip" in LSD_{25} takers produces an enhanced sense of reality, an increased sense of "itness" of the perceived objects (Huxley, 1959). On the other hand having a "bad trip" results very often in a feeling of unreality and depersonalization. The author of this paper also recorded that a "good trip" did not only produce an enhanced feeling of reality of the perceived world, but also a peculiar feeling that, when he was listening to a piece of music, he had a feeling, against his better judgment, that he was actively composing and performing that piece.

SUMMARY AND CONCLUSIONS

The contribution of a psychopathologist from his study of "depersonalization–derealization" to psychology of knowledge and perhaps to epistemology can now be summarized briefly

The strange syndrome of "depersonalization and derealization" suggests that:

1. There are two kinds of knowledge acquiring processes: that of an immediate perceptual knowledge and that of reflective conceptual knowledge, with the possibility of a conflict between the two kinds of knowledge.
2. The theories of perception based on the empiricist tradition in epistemology cannot explain a peculiar character of apparent reality or unreality of the perceived world.

3. The dimension of reality–unreality of perception, on the phenomenological level, may correspond, on the behavioural level, to a dimension characterized by the amount of active sensory-motor exploration of the environment. A hypothesis can be formulated that depersonalized subjects do not actively use their perceptual systems to extract information from the environment, or use them to a lesser extent than normal controls.

NOTES

1. The symptoms of *déjà vu* and *jamais vu* which are associated very often with the depersonalization—derealization syndrome pose also an interesting philosophical problem regarding human memory. In *déjà vu* subjects have an immediate experience of familiarity, recognition and having been acquainted with an object, a scene or a person, at the same time rationally believing to the contrary. In *jamais vu* objects which the subject recognizes as familiar using, rational judgment, appear in the immediate experience as being totally strange. Thus, memory seems to have two aspects, one perceptual, the other cognitive. There is, as it were, a quality of familiarity or strangeness which is perceived to reside in objects of the external world, independently, from the reflective judgment.

2. It is necessary to differentiate "phenomenological", meaning accessible to human conscious knowledge, in contrast to "noumenal", pertaining to the Kantian thing-in-itself, "phenomenological" as appearing in naive perception, "Phenomenological" as pertaining to a particular school of philosophy and psychiatry inspired by Husserl, and "phenomenalist" as pertaining to a particular epistemology identifying sensory data with ultimate reality. Since one of the features of Husserl's Phenomenology is a rejection of the limitations of human knowledge to phenomena and a belief in the absolute knowledge of the noumenal self and object, one should be very careful not to confuse these meanings. (In the essay when I refer to the Husserlian Phenomenology I use the capital *P*, while in the other cases I used small *p*).

3. For a discussion in English of "depersonalization—derealization" and related topics from the ontological, rather than from the epistemological point of view, adopted in the present essay, see Laing (1960).

4. Armstrong differentiates between immediate and mediate perceptions. Immediate perception is like traditional sense data, while mediate perception is direct knowledge of a seen object. Since he states that we are usually unconscious of our immediate perceptions, the question arises whether immediate perceptions exist at all, except on special occasions.

5. Discussing the same problems of perception from the Existential and Phenomenological point of view, although using a different idiom and not committing himself to an epistemological realism Merleau-Ponty (1962) comes to the same conclusions. The reality of external objects is given immediately to a "being-in-the-world" characteristic of an "involved consciousness" in contrast to a "positing consciousness."

6. The detached attitude of an introspectionist or an artist could be described as a passive reception of information from the environment with a minimum of active, constructive exploration. In the case of controlled day time imagination there could be mainly constructive activity with the feedbacks from memory and a conscious disregard of the environmental information. In the REM sleep dreams and hallucinations there could be a temporary or permanent incapacity to match the anticipatory schema with the incoming sensory information, because of breakdown of the feedback mechanism. A depersonalized patient is probably closest to the first category.

COMMENT ON WECKOWICZ PAPER

J. R. Royce

Dr. Weckowicz has offered an explanation of depersonalization in terms of perceptual deficiency. That is, he has put forward the hypothesis that such states are essentially introverted rather than extroverted with respect to the ecology; that the sense of irreality is due to "turning off" completely, or at least invoking a relatively passive perceptual attitude. The consequent psycho-epistemic-pathology is a diminishment or extinction of perceptual reality.

Is there a psychopathological opposite to depersonalization? Are there pathological consequences which might accompany what I will label perceptual overexposure? I am not thinking of the stress which occurs when input systems become overloaded, as in photic driving or audiogenic seizures, or even the consequences of information input overload. Rather, my focus is on the possible pathological consequence of over-commitment to perceptual reality. This is, when we have highly active, information extracting, invariant identifying (let us assume at least some degree of veridicality so that we do not get sidetracked into hallucinations, illusions, solipsism, and mysticism) perceptual systems dominating, while other cognitive modes (e.g., the conceptual) are seriously subservient.

BIBLIOGRAPHY

Armstrong, D. M., *Perception and the physical world*. New York Humanities Press, 1961.
Armstrong, D. M., *Bodily sensations*. London: Routledge and Kegan Paul, 1962.
Armstrong, D. M., A theory of perception. In *Scientific psychology*, Eds. B. B. Wolman and E. Nagel. New York: Basic Books, 1965.
Austin, J. L., *Sense and Sensibilia*. New York: Oxford Univ. Press, 1964.
Boring, E. G., *A history of experimental psychology*, New York: Appleton-Century-Crofts, 1957.
Brunswik, E., Reasoning as a universal behaviour model and a functional differentiation between "perception" and "thinking". Read at the *International Congress of Psychology*, 1954. Reproduced in *The psychology of Egon Brunswik*; Ed. K. R. Hammond, New York: Holt, Rinehart and Winston, 1966.
Campbell, D. T., Methodological suggestions from a comparative psychology of knowledge process. *Inquiry*, 1959, **2**, 152–182.
Cattell, J. P., Depersonalization phenomena. In *American handbook of psychiatry*, vol. III, Ed. S. Arieti, New York: Basic Books, 1966.
Descartes, R., *The Meditations*, (Second Meditation). In *The Philosophical Works of Descartes*, translated by Elizabeth S. Haldane and G. R. T. Ross. London: Cambridge Univ. Press, 1931.
Gibson, J. J., *The perception of the visual world*. Boston: Houghton Mifflin, 1950.
Gibson, J. J., Observations on active touch, *Psychological Review*, 1962, **69**, 477–491.
Gibson, J. J., *The senses considered as perceptual systems*. Boston: Houghton Mifflin, 1966.
Gibson, J. J., New reasons for realism, *Synthese*, 1967, **17**, 162–172.
Grize, Jean-Blaise, Genetic epistemology and psychology. In *Scientific psychology;* Eds.: B. B. Wolman and E. Nagel, New York: Basic Books, 1949.
Hebb, D. O. *Organization of behaviour*, New York: John Wiley, 1949.
Hume, D., *A treatise of human nature*, (Book one), London: Fontana Library, 1962.
Husserl, E., *Logische Untersuchungen*, Halle Niemeyer, 1900.
Huxley, A. *The doors of perception*, Harmondsworth, Middlesex: Penguin Books, 1959.
Inhelder, B. and Piaget, J., *The growth of logical thinking from childhood to adolescence*, New York: Basic Books, 1958.
James, W., *The principles of psychology*, New York: Henry Holt, 1890.
Kolers, P. A., The illusion of movement, *Scientific American*, 1964, **211**, 98–106.
Laing, R. D., *The divided self*. London: Tavistock Publications, 1960.
Mercury Project Summary, (including results of the fourth manned orbital flight.) Washington, NASA, D. C. 1963.
Merleau-Ponty, M., *Phenomenology of perception*, London: Routledge and Kegan Paul, 1962.
Miller, G. A., Galanter, E., and Pribram, K. H., *Plans and the structure of behaviour*. New York: Holt, Rinehart and Winston, 1960.
Neisser, U., *Cognitive Psychology*, New York: Appleton-Century-Crofts, 1967.
Penfield, W. and Rasmussen, T. *The cerebral cortex of man*. New York: Macmillan, 1955.
Perky, C. W., An experimental study of imagination. *American Journal of Psychology*, 1910, **21**, 422–452.
Piaget, J., *The origins of intelligence in children*. New York: International Universities Press, 1952.

Piaget, J., *The construction of reality in the child.* New York: Basic Books, 1954.
Piaget, J., Psychology and philosophy. In *Scientific psychology*, Eds. B. B. Wolman and E. Nagel, New York: Basic Books, 1965.
Pribram, K. H., A review of theory in physiological psychology. *Annual Review of Psychology*, 1960, **11**, 1–40.
Ryle, G., *The concept of mind.* Harmondsworth, Middlesex: Penguin Books, 1963.
Schilder, P., *Selbstbewußtsein und Persönlichkeitsbewußtsein*, Berlin: Julius Springer, 1914.
Weckowicz, T. E., Shape constancy in schizophrenic patients. *Journal of Abnormal and Social Psychology*, 1964, **68**, 177–183.
Weckowicz, T. E., Depersonalization. In *Symptoms of Psychopathology;* Ed. C. G. Costello, in press. New York: John Wiley, 1970.
Wexler, D., Mendelson, J., Leiderman, P. H. and Solomon, P., Sensory deprivation; a technique for studying psychiatric aspects of stress. *American Medical Association Archives of Neurology and Psychiatry*, 1958, **79**, 225.
Witkin, H. A. and Asch, S. E., Studies in space orientation. III Perception of the upright in the absence of visual field. *Journal of Experimental Psychology*, 1948a, **38**, 603–614.
Witkin, H. A. and Asch, S. E., Studies in space orientation. IV Further experiments on perception of the upright with displaced visual fields. *Journal of Experimental Psychology*, 1948b, **38**, 762–782.

XIV

NEUROLOGICAL NOTES ON KNOWING

Karl H. Pribram

Stanford University

INTRODUCTION

A discussion of the "neurology of knowing" presupposes some considerable knowledge about knowledge and about the way the brain functions. My thesis here is that we do in fact have available a great body of analysis and evidence; thus, matching the psychological against the neurological can effectively increase the relevance of both.

Let me define, for the purposes of this presentation, knowledge as codified information consensually validated. Lest the reader be turned off completely by this seemingly restrictive statement, let me add quickly that the definition portends not all what it seems to. It is derived from a long series of studies performed in my laboratories aimed at the problem of how the brain works while an organism is learning, remembering or forgetting. Again and again my experiments showed that how much may be learned or remembered—indeed even *what* may be learned or remembered—is at any moment determined as much by the context, the set and setting, in which an informative item is placed as by that item *per se*. Further, I found that we did not know how to manipulate the content-context relationship, or even how to think about it: We knew that somehow repetition was essential but knew little about which forms of repetition were effective and which were not. Finally, it became apparent that these patterns of repetition constitute codes and that cracking the codes would be tantamount to understanding how information storage and retrieval are best accomplished.

In short, my proposal is that the extent of learning, remembering and forgetting depends on the codes into which events are patterned—and that it is coding which determines knowledge. By this I do *not* want to convey just another statement of the Sapir-Whorf hypothesis. Rather I have in mind something similar to Charles Peirce's Theory of Meaning. But more of this in a moment.

CODES

First, what is a code? Not so long ago my laboratory came into the proud possession of a computer. Very quickly we learned the fun of communicating with this mechanical mentor. Our first encounter involved twelve rather mysterious switches which had to be set in a sequence of patterns, each pattern to be deposited in the computer memory before resetting the switches. Twenty such instructions or patterns constituted what is called the "bootstrap" program. After this had been entered we could talk to the computer—and it to us—via an attached teletype.

Bootstrapping is not necessarily an occasional occurrence. Whenever a fairly serious mistake is made—and mistakes were made often at the beginning—the computer's memory is disrupted and we must start anew by bootstrapping.

Imagine setting a dozen switches twenty times and repeating the process from the beginning every time an error is committed.

```
U U D D U U U D U D U D
U U U U U U U U U D D D
U U U U D U D U D U U U
U U D D U U U U U U U U
U U D D U U U D U U D D
D D U D D D U D D U U U
U D U D D U D U U D U D
U D U D U U U U U U D U
D U D D U U U U U U U U
D U U U U U U D D U U
```

and so on.

Imagine our annoyance when the bootstrap didn't work because perhaps on setting the 19th instruction an error was made in setting the eighth switch. Obviously, this was no way to proceed.

Computer programmers had early faced this problem and solved it simply. Conceptually, the twelve switches were divided into four triads and each combination of up down within each triad given an Arabic numeral. Thus

D	D	D	became	0
D	D	U	became	1
D	U	D	became	2
D	U	U	became	3
U	D	D	became	4
U	D	U	became	5
U	U	D	became	6
U	U	U	became	7

Conceptually, switching the first toggle on the right becomes a one, the next left becomes a 2, the next after this a 4 (and the next an 8 if more than a triad of switches had been necessary, i.e., if for instance our computer had come with sixteen switches we should have conceptually divided the array into quads). Thus the bootstrapping program now consisted of a sequence of twenty patterns of four Arabic numerals

e.g. 3 7 2 2
      0 0 1 4
      3 4 5 6
      2 2 1 3
      1 0 3 7

etc.,
and we were surprised at how quickly those who bootsrapped repeatedly, actually came to know the program by heart. Certainly fewer errors were made in depositing the necessary configurations—the entire process was speeded and became, in most cases, rapidly routine and habitual.

Once the computer is bootstrapped it can be talked to in simple alphabetical terms: e.g., JMP for jump, CLA for clear the accumulator, TAD for add, etc. But each of these mnemonic symbols merely stands for a configuration of switches. In fact, in the computer handbook the arrangement for each mnemonic is given in Arabic notation: e.g., CLA = 7200. This in turn is easily translated into U U U D U D D D D D D D, should we be forced to set the switches by hand because the teletype has gone out of commission.

Programming thus is found to be in the first instance the art of devising codes, codes that facilitate learning, remembering and reasoning. The logic of a computer is primarily a code, a set of signals which allows ready manipulation. The power of a program lies in the fact that it is a useful code.

29*

If you doubt this, try next month to check your bank statement against your record of expenditures and do it all using Roman rather than Arabic numerals. Can you imagine working out our national budget in the Roman system?

I have belabored this point because I believe that coding operations are central to what we call "knowing." I might even go so far as to suggest that knowing is coding.

What then are the forms coding can take? Here the results of research in brain function prove to be helpful. The nervous system, just as the computer, has as its primary signalling device an on-off type of process. The nervous system, just as the programmer, has to find ways by which to convert sequences of patterns of on-off events into usable, i.e., processable, codes. This is accomplished in the nervous system by the arrangement of inhibitory mechanisms which act to group signals and to allow time for depositing them. Grouping is accomplished by the process of lateral or surround inhibition through which the activity in one neuron causes a decrementing of activity in its neighbors; time for deposit depends on the process of neuronal self-inhibition through which a neuron relatively quickly decrements its own activity through negative feedback. Inhibitory mechanisms allow the occurrence of an alphabet of states to supplant the restrictions imposed by coding solely by on-off patterns of nerve impulses. Thus a simple neural alphabet (such as that composed of Arabic numerals in our initial bootstrap programming of the computer) can be manipulated by our input systems. A complex series of patterns of very simple on-off elements has been coded into a simpler series of patterns of somewhat more complex elements. The analogy with computer mechanisms can be carried even further: a hardware wiring diagram by which such transformations might be accomplished in a computer looks remarkably similar to a diagram of the organization of the retinal structure known to organize the living visual process. This exchange between a non-repetitive series of patterns made up of repetitive elements and a repetitive series of patterns made up of non-repetitive elements is the essence of coding.

One of the fascinating things we have learned about the operation of the brain is that, within any of its systems, information becomes distributed. Extensive removals and injuries impair performance remarkably little (until some critical point is reached). I have elsewhere detailed a type of mechanism (considered to be similar to that by which holograms are made) consonant with the known facts of neuroanatomy and neurophysiology which can accomplish such distribution of information (Pribram, 1966, 1969, and 1971).

IMAGES

Here it is sufficient to note that such a mechanism actually allows the construction and reconstruction of Images by a process in which only a limited number of variables need be coded. This then would be a degredation of the neural alphabet back into simpler components. However, these components are now no longer the presence or absence (on and off) of neural impulses but are indicators of relationships among them. Imaging therefore involves a *further* coding process by which the neural process can represent fully its origin. This isomorphism between environmental occurrences (events) and Image results from the fact that all of the transformations performed on the signalling events are completely reversible.

Composed as it is of few elements arranged in complex series of patterns, the Image thus resembles, as it should, the environmental pattern from which it originates. This is a resemblance only, however; as we have seen, the elements composing the Image represent relations between events rather than the events *per se*. That this is so, is most dramatically demonstrated by the experiments in which a subject is fitted with prism glasses which invert his entire visual field. As is now well known, reasonably rapid adjustment takes place so that the visual image is restored to its accustomed upright form (Held, 1968; Kohler, 1964).

Analysis of the brain's function has shown further that at least three different sorts of Images can be constructed. The first of these, already discussed, is initiated by and operates on sensory events generated at receptors which interface the organism with his physical and social environment—receptors located in the eyes, ears, nose, mouth, and skin. Another type of Image is constructed from events occurring deep in the central nervous system. Research over the past few decades has shown that the central core of the brain stem contains a variety of receptors, each sensitive to physico-chemical changes occurring in the organism's blood stream. Thus, cells sensitive to temperature, estrogens, androgens and adrenal steroids, osmotic equilibrium, blood glucose, sertonin, noradrenalin and the partial pressure of circulating CO_2 are located in a limited part of the brain surrounding the midline ventricular system and extending from just anterior to the hypothalamus to the lower part of the brain stem. These sensitive core-receptors regulate the production and conservation of heat, the sexual activities, thirst and hunger, the sleep and respiratory cycles of the organism (Pribram, 1960). Awareness of these processes must be based on some sort of Imaging. The Images constructed are, however, somewhat different from Images-of-Events of the world outside. Due to differences in receptor properties (e.g., core-receptors do not adapt) and differences in the organization of the neural processes engendered (e.g., there are probably no clearcut differences between lateral and self-inhibitory interactions), changes in the world-within are continuously monitored. Further, the neural mechanisms involved in the organization of the monitoring functions (e.g., the reticular formation in which the core-receptors are imbedded) are also sensitive to overall changes occurring in the world-outside. Monitor-Images therefore have the characteristic that they are induced by organismic state, i.e., by dispositions. Thus they are continuous rather than "thingy." Monitor-Images refer to subjective feelings whereas Images-of-Events make up the objective world of perceptions.

There is still another type of Image. The processes involved in its construction are movement-produced and movement-producing. Here again a large series of experiments is involved in making clear just what happens in the motor mechanism. Only a quarter of a century ago it was thought that the brain's motor cortex functioned as does a piano keyboard, that excitation of the appropriate neural element led to the contraction of a muscle or muscle group. Now we know that this is not so. Even at the simplest reflex level a large number of motor fibers (the α efferents) lead from the central nervous system not to muscles but to muscle spindles, receptors connected in parallel with muscle fibers. Excitation of these efferents to the spindle-receptors alters their activity—this is shown by changes which occur in the discharge of the afferent, sensory nerve fibers leading from the spindles to the central nervous system. The reflex mechanism can thus be activated either by operations performed on the muscle fiber (as when some external occurrence pushes or pulls) or by tuning the reflex to some new value via excitation or inhibition of the muscle spindle's activity. Research has shown that a good deal of the brain's control over movements is accomplished in this more subtle fashion (Miller, Galanter, and Pribram, 1960).

A corollary of the tuning process is the fact that such a mechanism is sensitive to the external forces which play on the muscles since they are hooked up in parallel with the spindles. Thus the sensory nerves from the spindles can relay information about force-fields to the brain—and in fact such sensory messages do reach the brain's cortex. Tracts from the periphery run rather directly to motor cortex where single cells (Malis, Pribram, and Kruger, 1953) have been found especially sensitive to the force necessary to perform an action (Evarts, 1967). Further, experiments have shown that a running record of changes in such force-fields allows a prediction to be made within millimeters of the extent and direction of the movement required next in order to continue effective action (Bernstein, 1967). These results have led me to call the Images constructed in the process of such endeavors, Images-of-Achievement.

Images-of-Achievement thus guide Actions (representations of such Images in the world external to the organism) rather than movements since these Images are composed of signals initiated by forces external to the organism. Images-of-Achievement guide movement, not by a piano keyboard type of process, but by tuning the reflex to accomplish an extrapolation of the "running record" (a wetware equivalent of a mathematical representation) of changes in the field of forces playing on the receptors which regulate the reflex. In this manner, Acts, representations of Images in the world-outside, are achieved.

IMMANENT KNOWLEDGE AND ACTION

Constructing Images thus constitutes three forms of knowing. We might call these the immanent forms. They are expressed in epistemology as Empiricism, Existentialism and Pragmatism, all rich in intuitive approaches to knowledge. All three hold that the criterion by which knowledge is known to be true is the *effect* such knowledge has: in Empiricism it is the effect on Images-of-Events; in Existentialism it is the effect on Monitor-Imaging; in Pragmatism it is the effect on Images-of-Achievement. Thus three forms of immanent knowing can be distinguished: knowing what, knowing that (in the sense, e.g., of obtaining carnal knowledge), and knowing how (see also Rozeboom's discussion of these forms in the present volume).

Despite the representational nature of these forms of knowing there remains the problem of the inherently personal nature of Imaging. The processes by which Images are constructed—though they employ constancies and other regularities recurrent in the brain's environment—occur entirely within the organism and thus tend to remain essentially private constructions. Polanyi (1960) has brought to our attention these personal processes. But, most analytical philosophers will insist that knowing must refer to something to be known and that this known cannot be ascertained without consensual validation. Consensual validation is not possible unless Actions, representations made in the organism's *environment*, are taken. The Acts necessary to establish knowledge are not simply come by. The neural mechanisms detailed in the next section show a rich intermeshing of Images-of-Achievement with those which produce Images-of-Events and Monitor-Images. Initially, as we shall see, these operations give rise to higher order (derived) knowledge. How then is immanence regained? Let me leave this topic for later and emphasize here the importance of Act to Knowledge, not in Brentano's sense but because to Act is to make a private process public. Thus, even though the process of Acting is highly personal and private, the Act once constructed becomes public. This accessibility of Action has major consequences.

SIGNS

Because of its privacy and also because of the richness of an Image similar to that found in uncoded "reality" there is considerable difficulty in sharing Immanent Knowledge directly. Other methods of coding do not share these difficulties. For instance, one process involves "decoding" the Image. Using this technique we identify aspects of the Image, assign them and work with these assignments. Neurologically, this process of identification is not yet fully explored. However, over the past two decades, studies performed in my laboratories and elsewhere have shown that those parts of the brain which had earlier been thought to serve associative functions, are more likely involved in the coding operations which lead to identifications of features of the Image (Pribram, 1960). These operations are similar to those already encountered in the production of neural signals from sensory events. In fact, the locus of operation may well be the same: We have evidence that the so-called cortical association areas of the brain work primarily to control input—in the visual and auditory modes, this control is exerted as far peripherally as the retina and the cochlear nucleus in the brain stem (Pribram, 1967; Spinelli and Pribram, 1966, 1967).

We found that this control is effected via structures in the brain which have motor functions (Reitz and Pribram, 1969). At first this presented us with an enigma; but on reflection it seemed less surprising. If motor mechanisms control movement by regulating muscle spindle receptors why is it odd that these same mechanisms should be found to control other receptor functions? Identification of features is after all an active process and the attaining of this perceptual skill is not that different from attaining a motor skill. The very same process which produces Images-of-Achievement must therefore come into play in decoding Images-of-Events.

Thus the very relationships to be Imaged are apparently under the influence of achievement control mechanisms. The processes which produce Images-of-Events and Images-of-Achievement are interdigitated to produce Signs. Significant (Sign-evoking) features of the Images-of-Events are enhanced when their identification is achieved through Action. We thus go about denoting: Indexing by means of Signs the universe which generated them.

Early in this manuscript we considered neural signals to be constructed into a primitive on-off alphabet of relationships among excitatory and inhibitory processes. The denotative Signs constructed by the cortical control mechanism can in a similar manner be viewed to represent neural words derived from higher order interactions coded when the processes which produce Images-of-Achievement operate on the processes which produce Images-of-Events. The alphabet constituted by neural inhibitory configurations would, therefore, correspond to the Arabic numerals used to determine the positions of each triad of switches. The Sign would correspond to the combinations of numbers used to bootstrap the computer.

In short, knowledge can be achieved through *Indexing* (categorization). Indexing goes beyond immanent knowledge by denoting, structuring the variety encompassed by the Image. In a sense meaning is imposed on the events by Indexing them; however, the imposition is derived from relationships among the events themselves. The knowledge which results is intrinsic if not immanent. As such it has the feel about it of being relevant though somewhat artificial—a code to be used to communicate about immanent knowledge but not to be confused with it. I can indicate to you by an identifying Sign that I know Jerome Bruner; neither you nor I confuse this indication as encompassing the richness and complexity of my Image of the person indicated.

SYMBOLS

One would expect a somewhat different result when the processes which generate Images-of-Achievement operate on, interact with, those which produce Monitor-Images. Evidence has accumulated that such interactions also occur. This evidence suggests, though somewhat indirectly, that Symbols are derived from such interactions. Symbols convey to the organism that his actions affect Monitor-Images, i.e., they engage his dispositions.

The evidence to which I refer is derived from the delayed reaction experiment. This task was devised by Hunter to show that young children and animals had ideas which could mediate in memory between an occurrence and its subsequent utilization (Hunter, 1913). While the subject watches, an experimenter hides a piece of chocolate or a peanut. The hiding place is then removed from view either by relocating the subject or by interposing a screen between subject and the hiding place. Some minutes (or even hours) later the hiding place is again exposed—the children and animals, of course, immediately search out the hidden tidbit. They show no difficulty with this task or any of its many modifications unless the frontal extremity of their brain is damaged. Only when the frontal cortex and a motor structure (the caudate nucleus) which lies deep to it are injured is this capacity to recall lost (Jacobsen, 1935; Rosvold and Szwarcbart, 1964).

Other considerations [anatomical and behavioral (Pribram, 1958)] show the frontal cortex to be intimately related to the core brain mechanisms which generate Monitor-Images. The question which has for decades puzzled investigators is the repeated finding that in the brain the mechanisms of recall and those dealing with appetites (or drives) are juxtaposed. (Initially the problem centered on the frontal cortex (Pribram, 1960); more recently the scene has shifted to limbic structures such as the amygdala (Bagshaw and Benzies, 1968; Bagshaw and Coppock, 1968; Bagshaw and Pribram, 1968; Pribram, 1967) and the hippocampus (Douglas, 1967; Douglas and Pribram, 1966); and now clinical evidence suggests that hypothalamic lesions markedly impair certain kinds of memory (Talland and Waugh, 1969).

These findings become less mysterious when the delayed reaction task is analyzed in terms of symbolic processing as conceived here. The problem can be altered slightly by using what is called the indirect method: a cue other than the tidbit itself can be used to indicate where the peanut or chocolate is to be hidden. Performance on the indirect is no different from that on the direct task. In the indirect case, however, the cue serves clearly as a token, a symbol of the action which will retrieve the tidbit. What cue is used is irrelevant—the token is arbitrarily associated to the disposition to retrieve the tidbit by the act of solving the problem.

The use of tokens has been explored using other techniques in chimpanzees. A Chimpomat was constructed on which the animal performed somewhat as people do on slot machines (Jacobsen, Wolfe, and Jackson, 1935). Chips were delivered upon appropriate action. These chips could later be turned in for a complement of peanuts. Chimps enjoy the Chimpomat—unless they are deprived of their frontal cortex. After such surgery tokens become meaningless, symbolic processes severely impaired.

Symbolization then, just as indexing, is a derivative of the interactions of processes which produce Images. In the case of Symbols the derivation is made from the interaction of the process which produce Images-of-Achievement with those which generate Monitor-Images. The Symbolic process involves Action, the construction of an external representation of what is going on in our brains. Symbols are thus expressions of feelings, expressions that come to represent the feelings in the world outside through use.

Symbols are thus different from indices: symbols are *not* isomorphic with the events they symbolize. As already noted symbols are constructed arbitrarily through use. Symbolic knowledge is thus paradoxically derived in large part from sources external to the events which they symbolize—they stem from the feelings to which they are addressed. A relationship is maintained between Feeling and Symbol—they are, as it were, grafted onto one another to produce a various and abundant crop.

DERIVATIVE AND LINGUISTIC KNOWLEDGE

Indexing and Symbolizing are therefore two ways of knowing that are considerably different from the Immanent mode. They are derived when Images are Acted upon. Indexing results from Action on Images-of-Events; Symbolizing occurs when Action concerns Monitor-Images. Since both Indexing and Symbolizing involve Action, the making of a representation external to the organism, derivative knowledge becomes quickly public and communicable.

In man this communicability appears to have taken a step beyond even the derivative knowledge of Signs and Symbols. Man manipulates Signs as Symbols: he uses signs arbitrarily. In the computer analogy we have been using, an alphabetical word is substituted for the numerical Sign word which indicates the switch position. This substitution brings about an increment of power at least equal to that provided by the initial coding operation. Now logical operations, rules, can be fashioned and applied since the relationship involved in Signing and Signifying can be made explicit. The very arbitrariness of the symbolic use (whether inductive or deductive) of Signs gives rise to the flexibility of language.

Man is also capable of using Symbols as Signs. He indexes symbolic representations by some sign or label, indicating their intrinsic attributes. Such signs become potent communicators when they code shared feelings. Human reasoning also may have its origin in this ability to index symbols, i.e., to provide them with the shared meaning.

Linguistic knowing is thus potent, but it is also remote from the occurrences about which knowledge is constructed. From these properties stem both the respect with which it is held by those who have tested the rewards of thoughtful analysis and the distrust with which it is viewed by those who prefer the immanence of the laboratory bench to the desk chair.

KNOWING AND MEANING, A NEUROEPISTOMOLOGY

To summarize: The results of experiments performed in my laboratories over the past two decades have led me to believe that the issue central to effective learning and remembering is coding. The nervous system turns out to be a magnificent instrument for efficient coding. The obvious suggestion is therefore that knowledge is a function of the brain's coding operations.

Several sorts of neural coding have been identified. A primitive code is composed of the excitatory and inhibitory interactions among neurons. From these elementary processes Images of three kinds are constructed: Events in the perceptual world initiate Images-of-Events; Monitor-Images deal with feelings; and Images-of-Achievement are concerned with Action. Through Action, Image constructions can yield Immanent Knowledge, personal, immediate and vital. More often, however, the intermeshing of the processes which give rise to Images-of-Events and Monitor-Images on the one hand and Images-of-Achievement on the other, gives rise to Signs and Symbols: Signs when perceptions are acted on, Symbols when action regards feelings. The derived knowledge of Sign and Symbols, though not as immediate, is public and can therefore be communicated readily.

A still more remote coding operation constitutes linguistic knowledge. Man, by indicating the significance of Symbols, indexing, labelling them, can communicate shared feelings. This facility proves to be a potent stimulus to expanding the communicative effort. Man can also make symbolic use of Signs, substituting Symbols arbitrarily until some "fit" is attained either to physical, biological or experiential disposition or through social usage. The power of the logical linguistic knowledge thus achieved is countered by its remoteness from that which is to be known. At its best therefore knowing becomes a web constituted of linguistic, derived and immanent knowledge processes, none of which are sufficient in and of themselves.

Should these views of the coding properties of our nervous sytem prove viable they would validate the main thrust of the argument expressed in Charles Peirce's theory of meaning (Peirce, 1934). Though I have freely used Peirce's nomenclature, my views were initially derived from neurobehavioral and neurophysiological data independently of any thorough reading of Peirce. Thus differences occur in systematic analysis and the uses to which I have put the nomenclature.

Despite this, Peirce's incisive thinking makes a good starting point for understanding. For example, Peirce makes the statement that "we are too apt to think that what one *means to do* and the *meaning of* a word are quite unrelated measurings of the word meaning." He points out that meaning is always related to doing, to the pragmatic in some way. However, he comes to this view in a long and tortuously reasoned argument which leaves unclear some felt relationships between tokens and icons and ends by stating that symbolic meaning is *the* essential form of meaning. In this way of taking on its pragmatic mantle knowing becomes overly expedient. My own analysis appears, to me at least, more straightforward and productive of a more balanced end. The fact that signs and symbols are derived in part through action brings to knowledge the dimension of intentionality, pragmatic but not expedient. Thus, for me, the pragmatic similarity of "what one means" and "what one means to do" centers on the intentionality of all meaning, the fact that significant and symbolic activity is forming, through the brain mechanisms involved in action, a representation of one's Imaging. Even the most abstract efforts of the mathematician concern his vision of relationships he can construct between occurrences. Even the most earthy of symbols, the phallic Hindu lingam, takes its impact from the imagery evoked by the stories of divine powers.

I would suggest, therefore, that both Indices and Symbols derive meaning to the extent that they can be employed to evoke Immanence. As in Peirce's theory of meaning, this gives primacy to an abductive form of reasoning: What I should today call hypothesis formation by analogy as against reasoning by deduction or induction. This is not to deny the importance of deduction and induction—only to deny them primacy.

The logic of abductive inference has received little formal study in Western philosophy. In science, however, abduction is now commonly used and takes the form of modeling. A fascinating example of the proper use of abductive reasoning was displayed by Watson and Crick in their discovery that the structure of DNA is a double helix (Watson, 1968). Careful study of such scientific endeavors should clarify the rules of legitimate abduction and its relationship to induction and deduction.

Until more is known there is little use in speculating about the possible neural mechanisms involved in abductive reasoning in all its complexity. It is likely, however, that because of the freshness of analogy, the novel call it makes on the familiar, the match and mismatch among expectancies, that a good beginning has been made in the study of the elemental processes involving the orienting reaction and its habituation (Bagshaw and Benzies, 1968; Pribram, 1969).

For epistemology the message of my view is clear. We have altogether too long and too exclusively focussed on the logical operations involved in deductive and inductive coding. We have paid only lip service to the external representations which can be constructed from these, and have not faced the key role of intentionality derived from Action in begetting Signs and Symbols. Further, only the intuitive philosopher has allowed himself the license of abduction and then only informally. For we have not clearly recognized abductive coding as a legitimate procedure. According to the analysis presented here, not only are abductive processes legitimate, they become essential if indices and symbols are to be made immanent and thus attain empirical, existential and pragmatic validity.

Ordinarily, in our concern with formal information processing, with rote indexing and with logical symbol manipulation, we have excluded abduction and therefore the path to immanence. On the other hand, immanence, whether empirical, existential or pragmatic, is not by itself, enough either. Though momentarily meaningful, immanent knowing will fail to provide the more enduring consensual ways of knowing unless the disciplines of Indexing and Symbolizing are also cultivated through Action to beget the power of linguistic operations. Knowledge is of a piece, linguistically potent, neurologically derived and beyond all that, Immanent.

SUMMARY AND CONCLUSIONS

The theme has been developed that knowing results from a complex of brain processes that are hierarchically arranged. The brain is so constructed that it continuously recodes signals. The initial recoding operations on input result in images. These are the representations that constitute immanent knowing. One form of immanence is that produced in the motor systems: an image of achievement that readily transforms into action. Acts are public and therefore subject to consensual validation. Thus a second level of knowing is derived when acts represent images of events in the world-out-there and when acts represent images that monitor the world-within-the-organism. These second level representations are here called signs and symbols. At the apex of the hierarchy stands the linguistic process which combines sign and symbol. Linguistic operations give rise to logically definable knowledge. Each level of knowing has its own strengths and limitations.

COMMENTS ON PRIBRAM'S PAPER

J. R. Royce

Let me begin with several comments on why I am impressed by Dr. Pribram's paper. First of all I'm impressed by the scope of his statement. As I see it, Professor Pribram is trying for nothing less than a general neuropsychology—and in this particular paper he puts the spotlight on the epistemological aspects of this general theory. Secondly, I am impressed by the conceptual ingenuity he has brought to bear in dealing with intransigent problems. Take, for example, the notion of coding as the key to knowing, and the hologram as the relevant underlying brain mechanism. Why should we be impressed by such a concept? Because nobody has known how to account for the fact that extensive brain damage impairs performance so little and because a hologram-like mechanism could resolve the dilemma of redundancy in coding. The hologram mechanism says that a small, but appropriate, sampling of the relevant elements is all that is required in order to reconstitute "organized wholes." This kind of concept introduces theoretical order in a domain of study where the pendulum has been oscillating between the poles of localization and mass action for over a hundred years, and if it holds up, it will constitute a conceptual breakthrough of the first magnitude. In spite of this possibility, I am primarily impressed by Professor Pribram's contribution because he is trying to spell out the underlying neurology of *constructionism*, and I must say that is a terribly difficult task. The point is that such an approach constitutes an attempt to get at the heart of the matter, namely the problem of *cognitive representation*, rather than play the more typical, safer, psychophysiological game of simply not bringing in mentalistic phenomena such as meaning, symbols, and image.

Let me now elaborate on what I believe is the heart of Pribram's neuropsychology—his effort to deal with the sign-symbol distinction. I will do this with two purposes in mind: (1) to provide an overall summary of his basic position, and (2) as a basis for asking a question. The summary is given in Table 1.

Now for the question. What is the relationship between your view of symbol and that of Cassirer? I'm reasonably certain your position is not inconsistent with his, but I wonder if you would offer a direct statement on this point. I ask it because the underlying neurology makes good sense in Cassirer's

TABLE 1 Summary of contrasting characteristics of sign and symbol as viewed by Pribram

Characteristic	Sign	Symbol
Type of Coding	Indexing	Symbolizing
Type of Meaning	Denotative	Connotative
Parallels to Peirce	Inductive-deductive	Abductive
Sample Behavior	Discrimination learning	Indirect delayed response
Neural Basis	Primary cortical projection areas and posterior association cortex	Frontal pole; Limbic system

context, and my own view is that Cassirer's (1953, 1955, 1957) philosophy of symbolic forms has not received the attention it deserves by either psychologists or philosophers. On the other hand, your criss-cross usage of sign and symbol on p. 459 was confusing, if not actually incompatible with Cassirer's conception.

There are inevitable problems of clarification—some of them semantic and some of a more conceptual nature. My most serious semantic difficulties hover around your usage of the word immanent. The most relevant dictionary definition of this word is "taking place within the mind of the subject, and having no effect outside of it." Having this in mind helped me at various points in the manuscript, but because I'm not clear regarding its usage, I've missed the full impact of your message in several crucial places. Two good examples are your last sentence in the paper where you claim that knowledge is, above all, immanent, and earlier (p. 455) where you allude to existentialism as one of three forms of immanent knowledge.

My problems with your meaning of "image" are of a more conceptual nature. I believe you have described yourself as a subjective behaviorist, and on top of that it is clear you are a non-reductionistic neuropsychologist. Given that kind of openness, what are the conceptual implications of the term image? Is it purely subjective? Is it merely a neural pattern? Or do images follow some kind of psychoneural isomorphism?

Toward the end of your manuscript you allude to the importance of abduction as a legitimate way of knowing. I happen to share this bias, but I do not see the basis for your claim. Can you elaborate on this? Why is abduction a valid mode of knowing? And why should psychology pay more attention to it?

Finally, a more philosophical issue which you may prefer to leave to the philosophers. As a psychologist interested in the neural basis for knowing, your working definition of knowledge as "codified information consensually validated" is acceptable. But it simply won't qualify as an adequate elaboration of truth criteria. For example, in the section on immanent knowledge you state that "knowledge is known to be true [by] the *effect* such knowledge has," and you point to different effects for the three epistemologies of empiricism, existentialism, and pragmatism. I am not suggesting that we initiate an infinite regress, but that you take us at least one step beyond consensual validation by spelling out the three different types of consensus which are implicit in your position.

DISCUSSION OF "NEUROLOGICAL NOTES ON KNOWING" BY KARL PRIBRAM

Kellogg V. Wilson

This paper is quite compactly written and I found it necessary to reread it several times and to take notes in order to understand it. Since I regard this paper as an important attempt to describe the brain as a macrosystem—a rare phenomena among physiological psychologists—and since this effort is quite consistent with some current trends in cognitive psychology and psycholinguistics, I would like to comment on two points on which I feel some misunderstanding is likely to arise. I do not feel there is any essential disagreement with Pribram's position but that these points deserve further emphasis and discussion.

First, I would like to consider the phenomena of "coding" in terms of formal grammars (Chomsky, 1963 in bibliography of my paper). Roughly, any grammar contains a set of rules for rewriting strings of symbols and so describes a coding operation. In a context-free grammar, the rules for rewriting any symbol are independent of the context in which the symbol appears whereas in a context-dependent grammar, at least some of the rewriting rules depend on the context of a symbol, usually adjacent symbols. In general, the recoding or rewriting operation in computer languages are usually context-free while natural language exhibits strong contextual dependencies—e.g. the exact meaning of a word will very frequently depend on its context which makes language translation based on word for word substitution inaccurate. Also, the Gestalt psychologists have often demonstrated that the interpretation of a particular contour can vary considerably with the context in which it is embedded. Pribram certainly recognizes the importance of contextual dependencies in coding when he states that "Again and again my experiments showed that how much may be learned or remembered— indeed even *what* may be learned or remembered—is at any moment determined as much by the context, the set and setting, in which an informative item is placed as by that item *per se.*" Yet his example of recoding of sets of three switch positions into numbers (which is essentially a conversion from base two to base eight representation of a number) is an example of a context-free grammar. Moreover, this recoding is based on rules (which he describes) so that only three rules (plus rules of arithmetic rather than eight) need be retained. This coding is essentially an extension of codes we have already learned as are the mnemonics he cites such as JMP for "jump" and CLA for "clear the accumulator."

My discussion of Pribram's example leads to a kind of apparent paradox. The recoding operations which are easily learned by humans involve mnemonics or rules which are extensions of already learned codes which involve a considerable reduction of the number of associations needed for arbitrarily assigned recoding operations, yet the coding operations involved in perception by the higher animals, at least, and in the use of language by humans seem to involve context dependent coding of a very complex sort. Of course, there are a variety of plausible explanations for this—among them that the recoding operations of language and perception are extremely overlearned in early life (perhaps during a maturationally determined period) so there is a strong predisposition to learn new recoding operations in terms of old ones. However, regardless of the position we take on the resolution of this seeming paradox, we have to introduce concepts regarding recoding operations that go a good deal beyond the more superficial interpretations of Pribram's example.

My second point concerns the use of the term *image* which has an unfortunate similarity to the term *imagery*. The traditional discussions of eidetic imagery emphasized the capacities of some individuals to reconstruct past visual experience in the form of an image so that detailed information, from a printed page for example, which was not initially attended to can be retrieved. However, this holistic kind of coding does not appear to be very common nor is it what Pribram has in mind. He states that Imaging involves "a process in which only a limited number of variables need be coded" and that the components of the code "are no longer the presence or absence (on and off) of neural impulses but are indicators of relationships among them." To me, this implies a considerable similarity to the Quillian type memory system described in my paper in which both properties and relationships are codified. In addition to the possibility of a reconstruction of the environmental event as coded, such coding permits the construction of combinations which have never been experienced, as can be vividly seen in the more creative imaginative play of children, artists and even (sometimes) scientists. Again, this involves no essential disagreement with what Pribram has said and is quite in key with the affective spirit with which he has said them. Insofar as there is disagreement it concerns what I feel is a somewhat arbitrary distinction between Images, Signs and Indices. I think it is correct to paraphrase Pribram as saying that Images are relational codings of experience, that Signs are relational codings of Images and that Indexing involves relational coding of Signs.

For reasons indicated in my paper, the extreme amount of interdigitation of relational codes in the Quillian memory would make such levels about as distinct as boundaries between academic subjects. Symbols may have a special status because of their relations to inner events—e.g. feelings—but I expect they are involved in this interdigitation as well. The assumption that a Quillian memory organization is as general as I have assumed may seem unwarranted, but it is more general than the hierarchy Pribram implies and it is a plausible model for a relational code involving discrete elements.

COMMENTS ON PROFESSOR PRIBRAM'S PAPER

William W. Rozeboom

There are few academic sports spectaculars quite so exhilarating as the sight of playmaster Pribram finger-tipping the ball in full sprint downfield. Yet if the game is not to degenerate into a shambles, someone must take responsibility for blowing the whistle on fouls.

Actually, my whistle chirps here will be rather timid, for while I have deep suspicions about much of the action in Pribram's performance, it all happens too fast for me to tell exactly what is going on. According to Pribram, the general sequence of cognitive events in an organism is for stimulus input to be first *coded* by the nervous system and then recoded into patterns of neural activity called *Images-of-Events*. Meanwhile, internal physio-chemical conditions give rise (via coding?) to *Monitor-Images* while images of a third kind, *Images-of-Achievement*, are representing *Actions* (i.e., external accomplishments). When these images-of-achievement interact with images-of-events on the one hand and with monitor-images on the other, *signs* and *symbols* respectively result. Finally, linguistic knowledge results when "man manipulates Symbols as Signs." All of this seems very profound—too much so, unfortunately, for me to understand very clearly. I do, however, find myself noting possible inconsistencies and wondering if Pribram has really addressed the definitive issues of cognition.

His theory of action, for example: I think I am safe in construing this to be very similar to Metzger's account (p. 244 ff. above). Certainly Pribram's statement that "Images-of-Achievement guide movement ... by tuning the reflex" (p. 455), i.e. that these set the equilibrium points in homeostatic lower-level motor processes, well fits this conception. But then I am at a loss to interpret his claim that images-of-achievement "are composed of signals [from muscular force fields] initiated by forces external to the organism" (p. 455), for this seems to imply that the reflex tuning so brought about is determined blindly by the organism's recent history of muscle events rather than by superordinate control from his cognitively intended goals. Very likely a simple rephrasing or word of clarification would allay my doubts on this point (as the final draft of Pribram's paper has already done for certain other qualms I had originally raised here). Considerably more than that, however, seems necessary to make public the substantive insights which I trust underlie the pyrotechnic dazzle of Pribram's account of cognition's afferent stages:

Consider, for example, his concept of "coding". Does this have any *psychological* implications beyond recognizing the obvious fact that since neural propagation of input signals cannot literally copy physical events at the receptor surface, central sensory processes must be transformations of their input precursors? I grant that Pribram is working towards a specific theory concerning what aspects of CNS activity are correlated in what way with input patterns, but he hasn't suggested what import this may have for a psychology which abstracts the functional properties of cognition from its neurophysiological substratum.

Again, we are told that the first stage of neural coding passes over into images[-of-events] through "a further coding process by which the neural process can represent fully its origin," (p. 453). I am unsure whether this is meant to imply that the pre-Image stage of coded input does not represent its origin as fully as does the Image, or merely that the two coding stages both fully represent their origin. Either way, Pribram's claims about "re-presentation" remain gratuitous at best (and beguiling at worse) until he clarifies what sort of representation is at issue here and faces up to the more important logical problems which remain for his account in this sense of the term. Does he really mean just that variable X "represents" variable Y when X-events are isomorphic to or statistically correlated with Y events? If so, then the Image can represent its origin no better than does the pre-Image stage of coding (since when the relation between variables X and Y is mediated entirely by variable(s) M, Y can be no more highly correlated with X than is M and will be less so if there is any error variance in the system); while by virtue of the reflexivity, transitivity, and (more roughly) symmetry of isomorphisms and correlations, the Image, pre-Image, and environmental origin all mutually represent one another as well as—most accurately of all—themselves. Surely Pribram intends "representation" to be more selective than this, so that an Image represents its external source *rather than* (instead of in addition to) itself or the pre-Image Coded input. Surely in an essay whose theme is the epistemic act of knowing and which purposefully makes free use of classical psychology's major cognitive concepts, the *of*-ness ascribed to Images-of-Events is intended to be the *cognitive* relation whereby an image Y represents an originating event (or between-event relation) X when Y is referentially *about* X. But then which among the events (or relations among events) in the causal sequence leading to Y is the one that Y represents, and by what analysis of aboutness can it be claimed that Y represents *that* particular X rather than some other one of its causal precursors? For example, if a photograph presents a viewer with retinal stimulation that arouses first-stage coded neural activity which in turn produces a recoded Image, is the originating event represented by this Image (1) the pre-image neural coding, (2) the retinal pattern, (3) the configuration of pigments on the photographic print, (4) something in the negative from which the print was made, or (5) the original scene to which this negative was first exposed? If Pribram elects (3) or (5), as I hope would be his preference, on what grounds can he argue that the viewer's Image represents the distally external event rather than its retinal or post-retinal consequence? Since he speaks of "resemblance" several times in this context, would he propose that the Image is literally more *like* (i.e., similar to) its distal origin than it is like mediating events at the sensory interface?

I am similarly uneasy about Pribram's treatment of "signs". We are told that these are produced by "decoding" or "indexing" images-of-events by much the same mechanism that produces images-of-achievement. Just how this occurs is not clear to me, for at one point (p. 456) the achievement-mechanism produces signs by modulating receptor action, which would control which images-of-events are formed in the first place rather than how the latter are subsequently Indexed; later, however, it is said that indexing "derive[s] when Images are Acted upon" (p. 459), while the "interdigitating" of images-of-events and images-of-achievements sounds more like an amalgam of these two image types than like a receptor bias on the first. But more important is what Indexing is conceived to accomplish. I interpret this to be a categorizing (*á la* Bruner) of images-of-events, that is, an abstractive identifying of their distinctive features. For this to be a genuine cognitive operation, however, the Image must have its identified attributes predicated of it in a propositionally structured process; whereas so far as I can make out, Pribram's Signs are simply reactions (central or otherwise) elicited by the Images so indexed. If so, his account of sign processes is nothing more than a neurophysiologically flavored paraphrase of traditional association-theoretic models (*á la* Staats and Kendler) which treat concept formation, abstraction, judgment, and other cognitive phenomena as convergent associations, i.e., as common labeling responses becoming attached to a variety of stimuli. I know Karl well enough by now to feel sure that he has something considerably more interesting than this in mind, but what that something-more may be remains at present a tantalizing mystery.

Pribram's use of the word *Symbol* to denote those "expressions of feeling" which derive from classifying Monitor-Images is strongly at odds with what most philosophers understand by this term, but I suppose that he is keying into the usage under which "symbols" (i.e., the Flag, Hamlet-seen-as-Everyman, firearms-seen-as-phallic, etc.) have an artsy-gutsy subjective/existential orientation *contra* the semantically pure external outlook of "signs." But are hormonal balances and the like then "the events [which symbols] symbolize" (p. 459)? If so, what is the nature of the relationship by which an indexed monitor-image is a symbol *of* a hormonal event? (Pribram emphasizes that it is not an isomorphism, but what then *is* it?)

Finally, to lessen the prospect of rotary agitation within Charles Peirce's grave, a *caveat* should be filed against the view that for Peirce, *abductive* reasoning is hypothesis formation by analogy (a claim which Pribram has now softened considerably since his original presentation but still not entirely abandoned). Peirce used the term "abduction" to describe whatever processes are responsible for a person's first thinking of a hypothesis prior to its subsequent confirmation or disconfirmation in one way or another (see Peirce, *Collected Papers* Vol. VI, p. 358). "Analogy" for him was a form of inference which *contrasted* with reasoning by hypothesis, while "abduction" was an aspect of the latter. In his own words,

> Argument is of three kinds: Deduction, Induction, and Abduction (usually called adopting a hypothesis). (*Collected Papers* Vol. II, p. 53.)

Peirce's concept of "argument" is broader than that of "inference," for it includes the acquiring of hypotheses in ways other than inference, namely, by abduction:

> Abduction must cover all the operations by which theories and conceptions are engendered. (*CP* V, p. 414)

For deriving conclusions from premises, on the other hand,

> non-deductive or ampliative inference is of three kinds: induction, hypothesis [whose premises may be given by abduction], and analogy. (*CP* VI, p. 31),

while

> analogy ... is a type of inference having all the strength of induction and more besides. (*CP* V, p. 411; the logical form of analogical argument is given in *CP* II, p. 310.)

Since Peirce treats analogy as distinct from though similar to induction, he should probably have included Analogy as a fourth kind of argument in the first quotation above.

REBUTTAL TO DISCUSSION
Karl H. Pribram

Back at the Center for Advanced Study in Theoretical Psychology I write this rebuttal to my three sometimes devastating and often insightful discussants just two years after my initial visit and one year to the day after my arrogant foray into neuroepistemology at Banff. I am, of course, grateful for the valiant attempts each of you made to have me become understandable and for "blowing the whistle on fouls." Let me, in this spirit of gratitude indicate in three separate sections (Sign and Symbol; Images; Ways of Knowing) the direction my thinking has taken over the past year and then, from this point of departure, to answer to the best of my present ability the specific questions posed.

SIGN AND SYMBOL

I begin with Kellogg Wilson's contribution. The heart of it concerns his statement that: "In general the recoding or rewriting operations in computer languages are usually context-free while natural language exhibits strong contextual dependencies ..." Wilson has spent his sabbatical this past year in my laboratories pounding away at this idea that we must distinguish between context-free and context-dependent constructions. He finally got through to me when with sudden insight while preparing another manuscript (What Makes Man Human, James Arthur Lecture, American Museum of Natural History, 1970) I realized that what I call signs are characterized by their context-free construction and that what I call symbols are characterized by their context-dependency. A sign is a deictic, denotive, indexing of events imaged. A monkey mastering a simple discrimination task learns that a + sign means peanut irrespective of the location or other stimulus dimension in which the + sign is embedded. In fact, learning to make discriminations or learning to make signs (as has Washoe the chimpanzee who communicates by means of American Sign Language) is to establish a context-free code.

Symbols, on the other hand, derive from context-dependent constructions. The delayed alternation task is the simplest example in primate experiments: Whether a monkey is to open the right or the left of two adjacent cups in order to obtain a reward is dependent on the context of where he had obtained the reward on the previous trial. In the delayed reaction task, the appropriate response is dependent on the context signalled during the predelay period. As an extension of the delay task, a hierarchy of contexts can be established in which each signal or reward becomes a token that establishes the context for the subsequent action. This is what was done with the Chimpomat during the 1930's and is currently being exploited by Premack with his chimpanzee Sarah.

Neurologically it makes sense that signs as context-free organizations are constructed by the activities of the primary projection systems and their associated areas of intrinsic cortex. Discrete, well structured, and fitted for a great deal of parallel processing, these systems allow the sorting out of constancies in the transformation of input. By contrast, the limbic systems of the forebrain are built with multiple self-reflecting loops within loops—just the sort of anatomical structure necessary to set up the sets of recursive functions necessary to the context-dependent constructions characteristic of symbols. Neurologically speaking, context dependency becomes state-dependency where state is a more or less temporary memory or motive setting. Thus, using the letters of the alphabet as signs is done when an index is made; using the letters of the alphabet as symbols occurs when words are made.

I believe that this modification of my earlier analysis of sign and symbol meets some of the difficulties encountered by my discussants. The use of the term symbol especially was obscure—now it falls more nearly in line with the usage given by Susan Langer and perhaps Cassirer and also, to some extent, Morris. I still differ with all of these earlier usages, however, in giving equal independent and parallel weight to the construction of sign and symbol and reserving for propositions the process of bringing the two together. In this respect my analysis is somewhat akin to that of Ayer's (1946). Thus, in direct answer to Kellogg Wilson's question, I think that hierarchies of signs are constructed by rewriting rules similar to those employed in computer languages and set forth in *Plans and the Structure of Behavior*; that hierarchies of symbols, on the other hand, are made more along the lines of a Quillian construction. Language uses both and this has given trouble in analysis. Nonetheless linguists and psychologists have felt the validity of the distinction. Psychologists have conceptualized it in terms of the difference between long-term and short-term memory (e.g. Atkinson, Bower); linguists in terms of the dimension simultaneity and successivity (e.g. Jacobsen).

Pribram	*Psychologists*	*Linguists*
Sign	Long Term Memory Process	Simultaneity
Symbol	Short Term Memory Process	Successivity

IMAGES

A second group of questions concerns the relationship between Image and the Neural Hologram. Here I can do less in the way of clarification since the issue runs squarely into the mind-brain problem. I have discussed my views on this issue extensively in the final chapter of *Languages of the Brain* (1971). Briefly, in reference to the present manuscript, the interpretation of what can be meant by the term Image depends on one's stance in the mind-brain dilemma. A monistic-pluralistic stance would either identify the brain process of neural hologram formation with Image formation or would point out that these are two ways of talking about the same set of events. The dualistic stance would suggest either that Images occur in parallel to neural holograms or that they intervene between the neurological process and subsequent related behaviors. Each stance has deficiencies and as a biologist I am awed, continue to wonder, and simply accept the mystery of the fact that I do perceive images which are altered when my brain processes are messed up.

I do so hope that my answer will be adequate to the questions posed by both Rozeboom and Royce, for I feel it important that science get away from a "know-it-all" attitude. There is a point at which analysis can go no further—the alternatives are adequately spelled out—and we can sit back and enjoy the mysteries of the natural world. I do not, of course, mean by this that we should be slovenly or slothful; nor do I mean by mystery some hazy shroud with which to envelop an issue. Quite the contrary. The feeling of mystery comes to me from having pushed hard-nosed analysis to its extremes and thus sharply illuminated the complementary facets of a complex issue. I am not claiming that I have reached this point in our discussions of Image, but I think sometimes there is a hidden agenda of a search for complete and absolute certainty when questions are asked in psychology, an agenda long ago given up when questions in physics are considered.

Given this framework, perhaps Rozeboom's and Royce's questions about the relationship between Images-of-Achievement and Images-of-Events can be answered, and also their more general query about the role of representations, internal and external. Taking the dualist stance, I would say that in writing this paper which you, Royce and Rozeboom can read, I have made an external representation of the neural process involved in my Images-of-Events over the past years. I have been able to do this by virtue of another set of neural processes—those which are involved in Images-of-Achievement. These neural processes have made it possible for me to write words and sentences with a pen on paper and to correct these scribblings until I have achieved a readable manuscript. The Images-of-Events and Images-of-Achievement on the one hand and the neural processes and this manuscript on the other, constitute two worlds—one private, one public (i.e., communicable), and both concern the scientist. There is a different and perhaps simpler and less provocative interpretation if I take a monistic-pluralistic stance: I would now claim that my brain states, this manuscript, and the final printed chapter are all embodiments of the same sets of experience I have enjoyed over the past years, experiences completely specifiable in terms of my observable interactions with the discussants and with others through talking and reading and writing.

The virtues of the multiple realization stance are obvious. Analysis is limited to that which is observable. A hard-headed precision and clarity can be achieved. What is sacrificed, however, is the intuitive reach of problems generated when the private world of experience is addressed independently and directly. For example, if the mechanism of pattern recognition is analyzed in terms of observables, the appropriate behavior can be generated to some considerable extent by a system of feature extractors preset to do the job. Actual human pattern recognition, on the other hand, is accompanied by a richness of Image unnecessary to the achievement of the recognition response. A decision must be made as to whether to ignore this richness. At times, for the purposes of simplicity and rigorousness, I am willing to temporarily shelve the problems posed by the private world. But over the long haul, as a psychologist, especially as a physiological psychologist, these problems must be faced in their own right for they are what make man human. And I am vitally interested in what constitutes the difference in man's brain that makes the difference.

WAYS OF KNOWING

Most of the remaining questions posed by my discussants refer to forms of knowing. Royce clearly formulates these questions in terms of the necessity for consensual validation and truth statements; Rozeboom centers his queries on my use of Peirce's term Abduction. In my paper I make the distinction between knowing and knowledge. I want to hold to that distinction. Knowing can be a private affair; knowledge is always public. In discussing this matter at length with Royce we came to the conclusion that when knowing is primarily dependent on Images-of-Events (percepts) and Monitor Images (feelings), the term "authenticity" is more appropriate than "truth." These forms of knowing I have called "immanent" and the definition given by Royce in his discussion describes what I mean. Immanent knowing is personal, private and may be difficult to communicate. Thus the criterion for knowing in the empiricist and existential modes is authenticity not truth.

The pragmatic mode, also, has nothing to do with truth. To know how to act is to be able to achieve the action. Achievement is the criterion for knowing. Knowing through achievement is partly a public and partly a private matter. One may look to others to determine (through extrinsic reinforcement) whether one has achieved or one may examine the match (intrinsic reinforcement) between act and intent, between the external representation achieved and the pre-existing representation of the Plan-for-Achievement in the Images-of-Achievement.

I believe from what I have so far learned from philosophers at this conference and from my readings since, that truth as a criterion for knowing comes in only when propositions are made. I use the term proposition to indicate constructions made by man when he uses signs symbolically, i.e., when he uses signs in a context-dependent fashion. This context dependency is, however, restricted and consistent. The context is predication, i.e., the truth or falsity (lawfulness?) of the way in which the sign is used. Thus the word boy may be used as a sign; the statement "this is (is not) a boy" can be taken as a proposition declaring "knowledge" which is potentially verifiable. Much of man's scientific effort is devoted to statements of procedures for verification.

In a similar manner, man uses symbols significantly. He does this when he reasons. Reasoning is accomplished by adopting temporarily a set of arbitrary rules which dispense with context dependency and thus momentarily free symbols from their ambiguity. Algebra or geometry are examples of "pure" reasoning.

Induction and Deduction are readily identifiable forms of reasoning as pointed out by Rozeboom. His question concerns abduction and the relationship between metapohr, analogy and abduction. My own view is that these terms denote a continuous dimension along which metaphor is the least, and abduction the most precise. Today we call abduction "model construction." Metaphor calls forth a feeling (Monitor-Image); analogy evokes a percept (Images-of-Events); and abduction, as I want to use the term in its present day model building definition, makes its demands on action (on the Image-of-Achievement). Since Peirce did not distinguish between types of Images, my usage of "abduction" differs from his but I believe that it is consistent with the spirit of his usage: As Rozeboom points out and substantiates in his quotations from Peirce, abduction gives rise to hypotheses, it is not directly involved in the reasoning process itself.

However, others might be less constrained in their use of the term reason—Wittgenstein for instance, points out that we rarely proclaim that an incorrect mathematical proof is unreasonable.

This is about as far as I now dare venture into the problems of the philosophy of knowing. The stimulus provided by the Center over the past two years has revealed a challenging vista, a world populated by neurophysiologists, traditional psychologists, behaviorists, cyberneticians, logicians and traditional philosophers. Perhaps I have as yet poorly identified just who is who, but, does this really matter so much? Though a search for how "who" knows may give direction to the search, the primary question does remain "how do *we* know?"

BIBLIOGRAPHY

Bagshaw, M. H. and Benzies, S., Multiple measures of the orienting reaction and their dissociation after amygdalectomy in monkeys, *Exp. Neurol.*, 1968, **20**, 175–187.

Bagshaw, M. H. and Coppock, H. W., Galvanic skin response conditioning deficit in amygdalectomized monkeys, *Exp. Neurol.*, 1968, **20**, 188–196.

Bagshaw, M. H. and Pribram, J. D., Effect of amygdalectomy on stimulus threshold of the monkey. *Exp. Neurol.*, 1968, **20**, 197–202.

Bernstein, N., *The Co-ordination and Regulation of Movements*. New York: Pergamon Press, 1967.

Douglas, R. J., The hippocampus and behavior (review), *Psychol. Bull.*, 1967, **67**, 416–442.

Douglas, R. J. and Pribram, K. H., Learning and limbic lesions, *Neuropsychologia*, 1966, **4**, 197–220.

Evarts, E. V., Representation of movements and muscles by pyramidal tract neurons of the precentral motor cortex. In M. D. Yahr and D. P. Purpura (eds.), *Neurophysiological Basis of Normal and Abnormal Motor Activities*, Hewlett, N. Y.: Raven Press, 1967, 215–254.

Held, R., in D. P. Kimble (ed.), *Experience and Capacity* (4th Conference on Learning, Remembering and Forgetting), New York: N. Y. Academy of Sciences, 1968.

Hunter, W. S., The delayed reaction in animals and children, *Behav. Mono.* 1913, **2**, 1–86.

Jacobsen, C. F., Functions of frontal association area in primates, *Arch. Neurol. and Psychiat.*, 1935, **33**, 558–569.

Jacobsen, C. F., Wolfe, J. B., and Jackson, J. A., An experimental analysis of the functions of the frontal association areas in primates, *J. nerv. ment. Dis.*, 1935, **82**, 1–14.

Kohler, I., *The Foundation and Transformation of the Perceptual World*, New York: International Universities Press, 1964.

Malis, L. I., Pribram, K. H., and Kruger, L., Action potentials in "motor" cortex evoked by peripheral nerve stimulation, *J. Neurophysiol.*, 1953, **16**, 161–167.

Miller, G. A., Galanter, E. H., and Pribram, K. H., *Plans and the Structure of Behavior*, New York: Henry Holt and Co., 1960.

Peirce, C. S., *Collected Papers*, Vol. I–VI, Cambridge: Harvard University Press, 1934.

Polanyi, M., *Personal Knowledge, Towards a Post-Critical Philosophy*, Chicago: University of Chicago Press, 1960.

Pribram, K. H., Psychosurgery in midcentury, *Surgery, Gynecology and Obstetrics*, 1960, **91**, 364–367.

Pribram, K. H., Comparative neurology and the evolution of behavior. In G. G. Simpson (ed.) *Evolution and Behavior*, New Haven: Yale University Press, 1958, 140–164.

Pribram, K. H., A review of theory in physiological psychology, *Annual Review of Psychology, Vol. II*, Annual Reviews, Inc., Palo Alto, 1960, 1–40.

Pribram, K. H., The intrinsic systems of the forebrain. In J. Field, H. W. Magoun and V. E. Hall (eds.), *Handbook of Physiology, Neurophysiology II*, American Physiological Society, Washington, 1960, 1323–1344.

Pribram, K. H., Some dimensions of remembering: steps toward a neuropsychological model of memory, In J. Gaito (ed.) *Macromolecules and Behavior*, New York: Academic Press, 1966, 165–187.

Pribram, K. H., How the brain controls its input. In L. Thayer (ed.) *Communication, Concepts and Perspectives*, Washington: Spartan Books, 1967, 191–295.

Pribram K. H., The new neurology and the biology of emotion: a structural approach, *American Psychologist*, 1967, **22**, 830–838.

Pribram, K. H., The neurophysiology of remembering. *Scientific American*, 1969, **220**, 73–86.

Pribram, K. H., Four R's of remembering. In K. H. Pribram (ed.) *On the Biology of Learning*, New York: Harcourt, Brace and World, 1969.

Pribram, K. H., *Languages of the brain*. Englewood Cliffs, N. J.: Prentice-Hall, 1971.

Reitz, S. and Pribram, K. H., Some subcortical connections of the inferotemporal gyrus of monkey. *Exp. Neurol.*, 1969.

Rosvold, H. E. and Szwarcbart, M. K., Neural structures involved in delayed-response performance, In J. M. Warren and K. Akert (eds.) *The Frontal Granular Cortex and Behavior*, New York: McGraw Hill, 1964, 1–15.

Spinelli, D. N. and Pribram, K. H., Changes in visual recovery functions produced by temporal lobe stimulation in monkeys, *Electroenceph. clin. Neurophysiol.*, 1966, **20**, 44–49.

Spinelli, D. N. and Pribram, K. H., Changes in visual recovery function and unit activity produced by frontal cortex stimulation, *Electroenceph. clin. Neurophysiol.*, 1967, **22**, 143–149.

Talland, G. A. and Waugh, N. C. (eds.), *The Psychopathology of Memory*, New York: Academic Press, 1969.

Watson, J. D., *The Double Helix*, New York: Atheneum Publishers, 1968.

AUTHOR INDEX

Aaronson, D.   *106*, 243–255
Abelson, R. P.   297, *343*, 372, 375, 379, 402, 406, *409*
Abruzzi, A.   *161*
Ach, N.   *161*
Achinstein, P.   *161*
Ackerman, R.   *161*
Agassi, J.   *161*
Alexander, H. G.   *161*
Alston, W.   105, *106*
Altman, J.   204, *212*
Ambrose, A.   *161*
Amerio, F.   *161*
Anderson, N. H.   303, *343*
Apfelbaum, B.   415, *427*
Arbib, M. A.   400, 401, 405, *409*
Aristotle,   90
Armstrong, D. M.   38, *106*, 437–439, *446*
Asch, S. E.   440, *447*
Ashby, W. R.   270, *282*
Atkinson, R. C.   179, *213*, 358, *362*, 474
Atkinson, R. M.   368, *410*
Attneave, F.   202, 203, *212*
Aubert, K. E.   157
Austin, G. A.   *106*, *343*
Austin, J. L.   67, *161*, 287, 437, *446*
Ausubel, D. P.   195, 196, 200, *212*
Ayer, A. J.   *161*, 437, 474

Bach, E.   *409*
Bagshaw, M. H.   458, 461, *479*
Bailey, D. E.   189, *214*, *346*
Ballachey, E. L.   180, 195, *213*
Bamber, D.   271, 275, *282*
Bar-Hillel, Y.   *161*
Barker, S. F.   *161*, *162*
Barron, F.   *106*

Bartley, W. W.   *162*
Bayle, P.   *162*
Beavin, J.   422, *428*
Békésy, G. von   258
Bennet, J. F.   62, *106*, *162*
Bentham, J.   11
Benzies, S.   458, 461, *479*
Berger, L.   415, 416, *427*
Bergson, H.   88, *106*, 156, *162*
Beritov, I. S.   204, 211, *212*
Berkeley, G.   *162*, 277, 437
Berlyne, D. E.   *162*, 192, 193, 199, 200, *212*, 272–275, 277, *282*
Bernstein, N.   455, *479*
Bertalanffy, L., von   90, *106*, 203, 209, *212*, 363, *428*
Beth, E. W.   *162*, 278, 279, *282*, 423, 425, *427*
Bhattacharya, K.   *162*
Binswanger, L.   *162*
Bischoff, N.   252, *264*
Björkman, M.   303, *343*
Black, M.   53, *106*, 119–121, 133, 136–138, 143, 144, 152, 155, 158–160, *162*, *163*
Blum, M. L.   179, *213*
Blumenthal, A.   406, 407, *409*
Bohm, D.   208, *212*, 270, 278, *282*
Bondi, H.   *163*, *175*
Boring, E. G.   436, 440, *446*
Bossom, J.   271, *282*
Bourbaki, N.   279, 423
Bower, G. H.   367, *409*
Bower, T. G. R.   271, *282*, 474
Boyle, P. J. R.   336, *344*
Brain, R.   258
Braithwaite, R. B.   *163*
Brehmer, B.   336, *344*

Brentano, F.   *163*, 229, 260, 262–264, 440
Brett, G. S.   62, *106*
Broad, C. D.   92, *106*, 137, 159, *163*
Broch, L.   *343*
Brown, G. S.   143, 159, *163*
Brown, J. S.   *213*, 267, 269, 271, 275, *282*
Brown, M. S.   *163*
Brown, R.   90, *106*
Bruner, J. S.   64, 67, *106*, 188, 192, 200, 207, 210, *212*, 272, 274, *282*, 287, *343*, 457, 471
Brunswik, E.   *163*, 187, *212*, 237, 286–289, 293, 318, 320, 321, 323, 327, 331, 332, 337, 340–*343*, 345, 355–357, 361, *362*, 439, *446*
Buchdahl, G.   *163*
Bunge, M.   155, *163*
Burger, J. F.   *410*
Burnham, C. A.   271, 275, *282*
Burt, C.   348, *362*
Bush, R. R.   *362*, *409*

Campbell, D. T.   23, *163*, 178, *212*, 288, 342, *343*, 431, *446*
Canon, L. K.   275, *282*
Carnap, R.   12–17, *23*, 54, 90, 92, *106*, 148, *163*, *164*
Carneades   121
Carrol, J. D.   372, 375, 379, *409*
Carroll, L.   78, *106*
Cassirer, E.   244, *264*, 422, *427*, 463, 464
Castañeda, H.   *164*
Cattell, J. P.   400, *446*
Chethimattam, J. B.   *164*
Chisholm, R. M.   *164*
Chomsky, N.   66, *106*, 207, *212*, 358, *362*, 373, 375, 379, 385, 388, 402, 406, *409*, 466
Clark, H. H.   347, 356, *362*
Cliff, N.   89, *106*, *409*
Cofer, C. N.   197, *212*
Cohen, M. R.   287
Colby, M. K.   375, 379, 402, 406, *409*
Collins, A. M.   400, 403, 406, 407, *409*
Cooper, F. S.   *410*
Coppock, H. W.   *479*

Courant, R.   157, *164*
Crick, F. H. C.   461
Cronbach, L. J.   92, *106*
Crutchfield, R. S.   178, 180, 195, *213*

Day, R. H.   271, *283*
Deese, J.   366, 370, 388, 400, *409*
Descartes, R.   434, *446*
DeSoto, C.   347, 356, 357, *362*
Deutsch, J. A.   198, *212*
Dingle, H.   *164*
Dirichlet   117
Dixon, T. R.   374, 385, *409*
Douglas, R. J.   458, *479*
Doyle, C. L.   178, *213*
Dreben, B.   23
Drever, J.   181, *212*
Duhem, P.   149, 159, *164*
Dulany, D. E.   37, *106*

Ebersole, F. B.   *164*
Edelheit, H.   423, 424, *427*
Edwards, P.   128–130, 133, 134, 159, *164*
Edwards, W.   39, *106*
Ekman, G.   243, *264*
Erikson, E. H.   419, *427*
Ernst, G. W.   400, 403, *409*
Euler   116, 156
Evarts, E. V.   454, *479*
Ewald, O.   *164*
Ezekiel, M.   333, *343*

Fant, C. G. M.   *409*
Fantz, R. L.   268, 271, 272, 275, *282*
Feigenbaum, E. A.   400, 403, *409*
Feigl, H.   92, *106*, *164*, 259
Feldman, J.   292, 327, 340, *343*, 400, 403, *409*
Feldman, S.   39, *106*
Ferrater, Mora, J.   *164*
Festinger, L.   195, 207, *212*, 238, 269, 271, 275, *282*
Feyerabend, P. K.   124, *164*
Fillmore, C. J.   407, *409*
Fitts, P. M.   32, *107*
Flavell, J. H.   191, 192, *212*, 366, *409*
Fodor, J. A.   42, 89, 92, 105, *107*, *212*
Forehand, G. A.   182, *213*

AUTHOR INDEX

Foster, M. H. *164*
Fowler, W. 183, *213*
Fox, K. E. 333, *343*
Frank, R. 361
Frankena, W. K. 53, *107*
Frege, G. 11, 72, 89, *107*
Freud, S. 234, 258, 413–417, 419–422, 424, 425, *427*
Frick, F. G. 327, *344*
Fritz, Ch., A., Jr. *164*
Furth, H. G. 64, *107*, 269, 270, 272, *282*, 417, 424, *427*

Gaarder, K. 275, *282*
Gagné, R. M. 66, *107*
Galanter, E. H. 179, 190, 198, *213*, *362*, *409*, *428*, 442, *446*, 454, *479*
Garner, W. R. 325, *343*
Gauss, C. F. 117
Gelb, A. 236
George, F. H. 4, 7, 177, 181, 184, *213*
Gerin, P. 268, 275, *283*
Gianonni, C. *164*
Gibson, E. J. *107*, 206
Gibson, J. J. 67, *164*, *165*, 195, 206, 215–218, 220–222, 227–237, *240*, 267, 268, 278, 282, 437, 438, 441, *446*
Gilbert, J. P. 379, *409*
Gill, M. M. 413, 423, 425, *427*
Gödel, K. 10
Goldberg, L. R. 325, 328, *343*
Goldney, K. M. 159, *172*
Gomulicki, B. R. 416, *427*
Goodman, N. 142–146, 148, 149, 159, *165*
Goodnow, J. J. 67, *106*, 287, *343*
Goss, A. E. 63, *107*, 194, *213*
Graefe, O. 243, 254, *264*
Granit, A. R. 417, *427*
Green, B. F., Jr. 303, *343*
Greenberg, J. H. 375, *409*
Grinker, R. R. 415, *427*
Grize, J. B. 432, *446*
Grohn, M. J. 387
Groner, R. 326–328, 331, 332, 334, 338–341, *343*, 347, 355, 358, 360, *362*

Grünbaum, A. *165*
Guilford, J. P. 373, *409*
Gullvåg, I., *165*, *173*
Gyr, J. W. 188, 190, 207, 210, 211, *213*, 231, 238, 267, 269, 271, 275, 280–*282*

Habermas, J. *165*
Halle, M. *409*
Hammond, K. R. 2, *165*, 285–288, 298, 304, 308, 320, 321–323, 326–328, 331, 335–338, 340, *343*, *344*, 345
Handel, S. 347, 357, *362*
Hanneborg, K. *165*
Hanson, N. R. 21, *23*, *165*
Harlow, H. F. 203, *213*
Harms, R. T. *409*
Harrison, J. *165*
Hartmann, E. 420, *427*
Hartnack, J. *165*
Hawkins, D. *165*
Hebb, D. O. 143, 159, 185–187, 200–204, 206, 211, *213*, 273, 277, *282*, *446*
Heidelberger, H. *165*
Hein, A. *213*, 269, 271, 272, *283*
Heisenberg, W. 208, *213*
Held, R. E. 207, *213*, 238, 269, 271, 272, *282*, *283*, 453, *479*
Helenius, M. 345
Helmholtz, H., von 224, 228, 242, 258, *264*, 437
Hempel, C. G. 84, *107*, *165*, 168
Hering, E. 236, *240*, *264*
Hesse, M. B. *165*
Hick, W. E. 327, *344*
Hilgard, E. R. 179, *213*
Hilpinen, R. *166*
Hintikka, J. *165*, *166*
Hoff, J. H. *166*
Hoffman, P. J. 328, *344*
Holland, J. N. 401, *409*
Holst, E., von 207, *213*, 238, 269, 271, 281, *284*
Holt, R. R. 415, 241, 423, *427*, *428*
Holzkamp, K. 254, *264*
Honigswald, R. *166*
Hopcroft, J. E. 405, *409*
Horton, D. L. 374, 385, *409*

31*

Howe, E. S. 89, *107*
Hull, C. L. 186, 192, 287, 299, 326
Hume, D. 10–12, 139, 140, *166*, 293, 436, 437, *446*
Humphrey, W. C. *166*
Hunt, E. B. 66, *107*, 360, *362*, 367, 387, *409*
Hunter, I. M. L. 348, 356, *362*
Hunter, W. S. 457, *479*
Husserl, E. 93, 228, 429–431, 435, 440, *446*
Hursch, C. 288, 298–300, 321, 328, 333, 335, 338, *344*
Hursch, J. L. 288, 298–300, 321, 328, 333, 335, 338, *344*
Hutt, M. L. 179, *213*
Huttenlocher, J. 356, 357, *362*
Huxley, A. 442, *446*

Ingarden, R. *166*
Ingle, D. 268, *283*
Inhelder, B. 269, *283*, 439, *446*
Isaacson, R. L. 179, *213*

Jackson, D. D. 422, *428*
Jackson, J. A. 458, *479*
Jacobsen, C. F. 458, 474, *479*
Jacobson, E. 273, *283*
Jacobson, R. 388, *409*
Jakobovits, L. A. *107*
James, W. 436, 437, *446*
Jaspars, J. F. M. 181, 182, *214*
Jaspers, K. *166*
Jeannerod, M. 268, 275, *283*
Jeffrey, H. *166*
Jeffrey, R. C. *166*
Johnson, A. B. 10–12, *23*
Johnson, D. M. 370, 385, *409*
Jones, L. V. 42, *107*
Jones, M. *410*
Juhos, B. *166*

Kant, I. 141, 194, 228
Kaplan, B. 45, 90, *109*
Kardos, L. 236
Katz, J. J. 42, 89, *107*, 139, 159, *166*, 374, 388, 400, *410*
Kelly, G. 197, *213*

Kemeney, J. G. *166*
Kendler, H. H. 179, 193, 194, 200, *213*
Kendler, T. S. 193, 194, *213*
King-Farlow, J. *166*
Klein, G. S. 413, 416, 421, 422, *428*
Kneale, W. *166*
Knouse, D. E. 297, *343*
Koffka, K. 195, 236, 430
Kohler, I. 453, *479*
Kohler, W. 240, 243, 257, 260–*264*, 430
Kolers, P. A. 436, *446*
Kopferman, H. 236, *240*
Korner, S. 93, *107*, *166*
Kotovsky, K. 360, *362*
Krech, D. 178, 180, 195, *213*
Kries, J., von 242, 258, *264*
Kruger, L. 454, *479*
Kubie, L. 415
Kuhn, T. S. 21, 124, *166*
Kyburg, H. E., Jr. 139, 159, *166*, *167*

Laing, R. D. 443, *446*
Lakatos, I. *167*
Landauer, T. K. 378, 408, *410*
Langer, S. K. 45, 90, *107*, 422, 425, *428*, 474
Lashley, K. S. 32, *107*, 186, *213*, 274, *283*
Lauenstein, L. 240
Leeper, R. W. 189, 190, 196–198, 200, 204, *213*
Leibniz, G. W. 141, 252
Leiderman, P. H. 440, *447*
Lenz, J. W. *167*
Leonard, H. S. 68, *107*
Lewin, K. 246, 254, *264*, 299
Lewis, P. J. 179
Liberman, A. M. 376, *410*
Lindman, H. 39, *106*
Locke, J. 92, 141, 218, 228, 437
Loevinger, J. 415, *428*
Loewenstein, R. M. *428*
London, M. 347, 356, 357, *362*
Lorenz, K. 414, *428*
Luce, R. D. *362*, *409*

MacCorquodale, K. *264*
Mach, E. 437

AUTHOR INDEX

MacLeish, A. 88, *107*
MacLeod, R. B. 194, 195, 200, *213*
Madden, E. H. *167*
Malis, L. I. 454, *479*
Maltzman, I. M. 194, *214*
Mandler, G. 183, *214*, 374
Manis, M. 184, *214*
Marais, E. N. 153, 160, *167*
Margolis, J. *167*
Marin, J. 360, *362*
Martin, J. 367, *409*
Martin, M. L. 93, 164
Martin, R. M. *107*
Massey, G. J. 84, *107*
Mates, B. 111, 157, *167*
McIntyre, R. *109*
Meehl, P. E. 92, *106*, 264
Melden, A. I. 104, *107*
Mendelson, L. 439, *447*
Merleau-Ponty, M. 223, 443, *446*
Metzger, W. 92, 233, *240*, 243, 257, 258, 260–*264*, 365, 469
Meyers, B. 271, *283*
Midgaard, K. *167*
Miller, B. A. 190, 198, *214*
Miller, G. A. 327, *344*, 358, 359, *362*, *410*, *428*, 442, *446*, 454, *479*
Mills, J. 437
Mills, J. S. 437
Miron, M. S. *107*
Mitchell, T. O. 304, *344*
Mittelstaedt, H. 271
Modell, A. H. *428*
Moore, T. V. 7
Morgan, C. 160
Morris, C. 56, 90, *107*, 474
Moroz, M. 206–209, 274, 361
Mowrer, O. H. 89, *107*
Müller, J. 218, 224, 228
Murphy, G. 63, *107*
McCleary, R. A. 271, *283*
McKeachie, W. J. 178, *213*
McNabb, D. G. C. *167*

Naess, A. 125, 127, 132, 136–140, 142, 149, 158–160, *167*, *168*, 331, *344*
Nagel, E. 92, *107*, 287
Natsoulas, T. 93, *107*

Naylor, J. 303, *344*
Neisser, U. 4, 7, 182, 183, 191, 197, 202, 203, 211, *214*, 416, 417, *428*, 436, 441, *446*
Neumann, J., von 277, *284*
Neurath, O. 19, *23*, 156
Newall, A. 400, 403, *409*
Newmann, M. *428*
Nicod, J. *168*
Nissen, H. W. 203, *214*
Nobel, C. E. 375, *410*
Norton, L. M. 402, *410*
Nyman, A. *168*

O'Connell, D. N. *240*
Ogden, C. K. 53, *107*
Oliver, W. D. *168*
O'Neil, Wm. 196, *214*
Ono, H. 212, 271, 275, *182*
Oppenheim, P. *168*
Osgood, C. E. 56, 89, *108*, 186, 187, 192, 193, 199, 200, 202, 211, *214*, 274, 366, 370, 374, 388, 400, *410*

Pap, A. 68, *108*, *168*
Papanoutsos, E. P. *168*
Paul, I. H. 416, 417, *428*
Peirce, C. S. 15, 16, 114, 157, *168*, 450, 460, 461, 472, 476, 477, *479*
Penfield, W. 439, *446*
Perky, C. W. 436, *446*
Pernier, J. 268, 275, *283*
Peters, R. S. 104, 105, *108*
Pettijohn, W. C. *168*
Peyton, J. D. 94, 98–101, 104
Phillips, L. D. 39, *106*
Piaget, J. 64, 97, *168*, 191, 192, 200–203, 207, *214*, 230, 269, 270, 272–275, 277–279, *282*, 283, 347, 360, *362*, 400, 404, 417–419, 421–425, *427*, *428*, 437, 439, 441, *446*, *447*
Pietarinen, J. *166*
Pikler, J. 245, *265*
Plato, 430
Platt, J. R. 270, 275, *283*
Plaus, F. X. 361, 426
Poincaré, H. 207, *214*, 270, 272, 278, *283*

Polányi, M.   21, *168*, 285, *344*, 454, *479*
Pollio, H. R.   374, 375, *410*
Pollock, J. L.   *168*
Polya, G.   *169*
Popper, K. R.   139, 159, *169*
Postal, P. M.   374, 388, 400, *410*
Potter, M. C.   189, *214*
Premack, D.   474
Pribram, J. D.   458, *479*
Pribram, K. H.   190, 198, 207, *214*, 257, 268, 270–272, 274, 280, 281, *283*, 376, 386, 407, 408, *410*, *428*, 439, 442, *446*, 447, 452–454, 456, 458, 461, 463, 464, 466, 468, 469–472, *479*, *480*
Putnam, H.   *169*
Pyrrho   121

Quillian, M. R.   6, 367, 387, 392, 395, 396, 400, 403, 405–407, *409*, *410*, 474
Quine, W. V.   23, 43, 93, *108*, 112, 157, *169*, 297, *344*

Radnitzky, G.   *170*
Ramsey, F. P.   *170*
Rapaport, D.   413, 419, 424, *428*
Rappoport, L.   288, *344*
Rasmussen, T.   439, *446*
Reichenbach, H.   139, 159, *170*
Reid, T.   436
Reitman, W. R.   363, *410*
Reitz, S.   456, *479*
Rescher, N.   *170*
Rey, A.   273, *283*
Richards, I. A.   53, *107*
Rickert, H.   *170*
Riemann, B.   116, 157
Riesen, A. H.   271, *283*
Rimland, B.   373, *410*
Riopelle, A. J.   204, *214*
Robinson, R.   68, 92, *108*
Rock, I.   271, 272, *283*
Rokeach, M.   39, 89, *108*
Rommetveit, R.   *170*
Rosthal, R.   *170*
Rosvold, H. E.   458, *480*
Rothman, M.   89

Royce, J. R.   97–100, *108*, *170*, 178, 203, 209, 210, *214*, *410*, 475, 476
Rozeboom, W.   26, 35–39, 51, 62, 67, 70, 71, 74, 77, 80, 84, 87–92, 94–97, 104, 105, *108*, *109*, *170*, 180, 181, 188, 198, *214*, 260, 263, 321, 325, 329, 335–339, *344*, 361, 391, 399, 400–407, *410*, 455, 475, 477
Rubinstein, B. B.   415, *428*
Ruch, F. L.   179, *214*
Russell, B.   11, 12, *109*, 112, 133, 134, 158, 159, *171*, 437
Ryle, G.   54, 91, *109*, *171*, 437, *447*
Rynin, D.   *171*

Sachs, J. M.   402, 407, *410*
Salmon, W. C.   139, 159, *171*
Sarbin, T. R.   189, *214*
Sasson, R.   402
Sayre, K. M.   *171*
Schackleton, B.   143
Schagrin, M. L.   *171*
Schank, R. C.   402, 404, *410*
Scheffler, I.   *171*
Schenk, E. A.   *344*
Schick, F.   *171*
Schifferli, P.   273, *283*
Schilder, P.   252, *265*, 433, *447*
Schjelderup, H.   159, *172*
Schmidt, S. J.   *172*
Schoenberg, J.   *172*
Schur, M.   *428*
Schwarcz, R. M.   403, *410*
Scriven, M.   *172*
Selberg, A.   157
Sellars, W.   45, 54, 91, 96, *109*, *172*
Shankweiler, D. P.   *410*
Shaw, J. C.   400
Sherrington, C. S.   215, 216, 258
Shiffrin, R. M.   358, *362*, 368, *410*
Shimony, A.   *172*
Simmel, G.   *172*
Simmons, R. F.   369, 371, 387, 403, *410*
Simon, H. A.   *172*, 360, *362*, 400
Singer, G.   271, *283*
Skinner, B. F.   56, *109*, 207
Skjervheim, H.   *172*
Skyrms, B.   *172*

AUTHOR INDEX

Slote, M. A. *172*
Smith, C. A. B. *172*
Smith, D. W. *109*
Smith, H. W. *172*
Smythies, J. R. 258
Snygg, D. 194, 195, *214*
Soal, S. G. 143, 159, *172*
Solomon, P. 440, *447*
Solnit, A. J. *428*
Spence, K. W. 188, *214*, 327
Sperry, R. W. 238, 269, *283*
Spilsbury, R. J. *172*
Spinelli, D. N. 456, *480*
Spitz, R. 419, *428*
Staats, A. W. 194, *214*
Stacy, R. *409*
Stebbings, L. S. 90, *109*, 348, *362*
Stegmüller, W. *164, 172*
Stern, D. 361
Stern, K. *172*
Stevens, S. S. 243, *265*
Stevenson, C. L. 52, *109*
Stone, P. J. 360, *362*, 367, *409*
Stratton, G. M. 224
Strawson, P. F. 122–130, 134, 135, 155, 158
Studdert-Kennedy, K. *410*
Suci, G. J. 366, *410*
Sudarshan, 136
Süllwold, F. 359, *362*
Summers, D. A. 300, 308, 320, 328, 338, *344, 345*
Summers, S. A. *345*
Suppes, P. *173*, 362
Swinburne, R. G. *173*
Szwarchart, M. K. 458, *480*

Taft, R. 189, *214*
Talland, G. A. 458, *480*
Tannenbaum, P. H. 366, 388, *410*
Tarski, A. 90, *109*
Taylor, R. 104, *109*
Tennessen, H. 158–160, *170, 173, 174*, 233
Terwilliger, R. F. 88, *109*
Tesler, R. C. 402, 410
Thompson, F. B. 371
Thomson, J. J. *174*

Titchener, E. B. 229, 436, 437
Todd, F. J. 304, 335, *345, 346*
Tolman, E. C. 188, 196, *265*, 293, *345*
Törnebohm, H. *174*
Trevarthen, C. B. 269, 271, 275, *283*
Tryon, R. C. *345*
Tucker, L. R. 303, 331, 335, 340, *345*
Tuomela, R. *174*
Twain, M. 361, *362*
Tyrrell, G. N. M. 143, 159, *174*

Überweg, F. 240, 265
Ullian, J. *174*
Ullman, J. D. 405, *409*
Ulmer, K. *174*
Underwood, B. J. 37, *109*
Unger, P. *109*
Urmson, J. O. 119

Van de Geer, J. P. 181, 182, *214*
Vendler, Z. *174*
Vigotsky, L. S. *174*
Vincent, R. H. *174*

Wald, A. *174*
Walker, D. E. 402, *410*
Wallace, J. R. *174*
Wallach, H. 236, *240*
Watkins, J. W. N. *174*
Watson, J. B. 193, 242, *265*
Watson, J. D. 461, *480*
Watzlawick, P. 422, 423, 425, *428*
Waugh, N. C. 458, *480*
Waxam, B. *409*
Weber, S. *410*
Weckowicz, T. *170*, 228, 257, 263, 433, 440, 445, *447*
Wepman, J. M. 42, *107*
Werner, H. 45, 90, *109*, 417, *428*
Werthermer, M. 430
Wexler, D. 439, *447*
Wheatley, J. *174*
Whiteley, C. H. *174*
Whittaker, J. O. 179, *214*
Whorf, B. L. *174*
Wilkins, M. 304, *344*
Will, F. L. 130–132, 159, *174, 175*

Willard, D. *109*
Willey, R. *213*, 267, 269, 271, 275, *282*
Wilson, K. V. 361, 367, 388, 394, 395, 405, *411*, 473, 474
Witkin, H. A. 440, *447*
Wittgenstein, L. 88, 159, *175*, 478
Wolfe, J. B. 458, *479*
Wolff, P. H. 418–421, 425, *428*
Woodward, P. M. 376, *411*
Woodworth, R. S. 198, 199
Wright, G. H., von 139–142, 159, *175*

Yarbus, A. L. 275, *284*
Yilmaz, Hüseyin, 23
Yngve, V. H. 358, *362*
Yourgrau, W. *175*

Zanstra, H. *175*
Zapffe, P. W. *175*
Zaporozhets, A. V. 273, 274, *284*
Ziff, P. *175*
Zivian, A. *213*, 267, 269, 271, 275, *282*

Øfsty, A. *175*

SUBJECT INDEX

Abduction 472, 476
Abductive reasoning 472
 primacy of 461
Aboutness 53, 60f.
Act of knowing 28f.
 the psycho-physical composition of the 29
Action 455f.
 and perceptual and cognitive processes 272f.
Activity
 and its logical-mathematical structure 273
Acts
 as representations of images 455
Acts of knowledge 456
Adaptive processes 269, 272
Ambient light 218
Ambient optic array 215, 219
 and correspondence of structure to environment 220, 221
 and invariant information in 221
 and perceptual information 269
Ampliation 114, 117, 118, 138, 140
Ampliative contentions 114f.
Ampliative inference 79f.
Ampliative knowledge 141
Ampliative knowledge claims 116f
 justification of 118
Analogy 461f.
Analyticity 20, 71, 123
Association theory
 and Quillian memory model 404f.
Associational structure 376–378
Associative structure 393–395
Automata theory 347, 399
Automatistic psychology 390
Automatistic theory of memory 395f.

Behavioristic psychology 242
Belief
 causal dynamics of 38
 compositional complexity of 37
 management 26
 psychological character of 36f
Belief justification 76
Belief strength 38, 39, 79, 86
 and subjective probability 76
Beliefs
 about the future 130–133
 logic of justifying one's 26
Bodies
 epistemology of 10, 11, 21
Bodily ego 243, 246–248
Brunswikian inference 355
Brunswik's lens model 287f.

Categorical coding 359
Codes 450f.
Coding
 contextual dependencies in 375f.
 and formal grammars 466
 psychological implications of 470
Cognition
 and acquisition of knowledge 201f.
 concept of 177f.
 continuum of types of 206
 existentialist dimension of 75
 and knowing 207
 mode of 46
 phylogeny of 209f.
 proximal-distal relations and 286f.
 psycho-philosophical research on 103
 singular vs. collective form of 180
 as used by psychologists 178–180
Cognitions
 as dispositional attributes 39

Cognitive
    as a kind of psychological process   182
    as a point of view   183
Cognitive acts   26
    psychology of   98
Cognitive arousal
    linguistic versus non-linguistic patterns of   100
Cognitive behavior
    discontinuation between 'simple' behavior and   202–204
Cognitive growth
    dynamic models of   66
Cognitive meaning   42, 54, 64, 72
Cognitive process
    as a categorized representational process   187–190
    as a conscious process   194–196
    as a constructed process   190–192
    as generalization   185
    as a mediating process   186
    as a mediating representional process   187
    as any nonemotional psychological process   184
    as a symbolic response   192 f.
    as a verbal mediating response   193 f.
Cognitive processes
    absolute vs. relational definition of   197 f.
    conscious vs. functional definition of   197
    criteria of   184 f.
    generality (or extent) of   199 f.
    inferential nature of   196
    mediating vs. determining function of   198 f.
    passive vs. active conception of   199
    towards a definition of   200–202
    and vicarious functioning   291
Cognitive psychology   36
Cognitive reference   61
Cognitive representation
    problem of   463
Cognitive structure   37
    Cognitive theory of psychology   209
    Cognitive tradition in psychology   188
    Cognize   181

Coherence theory of truth   436
Communication
    modes of   422
Community   21
Complete systems   10
Compositional structure   37, 44
Concept acquisition   65
Concept formation   48, 64 f., 66, 367
Concept-formative research paradigm   66
Concept learning   287
Concepts
    descriptive   51
    elementary sensory-perceptual features of   374
    evaluative   52, 64
    mentalistic   102
    origin of   65
    relational associations between   374
Conceptualist theory of meaning   62
Confirmation
    theories of   148
Consciousness   241 f.
Constative mode   135
Constructionism
    neurology of   463
Constructivist theory of knowledge   417 f.
Contemplative thought
    and language   46
Contentions
    ampliation vs. explicative   115
Correlator
    and the efferent-reafferent sequence   270
Correspondence principle of truth   49–50, 73
Critical phenomenal world
    and scientific findings   254
Critical realism   251, 255

Deductive inference   80
Deductive system
    claims within a   117
Definitions   68–71
    contextual   11, 14, 15
Denotation   70, 74 f., 93 n
Depersonalization-derealization syndrome   432
    definition and experience of   433, 434

SUBJECT INDEX

Depersonalization-derealization (*cont.*)
   physiological and experimental conditions of 439f.
   and problem of knowledge 432
Depth perception 223f
Descriptions 11
Developmental psychology
   contributions to logic and epistemology 431f.
Direct perception
   theory of 221
Direct realism 227, 237
Direct visual perception 215
Directed graph structure 387, 400

Ecological optics 217f.
Ecological physics 235
Efference
   and reafference 231
Efferent-reafferent correlations 271
Efferent-reafferent perceptual systems 232, 270
Empiricism
   and computer simulation 405–407
Empiricist psychology 228
Empiricist theory of perception 436f.
Environment
   active construction of a model of 441
   hypotheses and expectations about 269
   operations on 277
Epistemology 9f., 25, 77, 101, 227, 278, 413, 429f., 442, 461
   and the construction of images 455
   and an information-based theory of perception 227
   naturalized 10–13, 17–19, 21 f.
   relevance to psychology 94f.
   subject matter of 26
Evaluative terms
   in contrast to descriptive terms 64
Evolution 23, 247
   of behavior 209
Exafference 269
Experience
   drive determined organization of 422
Explanation
   nature of 431
Explicative knowledge claims 116f

Factor analysis 370
Feedforward mechanism 268
Focal vision 269
Form preferences 271
Formal logic 347f.

Genetic epistemology 431
Gestalt 19f.
Good reason
   standards of 128–130
Grammars 358, 373

Hierarchical list structure 366f, 370, 400
Hullian theory 70
Humanities
   knowing mode in the 100
Hypothesis
   projectibility of 144f

Illuminance
   extension of classical meaning of 218–221
Image 227, 464
   and imagery 467
   and the mind-brain problem 475
   as representation 470f.
Imagery 273
Images 453–455
Images-of-achievement 270, 455
Images-of-events 270, 453
Imaging
   and coding 453
   personal nature of 455
Immanent knowledge 461, 464
   and action 456
Impressions 10, 11
Indeterminacy of translation 16f, 22
Induction
   problem of 23, 113, 118f., 138
   problem of justifying 127, 128, 136–138, 142, 153
Inductionism 122f.
Inductive behavior 143f.
Induction cognition 285
   limits of 300
Inductive inference 113
   the problem of 119f.
Inductive interpersonal knowing
   a study of 303f.

SUBJECT INDEX

Inductive judgments
    double system parameters of   292–295
    single system parameters of   291, 292
    triple system parameters of   296, 297
Inductive knowing   287f, 320
    substantive and formal content of   296–299
Inductive practise   144
Inductive ratiocination   122
Inductive reason
    and reasonableness   126
Inference patterns   78f.
Information
    concept of   229
    and the optic array   235, 236
    sensory   218
    structural invariants as   217f.
Information processing models   37
Information retrieval
    and semantics   372f.
Information storage
    in hierarchial list structure   366f.
    in matrix structure   364–366
    in Quillian memory structure   367–370
    and retrieval   364, 449
Instinctual drives
    principle of   413f.
Intention
    content of   46, 60, 61
    mode of   46
    object of   60f.
Intentional aboutness   61
Intentional acts   45f, 60, 62, 102
    content of   43
    theory of   48
Intentional contents
    and relation to intentional objects   75
Intentional mode   38, 40, 69
Intentionality of belief   37
Intentionality of concepts   34
Interiorization   272–275
    as distinct from internalization   269f.
Inter-organism interaction processes   296f., 314, 318
Interpersonal communication   48, 73
Interpersonal learning   296f.
    cognitive systems in   314
Introspection   62f., 87

Knowing   364
    and coding operations   452
    concept of   126
    as construction of images   455
    as distinct from knowledge   476
    as experience   386
    as involving transforming and acting   270
    logic of   28f
    and meaning   459–462
    and modes of cognition   426
    problem of   111
    procedures for verification of   477
Knowing—it   32f.
Knowing—how   30–33
Knowing—that   30
Knowledge   25, 28, 94, 125, 193, 417
    and coding   449f, 459
    definition of   413, 449
    and drives   414
    and intentionality   461
    justification of   112
    objects of   28f.
    and sensory perception   432
    of skills   31
    as structuralization of experience   420f.
    types of   101
    verbal   364
Knowledge-by-acquaintance   30, 34, 438

Language
    as elicitor of cognitions   40f, 46–48
    psychology of   40
    and predication   273
    theories of   45
Language learning   68f.
Lens model   288
    mathematical logic of   288
    and types of systems and parameters   288–299
Lens model equation
    as a mathematical statement   298f.
    and system parameters   299–303
Linguistic knowledge   459
Linguistic reference
    and psychology   55

SUBJECT INDEX

Linguistic stimuli
   as distinguished from non-linguistic stimuli 43f, 95
Logical connectives and quantifiers 52
Logical empiricism 92n
Logical operations 277f.
Long-term memory
   and Quillian memory structure 373f.
Long-term memory organization 368

Mathematical group
   and habit family hierarchy 275
Mathematical structures
   and psychological concepts 279
Mathematics
   as a deductive system 117
   foundations of 9, 10, 12f., 71
Matrix structure memory 400
Meaning
   clarification of the concept of 41
   as internalized language 42
   and reference 50
   theories of 53f.
Memory
   automatistic models of 391
   drive determined organization of 415
   organization of information in 383
Memory organization
   directed graph structure of 387
   formal properties of 370f.
   multidimensional matrix structure of 386
Memory search processes
   and activation 404f.
Memory structure
   and inference processes 401f.
   and neurophysiology 376–378
Memory trace theory 396f., 416
Mental acts
   contents of 38, 43f.
Metabeliefs 77–79, 81–87, 93n
Metaphysics 17f
Modal operators 52
Monitor images 454
Motor exploration in perception 267
Motor mechanisms
   and the control of receptor functions 456
Motor theory of perception 281

Naturalism 17–19, 85
Nervous system
   and inhibitory mechanisms 452
Neurology of knowing 449
Non-demonstrative knowledge
   acquisition of 74
   justification of 149f., 156
Nonverbal thinking 47
Normative belief theory
   and empirical psychology 76
   and statistical inference 83

Objects
   logicalization of sensory processes and 243f.
Observation 80f
Observation sentences 12–15, 19–22, 125
Ontological induction 80
Operations
   interiorization of act leading to 274
Operations as data 277
Optative mode 135
Optic-array information
   distinguished from afferent information 217
Ordinary language philosophy 141
Organismic adaptation
   environmental model of 356f.
Organismic constructs
   and proximal-distal relations 285–286
Organismic-environmental interactions 288f., 318
   models of 207

Paragraph
   conceptual organization of 378f.
Paralogic 347f.
Paralogical operations 350
Paraphrases 11, 14, 77
Pattern perception 275
Perception 16–18, 215f., 225f.
   as active extraction of information 437f., 441
   as different from proprioception 216
   as distinct from cognition 437
   efferent-reafferent theory of 232
   epistemological implications of 270

SUBJECT INDEX

Perception (cont.)
  as immediate knowledge 438
  and issues in cognition and epistemology
    272–275
  and neural response mechanisms 280
  as a reafferent process 269–271
  sensation based theories of 221, 229
Perception
  copy theory of 65
  as sensory information 218
Perception of occlusion 222
Perception of the environment
  as different from perception of space
    223f.
Percepts
  phenomenal world of 246
Perceptual abilities 65
Perceptual aboutness
  causal analysis of 61f.
Perceptual beliefs
  cognitive beliefs as contradicting 439
Perceptual constancies 272
Perceptual development 268f., 272
Perceptual differentiation theory 67
Perceptual experience
  consciousness of and role of efference in
    271f.
Perceptual information 231
  and the optic array 238
Perceptual judgment 271
Perceptual learning 67f., 271
Perceptual organization
  and higher-order invariants 232
Perfect induction 287
Personal knowledge 140
Phenomenal objects
  constancy of 225
Phenomenal visual world 215
Phenomenal world 246f.
Phenomenalism 61f., 229, 254
Phenomenological movement 430
Phenomenology 443
Philosopher of science 155f.
Philosophical epistemology 27
Philosophical problems
  their relationship to scientific ones
    153f.
Philosophical reduction 254

Philosophical semantics 54, 70f.
Philosophy of knowledge 26, 82
Philosophy of mind 430
Philosophy of science 27
Phonology
  growth of 273
Primary process ideation
  structural mechanism of 420f.
Primary process thinking 414
Problem solving algorithm 349
Problem solving heuristics 351–355
Processing
  serial vs. parallel 400f.
Propositional attitude 99
Propositional information
  memory structure and 392
Propositional knowledge 33, 34, 97, 438
  as justified true belief 34f.
  logical features of 31
Propositional structure 37, 40, 44, 98,
    392
Propositions 17, 43
  truth value of 49
Proprioception 216
  as distinct from feedback 216–217
Protocol statement
  veridicality of 146f.
Proximal-distal relations 285
  substantive and formal representations
    of 286–287
Psychic energy
  neurological assumption of 415
Psychic structure 419
Psychoanalysis
  and epistemology 413
Psychoanalytic theory
  concepts of memory and 418
  concepts of representation and 416
Psycholinguistics 37, 41, 48
  and cognitive structure 379
Psychological activity
  hierarchical model of 202
Psychological processes
  phylogenetic continuity underlying 209
Psychological research
  assumption of 287
Psychologism 426
Psychologizing 25

SUBJECT INDEX

Psychology   13, 18f., 22f., 25, 83f., 89f.
   and cognitive processes   202–204
   epistemology of   431
Psychology of cognition   27, 44, 103
   and theory of knowledge   430
Psychology of inductive reasoning   67
Psychology of knowing   177
Psychology of knowledge   26, 429f., 442
Psychology of language   44f.
   requirements for a   56f.
Psychology of meaning   55
Psychopathology
   as an experimental discipline   432
Psycho-philosophy   25f., 53
Psycho-philosophy of knowledge   27f., 35f., 80
Psychosemantics   53, 56, 72
Pyrrhonism   121

Quillian memory
   and nominalism   404
Quillian memory structure   367–370
   and activation   373
   and belief systems   387
   limitations of   371f.

Rational belief
   traditional philosophic paradigm of   77
Rational reconstruction   13–15, 18f.
Rationality   82
   theory of   76
Reafferent process   268, 272
   and issues in cognition and epistemology   278
Reafferent theories of perception   274, 278
Realism   233, 239
Realist ontology   50
Reasoning
   forms of   477
Reduction forms   14f.
Reference   71, 74f.
   as distinct from meaning   54
   theory of   59
Relational codings   359, 467–468
Relational structures   385

Relational terms
   coding of   369
Representations   475
Representative design   356
Response
   concept of   247
Rules   66

Scepticism
   pyrrhonic formulations of   121
Scientific data analysis
   logic of   80
Scientific inference   77, 79
Scientific knowledge   154f.
Scientific psychology
   and philosophy   429
Scientific world orientation   154
Secondary process thinking   414
   differentiation and integration in   423f.
Semantic differential   366
Semantic hypotheses
   empirical testing of   127
Semantic structure   379f.
Semantic theory   63f.
Semantic veridicality   49
Semantical theories
   and ontology   50
Semantics   41, 50
   fundamental problems of   61
   psychological aspects of a theory of   51
   as a theory of aboutness   54
Sensationless perception   229
Sensations
   exteriorization of   242
Sense data   272
Sensoid concepts   64
Sensori-motor processes   270
Sensori-motor stage of development
   and concept of drive representations   418f.
Sentence   37
   as primary linguistic stimulus   43
Sentences
   organizational structure of   385f.
Short-term memory capacity   358
Signs   45, 270, 456f., 471
   as context free constructions   473f.
   symbolic use of   459

Skills   31
  integrated complexity of   31 f.
S–R theory
  ecological irrelevancy of   286
Statistical generalization   79
Statistical inference
  principles of   84
Stimulation   13, 17, 19, 20, 81, 84–86
Stimulation by light
  as distinguished from information in light   217
Stimulus
  concept of   246
Structural memory organization
  and verbal learning   21, 374
Structure
  problems of   32
Structure of cognition
  the verbal coding of   48
Structure of memory
  and asking questions   363
Structures of information
  from sentences   371, 376
Symbolic processes   193
Symbolic knowledge   458
Symbolic transformation   47
Symbolization   458
Symbolizing
  figurative aspects of   270
Symbol-referent asymmetry   56, 59
Symbols   45, 270, 457–459, 471
  as context dependent constructions   473 f.
  used as signs   459
Synonymy   72 f.
Syntactic structures   274
Syntax   48
Systems
  organism and environment as   288 f.
Superordinate cell assemblies   277 f.

Texture
  concept of   293
Theoretical concepts   68
  empiricist interpretation of   74
Theoretical psychology   279

Theoretical sentences   16 f.
Theories   15 f.
Theories of knowledge
  representational vs. constructivist   417
Theory of perception   267 f.
  and relativity theory   278
Thinking
  classificatory and relational   273
  coding process in   359 f.
  development of   420–422
  psychoanalytic theory of   414–416
Thought
  categories of   418
  discursive vs. nondiscursive   423
Trace memory model   407 f.
Translation of observation sentences   22
Transphenomenal reality   252–254
Tri-dimensional optic arrays   236
Truth
  degrees of   84 f.
  problems concerning   49 f.

Universal propositions   113

Verbal afferent processes
  semantic properties of   55 f.
Verbal images   41
Verbal knowledge   364 f., 386
Veridicality
  and perception   239
  principles of   50 f.
  and realism   237
Vienna Circle   16, 17, 19, 22
  thought model of   125
Vision
  as process of exploration in time   222
Visual Perception   215 f.
Visual proprioception   238
Visual sense
  as an active system   218
Visual system   267
Voluntary action   244 f.

Word meanings
  matrix ordering of   366 f.

BF
311
.B275
1969